Alexander Schall

The Principle of Unjust Enrichment

Alexander Schall

The Principle of Unjust Enrichment

DE GRUYTER

Professor Dr. Alexander Schall, M. Jur. (Oxford), Leuphana Universität Lüneburg

ISBN 978-3-11-075444-5
e-ISBN (PDF) 978-3-11-075445-2
e-ISBN (EPUB) 978-3-11-075458-2
DOI https://doi.org/10.1515/9783110754452

Library of Congress Control Number: 2024942830

Bibliographic information published by the Deutsche Nationalbibliothek
The Deutsche Nationalbibliothek lists this publication in the Deutsche Nationalbibliografie; detailed bibliographic data are available on the Internet at http://dnb.dnb.de.

The book is published open access at www.degruyter.com.
Printing and binding: CPI books GmbH, Leck

www.degruyter.com

MIX
Papier | Fördert gute Waldnutzung
FSC® C083411

Contents

A Introduction —— 1
I The principle of unjust enrichment as key to rationalise unjust enrichment in civil and common law —— **1**
II The (unorthodox) methodology of the book – exemplified by mistaken services —— **25**
III An aside on terminology —— **28**

B Main Part —— 31
I The central role of the enrichment principle for shaping the law —— **31**
1 From principle to law – general observations —— **32**
2 The enrichment claim: From principle to law – and back? —— **35**
3 The proposed answer: a general enrichment claim reduced to direct shifts of value —— **37**
II How the principles form unjust enrichment – the emergence of general enrichment claims —— **41**
1 The long and winding road to civilian enrichment law —— **41**
a) The development until the first codifications —— **41**
b) Germany: From Pomponius to Savigny —— **45**
c) France: back into the arms of Pomponius – but with eyes set on the *actio de in rem verso* —— **47**
d) The rift in civil law of unjust enrichment until present day —— **47**
2 The civilian-infused road to common enrichment law —— **49**
III The Roman foundations of enrichment law —— **56**
1 Overview —— **56**
2 The general development of the *condictiones* —— **57**
3 The “Mosaic” condictiones and the foundation of the enrichment principle —— **65**
a) The mothers of unjust enrichment claims: *condictio causa data causa non secuta* (D.12.4.) and failure of consideration —— **72**
b) The condictio ob turpem vel iniustam causam (D.12.5.) and extortion / duress —— **93**
c) The *condictio indebiti* and mistake —— **97**

4 The condictiones which were not transplanted via *Moses v Macferlan* — **103**
a) The condictio sine causa — **103**
b) The *condictio furtiva* – an important exception from "dare oportere" — **118**
5 The *negotiorum gestio* and unjust enrichment in civil law — **121**
a) The enrichment claim for prohibited interference — **122**
b) The enrichment claim for building on another's land — **127**
6 The *actio de in rem verso (utilis)* and unjust enrichment in civil law — **131**
a) The actio de in rem verso and the actio de in rem verso utilis in the Roman sources — **131**
b) The legal nature of the *actio de in rem verso* between *negotiorum gestio* and unjust enrichment — **134**
7 The *actio de in rem verso*, cloaked in the Pomponian principle, turns into hard French law — **139**
a) The earlier history of the *actio de in rem verso* in French law — **139**
b) The Crédit foncier case of 16 July 1889 — **145**
c) An aside: *Banque Financière* compared to Crédit Foncier — **151**
d) The "last stand" of the *negotiorum gestio* view: the Lemaire case of 16 July 1890 — **152**
e) The amalgamation of *actio de in rem verso* and general enrichment claim by the arrêt Boudier of 15 June 1892 — **157**
f) The doctrinal inconsistencies from amalgamating actio de in rem verso and unjust enrichment — **160**
8 Summary — **187**
IV The Pomponius-related extension beyond direct shifts of value and its incompatibility with English unjust enrichment — **191**
1 The irreconcilable contradiction of *Banque Financière / Menelaou* and *Costello* — **191**
a) *Banque Financière* — **191**
b) The acceptance of unjust enrichment against remote beneficiaries — **192**
c) The collision with *Costello v MacDonald* — **195**
d) The direct shift of value in *Lowick Rose v Swynson* — **198**
2 The origin of remoteness – *Lipkin Gorman v Karpnale* — **199**

3 The “equitable element” inherent in wide unjust enrichment: no gratuity at the expense of third parties — **200**

4 The equitable issues surrounding the restorations of gifts — **203**

a) Gifts and disenrichment – a marriage of old — **203**

b) Most reasons for reversing gifts are of equitable nature — **207**

5 Conclusions — **212**

6 Outlook on following part — **215**

7 Annex: A comparative view on *Lipkin Gorman* as a hybrid of personal action and *rei vindicatio* for a sum of money — **216**

a) The title to the money — **218**

b) The remedies available — **223**

c) Tracing and the principle of unjust enrichment — **225**

d) Final observations: Too narrow German Law — **228**

V The true shape of unjust enrichment: Savigny’s direct shift of value unlocks the rationale of restitution — **230**

1 The ousting of the Pomponian principle by the direct shift of wealth/value (unmittelbare Vermögensverschiebung) in Germany — **230**

a) The discovery of the direct shift of wealth/value concept by *Friedrich Carl von Savigny* — **230**

b) The adoption of Savigny’s direct-shift-of-wealth/value concept by the *Vorentwurf* and the *Erste Entwurf* — **235**

c) The direct shift of value dissolves the *condictio indebiti* in the general enrichment claim — **242**

2 The demise of the general enrichment claim in § 812 I 1 BGB – the rise of the *Trennungslehre* following *Walter Wilburg* and *Ernst von Caemmerer* — **254**

a) The doctrinal shift from *Einheitslehre* (= unity doctrine) to *Trennungslehre* (= separation doctrine) — **254**

b) The current structure of the law of unjustified enrichment in Germany — **257**

c) Fundamental criticism of the modern German approach to unjustified enrichment: the legacy of Wilburg’s fallacy — **260**

VI The normative foundation of unjust enrichment claims to reverse direct shifts of value — **262**

1 Party autonomy and *volenti non fit inuria:* the uniform foundation of enrichment claims for giving or taking value — **262**

2 The justification for equating money and money’s worth — **263**

3 Party autonomy and *volenti non fit iniuria* — **264**
4 The different challenges for performance-based and non-performance based enrichment claims ("giving value" and "taking value") — **265**
5 The purpose of transfers of value — **266**
a) The alignment of enrichment claims to the "performance" in Germany — **267**
b) The failure of purpose as the overall unjust factor — **268**
6 The enrichment claim for "taking value" — **273**
a) The basic principle at work — **273**
b) The superiority of the direct shift of value to the current approach of the *Eingriff in ein Recht mit Zuweisungsgehalt* (= violation of a right that allocates values) — **275**
c) *Der Fehlschluss vom Faktum auf die Norm* (= the fallacy to see the typical case as legal rule) — **279**
d) The example of the Bitcoin exchange raid — **280**
7 Direct shift of value, volenti non fit inuria and "imposed enrichment" (aufgedrängte Bereicherung) under the Aufwendungskondiktion and Rückgriffskondiktion — **282**
VII The normative foundation of defences under the direct shift of value approach — **284**
1 Direct shift of value and disenrichment — **284**
a) The extension to all *condictiones* under German law as explained by *von Kübel* — **284**
b) The original misconception of § 812 BGB (in particular: the *Saldotheorie*) — **286**
c) A modern normative justification of disenrichment — **295**
2 Security of receipts in three party situations: suum receipt / good consideration, disenrichment and other arguments — **303**
a) Disenrichment as an alternative to *suum receipt?* — **304**
b) The modern German solution: construction of a chain of enrichment claims (A – B and B – C) under a performance-based approach — **309**

C Conclusion: The principles of unjust enrichment — 324

Evans, Translation of Robert Joseph Pothiers Treatise on the Law of Obligations, or Contracts, Volume II, 1806 — 330

Sources Unjust Enrichment — 334

Table of Cases (Common Law) — 350

A Introduction

I The principle of unjust enrichment as key to rationalise unjust enrichment in civil and common law

This book is about the principle of unjust enrichment. That principle has shaped unjust enrichment in civil laws since medieval times. It subsequently entered the common law, first via the US in the 20th, then via England in the 21st century. Today, all major civil and common law jurisdictions contain a law of unjust enrichment.[1] The Third Restatement accepted it, as did the Supreme Court of the UK.[2] While enrichment laws differ profoundly in many respects, they share the same roots. The principle of unjust enrichment is the thread along which the storyline will be developed. It provides a new angle to comparative research and doctrinal analysis.

The principle of unjust enrichment has influenced all existing enrichment laws in one way or another. It is responsible for the vague and loose terminology of the general enrichment claims we find in jurisdictions like France, Germany, Italy, Spain and now also England: "enrichment"; "at the expense"; "unjust(ified)".[3] These actions cannot be applied by using a dictionary. In order to determine their content, it is necessary to get behind their wording. An apt test for this proposition is the "stamp case" that *Robert Stevens* has put forward in the course of his fundamental criticism of unjust enrichment.

---

1 Today, civilian enrichment law is often denominated as "unjustified "enrichment as opposed to common enrichment law as "unjust" enrichment cf. e.g. Goff & Jones, Unjust Enrichment, 10th edn. 2022, 1–16. But that must be questioned (for the reason see below, fn. 11 and sub III.). Therefore, and also for sake of legibility, the book will normally address all enrichment laws as unjust enrichment, following the seminal work of Eltjo Schrage (ed.), Unjust Enrichment – a Comparative Legal History of the Law of Restitution. 2nd edn. 1999.

2 *Banque Financière De La Cité v. Parc (Battersea) Ltd and Others* [1998] UKHL 7 = 1 AC 221, 227 (per Lord Steyn); *Barton v Morris* [2023] UKSC 3; *Samsoondar v Capital Insurance* Co Ltd' [2020] UKPC 33; cf. further *Benedetti v Sawiris and Others* [2013] UKSC 50, para. 10 (per Lord Clarke); *Barnes v Eastenders Cash & Carry Plc* [2014] UKSC 26 = [2015] AC 1; *Bank of Cyprus UK Ltd v Menelaou* [2015] UKSC 66; *HMRC v The Investment Trust Companies* [2017] UKSC 29; *Lowick Rose LLP v Swynson Limited and another* [2017] UKSC 32; for an account see Goff & Jones on Unjust Enrichment, 10th edn. 2022, 1–14 et seq.; Bant/Barker/Degeling (eds.), Research Handbook on Unjust Enrichment and Restitution, 2020.

3 Cf. *Samsoondar v Capital Insurance* Co Ltd' [2020] UKPC 33, para 18: "It has now become conventional to recognise … that a claim in the law of unjust enrichment has three central elements which the claimant must prove: that the defendant has been enriched, that the enrichment was at the claimant's expense, and that the enrichment at the claimant's expense was unjust."

https://doi.org/10.1515/9783110754452-001

A and B own the last two specimen of a rare stamp. By mistake, A destroys his own stamp. That multiplies the value of B's stamp, now being a unique.

B is enriched at the expense of A by mistake. Yet *Stevens* argues that no claim can lie, not in England nor anywhere else.[4] And he is eventually right. But why? The principle of unjust enrichment prohibits to benefit from another's loss. It had been formulated by the Roman jurist Sextus Pomponius and those who like a pun might assume that made him the "Principal of unjust enrichment". The two famous passages are D.50,17.206 and, in a slightly different version that does not mention wrongs, D.12.6.14.

D.50.17.206 (Pomp. 9 var. lec.):
"Iure naturae aequum est neminem fieri cum alterius detrimento et iniuria locupletiorem"

[Under natural law it is fair that nobody shall become enriched from another's detriment or injury.[5]]

D.12.6.14 (*Pomponius libro 21 ad Sabinum):*
"Nam hoc natura aequum est neminem cum alterius detrimento fieri locupletiorem."

[For it is naturally just that nobody shall become enriched from another's detriment[6]]

The principle had been codified by major civilian jurisdictions like France and Italy after prior acceptance by the case law of their Supreme Courts:

Art. 1303–1 Code civil (C.civ): "...celui qui **bénéficie d'un enrichissement injustifié au détriment d'autrui** doit, à celui qui s'en trouve appauvri, une indemnité ... ."
[...a person who is **unjustly enriched to the detriment of another** owes to the person who is impoverished compensation .... – Deep-L]

---

4 Robert Stevens, (2018) 134 LQR 574, at 578: "If we accept that no claim should succeed, and no legal system anywhere allows one in such a case something has gone wrong with the theory." Agreeing Lionel Smith, Restitution: A New Start?, in Devonshire/Havelock (ed.), 91, at p. 101. The stamp case is a variation on example built by D. Friedmann, Restitution of Benefits Acquired through Appropriation of Property or the Commission of a Wrong, 80 CoL Rev 504 (1980), 532 fn. 144.

5 According to the Digest translated by Scott the passage reads: "It is but just, and in accordance with the Law of Nations that no one, by the commission of an injury, can be enriched at the expense of another."
But the use of "Law of nations" does nor resonate with modern terminology. Also, the detriment need not necessarily stem from the commission of an injury, nor does the Latin text say that.

6 Scott: "For it is only in accordance with natural equity that no one should profit pecuniarily by the injury of another." Again, the translation by Scott is less appealing because of "injury" and also because from today's perspective, the central term "enriched" need not (must not?) be circumscribed as "profit pecuniarily".

Art. 2041 Codice Civile (CC): "Chi, senza una giusta causa, si **e' arricchito a danno di un'altra** persona e' tenuto, nei limiti dell'arricchimento, a indennizzare quest'ultima della correlativa diminuzione patrimoniale."

[A person who, without just cause, **has enriched himself to the detriment of another person** shall, within the limits of the enrichment, compensate the latter for the corresponding diminution of assets. – Deep-L]

In other civil law jurisdictions like e.g. Spain, the principle is accepted as binding law even though it remained in the realm of the courts.

Tribunal Supremo of 24/06/2020, STS 2072/2020 – ECLI:ES:TS:2020:2072, sub Cuarto, para. 1: "Los primeros escritos sobre el enriquecimiento sin causa, tal como ha llegado -como principio- a nuestros días, se hallan en sendos textos prácticamente idénticos de Pomponio recogidos en el Digesto: *nemo cum alterius detrimento locupletior fieeri debet* (nadie debe enriquecerse en detrimento de otro) (D. 12, 6, 14) *y iure naturae aequum est neminem cum alterius detrimento et iniuria fieri locupletiorem* (es equitativo por Derecho natural que nadie se enriquezca en detrimento y en daño de otro) (D. 50, 17, 206). Las Partidas[7] (7.a, 34, 17) recogen este principio: *ninguno non deve enriqueszer tortizeramente con daño de otro.*"

[The first writings on unjust enrichment, as it has come down to us as a principle, are found in two practically identical texts by Pomponius in the Digest: nemo cum alterius detrimento locupletior fieri debet (no one should enrich himself to the detriment of another) and iure naturae aequum est neminem cum alterius detrimento et iniuria fieri locupletiorem (it is equitable by natural law that no one should enrich himself to the detriment and harm of another). The Partidas recognized this principle: nobody must enrich himself tortiously from the detriment of another.]

Ibid. sub Cuarto, para. 4: "La doctrina jurisprudencial de esta Sala se mueve en esta dirección proclamando, a veces de modo explícito y terminante y otras de forma implícita, que la interdicción del enriquecimiento injusto tiene en nuestro ordenamiento jurídico el valor de un auténtico principio general del Derecho…."

[The jurisprudential doctrine of this Chamber moves in this direction, proclaiming, sometimes explicitly and categorically and sometimes implicitly, that the prohibition of unjust enrichment has the value of a genuine general principle of law in our legal system….Deep-L]

The Pomponian principle also lies at the core of the common law of unjust enrichment:

Banque Financière De La Cité v. Parc (Battersea) Ltd and Others [1998] UKHL 7 (per Lord Clyde):
"The basis for the appellants' claim is to be found in the principle of unjust enrichment, a

7 The Ancient Castilian Code that was completed under the reign of Alfonso X. ("el Sabio") of Castile (1252–1284).

principle more fully expressed in the Latin formulation, nemo debet locupletari aliena jactura."

Green v. Biddle, (U.S.) 8 Wheat. 1, 82–83 = 5 L Ed 547, 567 (1823)
"Thus it may happen that the occupant, who may have enriched himself to any amount by the natural as well as the industrial products of land ... is accountable for no part of those profits ..., in violation of that maxim of equity and of natural law, *nemo debet locupletari aliena jactura.*"

The principle formulated by Pomponius and adopted both by civil law and common law would call for restitution in the stamp case because B evidently benefits from the loss suffered by A. To deny the claim requires unlocking unjust enrichment. The key is retracing, deconstructing and redefining its principle. The topic at stake is far from academic. In the sixth issue of Volume 133 (2019–2020), the Harvard Law Review dedicated the annual "Developments in the Law" section to Unjust Enrichment. It laid bare considerable potential for enrichment claims in (US-American) legal practice: "Once we are equipped with a basic understanding of the principles of unjust enrichment, we begin to see missed opportunities everywhere."[8] And rightly so. For example, the Chapter four of that issue (*Aloha ʻĀina*) discusses native Hawaiian land restitution.[9] But there is no stopping there. Just think of the enormous shifts of wealth caused by climate change – or wars.

How does understanding the principle of unjust enrichment give us guidance to solve enrichment cases? The answer is: by reverse engineering. As the principle of unjust enrichment overlaid and shaped the law of unjust enrichment, it is the code to decipher and disentangle its components. Once that is done, the reasons for the current spread width of possible solutions to central issues will become transparent. This is true for both civil law and common law.

To start with civil law: The Pomponian principle of unjust enrichment hardened to law in France,[10] whereas it was rejected in Germany where instead the more precise principle of direct shifts of wealth was adopted following Friedrich Carl von Savigny.[11] Both decisions profoundly influenced the content of these superficially similar, yet so different enrichment laws. They led to a rarely noticed split between Germanic and French-infused enrichment laws, the most remarkable differences being: Only francophone jurisdictions allow enrichment claims

8 Developments in the Law, Introduction, 133 Harvard Law Review 2019–20) 2062, at 2066 referring to Voris v Lampert 446 P.3d 284 (Cal. 2019) – a case of wage theft (from one business associate by another through running down their company) that the Californian Supreme Court found itself unable to remedy under the tort of conversion.
9 Developments in the Law, Chapter 4, 6 Harvard Law Review 133 (2019–20) 2148.
10 The development culminated in the famous arrêt Boudier, see p. 155.
11 Zimmermann, pp. 872–873, 887.

against remote recipients. Only they have general (if subsidiary) enrichment claims based on the Pomponian principle that nobody be enriched from another's detriment.[12] In one word: **French enrichment law is wide. German enrichment law is narrow.**

The principle of unjust enrichment became the Godfather of the general enrichment claim in England. From the 19th century on, it has slowly but steadily diffused into common law.[13] The development got stuck in the US, but culminated in England with the acceptance of a general enrichment claim in *Banque Financière* (1998). Again, the principle of unjust enrichment appears as the culprit for the existence enrichment claims against remote recipients (*Menelaou; Lipkin Gorman*). The exercise of reverse engineering will lead back to *Moses v Macferlan.*[14] A combined consideration of the historic evolution and the general principles of private law will show that English enrichment claims rather be restricted to direct shifts of value, with the main paradigm being performances (= narrow enrichment law). Why would England accept the *actio de in rem verso* that is the heart and soul of French enrichment law?

To reach this conclusion, or even to see the question, we need go back into time and disentangle the web we weaved. Unjust enrichment started with the reception of Roman law in medieval Europe. Three different components have formed it. At the core were the ***condictiones sine causa.*** From a modern perspective, the *condictiones* could be subdivided further into claims arising from failed transfers ("giving value") and claims arising from wrongs ("taking value"). In addition, there was the ***actio de in rem verso (utilis).*** Finally, there was the above-cited statement by Pomponius that nobody shall be enriched from another's detriment. This was the original **principle of unjust enrichment.**

After the reception of Roman law, those three ingredients were mixed together and slowly but steadily cooked up civilian unjust enrichment. But on closer looks, they do not match very well. That led to countless frictions, twists and turns in civil laws. By contrast, English law only adopted the essential feature of the perfor-

---

12 That is why we should the French "enrichissement sans cause" should be seen as unjust enrichment, not as unjustified enrichment. This remains true even after the rebranding as "enrichissement injustifié" in the Civil Code of 2016 because that did not change anything in enrichment law but was only done in the context of eliminating the ancient French concept of "cause" from the Code Civil. This concept is similar to the consideration of common law and does not have decisive bearing on unjust enrichment, see Albers/Patti/Perrouin-Verbe (eds.), Causa contractus, 2022, in particular the contributions bei Perrouin-Verbe, "Causa and the Requirements of Valid Contracts" (p. 373) and Paturet, "La cause contractuelle aux confins de l'anthropologie et du droit" (p. 67).

13 Cf. Developments in the Law, Chapter 1, 133 Harvard Law Review (2019–20) 2077.

14 *Moses v Macferlan* (1760) 2 Bur 1005 = 97 ER 676.

mance-based *condictiones:* the "unjust factors" in *Moses v Macferlan.*[15] This could have led England to the narrow law of unjustified enrichment that Germany had tried to adopt following Savigny. Instead, Pomponius belatedly crossed the great divide, bringing all his baggage with him and causing disruption by pointing to wide enrichment law. Let us revisit this step by step.

Most ***condictiones sine causa*** concerned the **reversal of failed transfers.**[16] These actions are based on a clear rationale that resonates well with modern private law. They respond to the flaws of a transaction and are naturally located between the parties, and those parties only.

In addition, there was the ***condictio furtiva*** (D.13.1.).[17] In modern eyes, it looks like a case of **restitution for wrongs,**[18] but the emphasis was not really on the commission of the wrong, but on taking the value from another. To make the difference clear: Hong Kong's claim for the proceeds of the bribe to Reid in *Attorney-General of Hongkong v Reid* was about skimming off enrichment from a wrong, but not about restoring value taken from Hongkong.

By contrast, the *condictio furtiva* was about taking value. It had a complementary function to the *rei vindicatio* in the Roman system. The following example shows the way it worked: I steal your apple. You remain the owner. Based on your property right, you can claim back possession from under the *rei vindicatio* (= "vindicate" your property). Once I eat your apple, the *rei vindicatio* ceases to exist. The property right is lost with its substrate, and possession can no longer be returned. But the value I took from you by eating your apple can be recovered via the *condictio (furtiva).*[19]

---

15 This central thesis is based on Evans, A Treatise on the Law of Obligations, or Contracts, translated from Pothier, Vol. 2, 1806, pp. 328–331. Reprinted below p. 330.

16 *Condictio causa data causa non secuta,* D.12.4.; *condictio ob turpem vel iniustam,* D.12.5.; *condictio indebiti,* D.12.6. But the cases recited under the original heading of the *condictio sine causa* in D.12.7. also concerned flawed transactions.

17 Originally, the *condictio furtiva* (13.1.), but after the reception also the *condictio sine causa specialis* as developed by the Continental jurists.

18 Modern English law would not see that as unjust enrichment, Goff & Jones, Unjust Enrichment, 10th edn. 2022, 1–03–05; Burrows, A Restatement of the English Law of Unjust Enrichment, 2012, § 1 (3).

19 Under English law, the tort of conversion deals with both returning possession and accounting for the value. But under Roman law, a damages claim would not have brought back possession. Only the *condictio furtiva* could be used to recover either possession or the value taken – an exception made for practical purposes.

The ***actio de in rem verso*** (p. 131[20]) differed profoundly from the *condictiones.* The only common ground was the requirement of a benefit in the hands of the defendant ("enrichment"). Apart from that, it was not even an action in restitution. It did not result from a transaction *sine causa.* To the contrary, it was originally a claim to get paid for a contract of a family member from the *pater familias* as the "true" beneficiary – but only under the proviso that he actually benefitted. *That* was the function of the enrichment requirement in the *actio de in rem verso.*

The claim was designed to get around the "limited liability" of the *peculium,* just as piercing the corporate veil follows the pockets of shareholders of a company. The peculium was a separate fund of assets that enabled members of the household (typically sons or slaves) to trade on their own account despite being subject to the sole powers of the *pater familias.* The other party of the contract would normally bring the *actio de peculio* where enforcement was restricted to the *peculium.* In addition, that party could also proceed against the general estate of the *pater familias* under the *actio de in rem verso.* That claim was particularly useful if the peculium was exhausted ("nihil in peculio") because it allowed leapfrogging to the pockets of the *pater familias.*[21] But it was only available if the *pater familias* ("principal") had actually received a benefit from the dealings of family member ("agent").

Later, the *actio de in rem verso* was extended to "free" agents. As *actio de in rem verso utilis,* it now covered situations where a contract between an A and B produced a benefit for C. On grounds of having benefitted, C was deemed a "principal" and B his "agent", so that C became accountable to A for his profit. The **leapfrogging function** became the typical feature of the *actio de in rem verso* as opposed to the *condictiones.* However, some writers argued that the *actio de in rem verso* should be restricted to the insolvency of the agent because a general option to sue both agent and principal was overly beneficial.[22] This was not the pre-

---

20 In Germany, the term "*Versionsklage*" (= "version claim") became the standard translation for this Roman action. However, this was a misnomer because the word "versio" did not exist in classical Latin (Chiusi, p. 3 note 7). A fallacious term should not be transferred into English.

21 An open issue that was not resolved before Roman law had died out in Europe was whether the *actio de in rem verso* competed with the *actio de peculio* or whether it was barred before the peculium was exhausted. The latter view is reflected in the subsidiarity of the general enrichment claim of France and Italy.

22 Kupisch in Schrage (ed.), Unjust Enrichment, 2nd edn. 1999, p. 264 with fn. 114, citing J.A.T. Kind, Quaestiones forenses, 1792, vol 1, cap. 35: "Si quis igitur in ex meo per contractium tertii evadat locupletior, et tertius, qui mecum contraxit, non sit solvendo, contra eum, in cuius meum, licet mediate tantum versum est, in subsidium datur actio." [If, therefore, someone emerges from a third party's contract enriched by something that belonged to me, and the third party who contracted

dominant view at the time. But it became one of the two historic roots for the subsidiarity of the general enrichment claim.

France: Art. 1303–3 C.civ: "L'appauvri n'a pas d'action sur ce fondement lorsqu'une autre action lui est ouverte ou se heurte à un obstacle de droit, tel que la prescription." [The disenriched party has no action on this basis if another action is available to her or if she runs up against a legal obstacle, such as prescription.]

Italy: Art 2042 CC: "L'azione di arricchimento non è proponibile quando il danneggiato può esercitare un'altra azione per farsi indennizzare del pregiudizio subito." [The action for enrichment cannot be brought when the injured party can bring another action to obtain compensation for the harm suffered]. On this, see recently Corte di Cassazione, sezione III civile; ordinanza 20 febbraio 2023, n. 5222, Foro Italiano 3/2023, 719, 721.

Spain: Tribunal Supremo of 24/06/2020, STS 2072/2020 – ECLI:ES:TS:2020:2072, sub Cuarto, para. 11: "la acción de enriquecimiento deba entenderse subsidiaria, en el sentido de que cuando la ley conceda acciones específicas en un supuesto regulado por ella para evitarlo, son tales acciones las que se deben ejercitar y ni su fracaso ni su falta de ejercicio legitiman para el de la acción de enriquecimiento."

[The action for enrichment must be understood as subsidiary, in the sense that when the law grants specific actions in a case regulated by it to avoid it, it is these actions that must be exercised and neither their failure nor their lack of exercise legitimises the action for enrichment.]

In the course of time, the *actio de in rem verso* was extended to apply in simple two party situations, even though it was never restricted to those under the *ius commune.*[23] But the inclusion of two party situations produced a basic idea that became accepted in all civilian enrichment laws: I used my means for your benefit, so you have to account for it. Based on this rule, building on another's land calls as naturally for restitution as does cleaning another's windows. No request required, on closer looks not even an unjust factor.[24] As *Karl Solomo Zachariä* succinctly formulated:[25]

---

with me will not pay me, a subsidiary action will lie against him to share as much of mine as has been turned to his benefit.]

23 The early codifications followed that approach, see RG Judgement of 03.02.1880 IVa 502/79, RGZ 1, 159 on PrALR I 13 § 262. But see also p. 10.

24 This obsolete notion re-infiltrated German unjust enrichment in the 20th century as "Aufwendungskondiktion" and "Rückgriffskondiktion". It derailed the system of the *condictiones*-bases unjust enrichment in Germany, see p. 282.

25 Zachariä, Handbuch des französischen Civilrechts, Vol 3, 4th edn. 1837, § 576, at p. 430. On his influence on French unjust enrichment see below fn. 45. The lawyers of the ius commune had derived this rule from D.12.1.32. I will show in the main part why that may have been a misinterpretation.

"...dass derjenige, aus dessen Vermögen etwas in das Vermögen des Anderen verwendet worden ist, von diesem ... für die geschehene Verwendung Ersatz – mittels der *actio de in rem verso* – zu fordern berechtigt ist."

[... that the party from whose property[26] something has been used in the property of the other party is entitled to claim compensation from the other party ... for the use made by means of the *actio de in rem verso.* – Deep-L].

The third element of unjust enrichment was the **Pomponian principle of unjust enrichment.** Originally, it had not been a cause of action in its own right, neither in Rome nor in medieval Europe. But it was not merely the underlying rationale of the *condictiones* either. It soon became recognised as a moral principle of highest equity, almost akin to a religious commandment that resonated well both with scholastic and – later – natural lawyers. It took on the function of a "supereminent equity"[27] that could overcome strict law (*rigor iuris*) where medieval jurists thought apt. If written law left a party enriched at the expense of another, and this was deemed unjust, the higher principle was invoked to correct the law. For example, the mistake of law bar of the *condictio indebiti*, enacted in the later days of the Roman empire,[28] was overcome that way.[29]

Over time, the principle of unjust enrichment hardened into a **general enrichment claim.** When lawyers detect a general principle that is underlying a set of actions and remedies, the fundamental rule to **treat like cases alike** comes into play. This may either result in a sweeping clause for cases not covered by the specific actions or even in a general catch-all clause replacing the specific actions.

26 "Property" does not normally reflect "Vermögen" (wealth; fortune) accurately but seems apt here. "Aus dem Vermögen" means that A's money or money's worth is invested for the benefit of B, as will become clear in the following.

27 This very fitting term was coined by Lord Dunedin in *Sinclair v Brougham* [1914] AC 398, at 432: "The super-eminent equity was expressed by the Roman jurists in the brocard nemo debet locupletari jactura aliena."

28 CJ.1.18.10: Imperatores Diocletianus, Maximianus: "Cum quis ius ignorans indebitam pecuniam persolverit, cessat repetitio. per ignorantiam enim facti tantum repetitionem indebiti soluti competere tibi notum est." * diocl. et maxim. aa.Et cc. amphiae. * <a 294 d. v k. ian. cc. conss.>
[Where anyone, who is ignorant of the law, pays money which is not due, he cannot recover it; for you are well aware that only ignorance of fact confers the right to recover money which has been paid when it was not due.
Given on the sixth of the *Kalends* of January, during the sixth Consulate of the above-mentioned Caesars, 306.]

29 Kupisch in Schrage (ed), Unjust Enrichment, 2nd edn. 1999, pp. 241–243. Reference was also made to D.22.6.7. (Papinian 19 queast): "Iuris ignorantia non prodest adquirere volentibus, suum vero petentibus non nocet" [Ignorance of the law is not advantageous to those who desire to acquire it, but it does not injure those who demand their rights. Scott].

During the last bloom of Roman law in Europe (the *Usus Modernus Pandectarum*), prior to the codifications, we witness both. The legal authors assumed that the *condictio sine causa specialis*, was a sweeping clause to be applied in accordance with the Pomponian principle.[30] As *actio in factum ex aequitate*, it was a subsidiary claim that would only lie if no other remedy was available – the other of the two historic roots of the French and Italian rule of last resort. In addition to that, the *condictio sine causa generalis* was a catch-all-clause competing with every specific *condictio*. However, most jurists of the ius commune did not perceive the *actio de in rem verso* as manifestation of the Pomponian principle, but rather as a close relative of the *negotiorum gestio.*[31]

The evolution from moral principle to legal rule got derailed by the first wave of the great codifications. Neither the Preußische Allgemeine Landrecht of 1794 (ALR) nor the Code Civil of 1804 (C.civ) nor the Austrian Allgemeine Bürgerliche Gesetzbuch of 1812 (ABGB) contained a general enrichment claim based on Pomponius.[32] All three codes enshrined the *condictio indebiti*, making it the new paradigm of unjust enrichment. The Prussian and Austrian code also accepted the *actio de in rem verso,*[33] whereas France abstained ("cette action est inutile"[34]).

Against that background, the late German *Bürgerliche Gesetzbuch* of 1900 (BGB) could have rung the death knell of Pomponius in civil law jurisdictions. True, it contained a full-fledged law of unjust*ified* enrichment ("Ungerechtfertige Bereicherung"). But it had emphatically rejected both the principle of Pomponius and the *actio de in rem verso.*[35] Instead, the BGB only accepted the traditional

---

30 Kupisch in Schrage (ed.), Unjust Enrichment, 2nd edn. 1999, pp. 252–265.

31 von Tuhr, Actio de in Rem verso – zugleich ein Beitrag zur Lehre von der Geschäftsführung, 1895; Kupisch, Versionsklage, 1965, pp. 18 et seq.; id. in Schrage (ed.), pp. 249 .

32 Kupisch in Schrage (ed.), Unjust Enrichment, 2nd edn. 1999, p. 265–266. I beg to disagree with his view that the general enrichment claim was nevertheless part of Austrian and Prussian law of that time. While it is true that civilian codes cannot provide for everything, they surely aspire to contain the basic principles.

33 Both the Prussian and the Austrian provisions focussed on two party situations, see Kupisch in Schrage (ed.), Unjust Enrichment, 2nd edn. 1999, p. 268 (but note that the Reichsgericht ruled against restricting the *actio de in rem verso* to two party situations, RGZ 1, 159, see p. 138). The focus on two party claims coined Germanic legal systems' friendly attitude towards the above-mentioned "you benefit from my money"-rule as well as its hostility against leapfrogging.

34 Claude de Ferrière, La Jurisprudence du Digeste, Paris, 1677, annotations to D.15.3. Chiusi, p. 194.

35 Motive II, 829: "Die Vorschriften des Entwurfs über ... über die Schuldverhältnisse aus ungerechtfertigter Bereicherung (Kondiktionen) beruhen nicht auf dem ... allgemeinen Billigkeitssatze, Niemand dürfe sich mit dem Schaden eines anderen bereichern, noch auf dem ähnlichen, der Versionsklage des preußischen A.L.R. zugrundeliegenden Prinzipe..."

The provisions of the draft on ... on the obligations arising from unjustified enrichment (*condictiones*), are not based on the general principle of equity... that no one may enrich himself with

Roman *condictiones.* The codification was built on a new general principle that had been deduced by Friedrich Carl von Savigny from those *condictiones.* The Pomponian sentence had been discarded by Savigny as too vague and unfit for purpose on half a page (!) of his fundamental multi-volume treatise on Roman law in the 19th century.[36] Instead, he proposed a new, stricter enrichment principle. He concluded from the original case of the *condictio* (to demand repayment of a loan) that all *condictiones* were actions to reverse transfers of value.[37] The promise to repay the loan was substituted by the "unjust factors" of the *condictiones sine causa.*[38] As a consequence, German law of unjust enrichment was reduced to the *condictiones sine causa* that aimed to reverse a **direct shift of wealth** ("unmittelbare Vermögensverschiebung") that had taken place without a **legal ground** ("sine causa").

This innovative approach modernised enrichment law. It was no longer about unfair or "*unjust*" enrichment, like under the principle stated by Pomponius, but about "*unjustified*" enrichment. If values that were received without legal reason (*sine causa*) have to be returned, the existence of a legal reason will *justify* the benefit of the recipient. This rule can be explained as a direct consequence of party autonomy.[39] The codification of the §§ 812 et seq. BGB was based on this principle, and in the first half of the 20th century, it became the general test for all German enrichment claims. The commissioner Franz-Philipp von Kübel who was in charge with drafting the part on unjustified enrichment in the BGB adopted the new approach in his *Vorentwurf* (= "pre-draft"). He proposed seven specific condictiones that were performance-related and a sweeping clause to cover other "direct shifts

---

the loss of another, nor on the similar principle underlying the *actio de in rem verso* of the Prussian A. L. R. ..."

In the same sense already von Kübel, Motive Vorentwurf, p. 3.

36 Savigny, System des heutigen Römischen Rechts, Volume III, 1840, p. 451.

37 Savigny, System des heutigen Römischen Rechts, Volume V, 1841, pp. 511 et seq.

38 Savigny, System des heutigen Römischen Rechts, Volume V, 1841, p. 522 with reference to D.44.7.5.3. (Gaius 3 aur.) who focused on the *condictio indebiti:* "Is quoque, qui non debitum accipit per errorem solventis, obligatur quidem quasi ex mutui datione et eadem actione tenetur, qua debitores creditoribus: sed non potest intellegi is, qui ex ea causa tenetur, ex contractu obligatus esse: qui enim solvit per errorem, magis distrahendae obligationis animo quam contrahendae dare videtur." [Scott: He, also, who, through the mistake of the person who made the payment, received something to which he was not entitled, is bound as in the case of a loan, and is liable to the same action as that to which a debtor is liable to his creditor. It should not, however, be understood that he who is responsible in a case of this kind is bound by a contract; for anyone who pays money by a mistake does so rather with the intention of discharging an obligation than of contracting one.]

39 See below, pp. 18 et seq.

of wealth.[40] The *Erste Entwurf* (= First Draft) of the BGB, presented by the *Erste Kommission* (= First Commission), adopted this structure and merely reduced the number of the performance-related *condictiones* to five. However, the *Zweite Kommission* (= Second Commission) skipped the first draft and replaced it by a counter draft as basis of the §§ 812–822 BGB. The editorial purpose was to transform the principle of Savigny into one single catch all-clause that should head the chapter of unjustified enrichment and attach to every direct shift of wealth *sine causa.* This attempt was bound to fail – and eventually failed by the middle of the 20th century. It will be a central pillar of this book to show why this happened and how it could be avoided – otherwise, legal comparison would raise serious doubts about the viability of the general enrichment claim in England after its failure in Germany.

But irrespective of the predestined failure of its general enrichment claim, Germany never returned to Pomponius nor to the *actio de in rem verso.*[41] The only – indirect – concession of the codification to Pomponius and general equity had been the extension of the disenrichment defence to all *condictiones* (§ 818 III BGB). But the hostility towards the notion of a loose equitable remedy prevailed even here and German academics, led by *Werner Flume*, demystified, rationalised and considerably curtailed this so hard to grasp defence.[42] The gist of it being that the defendant must be kept to his spending choices (*Vermögensentscheidung*).[43]

Despite the afore-mentioned backlashes in all major codifications, the principle of unjust enrichment was not vanquished in civil law. It survived because it was resurrected by the Cour de Cassation. French jurists of the 19th century dearly missed the *actio de in rem verso.* Originally, they sought to "smuggle" the *actio de in*

---

40 § 27 Vorentwurf, picked up slightly modified in § 748 E I. The text is found below, at p. 20.
41 At least not openly. On closer looks, today's enrichment law relies on several outdated notions, most notably the two-party *actio de in rem verso* in the "Aufwendungskondiktion" and the "Rückgriffskondiktion" (see below, p. 21) and the principle "no benefit from a wrong" (Pomponius, D.50.17.206) as starting point of the "Eingriffskondiktion".
42 Flume, FS Niedermeyer, 1953, p. 103, at 154–155 [= Studien, p. 71–72].

By contrast, the jurisdiction of the Reichsgericht and the Bundesgerichtshof has always adhered to the view that equity governs the §§ 812 BGB more than other actions (BGHZ 55, 128 = NJW 1971, 609, 611: "Gebot der Billigkeit, dem das Bereicherungsrecht in besonderem Maße unterliegt" [The rule of equity, to which the law of enrichment is particularly subject]). This is seen particularly true for the disenrichment defence. In that respect, German judges accord with English judges, see recently *School Facility Managements Limited and others v Governing Body of Christ the King College and another* [2021] EWCA Civ 1053, paras. 34 et seq.
43 Flume, FS Niedermeyer, 1953, p. 103, at 154–155 [= Studien, p. 71–72]. See also Wilhelm, Rechtsverletzung und *Vermögensentscheidung* als Grundlagen und Grenzen des Anspruchs aus ungerechtfertigter Bereicherung, 1973; see also Goff & Jones, Unjust Enrichment, 10th edn. 2022, 4.34 et seq., 4.51 et seq.

rem verso into the Code Civil by arguing it was a consequence of an "abnormal" *gestion d'affaires* that had to be accepted as a non-written "supplement" of the express provisions in Art. 1372–1375 C.civ 1804. After this argument had encountered high profile criticism, the Cour de cassation changed the approach. In the arrêt Boudier of 1892, it introduced a general enrichment claim on the basis of the Pomponian principle as the new "cloak" to admit the *actio de in rem verso* to French law.[44] The general enrichment claim was derived from various specific actions and remedies in restitution scattered over the Code Civil of 1804. It was justified by the competence under Art. 4 C.civ. to close gaps in the law.[45] 124 years later, the development was perfected when the principle of unjust enrichment officially entered the revised Code Civil in Art. 1301 et seq.

Once the diverging developments concerning the principle of unjust enrichment in Germany and France have been brought to light, we recognise **two different answers to the stamp case** under the two paradigms of civilian enrichment law. To start with Germany:

> § 812 I 1 BGB: "Wer durch die Leistung eines anderen oder in sonstiger Weise auf dessen Kosten etwas ohne rechtlichen Grund erlangt, ist ihm zur Herausgabe verpflichtet."
>
> [Anyone who obtains something without legal cause through the performance of another or in any other way at the latter's expense is obliged to disgorge it to him.]

The wide wording covers the stamp case. The value increase is obtained by B at the expense of the misfortunate A. However, applying Savigny's modern principle it is obvious that there was **no shift of wealth.** Neither did A perform money or money's worth to B (*condictio indebiti*), not did B take money or money's worth from A (*condictio furtiva*). Even though German jurists of today do not apply § 812 I 1 BGB as a general enrichment claim with a "direct shift of wealth"- requirement any more, they would reach the same result by running through the specific *condictiones*, in particular the generally accepted cases covered by the sweeping clause for enrichments *in sonstiger Weise* (= "in any other way"), § 812 I 1 2. Alt. BGB. This would be argued as follows:

---

44 Cour de Cassation, Chambre des requêtes, 15 Juin 1892, Julien Patureau-Miran C. Boudier, D.P. 92.1.596. The Godfathers of the new enrichment approach of the arrêt Boudier were Charles Aubry and Charles-Frédéric Rau (p. 142). Their work was originally conceived as French translation of the German treatise on French private law by Zachariä (above p.8–9).

45 Kupisch in Schrage (ed.), Unjust Enrichment, 2nd edn. 1999, pp. 266–267 assumes, based on the corresponding provisions in Austria (§ 7 AGBG) and Prussia (§ 49 Einleitung ALR), that a general enrichment claim may have actually been part of Austrian and Prussian law. But this was never confirmed before courts and seems too bold a proposition, regarding the decades of contentious debate it took for the general enrichment claim to be admitted beyond the Code civil in France.

- There is no *Leistungskondiktion* under § 812 I 1 1. Alt. BGB because there is no performance by A.
- There is no *Eingriffskondiktion* under § 812 I 1 2. Alt. BGB because there was no wrong committed against A.
- There is no *Aufwendungskondiktion* under § 812 I 1 2. Alt. BGB because there is no voluntary investment by A.
- There is no *Rückgriffskondiktion* under § 812 I 1 2. Alt. BGB because A did not pay any debt of B.
- There is no exceptional *Direktdurchgriffskondiktion* under § 812 I 1 2. Alt. BGB because this is not a three-party-situation.

The **denial** of the stamp case is undisputed because German lawyers are safe in their knowledge that the Pomponian principle is not part of their unjustified enrichment. And this holds even true in the one case that arguably comes closest to granting an award in the stamp case: German law accepts claims in restitution for **enrichments** caused **by natural events.** A leading paradigm is the Roman *alluvio:* A flooded river washes away land of one which goes downstream and becomes adjacent to the land of another. According to the Roman jurist Ulpian, a *condictio* would lie to restore the value.[46]

Cases of enrichment by natural events have not played any role in practice, but they are unanimously approved in the German commentaries.[47] Other examples are a flock of sheep grazing off the pasture of the neighbour[48] or game moving from the hunting ground of A to that of B.[49] But even if we accepted those cases including the extremely dubious examples of the *alluvio* and the wildlife migration, the notable difference is the **shift** of wealth. The enrichment of B is always obtained by acquiring the substrate of A's property (or hunting right). Nature has taken value from A and given it to B. This differs from a mere causal link be-

46 D.12.1.4.2. (Ulpian libro 34 ad Sabinum): "Ea, quae vi fluminum importata sunt, condici possunt." See also Gaston Rau, p. 118; Zimmermann, p. 841 with fn. 48.

47 Staudinger/Lorenz, § 812 Rn. 22 et seq., 30; BeckOKBGB/Wendehorst, 1.8.2023, § 812 Rn. 30 and Rn. 121; Erman/Buck-Heeb, § 812 Rn. 82; NK-BGB/Prinz von Sachsen Gessaphe, § 812 Rn. 76; Koppensteiner/Kramer, Ungerechtfertigte Bereicherung, 2nd edn. 1988, p. 69.

48 NK-BGB/Prinz von Sachsen Gessaphe, § 812 Rn. 76. This is an ancient mishap that was already regulated in § 57 Code of Hammurabi: "If a shepherd have not come to agreement with the owner of a field to pasture his sheep on the grass; and if he pasture his sheep on the field without the consent of the owner, the owner of the field shall harvest his field, and the shepherd who has pastured his sheep on the field without the consent of the owner of the field, shall give over and above twenty GUR of grain per ten GAN to the owner of the field." Sourced from the Harper translation, https://en.wikisource.org/wiki/The_Code_of_Hammurabi_(Harper_translation).

49 BeckOKBGB/Wendehorst, 1.8.2023, § 812 Rn. 30.

tween getting poorer and getting richer, as in the stamp case or every time share prices rise or fall depending on a decrease or an increase of the interest rate. A mere causal link of enrichment and detriment will only suffice under the too wide Pomponian principle of unjust enrichment. Accordingly, the solution of the stamp case must be argued differently in France where the Pomponian principle has become the direct legal basis for the general enrichment claim.

Again, the wording indicates an enrichment claim of A against B. How could an award be denied in France? Since the true colour of French enrichment law is the *actio de in rem verso*, the first and foremost answer is that the stamp case does not concern any failed investment of A for the benefit of B, but an enrichment from an accident. Evidently, there is no leapfrogging involved either. However, the dismissal of the stamp case claim is more difficult to argue in France since the Pomponian requirements of "enrichissement" of one caused by the "detriment" of another directly translate into an award. The amalgamation of Pomponian unjust enrichment and *actio de in rem verso* blurred the profound doctrinal differences. This contradicts the clairvoyant demand of Marcel Planiol in the 19th century:[50]

> "Il y a un intérêt de premier orde a maintenir aussi pures que possible les notions scientifiques du droit. C'est le seul moyen de ne pas laisser acculer à des consequences inadmissibles, auxquelles on ne peut plus échapper que par des decisions contradictoires."
>
> [There is a vital interest in keeping the scientific notions of law as pure as possible. This is the only way of avoiding inadmissible consequences that lead to contradictory decisions.]

Disguising the *actio de in rem verso* under the veil of the principle of unjust enrichment has led to ambiguity. French jurists may on principle agree with Germans that unjust enrichment is not supposed to serve vague palm tree justice. Also, they have put safeguards in place to contain the reach of unjust enrichment, most notably the subsidiarity principle. But this is not a bar against the stamp case. It merely disguises the judicial discretion at work (below p. 23).

How is all this relevant for English unjust enrichment? The answer is that *Banque Financiére*[51] is the arrêt Boudier of English law. The House of Lords deduced the general enrichment claim from the various action and remedies in res-

50 D. P. 91.1.49 (annotation of Cour de cassation of 16 July 1890). In that passage, Planiol demanded a clear distinction between unjust enrichment and *negotiorum gestio* (in France: *gestion d'affairs*, Art. 1303-1-1303-5 C.civ 2016; previously Art. 1371-1375 C.civ 1804). His flamboyant critique paved the way to the famous arrêt Boudier of 1892. But the same clarity must be applied to unjust enrichment itself.

51 *Banque Financière De La Cité v. Parc (Battersea) Ltd and Others* [1998] UKHL 7

titution in a similar way as the Cour de cassation. In doing so, it also relied on the Pomponian principle. As shown above, Lord Clyde – in line with the majority of modern common lawyers – saw it at the heart of unjust enrichment.

The stupend consequence is that *Banque Financière* and later *Menelaou* allowed leapfrogging claims against indirect recipients that are so well known to French or Italian law but out of question for German law and completely at odds with English law that has hardly ever heard of, let alone desired any claim akin to the *actio de in rem verso. Banque Financière* even has a hundred years older French twin case![52]

There is a sound argument that English law chose an ill-fitting principle because "no benefit from another's detriment" is too wide and too vague. Germany has been there, and England might have to go there, too. At the heart of *Moses v Macferlan* were unjust factors that were directly transplanted from the corresponding *condictiones sine causa* into the English action of money had and received for the use of the plaintiff. Both the actio for money had and received and the old Roman form of action named *condictio* provided neutral legal bases to claim (back) money from another. By adopting the causes of action of the most prominent *condictiones sine causa,*[53] Lord Mansfield transplanted their characteristic feature into English law: a direct shift of value effected under flawed consent. That is why the standard argument that English law has not accepted the *condictio indebiti*[54] falls short. The "Mosaic *condictiones*" have shaped English law of unjust enrichment, whereas other civilian instruments like the general sweeping clause *condictio sine causa specialis,* the *actio de in rem verso* and the *negotiorum gestio* never played any role. Nor should Pomponius ever have.

This restriction to the *condictiones* is similar to the law of unjustified enrichment in §§ 812 BGB. The core cases were the same – and so is the underlying principle. That explains the amazing fact that English Courts developed the "direct shift of value" test a hundred and fifty years after Friedrich Carl von Savigny's "unmittelbare Vermögensverschiebung" (= "direct shift of wealth"). Conversely, applying the wrong principle can lead the law astray. Lawyers will not be able to "keep the scientific notions clean" and "avoid inadmissible consequences and contradictory decisions". This point will be underscored by reference to the hardly reconcil-

---

52 Cass req DP 89.1.393 (Crédit foncier v Arrazat).

53 The *condictio causa data causa non secuta* (failure of consideration); the *condictio indebiti* (= mistake); the *condictio ob turpem vel inustam causam* (illegality, oppression).

54 Recently reiterated in *School Facility Managements Limited and others v Governing Body of Christ the King College and another* [2021] EWCA Civ 1053, para 75 (per LJ Popplewell).

able cases of *Banque Financiere*[55] and *Swynson*,[56] *Menelaou*[57] and *Costello*[58], as well as the mystic decision of *Lipkin Gorman v Karpnale.*[59]

Would it have been wiser to follow the example of **US law** and **abstain from a general enrichment claim?** Prima facie, the answer seems to be yes. But as shown above, specific actions were the starting point of both Roman and English unjust enrichment. In the end, the principle of unjust enrichment overlaid them to produce the general enrichment claim. This is the logical consequence of the commandment to treat like cases alike. Caution against general claims is therefore not the (sole) remedy. It is not enough to frame "no benefit from another's detriment" as a moral principle that may explain rules of restitution but cannot be applied directly. The Third Restatement supports almost every specific claim or remedy in restitution with the argument that the defendant must not be unjustly enriched at the expense of the claimant. If this is true, why not in the stamp case? Apart from hiding behind the impermeable walls of judicial discretion, would American law have an answer to this?

The Third Restatement's numerous references to the principle not to be unjustly enriched from another shed light on its far bigger role under common law. The principle of unjust enrichment has inter alia been a normative vehicle for creating intellectual property rights in the INS case.[60] It is now widely used to explain a wide range of traditional legal instruments and remedies, like e.g. subrogation, contribution, following and tracing, constructive or resulting trusts, rescission etc. By contrast, codified systems do not have to justify the provisions of their codes other than by saying: This is enacted, so this is the law and we are bound to it. That narrows down the scope for a law of unjust enrichment from the outset. Specifically regulated issues like contribution, subrogation and rescission or their functional equivalents are not included, neither doctrinally nor on a philosophical level. This used to be different under the *ius commune* where unjust enrichment foundations had been discussed for many remedies in a similar way.[61]

---

55 *Banque Financière De La Cité v. Parc (Battersea) Ltd and Others* [1998] UKHL 7.

56 *Lowick Rose LLP v Swynson Limited and another* [2017] UKSC 32.

57 *Bank of Cyprus UK Ltd v Menelaou* [2015] UKSC 66.

58 *MacDonald Dickens & Macklin v Costello* [2012] QB 244.

59 *Lipkin Gorman v Karpnale Ltd* [1991] 2 AC 584.

60 International News Service v. Associated Press, 248 U.S. 215 (1918)

61 Cf. Antonin Pavlicek, Zur Lehre Von Den Klagen aus Ungerechtfertigter Bereicherung 1878, p. 2–3: "Ja man ging in der Anwendung des Satzes soweit, dass man ihn als allgemeines Rechtsprinzip darstellte, woraus in jedem Fall der Bereicherung des einen auf Kosten eines anderen, wo nicht aus einem besonderen Rechtsgrunde dem Verkürzten ein Rechtsmittel gegeben ward, eine subsidiäre Bereicherungsklage abgeleitet wurde. ... dass nach römischem Rechte aus diesem

The book will not deal with all the instruments that are viewed as enrichment-related by modern common law doctrine. But it must caution against "overloading" the principle of unjust enrichment. There are many legal tools in common law that seem perfectly justifiable without reference to unjust enrichment. For example, rescission is not based on a simple unilateral mistake. Thus, it *cannot* be an application of the principle of unjust enrichment.[62] The right to sue every joint debtor for the full amount serves the interests of the creditor. It is not designed as lottery to discharge other debtors. That is why the paying debtor can demand contributions from the others. The crutches of Pomponius should not be necessary to explain such rules in modern legal systems. This so much more since they have proven their subversive power to unravel the law throughout legal history.

To conclude: the mission of the book is **to rationalise unjust enrichment by demystifying the Pomponian principle of unjust enrichment** and present the **superior normative foundation** of the alternative system focussed on the **direct shift of value *sine causa***, as first laid out by Savigny. It will be shown that neither the *condictiones* nor *Moses v Macferlan* rest on the prohibition to benefit from another's loss. Rather, these claims refer to direct shifts of value and share a clear rationale that flows directly from party autonomy. *Samuel Stoljar* has said:[63]

> "Indeed a basic theme running through our law is that . . . *things or money cannot validly pass from one person to another without the former's sufficient consent* either before or after the event."

Add to this *Friedrich Carl von Savigny* who said:[64]

Billigkeitsprincipe nicht bloss das ganze Institut der Condictionen, sondern überhaupt alle jene Rechtsinstitute, welche die Rescission der Bereicherung des einen auf Kosten eines anderen bezwecken, abzuleiten seien."

["Indeed, one went so far in the application of the sentence that it was represented as a general principle of law out of which any enrichment at the expense of another, when no particular remedy based on a specific legal ground / reason was granted to that other party, a subsidiary enrichment claim was derived. ... that, pursuant to Roman law, from this principle of fairness, not merely the institute of unjust enrichment, but indeed all legal institutes are derived which serve the purpose of rescission of an enrichment at the expense of another."]

62 In the same sense, if from a different angle, see ALI, The Restatement of Restitution and Unjust Enrichment (Third), Vol 1, p. 480: "Rescission has sometimes been called "restitution" because is function is clearly to restore, but enrichment is not a requirement of the remedy."

63 Stoljar, Quasi-Contract, 2nd edn 1989, p. 6.

64 Savigny, System des heutigen Römischen Rechts, Vol. V, 1841, p. 523, referring to D. 12.6.26.12 (Ulpianus ad edictum). See also below pp. 101 and 233.

> "Ja sogar eine Arbeit, die geleistet wird, weil man dazu irrigerweise verpflichtet zu sein glaubte, kann die Kondiktion begründen, insofern sich die Arbeit auf einen bestimmten Geldwert zurückführen, also mit einer gezahlten Geldsumme vergleichen lässt."
>
> ["Indeed, even **works which were conducted because one erroneously believed an obligation to exist** to this effect can **give rise to a condictio**, insofar as the works were linked to a particular **pecuniary value**, which is to say that **they can be compared to a particular sum of money.**"]

Both statements combined, "money and property" in Stoljar's seminal sentence are replaced by "money and money's worth".

> **Money or money's worth cannot validly pass from one person to another without the former's sufficient consent.**

That rule explains the enrichment actions to recover direct shifts of value *sine causa* for both common and civil law. Vitiation or lack of consent *per se* commands the reversal of the transfer or the usurpation of the value. This is not contingent on any (mis)conduct of either party. The law simply corrects the wrongful state that it disapproves. Restitution springs directly from the flawed shift of value. Imagine it as that one moment captured by Michelangelo's "Godly spark": The payment, the conveyance of property, but also the haircut, the song of the singing flower, the use of the hired car or building, in short, **every performance of money or money's worth is a direct shift of value** from the provider to the recipient in the eyes of unjust enrichment, As the *Erste Kommission*, following *Franz Philipp von Kübel*, had proposed for the BGB,[65] restitution is restricted to the parties of the failed performance and to the money or money's worth transferred or taken.[66]

There is no "natural" transfer of value that exists independent of and may differ from the act of "performance". To assume otherwise was the very misconception that brought the direct shift of wealth approach in Germany down. To overcome this long-lasting error is a core argument of the main part. In a nutshell: The same natural act of painting a house can either be *one* performance = transfer of value (from the painter to the owner) or *many* performances = transfers of value (from an employee to his employer who is subcontractor to the main con-

65 Cf. the *condictio indebiti* under § 737 E I: "Wer zum Zweck der Erfüllung einer Verbindlichkeit eine Leistung bewirkt hat, kann wenn die Verbindlichkeit nicht bestanden hat, von dem Empfänger das Geleistete zurückfordern." [A person who has rendered a performance for the purpose of discharging a liability may, if the liability did not exist, reclaim from the recipient what has been rendered.]

66 For a performance-based approach under English law Stevens, The Laws of Restitution, 2022, p. 29 et seq., id. LQR (2018) 573.

tractor who has been charged by the tenant who was obliged to do so under his tenancy agreement with the landlord who may be owner on freehold or leasehold). Any search for a "natural" shift of value in this setting would be misguided. Thus, to state that this approach is wrong is correct[67] but does not disprove the shift of value approach because it misses its point.

But why then dissolve the requirement of a performance within the abstract concept of a shift of value at all? Would it not be enough to reverse failed performances? For 19th century Germany, the answer surely had to be no because of the above-mentioned cases of "taking value" (*condictio furtiva*). Moreover, recognising each performance as direct shift of value leads to the apt test: If objective value has been taken, it has to be restored to the person with whom the usurper should have bargained for the benefit, so to say: the "meant-to-be performance". Under English law, a similar notion is linked with Wrotham Park damages,[68] but in truth, it (also) belongs to unjustified enrichment. The main part will develop following equation: performance = direct shift of value = "meant-to-be performance". This will be the normative framework of true unjust enrichment. It will determine precisely where the actions should lie.

In the world of *Savigny*, restitution for unjust enrichment *sine causa* rested solely and unilaterally on the vitiation or lack of consent of the claimant. The vitiation of consent has been more precisely defined by the **failure of the purpose of a performance** under the approach adopted by *Franz Philipp von Kübel* and the *Erste Kommission*, as for example seen in § 737 E I:

> "Wer zum Zweck der Erfüllung einer Verbindlichkeit eine Leistung bewirkt hat..."
>
> [= A person who has rendered a performance for the purpose of discharging a liability].

The doctrinal and philosophical foundations of this approach reach back to the *ius commune*. They have been elaborated by the *Zwecklehre* (= doctrine of purpose):[69] *Nihil est sine ratione* = Nothing happens without a reason. There are prime reasons for people to make transfers to others, namely to acquire (*acquirendi causa*), to discharge (*solvendi causa*) and to make a gift (*donandi causa*). The law accepts the failure of these typical purposes of performances as ground for restitution, thereby distinguishing as irrelevant other motives and one-sided expectations.

Conversely, the achievement of the purpose circumscribes the **subjective side** of the concept of *Rechtsgrund* / *causa* (= legal reason). It validates the transfer for

67 Stevens, The Laws of Restitution, p. 35–36.

68 *Morris-Garner v One Step (Support) Ltd* [2018] UKSC 20.

69 See the account Ehmann, Zur causa-Lehre, JZ 2003, 702, a leading proponent of this school of thought founded by Hugo Kreß.

good. But it only relates to wilful transfers (= performances). They have a legal reason if their purpose is achieved. Then there can be no recovery. In addition, there also exists an **objective side** of the concept of *Rechtsgrund / causa.* While valid consent justifies every transfer, this does not mean that lack of valid consent will necessarily lead to restitution. The enrichment claim can also be defeated if there is an objective justification to uphold the enrichment.[70]

Once it is recognised how this system works, the reservations against the German "failure of basis" approach become invalid.[71] It is not up to the defendant to "justify" his enrichment. Under German procedural law, it is the task to the claimant to prove the requirements of his claim,[72] that is the lack or loss of the *Rechtsgrund/causa.* The claimant will have to make a case under one of the specific bases of a claim, e. g. the *condictio indebiti* for failure of the *causa solvendi* (§ 812 I 1 1. Alt. BGB), the *condictio ob rem* (§ 812 I 2 2. Alt. BGB) for failure of any other agreed purpose of his performance ect.

Against this background, the claim that German law does not require unjust factors proves more or less misconceived.[73] Admittedly, there is some truth to it in the fringe areas of the *Aufwendungskondiktion* and the *Rückgriffskondiktion.* But this is only because German post-war doctrine, in its exaggerated apostation from Savigny, has forgotten about the "no consent" requirement of the *condictio sine causa specialis* and fell back to the outdated notion of the *actio de in rem verso* in two party situations that simply stated: You have my money so you owe me. Contrast this to the original provisions of the pre-draft and the First Draft:

> § 27 Vorentwurf von Kübel: "Derjenige, aus dessen Vermögens etwas **ohne seinen Willen** in das Vermögen eines anderen gekommen ist, kann, wenn ein rechtlicher Grund hierzu von Anfang an nicht vorhanden war oder derselbe später weggefallen ist, von letzterem Rückerstattung verlangen."
>
> [The person from whose property something has come into the property of another **without his "will" (better: consent)** may, if a legal reason for this did not exist from the beginning or if this reason has subsequently ceased to exist, demand restitution from the latter.]

---

70 E. g. prescription, see Goff & Jones, Unjust Enrichment, 10th edn. 2022, 2.14. For the ius commune, see Hallebeek in Schrage (ed.), Unjust Enrichment, 2nd edn. 1999, p. 112–113, also referring to the similar concept of usucaption.

71 Paradigmatic Goff & Jones, 1–23 et seq., relating to the discussion – and rejection – of the Birksian absence of basis approach, see Birks, Unjust Enrichment, pp. 101 et seq, 129 et seq., inspired by Sonja Meier, Irrtum und Zweckverfehlung, 1999.

72 As to the general maxime *ei incumbit probatio qui dicit* Stevens, The Laws of Restitution, p. 353.

73 Correctly Stevens, Restitution, p. 105.

§ 748 E I: "Derjenige, aus dessen Vermögen nicht kraft seines Willens oder kraft seines rechtsgültigen Willens ein anderer bereichert worden ist, kann, wenn hierzu ein rechtlicher Grund gefehlt hat, von dem anderen die Herausgabe der Bereicherung fordern."

[The person from whose property another person has been enriched **not by virtue of his will (consent) or by virtue of his legally valid will (consent)** may, if there was no legal ground / reason for doing so, demand the restitution of the enrichment from the other person.]

The oblivion of the "no consent"-requirement is the only justification to the claim that there are no unjust factors in Germany. It is an error that German doctrine made in the 20th century and has preserved to date.[74] This mistake cannot be held against the flawless system devised by Savigny and von Kübel who presented a coherent and persuasive normative foundation of unjust enrichment. Under their regime, the claimant must show either the failure of the purpose of his performance or the lack of consent to an act of taking value from him, in other words: the existence of unjust factors giving rise to a restitutionary claim. The book will argue that this system can provide guidance for English law because its parameters have been imported by *Moses v Macferlan.* For example, a payment on a non-existing debt will always trigger a claim in unjust enrichment not because there is any "absence of basis", but because the consideration (= the discharge of the debt) has totally failed (see pp. 98, 108 and 272).

Under this modern, party-autonomy based view of unjust(ified) enrichment, the vague language of general enrichment claims loses any threat to legal certainty. No strange cases about gains and losses from stamps, capital markets, flooded rivers or climate change come up. By contrast, the "super-equitable" principle not to profit from another's harm surely sounds fair and nice. But it is at odds with modern ideas of personal freedom. In a market economy, one's gain will always be another's loss.[75] The times when this was held unjust are long gone. Back then, peripatetic thinkers also believed that every asset under the sun had one just and fair price.

It is doubtful whether "no benefit from another's harm" can be accepted as moral principle in our modern world at all. But it is certainly not fit for direct application as legal rule. This is what Savigny said. It is what the Continental legislators in the 18th and 19th century had recognised. It is confirmed by the stamp case. It is supported by profound analysis of the implications Pomponius has caused over time, mainly in France. The common law has a proud history of consulting legal

74 For the criticism see Schall, Leistungskondiktion und Sonstige Kondiktion auf der Grundlage des einheitlichen gesetzlichen Kondiktionsprinzips, 2003, pp. 83 – 91.

75 For this argument see *Savigny*, System des heutigen Römischen Rechts, Volume III, 1840, p. 451.

comparison.[76] It cannot be satisfied with having overlooked the massive reservations that civil law has been harbouring against Pomponius and the alternative explanation of unjustified enrichment put forward by Savigny.[77]

The moral appeal of Pomponian unjust enrichment became the vice and virtue of unjust enrichment, the reason for its stunning success as well as the source of deep-rooted problems that are epitomised by the stamp case. The principle was supposed to serve (a) as the rationale of legal actions and (b) as a "supereminent equity" to overcome strict law at the same time. But there exists an **eternal antagonism of law and equity**, known to all civil and common lawyers and aptly described in the Latin phrase "summum ius, summa iniuria". The principle of unjust enrichment wants to play on both sides of that perennial battle field. This is the **paradox of unjust enrichment** that surfaces wherever the law follows Pomponius. He drowned enrichment law in a "Nebelmeer" (= sea of fog). Take France and Italy where the enrichment claim is subsidiary, that is to say it only applies where no other action or remedy is available. In the stamp case, this rule is useless because it is obvious that there is no other remedy at hand. Since the legislator can always decide to leave a loss where it falls, "casum sentit dominus", the true task is to divine if the lack of a remedy is to be accepted as the law, or if it shows a gap in the law that needs to be closed.[78] Following Pomponius, the answer is removed from the law and delegated to the wisdom of the judges.[79] We are left to accept what is decreed by the oracles of the law.

---

76 For a glorious example see the causation issue in *Fairchild v. Glenhaven Funeral Services Ltd* [2002] UKHL 22 where it was clear several parties had breached their duties, but unclear which breach eventually caused the harm.

77 One reason may be that John P. Dawson, Unjust Enrichment, 1951, p. 90 with fn. 83 relied on the work of Moritz Wellspacher, Versio in rem, 1900, cf. Kupisch in Schrage (ed.), Unjust Enrichment, 2nd edn. 1999, p. 268 with fn. 9. Wellspacher viewed the *actio de in rem verso* as enrichment claim in accordance with Pomponius, as was the law in France. But both instruments had been rejected by the BGB and called outdated and obsolete by the First Commission (Motive II, 829). Dawson simply picked the wrong source.

78 *Dargamo Holdings Ltd and another v Avonwick Holdings Ltd and others* [2021] EWCA Civ 1149, para. 75 (per LJ Carr), citing Frederik Wilmot-Smith, Contract and Unjust Enrichment in the High Court of Australia, 136 LQR (April) 2020, 196–201: ""Since a court can… always let gains and losses lie where they fall, there is never a true "gap": it follows that there is only ever a "gap" if (for independent reasons) one concludes that there should be a restitutionary claim."

79 For a recent example from practice, on a particular aspect (the relation between the defences of change of position and counter-restitution) *School Facility Managements Limited and others v Governing Body of Christ the King College and another* [2021] EWCA Civ 1053, at para 85 (per LJ Popplewell): "I am inclined to think that there can be no inflexible rule that one defence trumps the other, and that the defences can be applied on a case-by-case basis to produce a just outcome on

For sake of accuracy, it is fair to add that it was not the principle of Pomponius, but the language of Lord Mansfield that first laid the ground for the suspicion that English law of unjust enrichment or restitution (as it then was) might be a loose equitable concept.[80] But this assumption has never been well founded. It can be explained and rejected, starting with the fact that *Moses v Macferlan* was decided at law. The dissolution of the boundaries between law and equity only became inevitable when the law adopted the equitable brocade "nobody must benefit from another's detriment" as a rule and built unjust enrichment on it.

English law denies this.[81] But this is a *protestatio facto contraria.* There is no persuasive doctrinal foundation for such a statement, starting from the fact that the supporting references go straight back to *Lipkin Gorman* where Lord Goff elaborated at length on the equity and fairness of enrichment and disenrichment.[82] In truth, English law has adopted a general enrichment claim on the same equitable terms as France. It accepts "no benefit from a wrong" as rationale like France (and the US). It has awarded claims against remote recipients like France. But England did not even introduce the French subsidiarity rule.[83] How could it deny the stamp case? Which rule would it conjure up against the claimant? Oh, what a tangled web we weaved because Pomponius hath us deceived!

particular facts, which may vary greatly. Some change of position defences may be capable of being analysed in terms of enrichment or disenrichment, others may not."

80 Cf. Eg *Roxborough v Rothmans of Pall Mall Australia Ltd* (2001) 208 CLR 516, Rn 83–89 (per Gummow J).

81 *Dargamo Holdings Ltd and another v Avonwick Holdings Ltd and others* [2021] EWCA Civ 1149, para. 59: "An unjust enrichment claim is not based on a wide ranging and open-ended assessment of fairness (or justice) in the round. Rather, it is a common law remedy requiring a claimant to make out an established category of "unjust factor" in order to trigger the claim." For the chain of references see *School Facility Managements Limited and others v Governing Body of Christ the King College and another* [2021] EWCA Civ 1053, para 33: *HMRC v The Investment Trust Companies* [2017] UKSC 29, para 39 (per Lord Reed), referring to Lord Goff of Chieveley in *Lipkin Gorman v Karpnale Ltd* [1991] 2 AC 548, 578.

82 E.g. *Lipkin Gorman v Karpnale Ltd* [1991] 2 AC 548, 579: "The answer must be that, where an innocent defendant's position is so changed that he will suffer an injustice if called upon to repay or to repay in full, the injustice of requiring him so to repay outweighs the injustice of denying the plaintiff restitution." In the same vein *School Facility Managements Limited and others v Governing Body of Christ the King College and another* [2021] EWCA Civ 1053, at paras. 83–85, assimilating counter-restitution to equitable sett-off.

83 *Dargamo Holdings Ltd and another v Avonwick Holdings Ltd and others* [2021] EWCA Civ 1149, para. 75 (per LJ Carr).

II The (unorthodox) methodology of the book – exemplified by mistaken services

The case for the book is herewith made. The main part will deliver the foundation of the claims made in this introduction. It uses unorthodox methodology to show its points: the comparative and historical and doctrinal analysis of a legal principle. The aim is "helping towards a deeper, a more intellectual understanding of the law".[84]

For that purpose, the book illuminates the roots of unjust enrichment, but it is not addressed to legal historians because it does not attempt to analyse the past itself. The reason is that unjust enrichment has been shaped by what the elders thought and not by what they should have thought. That is why the book relies on the existing, profound accounts[85] and puts the emphasis on how the Roman roots have been connected and modified over the centuries in order to the present laws. Also, the book uses legal comparison, but it is not a standard comparative law book[86] because it is not primarily interested in the solutions of cases like paying another's debt or building on another's land.[87] For the book, there is no satisfaction in showing that *Banque Financière* or *Menelaou* would technically not be subject to §§ 812 BGB because there are no invalid contracts involved. But it is interested in showing how the wrong principle helped to "smuggle" leapfrogging into English law. Finally, the book makes use of doctrinal arguments. But it is less interested how well any given court decision sits within its national framework. Common law knows authority and persuasive authority, but it is for common lawyers to judge whether authority is persuasive.[88] The book merely likes to offer some tentative conclusions by regarding the different bases on which French, German and English law have erected the edifices of their law of unjust enrichment.

---

84 Cp. Stoljar, *Mistake and Misrepresentation: A Study in Contractual Principles* (1986), Preface.
85 Most notably the preparatory works for the BGB by Franz Philipp von Kübel, Motive zum Vorentwurf, and the Erste Kommission, Motive zum Ersten Entwurf; further Eltjo Shrage (ed.), Unjust Enrichment, 2nd edn. 1999; Reinhard Zimmermann, The Law of Obligations, 1996, pp. 834 et seq.
86 As to legal methodology of comparative law in general, see Basil Markesinis, Foreign Law and Comparative Methodology: A Subject and a Thesis, 1997.
87 To that end, see e. g. v.Bar/Swann, Principles of European Contract law: Unjustified Enrichment, 2010; Johnston & Zimmermann, Unjustified Enrichment – Key issues in Comparative Perspective, 2002; Zimmermann, Unjustified Enrichment – the Modern Civilian Approach [1995] 15 OJLS 403.
88 Cp. *Great Peace Shipping Ltd v Tsavliris (International) Ltd* [2002] EWCA Civ 1407 disposing of *Solle v Butcher* [1950] 1 KB 671.

The example of mistakenly delivered services ("cleaning another's shoes"[89]) demonstrates how the book argues. Legal history offers not only one, but even two explanations for the solution under civil law doctrine. The first is linked to the *actio de in rem verso* and has been introduced above. My money came to you, so you owe me. An alternative, more accurate explanation can be derived from two basic features of the Roman *condictiones* as elaborated by Savigny. First, the *condictiones* were triggered **unilaterally** by the flawed or non-existent consent of the claimant. Second, they covered **both the transfer of money and money's worth** (services). Therefore, mistakenly cleaning another's shoes or windows justifies an enrichment claim principally in the same way as a mistaken payment. The objective value of the service must be returned, subject to the defence of disenrichment / change of position that will depend on the existence or not of a spending choice that must be upheld.[90] The different approach of English doctrine is likewise rooted in legal history. The unilateral unjust factors of the "Mosaic *condictiones*" were only implanted into an action to recover money transferred to the defendant. The recovery of services was governed by *quantum meruit.*[91] This action has always been contingent on a prior request by the defendant. The reason was principally sound. Services cannot be returned in kind. You cleaning my window cannot be returned by me cleaning your window. That is why restoration equates to payment. But payment for services requires a prior agreement because human conduct cannot unilaterally be imposed on others as valuable (or else any annoying busker in the underground could sue the passengers).[92] Conversely, if the human conduct is requested, *quantum meruit* will reward it even if no specific fee was agreed. The same rule exists in German law: § 612 BGB for services (*Dienstvertrag*) and § 632 BGB for services to an end (*Werkvertrag*). However, this is apparently a contractual claim based on the assumption that the normal fee was agreed. By using *quantum meruit* instead of money had and received as basis for enrichment claims concerning services, English law erected a bar to the recovery of misdirected services that does not exist for the recovery of misdirected payments.

---

89 *Taylor v Laird* (1856) 25 LJ Ex 329, 333 (per Pollock C B); Stevens, The Laws of Restitution, pp. 5 and 37–38. The issue is discussed under the heading of "free acceptance" and is of relevance both as a test for enrichment and as unjust factor, cf. further Goff & Jones, 10th edn. 2022, 4–53 at seq and Chapter 17; Burrows, "Free Acceptance and the Law of Restitution" (1988) 104 LQR 576; Mead, "Free Acceptance: Some Further Considerations" (1989) 105 LQR 460.

90 In that case by what English enrichment lawyers would call subjective devaluation, cf. e.g *Benedetti v Sawiris* [2013] UKSC 50, para. 15–26 (per Lord Clarke).

91 Baker, in Schrage (ed.), Unjust Enrichment, 2nd edn. 1999, Unjust Enrichment, pp. 35–41.

92 Cf. Stevens, The Laws of Restitution, pp. 46–48.

Legal history explains why the restitution of services requires a request in England, but not on the Continent. But it can do more. It also indicates that a general enrichment claim based on the Pomponian principle would have to lie regardless of the request. The reason is that objective value in the form of a payable service (window cleaning) has been shifted.[93] The transfer by the claimant was flawed by an unjust factor (mistake), and the defendant would thus unjustly be enriched at the expanse of the service provided. Alternatively, if Pomponius was rejected, Savigny would say the same. The principle to return failed performances demands the same outcome for money and services – unless there was a sound justification to treat money differently from money's worth. The Romans thought not, and Savigny thought not. But that is not to say that they were right. If a transfer of money is flawed by unjust factors, it can actually be undone by an enrichment claim. By contrast, as has just been shown, the return of a service is impossible. Work done cannot be "unworked". The return of the value means paying for the service like under a contract. From that angle, it is defensible to demand a request to procure a factual meeting of minds[94] and to bar recovery otherwise.[95]

This example is paradigmatic for the way in which the book pursues its agenda. It does not seek to give a final answer to the services case, but only to deepen the understanding. The law of unjust enrichment sprang from the same roots, but wears different looks dependent on the choices jurisdictions have made over time, like e. g. whether or not to adopt the principle of unjust enrichment as general enrichment claim, the *actio de in rem verso* or the *negotiorum gestio.* Within these frameworks, the evolution of unjust enrichment followed the laws of logic because the law is reason – albeit confined by path dependence. I am however convinced that the laws of logic demand the abdication of Pomponius and the enthronement of Savigny's narrow enrichment for English law. Then we can all be the *Wanderer über dem Nebelmeer.*[96]

93 Rightly Burrows, The Law of Restitution, 3rd edn. 2011, pp. 46–47.

94 For the relevance of the factual agreement see *Dargamo Holdings and others v Avonwick Holdings and others* [2021] EWCA Civ 1149 at para 132 (per LJ Carr), following Frederick Wilmot-Smith in *Replacing Risk-Taking Reasoning* 127 LQR (October) 2011, 610, at p. 620–623.

95 Adamantly in that sense Stevens, pp. 37–38.

96 The "Wanderer above the Sea of Fog" is a famous painting by Caspar David Friedrich that I have always felt captures very well the situation of unjust enrichment lawyers, https://de.wikipedia.org/wiki/Der_Wanderer_%C3%BCber_dem_Nebelmeer. According to the caption in the Times, 12. January 2024, it is "arguably the most famous painting Germany has produced.", https://www.thetimes.co.uk/article/caspar-david-friedrichs-art-lost-in-a-sea-of-woke-fog-t6mfh5zbk

III An aside on terminology

Law is based on language. The language must be exact and precise. Legal terminology is vital to create, understand and explain the law. However, since the days of Babel, language also erects barriers and impedes mutual understanding. This is burdensome for comparative law, particularly if comparative law is perceived with *Konrad Zweigert* as a "universal method of interpretation".[97] The book will therefore have to thread on a thin line. It will carefully try to avoid the establishment of new terminology and doctrinal categories that are not accepted yet. But it will and must also abstain from some established labels that it cannot subscribe to. This namely concerns the widespread distinction between civilian *unjustified* enrichment and English *unjust* enrichment. This taxonomy disguises the recognition that the enrichment laws of England and Germany are closer to each other because of their narrow view of unjust enrichment ("direct shift of value") than the civilian jurisdictions of France / Italy / Spain that adhere to wide Pomponian enrichment *that* would rather be called "unjust" even though France now speaks of *enrichissement injustifié*. To underpin this point, the book generally speaks of unjust enrichment and only occasionally of unjustified enrichment, which is the exact translation of the legal term that the German Code uses when speaking of the actions pursuant to the §§ 812 BGB (*ungerechtfertigte Bereicherung*). Also, the translation of *Rechtsgrund* with legal ground, even though widely accepted, seems less accurate than legal reason (p. 62).

Another issue of high relevance for the book is the distinction of strict law and equity. It is in the flesh and blood of every common lawyer. But the difference between strict legal rules and vague equitable remedies (*rigor iuris* vs. *aequitas*) was equally well known to Roman law and the ius commune.[98] Indeed, the law of unjust enrichment has been caught between strict law and equitable remedy for the better part of its existence in both civil and common law. That is the reason for much of the debate and has constantly fuelled the fierce criticism of the concept of unjust enrichment. The book will reiterate this observation in the course of reverse engineering again and again. The reader will recognise when terms like "equity" / "equitable" refer to the English law of equity and when they refer to

---

97 Zweigert, Rechtsvergleichung als universale Interpretationsmethode, RablesZ 15 (1949/50), 5. On taxonomy of comparative unjust enrichment see Helen Scott, in Bant/Barker/Degeling, ch8, pp. 145 et seq.

98 See only Savigny, System, Vol. V, § 218 Arten der Klagen. Iudicia, arbitria. Stricti juris, bonae fidei", at pp. 101 et seq. However, the Roman meanings must not be equated with today's taxonomy even though they clearly infused it. Take for example the distinction between "arbitrary" and "bona fide" actions.

the general concept of higher law correcting strict law for considerations of fairness ("aequitas" / équité") that is of particular relevance for civil lawyers when interpreting general clauses like "bonae mores" or "good faith".[99]

Finally, the introduction made clear that the book perceives the principle on which the "true" narrow English enrichment is based as the same as the one that had been deduced by Savigny from the Roman *condictiones.* However, there is a slight difference in terminology that must be observed. Savigny spoke of the *unmittelbare Vermögensverschiebung. Vermögen* means the compound value of all your assets. The French word is *patrimoine.* There is no perfect equivalent to it in English. The "assets" is a term often used synonymously. But it does not cover the same ground because it refers to the individual rights as such, not to the sum of their value including intangible values like goodwill. The former, not the latter is shown in the traditional balance sheet. The English word closest to *Vermögen* seems to be wealth. Accordingly, the book uses it to describe Savigny's theory and to mark the distinction from English unjust enrichment while still expressing that his principle is equivalent, even though it was less precisely formulated.

On closer looks, a shift of wealth is not necessarily a shift of value – and vice versa. In the stamp case, wealth is shifted because the same event sinks the "market value" of A and raises that of B. But no value was shifted. Conversely, a haircut leaves the balance sheets of hairdresser and customer untouched. But the service rendered was money's worth, so value was shifted. The more precise term is therefore the shift of value / *Wertverschiebung.*[100] This was also meant by Savigny. Evidence is his equation of transfers of money and money's worth.[101] Unfortunately, the less precise term *Vermögensverschiebung* caused two fallacies: (a) that unjust enrichment only referred to shifts of assets (which a haircut is not) – *gegenständliche Vermögensverschiebung,*[102] and (b) that enrichment claims would always have to follow the actual transfer of the asset – i.e. in the example of bank transfers from the customer's bank to the recipient. These two misinterpretations eventually brought Wilburg and von Caemmerer to discard Savigny's principle. A major con-

99 On this in general see e.g. Sirks/Mausen (eds.), Aequitas, équité, equity, 2015.
100 In a similar vein, but restricted to performances, MünchKomm/Schwab, Vol 7, 9th edn. 2024, § 812 mn. 47: *(zweckgerichtete) Hingabe von Vermögensvorteilen = (purposive) surrender of benefits*; BeckOK/Wendehorst, 1.5.2024, § 812 mn. 38: *Verschaffung eines Vorteils = providing a benefit.*
101 *Savigny,* V, p. 523; see in more detail below, pp. 233–234. Cf. further pp. 263–264.
102 *Ellger,* Bereicherung durch Eingriff, 2002, p. 58: "Die strikte Einhaltung dieses Erfordernisses schließt den Bereicherungsausgleich aus, in denen es um die Bereicherung aus nichtkörperlichen Gegenständen geht"; in the same sense *Maximilian Wolf,* Bereicherungsausgleich bei Eingriffen in höchstpersönliche Rechtsgüter, 2017, pp. 112.

tributory factor is the formulation of Savigny's original principle not being exact enough. It was aggravated by adopting the even less precise term "at the expense" in the final version of § 812 BGB. The book will elaborate this important point in great detail below, pp. 247 et seq.

B Main Part

I The central role of the enrichment principle for shaping the law

Today, all major jurisdictions contain enrichment laws. Nevertheless, there is remarkable divergence regarding the existence or not of a general claim to reverse unjust(ified) enrichment. France, Italy and the UK have it, the US and – despite the apparent wording of § 812 BGB – Germany do not. In jurisdictions that have a general enrichment claim, there is a follow up distinction. The general claim may come as a "small" sweeping clause that merely supplements the set of more specific enrichment actions (like e.g. *condictio indebiti*). Such sweeping clauses are typically reduced to a subsidiary remedy of last resort (France, Italy, Spain).[103] Alternatively, the general enrichment claim may replace the specific enrichment actions which are immersed into one single catch-all cause of action. That was the original, now abandoned concept of the German BGB. It appears to be the law of England, too.

This picture replicates multiple times if we take into account smaller jurisdictions like e.g. Switzerland (general sweeping clause), Austria (no general enrichment claim), Greece (general sweeping clause) or Scotland (no judicial acceptance of a general enrichment claim yet). These differences lead back to the quest for the principle of unjust(ified) enrichment. They mirror the struggle to define a uniform enrichment principle and cast it into a general enrichment claim. The principle of unjust(ified) enrichment is the key to understand the law. This is true for civil law, but also for common law, notwithstanding the scepticism expressed by Gummow J in *Roxborough v Rothmans* (at [72]):

> "Considerations such as these, together with practical experience, suggest caution in judicial acceptance of any all-embracing theory of restitutionary rights and remedies founded upon a notion of "unjust enrichment". To the lawyer whose mind has been moulded by civilian influences, the theory may come first, and the source of the theory may be the writing of jurists not the decisions of judges. However, that is not the way in which a system based on case law develops; over time, general principle is derived from judicial decisions upon particular instances, not the other way around."

With respect, this statement does not seem entirely persuasive with regard to the evolution of unjust enrichment. Both civilian unjustified enrichment and English

103 See pp. 162–168.

https://doi.org/10.1515/9783110754452-002

unjust enrichment emerged from a general principle that was extracted from existing cases and, over time, hardened into law. As will be shown, the main problem of the development in unjust enrichment was not to find a principle at all, but to find the correct principle or "maxim", as Christopher St. German named it in *Doctor and Student*, p. 59:[104]

> "And such maxims be not only holden for law but also other cases like unto them and all things that necessarily followeth upon the same ... And therefore most commonly there be assigned some reasons or consideration why such maxims be reasonable and ought reasonably to be observed as maxims to the intent that other cases like may the more conveniently be applied to them and judged by the same law."

Both civil law and common law must respect a legal principle once it is established. Like cases must be treated alike. This has always been the mantra in the teaching of Peter Birks. And rightly so. The ensuing observations will confirm that the hardening of a principle into law, while surely rare, is as familiar to common law as it is to civil law.

1 From principle to law – general observations

Legal principles are the underlying of legal rules. But they are not normally legal rules themselves. Most principles are too abstract, vague and "lofty" to be directly applied in order to solve cases. Take for example "pacta sunt servanda", "volenti non fit iniuria" or "neminem leadere". As Coke said with regard to the principles of natural law: "Such generalities never bring anything to a conclusion."[105]

However, sometimes such principles can be sufficiently substantiated to be applied as legal rules. This is a necessary process to develop the law because "common law is extended by equity[106] that whatsoever falleth under the same reason will be found the same law."[107] Common lawyers may still speak of a principle, or

104 As to the context within the conception of common law that was shared by Coke, Davies and others cf. Postema, Classical Common Law Jurisprudence, Part 1, 2 OUCLJ (2002), 155, at pp. 171–172.
105 Coke, The Reports of Sir Edward Coke, in Thirteen Parts, Moore Dublin 1796, 6th Report, Preface.
106 To be understood as analogy, see Postema, Classical Common Law Jurisprudence, Part I, 2 OUCLJ (2002), 155, at. p. 171.
107 Thomas Hedley in his famous speech before parliament, 85 Proceedings in Parliament 1610, edited by Elisabeth Read Foster (1966), Yale University Press, at p. 176.

of a doctrine,[108] or a maxime.[109] German lawyers would generally prefer the term "Prinzip". The taxonomy used in English academic writing is not consistent. Often, the terms principle and doctrine seem to be used synonymously to simply describe the general claim in unjust enrichment under the four-stage-test.[110] Those works usually miss the core of the issue: the way that the two competing principles underlying unjust enrichment shaped the requirements of the general action. That is why they cannot explain the deep-rooted doctrinal differences between narrow and wide enrichment.[111] In a more fitting manner, Lionel Smith and Samuel Beswick speak of "Unjust Enrichment: Principle or Cause of Action?"[112] However, that seems to presuppose that "principle" *only* means the underlying, generic rationale.[113] This understanding would not reflect the (rare) process where such principles harden into law, i. e. are directly applied. It is exactly this process that the book

---

108 *Prest v Petrodel Resources Ltd* [2013] UKSC 34 spoke of the "doctrine" of piercing the veil. See also *Orakpo v. Manson Investments Ltd* [1978] AC 95 (HL), at 104 (per Lord Diplock): "My Lords, there is no general doctrine of unjust enrichment recognised in English law."

109 Christopher St. German, *Doctor and Student,* p. 59 (see above p. 31).

110 Cf. e. g. Graham Virgo, The Principles of the Law of Restitution, 3rd edn. 2015, Chapter 3: The Principle of Unjust Enrichment, pp. 45–61; W. *Friedman. 'The Principle of Unjust Enrichment* in English Law' (1938) 16 Can Bar Rev 243 (Part I) and 365 (Part II); Charles Manga Fombad, The principle of unjust enrichment in international law, The Comparative and International Law Journal of Southern Africa Vol. 30, No. 2 (JULY 1997), pp. 120–130; Rai, Ruchir, The Principle of Unjust Enrichment (April 16, 2012). Available at SSRN: https://ssrn.com/abstract=2353502; more aptly titling e. g. H Gutteridge and RJA David, The doctrine of unjustified enrichment (1933–1935) 5 CLJ 204–229.

111 Take e. g. W. *Friedman. 'The Principle of Unjust Enrichment* in English Law' (1938) 16 Can Bar Rev 243, 253–254 (simply equating German and French unjust enrichment): "The German Law of unjust enrichment is codified in arts. 812–822 of the Civil Code and therefore did not have to be freely developed by law Courts as in France. It is all the more interesting to see that the results achieved are largely the same." Misfortunately, this broad brush approach is sometimes still adopted in comparative law cf. eg. "Developments in the Law: Unjust Enrichment" 133 HarvLR [2022] 2062, at 2079 with fn. 21; Gordley in Bant/Barker/Degeling, p. 41.

112 Lionel Smith and Samuel Beswick, Unjust Enrichment: Principle or Cause of Action? (September 29, 2021). Restitution 2021, pp. 1.1.1–1.1.15 (Vancouver: Continuing Legal Education Society of British Columbia, 2021), Available at SSRN: https://ssrn.com/abstract=3942665. In a similar vein Zimmermann, p. 852: "What was the general principle that had justified the granting of specific enrichment actions ...?"

113 As to that widespread understanding cf. e. g. Pascal in the beginning of his book review THE DOCTRINE OF UNJUSTIFIED ENRICHMENT IN THE LAW OF THE PROVINCE OF QUEBEC [McGill Legal Studies No. 2], by George S. Challies. Wilson and Lafleur, Limited, Montreal, 2d ed. 1952, pp. xii, 216] in the Louisiana Law Review Volume 14 | Number 3, April 1954 – https://digitalcommons.law.lsu.edu/lalrev/vol14/iss3/30:

"The principle of unjustified enrichment, that no one should be enriched at the expense of another without justification, is the foundation for much that is in any system of law, for it is a corollary of the virtue of justice."

is interested in. The decisive point is to understand that a generic normative principle can turn into hard law and become directly applicable. Even if no generally accepted taxonomy describes this rare process, it is clear it exists.

Instances of the process of a principle becoming directly applicable law can be found in civil law as well as in common law. One example well known to comparative lawyers is French tort law where the principle of "neminem laedere" has been cast into a general tort claim. Any person who *causes damage to another intentionally or negligently* will be liable to compensation.[114]

> Art 1240 C.Civ. (= Art 1382 old C.Civ): Tout fait quelconque de l'homme, qui cause à autrui un dommage, oblige celui par la faute duquel il est arrivé à le réparer.
>
> [Any act of man, which causes damage to another, obliges the person by whose fault it was done to repair it. – according to Deep-L).

An example from common law world is the English tort of negligence. It was cast into its current shape by *Donoghue v Stevenson.*[115] Prior to this landmark case, there were only scattered cases of liability for negligent acts. The law was uncertain. Hardly reconcilable cases stood in the way of a clear rule. This changed when Lord Atkin developed the liability tests of reasonableness and foreseeability for acts that harmed others. The process has later been described by Lord Reid in the case of the useless Borstal boys:[116]

> About the beginning of this century most eminent lawyers thought that there were a number of separate torts involving negligence each with its own rules, and they were most unwilling to add more. They were of course aware from a number of leading cases that in the past the Courts had from time to time recognised new duties and new grounds of action. But the heroic age was over, it was time to cultivate certainty and security in the law: the categories of negligence were virtually closed. ... In later years there has been a steady trend towards regarding the law of negligence as depending on principle so that, when a new point emerges, one should ask not whether it is covered by authority but whether recognised principles apply to it. *Donoghue* v. *Stevenson* [1932] AC 562 may be regarded as a milestone, and the well-known passage in Lord Atkin's speech should I think be regarded as a statement of principle. It is not to be treated as if it were a statutory definition. It will require qualification in

114 Contrast however Germany that preferred to create three more specific headings of liability: The violation of certain "absolute" rights or goods like life, body, health, freedom, property ("Rechtsgutsverletzung") under § 823 I BGB, the violation of laws designed to protect another ("Schutzgesetzverletzung") under § 823 II and, as a "small sweeping clause", the intentional and immoral causation of harm to another ("Vorsätzliche sittenwidrige Schädigung") under § 826 BGB. In that case, "neminem leadere" is not directly applicable but serves as an overarching moral principle.
115 *Donoghue v Stevenson* [1932] AC 562.
116 *Home Office v Dorset Yacht Co Ltd.* [1970] UKHL 2.

> new circumstances. But I think that the time has come when we can and should say that it ought to apply unless there is some justification or valid explanation for its exclusion.

The observations of Lord Reid can be generalised. *Banque Financière* is the *Donoghue v Stevenson* of unjust enrichment. Since that decision, unjust enrichment has given rise to a remedy in restitution unless there is some justification no to do so. There is a test for liability (the four-stages-test) to be passed.

> Cf. e.g. *Benedetti v Sawiris* [2013] UKSC 50, [2014] AC 938, at para. 10:[117] " When faced with a claim for unjust enrichment, a court must first ask itself four questions: (1) has the defendant been enriched? (2) was the enrichment at the claimant's expense? (3) was the enrichment unjust? (4) are there any defences available to the defendant?

But following Lord Reid, this is not to say that the courts are strictly bound by that test like they were by an Act of Parliament. Rather, they have the power to develop case by case exceptions from the general rule if there is a valid justification.[118] To do so, it is indispensable to know the exact content of the principle. This cannot be an easy task for the common law, bearing in mind that the issue has haunted civil law for centuries and the debates have provided more than one answer.

2 The enrichment claim: From principle to law – and back?

Unjust enrichment is paradigmatic for an evolution from principle to law. This is true for both civil law (France) and common law (England). But in a unique contrast, it is also paradigmatic for the failure of an evolution from principle to law. This is also true for civil law (Germany) and common law (US).

---

117 Cf. further *Barton v Morris* [2023] UKSC 3, at para. 77 (per Lady Rose) and at para. 228 (per Lord Burrows); *Investment Trust Companies v Revenue and Customs Comrs* [2017] UKSC 29; [2018] AC 275, paras 24, 39–42; *Samsoondar v Capital Insurance Ltd* [2020] UKPC 33, [2021] 2 All ER 1105, paras 18–20; *Dargamo Holdings Ltd v Avonwick Holdings Ltd* [2021] EWCA Civ 1149, [2022] 1 All ER (Comm) 1244), paras 51–63 (per LJ Carr).

118 Cp. *Dargamo Holdings Ltd v Avonwick Holdings Ltd* [2021] EWCA Civ 1149, [2022] 1 All ER (Comm) 1244), at para 56 (per LJ Carr): "Originally this four-stage approach was considered to be rigid. Each question was to be applied uniformly in individual cases (see *Banque Financière de la Cité v Parc (Battersea) Ltd* [1988] UKHL 7; [1999] 1 AC 221 (at 227)). However, more recently the courts have cautioned against an inflexible approach (see for example *Swynson Ltd v Lowick Rose Llp* [2017] UKSC 32; [2018] AC 313 ("*Swynson*") at [22]). As Lord Reed stated in *ITC* at [41]: '...the questions are not themselves legal tests, but are signposts towards areas of inquiry involving a number of distinct legal requirements.'

The principle of Pomponius turned to into a general enrichment claim in France, Italy and Spain. It even became codified in Italy and France. The result is a wide enrichment claim that has two distinctive features. It addresses remote recipients because it embraces the *actio de in rem verso* (pp. 131–191). And it is an equitable remedy of last resort with the power to overcome strict law (p. 9).

By contrast, Germany rejected both Pomponius and the *actio de in rem verso.* Instead, Savigny developed an alternative principle that took the stage and turned into law, too.[119] It formed the general enrichment claim in § 812 I 1 BGB. But this enrichment claim was narrow because it was restricted to "direct shifts of wealth" and did not address remote recipients. It was *not* conceived as an equitable remedy that lay in the discretion of the judge ("Billigkeitsrecht"). The demise of the Pomponian principle in Germany and other late Codes (e.g. Switzerland, Greece). split the civil law world into two halves.

At first, Savigny succeeded where Pomponius had failed. But then, the newly found general enrichment failed, too. Following the works of *Walter Wilburg* and *Ernst von Caemmerer*, it was replaced by the modern German *Trennungslehre* (pp. 254–261). Together with the general claim, the uniform principle was vanquished.

A similarly ambivalent picture emerges under common law. The principle of Pomponius was first recognised in the US. The First Restatement of Restitution, published by the ALI in 1937, accepted the prevention of unjust enrichment as cornerstone of American law. But the underlying principle never matured into a general enrichment claim. This failure is in stark contrast with UK common law where unjust enrichment was recognised much later but eventually produced a general enrichment claim in *Banque Financière* (1998).

The development in England is of utmost interest. This is obviously, but not only, so because the emergence of a new law of unjust enrichment is a singularity that is bound to attract attention by comparative private lawyers. It takes us on an imaginative journey in a time machine back to the old days of the civilian *ius commune* when Pomponius started to take over unjust enrichment.

But even more intriguing is the result. England produced a strange hybrid between French and German enrichment law. Like French enrichment law, it is based on the principle of no benefit from a loss. The general enrichment claim is therefore wide and can reach out to remote recipients. But unlike in France, it is not an equitable remedy of last resort but an action of strict law. There is no rule of sub-

119 Zimmermann, pp. 872–873 and 887–891. See below, pp. 230 et seq.

sidiarity.[120] Moreover, the requirement of a "direct shift of value" is equivalent to Savigny's direct shift of wealth (on the precise terminology see pp. 29–30).

This prelude shows the complexity of the tasks ahead. Unjust enrichment is accepted by the courts of England. But it is also harshly criticised. One would like to know: Does the positive evolution of the general enrichment claim in France, Italy and Spain confirm the English way. Or does the failure of not one but even two enrichment principles and their general claims in Germany indicate that English law is doomed? The answer is as complex as the comparative outlook indicates.

3 The proposed answer: a general enrichment claim reduced to direct shifts of value

The book will propose a narrow concept of unjust enrichment for England. The general enrichment claim can be handled if applied in accordance with the principle of "direct shift of value". That unites English unjust enrichment and German unjust enrichment. It brings to an end what was already inherent in the two equivalent concepts of failure of consideration and failure of purpose. As Ibbetson rightly said:[121] "This idea of consideration is English lawyers' analogue of the civilian idea of *causa*, and its application could produce very similar results to the civilians' ... *condictio indebiti.*"[122]

It must be noted that in recent times, the traditional term "failure of consideration" has been replaced by "failure of basis" in England.[123] We will come back to that in more depth below (pp. 87–92). Suffice to say here that the confusion with the notion of consideration as requirement for the formation of contracts is not to be feared. [124] Rather, it confirms the analogy to *causa* that has the same double meaning in civil law.[125] This duplication rests on the similar function: consideration makes the promise binding and the performance permanent. Civil

---

120 Cp. the Court of Appeal in *Dargamo Holdings Limited v Avonwick Holdings Limited* [2021] EWCA Civ 1149, at paras. 75–76 (by Lady Justice Carr).

121 Ibbetson in Schrage (ed.), at p. 140. See also below p. 70.

122 The notion of failure of purpose can also explain restitution of payments on non-existing debts, thus dispensing from the need to show mistake, see p. 98 and pp. 268–270.

123 Cf. e.g. *Barton v Morris* [2023] UKSC 3, at paras. 231–232 (per Lord Burrows); *Dargamo Holdings Ltd v Avonwick Holdings Ltd* [2021] EWCA Civ 1149, [2022] 1 All ER (Comm) 1244, at paras. 77–80 (per LJ Carr).

124 Contrast *Barton v Morris* [2023] UKSC 3, at paras. 231 (per Lord Burrows): "The terminology of failure of consideration invites confusion with consideration as a requirement for the formation of a contract; ..."

125 Albers/Patli/Perrouin-Verbe (eds.), Causa contractus, 2022.

law has dropped the former, but not the latter function of *causa*. According to the *Zwecklehre* (*causa*-doctrine), the failure of the *causa acquirendi* is one of only three primary purposes[126] of performances the failure of which triggers restitution. If this is true, **all performance-based enrichment claims rest on qualified consent.**

Two obvious objections against the strict reduction to direct shifts of value can be raised. Why rely on Savigny even though he failed at home? Why not choose the French enrichment claim instead which is alive and kicking in France and elsewhere? The rejection of these objections requires a structured argument that is not easily accessible and must therefore be explained in advance. The crucial point is that Savigny's principle explains both the Roman *condictiones* and the English claims in restitution after *Moses v Macferlan.* His explanation allows to understand the rationale of unjust enrichment as "repair works" for value transfers that violate party autonomy.

Dargamo Holdings Ltd v Avonwick Holdings Ltd [2021] EWCA Civ 1149, at para. 52 (per LJ Carr): The purpose of the claim is to correct normatively defective transfers of value, usually by restoring the parties to their pretransfer positions (see *Menelaou v Bank of Cyprus Plc* [2015] UKSC 66; [2016] AC 176 (at [23]) and *Investment Trust Companies v HMRC* [2017] UKSC 29; [2018] AC 275 ("*ITC*") (at [42])

The prospective harmony of English and German unjust enrichment is based on the fact that Lord Mansfield imported the unjust factors of the most important *condictiones*, and that Savigny formulated a better principle than Pomponius had done. From the same roots spring the same trees.

Still, the failure of Savigny in Germany must be explained. It will be explained by a fallacy that started as a "technical error" in an ill-advised and subsequently half-abandoned attempt to produce a general enrichment claim for all actions in restitution. This has led the interpretation astray (pp. 242–261).

By contrast, the general enrichment claims of France or Italy cannot be called into the witness box to speak in favour of English unjust enrichment. The first reason is that the Pomponian principle gives rise to an equitable remedy at the discretion of the judge. The air of higher (Godly) justice appealed to legal philosophers and theologists ("Iure naturae aequum est..."). But it blurred the rationale of unjust enrichment and made it look like a vague and loose remedy prone to "well-meaning sloppiness of thought."[127] It was (ab)used to correct the strict law

126 The other two being *the causa solvendi* and the *causa donandi*, see pp. 271–272.
127 Originally coined by Scrutton LJ in *Holt v Markham* [1923] 1 K.B. 504, at p. 513, the term became a code word for unjust enrichment critics like e.g. Peter Watts, "'Unjust Enrichment' – the Potion that Induces Well-meaning Sloppiness of Thought", *Current Legal Problems*, Vol. 69, No. 1 (2016), 289.

("rigor iuris") where lawyers thought apt.[128] Therefore, it had to be strictly contained in order not to undermine the strict law. This has been achieved in France, Italy and Spain by the subsidiarity principle. However, English law does not understand unjust enrichment as an equitable remedy but strict law.

> *Barton v Morris* [2023] UKSC 3, at paras. 231–232 (per Lady Rose): "The analysis proposed by Mr Barton appears to be at base, an appeal to what Lord Reed deprecated in Investment Trust Companies v Revenue and Customs Comrs [2017] UKSC 29, [2018] AC 275, para 39 as a claim based on perceived requirements of fairness applied on a case-by-case basis (see also the authorities to similar effect in Dargamo paras 60 onwards). I would reject that analysis and hold that the claim in unjust enrichment also fails."
>
> Further authorities cited by LJ Carr in Dargamo stem from Australia: *Pavey & Matthews Pty Ltd v Paul* (1987) 162 CLR 221 at 256–257 (per Deane J): "To identify the basis of such actions as restitution and not genuine agreement is not to assert a judicial discretion to do whatever idiosyncratic notions of what is fair and just might dictate..."
>
> *David Securities Pty Ltd v Commonwealth Bank of Australia* (1992) 175 CLR 353, at 379: "Accordingly, it is not legitimate to determine whether an enrichment is unjust by reference to some subjective evaluation of what is fair or unconscionable. Instead, recovery depends upon the existence of a qualifying or vitiating factor such as mistake, duress or illegality."

Since unjust enrichment is not seen as an equitable remedy, any subsidiarity rule is rejected.[129] Notwithstanding that the power of subsidiarity rules must be challenged on principle anyway (pp. 162–168), this excludes a valuable judicial tool that France, Italy and other jurisdictions have at hands to curtail unjust enrichment and prevent ludicrous claims.

The second reason is that the principle of Pomponius was not introduced in France on its own merits (that have always been questionable) but as a much-needed new cloak for the *actio de in rem verso utilis* that allowed enrichment claims against remote recipients. The original line of cases of the 19th century were students who derived benefits from their private education by teachers whom the bankrupt parent(s) could not pay afterwards (see below p. 140). But English law never relied on direct authority from the Roman sources. Nor did it have

---

128 Cf. e. g.: pp. 122, 124–127, 127–130; Zimmermann, pp. 873–874, 876, 878. For a modern variation of this function Jan Smits, The Principle of Unjust Enrichment and Formation of Contract: The Importance of a Hidden Policy Factor, European Review of Private Law (2006) pp. 423–435 in a paper written in honour of Eltjo Schrage to whose fundamental book *Unjust Enrichment* this book is particularly indebted.

129 *Dargamo Holdings v Avonwick* [2021] EWCA Civ 1149, at paras. 75–76. But contrast "Developments in the Law: Unjust Enrichment" 133 HarvLR (2020) 2062, at 2078 as to diverging tendencies in the US. But cf. also Baker in Schrage (ed.), at p. 52, mentioning ancient "English versions" of subsidiarity rules in English law that never made it into modern times.

any comparable line of cases to be furnished with a coherent doctrinal explanation retrospectively. Quite to the contrary, it was only the introduction of "no benefit from a loss" that opened the door for enrichment claims against remote recipients. *Banque Financière* immediately produced a twin case to a French *actio de in rem verso* case of 1871.[130] For a variety of reasons, such claims militate against basic principles of private law – unless they are restrained to gratuities like those sanctioned by the *actio Pauliana.* This principle has always held **remote recipients of gratuities** to account if their benefit was received at the expense of another.

To support these arguments, we will first look at a rough sketch of the evolution from principle to law under civil and common law. We will then introduce all Roman bases of civilian enrichment law and link them to today's laws. We will start with the *condictiones* to show where they accord with and where they diverge from English law of restitution after *Moses v Macferlan* (1760). A major difference between the *condictiones* and English unjust enrichment can be explained by the fact that Lord Mansfield did not import the dubious *condictio sine causa* (see pp. 103–118) that served as catalyst for the general enrichment claim in civil laws. That is why the general principle took much longer to emerge in England.

After the *condictiones*, we will look at other Roman law institutions that have shaped civilian unjust enrichment: the *negotiorum gestio* (p. 121) and the *actio de in rem verso* (p. 131). The focus will be on the role of the principle of unjust enrichment in this process. It took on the function of a super-equity to trump any harshness of the strict law as tradited in the Digest. But this corrective function as "higher law" clearly clashes with the (later) role of the Pomponian sentence as principle of all *condictiones* and general sweeping clause for cases not explicitly covered. The *condictiones* have always been strict law actions[131] – just like the action for money had and received.

After the review of the Roman bases, we will learn about the evolution in France. The reference to the old cases will underpin the thesis that French lawyers merely used Pomponius to "smuggle" the general *actio de in rem verso utilis* into the Code civil. Other cases will show the dangers of the vague principle not to benefit from another's loss. The attempt to defuse this problem via a subsidiarity rule will be questioned.

The next step is to introduce the diverging development in Germany. We will see in great depth how Savigny extracted the direct shift of wealth from the *condictiones* in the Digest, how Franz Philipp von Kübel picked up and refined the notion to propose a law of unjust enrichment, how this was adopted by the First Com-

---

130 The Crédit foncier case, Cass req DP 89.1.393. See pp. 145–152.

131 Savigny, System des heutigen Römischen Rechts, Vol. V, p. 106; Zimmermann, p. 853.

mission but dropped by the Second Commission, and most importantly, how Savigny's theory gave us the key to the true rationale of unjust enrichment and how German lawyers threw this key away and kept unjust(ified) enrichment locked up in the prison of legal uncertainty.

We will constantly contrast the irreconcilable results achieved under a general claim based on "no benefit from a loss" under English law with the clear-cut solutions provided by a strict direct-shift-of-value-approach.

II How the principles form unjust enrichment – the emergence of general enrichment claims

The following passage will first present an overview of the evolutions of civilian and common law enrichment in a nutshell. The starting point of the evolution was the same in civil law and common law. Unjust enrichment began with a "marriage of cause and action". Both Roman law and English law had "neutral" forms of action to claim money from another. Here the *condictio*, there the *indebitatus assumpsit*. Over time, these actions became linked to causes of action in restitution: the *condictiones causa data causa non secuta* and *indebiti* of civil law were mirrored by the action for money had and received in case of mistake or failure of consideration (pp. 72, 97). Lines of cases built up and sparked the search for an underlying principle. But they did so in very different ways at very different times.

1 The long and winding road to civilian enrichment law

a) The development until the first codifications

Civil law starts with the Digest, and so does unjustified enrichment. This is therefore where the observations begin. The development of the *condictiones* prior to the Digest, in the classical period of Roman law, remains a subject of legal history that may be of interest to some but does not further the purposes of this book.[132] The Digest contained following *condictiones* based on causes of action in restitution:

- The condictio causa data causa non secuta (D.12.4.)
- The condictio ob turpem vel iniustam causam (D.12.5.)

132 As to this cf. e.g. Zimmermann, pp. 838–857; Liebs, The History of the Roman condictio up to Jusitinian, in MacCormick/Birks (eds.), The legal mind – essays for Tony Honoré (1986) 163; Saccoccio, Si certum petetur. Dalla condictiones dei veteres alle condictiones giustinianee, 2002. See also below, pp. 58 et seq.

- The condictio indebiti (D.12.6.)
- The condictio furtiva (D.13.1)

The Digest also contained the *condictio sine causa* (D.12.7.) and the Pomponian sentence (D12.6.14 and D.50.17.206). The chapter of the *condictio sine causa* served as a kind of catch-all heading to collect cases that could not clearly be attributed to the specific *condictiones.*[133] It contained only four references, none of which dealt with the cases that were classified as *condictio sine causa* (*specialis*) in later times.

The sentence of Pomponius overarched the *condictiones* under the Justinian Code. It is the originator of unjust enrichment. As Werner Flume put it:[134]

> "Das Kondiktionsrecht der Justinianischen Kompilation steht unter dem Gedanken der Bereicherungshaftung. Der Satz von D.50.17.206: *iure naturae aequum esse neminem cum alterius detrimanto fieri locupletiorem,* ist die Signatur des justinianischen Kondiktionsrechts."
>
> [The Justinian compilation's law of *condictiones* is based on the idea of liability for enrichment. The sentence of D.50.17.206 ... is the signature of Justinian law of *condictiones.*

However, it must be understood that the Pomponian sentence was not the basis of an action itself.[135] Nor did it subject all *condictiones* to a general defence of disenrichment.[136] These were developments that materialised centuries later. In the Justinian Code, the sentence merely stated a generic moral principle that was understood as the rationale of the *condictiones.*[137] Wolfgang Ernst has astutely described the effect that inserting this generic moral principle had on the traditional *condictiones.*[138]

> "Nachdem die Gesetzgebung Justinians die römischen Kondiktionen mit einem gleichsam naturrechtlichen Bereicherungsverbot überwölbt hatte, konnte die Handhabung der Kondiktionen von dem sie begleitenden "Prinzip" des Bereicherungsverbots nicht unberührt bleiben."
>
> [After Justinian's legislation had overarched the Roman *condictiones* with a prohibition of enrichment under natural law, as it were, the handling of the *condictiones* could not remain unaffected by the accompanying 'principle' of the prohibition of enrichment. – based on DeepL]

---

133 Zimmermann, p. 856. This function continued over time, cp. the §§ 23–27 in Chapter IV. of the *Vorentwurf* of the BGB by Franz Philipp von Kübel that was named "Rückforderung wegen grundlosen Habens" (= restitution for having without reason).
134 Flume, FS Niedermeyer, 1953, 103, at p. 129.
135 Zimmermann, p. 852 and 873.
136 Flume, FS Niedermeyer, 1953, 103, at p. 129.
137 Zimmermann, pp. 851–854.
138 Ernst in Flume, Studien, Einleitung, p. 5.

The principle formulated by Pomponius was however much more than just the "underlying" of the *condictiones sine causa.* It was also used to explain specific solutions. One illuminating example of this explanatory function ascribed to the prohibition of unjust enrichment was the first recital of the Pomponian sentence in the Digest, i. e. the reference in D.12.6.14.[139] It has been assumed that the reference had been inserted to explain the solution in the antecedent passage of D.12.6.13.1. In this passage, it was stated that a minor who had taken up a loan and paid it back after acquiring legal capacity cannot recover the repayment (even though the loan had been invalid at the time):[140]

> D.12.6.13.1. (Paulus ad Sabinum): Item quod pupillus sine tutoris auctoritate mutuum accepit et locupletior factus est, si pubes factus solvat, non repetit.
>
> ["Moreover, where a ward borrows money without the authority of his guardian, becoming more wealthy thereby, and pays the same after he reaches puberty, he cannot bring an action for its recovery." Scott]

From a modern day perspective, the solution could have well been explained as a ratification of the prior contract by the minor after his coming of age.[141] But it *was* explained by the prohibition of unjust enrichment because recovery of the loan repayment would have revived the unjust enrichment of the *pupilllus.*[142] This passage is so much the more of interest because enrichment claims against minors are one of the two core cases (the other one being invalid gifts between spouses) where the disenrichment defence has always been applied under Roman law and where it was justified due to the lack of a spending decision.[143]

The explanatory function[144] of the Pomponian principle is a characteristic feature that promoted its rise over the centuries. It has already been well understood

139 D.12.6.14 (*Pomponius libro 21 ad Sabinum):* "Nam hoc natura aequum est neminem cum alterius detrimento fieri locupletiorem." (for the translation see above in the Introduction).
140 Hallebeek in Schrage (ed.), at p. 63 – 64.
141 Cp. § 108 Abs. 3 BGB: "Ist der Minderjährige unbeschränkt geschäftsfähig geworden, so tritt seine Genehmigung an die Stelle der Genehmigung des Vertreters." [If the minor has acquired full legal capacity, his or her authorisation shall take the place of the authorisation of the representative. Deep-L]. It must be noted that under Roman law, impuberes acquired some legal powers despite not having full legal capacity yet.
142 Hallebeek in Schrage (ed.), at p. 63 – 64: The basis for this assumption was the usage of the explanatory conjunction "nam" (= for/because) in D.12.6.14.
143 Cf. Flume, FS Niedermeyer, 1953, 103, at pp. 124 et seq. = Flume, Studien, at pp. 45 et seq. on the deductions for rationale and scope of the disenrichment defence.
144 Zimmermann, p. 873 speaks of a "formative force behind a variety of rules and institutions of positive law".

by the medieval glossators[145] and became a recurring pattern that was used in many other cases. On the one hand, it was a welcome tool to explain many unspecified references scattered across the Digest that simply said that "a *condictio* would lie" to grant recovery in this or that case. On the other hand, and more importantly, it was even used as a driver to overcome "inconvenient" rules of strict Roman law, thus creating the air of unjust enrichment as equitable remedy that prevails over strict law ("rigor iuris"), e.g. with a view to building on another's land and officious intermeddling. The man to be named here foremost is Martinus Gosia (p. 125).

The analysis by the glossators marked the beginning of unjust enrichment.[146] Originally, the Digest had merely assigned a limited role to the *condictio sine causa* and the Pomponian sentence. But both rose to prominence after the reception of Roman law in medieval Europe. Over time, a growing number of jurists conceived the principle itself as the justification for granting the remedy.[147] They identified the sentence of Pomponius as the principle of the *condictio sine causa* that they had found in the Digest. It was applied as the basis of the *condictio sine causa* (*specialis*).[148]

But the success of Pomponian sentence rested on a broader basis. As a high moral principle of general equity, it resonated well with Canon lawyers and (later) natural lawyers in the wake of enlightenment (most notably Hugo Grotius[149]). The theological doctrine of restitution (*Lehre von der Restitution*) demanded restitution as a moral duty to God to make good injustice.[150] According to Nils Jansen, the Canon law doctrine became the second root ("zweite Wurzel") of unjust enrichment.[151] Against this background of broad acceptance, the uniform enrich-

---

145 Hallebeek in Schrage (ed.), p. 64, referring inter alia to the Azo Portius' Apparatus ad D.50.17.206, Biblioteca Vaticana vat. Lat. 966: Si pupillus mutuam acceperit pecuniam et locupletior ex ea factus, soluat, non repetit. "Nec enim est equum ipsum cum damno alterius locupletari ut supra de condict in 1. Naturaliter (D.12.6.13.1.) et 1. Nam hoc (D.12.6.14)..."

146 Cf. Ernst, in Flume, Studien, Einleitung, p. 5; Jansen, AcP 216 (2016) 112, 132 et seq.

147 Hallebeek in Schrage (ed.), at p. 64.

148 *Glück*, Die Pandecten nach Hellfeld, Vol. 13.1, p. 185–186; Jansen, AcP 216 (2016), 112, at p. 139.

149 Hugo Grotius, De iure belli, II, III, §§ 2–12. Cf. Zimmermann, pp. 885–886 arguing that he was the first proponent of a general enrichment claim. However, he failed to convince the Natural Law Codifications.

150 Cf. E.g. Petrus Lombardus, Senetntiae Lib. IV, dist. 15, cap. 7 nr. 9; Thomas Acquinas: Summa Theologiae, II-II, q 62; Schrage and Nicholas in Schrage (ed.), p. 12; Hallebeck in Schrage (ed.), pp. 59–60; Weinzierl, Die Restitutionslehre der Frühscholastik, 1936.

151 Jansen, AcP 216 (2016) 112, pp. 135–138; sceptical however Schrage and Nicholas in Schrage (ed.), p. 12: This Canon law concept of restitution however is of a definitely distinct nature from the Civil law concept.

ment principle seemed well equipped to harden into law. But the process stalled when the first codifications emerged. The reason was the flip side of its appeal as higher law. Such lofty principles have the potential to stir up strict law and run a coach and horses through legal certainty. That primeval conflict lies at the heart of the legal order. Even if it is true that "equity shall prevail", this must not result in arbitrary palm tree justice.

Faced with the conflict at hand, the first jurisdictions that subscribed to the new idea of national codifications opted for restraint. Neither the Prussian Allgemeine Landrecht of 1794 nor the French Code Civil of 1804 nor the Austrian Allgemeine Bürgerliche Gesetzbuch (ABGB) of 1812 enshrined a general enrichment claim. Instead, they contained the clearly defined (and confined) *condictio indebiti.*[152] However, these first Codes also contained several provisions that circumscribed specific cases of the *actio de in rem verso* (p. 137). This held at least the door open for the later acceptance of the general principle, as happened decades later in France.

b) Germany: From Pomponius to Savigny

Nineteenth-century-Germany went further and rejected Pomponius outright. It closed the door once and for all. The starting point was the great work of Friedrich Carl von Savigny: *System des heutigen Römischen Rechts* where he delivered a profound doctrinal analysis of Roman law. His programme can be described as "back to the sources". He disregarded the centuries of writing by the glossators, post-glossators and the jurists of the ius commune.[153] Savigny only considered the original Pandects, i.e. the part of the Corpus Iuris Civilis that contained the collection of legal opinions of classical Roman jurists. Even though this collection had been assembled by the compilators of emperor Justinian, he saw in it the true "spirit of the people" ("Volksgeist") as it had grown since time immemorial. This represented Savigny's idea of what the law is and why it binds us. This new methodology was the signature of his *Historische Rechtsschule*[154] and became highly influential, even though it has remained contentious throughout.[155] Without taking sides in that general debate, it is noteworthy that it resonates well with the theory of com-

152 Hallebeek in Schrage (ed), at p. 67–68.

153 Flume, FS Niedermeyer, 1953, 103, at p. 140 = Studien, at p. 59: "Die neuere Romanistik hat die Literatur zum Bereicherungsrecht von den Glossatoren bis zum Ende des gemeinen Rechts unberücksichtigt gelassen."

154 The name of the school of thought founded by Savigny.

155 Cp. e.g. Coing: Europäisches Privatrecht 1800–1914, § 4, p. 45–46; Wieacker: Privatrechtsgeschichte der Neuzeit unter besonderer Berücksichtigung der deutschen Entwicklung, 2nd edn. 1967, p. 385.

mon law. True, there is the difference that classical Roman law was only mirrored indirectly by the writings of jurists like Ulpian, Pomponius or Papinian, not directly by reported judgements of the courts. But that is not to say that those writers "made" the law. They commented on the law, often enough because they taught it. Many ran law schools that worked similar to Inns of Court. They were "persuasive authority" to the practitioners they trained, just as the work of Peter Birks was for generations of common lawyers. So the law that developed from these sources was customary or "common" law.

It is necessary to understand Savigny's influence on German unjust enrichment because his back-to-the-roots-approach can be replicated for English unjust enrichment. His methodology is closer to that of a common lawyer than that of a modern civil lawyer who primarily attempts to make sense of the words of his code. Savigny's search for the principle of unjust enrichment corresponds to the quest of Peter Birks, and it was done for the same reason: Treat like cases alike. By applying his methodology to the original bases of unjust enrichment in the Digest, Savigny derived a principle that deviated from Pomponius. To get there, he disregarded later interpretations by the medieval and modern lawyers of the ius commune as well as the findings of natural law or the content of the emerging national Codes.[156] That gave him a clean slate where he could start his interpretation of Roman law afresh, unburdened from centuries of dialectics, fallacies and aberrations that grew from the middle-ages over enlightenment into the first natural law codifications.

The back-to-the-roots-approach was particularly helpful for unjust enrichment because it allowed Savigny to overcome both the Pomponian principle and the closely interwoven *actio de in rem verso utilis.* He dismissed the Pomponian sentence as to wide and vague to be applied as law (p. 230). He ignored the *actio de in rem verso utilis* because it was merely a later extension of the classical *actio de in rem verso* by Roman Imperial Law.

The overcoming of both the principle of Pomponius and the *actio de in rem verso utilis* relieved Roman legal doctrine from a millstone that had threatened to drown unjust enrichment in a contourless sea of vagueness for centuries. Now the door was open to define a new, more precise and persuasive principle of the *condictiones.* According to Savigny, the common ground of all *condictiones* was a "direct shift of wealth/value". That principle became the backbone of German law. The existence of a uniform principle meant that there could still be a gen-

156 On the work of Savigny see Hermann Klenner, Savigny's Research Program of the Historical School of Law and Its Intellectual Impact in 19th Century Berlin, The American Journal of Comparative Law, Vol. 37, No. 1 (Winter, 1989), pp. 67–80; cf. further

eral enrichment claim – although Savigny very wisely did not advocate one. But that claim was not to be based on the enrichment from another's loss (Pomponius), but on a direct shift of wealth that was "unjustified" (= *sine causa*). It was the backbone of a law of unjust enrichment that was narrowly restricted to the persons involved in the transfer.

The BGB-Redaktor Franz Philipp von Kübel adopted Savigny's principle in his *Vorentwurf* (= pre-draft) as basis of German law of unjust enrichment (pp. 235–242). The First Commission essentially adopted the pre-draft, even if slightly streamlined.[157] The Second Commission changed the formal structure of German enrichment law completely. It intended to create a general enrichment claim catching both performance and non-performance cases in § 812 I 1 BGB. But it also adhered to Savigny's principle. As a result, the German enrichment claim was not based on the enrichment from another's loss, but on a direct shift of wealth/ value that had taken place without a legal ground / reason.[158] So on the first of January 1900, Germany had a coherent law of unjustified enrichment – unlike the older codes of France and Austria.

c) France: back into the arms of Pomponius – but with eyes set on the *actio de in rem verso*

However, just when it seemed that the Pomponian prohibition of enrichment from another's loss had been laid to rest for good, French law took a different turn. The arrêt Boudier of 1892 accepted the old principle as part of French law – even though it had *not* been codified in 1804 (pp. 139–191). That apparently defeated Savigny's claim of the Pomponian sentence being too wide and too vague to be applied as law. But of course, as argued in the introduction, the true principle on which the arrêt Boudier rested was the *actio de in rem verso (utilis)* which the French jurists – unlike the Germans – eventually identified with the general enrichment claim.

d) The rift in civil law of unjust enrichment until present day

From the arrêt Boudier in 1892 on, the civilian jurisdictions were split. The French example emboldened other Francophile jurisdictions like Italy and Spain to adopt the general enrichment claim along the lines of the Pomponian sentence. The ex-

157 The number of performance-based claims was cut down from 8 to 4: § 737 E I (condictio indebiti); § 742 E I (condictio causa data causa non secuta); § 745 (condictio ob causam finitam); § 747 E I (condictio ob turpem vel iniustam causam).

158 As to the terminology, see below p. 62.

ample of Spain, embodied in the recent restatement delivered by the Tribunal Supremo in 2020, has already been referred to in the introduction (p. 3)

Italy was the first major jurisdiction where the principle was enshrined in a Code after its acceptance by the courts. This happened when the Codice Civile was recast in 1942.[159] In the "motherland" France, the codification of the general enrichment claim took much longer. In 2016, the thoroughly revised Code Civil finally received the enrichment claim.[160] In those jurisdictions, enrichment law embraces the version claim and reaches out to remote beneficiaries (**"wide unjust enrichment"**). By contrast, German enrichment law, solely based on the condictiones, does not reach beyond the direct recipient of a benefit on grounds of principle (**"narrow unjust enrichment"**).[161]

This distinction is glossed over by the common language of enrichment law. It creates the impression of a unifying bond between all civilian jurisdictions. There are two main reasons for that. The first is that German jurists, despite overcoming the Pomponian sentence, accepted the idiosyncratic defence of "Entreicherung" (= disenrichment) for *all* enrichment claims (§ 818 Abs. 3 BGB).[162] The justification was the (alleged) equitable nature of these claims "ex aequo et bono".[163] But while that explanation reflected the state of the art at that time, it is hard to see how unjustified enrichment could simultaneously be of "equitable nature" but not arbitrary "Billigkeitsrecht". It took the groundbreaking work by Werner Flume to rationalise disenrichment and show that the defence of disenrichment has never truly been based on loose and sloppy fairness notions.[164]

The second reason for the superficial similarity of civilian enrichment laws is the watering down of Savigny's requirement "aus dem Vermögen" (= out of the assets / the wealth) to the generic "auf Kosten" (= at the expense) by the Second Commission.[165] This was part of a series of undercooked editorial changes on the way to the final version of § 812 I 1 BGB. These produced ambiguities that made unjustified enrichment to one of the most debated and most difficult areas of German private law. The dissolution of these ambiguities rightly brought the interpretation

159 Art. 2041 Codice Civile.

160 Art. 1303 C.civ.

161 It must be noted that there is an exception to that rule in § 822, but it reduced to dead letter law by an extremely narrow interpretation, see p. 228.

162 While this accorded with the predominant view of 19th century jurist, it had been highly contentious in earlier times. Most notably, the condictio indebiti would not allow the defence when repayments or retransfers in kind were sought, cf. pp. 284–286.

163 Von Kübel, Motive, p. 38; as to the similar argument under common law Edelmann, Boston Law Review [2012] 1009, at 1021 et seq.

164 Flume, FS Niedermeyer, 1953, 103.

165 See below, pp. 247–250.

of § 812 I 1 BGB as general enrichment claim to an end. But unfortunately, this also killed the clear and persuasive rationale of Savigny's enrichment principle that went down with it (pp. 260–262).

2 The civilian-infused road to common enrichment law

Common law of unjust enrichment starts with *Moses v Macferlan* (1760). In this seminal case, Lord Mansfield essentially transferred the core triggers of the *condictiones* as legal transplants into English law (pp. 65–103). This thesis reiterates the sound arguments by David William Evans in the second volume of his translation of Robert Joseph Pothier's Treatise on the Law of Obligations, or Contracts, 1806. The respective pages are attached in the appendix, and there is nothing more to add.

To be sure, there had already been remedies in cases of extortion,[166] mistake[167] or failure of consideration[168] prior to *Moses v Macferlan.* Also, while the old remedies varied with respect to the jurisdiction and the actions, the action for "money had and received for the use of the plaintiff" had already begun to take over those restitutionary functions by way of "covert extension".[169] The underlying notion is an enforceable "trust of money".[170] This idea is basically the same as that of the *condictio* which lies to enforce the "credit" (= trust) given to the debtor.[171] But it was Lord Mansfield's categorisation of "unjust factors" and their attachment to the action for money had and received that took on the role that the *condictiones* of the Digest had played for the civilian jurists. In the following centuries, the action for money had and received flourished with the unjust

166 *Astley v Reynolds* (1731) 93 E.R. 939 (the action for money had and received).
167 *Bonnell v Fowke* (1657) 1 Sid. 4, the first case brought under money had and received for mistake, according to Baker in Schrage (ed.), at p. 49–50; cf. further Ibbetson in Schrage (ed.), at p. 139 referring to *Framson v Delamere* (1595) Cro El. 458, Moo 407 as very first English case of mistake.
168 See in great depth Ibbetson in Schrage (ed.), at pp. 125 et seq. 129: "It is hard to avoid the conclusion that in the fourteenth century English law generally recognised a remedy based on unjust enrichment analogous to the Roman *condictio causa data causa non secuta*.... The picture in the fifteenth century is similar... we find claims for the return of money paid to a ploughman who had failed to plough and a builder who had failed to build..."Cf. further Baker in Schrage (ed.), at p. 53.
169 Baker in Schrage (ed.), at p. 48–49, explaining the difficulty to find evidence "because the formula of the count ("money had and received for the use of the plaintiff") remains unchanged while its legal ambit widens."
170 Baker in Schrage (ed.), at p. 48 with fn. 91, noting that the common law accepted equitable interests in money which eventually made it necessary to distinguish the action for money had and received from equitable trust of money, citing e.g. *Case v Roberts* (1817) Holt N.P. 500.
171 Savigny, System des heutigen Römischen Rechts, Vol. V, pp. 512 et seq.

factors of *Moses v Macferlan*, e.g.: mistake (*Kelly v Solari*[172]), failure of consideration (*Fibrosa v Fairbairn*;[173] *Rowland v Divall*[174]), duress (*Barton v Armstrong*[175]) or undue influence (*Allcard v Skinner*[176]).

Soon after *Moses v Macferlan* was decided, first attempts to detect an underlying principle were made.[177] However, the seeds of *Moses v Macferlan* would not grow into a law of unjust enrichment yet. First of all, the notion of an implied contractual promise to repay proved resilient and left Lord Mansfield's visionary classification as a "debt implied by law" as "*vox clamantis in deserto*".[178] Moreover, while the triggers of the specific, performance-based *condictiones* had been transplanted, the generic *condictio sine causa* and its underlying, the Pomponian sentence, were not. Thus, there was no holder to attach any doctrine of disenrichment under English law.[179] The situation markedly differed from civil law where the authority of the Digest had been accepted in total. Even without reference to Pomponius, the Digest contained several hints that restitution from bona fide recipients should only mean skimming off enrichment and in turn be limited by disenrichment.[180] The juristic debate in the *ius commune* concentrated on the question whether this doctrine related to *all* restitutionary actions or whether it was restricted to defendants who had to return an asset *in specie* (= specific performance) and this specific asset was destroyed by *force majeur*. This debate took its while. As we have seen, civil law itself was far from recognizing a coherent law of unjust(ified) enrichment at the time of *Moses v Macferlan*. This is why the *condictio indebiti* in the older Codes of France and Austria is not subject to a general defence of disenrichment.[181]

172 (1841) 9 M&W 54, 152 ER 24.
173 [1943] AC 32 containing countless references starting with *Giles v Edward* (1797) 7 Term rep 181, *Taylor v Caldwell* (1863) 3 B. & S. 826 or "coronation cases" like *Chandler v Webster* [1904] 1 K.B. 493.
174 [1923] 2 KB 500.
175 [1976] AC 104. This unjust factor is of ancient origin, cp. Ibbetson in Schrage (ed.), at pp. 135 et seq.
176 (1877) LR 36 Ch D 145.
177 See below p. 69.
178 Jones in Schrage (ed.), at p. 150.
179 *Baylis v Bishop of London* [1913] 1 Ch 127.
180 Flume, FS Niedermeyer, 1953, pp. 103 et seq (however contending their impact). See e.g. also the citations of Ulpian 28 ad ed D.13.6.1.2 and 13.6.3. ("Sed mihi videtur, si locupletior pupillus factus sit, dandam utilem commodati actionem…") and D.26.8. ("naturaliter tamen obligabitur in quantum locupletior factus est") in *Sinclair v Brougham* [1914] AC 398, at pp. 434–435 (per Lord Dunedin).
181 See Art 1352 C.civ. contrasted with Art 1303 C.civ. for France; § 1437 ABGB in conncetion with §§ 329 et seq. ABGB for Austria.

The second stage of the growth process from "consimili casu" to a general principle that would eventually turn into hard law was not ignited before the 20th century. It began with a setback. *Sinclair v Brougham* nearly "closed the door" for a separate law of restitution or unjust enrichment.[182] Instead it strictly followed the longstanding contract-tort dichotomy[183] and upheld the Common Law approach to imply promises to repay that had its roots in the old forms of actions.[184] But these "ghosts of the pasts clanking their medieval chains" were robustly rejected by Lord Atkin in *United Australia*:

> *United Australia v Barclays Bank* [1941] AC 1, at pp. 27–29: "The cheat or the blackmailer does not promise to repay to the person he has wronged the money which he has unlawfully taken: nor does the thief promise to repay the owner of the goods stolen the money which he has gained from selling the goods. Nevertheless, if a man so wronged was to recover the money in the hands of the wrongdoer, and it was obviously just that he should be able to do so, it was necessary to create a fictitious contract: for there was no action possible other than debt or assumpsit on the one side and action for damages for tort on the other. ... The alleged contract by the blackmailer and the robber never was made and never could be made. The law, in order to do justice, imputed to the wrongdoer a promise which alone as forms of action then existed could give the injured person a reasonable remedy. ... These fantastic resemblances of contracts invented in order to meet requirements of the law as to forms of action which have now disappeared should not in these days be allowed to affect actual rights. **When these ghosts of the past stand in the path of justice clanking their medieval chains the proper course for the judge is to pass through them undeterred.**"

Building on that, the notion of implied promises to repay was finally laid to rest by Lord Wright in *Fibrosa v Fairbain:*

> *Fibrosa Spolka Akcyjna v Fairbairn Lawson Combe Barbour Ltd* [1943] AC 32, at pp. 63–64: "Yet the ghosts of the forms of action have been allowed at times to intrude in the ways of the living and impede vital functions of the law. Thus in *Sinclair v. Brougham*, Lord Sumner stated that "all these causes of action [sc. for money had and received] are common species of the genus assumpsit now rest, and long have rested, upon a notional or imputed promise to repay." This observation, which was not necessary for the decision of the case, obviously does not mean that there is an actual promise of the party. The phrase "notional or implied promise" is only a way of describing a debt or obligation arising by construction of law. The claim for money had and received always rested on a debt or obligation which the law implied or more accurately imposed ... This agrees with the words of Lord Atkin which I

182 *Sinclair v Brougham* [1914] AC 398.
183 As to the law between 13th to 16th century, Ibbetson in Schrage (ed.), at p. 121.
184 *United Australia v Barclays Bank* [1941] AC 1, at pp. 26 et seq. (per Lord Atkin) and at pp. 41 et seq (per Lord Porter); *Fibrosa Spolka Akcyjna v Fairbairn Lawson Combe Barbour Ltd* [1943] AC 32, at pp. 63–64 (per Lord Wright); Lord Wright of Durley, "Sinclair v Brougham", in: Legal Essays and Addresses, CUP 1939, at pp. 1 et seq.; Baker, in Schrage (ed.), p. 31, at pp. 33 et seq.

> have just quoted, yet serious legal writers have seemed to say that these words of the great judge in *Sinclar v. Brougham* closed the door to any theory of unjust enrichment in English law. I do not understand why or how. It would indeed be a reductio ad absurdum of the doctrine of precedents. In fact, the common law still employs the action for money had and received as a practical and useful, if not complete or ideally perfect, instrument to prevent unjust enrichment, aided by the various methods of technical equity which are also available, as they were found to be in Sinclair v. Brougham."

Fibrosa established the law of restitution (as it then was) as a third source of obligations, independent of contract or tort, that arose by operation of law and aimed to prevent unjust enrichment. However: "It was not until 1966 when Robert Goff and Gareth Jones (as they then were) published their ground-breaking work, *The Law of Restitution* (1st edn.), that English law sought to recognise a principled basis for the law of restitution based on reversing unjust enrichment."[185] Inspiration for this development came from John P. Dawsons "Unjust Enrichment – a comparative Analysis" 1951 as well as from the first "Restatement of Restitution", released by the American law Institute in 1937 which stated in its s.1:

> "A person who has been unjustly enriched at the expense of another is required to make restitution to the other."

The formulation "at the expense" is the same as in § 812 I 1 BGB. However, for common lawyers, the Pomponian sentence is the underlying principle of unjust enrichment. The beginning is found in US law after the secession. As early as 1823, the Pomponian principle had been used in a slightly different version as one of a number of arguments to decide a case. In Green v. Biddle, the US Supreme Court used the maxime "*nemo debet locupletari aliena jactura*" and held it against an Act of Kentucky that allowed the occupants of land to claim compensation from the owner for the value of all improvements ever made, while they would have to disgorge the profits only from the time the lawsuit was brought.[186] Apparently, it has not been questioned then or ever after that the Pomponian sentence formed part of American law. We do not find any fundamental criticism of the Pomponian sentence comparable to that of Lord Dunedin in *Sinclair v Brougham.* To the contrary, unjust enrichment based on the Pomponian sentence grew after it had been pro-

---

185 *Dargamo Holdings Limited v Avonwick Holdings Limited* [2021] EWCA Civ 1149, at para. 51 (by Lady Justice Carr); Goff & Jones, 1–01.

186 Green v Biddle (U.S.) 8 Wheat. 1, 83 = 5 L Ed 547, 567 (1823).

moted by the First Restatement and the great work of J.P. Dawson[187] and ignited the evolution in England.[188]

However, at the crossroads of turning the principle into hard law, the US and the UK went different ways. In the US, the evolution came to a halt not dissimilar to that witnessed in the first Civilian codifications. As of today, the Third Restatement accepts the Pomponian principle "no benefit from another's loss" as the equitable rationale of unjust enrichment and deduces the defence of change of position from it.[189] However, it does not favour a general enrichment claim but adheres to the specific actions and remedies of the law of restitution.

English law went further. Disenrichment, in the guise of change of position, was accepted in *Lipkin Gorman* (1991).[190] In *Banque Financière* (1998), the principle was finally turned into law.[191] The four-stage-test was introduced to decide whether restitution was awarded:

(1) Has the defendant been enriched?
(2) Was the enrichment at the expense of the claimant?
(3) Was the enrichment unjust?
(4) Are there any defences?[192]

---

187 Dawson, Unjust Enrichment – a Comparative Analysis, 1951; reprinted 1999. Cf. further "Developments in the Law: Unjust Enrichment, HarvLR 133 [2020] 2062, at 2084 et seq.

188 Birks, Unjust Enrichment, 2005, p. 4; Andrew Kull, James Barr Ames and the Early Modern History of Unjust Enrichment, 25 OXFORD J. LEGAL STUD. 297 (2005).

189 Section 65 Restatement (Third): "If receipt of a benefit has led a recipient without notice to change position in such manner that an obligation to make restitution of the original benefit would be inequitable to the recipient, the recipient's liability in restitution is to that extent reduced."

190 *Lipkin Gorman v Karpnale Ltd* [1991] 2 AC 584.

191 *Banque Financière De La Cité v. Parc (Battersea) Ltd and Others* [1998] UKHL 7 = 1 AC 221, 227 (per Lord Steyn); subsequently *Benedetti v Sawiris and Others* [2013] UKSC 50, Rn 10 (per Lord Clarke); *Barnes v Eastenders Cash & Carry Plc* [2014] UKSC 26 = [2015] AC 1; *Bank of Cyprus UK Ltd v Menelaou* [2015] UKSC 66; *HMRC v The Investment Trust Companies* [2017] UKSC 29 (Vorinstanzen: *Investment Trust Companies v HMRC* [2015] EWCA Civ 82; [2012] EWHC 458 (Ch), Rn 38 (per Henderson J.); *Lowick Rose LLP v Swynson Limited and another* [2017] UKSC 32 (Vorinstanz: *Swynson Ltd v Lowick Rose LLP* [2015] EWCA Civ 629); *Relfo Ltd v Varsani* [2014] EWCA Civ 360; *TFL Management Services v Lloyds Bank Plc* [2013] EWCA Civ 1415; for the earlier view against a claim in unjust enrichment see e.g. *Orakpo v Manson Investments* [1978] AC 95, 104 (per Lord Diplock).

192 Referring primarily but not exclusively to change of position, see in detail Dyson/Goudkamp/Wilmot-Smith, Defences in Unjust Enrichment, 2016.

A general enrichment claim under the four stage test has since formed part of the laws of England.[193] But a fierce debate is still raging,[194] while other members of the common law family reject a general enrichment claim (US) or even unjust enrichment as an independent subject of law (Australia).[195] The relatively new development[196] is not settled yet. Following points are of particular interest for the purposes of the book:

- The introduction of the direct shift of value as basic rule.[197]
- The recent innuendos that the four-stage-test may not be conclusive for the award in restitution.[198]
- The uncertainty about the contours of failure of consideration / basis.[199]

---

193 *Barton v Morris* [2023] UKSC 3, at para. 77 (per Lady Rose) and at para. 228 (per Lord Burrows); *Benedetti v Sawiris* [2013] UKSC 50, [2014] AC 938, at para. 10; *Investment Trust Companies v Revenue and Customs Comrs* [2017] UKSC 29; [2018] AC 275, paras 24, 39–42; *Samsoondar v Capital Insurance Ltd* [2020] UKPC 33, [2021] 2 All ER 1105, paras 18–20; *Dargamo Holdings Ltd v Avonwick Holdings Ltd* [2021] EWCA Civ 1149, [2022] 1 All ER (Comm) 1244), paras 51–63 (per LJ Carr).

194 Cf. e.g. Stevens, The Unjust Enrichment Disaster, (2018) 134 LQR 574; id., The Laws of Restitution, 2023; see already id., "Is there a law of unjust enrichment?" in: Degeling/ Edelman (Hrsg.) *Unjust Enrichment and Commercial Law*, 2008; Lionel Smith, "Restitution: A New Start?", in Devonshire/Havelock (eds.), The Impact of Equity and Restitution in Commerce, 2018, 91; contrast Burrows, In Defence of Unjust Enrichment, 78 (3) CLJ 521 (2019); cf. further P. Watts, "'Unjust Enrichment' – the Potion that Induces Well-meaning Sloppiness of Thought", *Current Legal Problems*, Vol. 69, No. 1 (2016), 289; 'Property and "Unjust enrichment": Cognate Conservators' [1998] NZ Law Rev 151; 'Review: Unjust Enrichment' (2005) 121 LQR 163.

195 *Australian Financial Services and Leasing Pty Ltd v Hills Industries Ltd* [2014] HCA 14, (2014) 253 CLR 560; zuvor *Roxborough v Rothmans* of *Pall Mall Australia Ltd* [2001] HCA 68; *Farah Constructions Pty Ltd v Say-Dee Pty Ltd* [2007] *HCA 22; Lumbers v* W *Cook Builders* Pty Ltd (in liquidation) [2008] HCA 27; *Bofinger v Kingsway Group* Limited [2009] HCA 44; but see also the criticism by Burrows, "The Australian Law of Unjust Enrichment: Has the High Court Lost its Way?" in E Bant and M Harding (eds), Exploring Private Law (CUP 2010) ch 3.

196 *Dargamo Holdings Limited v Avonwick Holdings Limited* [2021] EWCA Civ 1149, at para. 51 (per Lady Justice Carr).

197 *The Investment Trust Companies v HMRC* [2017] UKSC 29, at para. 37 seq; 46 et seq.; *Relfo Ltd (in liq) v Varsani* [2014] EWCA Civ 360; Dargamo Holdings Limited v Avonwick Holdings Limited [2021] EWCA Civ 1149: "The purpose of the claim is to correct normatively defective transfers of value."

198 *Dargamo Holdings Limited v Avonwick Holdings Limited* [2021] EWCA Civ 1149, at para. 56 (per Lady Justice Carr), referring to *Swynson Ltd v Lowick Rose Llp* [2017] UKSC 32; [2018] AC 313 ("*Swynson*") at para 22 and Lord Reed in *The Investment Trust Companies v HMRC* [2017] UKSC 29, at para. 41: "...the questions are not themselves legal tests, but are signposts towards areas of inquiry involving a number of distinct legal requirements.

199 *Barton v Morris* [2023] UKSC 3, at paras. 77 et seq.; *Dargamo Holdings Limited v Avonwick Holdings Limited* [2021] EWCA Civ 1149, at paras. 77 et seq.

Those points support the initial suspicion that common law has chosen the wrong principle. The issues are contentious and unresolved to date because the common law debate on unjust enrichment is focussed on Pomponius and neglects Savigny. It is the involvement of Pomponius that causes the much criticised feature of a loose equitable remedy that undermines strict law and produces "well-meaning sloppiness of thought". Unjust enrichment must be tamed by strict directness in order to work out a clear rationale. Claims against remote recipients should not be allowed, or at least they should not be allowed on the vague principle of Pomponius because this leads to irreconcilable cases (see in detail pp. 191–199).

In the edifices of civil enrichment laws, there are more strings of thought that have the potential to enrich common law. It is certainly true that English unjust enrichment developed differently in various ways within its unique common law environment. Take e.g. the laws of following and tracing,[200] constructive and resulting trusts[201] or subrogation,[202] to name just a few. But beyond these "natural" differences, it is also true that the "Scalian" moment of *Moses v Macferlan* freeze-framed those parts of the civilian enrichment law that Lord Mansfield accepted as the state of the art of mid-eighteenth century. Just as the American revolution cut the ties to the English Common Law in 1789, English enrichment law got separated from the further development on the Continent after 1760. This was misfortunate because civilian enrichment law had still been underdeveloped at that time. The premature transplantation impeded and delayed solutions that were found elsewhere but could also have been found in England because they were logical deductions from the basis that had been imported into common law. This is particularly true for the *condictio sine causa* and the no-consent cases, but also for the relation of mistake and failure of consideration. But the gap can be bridged. Past and present civil law solutions can be considered under common law as far as the same doctrinal foundations are at work.

200 Goff & Jones, 7–19 et seq.; 7–26 et seq.

201 Goff & Jones, 38–06 et seq.

202 *Banque Financière de la Cité v Parc (Battersea) Ltd* [1998] UKHL 7; Goff & Jones, 39–01 et seq.

III The Roman foundations of enrichment law

1 Overview

Unjust enrichment is a child of Roman law. The two main bases are the *condictiones* and the Pomponian prohibition to benefit from another's loss as their overarching moral principle. They are the centrepiece of the evolution from principle to law. That process had already started in ancient Rome when the *condictio*, initially a form of action to recover loans, i.e to enforce "trusts of money", (cp. D. 12.1.), was combined with causes of action in restitution, most notably the *condictio causa data causa non secuta* (D.12.4) and the *condictio indebiti* (D.12.6.).[203]

When Lord Mansfield decided *Moses v Macferlan* (1760), he transferred the triggers for restitution of some (but not all) Roman *condictiones* to the English action for money had and received. These "Mosaic condictiones" laid the ground for common law unjust enrichment (pp. 65–102). With a certain delay, the principle not to benefit from another's loss followed suit.

However, the roots of civilian enrichment laws are also closely intertwined with the *negotiorum gestio* that "rewards" officious intermeddling (p. 121). This connection has shaped some peculiar aspects of civilian as opposed to common law enrichment. Common law takes a profoundly different, principally unsympathetic approach to unwarranted interference in other people's affairs and is equally cold with regards to any enrichments springing from such doing.

Finally, the *actio de in rem verso utilis* must be accounted for (p. 131). It is probably the biggest "unknown unknown" marker to distinguish between civilian and common law enrichment. It has rarely been mentioned in comparative work[204] even though it is at the very heart of French enrichment law. This may be due to the fact that even within civil law, its position has never been clearly settled. Some lawyers of the *ius commune* regarded it as an enrichment claim, while others would see an agency-related instrument. This disagreement ended up in a split between the leading civil law jurisdictions: In Germany, the *actio de in rem verso* was completely ousted. Neither was it included within the law of unjustified enrichment in the §§ 812–822 BGB[205] nor did it enter the Code as a separate claim.[206]

203 Zimmermann, pp. 835–839, 851–854.

204 But see Zimmermann, pp. 878–884; Hallebeek in Schrage (ed.), pp. 103–106.

205 The doctrinal argument was that unjustified enrichment based on Savigny's direct shift of wealth excluded the *actio de in rem verso*, see von Kübel, Motive zum Vorentwurf, p. 11–12; Motive II, 829 and 872. Interestingly, this argument is still generally accepted to explain why the wide wording of § 812 BGB must not accommodate the version claim even though Savigny's principle itself is thought to be overcome.

By contrast, the French Cour de cassation adopted it as general enrichment claim even though the Code civil 1804 had deliberately abstained from codifying it (above p. 10).

This historic divide coins these two legal systems to the present day. In Germany, enrichment law consists only of the *condictiones* (§§ 812–817 BGB).[207] In France, the general claim to return an *enrichissement injustifie* (previously: *sans cause*) under Art. 1303 C.civ. is distinguished from the *condictio indebiti* = *repetition de l'indu* in Art. 1302 C.civ (= Art. 1376 old C.civ of 1804) and follows different rules on disenrichment.[208] While they differ from the traditional rules of the *condictiones* under the ius commune,[209] their common feature is the lack of a general defence of disenrichment.[210] This division creates a fosse that cuts right through the heart of civilian enrichment law. The contested questions are whether or not there is a general claim of unjust enrichment, and if so, on which principle it is based: the Pomponian sentence or Savigny's shift of wealth? That same question must be answered for the general enrichment claim of English law, too.

2 The general development of the *condictiones*

The starting point is the great compilation known as the Digest. It was commissioned by the Byzantine Emperor Justinian who reigned from 527 to 565 a.D. He had – without lasting success – tried to rebuild the Western part of the Roman Empire that had crumbled after the fall of Rome in 476. In addition, displaying a characteristic appetite of conquerors to leave their mark on the law, he aimed to have the enormous body of Roman law restated authoritatively by his crown jurists.[211]

---

206 The reasons for this separate decision are elaborated by the First Commission, Motive II, 871–872.

207 § 822 BGB is seen as a very narrow exception and practically dead letter law, see p. 228.

208 Art.1302–3 C.civ in connection with Art. 1352–1352–9 C.civ.

209 As to those see Flume, FS Niedermeyer, 1953, 103, at pp. 127–136 = Studien, pp. 48–55; Zimmermann, pp. 896–900.

210 In particular, claims for restitution of money are not subject to disenrichment at all (Art. 1302 C.civ. "La restitution d'une chose **autre que d'une somme d'argent** a lieu en nature ou, lorsque cela est impossible, en valeur, estimée au jour de la restitution.", with the following Articles reducing the obligation to answer for the value in favour of bona fide recipients.)

Also, services will always be "restored" by paying for their objective value at the time of receipt (Art 1352–8: "La restitution d'une prestation de service a lieu en valeur. Celle-ci est appréciée à la date à laquelle elle a été fournie.").

211 It is said that only a quarter of the sources of Roman law survived while the others were discarded as heresy, consequently destroyed and are forever lost.

The result is known as Corpus Juris Civilis. Like Cesar's Gaul, it was divided into three parts. The first part were the Institutiones, a classical textbook to train lawyers. The second part were the laws enacted by Emperor Justinian. The third and most prominent part were the "Digest" or "Pandects" (*digesta seu pandectae* = arrangement of the all-containing), a compilation of fifty books that contained a collection of sources on the entire Roman law as it then was, with all its actions, remedies and defences explained by extracts from books, commentaries and opinions of classical Roman lawyers like e. g. Ulpinianus, Papinianus, Julianus, Paulus or, last but not least, Sextus Pomponius.

This "Code" sank into oblivion for centuries. The resurrection of the Roman Empire in the Western parts was short-lived. When it had finally fallen for good, dark and mystic ages of rare literacy ensued in this part of the world. Meanwhile in the surviving Eastern Roman Empire with its capital Constantinople, the Latin language was superseded by Greek. Roman law abdicated. But it had a glorious come back.

When a complete handwritten copy of the Digest, today known as the "littera Florentina", was retrieved in Northern Italy by coincidence in 1070, it found its way to Bologna where the medieval scholars, first and above all the famous *Irnerius*, known as "lucerna iuris" (= the "lantern of the law"), and his disciples started to analyse the enormous body of texts by applying latest scholastic methodology. They laid the foundation for the glorious law school of Bologna that began to spread these ancient rules across the new, Frankonian Europe, dominated as it was by the Holy Roman Empire and France. Civil Law was born.

With Civil law originated the law of unjust enrichment. The Digest contained the *condictiones sine causa.* The *condictiones sine causa* have always been the heart of unjust enrichment. They are the generally accepted centre-piece of unjustified enrichment. These causes of action survived the centuries essentially unchanged[212] before they were translated into the national languages to enter the European codifications, last but not least the German BGB. Therefore, if we look at the original *condictiones* of the Digest, we can recognise astonishing mirror images of today's enrichment claims. These specific claims have always been essential for the quest for any principle of unjust enrichment.

The main causes of action were compiled at the beginning of the second book of the old Digest ("Secunda pars digesta veteris"), although it must be noted that many other cases were found scattered all over the Digest.[213] By the time of the

212 Zimmermann, pp. 857–873. However, the role of the *condictio sine causa* grew and grew.

213 The reason ist that classical Roman Law did not distinguish different *condictiones* but applied the (abstract) *condictio*, cp. Zimmermann, pp. 835–836 and 839. See also below, p. 111.

Justinian compilation, the *condictio* had already come a long way. It is rooted in the lex Silia (for money) and the lex Capurnia (for specific assets).[214] These laws date back to the early days of the Republic, about 250 B.C.[215] We know about it due to another, almost incredible coincidence: the discovery of the Institutiones of Gaius[216] by the Prussian civil servant and scholar *Barthold Georg Niehbur* in Verona in 1816, en passant on a diplomatic mission to Rome where he was to become ambassador at the Holy See.[217]

Originally, the *legis actio per condictionem* was a form of action in the old Republic that allowed the plaintiff to seek redress in trial before a judge. There would be a follow-up meeting in Court ("in iure") within 30 days.[218] The verb "condicere" was used in the sense of fixing or determining this date, i.e. the claimant could impose it on the defendant. The complete formula became known after another trove in Egypt in 1933.[219] It was described in book 4 of the Institutiones of Gaius:

> Gaius 4.17b: "Per condictionem ita agebatur: AIO TE MIHI SESTERTIORUM X MILIA DARE OPORTERE: ID POSTULO, AIAS AUT NEGES. Adversarius dicebat non oportere. Actor dicebat: QUANDO TU NEGAS, IN DIEM TRICENSIMUM TIBI IUDICIS CAPIENDI CAUSA CONDICO. Deinde die tricensimo ad iudicem capiendum praesto esse debebant. Condicere autem denuntiare est prisca lingua."
>
> [Via the condictio was sued thus: I CLAIM THAT YOU MUST GIVE ME TEN THOUSAND SESTERCES. I CHARGE THEE TO ADMIT OR DENY THIS. The Adversary said, he was not bound. The plaintiff said, SINCE YOU DENY, I SAY TO YOU THE THIRTIETH DAY, THEN TO RECEIVE A JUDGE. Thereupon they had to be present on the thirtieth day to receive a judge. And indeed 'to announce' (condicere) in the former language is as much as 'to proclaim'.

---

214 Gai. 4,19: "Haec autem legis actio constituta est per legem Siliam et Calpurniam, lege quidem Silia certae pecuniae, lege uero Calpurnia de omni certa re." [This form of judicial procedure was established by the *Lex Silia* and the *Lex Calpurnia*; by the *Lex Silia*, to receive a certain sum of money, and by the *Lex Calpurnia*, to recover any other property which was certain. – translated by L.P. Scott]

215 Kaser/Hackl, Das Römische Zivilprozessrecht, 1996, § 10 III, p. 69; *Kaser*, SZ 101 (1984), 52; *Pernice*, p. 233.

216 On Gaius, see e.g. György Diósdi, "Gaius der Rechtsgelehrte", in: Hildegard Temporini at al. (eds.), Aufstieg und Niedergang der Römischen Welt – Rise and Decline of the Roman World, Vol 15: Recht (Methoden, Schulen, einzelne Juristen, 1976, pp. 605 et seq.

217 For a complete account of the story, a veritable thriller including ensuing libel claims against a fierce critic, see Varvaro, Der Glücksstern Niehburs und die Institutionen des Gaius, 2nd edn. 2014, https://www.jura.uni-heidelberg.de/md/jura/mat/band_2_der_gluecksstern_niebuhrs_varvaro.pdf.

218 There was no need for a *vademonium* to secure the appearance of the counter party in the case of the *legis actio per condictionem*, see Kaser/Hackl, Das Römische Zivilprozessrecht, 1996, § 10 III., p. 69.

219 Manthe, p. 17. Therefore, it is not covered in the translation by Scott.

[Edited version of the translation by www.DeepL.com/Translator (free version) into English from the German translation of Ulrich Manthe.[220]]

This ancient form of action was not linked to a specific cause of action. The reason why the defendant should be obliged was not expressed in the solemn formula the claimant had to recite.[221] With the end of the old Republic in the 1st century BC and the dawning of the Imperial Age, the famous "classical period" of Roman law began. A visible sign of this transition was that the use of the oral, and thus error-prone, formulas had been abolished. They were superseded by written formulas.[222] This procedural evolution did however not alter the fact that the *condictio* remained an abstract obligation.[223] The defendant was required to pay a specified sum or transfer a specified asset at a given date.

One might compare the reasons of this development with the turn English law took after Slade's case[224] that was the starting point to replace the ancient action in debt with the handier *debitatus assumpsit.*[225] The effects with respect to unjust enrichment were similar, too. The action of *debitatus assumpsit* originally required but a promise to pay. This could also be implied.[226] That made it an abstract claim that could be combined with various causes of actions. The same is true for the *condictio* that originally lay to recover loans (D.12.1.: *de rebus creditis si certum petetur et de condictione*).[227] Following Peter Birks, we could speak of "contrac-

---

220 Manthe, Gaius Institutiones – Die Institutionen des Gaius, 2nd edn. 2015.

221 *Kaser/Hackl*, p. 111; *Zimmermann*, p. 835;

222 Gai 4.30: Sed istae omnes legis actiones paulatim in odium uenerunt. namque ex nimia subtilitate ueterum, qui tunc iura condiderunt, eo res perducta est, ut uel qui minimum errasset, litem perderet; itaque per legem Aebutiam et duas Iulias sublatae sunt istae legis actiones, effectumque est, ut per concepta uerba, id est per formulas, litigaremus. [All these forms of judicial procedure, however, gradually became unpopular on account of the extreme subtlety of the ancient legal authorities, so that the result was that anyone who committed the slightest error lost his case. Hence, by the *Lex Aebutia* and the two *Leges Julia*, proceedings under this law were abolished, and another form was substituted for them; so that at present in litigation we make use of written instructions, that is to say, formulas, for that purpose. – translated by LP Scott].

223 Zimmermann, p. 835.

224 *Slade v Morley* (1602) B. & M. 420.

225 Ibbetson, Sixteenth Century Contract law: Slade's Case in Context, OJLS (1984) 295; id., Assumpsit and Debt in the early Sixteenth Century: the originis of the Indebitatus Count, CLJ (1982) 142; Baker, New Light on Slade's case, CLJ (1971) 51; Ames, The History of Assumpsit, Harv. L. R. 2 (1888–1889) 1. Dawson, p. 42 perceives the *condictio* as "the Roman general assumpsit".

226 See Baker in Schrage (ed.), pp. 33 et seq.

227 Savigny V, pp. 512 et seq., 576 et seq.

tual restitution".[228] Due to its abstract nature, the *condictio* proved useful for causes of action in restitution. It developed into a legal tool to recover values that the claimant had lost and claimed back. This is similar to how "debitatus assumpsit" under the count of "money had and received for the use of the plaintiff" became the vehicle of English unjust enrichment in *Moses v Macferlan* (1760). This extension created the same notion of "quasi contract" as the *condictio* because both were based on a fictitious promise to (re)pay.[229]

The *condictio* was generally not available if the claimant still held the title.[230] Thus, if transactions were flawed in a way that invalidated the transfer of title to the recipient, restitution could simply be achieved by reclaiming possession under the *rei vindicatio.* But unlike the tort of conversion, the *rei vindicatio* ceased to apply when possession was lost. That necessitated a complementary *condictio.* This substitute function for the lost *rei vindicatio* is described with the term "Vindikationsersatzfunktion" by German lawyers.[231] It is an important function and shows that civilian unjust enrichment is not restricted to failed transactions but embraces the "no consent"-cases, too.[232]

The reasons that triggered recovery under the various transfer-related *condictiones* can be summarised by lack (or loss) of the *causa.* The Romans recognised that transfers were made for a reason (Latin: *causa*). This reason had to be met. To keep the benefit, the recipient had to show *iusta causa.*[233] The exact notion of *causa* has been contentious over the centuries. It had not been settled as long

---

228 Birks, Unjust Enrichment, 205, p. 11 and 25. Under modern law, the existence of a thing called "contractual restitution" is however controversial, contrast Burrows, The Law of Restitution, 2011, pp. 12–13.

229 See Baker in Schrage (ed.), pp. 33 et seq.

230 D. 13.3.1.1. (Ulp 27 ad ed): Rem autem suam per hanc actionem nemo petet, nisi ex causis ex quibus potest, veluti ex causa furtiva vel vi mobili abrepta.

[No one can, by means of this action, bring suit for his own property, except where he is permitted to do so in certain cases; as, for instance, in an action based on theft, or where movable property has been taken away by force. – Scott]

Gai IV.5: Appellantur autem in rem quidem actiones uindicationes, in personam uero actiones, quibus dari fieriue oportere intendimus, condictiones. [Moreover, real actions are styled suits for the recovery of property, but personal actions, by which we assert that something must be given, or some act be performed, are called *condictiones.* – LP Scott]; cf. further on the passage by Gaius Savigny V, pp. 587 et seq.

231 Cf. Savigny V, pp. 109 et seq., 515, 518; Jansen, AcP 216 (2016) 112, at p. 140.

232 Cf. also Zimmermann, pp. 839–841 and 854. But see for the difficult acceptance of this category of cases next to performance-based *condictiones* Jansen, AcP 216 (2016) 112, at p. 143–144.

233 Cf. Ulpian D.12.7.1. (ad Sabinum): .... Constat id demum posse condici alicui, quod vel non ex iusta causa ad eum pervenit..." [It is settled that by the condictio, from anyone can be recovered what gets to him without just cause.]. See also Zimmermann, pp. 854–857.

as the *ius commune* was alive.[234] But surely, the causa was not identical with a (valid) contract. This can be drawn from the illuminating case of the *fullo* and the *toga* that was lost and found (pp. 107–108).

In my view, there is no more gain in revisiting the analyses into the meaning of "causa" in the Digest. The German codification has made a decision that captures the essential meaning. It translated the "causa" as "Rechtsgrund". At first sight, it seems and sounds that this directly translates into English as "legal ground". However, that translation would not be accurate because of the double meaning of "ground" that can be understood either as "reason" ("on grounds of") or as "basis". Indeed, comparative law seems to have led common law to understand "legal ground" as "basis", as the discussions about the unjust factors of "absence of basis" corresponding to *sine causa* and "failure of basis" corresponding to *causa data causa non secuta* indicate. But that was the wrong choice. The "legal ground" is not the "soil" on which the transaction firmly rests but the reason why the transaction was made. This is of particular interest because the new language of failure of basis is prone to confusion (pp. 87–92).

More generally speaking, the legal reason is the explanation why the shift of value is allocated to the defendant. Lack of a "legal ground" does not mean that there is no basis for the transaction but that there is no reason to validate and perpetuate the transaction. That is why German law speaks of unjustified enrichment, not of unfounded enrichment. It follows that *Rechtsgrund* / *causa* is to be understood in the sense of "reason", not of "basis". The book will proceed on this taxonomy. The legal reason of a value shift can be imposed by the law objectively (Example: a debtor must accept the foreclosure of his land even though it is against his will). Alternatively, it can be based on the subjective will of the transferring party: "volenti non fit inuria". But there are instances where the will of the party is flawed in the eyes of the law, either ab initio or by subsequent events, in a way that renders the transfer reversible. The relevant cases must be distinguished from one-sided motives that must always be irrelevant at private law, even if known to the other party. The German *Causa-Lehre* (= causa doctrine) or *Zwecklehre* (purpose doctrine) has developed a persuasive concept to achieve this task (below pp. 92, 270–272). The common ground for all recoveries of vitiated transfers is a failure of purpose.[235] That is not far from the original meaning of "consider-

234 See the account by von Kübel, Motive VE, pp. 5–7.

235 As to the causa-doctrine Ehmann, Zur causa-Lehre, 2003; id., Der Zweck der Leistungen und Leistungsversprechen, 2019. This doctrine is closely linked with the (controversial) subjective understanding of "ohne Rechtsgrund" (= without legal reason) in § 812 I 1 BGB as failure of purpose. The subjective theory of legal ground / reason is little explored by comparative lawyers. But see

ation", as explained by Peter Birks:[236] the consideration of the transferor why to make the transfer. Indeed, the English concept of failure of consideration appears to be parallel to the failure of purpose.[237] We will come back to that (below pp. 72 et seq., 91–92). But we will bypass the related, but slightly differing concepts of "consideration" and *causa* (*contractus*) in relation to the formation of binding contracts because their doctrinal function as well as their content is different.[238]

The Digest contained various situations and circumstances where the law recognised a case for restitution because there was no *causa*, either because the *causa* of a transaction did not materialise, got lost, lacked from the outset or was immoral. However, as pointed out above, the *condictiones* also covered restitution of values taken from the plaintiff against or without his will. In particular, the *condictio furtiva* (D 13.1.) could be brought against thieves. This kind of restitution for wrongs would not be classified as unjust enrichment by English restitution lawyers. But the inclusion of these cases is defensible, and will indeed prove pivotal for the completeness of the underlying legal principle.

The Roman *condictiones* already show the dichotomic structure of failed transfers and other enrichment cases that resurfaced in modern German enrichment law. The *condictio causa data causa non secuta*, the *condictio ob turpem vel iniustam causam*, the *condictio indebiti* and, with respect to the few cases explicitly mentioned sub D.12.7., even the *condictio sine causa* concerned failed transactions. By contrast, the *condictio furtiva* aimed at the restitution of stolen value. Moreover, as Savigny elaborated in the 19th century, **all** condictiones were restricted to the immediate parties of the flawed shift of wealth, which normally took place between

---

Helen Scott, "Restitution of Extra-Contractual Transfers: Limits of the Absence of Legal Ground", 14 RLR 93 (2006); Du Plessis, Edin LR (2014), 416; Meier, Irrtum und Zweckverfehlung, 1999.

236 Birks, Unjust Enrichment, 2005, p. 117.

237 In the same sense Ibbetson in Schrage (ed.), at p. 140, referring further to Simpson, A History of the Common Law of Contract, 1975, pp. 327–405, but also to the caveats drawn by Barton, Book Review (1977) 27 Univ Toronto LJ 373, 379–381. Cf. further Robert L Henry, "Cause in the Civil Law and Consideration in the Common: Much Ado About Nothing", 29 Kentucky Law Journal 4 (1941), 369: "Cause in the Civil Law corresponds to consideration in the Common. They are essentially the same in conception."

238 For the distinction of the two meanings within the common law *Fibrosa v Fairbairn* [1943] AC 32, at p. 48 (per Viscount Simon VC): "In English law, an enforceable contract may be formed by an exchange of a promise for a promise, or by the exchange of a promise for an act–I am excluding contracts under seal–and thus, in the law relating to the formation of contract, the promise to do a thing may often be the consideration, but when one is considering the law of failure of consideration and of the quasi-contractual right to recover money on that ground, it is, generally speaking, not the promise … but the performance of the promise."

For a current comparative account on the causa contractus, see Albers/Patti/Perrouin-Verbe, Causa contractus, 2022. As to the important role of the jurisconsulte Jen Domat in France, see p. 182.

payor and payee, but likewise between the owner and the thief consuming the good.

The categories of the *condictiones* were not only distinguished by their causes of action (*indebiti*; *causa data causa non secuta* etc.), but also by the award the claimant tried for: a claim for money was brought under a *certi condictio*, other assets were claimed under the *Triticaria condictio*, which in the case of non-specified goods was known as *incerti condictio.*[239] The categorisation of the *condictiones* in the Digest was additionally complicated by the fact that the *certi condictio* was simply referred to by that name, whereas the causes of action were only mentioned where the *incerti condictio* lay.[240] That said, the relevant *condictiones* to watch are:

- The *condictio causa data causa non secuta* (D.12.4.)
- The *condictio ob turpem vel iniustam causam* (D.12.5.)
- The *condictio indebiti* (D.12.6.)
- The *condictio since causa* (D.12.7.), including the *condictio ob causam finitam*
- The *condictio furtiva* (D.13.1.).

They were at the heart of unjust enrichment in the *ius commune* and shaped the search for the principle by canon and natural lawyers. With the rise of contract, the *condictio indebiti* emerged as the most important action.[241] It catered for restitution where the contract was invalid, while otherwise, contractual remedies would apply. The *condictio indebiti* was therefore the only obvious enrichment claim to make it into the first great codifications. But that changed with the revival

---

239 D.13.3.1. (Ulp 27 ad ed.): Qui certam pecuniam numeratam petit, illa actione utitur "si certum petetur": qui autem alias res, per triticariam condictionem petet. et generaliter dicendum est eas res per hanc actionem peti, si quae sint praeter pecuniam numeratam, sive in pondere sive in mensura constent, sive mobiles sint sive soli. quare fundum quoque per hanc actionem petimus et si vectigalis sit sive ius stipulatus quis sit, veluti usum fructum vel servitutem utrorumque praediorum.

[He who brings suit for a certain sum of money must make use of the action to which the clause, "Where a certain demand is made," refers: but a party who sues for any other kind of property must do so by means of a Triticarian Action. And, generally speaking the property to be sued for in this action is anything except a definite sum of money, whether it is established by weight or by measure, and whether it is movable or a part of the soil. Therefore, we may also bring suit for a tract of land, whether it is under perpetual lease, or whether anyone has stipulated for a right, as, for instance, an usufruct, or a servitude attaching to either kind of estate. – Scott]

See Savigny, V, pp. 610 et seq., p. 626.

240 Savigny, V, p. 631.

241 Zimmermann, p. 838, assumes that this was promoted by the Institutiones of Gaius and Justinian where the *condictio indebiti* served as prominent paradigm.

of Roman law by the *Historische Rechtsschule* in Germany.[242] As a result, all of the above-mentioned *condictiones* of the Digest found their way into the BGB[243] and remained of relevance to the present day. By contrast, only some of those *condictiones* were transplanted by *Moses v Macferlan* (1760).

The following introduction of the *condictiones* is divided into two parts. The first part refers to the *condictiones* that made it into English law as unjust factors: *causa data causa non secuta, ob turpem vel inutam causam* and *indebiti.* Since they were firmly established for the first time by *Moses v Macferlan* (1760), we might speak of the "Mosaic" *condictiones.* The second part concentrates on those that were left behind, namely the *condictio sine causa,* in an attempt to shed light on "what went missing".

As regards the methodology of the following chapters, it must be emphasised that the Digest are not a codification but an edited compilation of relevant legal opinions and commentaries of Roman lawyers. They may come either as abstract statements of principles and rules or as discussions on the solution of concrete cases. They contain ambiguities and contradictions that civilian jurists have tried to come to terms with for centuries after the reception. The enormous material of the Digest continues to be researched and debated by Roman legal historians to the present day. The purpose of this book is not, and cannot be, to contribute to those debates. The justification for this is that history has taken its course and the *condictiones* are immersed in the codes, most notably the §§ 812 BGB. That said, it nevertheless seems not only appropriate, but even necessary to insert a wide range of original passages from the Digest (cited in the original Latin version as well as translated). This is done to illuminate the origins of the two competing principles of unjust enrichment. The gain of approaching Roman legal thinking and recognising similarities and differences in the evolution of the concepts of restitution from then to now by comparison should weigh up potential losses from "glossing over" the stupend number of issues and depth of research, e. g. as to the *actio de in rem verso.*

3 The "Mosaic" condictiones and the foundation of the enrichment principle

In *Moses v Macferlan* (1760), Lord Mansfield famously stated where restitution under the action for money had and received would be available:

---

242 See above p. 45.

243 See pp. 257 et seq.

> "This kind of equitable action to recover money, which ought in justice to be kept, is very beneficial, and therefore much encouraged. It is only for money which, ex aequo et bono, the defendant ought to refund. It does not lie for money paid by the plaintiff, which is demanded of him as payable in point of honour and honesty, though it could not have been recovered from him by any course of law as in payment of a debt, barred by the statute of limitations or contracted during his infancy. It lies for money paid by mistake or upon a consideration that happens to fail or for money got by imposition, express or implied, or extortion, or oppression, or an undue advantage taken of the plaintiff's situation, contrary to laws made for the protection of persons, under these circumstances. In one word the gist of this action is that the defendant is obliged by the ties of natural justice and equity, to refund the money."

According to *Evans*, "it will be hardly contended that he [Lord Mansfield] found the materials of his exposition in any preceding volume of Reports; whereas a very slight comparison will evince the source of it to have been the judicial wisdom of ancient Rome."[244] Evans shows meticulously that Lord Mansfield uses passages of the Institutiones and the Digest, and also of the 17th century commentary on the Institutiones by the great Dutch jurist *Arnoldus Vinnius.*[245] In essence, Lord Mansfield had recognised the causes of action of the *condictio indebiti* (mistake), the *condictio causa data causa non secuta* ("failure of consideration") and the *condictio ob turpem vel iniustam causam* ("imposition, extortion, oppression, undue advantage" etc) as English law.

Lord Mansfield did not cite any references to English precedents for his propositions. That does not mean that there were none. For example, 30 years before *Moses v Macferlan*, the extortion case *Astley v Reynolds*[246] had been decided. Also, the path from fraud to "equitable fraud" to today's unjust factor of undue influence[247] had already been laid.[248] More importantly, David Ibbetson has shown that remedies for failure of qualified transactions, analogues to the Roman *causa data causa non secuta,* have been well accepted for a long time in medieval

244 Evans, at p. 328 (for the reprint of the whole passage, see the appendix)

245 Arnolius Vinnius, *In quatuor libros institutionum imperialium commentarius academicus et forensis*, Herbornae, 1699; online http://tudigit.ulb.tu-darmstadt.de/show/51-4583/0001/thumbs. See also id., *Selectarum Quaestionum Juris libri II quibus additaë sunt Simonis Vinnii Arnoldi filii orationes duae,* Rotterdam 1672

246 *Astley v Reynolds* (1731) 93 E.R. 939; see also Ibbetson in Schrage (ed.), at. p. 138 with several references to 15th century cases in Fn. 91. But see also Blackstone, Commentary, Vol 4, Ch. 10, p. 141 (qualifying extortion as a public wrong committed by office holders).

247 Called "undue advantage" in *Moses v Macferlan.*

248 Gareth Jones in Schrage (ed.), p. 149, at p. 154 points to Lord Hardwicke in *Morris v Burroughs* (1737) 1 Atk. 398 and beyond (ibid fn. 25 and 26).

English law.[249] During that time, they shifted from Common Law to Equity before returning in the 16th century via the action of debt, to be eventually superseded by indebitatus assumpsit in the 17th century. However, explicit remedies for mistakes beyond fraud or duress were scarce and maybe even non-existent before the 16th century,[250] the first probably being *Bonnel v Fowke* (1657).[251] Moreover, a principled basis for a substantive law doctrine could hardly be found in the old cases and remedies. This was probably due to the predominantly procedural approach of primeval Common Law that was subject to the haphazard interventions of Equity.[252]

After substantive English law had begun to consolidate in the 17th and 18th century, it was Lord Mansfield who first summarised and rationalised the triggers of restitution under money had and received, and he did so drawing from Roman law.[253] It has been assumed that, being of Scottish origin, he may have been motivated by the acceptance of unjust enrichment as Scots law.[254] Apparently, there had been a special connection between his work with the treatise on the Principles of Equity, written by Henry Home, Lord Kames, that is witnessed in the preface of the second edition.[255] He may well have had a look at his *Pothier*, too, as many English

249 Ibbetson in Schrage (ed.), p. 121, at pp. 125 et seq, in particular 131–132, summarising: "The general conclusion must be clear: medieval English law consistently allowed a remedy to reverse the effect of a qualified transaction, ..."

250 Ibbetson in Schrage (ed.), at p. 139: "...the fact that we do not find cases of mistake as ground for petitioning relief in the Chancery is very telling and suggests that the fortunate recipient was allowed to keep the property or money given to him."

251 2 Sid. 4; BL MS. Lansdowne 1109, fo. 135, record: KB 27/1797, m. 628; see in detail Baker in Schrage (ed.), at pp. 49–50 (with Fn. 95). It was a remarkable case of a payment to the wrong public officer. The payment was a rent for the office of coal meter and it was made to the Lordmayor (upon his explicit demand!) instead of the chamberlaine who subsequently required to be (and was) paid. According to Baker, at p. 50, the claim in restitution against the Lordmayor succeeded (as it really had to) and restitution for payment by mistake was never questioned again.

However, it is hard to see why a payment to the wrong officer is not a mistake of law which would not have granted restitution at the time, resubmitting the case to the unjust factor of extortion.

252 On the various difficulties that research into the matter is confronted with see e. g. Baker in Schrage (ed.), pp. 32–34 and Ibbestson in Schrage (ed.), at pp. 121–125.

253 Critical to this mainstream assumption however Cohen 45 Harv. L. Rev. 1333 et seq. (1932). But even if the development would have been the same without *Moses v Macferlan* (1760), as he argues, this would in my view only indicate that there had been earlier side glances to the Continent.

254 See the account by MacQueen/Sellar in Schrage (ed.), pp. 289 et seq.; cf. further Viscount Stair, Institutions of the Laws of Scotland, 1681 (1981 edn), p. 158; Lord Bankton, An Institute of the Laws of Scotland in Civil Rights, vol I (1751), at p 357; Henry Home, Lord Kames, The Principles of Equity, 2nd edn. 1767, at pp. 71, 144 for condictio indebiti and causa data causa non secuta.

255 See preface of the 2nd edn. 1767; in great detail MacQueen/Sellar in Schrage (ed.), p. 289, at pp. 314 et seq.

judges have done over time.[256] But the decisive point is that, as Evans has shown, Lord Mansfield has read the Roman sources directly and also consulted *Arnoldus Vinnius.* That being so, the question is: Did he transplant the unjust factors of three specific *condictiones causa data causa non secuta, indebti* and *ob turpem vel iustam causam* into English law? The answer must be: yes! With respect to the "evidence" provided by Evans, I cannot agree with J.H. Baker who assumes that the term "quasi-contract" was the only specific borrowing from Roman Law.[257]

To be sure, the action of money had and received was a pure common law claim that had no links to the Roman *condictio* and did not indicate any defence of disenrichment – which may well explain why it took until 1991 before change of position was accepted in *Lipkin Gorman.* Money had and received was one of the "four counts" of "indebitatus assumpsit" that indicated the reason (or causa, if you wish) for assuming the obligation to pay in the opening pleadings.[258] It had developed under common law as a kind of "trust" (at law!) for money that had been received by the defendant "for the use" of the claimant.[259] But the different procedural background of the common law action is not the relevant point because both the Roman and the English action shared the most important feature. They were sufficiently "neutral" bases to claim (or reclaim) money from another.[260] While the former worked on the fiction of a loan, the latter worked on the fiction of a trust. Both fictions resulted in a duty to repay. This made them appropriate vessels to be extended to payment obligations that had their reason, their cause of action, in a ground for restitution.

The all-important part of *Moses v Macferlan* was therefore the planting of the Roman causes of action into English soil. Even though Lord Mansfield picked only

256 For example *Sinclair v Brougham* [1914] AC 398, at p. 435 (per Lord Dunedin).

257 Baker in Schrage (ed.), at p. 53. I do however agree with his statement that "posterity came to regret the choice of name".

258 Baker in Schrage (ed.), at p. 35 (the others being: goods sold, work done and money paid/laid out).

259 See the thorough account by Baker in Schrage (ed.), p. 31, in particular at pp. 47 et seq., tracing this claim to the early 17th century. Baker (ibid fn. 88) cites *Gilbert v Ruddeard* (1607) Dyer (Treby edn.) 272n with a literal paradigm: Debtor T delivered money to D to be delivered to P. P can sue D on an implied assumpsit for the money because, due to the debt of T to D, the delivery to P cannot be countermanded. The money was had and received by D for the use of P (the "beneficiary" of the "trust").

260 According to Baker in Schrage (ed.), at p. 54, the count of "money paid" would have been closer to the civilian view of the *condictiones sine causa* as "quasi-loans" in based on a relationship of "trust" as well ("creditor"), cp. Savigny, V, pp. 512 et seq.

some, while leaving others (particularly the *condictio sine causa*),[261] he managed to catch the essence of what was at the heart of the *condictiones sine causa:* the will of the claimant who had paid over money to another was vitiated (by initial flaws or subsequent failures) in a way that the transaction could no longer stand. The principle "volenti non fit inuria" was overcome and restitution granted.[262] The acceptance of the triggers of the Roman *condictio causa data causa non secuta*, the *condictio indebti* and the *condictio ob turpem vel inustam causam* as causes of action for money had an received turned them from (at best[263]) persuasive into actual authority.[264]

After *Moses v Macferlan*, the English soil was fertilized. The principle of unjust(ified) enrichment could be deduced on a *consimili casu* basis. As first witness of this effect, William Blackstone can be named:

> Blackstone, Commentaries, Book 3, Ch. 9, p. 162:[265] "A third species of implied assumpsit is when **one has had and received money of another's, without any valuable consideration given on the receiver's part:** for the law construes this to be money had and received for the use of the owner only; and implies that the person so receiving promised and undertook to account for it to the true proprietor. And, if he unjustly detains it, an action on the case lies against him for the breach of such implied promise and undertaking; and he will be made to repair the owner in damages, equivalent to what he has detained in such violation of his promise. This is a very extensive and beneficial remedy, applicable to almost every case where the defendant has received money which ex aequo et bono he ought to refund. It lies for money paid by mistake, or on a consideration which happens to fail, or through imposition, extortion, or oppression, or where undue advantage is taken of the plaintiff's situation."

As can be seen, Blackstone rightly saw the overarching principle of the remedy in the failure of consideration (= purpose) and restricted restitution to payor and

---

261 As to the possible reasons p. 103.

262 *Astley v Reynolds* 93 E.R. 939. As to volenti non fit inuria, see also the restriction of the *condictio sine causa* to shifts of wealth without the will of the claimant in the earlier German drafts, below pp. 240–241.

263 In general, the views on the persuasiveness of Civil law appear to be mixed and depend on the personality of the judge. For a positive attitude see e.g. Blackburn J. in *Taylor v Caldwell* [1863] EWHC QB J 1: "Although the Civil law is not of itself authority in an English Court, it affords great assistance in investigating the principles on which the law is grounded. And it seems to us that the common law authorities establish that in such a contract the same condition of the continued existence of the thing is implied by English law."

264 Cf e.g. *Woolwich Building Society v Commisioners of Inland Revenue* [1993] AC 70, (per Lord Jauncey of Tullichettle).

265 Online available https://avalon.law.yale.edu/18th_century/blackstone_bk3ch9.asp.

payee (= direct shift of value). A similarly narrow principle was recognised by Lord Haldane.

> *Royal Bank of Canada v The King* [1913] A. C. 283 (P.C.), at p. 296 (per Lord Haldane L.C.):[266] "It is a well-established principle of the English common law that when **money has been received by one person which in justice and equity belongs to another**, under circumstances which render the receipt of it a receipt by the defendant to the use of the plaintiff, the latter may recover as for money had and received to his use."

The dicta emphasised in fat print are basically in line with Savigny's concept of unjustified enrichment as a direct shift of value without legal reason. Blackstone appears closer by pointing to the lack of consideration, bearing in mind that Scott used "consideration" equivalent to "causa" throughout in his translation of the Digest.[267] Compared to that, "money that in justice and equity belongs to another" surely sounds more generic. But in a sense, it merely describes the lack of legal reason to keep a benefit from the opposite side, as a legal reason to return a benefit.

These early indicators of a narrow principle sit well with the fact that Lord Mansfield did not refer to the Pomponian sentence explicitly. The reason may have been a fear that its vivid language pointed straight to Equity ("iure naturae aequum est…") while the case in front of him was to be solved at law. This is an imminent danger of Pomponius' principle, as was rightly recognised by Lord Dunedin in *Sinclair v. Brougham*:

> *Sinclair v. Brougham* [1914] AC 398, at 434: "It will suffice if there is an equitable remedy. … Now, the Roman law met the situation by recognizing that there was the super-eminent equity … The super-eminent equity was expressed by the Roman jurists in the brocard nemo debet locupletari jactura aliena."

In *Moses v Macferlan*, Lord Mansfield used language very close to Pomponius. In a later case, his reference to equity became even clearer:

266 Referred to in *Fibrosa v Fairbairn*, [1943] AC 32, at p. 65 (per Lord Wright).

267 E. g. D.12.4. Concerning a suit for the recovery of property given for a consideration which does not take place.; D.12.5. Concerning a suit for the recovery where the consideration is immoral or injust; D.12.7.1. There is also the following kind of a personal action for recovery where anyone makes a promise without consideration, or where he pays something that was not due. Where a party makes a promise without consideration, he cannot bring an action for an amount which he did not give, but only for the obligation itself. Contrast however the heading of D.12.7. Concerning an action for recovery without ground. Scott's language confirms that "consideration" means "reason", see below, p. 105.

> *Clark v Shee and Johnson* (1774) 1 Cowp. 197, 199: "This is a liberal action in the nature of a bill in equity; and if, under the circumstances of the case, it appears that the defendant cannot in conscience retain what is the subject matter of it, the plaintiff may well support this action"

That language may well have been borrowed from civil law that was at the time in a similar state of confusion about the legal or equitable nature of unjust enrichment in general and the *condictiones* in particular. The effect was that the clear-cut remedy of money had an received to recover failed payments evaporated into the nebulous realm of equitable unjust enrichment. That had already been felt and said by Lord Dunedin:

> *Sinclair v. Brougham* [1914] AC 398, at 431: "I think one cannot help feeling that this action was truly the putting of an equitable doctrine under a legal form."

When the enrichment principle of Pomponius belatedly entered the common law through the backdoor of separated US law, it continued to mislead unjust enrichment into this direction[268] and was criticised for exactly that (p. 38: "well-meaning sloppiness of thought"). Today, English law is adamant that unjust enrichment is not a vague equitable concept. In a much-cited passage from Goff & Jones, it is said that:[269]

> "the 'unjust' element in 'unjust enrichment' is simply a 'generalisation of all the factors which the law recognises as calling for restitution' [a citation from the judgment of Campbell J in Wasada Pty Ltd v State Rail Authority of New South Wales (No 2) [2003] NSWSC 987 at [16], quoting Mason & Carter, Restitution Law in Australia (1995), 59–60]. In other words, unjust enrichment is not an abstract moral principle to which the courts must refer when deciding cases; it is an organising concept that groups decided authorities on the basis that they share a set of common features, namely that in all of them the defendant has been enriched by the receipt of a benefit that is gained at the claimant's expense in circumstances that the law deems to be unjust. The reasons why the courts have held a defendant's enrichment to be unjust vary from one set of cases to another..."

English law declares unjust enrichment not to be a loose equitable remedy. This is as it should be. However, this statement is only valid if the generic "no benefit from a loss" is replaced by the direct shift of value. As long as "no benefit from another's loss" governs, it will produce a wide enrichment. The reason is that unjust factors are merely relevant to the parties to the direct shift of value. They justify neither

268 "Developments oft he Law: Unjust Enrichment", 133 HarvLR (2019–2020), at 2077 et seq.
269 Goff & Jones, 1–08; cited with approval in *Barnes v Eastenders Cash &Carry* plc [2014] UKSC 26, [2015] AC 1, at para. 102 (per Lord Toulson); *Barton v Morris* [2023] UKSC 3, at para. 81 (per Lady Rose); *Dargamo Holdings Limited v Avonwick Holdings Limited* [2021] EWCA Civ 1149, at para. 62.

restitution nor retention of benefits by remote recipients. Wide enrichment claims lead to contradictory and irreconcilable decisions, as will be shown in detail below, pp. 191 et seq. That is why a judicial say-so does not suffice to settle the matter here. Authority does not work as a wishing well. It cannot erase the irresolvable conflict that arises if strict legal actions are wrongly deduced from a vague equitable principle that has matured into hard law. The only way out is to reduce enrichment claims strictly to direct shifts of value

But meanwhile, let us look at the three *condictiones* that are replicated by the action for money had and received because Lord Mansfield transplanted the causes of action into English law.

a) The mothers of unjust enrichment claims: *condictio causa data causa non secuta* (D.12.4.) and failure of consideration

aa) *The condictio causa data causa* and common law

The *condictio causa data causa non secuta* (also: *condictio ob rem;*[270] *condictio ob causam datorum*) concerned conditional payments that were made by the payor to achieve a certain outcome. If that outcome did not materialise, the payment could be recovered. The payor wanted to induce a certain conduct by the payee without the latter being obliged to do so, like e.g. to free a person from the powers of the *pater familias* (emancipation of a son; manumission of a slave) or to refrain from bringing an action.

> Dig. 12.4.1pr. (Ulpianus 26 ad ed.):
> Si ob rem non inhonestam[271] data sit pecunia, ut filius emanciparetur vel servus manumitteretur vel a lite discedatur, causa secuta repetitio cessat.

---

270 Note that there are passages in the Digest where a distinction is drawn between the "causa" and the "res" as the purposes pursued by the payor, cf. e.g. D.12.5.1.pr (below sub c) and D.12.6.52 (Pomp. 27 ad Q. Muc.): "Damus aut ob causam aut ob rem: ob causam praeteritam, veluti cum ideo do, quod aliquid a te consecutus sum vel quia aliquid a te factum est, ut, etiamsi falsa causa sit, repetitio eius pecuniae non sit: ob rem vero datur, ut aliquid sequatur, quo non sequente repetitio competit."

But these passages are even less clear than the meaning of causa itself and do not warrant further consideration. For example, D.12.6.52 seems to indicate that "ob causam" relates to reasons in the past ("praeteritam") whereas "ob rem" relates to future acts – which evidently contradicts the notion of "causa data causa non secuta".

271 The legitimacy of the purpose / *causa* ("non inhonestam") distinguishes the *condictio ob rem* from the *condictio ob turpem vel iniustam causam.* This distinction also explains the term "repetitio cessat" because in the case of a prohibited purpose, the *condictio* survived the achievement of the outcome

It also covered upfront payments for works that were not performed.

> See e. g. D.12.4.11 (Julian): Si heres arbitratu liberti certa summa monumentum iussus facere dederit liberto pecuniam et is accepta pecunia monumentum non faciat, condictione tenetur.
>
> [If a heir has given money to a freedman who shall, according to his discretion, build a monument[272] at a certain price, and if he does not build the monument despite having accepted the money, he will be subject to the *condictio.*]

Many of these situations would be covered by contractual remedies in modern jurisdictions. In ancient Roman law however, contract law was underdeveloped in manifold ways. For example, services were seldom contracted for because they were typically owed by virtue of personal legal ties (family; slavery). In our context, it is of particular importance that the enforcement of contracts was limited by strict formal requirements that were not available in many situations of everyday life.[273] Purely consensual agreements were not normally actionable. That only began to change in the classical period of Roman law, with the rise of the so-called *Innominatkontrakte* = innominate contracts.[274] Prior to that time, the availability of the *condictio* was essential. Since neither the performance nor damages for breach could be enforced against the other party, getting the money back was the only help available.

The reason for restitution is that the *causa* of that transfer had failed. The German Causa-doctrine would speak of a *Zweckverfehlung* (= failure of purpose), in this case concerning the *Erwerbszweck* = *causa acquirendi* (see in more detail pp. 270 – 272). For English lawyers, this is a failure of consideration / basis.

Today, the *condictio indebiti* may widely be regarded as the paradigm case of unjust(ified) enrichment.[275] But the *condictio causa data causa non secuta* was the "mother of unjust enrichment" because it described the primeval and most pressing case for restitution: not getting what one had bargained for. The *condictio indebiti* is only a prominent part of that parcel. It remedies the failed bargain for the discharge of the debt. It has been said that in mistake cases, the intent of

---

272 Monument is used in the sense of a tomb here, like those that still can be seen along the ancient Via Appia before the gates of Rome.

273 Cf. e. g. Zimmermann, The Law of Obligations, pp. 82 et seq. and 843 – 844; Honsell, Römisches Recht, 3 edn., § 54, pp. 134 et seq.

274 Zimmermann, pp. 857– 858; also pp. 860 – 862 to the demise of innominate contracts. Cf. also Schall in Beck OGK BGB, § 346 mn. 3.

275 Ernst in Flume, Studien, Einleitung, p. 2 with fn. 1.

the payor is vitiated, whereas in failure of consideration cases, it is qualified.[276] But this is misleading. Once the failure of purpose is recognised as the overarching trigger for restitution, it turns out that intent of the payor is qualified in both cases. The difference is only that in one line of cases, the purpose fails from the outset (liability mistakes being the most prominent, but not the only example) whereas in the other line of cases, the purpose fails due to subsequent events. This does not change the fact that the intent was qualified by a condition in both cases. The failure of the condition is the flaw of the transaction (payment, conveyance, "performance", etc.) that calls for restitution. But even if the purpose fails from the outset, it does not "vitiate" the intent of the performing party. The unilateral mistake of the payor cannot suffice to vitiate = invalidate the transaction – just as it does not suffice to invalidate a contract. Lord Toulson rightly said "it should not be thought that mere failure of an expectation which motivated a party to enter into a contract may give rise to a restitutionary claim."[277] The almost impossible difficulty to distinguish relevant unilateral mistakes from irrelevant unilateral motivations[278] dissolves immediately with the emergence of the failure of the purpose (*causa solvendi*; *causa acquirendi*). This recognition allowed German law to overcome the peculiarities of mistake and find a more coherent solution (see pp. 270–272).

The fundamental answer to any failed bargain has always been: "money back". The remedy is of great ancientness. It was testified more than 3800 years ago. § 278 of the Code of Hammurabi provided:

> "If a man sell a male or female slave,[279] and the slave have not completed his month, and the bennu fever[280] fall upon him, he (the purchaser) shall return him to the seller and he shall receive the money which he paid."[281]

---

276 *Dargamo Holdings Limited v Avonwick Holdings Limited* [2021] EWCA Civ 1149, at para. 79 (per LJ Carr), referring to Burrows, The Law or restitution, 3rd edn. 2011; cited with approval in *Barton v Morris* [2023] UKSC 3, at para. 79 (per Lady Rose).

277 *Barnes v Eastenders Cash & Carry plc* [2014] UKSC 26, [2015] AC 1, at para. 115.

278 On the critical debate on "mistake" see in particular Meier/Zimmermann, "Judicial Developments of the Law: *Error Juris*, and The Law of Unjustified Enrichment- A View from Germany' (1999) 115 LQR 556, 561 et seq. Opposing mistake outright Stevens, pp. 71 et seq..12.75.

279 I am fully aware that any kind of slavery is absolutely inhumane and that therefore, bringing this example may be perceived as problematic and even hurtful by some. But it makes an important point as to the evolution of legal thinking that took place in a past very long gone. This shall not imply or invite any positive view on slavery to any time in any place in the world.

280 = epilepsy.

281 Sourced from the Harper translation, https://en.wikisource.org/wiki/The_Code_of_Hammurabi_(Harper_translation)

The Code of Hammurabi granted a claim for restitution that is subject to counter-restitution. The reason for restitution is that the buyer does not get what he bargained for. This rule predates the emergence of the law of contract with remedies like damages or repudiation. Enforceable promises undoubtedly facilitated trade and made modern market economy possible. But humans never needed enforceable claims to exchange goods. This can still be observed today. Every day, there are millions of sales in the shops and markets of the UK – but far less contracts to sell.[282] If exchanges fail, getting the money back is the simple and obvious remedy.

Over the course of the millennia, this basic notion has remained the same while more refined remedies (and defences[283]) were created as contract law developed, starting from the Roman *actio redhibitoria* and *actio quanta minoris* via the Sales of Goods Act 1979 to the Consumer Protection Directive 1999/44/EC with its priority right to have faulty goods repaired or replaced (Art. 3(3)). One reason may have been that money back is a crude rule that does not cater for the various degrees of faultiness of goods. That makes it reasonable to leave restitution for (total) failure of consideration out of the picture in that context. But English law has always allowed restitution for (total) failure of consideration.[284] And it kept this rule alive besides the availability of contractual remedies.[285] Money given for nothing can be recovered, be it for a title that did not pass (*Rowland v Divall*[286]) or for works that never materialised (*Fibrosa v Fairbain*[287]), like the case of the freedman and the tomb in D.12.4.11. The leading cases of modern times[288] are *Barnes v Eastenders Cash & Carry* plc[289] and *Roxborough v Rothmans.*[290] These cases were the points of reference when *Barton v Morris* relabelled "failure of consideration" as "failure of basis". That must be looked at closer below because it is connected to the shared origin of the claims (pp. 87–92).

---

282 Cf. s.2(4) and (5) Sales of Goods Act 1979. See also below, p. 271.

283 Last not least "Caveat emptor", cf. Zimmermann, pp. 307–308.

284 Ibbetson in Schrage (ed.), at pp. 125–132 with numerous references. Ibbetson distinguishes between gifts for a purpose that did not eventuate (p. 126, e.g. in anticipation of a marriage, *matrimonii causa*), contracts that failed for circumstances that were beyond the parties (p. 127) and breaches of contract (p.128). For modern criticism of "total" see Stevens, pp. 115–116.

285 According to Ibbetson in Schrage (ed.), at p. 128, this dualism can be traced way back in legal history (he cites a remark in a year book case of 1294).

286 [1923] 2 KB 500.

287 *Fibrosa Spolka Akcyjna v Fairbairn Lawson Combe Barbour Ltd* [1942] UKHL 4.

288 So declared by Lady Rose in *Barton v Morris* [2023] UKSC 3, at para. 79.

289 [2014] UKSC 26, [2015] AC 1.

290 *Roxborough v Rothmans of Pall Mall Australia Ltd* [2001] HCA 68, (2001) 208 CLR 516.

According to orthodoxy, at least for the time being, such failure of consideration claims will lie irrespective of the validity of the contract. The ground for this had been laid in *Fibrosa v Fairbain*[291] where Viscount Simon LC said (at p 48):

> In English law, an enforceable contract may be formed by an exchange of a promise for a promise, or by the exchange of a promise for an act— I am excluding contracts under seal -and thus, in the law relating to the formation of contract, the promise to do a thing may often be the consideration, but when one is considering the law of failure of consideration and of the quasi-contractual right to recover money on that ground, **it is, generally speaking, not the promise which is referred to as the consideration, but the performance of the promise.** The money was paid to secure performance and, if performance fails the inducement which brought about the payment is not fulfilled.

This is persuasive because the validity of the contract does not prevent the failure of the consideration or *causa acquirendi* – which is the very *raison d'être* of restitution (see below pp. 91–92). The performance of the promise is typically the counter-performance. It would not make sense to require that the contract be wiped out (by rescission etc.) before restitution can take place because this would bring down contractual damages claims and undeservedly help the other party who committed the breach of contract (if there is one).[292] Conversely, the binding promises under the valid contract are not required to explain or justify restitution. Therefore, this is not a contractual claim either.[293]

The dictum by Viscount Simon is however too narrow in another sense. According to him, failure of consideration means failure of the counter-performance that had been *promised under the contract* (see bold print).[294] As will be shown, the *condictio causa data causa non secuta* covered mainly payments that were made

291 *Fibrosa Spolka Akcyjna v Fairbairn Lawson Combe Barbour Ltd* [1942] UKHL 4, [1942] AC 32; followed e.g. by *Dargamo Holdings Limited v Avonwick Holdings Limited* [2021] EWCA Civ 1149, at para. 80.

292 This was acknowledged by the great reform of German law of obligations in 2002. Since then, § 325 BGB expressly allows the cumulation of “Rücktritt” (a sort of rescission, triggering contractual restitution under § 346 BGB) and damages claims.

293 The contrasting views of many authors seem primarily motivated by a desire to clip out the disenrichment defence. But that outcome can be achieved by unjust enrichment, too, see below p. 284.

294 Contrast *Dargamo Holdings Limited v Avonwick Holdings Limited* [2021] EWCA Civ 1149, at para. 80 (per LJ Carr): “It is common ground that the meaning of failure of basis extends beyond failure of promissory consideration payable under a contract or a failure of contractual counter-performance (see *Fibrosa Spolka Akcyjna v Fairburn Lawson Combe Barbour Ltd* [1943] AC 32 at 48)”

But the cited passage does not say the latter.

conditional on a *quid pro quo* but could not be enforced because of the lack of a binding obligation to perform. In recent times, the common law has moved the claim for failure of consideration into the same direction and combined the move with a shift of terminology from "failure of consideration" to "failure of basis". We will come back to that below.

bb) The condictio causa data causa non secuta and civil law

Civil law has taken a different route though. With the constant rise of contract in modern times,[295] the formerly central role of the *condictio causa data causa non secuta* was steadily diminished. At the same time, the importance of the *condictio indebiti* grew. It provides restitution where the contract is invalid, whereas in other cases of default, only contractual remedies (damages, repudiation etc.) are at hand. That development significantly reduced the scope for the *condictio ob rem.* It was furthered by a strict adherence to the principle of "pacta sunt servanda". Reclaiming the money means turning away from the contract. And that would not be permitted under Civil Law, not even in case of breaches. That situation only changed when the codifications devised statutory rights to withdraw from contracts.[296]

The civilian shift of the failure of the *causa acquirendi* into the realm of contract started with sales law. The curule aediles, in charge of Roman markets, accepted restitution for failure of the purchased good (slave) in the same way as the Code Hammurabi had done. They developed the *actio redhibitoria* and added the *actio quantis minoria* to reduce the price if the good was kept.[297] These remedies became central pillars of civilian sales law. From a doctrinal perspective, they had never been part of unjust enrichment, but contractual remedies. As such, they entered the European codifications and became gradually extended to cover various sorts of breaches of contract.[298] For example, the German *Rücktrittsrecht* under §§ 346–354 BGB[299] provides for a right of restitution and counter-restitution, orig-

---

295 Zimmermann, pp. 860–862, 866–868. In depth Sorge, Verpflichtungsfreier Vertrag, 2017. It may be that the rise of contract will come to a halt for the first time in legal history. The emergence of "smart contracts" based on the blockchain technology makes enforceable obligations redundant.

296 Take for example the German Rücktrittsrecht in § 346 BGB. For the development, see Leser, Der Rücktritt vom Vertrag, 1975, pp. 1 et seq.; Schall in BeckOGK, § 346 mn. 2 et seq.

297 Zimmermann, pp. 311 et seq.; Harke, AcP 205 (2005), 67, at pp. 68–71.

298 See for example Art. 1217 Code Civil or §§ 437 n° 2, 440 and 441 BGB in conjunction with § 346 BGB.

299 This is a right to "undo" the contract and trigger restitution of any performances already made. It can be seen as functional equivalent of rescission. It inter alia covers classical failure of consideration cases, however subjecting restitution to a prior declaration of *Rücktritt* (= "rescission or "termination" of the contract).

inally construed along the lines of the *actio redhibitoria*, before a major overhaul in 2002. Unlike unjustified enrichment, the provisions of the *Rücktrittsrecht* require the existence of a valid contract. They cease to apply if the contract is avoided ab initio.[300] The declaration of the *Rücktritt* itself is assumed not to eliminate the contract but merely to reverse the contractual obligations so that a restitution contract comes into existence (*Rückgewährschuldverhältnis*).[301] The upshot of the doctrinal classification as contractual remedy is that there is not defence of disenrichment available against the claim for restitution and counter-restitution which is an outcome desired by many common lawyers as well.[302]

Nevertheless, the clothing of sales law as contractual remedy is primarily due to path dependence. The notion that the buyer of the faulty good has still got what he bargained for may have marked the difference to the builder who does not build. Caveat emptor! The same notion prevails under common law. Lord Atkin explained it in *Bell v Lever Bros*:[303]

> A buys B's horse; he thinks the horse is sound and he pays the price of a sound horse; he would certainly not have bought the horse if he had known, as the fact is, that the horse is unsound. If B has made no representation as to soundness and has not contracted that the horse is sound, A is bound and cannot recover back the price. A buys a picture from B; both A and B believe it to be the work of an old master, and a high price is paid. It turns out to be a modern copy. A would never have entered into the bargain if he had known the fact. A has no remedy, and the position is the same whether B knew the facts or not, so long as he made no representation or gave no warranty.

For this reason, the sale of faulty goods has never been perceived as a case of *causa data causa non secuta*. Nevertheless, the overarching trigger of restitution in all those cases, from the non-completed tomb via the faulty goods to *Rowland v. Divall*,

---

300 For the comparison of the two instruments that both cover parts of the ground of common law rescission cf. *Schall* in BeckOGK BGB, § 346 mn. 35 et seq.

301 BGHZ 174, 290 = NJW 2008, 911, at para. 10; Leser, Der Rücktritt vom Vertrag, 1975, pp. 150 et seq.; E. Wolf, AcP 153 (1954), 97, at pp. 103 et seq. But contrast German academics assuming that the true nature of restitution after the declaration of a *Rücktritt* is unjust enrichment: Soergel/*Lobinger*, Vor § 346 mn. 15 and 18 et seq.; *Kohler* JZ 2002, 682, 684 et seq. id., AcP 208 (2008), 417, 430 et seq. Contrary to the fears of the prevailing opinion, this classification would not lead to widespread allocation of the disenrichment defence because following *Flume* (below p. 85 and 301), no disenrichment defence for expenses made can be held against the return of upfront payments anyway. The same rule applies to common law (*Fibrosa v Fairbairn*).

302 See also Stevens, p. 10, who bases the claim on an agreement. For a contractual classification of the *condictio causa data causa non secuta* see also BeckOK/Wendehorst, § 812 para. 85, id. in Zimmermann, Grundstrukturen eines Europäischen Bereicherungsrechts, 2005, 47, 81 f.; cf. further Thomale, Leistung als Freiheit, 2012, 197 f.

303 *Bell v Lever Bros* [1931] UKHL 2, [1932] AC 161, 218 et seq.

is that the buyer does not get what he bargained for, i. e. the failure of the "*causa acquirendi*" (= the consideration). This is confirmed by the qualification of German sales law in 2002 where the duty of the vendor had been expanded to encompass delivery (transfer of title and possession) to a flawless good.[304]

A learned guess may suggest that the separate treatment of sales of faulty goods inhibited the proper development of the *condictiones.* It certainly showed that the Romans were aware of the need to make counter restitution when reversing a failed exchange. But the most prominent line of cases simply was not enrichment law to them. Had it been, there is no reason to assume that they would have allocated the risks of restitution differently. Civil laws would not have to be afraid of disenrichment when reversing contracts where the *causa acquirendi* had failed. But they were, and as a consequence, the law of contract grew and grew while the *condictio causa data causa non secuta* shrank into oblivion. It was not even enshrined in the Codes of France and Austria, whereas in Germany, it entered the BGB in § 812 I 1 2nd alternative BGB but was reduced to a subsidiary remedy for rare cases beyond regular contracts, where a payment is made to induce the recipient to some act or omission to which he is not legally obliged. Take the following example:

> A has committed a minor offence against B. A gives B 500 £ not to report him to the police. B accepts the money, but then changes his mind and reports A to the police.

In modern jurisdictions, cases like this are usually governed by contract. Common lawyers would construe a non-disclosure agreement (NDA). The payment would be made in return for the promise by B to abstain from reporting. Provided there are no public policy reasons invalidating the agreement,[305] B will be obliged not to re-

---

304 For example, German sales law of 2002 added a new sentence: "Der Verkäufer hat dem Käufer die Sache frei von Sach- und Rechtsmängeln zu verschaffen." [The seller must provide the buyer with the item free of material defects and defects of title. – DeepL].

305 Under common law, the line for the validity of NDAs is normally drawn at crimes. It may even be that an early example could be found in the Digest itself. Recovery of the payment that should secure non-reporting was allowed regardless of compliance by the recipient in a case where a slave had given money not to be reported for his theft, Julian D. 12.5.5 (3 ad Urs. Fer.): "Si a servo meo pecuniam quis accepisset, ne furtum ab eo factum indicaret, *sive indicasset sive non*, repetitionem fore eius pecuniae, Proculus respondit." Cf. further Christian Friedrich von Glück, Die ausführliche Erläuterung der Pandekten nach Hellfeldt, Dreizehnten Teils erste Abteilung, 2nd edn. 1843, p. 61.

However, this can only serve as example for an early public policy restriction if we assume that the not-to-be-reported theft by the slave had been committed against the recipient. But the text is ambiguous here. If we instead assume that the theft had been committed against the owner of

port A. If B nevertheless reported A, this would be a breach of contract and trigger damages.

But it is not necessary to create obligations under a confidentiality agreement in order to recover the payment. Without the conclusion of a confidentiality agreement, B may not be *obliged* not to report. However, if B accepted the money offered and then chose to go to the police all the while, this would be answered by a restitutionary claim on grounds of the failure of the mutually agreed[306] purpose of the payment: *causa data causa non secuta!* This is a German textbook example for recovery under § 812 I 2 2. Alt. BGB.[307] The same solution should be achieved under failure of consideration. An example is the breach of the promise not to sue in *Moses v Macferlan* (see below p. 110).

The alternative between a mere *condictio ob rem* and an obligation to abstain from action was already known to the Romans:

> D.12.4.3pr. (Ulpianus 26 ad ed.)
> Dedi tibi pecuniam, ne ad iudicem iretur: quasi decidi. an possim condicere, si mihi non caveatur ad iudicem non iri? et est verum multum interesse, utrum ob hoc solum dedi, ne eatur, an ut et mihi repromittatur non iri: si ob hoc, ut et repromittatur, condici poterit, si non repromittatur: si ut ne eatur, condictio cessat quamdiu non itur.
>
> [(Scott): I paid you a certain sum of money to avoid your bringing me into court; and, hence I, as it were, disposed of the matter. Can I bring suit for recovery, if security is not furnished me that judicial proceedings will not be instituted? It is true that it makes a great deal of difference whether I paid the money for no other purpose than to avoid being brought into court, or that I should be promised that this would not be done; but if this was the consideration, namely, that I should be promised, I can bring suit to recover the money if the promise was not given; but if the understanding was merely that judicial proceedings should not be undertaken, no action for recovery will lie as long as this is not done.]

The passage highlights the difference between bargaining for a contract to abstain ("repromittatur" = the "promise back" or "counterpromise") and bargaining for the omission itself, without any promise made. In the first case, the money can be reclaimed as soon as it is clear that the promise not to sue will not be made, whether or not the defendant actually brings the claim. By contrast, in the second case, there is a constellation that is close to what has been described as "unilateral con-

---

the slave and was merely witnessed by the recipient of the payment, the case is clearly based on the immorality of this bribe that would incite obstruction of justice at the expense of the owner.

306 In this example, the payment is mutually agreed. But note that this need not be so to found the claim, see below p. 83.

307 BeckOK BGB/Wendehorst, § 812 para. 88.

tract" in *Barton v Morris.*[308] The difference is that in a *causa data causa non secuta* situation the payment is advanced beforehand so that there is no duty at all, neither for the one party to perform nor for the other to make the payment afterwards. Instead, the rule is that recovery of the advance will be barred as long as the defendant does not bring the claim, whether or not he promises not to do so. The second part raises some tension with a subsequent passage in D.12.4.3.2. according to which the payor will not only be able to reclaim the money in case of failure of the purpose, but also if he has second thoughts himself and rues the payment.[309] This is consequential because it confirms the complete lack of obligation on both sides. But it need not be delved into here because it is no more the law under § 812 BGB.

The gist of D.12.4.3. is: A payment can be made conditional unilaterally by the payor, to motivate the recipient to commit or omit a certain act, without creating an obligation. The "consideration", i. e. a *quid pro quo* for the payment is typically the respective act or omission itself. But it can also be an outcome that is dependent on a contribution by the other side, but cannot be guaranteed. The other party retains freedom to perform or not to perform the act or to omit or not to omit even when accepting the payment. If the party chooses not to comply, it will not liable for a breach, but it cannot "earn", that is retain the payment. But if it earns the payment by the act or omission, the payment will be made *cum causa,* i. e. for good consideration.

This construction of the transaction makes particular sense where the payor is not able to enforce the consideration he seeks by specific performance or damages claims, for example if the other party is yet to enter into a contract with him or if a contract cannot be concluded because the recipient cannot promise the act or omission. This may be for the example the case where the recipient cannot contract out of his right to file a complaint, report a crime or bring a lawsuit. Unlike NDAs not to report crimes, such payments would arguably not violate public policy because the victim is still free to choose to report and simply return the money,

308 *Barton v Morris* [2023] UKSC 3, at para. 17: "Mr Barton was not under any obligation to make an introduction of a potential buyer to Foxpace in the sense that if, after he had concluded the agreement with Foxpace, he had decided for whatever reason not to disclose Western's name to Foxpace, he would not have been in breach of any contractual obligation. But if he did make the introduction and if Foxpace did sell Nash House to Western for £6.5 million, then Foxpace would be in breach of the express terms of the agreement if they failed to pay him £1.2 million. That was the extent of the express agreement reached by the parties."

German law would speak of "*einseitig verpflichtender Vertrag*". Brokerage agreements under § 652 BGB are a typical example. On agreements beyond contract see also Stevens, pp. 111–115.

309 12.4.3.2. (Ulp 26 ad ed): "Sed si tibi dedero, ut stichum manumittas: si non facis, possum condicere, aut si me paeniteat, condicere possum." Cf. further Zimmermann, p. 858.

without any threat of becoming subject to choking damages claims.[310] Another example would be a situation where the payor seeks an outcome that the other party can only initiate but not guarantee because it is beyond its competences, for example the procurement of a certain permission that the other party can apply for to be granted by a public authority.

Barnes v Eastenders fits this pattern. The Crown Court appointed a management receiver on application of the Crown Prosecution Service (CSP) under the Proceeds of Crime Act 2002. The Court order was later squashed. As a consequence, the receiver was not entitled any longer to cover his costs from the assets of the company. The receiver had been employed by the CSP. The consideration for his services was supposed to be the right to cover the costs from the assets of the managed companies. It could not be delivered by the CSP because it had to be ordered by the Court. The CSP could only initiate the process to get the Court order – which it originally did successfully. When the Court order was squashed later on, the consideration for the services failed. The receiver had bargained for nothing, the *causa acquirendi* of his services was not achieved. *Causa data causa non secuta!* It was rightly held that that a *quantum meruit* would lie against the CSP that had requested the services. It does not matter that the contractual obligations had been fulfilled at the time. One must bear in mind that contractual obligations are just means to facilitate the exchange of goods and services. They cannot prevent that those exchanges actually fail.

Also, smart contracts may open a modern field of application for "ob rem" cases. Their trick is to execute exchanges automatically by crypted codes, without creating antecedent contractual obligations. This disposes of the need for contractual enforcement. But it will not prevent exchanges from failing in the real world, and when they do, *ob rem* actions like § 812 BGB or failure of consideration will have to step in.

An important observation about the *condictio causa data causa non secuta* is the **unilateral foundation** of the claim. The *causa* of the payment is set by the payor, and restitution is simply ordered because that given causa does not follow suit. To be sure, the clearest case for restitution is a purpose that is not achieved after it had been *mutually* agreed by the parties, as was the case with the non-completed tomb in D.12.4.11. Conversely, serious doubts will always be raised if claims are to be imposed on the defendant unilaterally.[311] For example, unsolicited goods need neither be paid nor returned. They are treated as a gift by common law for

---

310 Sed query whether a payment meant to dissuade the recipient to report a crime can be recovered because it may be seen as violating public policy as well as the NDA.

311 In general, see Stevens, pp. 9–10, 46, 81, 111.

good reason. Art. 27 of the Consumer Rights Directive has spread this rule over Europe. Also, it is generally far more difficult to distinguish relevant purposes from irrelevant motives without recourse to an agreement between the parties. But notwithstanding that, a valid agreement on the purpose of the performance is not a precondition of the *condictio causa data causa non secuta.* It suffices that the outcome is sought by the performing party – and fails. To go back to the above example: If A pays B not to report his offence, but B mistakes the payment as a gift of regret or compensation for immaterial harm, the purpose is not mutually agreed, but there must be a claim in restitution. It does not matter whether the outcome sought by A is not achieved because it was agreed but failed (B reports nevertheless, see above) or because the parties even failed to agree. In both cases, the transfer was not intended as a gift and the defendant can make no case to keep it. In line with that, the second alternative of § 812 I 2 BGB orders restitution if "the outcome sought by a performance according to the content of the legal act does not materialise" ("der mit einer Leistung nach dem Inhalt des Rechtsgeschäfts bezweckte Erfolg nicht eintritt").[312]

It must be mentioned that it was not entirely clear in the Digest whether the *condictio causa data causa non secuta* required that the outcome to be achieved (= the "causa non secuta") had been agreed upon, or whether it could be set unilaterally by the payor. The text ("causa data") seemingly indicates that the purpose of the payment was set as a one-sided octroi by the payor. By contrast, the historic evolution from the loan might suggest a situation where the parties agreed to achieve a purpose and imply a promise to repay in case of failure "as if the parties had agreed on a loan" – the payment would be made on a preliminary basis, and the subsequent achievement or failure of the agreed purpose would decide whether the payment turned into the price paid on a permanent exchange or remained a loan to be returned. Convertible bonds on the capital markets are construed in a similar way.

But the open issue of the unilaterality of the *condictio causa data causa non secuta* in D.12.4 does not call into question the unilateral foundation of the *condictiones* for the failure of the purpose set by the payor. If D.12.4. was not applied due to lack of an "acceptance" by the payee, this would not deny restitution to the payor. Rather, the *condictio sine causa* would be available instead (D.12.7.). That is why we can deduce that the decisive trigger for restitution under all performance-based *condic-*

312 Note that the term "Inhalt des Rechtsgeschäfts" does not indicate an agreement, because German law also knows unilateral "Rechtsgeschäfte" (thus better translated as legal act than legal transaction). On example is the performance. Another one is the granting of power of attorney ("Vollmacht") under §§ 164, 167 BGB

tiones is the disappointment of the claimant. This is the failure of purpose approach adopted by the German codification that will be elaborated in great detail below (pp. 245–246, 266–272). The same picture emerges under Common Law if "consideration" is not understood in the too narrow meaning of counter-performance, but quite literally as the "expected return" of the performance (see in more detail pp. 91–92).[313] In that broader sense of the *quid pro quo*, it becomes the reason for the decision-making to shift value to the other party. That is how William Blackstone saw the law after *Moses v Macferlan.*[314] The civilian language would call this reason to make the payment the *causa acquirendi.*[315]. The expected return is the primary purpose for the performing party to make the payment. It is therefore the only purpose the failure of which is relevant for restitution, as distinguished from all other possible expectation and assumptions that may be disappointed (I was sure the shares would rise). Nevertheless, it is unilateral. It need not be agreed because failure of reaching an agreement does not leave the performance where it is but is the first reason why the purpose failed and it must be given back. That is why the action for money had and received facilitated the unilateral approach.

Robert Stevens says about the English laws of restitution:[316]

> It is not the case, nor should it be, that the justification for recovery can be wholly plaintiff sided.

From the perspective of legal philosophy, that is a strong statement. But it cannot be denied that the basic justification of the Roman *condictiones sine causa* is unilateral foundation. Generally speaking, common law has always had its own ways, but since Lord Mansfield transplanted the triggers of the Roman *condictiones*, the reasons for restitution are unilateral as well. However, civil lawyers were well aware that the unilateral foundation of the claim required higher protection for innocent defendants. It was found in the defence of disenrichment. That is why the introduction of the *condictio ob rem* concludes with a side note on disenrichment.

Classic Roman law did not accept a defence of disenrichment/change of position if the *condictio* sought to recover a payment.[317] Thus, like in *Fibrosa*, the freed-

313 Birks, Unjust Enrichment, 2005, pp. 117 et seq.
314 See above, p. 69.
315 For the detailed explanation of the three purposes (causae) the failure of which triggers restitution see pp. 270–272.)
316 Stevens, p. 46; but contrast Burrows, In Defence of Unjust Enrichment, 78 (3) CLJ 521 (2019).
317 Zimmermann, pp. 896–900; Flume, FS Niedermeyer, 1953, 103 et seq., 130 = Studien, p. 50; Erxleben, Die Condictiones sine Causa, Vol I, 1950, pp. 182 et seq.

man of D.12.4.11 would not have been able to set off any expenses. The defence of disenrichment was decisively promoted by the Justinian codification with the Pomponian principle. Interestingly, German lawyers of the 19th century generalised the disenrichment defence to cover *all* recovery claims based on a *condictio*, be it for money, generics or specifics, while at the same time rejecting the equitable principle of Pomponius as basis of unjust enrichment. To dissolve this contradiction, another rationalisation of disenrichment had to be found and was found eventually. Werner Flume sought the rationale of disenrichment in the trust on the receipt of the performance caused by the performing party (see p. 297). By doing so, he made a major contribution to the liberation of unjustified enrichment from the historic claws of *Billigkeitsrecht*. In the context of *causa data*, Flume argued there can be no deduction of the expenses from the upfront payment because the defendant would have suffered the same loss if he had not received any advance payment. That is why there was no direct causal link of the payment and the expenses.[318] The argument is taken from BGH II ZR 295/51,[319] a twin decision of *Fibrosa v Fairnbairn*:[320] The defendant had been charged with the delivery of machines to produce ammunition. He received an upfront payment. Delivery was not made due to war events. The claimant demanded refund of his prepayment. The defendant objected that the machines were practically ready and all money spent on them. The Bundesgerichtshof did not hear this defence.

The decision is persuasive. One should add that the deduction would undermine the contract that required delivery for the payment to be earned. That argu-

318 Flume, FS Niedermeyer, 1953, 103, 162–163 in justification of the decision BGH II ZR 295/51, BeckRS 1952, 31203092. Such claims for partial payments could arise from contractual agreements, but also from counter-claims based on a *negotiorum gestio* under §§ 683, 670 BGB or on unjustified enrichment under § 812 BGB (provided the other party has received value from the expenses made).

319 BGH BeckRS 1952, 31203092: "Die Bereicherung die die Beklagte durch die nicht zu einer Lieferung führende Anzahlung der Klägerin erhalten hat und der Vermögensverlust durch den Abtransport der Maschinen stehen in keinerlei ursächlichem Zusammenhang. Die Beklagte hätte den eingetretenen Verlust auch erlitten, wenn keinerlei Anzahlung von einem Abnehmer erfolgt wäre, so wie es zweifelsfrei bezüglich anderer Halbfabrikate auch der Fall ist."

[The enrichment that the defendant received through the advance payment from the plaintiff, which did not lead to a delivery, and the loss of assets through the removal of the machines are not causally connected in any way. The defendant would also have suffered the loss incurred if no advance payment had been made by a customer, as is undoubtedly the case with other semi-finished products.]

320 *Fibrosa Spolka Akcyjna v Fairbairn Lawson Combe Barbour Ltd* [1942] UKHL 4.

ment is made by Robert Stevens for English law.[321] This is in line with a recently emerging line of judicial speeches that although unjust enrichment can bite when contracts are valid, it must not undermine the contractual obligations and risk allocations.[322] One qualification should however be added: if the other party indeed receives an actual value from the "half-performance", it must account for it in unjust enrichment, too. For example, if the builder leaves the owner with a pitch-perfect fundament before going bankrupt and being unable to complete the house.[323]

But it also should be noted that the diverging solution of the Frustrated Contracts Act to cater for expenses in cases of frustration irrespective of any value received by the claimant[324] is still possible in Germany. Tellingly, it is now based on the purely equitable institute of *Wegfall der Geschäftsgrundlage* under § 313 BGB. This rule codified long-established case law.[325] The German term translates along the lines of lack / loss or cessation of the basis of the transaction. This makes it necessary to compare this German legal institute with (and distinguish it from) the new terminology of failure of basis that has been adopted under English unjust enrichment in lieu of failure of consideration (p. 87).

The rule in § 313 BGB covers the situations of the Law Reform (Frustrated contracts) Act 1943[326] and rose to prominence in the recent Pandemic,[327] but it would also go further and provide relieve in the now abandoned *Solle v Butcher*[328] scenarios of common equitable mistake. The traditional textbook example of the "Kar-

321 Stevens, pp. 359–360; id, LQR (2018), 573, at p. 587: A defence of change of position is, in such circumstances, inconsistent with the agreement made, and incompatible with the reason for the claim.

322 *Barton v Morris* [2023] UKSC 3, at paras. 90–91 (per Lady Rose) referring to the "impeccable authority of *Pan Ocean Shipping Co Ltd v. Creditcorp Ltd (THE "TRIDENT BEAUTY")*. [1994] 1 Lloyds Report 365; *Dargamo Holdings v Avonwick Holdings* [2021] EWCA Civ 1149, at paras. 65–76 (per LJ Carr). See also *Regalian Properties Ltd v. London Docklands Development Corp* [1995] 1 WLR 212; Stevens, pp. 114–115.

323 Normally, service contracts provide for such situations by milestones triggering instalments. In that case, recourse to unjust enrichment is not necessary.

324 Cf. s.1(2) Law Reform (Frustrated Contracts) Act 1943.

325 This is a former case law concept developed by the Reichsgericht to provide relief in the times of the hyperinflation of the 1920ies, see Schall, JZ 2020, 388, 389–390.

326 On the notion of "frustration" cf. further *Panalpina (Northern) Ltd [1981] AC 675* at 700 (per Lord Simon).

327 BGHZ 232, 178; critical however, arguing for "legal impossibility" under §§ 275, 326 BGB Köndgen, JZ 2022, 990 et seq; in the same vein, prior to the supreme court judgement, already Schall, JZ 2021, 455 et seq. As to the legal concept of impossibility, see also the judgement of Blackburn J. in *Taylor v Caldwell* [1863] EWHC QB J 1.

328 *Solle v Butcher* [1950] 1 KB 671, overruled by *Great Peace Shipping Ltd v Tsavliris (International) Ltd* [2002] EWCA Civ 1407, see p. 90.

nevalszugfall",[329] an equivalent to the coronation cases,[330] would be solved under § 313 BGB as follows: no rent will be due for the window seat to watch the cancelled pageant, but expenses made by the landlord for the provision of ancillary services like a buffet or a dinks reception should be paid. The provision of § 313 BGB is not a strict rule, but an equitable remedy that depends on a thorough balancing exercise subject to the merits of each individual case. For example, with regard to the question how much rent (if any) was due under business leases frustrated by CoViD-lockdowns, a wide range of factors including the financial situation of both parties (!), the availability of alternative uses etc had to be taken into account.[331]

cc) An aside: Failure of basis or failure of consideration?

Recently, English Courts preferred the term "failure of basis" to the traditional "failure of consideration". The development culminated in *Barton v Morris*[332] where the shift of terminology in the "scholarly judgment" of LJ Carr in *Dargamo Holdings*[333] was "officially" approved by Lady Rose.[334] LJ Carr (who followed Goff & Jones) had pointed out:

> 77. ... Whilst long-established, it is generally accepted that the terminology of "failure of consideration" is apt to lead to confusion. In particular, as set out below, the term "consideration", when used in the phrase "failure of consideration" as a basis for a restitutionary claim, does not carry the same meaning as it does when considering whether there is sufficient consideration to support the formation of a contract (see *Barnes* at [104]).
>
> 78. I prefer to adopt the terminology of "failure of basis" suggested by *Goff and Jones* at 12–10 to 12–15. However, whichever terminology is used, the legal content is the same ...

329 People tend to rent window places to watch the famous annual Karnevalszüge (pageant) that take place in Köln, Düsseldorf and Mainz on Rosemontag (the day before Shrove Tuesday). Sometimes however, these events are cancelled on short notice, just as was the original coronation date of Edward VII on 26 June 1902.

330 *Krell v Henry* [1903] 2 KB 740; *Chandler v Webster* [1904] 1KB 493 (CA); cf. Stevens, pp. 138–140.

331 BGHZ 232, 178; Schall, JZ 2020, 388.

332 *Barton v Morris* [2023] UKSC 3, at para. (per Lady Rose) 78 and at para. 231 (per Lord Burrows).

333 *Dargamo Holdings Limited v Avonwick Holdings Limited* [2021] EWCA Civ 1149.

334 *Barton v Morris* [2023] UKSC 3, at para. (per Lady Rose) 78; the same point is made by Lord Burrows in *Barton*, at para 231: "The terminology of failure of consideration invites confusion with consideration as a requirement for the formation of a contract;..."

The need to distinguish consideration in enrichment from consideration in contract has been felt for a longer while in England.[335] It can be traced back as far as to *Fibrosa v Fairbairn* where Viscount Simon explained:[336]

> "In English law an enforceable contract may be formed by the exchange of a promise for a promise or by the exchange of a promise for an act...but when one is considering the law of failure of consideration and the quasi-contractual right to recover money on that ground, it is, generally speaking, not the promise that is referred to as the consideration but the performance of the promise."

However, despite the contrary assumption of LJ Carr (at para. 78), the new terminology seems to have a bearing on the meaning because it resonates better with the definition that Peter Birks had proposed for failure of consideration in the past and that has become adopted by the Courts of England.[337]

> Failure of the consideration for a payment...means that the state of affairs contemplated as the basis or reason for the payment has failed to materialise or, if it did exist has failed to sustain itself.

For a comparative lawyer from Germany, this definition brings the concept of failure of basis in a dangerously close resemblance to the equitable concept of *Wegfall der Geschäftsgrundlage* with its Roman precursor of *clausula rebus sic stantibus.* The functional equivalent may be the law of frustration. But the accurate translation of the term *Geschäftsgrundlage* would be "basis of the transaction". The legal definition is now found in § 313 BGB. It is under the official heading *Störung der Geschäftsgrundlage.* This move away from the traditional language is meant to indicate that the *Geschäftsgrundlage* can either be lost or lack from the outset (cp. § 313 II BGB). § 313 S. 1 reads:

> Haben sich Umstände, die zur Grundlage des Vertrags geworden sind, nach Vertragsschluss schwerwiegend verändert und hätten die Parteien den Vertrag nicht oder mit anderem Inhalt geschlossen, wenn sie diese Veränderung vorausgesehen hätten, so kann Anpassung des Vertrags verlangt werden, soweit einem Teil unter Berücksichtigung aller Umstände des Einzelfalls, insbesondere der vertraglichen oder gesetzlichen Risikoverteilung, das Festhalten am unveränderten Vertrag nicht zugemutet werden kann.

---

335 Cf. e.g. *Sharma v Shimposh*, [2011] EWCA Civ 1383, at para 23 (per LJ Toulson as he then was); *Barnes v Eastenders Cash &Carry* plc [2014] UKSC 26, [2015] AC 1, at para. 104 (per Lord Toulson).

336 *Fibrosa Spolka Akcyjna v Fairbairn Lawson Combe Barbour Ltd* [1943] AC 32, at p. 48.

337 Birks, Introduction to the Law of Restitution, 1989, at p. 223; cited with approval by LJ Toulson (as he then was) in *Sharma v Shimposh*, [2011] EWCA Civ 1383, at para. 24 and by Lord Toulson in *Barnes v Eastenders Cash &Carry* plc [2014] UKSC 26, [2015] AC 1, at para. 104; see also LJ Carr in *Dargamo Holdings Limited v Avonwick Holdings Limited* [2021] EWCA Civ 1149, at para. 80.

> [If circumstances that have become the basis of the contract have changed significantly after the contract was concluded and the parties would not have concluded the contract or would have concluded it with different content if they had foreseen this change, the contract may be amended if one party cannot reasonably be expected to adhere to the unchanged contract, taking into account all the circumstances of the individual case, in particular the contractual or statutory distribution of risk. Translated with DeepL.com (free version)]

The "circumstances that have become the basis of the contract" bear close resemblance to the "state of affairs contemplated as the basis or reason for the payment" in the definition of Peter Birks. Take the example of the wedding ring. If the spouse is jilted at the altar, it is obvious that the state of affairs contemplated by the parties has fundamentally changed. But this is not a reason for the law to allow the return of the ring. This is because the law shifts this risk to the buyer. Even German law that generally accepts the instrument *Störung der Geschäftsgrundlage* subjects it to the "statutory distribution of risks". So much the more common law has to.

The modern concept of failure of basis nears it to frustration. But failure of consideration is different from frustration. The definition and the subsequent relabeling to failure basis seems too wide and carries an inherent danger of being misleading. This observation is not only based on comparative law. In *Bell v Lever Bros*,[338] Lord Atkin said cautionary words when explaining the common law doctrine of frustration / mutual mistake:

> Sir John Simon formulated for the assistance of your Lordships a proposition which should be recorded: "Whenever it is to be inferred from the terms of a contract or its surrounding circumstances that the consensus has been reached upon the basis of a particular contractual assumption, and that assumption is not true, the contract is avoided: i. e., it is void ab initio if the assumption is of present fact and it ceases to bind if the assumption is of future fact.
>
> I think few would demur to this statement, but its value depends upon the meaning of "a contractual assumption". And also upon the **true meaning to be attached to "basis", a metaphor which may mislead.**

Bell v Lever Bros concerned a case of a golden handshake to two employees. Later, it transpired that both could have been dismissed without compensation for gross misconduct (forming a cocoa cartel). Lever Bros (who later became Unilever) sought rescission of the compensation package and restitution of the amount paid. The lower Courts had granted the claim. The House of Lords reversed it and upheld the agreement. The sceptical verdict of Lord Atkin on "basis" and "contractual assumption" must be read against that background. How right he was can be understood from the dicta in the lower Courts. They were meticulously present-

338 *Bell v Lever Brothers* [1931] UKHL 2, at 34.

ed in *Great Peace Shipping*[339] where the Master of the Rolls, Lord Philipps, buried *Solle v Butcher*[340] because it contradicted *Bell v Lever Bros.* Take for example the judgement of LJ Scrutton in the Court of Appeal (allowing rescission of the compensation agreement).

> "In my opinion, the present law is that where at the time of making the contract **the circumstances are such that the continuance of a particular state of things is in the contemplation of both parties fundamental to the continued validity of the contract**, and that **state of things substantially ceases to exist** without fault of either party, the contract becomes void from the time of such cessation, the loss falling where it lies. This may be put either on implied contract or on destruction of the foundation or root of the contract before its term of performance has expired. The contract is valid when made, for its implied foundation then exists, but becomes void when during the term the foundation ceases to exist.
>
> Now consider the case where the **implied foundation is assumed by both parties** to exist at the time of making the contract, but does not in fact exist. One may describe the result as either that the contract is void because of an implied term that its validity shall depend on the existence at the time of the contract, and during its term of performance, of a particular state of facts, or (which is only another way of putting the proposition) that there is a mutual mistake of the **parties**, who make the contract **believing that a particular foundation to it exists, which is essential to its existence, a fundamental reason for making it.** In either case the absence of the assumed foundation makes the contract void."

There is little to distinguish the dicta in bold print from the definition of failure of consideration above. And there is little to distinguish the disapproved *Solle v Butcher* from the reasoning by Gummow J in Roxborough. In *Solle v Butcher*, the later Master of the Rolls Lord Denning had formulated the doctrine of "equitable mistake" that was said to render contracts voidable:[341]

> A contract is also liable in equity to be set aside if the parties were under a common misapprehension either as to facts or as to their relative and respective rights, provided that the misapprehension was fundamental and that the party seeking to set it aside was not himself at fault.

In that case, the parties had agreed on a lease under the shared mistake that the tenancy was not covered by the restrictions under the Rent Acts 1920 and 1938. In fact it was, and therefore the Court of Appeal allowed rescission of the contract. In the Australian case *Roxborough v Rothmans*, New South Wales had imposed a "licence fee" on the sale of cigarettes to under the Business Franchise Licences (To-

339 *Great Peace Shipping Ltd v Tsavliris (International) Ltd* [2002] EWCA Civ 1407
340 *Solle v Butcher* [1950] 1 KB 671.
341 *Solle v Butcher* [1950] 1 KB 671, at 693 (per LJ Denning as he then was); cfd. in *Magee v Pennine Insurance Co.* [1969] 2 QB 507, at 514 (per Lord Denning).

bacco) Act 1987. Retailers did not have to pay the fee to the State if the wholesaler had already paid it on the tobacco product in question. This allowed an efficient centralization of the process. The wholesaler (Rothmans) paid the fee and passed it on to the retailers as part of the sales price ("tax component"). When the licence fee was ruled illegal for violation of federal law, the retailer Roxborough successfully claimed their money for failure of consideration. Gummow J explained that the retailers "had paid moneys on a basis that later became falsified; the state of affairs presented ... by the operation of the Business Franchise Licences (Tobacco) Act 1987 (NSW) in respect of the future licence periods ... failed to sustain itself." He argued for failure of consideration as follows:

> "Here, 'failure of consideration' identifies the failure to sustain itself of the state of affairs contemplated as a basis for the payments the appellants seek to recover"

This statement reads as if the existence of the duty to pay the licence fee was the basis of the contractual obligation, and that the failure of *that* basis or "state of affairs" founded the claim for failure of consideration / basis. But this reasoning begs the question: If *Bell v Lever Bros* ruled that – beyond the narrow concept of common mistake – common misapprehensions / assumptions as to the "basis" of the transactions are irrelevant both at law and equity, how can such misassumptions on the state of affairs still trigger claims in unjust enrichment?

The answer is: They cannot. Failure of basis / consideration is not the failure of circumstances that are of fundamental importance for the transaction. It is not concerned with the existence of the licence fee or the scope of regulation under the Rents Acts or the wedding taking place. It is exactly the failure of the ***quid pro quo*** of the performance. This point has been made by LJ Toulson in *Sharma v Simposh*,[342] referring to Goff & Jones (in a prior edition):[343]

> In most of the situations, however, the **ground of recovery is that the expected return for the payment**, or consideration, as it is confusingly called, **has failed.**

The "**expected return**" is the reason why the performance was made, the *quid pro quo* of the performance, the "consideration". In the language of the *German Zwecklehre* (failure of purpose doctrine), this is the *causa acquirendi*. It is *not* the general background, the state of affairs, that has motivated the transaction. To come back to the example of the wedding ring. The consideration is the ring itself, and the

342 *Sharma v Simposh Ltd* [2011] EWCA Civ 1383, at para. 22.

343 In that case the reference was made to the previous edition, Goff & Jones, The Law of Restitution, 7th edn. 2007, 19–002.

ring only. It is not the state of affairs, i. e. the wedding taking place. And this is true even if that state of affairs was the fundamental motivation for the transaction.

The long-lived uncertainty about the meaning of consideration seems to be caused by a gap between the "normal case" and the legal rule. The expected return for a performance is normally the counter-performance. But this is not necessarily the case. In *Barnes v Eastenders*, the expected return was the right to draw the renumeration from the assets of the managed companies. This was not a counter-performance to be delivered by the CSP. But it was the *quid pro quo*, the **return for the payment.** This return also made the contract between CSP and the receiver binding even though the CSP could not promise to deliver the right. Contractual consideration is always the *quid pro quo* or **return for the promise.** Again, this return will normally be a promise of a counter-performance by the other party (payment). But it need not be so. The return can be fairly little (*Carbolic Smokeball*). That is why the "conditional gift" of German law (§ 525 BGB) may not be a gift at all under English law (see p. 211).

Apparently, the legal rule is wider than the normal case. If the legal rule is formulated wide enough, consideration covers both promises and performances. The expected return for a promise or a performance is the consideration. Delivery of it makes the promise binding and the performance permanent.

The clarification by Goff & Jones also helps to set the terminology under civil law straight. The *condictio causa data causa non secuta* does not qualify the *causa* more precisely. But where the Romans failed, the German *Causa-doctrine/Zwecklehre* succeeded. It defined three primary purposes of transfers: the *causa acquirendi*, the *causa solvendi*, and the *causa donandi.* They are distinct from one-sided or shared assumptions about the circumstances of the transaction. This is important because only their failure invalidates the will of the performing party in a way that restitution is triggered, whereas other motives are irrelevant (for a more through explanation of this doctrine see pp. 270–272). With a view to what has been said hitherto, the failure of the *causa acquirendi* should be the only relevant trigger for *causa data causa non secuta*, and with a view to the shared Roman roots of English enrichment, it should be the only trigger for failure of consideration. The equivalent to "consideration" is therefore not simply the *causa*, but more precisely the *causa acquirendi.*

b) The condictio ob turpem vel iniustam causam (D.12.5.) and extortion / duress

The *condictio ob turpem vel iniustam causam* ordered the restitution of benefits which were immorally or unjustly obtained by the recipient,[344] see e.g.:

> Dig. 12.5.6 (Ulpianus 18 ad Sabinum)
> Perpetuo Sabinus probavit veterum opinionem existimantium id, quod ex iniusta causa apud aliquem sit, posse condici: in qua sententia etiam Celsus est.
>
> [(Scott): Sabinus always approved of the opinion of the ancient authorities, namely, that where anything is in the hands of a party illegally, it can be recovered by a personal action; and Celsus also concurs in this opinion.]
>
> D.12.5.7. Pomponius 22 ad sab.
> Ex ea stipulatione, quae per vim extorta esset, si exacta esset pecunia, repetitionem esse constat.
>
> [(Scott) Where money has been obtained through a stipulation which was extorted by force, it is established that an action will lie for its recovery.]

Following Evans, we discover the *condictio ob turpem vel iniustam causam* behind Lord Mansfield's dictum "…or for money got by imposition, express or implied, or extortion, or oppression, or an undue advantage taken of the plaintiff's situation, contrary to laws made for the protection of persons, under these circumstances."[345] It was the originator of the unjust factors of undue influence and duress that produced notable cases[346] and a wide range of doctrinal questions (economic duress; unconscionable transactions). Even the real underlying is up to debate (vitiated consent or abuse of power). On closer looks, a similar uncertainty was already rooted in Roman law.

In the introductory passage of D.12.5.1, the *condictio ob turpem vel iniustam causam* was explained as "antithesis" to the *condictio ob rem:* if the purpose was legitimate, the condictio would cease when the outcome was achieved. If the purpose was illegitimate, the *condictio* would still lie even though the outcome was achieved:

> D. 12,5,1pr.–2 (Paul. 10 ad Sab.):
> Pr. Omne quod datur aut ob rem datur aut ob causam, et ob rem aut

344 Zimmermann, pp. 844–845, 862.
345 See Evans, p. 329, also referring to Arnoldi Vinnii JC., De quæstionibus juris selectis libri duo, 1844, at p.140: "Si quis dolo malo aliquem induxerit, aut metu illato cuegerit, ut promitteret non possum adduci ut credam, solutum ex his causis retineri posse." St the said passage, Arnold Winnen used D.12.5.7 to underpin his view that in case of extortion, the error iuris bar would not apply.
346 Most prominently *Allcard v Skinner* (1887) 36 ChD 145.

turpem aut honestam: turpem autem, aut ut dantis sit turpitudo, non accipientis, aut ut accipientis dumtaxat, non etiam dantis, aut utriusque.

1. Ob rem igitur honestam datum ita repeti potest, si res, propter quam datum est, secuta non est.
2. Quod si turpis causa accipientis fuerit, etiamsi res secuta sit, repeti potest.

[Scott: Everything which is given is parted with either with some purpose in view or for a consideration; and where it is given for some purpose it may be either immoral or honorable, and where it is immoral, the immorality may either attach to the giver and not to the receiver, or it may attach to the receiver and not the giver, or it may attach to both.

(1) Hence where anything is given for an honorable purpose, an action can be brought for its recovery only where the purpose for which it was granted was not accomplished.

(2) Where, however, the receiver is the one guilty of immorality, even though the purpose be accomplished, an action can be brought for the recovery of the gift.]

This seems to deviate from the unilateral explanation of the *condictio sine causa* from the disappointment of the payor. The achievement of the purpose is irrelevant if it was immoral. Restitution will be ordered anyway. That resonates with a public policy rationale along the lines of: "Illicit transactions cannot stand". But why should the payor become the private attorney of the public interest, in particular if the illicit outcome was sought by him? The answer is that he is not. The rationale of this action is *not* to undo illicit transactions. This is confirmed by the most important and characteristic feature of the *condictio ob turpem vel iniustam causam:* the bar to recovery erected by the "in pari delictu" rule.

Dig. 12.5.3 (Paulus 10 ad Sabinum).
Ubi autem et dantis et accipientis turpitudo versatur, non posse repeti dicimus: veluti si pecunia detur, ut male iudicetur.

[Scott: Where both the giver and the receiver are guilty of immoral conduct, we hold that suit cannot be brought for the recovery of the donation; as, for instance, where money is paid in order that an unjust judgment may be rendered.]

The "in pari delictu" or "particeps criminis"[347] rule is better known from tort law. But as Papinian put it succinctly: In equal fault, possession prevails. If the law does not intervene to correct the (illegitimate) shift of wealth, the loss lies where it falls.

347 *Astley v Reynolds* (1731) 93 E.R. 939. Very critical on this rule Zimmermann, pp. 846–871 and particularly pp. 863–866 ("Sinister" and "disastrous" results).

Dig. 12.7.5pr. (Papinianus 11 quaest.)
... Dixi, cum ob turpem causam dantis et accipientis pecunia numeretur, cessare condictionem et in delicto pari potiorem esse possessorem:...

[Scott: ... I said that where money was paid for some immoral consideration which affected both the giver and the receiver, an action for recovery would not lie, and where both of them are equally culpable, the possessor has the advantage;...]

In England, the rule was already known before *Moses v Macferlan* (1760). In *Astley v Reynolds* (1731),[348] it was accepted by all sides, but held not to lie on the facts of the case. The flipside is the rule *ex turpi causa non oritur actio*[349] which has lately been based on the principle "no benefit from a wrong" by the Supreme Court in *Patel v Mizra.*[350] This venerable principle is also enshrined in the second part of the Pomponian sentence (D.50,17.206: "...neminem fieri cum alterius detrimento **et iniuria** locupletiorem."). On that footing, it would by the way qualify restitution for wrongs as unjust enrichment.

In Germany, the *condictio ob turpem vel iniustam causam* was codified in § 817 BGB. The first sentence contains the action, the second sentence orders the bar for recovery *in pari delictu.* Since immorality or illegality usually invalidate any contract, agreement or transfer, with the consequence of triggering a *condictio indebiti*, the additional cause of action in sentence 1 is of no consequence. Far more important is the bar for restitution if the claimant himself was guilty of immorality or injustice, be it solely or together with the payee. Not only does it bar restitution under the *condictio ob turpem vel iniustam causam* (§ 817 Satz 1 BGB), but it also cancels all other enrichment actions including the *condictio indebiti.*[351]

However, even though the bar for *in pari delictu* is codified in § 817 Satz 2 BGB, lawyers have found it difficult to accept in cases of mutual immorality or illegality. Take the example of moonlighting where it is neither pleasant to award nor to deny payment for the works or remedies for faulty performance. That is why the German Supreme Court and the prevailing doctrine have devised an additional test. They will look at the purpose of the law that makes the transaction illegal to

348 *Astley v Reynolds* (1731) 93 E.R. 939.

349 *Holman v Johnson (*1775) 1 Cowp 341, 343 (per Lord Mansfield); see *Patel v Mirza* [2016] UKSC 42; cf. further *Stone & Rolls Ltd v Moore Stephens* [2009] UKHL 39 (applying the directing mind and will doctrine – which was interpreted as a case of piercing the corporate veil by Lady Hale (para. 95) and Lord Walker (para. 106) in *Prest v Petrodel* [2013] UKSC 34.

350 *Patel v Mirza* [2016] UKSC 42, at para. 99 (per Lord Toulson).

351 Prevailing opinion in Germany, RGZ 161, 52; BGHZ 35, 103 = NJW 1961, 1458, 1459; BGHZ 36, 395 = NJW 1962, 955, 958; MünchKommBGB/Schwab, § 817 para. 11; BeckOK BGB/Wendehorst, § 817 para. 11.

decide whether or not recovery should be barred.[352] Similar issues have haunted English law,[353] which has led to *Patel v Mirza*[354] producing a new test comparable to the German one.[355] By contrast, the exclusion of recovery is generally accepted where *only* the payor is guilty of immoral or illegal conduct. Unlike in the case of shared immorality / illegality, this is an evident and clear-cut application of *ex turpi causa.* The payor must not invoke his own misdeed to claim recovery. For Ulpian, the bar to restitution in case of unilateral immorality was even placed on a different rationale ("nova ratione"):

> Dig. 12.5.4.3 (Ulpianus 26 ad ed.)
> Sed quod meretrici datur, repeti non potest, ut labeo et Marcellus scribunt, sed nova ratione, non ea, quod utriusque turpitudo versatur, sed solius dantis: illam enim turpiter facere, quod sit meretrix, non turpiter accipere, cum sit meretrix.[356]

The *in pari delictu*-bar to recovery defeats any policy rationale of "immoral transactions cannot stand" – because they do. The *condictio ob turpem vel iniustam causam,* too, is founded **unilaterally** on the protection of the claimant. In this case, the concern is not with his disappointment by "frustration" of the purpose, but about the undermining of his free will. If I force or trick you to hand over your wallet, you will achieve your "purpose" to give me the wallet as soon as I have it. But of course, the law will let you to recover it because you did not choose this purpose freely. English law has grasped this central notion of the *condictio ob turpem vel iniustam causam* and built wisely on it. This was of particular importance to achieve the invalidation of gifts because, unlike in civilian jurisdictions, they are not covered by the rules of contracts under common law. That is why

---

352 MünchKommBGB/Schwab, § 817 para. 22; BeckOK BGB/Wendehorst, § 817 para. 23. But note that the Supreme Court has given up his former jurisdiction relating to moonlighting (BGHZ 111, 380) and applies the bar now without the prior reservation, BGHZ 201, 1 = NJW 2014, 1805; BGH NJW 2015, 2406; approving MünchKommBGB/Schwab, § 817 para. 28.

353 Notably *Tinsley v Milligan* [1993] UKHL 3.

354 *Patel v Mirza* [2016] UKSC 42 overruling the formal(istic) approach of *Tinsley v Milligan* [1993] UKHL 3

355 Like in Germany, the test in *Patel v Mirza* [2016] UKSC 42 (per Lord Toulson) takes into account, inter alia, the purpose of the prohibition which has been transgressed, and whether the purpose would be enhanced by the denial of the claim.

356 Note however that a highly contentious distinction was made here. It was held that it is only immoral to *be* a prostitute (and perform sexual acts) but that the acceptance of the money as such is *not* immoral. But does that not amount to saying that *being* a hitman is illegal, but accepting money for a hit is *not?* Note further the similar debate on a comparable argument made by Papinian in D.12.7.5 in relation to money given for a prohibited marriage of close relatives, see p. 110. See also Zimmermann, p. 846 with fn. 82 and p. 847 with fn. 91.

the necessary lines are drawn directly within the unjust factor, and not in remedies like avoidance or rescission for misrepresentation etc. (see pp. 203 et seq.).

c) The *condictio indebiti* and mistake

The *condictio indebiti* (D. 12.6.) allowed the payor to recover from the payee payments made on a non-existing liability. The first description at the head of the chapter is delivered by Ulpian.

> Ulpian D. 12.6.1 (ad edictum.): "Et quidem si quis indebitum ignorans solvit, per hanc actionem condicere potest: sed si sciens se non debere solvit, cessat repetitio."
>
> [Scott: And, indeed, if anyone ignorantly pays what is not due, he can recover the same by means of this action; but if he paid it being aware that he did not owe it, an action for its recovery will not lie.]

The two parts of the sentence constitute the heart of the *condictio indebiti.* The first half grants restitution for a performance made under a liability mistake ("indebitum ignorans"), while the second half bars restitution if the payor knew that he was not obliged ("sciens se non debere").

For a long time, civil lawyers have got the relation between the two sentences wrong. If you look at the first sentence in isolation, it appears to be the case that the claimant must prove his error. That has indeed been the law of old.[357] It is also the rule under Common Law. However, on closer looks, the second sentence bars the claim only where the claimant *knew* that he was not obliged. Uncertainty or chancing is not enough.[358] This is the better solution. It has been adopted in France despite the ambiguous wording of Art. 1376 of the old Code Civil (now – unchanged – Art 1302–1 C.civ, see ensuite in the text).[359] And it was expressly laid down in accordance to the modern view in Germany where it entered the codification in § 814 BGB. As a result, the claimant does no longer have to *prove* that he erred

357 Still discussed in depth and upheld by Savigny, III, at pp. 360–362 and 447 et seq. by the middle of the 19th century. For a succinct account of this "single most disputed area of Roman Law of unjustified enrichment" Zimmermann, pp. 849–851.

358 Cp. Cass soc. 14 oct. 1993, n° 91–12.974 P in a case where there was a legal controversy about the interpretation of the basis of the payment going on. By contrast, common law excludes restitution in cases of doubt, *Kleinwort Benson v Lincoln City Council* [1999] 2 AC 349 (HL) 408 (per Lord Hope); *Marine Trade A v Pioneer Freight Futures Co Ltd BVI* [2009] EWHC 2656, paras. 62–77; also approving Stevens, p. 77.

359 Cass soc. 14 oct. 1993, n° 91–12.974 P = Bulletin 1993 V N° 236 p. 161: "les articles 1235 et 1376 du Code civil ne faisant pas de l'erreur une condition nécessaire de la répétition de l'indu"; cf further, containing numerous references, Dalloz, *Le nouveau droit des obligations et des contrats 2019/2020,* 2nd edn. 2018, n° 10: "Erreur du solvens non requise (indu objectif)."

with respect to the existence of the debt. As a consequence, the burden of proof shifted from the claimant (for his error) to the defendant (for the knowledge of the claimant). This was an important development that also disposed of the mistake of law bar. It was facilitated by the recognition of the failure of purpose of the performance as overarching "unjust factor".[360] English law could likewise overcome the problematic "mistake". Since discharge of a debt is good consideration (*Barclays v Simms*; *Lloyds v Independent*), not achieving that discharge must lead to failure of consideration (see further p. 108 and as to gifts pp. 207 et seq).[361]

In modern times, the *condictio indebiti* became the paradigm of Civilian enrichment law. The constant rise of contract, in particular of contracts that become binding by mere meeting of minds without additional formal requirements, led to a situation where contractual agreements are construed as underlying of almost all transfers. If the transaction is flawed in a way that invalidates the contract, the exchange of goods will be undone by the *condictio indebiti.* By contrast, if the contract remains valid, default in the transaction will be dealt with by contractual remedies (e. g. damages claims). That being so, French law even assumed that the *condictio indebti* was the only enrichment claim worth codifying (see below)

> Art 1302–1 C.civ.: Celui qui reçoit par erreur ou sciemment ce qui ne lui est pas dû doit le restituer à celui de qui il l'a indûment reçu.

This is built on the premise that every payment relates to an obligation (a doubtful premise with a view to the conditional payments covered by the *condictio causa data causa non secuta*).

> Art. 1302 C.civ.: Tout paiement suppose une dette; ce qui a été reçu sans être dû est sujet à restitution.

But already in Roman times, the *condictio indebiti* played a distinguished role. Its function was to reverse transfers that been performed as *solutio indebiti.*[362] The

---

360 Von Kübel, pp. 16–19; Saving, III, pp. 447 et seq. had defended the mistake of law – bar in vain and according to Zimmermann, pp. 870–871, wrongly as far us classic law was concerned; contrast Kupisch in Schrage (ed.), pp. 241–243.

361 Cf. Meier, Irrtum, pp. 371 et seq.; Meier/Zimmermann, "Judicial Developments of the Law: *Error Juris*, and The Law of Unjustified Enrichment- A View from Germany' (1999) 115 LQR 556, 561 et seq. Opposing mistake outright Stevens, pp. 71 et seq.

362 Adolfe Wegmann Stockebrand, In re obilgata, p. 146–149, referring to the Institutiones Gai, 3, 91.

solutio concerned an *indebitum* if the debt did not exist or if the payor was not the true debtor although he had thought to be.

> D.12.6.65.9 (Paulus 17 ad Plautius): "Indebitum est non tantum, quod omnino non debetur, sed et quod alii debetur, si alii solvatur, aut si id quod alius debebat alius quasi ipse debeat solvat."
>
> [Scott: Payment is not due, not only where it is absolutely not owing, but also where it is owing to another and is paid to a third party, or where what one man owes another he pays as if he himself owed it.]

The need for the condictio in these cases arose from the fact that transfers (of money or goods) that were made to discharge an obligation (*solutio*) were valid even though the debt did not exist or was not owed by the transferor.[363] This was due to the specific construction of the *solutio*. Normally, valid transfers required a *iusta causa* to stand.

> Paulus, D.41.1.31 (ad edictum): "Numquam nuda traditio transfert dominium, sed ita, si venditio aut aliqua iusta causa praecesserit, propter quam traditio sequeretur."[364]
>
> [Scott: The mere delivery of an article does not transfer its ownership, for this takes place only where a sale or some other just cause precedes delivery.]

At first sight, it seems to follow that the transfer was invalid if the debt did not exist. There would have been no "*datio*", and the *rei vindicatio* would have to lie instead of the *condictio*. However, in the case of discharges, the act of *solutio* as such was seen as the *causa*. That is why the transfer was valid even if the debt to be discharged did not exist so that the *solutio* referred to an *indebitum*.[365]

The validity of the *solutio* despite the lack of an obligation was a paradox that haunted German lawyers in the 19th century. How could a transaction be valid enough to transfer the title but flawed enough to call for restitution?[366] The answer to this was found in what Germans call the *Trennungs-* and *Abstraktionsprinzip*.[367] This doctrine describes the legal distinction that German law draws between the contract which creates the mutual duties to perform and the agreements that may be necessary to actually transfer the title to money/goods/rights etc. in order to discharge those duties. Under this twin principle, the validity of contracts

363 Zimmermann, pp. 841–842, 848.
364 Stockebrand, p. 148; Kaser, 1961, pp. 61 et seq.
365 Stockebrand, p. 148–149. As to the question whether a datio was a necessary requirement of all condictiones, see in the negative pp. 232–233.
366 Von Kübel, pp. 3–12; Zimmermann, p. 867 with fn. 200.
367 Von Kübel, pp. 15–16; Zimmermann, pp. 862–868.

is judged separately from the validity of transfers related to those contracts (as common law does, but not e.g. Austria or France). For example, the contract to sell under § 433 BGB only creates the obligation to transfer the title to the good. The transfer of the title itself is effected by an *Übereignung* (= conveyance) under § 929 BGB.[368] The *Übereignung* is a separate transaction that consists of offer, acceptance and handing over of possession. The point of the principle is that the validity of this separate transaction is independent of the validity of the contract. As a consequence, property can be transferred under an invalid contract. The *rei vindicatio* is defeated because the title is lost, but the *condictio indebiti* will step in and allow recovery of the property (working as a "ius ad personam", not "ad rem").

The principle is designed to prevent an eventual invalidity of the contract from affecting the validity of the transfer of title for the sake of commercial certainty.[369] As a consequence, personal claims for restitution will lie instead of proprietary claims to reverse transactions based on invalid contracts. It is controversial whether or not Roman law separated (the validity of) contract and transfer of title to the same extent as German law does.[370] But they surely understood that the acquisition of the title, while allowing the recipient to dispose of the asset, did not spare him from an obligation to return it. This lesson could be learned from the paradigmatic case of the loan (D.12.1.). To explain the duty to restore by the reference to natural justice ("ex aequo et bono")[371] did therefore not mean that the *condictio* must be shifted from strict law to the equitable remedies. The same is true for English law – even though there *are* parallel ideas underlying both the emergence of the trust from the use and of restitution claims from money had and received for the use of the plaintiff (p. 49).

The *condictio* allowed the claimant to demand from the defendant to retransfer the specific good ("ipsum"), or, in case of money or fungible items ("res que pondere numero mensura constant"), to transfer an equivalent amount ("tantundem"),[372] in England: Quantum valebat.

> D.12.6.7. (Pomponius 9 ad Sabinum): "Quod indebitum per errorem solvitur, aut ipsum aut tantundem repetitur."

---

368 For sake of accuracy it should be mentioned that § 929 BGB only refers to the transfer of chattles, whereas the conveyance of land is called "Auflassung" and governed by §§ 873, 925 BGB. The assignment of claims is covered by § 398, of other intangible rights by §§ 413, 398 BGB.

369 See the fundamental book by Astrid Stadler, Gestaltungsfreiheit und Verkehrsschutz durch Abstraktion, 1996.

370 Zimmermann, p. 867 with fn. 200.

371 E.g. D.12.6.6.66 (Papinian 8), below p. 112; von Kübel, p. 16.

372 Stockebrand, p. 148 with Fn. 179.

[Scott: Where money which is not due is paid through mistake, suit may be brought for the recovery of the same money, or of an equal amount.]

Moreover, it also covered the restitution of user and services. The relevant passages are found in D.12.6.26.12 (Ulp 26 ad ed.) The Romans were aware of the difference between money or goods and such intangible values that could not be returned in natura. But they also understood that services of money's worth (*operae fabriles* as opposed to *operae offciales* that were owed by freedmen to their former masters[373]) could be estimated and accounted for under the *condictio* because this action was not restricted to give back "in natura" exactly what had originally been received (the labour done and time gone by).[374] The reference paves the way to the decisive argument that was later found by Savigny: Every performance of money's worth (services; works; user) constitutes *per se* a direct shift of wealth/value (pp. 233–234).

Finally, it is worth noting a passage where Julian held that a *condictio indebiti* would not lie if there was no prior transaction ("negotium") between the parties. It deals with building on another's land.

Dig. 12.6.33 (Iulianus 39 Dig.)

Si in area tua aedificassem et tu aedes possideres, condictio locum non habebit, quia nullum negotium inter nos contraheretur: nam is, qui non debitam pecuniam solverit, hoc ipso aliquid negotii gerit: cum autem aedificium in area sua ab alio positum dominus occupat, nullum negotium contrahit. sed et si is, qui in aliena area aedificasset, ipse possessionem tradidisset, condictionem non habebit, quia nihil accipientis faceret, sed suam rem dominus habere incipiat. et ideo constat, si quis, cum existimaret se heredem esse, insulam hereditariam fulsisset, nullo alio modo quam per retentionem impensas servare posse.

[Scott: If I build on your unoccupied land, and you obtain possession of it afterwards, there will be no ground for an action for recovery, because no business contract was made between us; for he who pays money which is not due, by this act transacts business to a certain extent, but when the owner of land takes possession of a building erected thereon by another, no business transaction takes place; for, in fact, even if a person who built upon the land of another should himself deliver possession, he would not have a right of action for recovery, because he would not, in any respect, have transferred the property to him who received it, as the owner would merely have obtained possession of what was already his. Therefore it is established that if the party who thought himself to be an heir should prop up a house

373 On this distinction see Mitteis, Operae officilaes and operae fabriles, ZRGRA 23 (1902), 143 et seq.; cf. further Christian Schnabel, Der solutionis causa adiectus im Römischen Recht, 2015, pp. 107 et seq.

374 D.12.6.26.12 (Ulp. ad ed.) and D.12.6.65.7 (Paul 17 Plaut.); see Flume, FS Niedermeyer, 1953, 103, at pp. 111–112 = Studien, pp. 34–35.

which was part of the estate, he could be reimbursed for his expenses in no other way than by retaining the property.]

The view of Julian is interesting because his solution is much more in line with English law that generally opposes restitution for unilaterally imposed benefits (p. 84) than with Civil laws which principally grant recovery for building on another's land.[375] We will see below how D.12.6.33 became gradually obsolete (p. 120). Two arguments developed considerable force: the extension of the *negotiorum gestio* to unsolicited officious intermeddling and the "super-eminent equity"[376] of the Pomponian enrichment principle. The extension on enrichments that occurred without the will of the claimant fell on fertile ground because the *condictio furtiva* had never required a transaction.[377] This may well explain why English law has not developed into the same direction yet. It has neither accepted a general principle of *negotiorum gestio* nor the *condictio sine causa* and is therefore struggling with imposed enrichments and non-consent cases. If English law can be explained in that way by path dependence, this may indicate that will change with the acceptance of a general enrichment claim.

Another similarity between Roman and English law can be recognised on the question whether restitution is based on the "unjustness" of the transfer, or of the receipt, or of the retention of the benefit. The question becomes academic once the uniform reason for restitution is ascertained: the flawed consent of the claimant to the shift of value. However, it is still interesting to note that the Romans had similar, and similarly competing views on the issue. The references in the Digest emphasise in varying ways the transfer ("datum"), the receipt ("accipit", "ad eum pervenit"), the retention ("deprehenditur") or simply the having of the benefit *sine causa* ("apud aliquem sit"), cf. the following references (with emphasis, but without translation):

D.12.6.66 (Papinianus 8): "Haec condictio ex bono et aequo introducta, quod alterius apud alterum **sine causa deprehenditur**, revocare consuevit."

Dig. 12.5.6 (Ulpianus 18 ad Sabinum)
Perpetuo sabinus probavit veterum opinionem existimantium id, **quod ex iniusta causa apud aliquem sit**, posse condici: in qua sententia etiam celsus est.

D.12.7.4. (Africanus): "Nihil refert, utrumne ab initio **sine causa quid datum sit** an causa, propter quam datum sit, secuta non sit."

---

375 v.Bar/Swann, Principles of European Contract law: Unjustified Enrichment, 2010, at p. 378 et seq. *Yeoman's Row v Cobbe* [2008] UKHL 55: only proprietary estoppel or quantum meruit (request!).
376 So named in *Sinclair v Brougham* [1914] AC 398, at p. 433 (per Lord Dunedin)
377 In the same sense, Zimmermann, p. 854.

Dig. 44.7.5.3 (Gaius 3 aur.)
Is quoque, **qui non debitum accipit per errorem solventis**, obligatur quidem quasi ex mutui datione et eadem actione tenetur, qua debitores creditoribus:

Dig. 12.7.1.3 (Ulpianus 43 ad sab.):
Constat id demum posse condici alicui, **quod vel non ex iusta causa ad eum pervenit** vel redit ad non iustam causam.

With that observation, we can close the introduction of the "Mosaic condictiones" and turn to those pillars of civilian enrichment law that have not been adopted by Lord Mansfield.

4 The condictiones which were not transplanted via *Moses v Macferlan*

English unjust enrichment has been shaped by the three specific Roman *condictiones ob rem, indebiti* and *ob turpem causam* transplanted in *Moses v Macferlan* (1760). But it is also determined by what Lord Mansfield did not import: the *condictio sine causa* (D.12.7.), the *condictio furtiva* (D.13.1) and the Pomponian sentence (D.12.6.14 and D.50.17.206). They will be presented hereafter.

The omissions of those *condictiones* go hand in hand with the non-recognition by English law of the *negotiorum gestio* and of the *actio de in rem verso utilis.* These instruments played a pivotal role for the evolution of civilian enrichment law, too. They are the key to the differences between English and Civilian unjust(ified) enrichment and will be presented in separate chapters en suite.

a) The condictio sine causa

The *condictio sine causa* was described in Digest 12.7. It gained vital importance as basis for the general enrichment claim that contained the underlying principle (first the Pomponian sentence, later the direct shift of wealth according to Savigny). In a sense it could be said that the *condictio sine causa* impersonated unjust enrichment. This central function is somewhat at odds with the rather limited role of the original chapter in the Digest. That part only contained a few cases of which the compilators, for some reason or another, had assumed that they were not covered by the specific *condictiones*, but where they held that restitution should be granted nevertheless. The main point of the cases in D.12.7. was the extension of the *condictio* beyond the specific settings of *causa data causa non secuta* and *indebiti* to situations where the causa either lacked from the outset (*sine causa*) or got lost subsequently (*causa finita*).

Moses v Macferlan (1760) did not transplant the *condictio sine causa.* We can only speculate about the reasons. But it is safe to say that a core function of the *condictio sine causa* (and the insofar closely related *condictio furtiva*) was to complement the *rei vindicatio* when the property of another is used up or sold on. This function was not of interest in England where the tort of conversion, having replaced detinue and "case", would cover both objects of restitution, the return in kind as well as damages. Also, the *condictio sine causa* had become a generic catch-all device in the *ius commune* by the time of the mid-eighteenth century. It could not be pinned to specific reasons for restitution, but was applied under the vague terms of the Pomponian sentence. That may have had as little appeal to Common Lawyers back in the day as the "absence of basis" approach has today – so much the more since the attractiveness of this catch-all clause to the Civil Lawyers of the time was limited as well, as the first codifications show.

However, the omission of the *condictio sine causa* was the reason why an important train of thoughts to understand the principle of restitution for unjust enrichment more precisely than Pomponius were lost on the Common Law. This is in particular true for the *condictio ob causam finitam* that explained restitution for a subsequent loss of *causa* in a clear and comprehensible way by the example of the *fullo* (bleacher) and the lost toga. But it is also visible in the argument on the initial lack of a *causa* with which the chapter D.12.7. starts.

aa) The initial lack of a *causa*

For the Roman lawyers, the following conclusion was settled: If there was a *condictio* in case the *causa* of the transaction did not materialise (*non secuta*) or the debt to be paid did not exist (*indebiti*), there also had to be a *condictio* if there was no valid *causa* for the transaction from the outset (*sine causa*).

> D.12.7.4. (Africanus): "Nihil refert, utrumne ab initio sine causa quid datum sit an causa, propter quam datum sit, secuta non sit."
>
> [It does not make a difference whether something was given without causa ab initio or whether the causa for which it was given hat not materialised]

See also D.12.7.1.2–3 (Ulpianus 43 ad sab.), including the *causa finita* but referring mainly to promises given *sine causa*.[378]

---

378 The upshot of this reference to Ulpian, starting with D.12.7.1.prologue, was that also a mere promise, given sine causa, could be claimed back with the condictio, cf.: D.12.7.1pr. (Ulpianus 43 ad sab.): "Est et haec species condictionis, si quis sine causa promiserit vel si solverit quis indebitum. qui autem promisit sine causa, condicere quantitatem non potest quam non dedit, sed ipsam obligationem." But en passant, it also provided authority for the condictio sine causa.

(2) Sive **ab initio sine causa** promissum est, sive fuit causa promittendi quae finita est vel secuta non est, dicendum est condictioni locum fore.

(3) Constat id demum posse condici alicui, **quod vel non ex iusta causa ad eum pervenit** vel redit ad non iustam causam.

[(2)Be it something is promised without "causa" ab initio, be it the causa for the promise if terminated or did not follow suit, it must be said that the *condictio* will lie.

(3) Finally, it is established that a condictio can be brought against someone because something did get to him without a just "causa" or something was given back to him without a just "causa".]

NB: The translation of **Scott equates "causa" with "consideration"**. That is true if we perceive it in the sense of reason, like Birks, p. 118 and Stevens, p. 109. See also above p. 62 and 70.

[Scott: (2) Whether the promise was made without consideration in the beginning, or in consideration of a promise which is terminated, or did not take effect, it must be said that there will be ground for an action for recovery.

(3) It is established that a suit for recovery can be brought against the party only where the property came into his possession without a valid consideration, or for some consideration which has ceased to be valid.]

The *condictio sine causa* was inter alia assumed to lie when the transfer was intended for a certain purpose, but the parties failed to agree on that purpose. That appears to be a case of the *condictio causa data causa non secuta*, but it could also be argued that this was not the case of because what failed is not the (agreed) causa, but already the agreement (of the causa). But since that does not strengthen the case of the recipient to retain the benefit in any way, it was clear to the Romans that a *condictio sine causa* would have to lie.[379]

We can underpin the logic of this argument by "transferring" the Roman *condictiones* into the framework of modern law. As seen above, German lawyers would construe any sale under § 433 BGB, even those over the counter, as a contract giving rise to mutual obligations to deliver and to pay. It follows that any exchange of performances under a void *Kaufvertrag* could be caught by the *condictio indebiti*. In order to understand the necessity that the Romans felt for accepting the *condictio since causa* next to the *condictio indebiti*, it is better to have a look at English sales law because there is a distinction that is vital to understand what happened in the Digest. A "contract of sale" can either come as an "agreement to sell" (s.2(5) Sale of Goods Act 1979) or as a "sale" (s.2(4) Sale of Goods Act 1979). In the first case, the contract gives rise to an obligation to deliver, like its German counterpart, the *Kaufvertrag* under § 433 I 1 BGB. In the second case however, the

379 v. Glück, Die Pandecten nach Hellfeldt, Vol 13/1, p. 200.

parties immediately exchange money for goods. No obligations arise. They are simply not necessary because the exchanges are carried out immediately and therefore, no party needs to be forced to perform by creation of an obligation.

English law treats both kinds of contracts of sale equal under s.2(1) Sales of Goods Act 1979) – instead of denying any difference by construing "immediately discharged promises" (as German lawyers do). This equal treatment is persuasive because the essence of the transaction as a sale is not altered by the creation or not of antecedent obligations. They are only a means to facilitate the exchange. Therefore, the equal treatment of sale and contract to sell must be mirrored in unjust enrichment. It is evident that from the perspective of restitution, too, there can be no difference whether the invalid contract under which the money and the goods were exchanged was construed in a way that, had it been valid, it would have given rise to antecedent obligations or not. If an agreement to sell was void, the parties would have performed on non-existing duties. Restitution of both goods and money would be covered by the *condictio indebiti.* But under a sale, without antecedent obligations, no payment could have been made on the (presumed) obligations. If a sale was void, the *condictio indebiti* would technically be unavailable. But there would still be no case for the defendant to keep the benefit. That is why the *condictio* had to be extended to the *sine causa ab initio* setting.

Restitution for absence of a *causa* resembles restitution for absence of basis – and it led to the same problems of uncertainty. But it also had advantages. The extension to the *condictio sine causa* allowed equal treatment of all transfers lacking a valid legal reason. The cases of the *condictio indebiti*, the *condictio causa data causa non secuta* and the *condictio ob turpem vel iniustam causam* could all be brought to the common denominator of transfers *sine causa.*[380] This abstraction may only have started in the Digest. But centuries later, after the reception, the lawyers of the *ius commune* had worked out that the *condictio sine causa* was an appropriate heading for a general enrichment claim. It covered the scope of all specific *condictiones.* Moreover, it was not restricted to failed transactions. This led to the recognition of the law of unjust enrichment. At the same time, it begged the question where restitution should lie. For quite a while, the answer was thought to be given by Pomponius in D.12.6.14 and D.50.17.206. We will come back to that in due course. But before that, the *condictio ob causam finitam* deserves attention.

bb) The *condictio ob causam finitam*

The *condictio ob causam finitam* concerned transfers that were originally made for a valid *causa*, but that *causa* became annihilated by subsequent events. The logic to

380 Zimmermann, pp. 871–873.

cover those cases is persuasive, as the explicit example of a *causa finita* provided by the Digest shows.

> Ulpian 12.7.2. (ad ed.): “Si fullo vestimenta lavanda conduxerit, deinde amissis eis domino pretium ex locato conventus praestiterit posteaque dominus invenerit vestimenta, qua actione debeat consequi pretium quod dedit? Et ait Cassius eum non solum ex conducto agere, verum condicere domino posse: ego puto ex conducto omnimodo eum habere actionem: an autem et condicere possit, quaesitum est, quia non indebitum dedit: nisi forte quasi sine causa datum sic putamus condici posse: etenim vestimentis inventis quasi sine causa datum videtur.”
>
> [Scott: Where a fuller made a contract to clean some clothes, and the clothes being lost, he is sued on the contract and pays their value to the owner, and the owner afterwards finds the clothes; what kind of an action must the fuller bring to recover the amount which he paid? Cassius says that he not only can bring an action on contract, but also one for recovery against the owner. I think that he has, at all events, a right of action under a contract, but with respect to the suit for a recovery there is a question, because he did not pay what was not due; unless, indeed, we can hold that an action for recovery can be brought on the ground that the money was paid without any consideration (“causa”), for the clothes having been found, this would seem to be the case.]

If clothes were brought to the laundry, or rather, the bleachery (“fullonica”)[381] and got stolen there, the bleacher or fuller (“fullo”) would have to pay damages to the owner (“domino pretium praestiterit”). If the owner later managed to retrieve his stolen “clothes (“posteaque dominus invenerit vestimenta”), the damages payment lost its *causa* and the *condictio* would lie *ob causam finitam.* But the condictio had to surmount one major objection. At the time when the damages were paid, they were actually owed and the payment was made on a *debitum* (“an autem et condicere possit, quaesitum est, quia non indebitum dedit.”). The answer of Ulpian was that after the clothes were retrieved, the damages “looked as if given sine causa”. Although this sounds like a fiction (“quasi sine causa datum videtur”), it is not because the underlying judgement is sound. It is evidently reasonable that the payment cannot be kept after the damage it was supposed to cover had vanished.

In my view, this passage is key to unlock unjust enrichment. It illuminates the concept of (lack of) causa better than previous attempts that basically equate *causa*

381 The standard garment of the Roman was the toga. This exquisite long white piece of cloth had to be bleached by the “fullo” on a regular basis to be shining white again. The natural bleach used for this purpose was urine, making the bleaching business a fetid affair. The tax on this valuable asset was imposed by Emperor Vespasian who is said to have justified it with the famous words “pecunia non olet.” The best preserved “Fullonica of Stephanus” was unearthed in Pompeji 1912–1914.

with a valid contract. The *causa* cannot be the obligation of the *fullo* to indemnify the *dominus* because that debt had existed and been discharged when the payment was made – and yet the owner cannot keep the payment. Nor can the causa be found in the contract between the fullo and the owner of the toga. This contract was not invalidated by the events – and yet the owner cannot keep the payment.

This shows that causa simply means the "reason" or "purpose" of the payment. The aim can be expressed as causal or as final. The purpose the payor seeks to achieve equals the reason the payment is made. The reason/purpose of the payment of the *fullo* was to mitigate the damage suffered by the owner. It follows that **compensation is the *causa* of damages.** When the toga reappeared, the damage dissolved and the compensatory reason for the payment fell away: *causa finita!* We might as well say: the purpose of the payment was frustrated. The purpose of the performance became indeed the terminology of German law. The concept has been explained and further elaborated by the so-called *Zwecklehre*/Causa-doctrine (pp. 270–272). D.12.7.2. helps us understand why initial lack and subsequent loss of the *causa* rank equal. The disappointment of the claimant by the groundlessness/frustration of the purpose are the same. That is also the reason why an error on the existence of the debt cannot be a prerequisite for restitution. Only knowledge of the non-existence founds the bar because only then, the payor makes a gift. This is different in cases of compulsion. But compulsion excludes knowledge because the payor knows both about the diverging opinion of the presumed creditor and that only a Court can decide. That is why Germans would not apply § 814 BGB.

Moreover, D.12.7.2. confirms what I have explained above with respect to the sale and the contract to sell. The existence of legal obligations can duplicate the *causae* of the performance, i.e. the reasons why we perform = the purposes we seek with our performance. We pay to discharge our debt (*causa solvendi*). But in most cases, we also pay for why the debt exists, e.g. to receive the counter-performance (*causa acquirendi*) or, as here, to compensate damages (we might call it *causa compensandi*). Such obligations are called "causal obligations" in Germany. They are distinguished from exceptional "abstract obligations". Those are "naked" obligations that arise from a mere contract to pay without declaring whether the payment is made on a sale, a lease, a loan etc. Abstract obligations in this sense are promissory notes like *abstraktes Schuldversprechen* (§ 780 BGB = abstract promise of debt), *abstraktes Schuldanerkenntnis* (§ 781 BGB = acknowledgement of debt), *Scheck* (cheque) and *Wechsel* (bill of exchange). German law does accept naked obligations, but it does not accept them as *causa* to keep the benefit. The rule is enshrined in § 812 Abs. 2 BGB:

"Als Leistung gilt auch die durch Vertrag erfolgte Anerkennung des Bestehens oder des Nichtbestehens eines Schuldverhältnisses."

["Performance is also the recognition by contract of the existence or non-existence of a debt relationship." – by Deep-L]

This rule marks two points. First, it confirms that promises are subject to restitution (see below in the text). Second, it shows that a naked obligation will not normally suffice to justify a transfer. German courts will always look for an underlying causa to determine why an abstract obligation was created and whether the payment made under it can be kept by the recipient. If there is no valid causa underlying the creation of the abstract debt, it will either be barred by the plea of unjustified enrichment under § 821 BGB or, in case that plea is not available in the respective court procedure,[382] the payment made will be subject to restitution under §§ 812 Abs. 1 and 2 BGB. The only exception to the rule that all abstract obligations are subject to restitution if they lack a *causa* is provided for by securities law. If cheques or bills of exchange are assigned by the first drawee to subsequent holders, all pleas from the underlying causa will get lost in a bona fide purchase for value (Art. 22 ScheckG; Art 17 WG).

The splitting up of abstract obligations and underlying causal transaction delivers further evidence on the duplication of purposes thesis (cf. p. 272).

That promises can be subject to restitution under the condictio was well settled in Roman law. In the chapter on the *condictio sine causa*, it was stated: If a promise was given sine causa, the *condictio* would relieve the claimant from the resulting obligation.

Ulpian, D.12.7.1. (ad Sabinum): "Est et haec species condictionis, si quis sine causa promiserit vel si solverit quis indebitum. Qui autem promisit sine causa, condicere quantitatem non potest quam non dedit, sed ipsam obligationem."

[Scott: There is also the following kind of a personal action for recovery where anyone makes a promise without consideration, or where he pays something that was not due. Where a party makes a promise without consideration, he cannot bring an action for an amount which he did not give, but only for the obligation itself.]

Julian, D.12.7.3. "Qui sine causa obligantur, incerti condictione consequi possunt ut liberentur: …"

[Where parties oblige themselves *sine causa*, they can pursue to be liberated under a *condictio incerti*…]

382 This is e.g. the case in a Wechselprozess (§§ 602, 592, 598 ZPO).

Here, the Digest give an affirmative answer to a question is debated under English law, too, namely whether promises, i. e. the creation of obligations, amounts to a shift of value that can become subject to restitution.[383] But I would like to add the qualification that only the recovery of abstract obligations is possible because only they can exist isolated from the underlying causal contract. If the obligation springs directly from a causal contract, isolated recovery does not seem to make sense. If I promised the builder to pay for works that he has not performed yet, I do not have to recover my obligation towards him because I will not be bound to pay anyway. But if I transfer a promissory note on a sale and the consideration fails, I can recover the claim. In *Moses v Macferlan* (1760), the promise not to sue was the most important consideration because without it, the transaction was economically useless for Moses. When that promise was broken, the transfer of the note / abstract claim had to be unwound for failure of consideration.

The final reference in D.12.7. concerned the distinction between the *condictio sine causa* and the *condictio ob turpem vel iniustam causam.*[384] Papinian explained that a dowry given for a prohibited marriage (between close relatives) could be recovered without being barred by immorality of both parties. This was so because

383 In the affirmative Burrows, The Law of Restitution, p. 17.

384 D.12.7.5. (Papinianus 11 quaest.: pr. Avunculo nuptura pecuniam in dotem dedit neque nupsit: an eandem repetere possit, quaesitum est. Dixi, cum ob turpem causam dantis et accipientis pecunia numeretur, cessare condictionem et in delicto pari potiorem esse possessorem: quam rationem fortassis aliquem secutum respondere non habituram mulierem condictionem: sed recte defendi non turpem causam in proposito quam nullam fuisse, cum pecunia quae daretur in dotem converti nequiret: non enim stupri, sed matrimonii gratia datam esse.

1. Noverca privigno, nurus socero pecuniam dotis nomine dedit neque nupsit. Cessare condictio prima facie videtur, quoniam iure gentium incestum committitur: atquin vel magis in ea specie nulla causa dotis dandae fuit, condictio igitur competit.

[Scott: Where a woman who was about to be married to a maternal uncle, gave a sum of money as dowry, but did not marry him, the question arose whether she could bring an action for the recovery of the money? I said that where money was paid for some immoral consideration which affected both the giver and the receiver, an action for recovery would not lie, and where both of them are equally culpable, the possessor has the advantage; and that anyone who adopted this principle perhaps would answer that the woman could not bring an action for recovery; but, on the other hand, it could be justly maintained that the question to be considered was not so much that the consideration was immoral, as that there was no consideration at all; since the money which was paid could not be converted into a dowry, as it was paid not for the purpose of unlawful cohabitation but on account of matrimony.

(1) A stepmother paid a sum of money as dowry for her marriage to her stepson, and a daughter-in-law also did this for her marriage to her father-in-law, and neither marriage took place. It would seem at first view that an action for recovery of the money would not lie, since an union of this kind is incest by the Law of Nations; still, in such instances it is the better opinion that there was no consideration for giving the dowry, and thus an action for its recovery will lie.]

the money was not given for the immoral purpose of prohibited sexual intercourse, but for the principally “honest” purpose of the marriage that however could never materialise under these circumstances (“non enim stupri, sed matrimonii gratia datam esse”). Alas, it was made *sine causa*.[385]

cc) The *condictio sine causa* as catch-all clause of Pomponian unjust enrichment

The references listed in D.12.7 only concerned exceptional cases where transactions had failed but recovery was not, or at least not readily available under the specific headings of the condictiones *causa data causa non secuta, ob turpem vel iniustam causam* or *indebiti*. However, the *condictio sine causa* did not remain restricted to this rudimentary and marginal state. Its importance grew steadily during the time after the reception to become the general enrichment claim at last.

The emergence of the *condictio sine causa* was supported by the fact that many other cases of *condictiones* could be found scattered over the whole body of the Digest. Often, there would only be statements like “condicere possit” etc. To give but one example: In D.19.1. the actions arising from a sale are reported (“de actionibus empti venditi”). But in D.19.1.11.6. Ulpianus (32 ad edictum) reported on a case for the *actio ex empto* where the *condictio* could be brought, too. Normally, things transferred as deposit (“arrha”) to secure the conclusion of the contract had to returned when the sale was concluded. But what if the recipient did not oblige. Ulpianus supplements the answer given by Julianus: “Et Iulianus diceret ex empto agi posse: **certe etiam condici poterit**, quia iam sine causa apud venditorem est anulus.” This is either a *condictio causa data causa non secuta* or a *condictio sine causa*, depending on whether an agreed purpose is required for the former. The jurists of the *ius commune* would often count references to the *condictio* in other parts of the Digest to the *condictio sine causa*.[386] Moreover, there were references that would not even specify the action that would lie. One famous example is found in the Codex of Justinian (C.4.26.7.3.). Today, it is widely understood as *actio de in rem verso utilis* (p. 131). But at the time of the *Glosse*, others saw a *negotiorum*

---

385 But note that the argument of Papinian was far from generally accepted. Since the bride and groom to be were close relatives, a “honest” marriage was not possible but prohibited from the outset. Therefore, it was hard to understand why an exception from the general rule of the *condictio ob turpem vel iniustam causam* should be made in this specific case, see v. Glück, Die Pandecten nach Hellfeld, Dreizehnten Teils Erste Abteilung, (1811) p. 188–189.

386 Cf. v. Glück, Die Pandekten nach Hellfeldt, Dreizehnten Teils erste Abteilung (Vol 13/1), pp. 186 et seq. and pp. 204–205 as to the arrha; however, there were often widely differing views amongst the commentators, see Hallebeek, in Schrage (ed.), Unjust Enrichment, pp. 66 et seq. The reason is the abstractness of the original *condictio*, Zimmermann, pp. 835–836, 839.

gestio, but we also find a first interpretation as a "*condictio sine causa ex equitate*" (analogous to D.12.1.32, p. 115).[387]

Over time, Continental jurists recognised that the *condictio sine causa* could serve as a general claim that covered every enrichment case.[388] All failed payments and transactions that were addressed by the specific *condictiones* could be analysed on a more general level as transfers made *sine causa*. An early testimony of this approach can be seen in the following dictum of Papinian. It is reported in the chapter relating to the *condictio indebiti* (D.12.6) but it expresses a more general thought:

> D.12.6.66 (Papinian 8): "Haec condictio ex bono et aequo introducta, quod alterius apud alterum sine causa deprehenditur, revocare consuevit."
>
> [This condictio, introduced ex aequo et bono, allows to recover what one retains from another sine causa]

Based on this recognition, a doctrinal distinction was introduced between the *condictio sine causa generalis* and the *condictio sine causa specialis*.[389] The *condictio sine causa generalis* was said to stand beside the specific enrichment actions (*causa data causa non secuta, indebiti* etc.) and to compete with them, while the *condictio since causa specialis* was said to cover cases that were beyond the scope of the traditional claims.[390]

The basis of the *condictio sine causa specialis* was found in the Pomponian sentence that nobody shall be enriched from another's detriment.[391]

> D.12.6.14 (Pomponius libro 21 ad Sabinum):
> "Nam hoc natura aequum est neminem cum alterius detrimento fieri locupletiorem."
>
> [For it is naturally just that nobody shall become enriched from another's detriment][392]

---

387 Hallebeek, in Schrage (ed.), Unjust Enrichment, at p. 66 names Jacques de Révigny for this view.

388 Cf. von Glück, Die Pandecten nach Hellfeld, Vol 13/1, p 184: Es ist ferner zu bemerken, dass in all den Fällen ... mit Recht gesagt werden kann, der Beklagte besitze das, was von ihm zurückgefordert werde, sine causa, oder non ex iusta causa, d.i. ohne gültigen Rechtsgrund.

389 v.Glück, Die Pandecten nach Hellfeldt, p. 185.

390 v.Glück, Die Pandecten nach Hellfeldt, pp. 185–186; Zimmermann, pp. 871–873.

391 Cf. e.g. v.Glück, Die Pandecten nach Hellfeldt, pp. 185–186; see further *Chiusi*, Die actio de in rem verso im römischen Recht, 2001, p. 25, 29; Jansen, 'Farewell to Unjustified Enrichment?' (2016) 20 Edin L J 123, 130 and n. 28 (however claiming that Pomponius wanted to exclude the claim rather than justify it, see also Jansen, SZ (RomA) 120 (2003), 106, 118 et seq).

392 According to Scott: "For it is only in accordance with natural equity that no one should profit pecuniarily by the injury of another." That does not appear exact, above p. 2 with fn. 5 and 6.

D.50.17.206 (Pomp. 9 var. lec.):
"Iure naturae aequum est neminem fieri cum alterius detrimento et iniuria locupletiorem"

[Under natural law it is fair that nobody shall become enriched from another's detriment or injury.][393]

This statement of Pomponius had not played a central role yet in classic Roman law. It certainly did not describe a general cause of action that would be applied beyond the tradited cases to cover every possible unjust enrichment.[394] However, it may have already been used as an argument to support specific actions. One example is provided by Ulpian in D.2.15.8.22: "*...nec enim debet ex alieno damno esse locuples.*" [because nobody must be enriched with another's damage].[395] Another example might be the first citation of the Pomponian sentence in D.12.6.14. Arguably, the Justinian compilators placed it there to support the claim in D.12.6.13.1.[396]

After the reception of Roman law, the role of the Pomponian principle gradually changed from a marginal note to the central pillar of the *condictiones*. While the glossators had recognised the existence of the prohibition to benefit from another's loss, it is uncertain in how far they considered it a rule of law.[397] Their inbuilt methodological restrictions kept them from developing a broader general rule. But these boundaries were overcome, first with the help of Canon law, then by natural law. Pomponius had pronounced a sublime moral principle that resonated with natural lawyers. The language of "natural justice" made it sound like a commandment. It could be linked to the Canon law principle of restitution that was attached to the commandment "thou shalt not steal" – a rule that could well be understood in the wider sense of "do not keep what is somebody else's".[398]

While Canon law paved the way, the humanist and natural lawyer Hugo Grotius is acclaimed to be the first European jurist who has pronounced unjust enrichment as a separate category among the sources of obligation in his systematic approach to natural law.[399] In doing so, he drew from the systematic categorisation

---

393 According to Scott: "It is but just, and in accordance with the Law of Nations that no one, by the commission of an injury, can be enriched at the expense of another." That seems too freely translated, above p. 2 with fn. 5.
394 Hallebeek in Schrage (ed.), p. 62.
395 Hallebeek in Schrage (ed.), p. 63.
396 Hallebeek in Schrage (ed.), p. 63–64.
397 Hallebeek in Schrage (ed.), pp. 64 et seq.
398 Schrage/Nicholas, Unjust Enrichment: A Historical and Comparative Overview, in: Schrage (ed.): Unjust Enrichment and the Law of Contract, at p. 1, 3.
399 Feenstra in Schrage (ed.), pp. 197 et seq.; De Groot (Grotius), Inleydinge tot de Hollantsche rechtsgeleertheit, Book III, 1631, XXX, S. 1ff.; cf. Visser in Feenstra/Zimmermann, Das römisch-holländische Recht: Fortschritte des Zivilrechts im 17. und 18. Jahrhundert, at pp. 371 et seq.; Zimmer-

achieved by the Aristotelean approach of the Spanish scholastics.[400] The School of Salamanca had developed a pioneering system based on concepts of natural law when commentating on the *Summa Theologiae* of St. Thomas Aquinas[401] – the interpretation of Aristoteles that had elevated him to be (one of) the most important philosopher(s) of the High Middle Ages. These fundamental developments have coined unjust enrichment. The philosophical discussion within the parameters of corrective justice has continued to fascinate,[402] these days mostly common lawyers.[403] Moreover, the close link to "Godly justice" became a further important aspect that fed the notion of unjust enrichment as an equitable concept where *aequitas* surpassed the limitations of *rigor iuris* (strict law).[404]

The acceptance by Canon law and natural law empowered the Pomponian principle and promoted its rise of into the law of unjust enrichment. However, the principle was also loose and vague and thus, to put it mildly, not easy to apply. This has been demonstrated in the beginning by reference to the stamp case of Robert Stevens. It is confirmed by an old case that had been submitted to the then existing law faculty of Helmstedt in the year 1717. It was reported by Augustin Leyser, like Arnoldus Vinnius a famous jurist of the usus modernus Pandectarum:[405]

> A extends a loan to house owner B.[406] B uses the funds to pay off his mortgage to C and subsequently sells the house (now unencumbered) to D. B becomes bankrupt. A sues D for repayment. D objects that he did not contract with A.

---

mann, p. 885; Aguirre, Hugo Grotius and the Scholastic Tradition, Espíritu LXXI (2022), n.º 163, pp. 63 et seq.; Mélodie Combot, Quasi-contrat et enrichissement injustifié, 2023, pp. 52 - 54 and 73–75.

400 Aguirre, Hugo Grotius and the Scholastic Tradition, Espíritu LXXI (2022), n.º 163, pp. 63–78.

401 Cf. e.g. Aguirre, Restitution and corrective justice in the Aristotelian scholastic tradition: The contribution of Francisco Suárez (1548–1617), CAURIENSIA, Vol. XV (2020) 221–254; Hallebeek in Schrage (ed.), pp. 59–60.

402 Aguirre, Restitution and corrective justice in the Aristotelian scholastic tradition: The contribution of Francisco Suárez (1548–1617), CAURIENSIA, Vol. XV (2020) 221–254

403 See e.g. the Supreme Court of Canada, Kingsway Investments v New Brunswick (Department of Finance) [2007] 1 SCR 3, para 32; Ribstein in Chambers/Ch.Mitchell/Penner (eds.), The Philosophical Foundations of the Law of Unjust Enrichment, 2009, Ch. 2, pp. 31 et seq.; discussed by Matthew Doyle, Unjust enrichment and Corrective Justice, (2012) 62 Toronto law Journal 229.

404 Schrage, p. 12.

405 Augustin Leyser, Meditationes ad pandectas II, 1723, pp. 636–7; see also Wieling/Finkenauer, Bereicherungsrecht, 2nd edn. 2020, § 4 para. 3, at pp. 52–3; Reuter/Martinek, Ungerechtfertigte Bereicherung, 1983, at p. 18.

406 In truth, the name of the house owner was Oppermann. The other names are not reported.

The claimant succeeded "weil die Klage... sowohl in den Römischen Gesetzen, als auch in der allgemeinen aus dem natürliche Rechte genommenen Regul ‚ne quis locupletoir fiat cum alienus damno' begründet ist"[407] [because the action is founded ... both in the Roman laws, and in the general rule taken from the natural law that nobody be enriched from another's detriment].

The case has the outer appearance of an *actio de in rem verso* or "Versionsklage" (p. 131).[408] But the award was based on unjust enrichment. It shows the close relation between the two instruments under the Pomponian sentence which only got cut off when the German law of unjustified enrichment was codified on the basis of Savigny. The idea to reclaim the loan from a remote beneficiary was not solely based on the *actio de in rem verso* of D.15.3., but was supported by a passage from the "primeval" *condictio* to recover loans (D.12.1. De rebus creditis si certum petetur et de condictione). As Augustin Leyser put it, the *condictio* came together with the *actio de in rem verso* ("*convenit*").[409]

D.12.1.32 (Celsus 5 Dig.)
Si et me et Titium mutuam pecuniam rogaveris et ego meum debitorem tibi promittere iusserim, tu stipulatus sis, cum putares eum titii debitorem esse, an mihi obligaris? subsisto, si quidem nullum negotium mecum contraxisti: sed propius est ut obligari te existimem, non quia pecuniam tibi credidi (hoc enim nisi inter consentientes fieri non potest): **sed quia pecunia mea ad te pervenit, eam mihi a te reddi bonum et aequum est.**

[Scott: If you request Titius and myself to lend you money and I order a debtor of mine to promise to furnish it to you, and you make a stipulation believing that he is the debtor of Titius, will you be liable to me? I am in doubt on this point, if you did not enter into any contract with me, but I think it is probable that you are liable; not because I lent you money (for this cannot be unless the parties consent); but because my money came into your hands, and therefore it is proper and just that you should repay it to me.]

At first sight, that passage seems to support the view that the loan can be recovered from a remote beneficiary who did not contract with the claimant ("non quia pecuniam tibi credidi") because the defendant had benefitted from the money of the claimant ("sed quia pecunia mea ad te pervenit").[410] However, a closer look to the complicated situation shows a different picture. The defendant had

407 Augustin Leyser, Meditationes ad pandectas II, 1723, pp. 636–7.
408 Reported as such by Wieling/Finkenauer, Bereicherungsrecht, 2nd edn. 2020, § 4 para. 3, at p. 52–3.
409 Augustin Leyser, Meditationes ad pandectas II, 1723, p. 636: Habent jam actionem utilem de in rem verso, cumqua condicio illa ex L. 32. de Rebus creditis exactissime convenit.
410 This was indeed a view taken by some interpreters of the Digest, see Hallebeek, in Schrage (ed.), p. 66; Zimmermann, pp. 853–854 and 874.

asked both the claimant and one Titius for a loan ("et me et Titium mutuam pecuniam rogaveris"). The claimant made his own debtor promise the money to the defendant in order to enter into a loan contract with the defendant ("ego meum debitorem tibi promittere iusserim"). But the defendant assumed he had received the promise from a debtor of Titius ("tu stipulatus sis, cum putares eum Titii debitorem esse"). As a result, the defendant had entered neither into a contract with the claimant (with whom he did not assume to contract) nor with Titius (who was not aware of any contract). But that is not to say that there was no prior "negotium". The intended "negotium" merely failed owing to the dissenting assumptions about which principal extended the loan. The recovery of the payment should therefore have been recognised as a straight case of the *condictio sine causa* or, if no agreement is required on the failed purpose that had been pursued with the payment, a *condictio causa data causa non secuta* by the claimant. But this is not the way the passage had been viewed over the centuries by the jurists of the *ius commune*. Instead, it was taken for the principle highlighted in the citation above: "Because my money has reached you, it is just and equitable that you refund it to me" ("sed quia pecunia mea ad te pervenit, eam mihi a te reddi bonum et aequum est.").[411] This idea may also have been the bottom line of *Lipkin Gorman v Karpnale.*[412] It was a powerful facilitator to overcome the "negotium"-requirement in order to extend the general enrichment claim beyond failed transactions and the rule of D.12.6.49 ("His solis pecunia condicitur, quibus quomodo solute est, non quibus proficit").[413]

The example from Helmstedt highlights the danger that wide enrichment claims pose to commercial certainty. The Pomponian principle only looked for detriment on the side of the claimant and causal gain on the side of the defendant. It provided no reliable tool to contain claims against remote beneficiaries like D or, for that matter, C who might as well have been sued for his enrichment. In particular, the enrichment claim is not necessarily defeated by the contract between B and D.[414] Unlike the specific *condictiones*, the Pomponian sentence did not mention the lack of a *causa* or any other "unjust factor". The injustice was seen simply in the benefit from another's detriment. But that extension also blurred the rationale and sparked endless doctrinal controversies. They overshadowed the *condictio sine*

411 See Hallebeek in Schrage (ed.), at p. 108 with Fn. 209; Zimmermann, p. 847.

412 *Lipkin Gorman v Karpnale Ltd* [1991] 2 AC 548. See pp. 216 et seq.

413 Cf. Hallebeek in Schrage (ed.), at pp. 66–67, at p. 92 with fn. 151, at pp. 108 et seq and at p. 119–120. Zimmermann, p. 873–874.

414 The justification via contracts is the approach adopted by French law (see p. 168). See also Wieling/Finkenauer, Bereicherungsrecht, 2nd edn. 2020, § 4 para. 3, at p. 53 (assuming that the jurists overlooked that aspect).

causa (specialis) before Savigny's approach took hold.[415] These uncertainties made many jurists refuse a general enrichment claim. Following suit, the first codifications abstained from it, too, and kept themselves with more precise provisions. Von Kübel discarded the Pomponian sentence and based the German codification on Savigny (pp. 235 et seq.). But notwithstanding those controversial uncertainties, it was widely acknowledged by the end of the seventeenth century that the Pomponian sentence (a) was the underlying principle of the specific *condictiones*[416] and (b) was the apt test for the *condictio sine causa specialis.*[417]

Once the *condictio sine causa* had been established as general claim, it covered the whole range of unjust enrichment cases. While the references in D.12.7. had only concerned failed transactions, the *condictio sine causa* of the *ius commune* covered mainly **non-consented shifts of values**, too, e.g. where the defendant was enriched by stealing or otherwise taking value from the claimant without the latter's will.[418] This was necessary because of the so-called "*Vindikationsersatzfunktion*", i.e. the taking over of the *condictio* when the *rei vindicatio* has ceased to apply (see next, pp. 118–119). This is a feature that English law does not require due to the tort of conversion – a potential explanation why unjust enrichment in non-consent cases has hardly developed and always remained in the shadows of restitution for wrongs.

The expansion to the non-consent cases resulted in a two-tier system, consisting of performance-based enrichment and enrichment in other ways. By the time of the German codification, the doctrinal dichotomy had been perfected (see p. 241). The original cases of D.12.7. with their transactional context had been completely immersed within the performance related enrichment claims, the *Leistungskondiktionen,*[419] while the *condictio sine causa (specialis)* covered the other enrichments. This action replaced and extended the classical Roman *condictio furtiva* (see next). Both the *Vorentwurf* (= pre-draft) of Franz-Philipp von Kübel and – following him – the *Erste Entwurf* (= First Draft) of the BGB suggested to introduce the *condictio sine causa* into the BGB as a "small" sweeping clause for non-

415 On those doubts cf. e.g. v. Reinhard, AcP 29 (1846), 233, 234 et seq.
416 Cf. e.g. (to the Austrian condictio indebiti) Zeiller, Commentar über das ABGB, 1813, p. 156, As to France, Gaston Rau, p. 2 et seq.
417 v. Glück, Die Pandecten nach Hellfeld, Vol 13/1, p. 209; Rabel, Grundzüge des römischen Privatrechts, § 76, p. 119; Staudinger/Martinek, Eckpfeiler des Zivilrechts, Ungerechtfertigte Bereicherung und GoA, para. 9.
418 Savigny, V, p. 518; v.Glück, Die Pandecten nach Hellfeldt, Vol 13/1, pp. 191 et seq.
419 The *condictio ob causam finitam* is covered by § 812 I 2 1. Alt. BGB ("Wegfall des rechtlichen Grundes" = loss of legal reason), whereas the *condictio sine causa* and the *condictio indebiti* are amalgamated in § 812 I 1 1. Alt. ("ohne rechtlichen Grund" = lack of legal reason). See in more detail below, pp. 254 et seq.

performance related enrichments.[420] It was drafted according to Savigny's direct shift of value principle and thus liberated from the uncertainties of the past. But it applied only to those shifts of value that had occurred without or even against the will of the claimant.[421] It mirrored exactly the underlying principle and will therefore become of vital importance for our analysis. But unfortunately, the clear distinction got lost with "editorial changes" on the way to the final version of § 812 I 1 BGB. As a consequence, the systematics got lost and German enrichment law derailed. When it was put back on tracks by Walter Wilburg and Ernst von Caemmerer, the clarity of once could not be restored, only shadows on the wall (see in great detail below, pp. 254 et seq.).

b) The *condictio furtiva* – an important exception from "dare oportere"

The *condictio furtiva* (D.13.1.) was an exceptional action. It was the only *condictio* that competed with the *rei vindicatio.* Normally, the *condictio* would not be available for the owner to recover his property:

> D.13.1.1. (Ulpianus 18 ad Sabinum): "In furtiva re soli domino condictio competit".
>
> [The owner has a competing condictio only for a stolen thing]
>
> D.7.9.12 (Ulpianus 18 ad Sabinum): "...et proditum est neminem rem suam nisi furi condicere posse.
>
> [...and it has been passed down that nobody can reclaim his own thing by the *condictio* but from the thief.]

The claimant could not bring the *condictio* in order to recover things that still belonged to him. The *rei vindicatio* and the *condictiones* did not compete, but excluded each other. The reason was the "dare opportere" as the legal consequence of a *condictio.* The defendant was forced to make a "datio" to the claimant, i. e. to transfer the title to him, be it to money or to assets.[422] This was impossible if the claimant already held the title to the asset he wanted to recover from the defendant. In that case, the defendant could not be obliged to a "datio". He was only liable to restore possession to the claimant.[423] It followed that as long as the *rei vindicatio* was

420 § 748 E I; § 27 VE. See in detail below, pp. 230 et seq.

421 This is no longer visible in § 812 I 1 2. Alt. BGB, but was clearly expressed in the respective provision of the First Draft, § 748 E I, likewise in the predraft, § 27 VE.

422 Note that this did not necessarily mean that the benefit had been received by way of a datio. See below, p. 120. In the same sense Zimmermann, p. 854.

423 Above p. 59. The term used for this was "restitutere", D.6.1.9 (Ulp. 16 ad ed.). Note that this terminology is slightly at odds with the equation of unjust enrichment and restitution.

available, the claimant had to bring it. Only when the *rei vindicatio* ceased to apply, he could resort to the *condictio* instead.[424] From that angle, the *condictio* was the substitute of the *rei vindicatio*. The German term for the complementary role of the *condictio* is "***Vindikationsersatzfunktion***". It belongs to the common knowledge of German lawyers.

The exceptional feature of the *condictio furtiva* was that it could be brought by the owner despite the fact that he still held the title so that the defendant could not be forced to "dare opportere" to transfer the title, but only to "restituere" with regard to the possession.[425] This exception was designed as a privilege for the benefit of the victim of a theft.[426] To win an award under the *rei vindicatio*, the owner would have to show that the defendant was either still in possession or had disposed of his possession *dolo malo* (= mala fide). By contrast, the *condictio furtiva* would lie even if the possession had been lost without any proof of *dolo malo*.[427] The owner would not lose his claim merely because the defendant lost possession of the stolen good. The defendant could not object that somebody else had dispossessed him. That closed the door for unmeritorious defences that would have been hard to disproof. That is why Roman law allowed the owner to bring the *condictio furtiva* against the thief in competition with the *rei vindicatio*.

The exceptional feature of the *condictio furtiva* was only its *simultaneous* application competing with the *rei vindicatio*. The fact that a *condictio* stepped in as soon as the thief had used up the stolen property was not exceptional, but consequential in light of the *Vindikationsersatzfunktion*, as pointed out above. It is easily understood. If I drink up your beer or eat up your bread, I will have to pay for the value since I cannot return "in natura" what I took from you. Under Common law, this rule is enforced by damages under the tort of conversion. But under Civil law,

---

424 v. Glück, Die Pandecten nach Hellfeld, Vol 13/1, pp. 183–184. One once well-known example for this relation between rei vindicatio and condictio is the recovery of gifts between spouses. Those gifts were invalid under Roman law, cf. D.24.1.1. (Ulpianus 32 ad Sabinum): "Moribus apud nos receptum est, ne inter virum et uxorem donationes valerent." If the wife was still in possession of the present, the *rei vindicatio* would lie. By contrast, the *condictio (sine causa)* would apply if she had consumed the gift and enriched herself by that, v. Glück, Die Pandecten nach Hellfeld, Vol 13/1, pp. 183–184; Georg Friedrich Puchta, Vorlesungen über das heutige römische Recht, Band 1, 1847, § 425, p. 269.

425 Zimmermann, p. 839. This was the prevailing doctrinal view, v. Glück, Die Pandecten nach Hellfeld, Vol 13/1, pp. 215–217, also containing references to authors who tried various arguments to align the condictio furtiva with the datio requirement.

426 Savigny, V, p. 553; v. Glück, Die Pandecten nach Hellfeld, Vol 13/1, pp. 211 et seq.

427 v. Glück, Die Pandecten nach Hellfeld, Vol 13/1 p. 213, pointing to the other advantage that the claimant did not normally have to prove his ownership but just the theft (but different in case of competing claimants).

the loss of possession defeats the *rei vindicatio*, while tort law will not be applied vis-a-vis a *bona fide possessor* (see § 993 Abs. 1 BGB). The *condictio* must fill the gap and grant recovery of the value that was taken from the owner.[428] This was seen as consumption and gave rise to a *condictio*. Another old paradigm was the intrusion of cattle (sheep, cows) on another's land where they were grazing without consent. This ancient mishap has already been regulated in the Code Hammurabi.[429]

The *condictio furtiva* allowed the *condictio possessionis* even though the **defendant** could not be obliged to perform a "dare opportere" (since the claimant already held the title). But that is not to say that there had to be a "datio", i. e. a transfer of title, from the claimant to the defendant. True, the *condictiones* would typically cover situations where title to an asset (money, goods) had been vested in the recipient. This would mostly happen in the cases of the *condictio indebiti* because the *solutio* led to a valid "datio" to liberate the (apparent) debtor from his "dare opportere". Moreover, D.12.6.33 (Iulianus 39 Dig.) undoubtedly required a *negotium* as basis for a *condictio*. But this prerequisite had been overcome by the interpreters of the *ius commune*.[430] The initiator for this development was the *negotiorum gestio* in cooperation with the Pomponian sentence, later also the *actio de in rem verso*. But even if we follow the back to the roots approach of the *Historische Rechtsschule* in the complete disregard of academic analysis from the glossators onwards, we must note that Roman law allowed the *condictio* for the value of services. Apparently, the presumed requirement of an antecedent *datio* provides yet another example of the recurring (see p. 279) fallacy to deduct a legal rule from the "normal cases" (loan; *solutio*). It cannot be stressed enough how damaging the insistence on a "gegenständliche Vermögensverschiebung" (best translated as "transfer of a tangible asset") has been for German law of unjustified enrichment. It was wrong and led the law so far astray that the sound principle of Savigny was buried with it (p. 260).

---

428 So for example if another's money was paid to an innocent recipient ("inscio vel invito domino") and was mixed with his own, D.46.3.78 (Iaviolenus 11 ex Cassio): "Si alieni nummi inscio vel invito domino soluti sunt, manent eius cuius fuerunt: si mixti essent, ita ut discerni non possent, eius fieri qui accepit in libris Gaii scriptum est, ita ut actio domino cum eo, qui dedisset, furti competeret." Cf. further Herbert Hausmaninger/Richard Gamauf, A Casebook on Roman Property Law, 2012, p. 199 (including a translation); Gamauf, Vindicatio Nummorum, 2001, pp. 149–166.

429 § 57 Code of Hammurabi: "If a shepherd have not come to agreement with the owner of a field to pasture his sheep on the grass; and if he pasture his sheep on the field without the consent of the owner, the owner of the field shall harvest his field, and the shepherd who has pastured his sheep on the field without the consent of the owner of the field, shall give over and above twenty GUR of grain per ten GAN to the owner of the field." Sourced from the Harper translation, https://en.wikisource.org/wiki/The_Code_of_Hammurabi_(Harper_translation).

430 Zimmermann, p. 854. Cf. above, p. 101.

At the end of the day, while it was typical for the *condictio* to reverse a transfer of title *sine causa*, such a "*datio*" was no mandatory prerequisite of the *condictiones*. Regularly, it would be found. But the *condictio* to recover taken or "stolen" values was not based on a wilful "datio" of the claimant. It was a "condictio sine datione".[431] And this became true not only for the exceptional *condictio furtiva*, but also for the general *condictio sine causa specialis*. To make this point, we revert to the recovery of the invalid gift to the wife. Since the gift was invalid, there was no title transferred and the *rei vindicatio* would lie to claim repossession. This only changed when the gift was consumed by the wife (D.24.1.5.18 Ulp 32 ad Sab). But the consumption of another's property is not a transfer of value, but a taking of value. The same is true for the stolen money mixed and paid away by the thief.

To sum up: all *condictiones* but the *condictio furtiva* required a "dare oportere" *from the defendant to the claimant*, i.e. a "(red)datio" to return the value in question. But that was not to say that they did require a prior "datio" of that value from the claimant to the defendant. Such a requirement had been stated in another passage that dealt with the consequences of erroneous building on another's land. But it was already overcome in the course of the Middle Ages. As a consequence, it was settled that the *condictiones* did not only cover flawed transfers of titles or values, but also the taking of values without consent of the claimant. This dichotomy of enrichment claims was clearly recognised by Savigny, incorporated into his concept of direct shift of value and taken up by *Franz Philipp von Kübel* in the pre-draft of the BGB (pp. 230 et seq.).

5 The *negotiorum gestio* and unjust enrichment in civil law

The *negotiorum gestio* was a concept of Roman law[432] that has been received by Civilian jurisdictions,[433] but firmly rejected by Common Law.[434] This difference had profound effects on the shape of the respective enrichment laws. The *negotiorum gestio* played a vital role in extending the enrichment claims from failed

431 Adolfo Wegmann Stockebrand, Obligatio re contracta, 2014, p. 149 (with more references in footnote 185).

432 For an account see Zimmermann, pp. 433 et seq.; Sheehan, Negotiorum gestio: A Civilian Concept in the Common Law?, The International and Comparative Law Quarterly, 55 (2006), 253, at pp. 255 et seq.

433 Germany: §§ 677–687 BGB; France: Art. 1301–1301–5 C.civ.; Italy: Art. 2028–2032 C.C.

434 See only Dawson, "Negotiorum Gestio": The Altruistic Intermeddler, HarvLR, 74 (1961), 817; Jeroen Kortmann, Altruism in Private Law: Liability for Nonfeasance and Negotiorum Gestio, 2005, Chapter 11, p.99 et seq; Stevens, pp. 173 et seq.

transactions to enrichments in other ways (non-consent cases). It was the "natural" remedy to surpass the requirement of a *negotium* since it dealt *per definitionem* with situations without the consent of the principal. Due to England's agnostic stance towards the *negotiorum gestio*, English unjust enrichment of today appears to some extent closer to the transaction-related *condictiones* than Civilian unjustified enrichment.

Two examples are particularly illuminating of the different path taken by civilian enrichment law: the claim to skim off enrichment from a ***negotiorum gestio contraria***, i.e. prohibited interference with another's affairs, and the enrichment claim for **building on another's land.** Together with the *actio de in rem verso*, they exemplify the wide civilian enrichment claim in the wake of the Pomponian sentence.[435] But they are also key to understand why unjust enrichment is so difficult to classify as strict law or equity. Their distinctive feature is that they had to be developed *against* the authority of the Corpus Juris Civils. The Justinian Code contained an explicit prohibition of any claims for the benefit of prohibited intermeddlers (CJ.2.18.24), while the Digest denied the builder on another's land a claim for compensation (D.12.6.33). Both rules were overcome by recourse to the Pomponian prohibition to benefit from another's loss. That created a conflict between strict law (*rigor iuris*) and the principle of unjust enrichment. That is why the principle of unjust enrichment appeared to belong to equity, while the *condictiones* were clearly strict law. Ridding enrichment law of Pomponius is one way to counter the sloppiness of thought criticism.[436]

a) The enrichment claim for prohibited interference

The *negotiorum gestio* itself is no obvious case of unjust enrichment. The link only gets "activated" in case of a **prohibited** interference with another's affairs, the *negotiorum gestio contraria*. In the normal case of a legitimate *negotiorum gestio*, the affairs of another are managed in accordance with the interests and the presumed will of the principal. The "gestor" (or: "gerens") is reimbursed for his useful expenditure as if he had acted as an authorised agent. An agent's claim for reimbursement does not require that the principal is enriched. It is not designed to skim off unjust profits, but to compensate the agent for his layout. This is illustrated in the German code. Under § 683 BGB, the *gestor* can claim reimbursement for his necessary expenditure ("Aufwendungsersatz") like a mandatary ("wie ein Beauftragter")

435 Zimmermann, p. 875–883.
436 Another way is to curtail the claim to a subsidiary remedy of last resort, p. 162.

under § 670 BGB. As a rule, this does *not* include a remuneration for the work of the *gestor*.[437]

§ 683 Satz 1 BGB:
"Entspricht die Übernahme der Geschäftsführung dem Interesse und dem wirklichen oder dem mutmaßlichen Willen des Geschäftsherrn, so kann der Geschäftsführer wie ein Beauftragter Ersatz seiner Aufwendungen verlangen."

[If the assumption of the management of the business corresponds to the interest and the real or presumed will of the principal, the gestor may claim reimbursement of his expenses like a mandatary]

§ 670 BGB:
"Macht der Beauftragte zum Zwecke der Ausführung des Auftrags Aufwendungen, die er den Umständen nach für erforderlich halten darf, so ist der Auftraggeber zum Ersatz verpflichtet".

[If the agent incurs expenses for the purpose of executing the mandate, which he may consider necessary under the circumstances, the principal shall be obliged to reimbursement.]

The legal situation changes however if the *gestor* does *not* act in accordance with the presumed interest or even *against* the express wishes of the principal (unjustified or prohibited interference). In that case, he will only be allowed to skim off the unjustified enrichment of the principal. The rule is stated in § 684 BGB that further refers to § 812 BGB.

§ 684 Satz 1 BGB:

Liegen die Voraussetzungen des § 683 nicht vor, so ist der Geschäftsherr verpflichtet, dem Geschäftsführer alles, was er durch die Geschäftsführung erlangt, nach den Vorschriften über die Herausgabe einer ungerechtfertigten Bereicherung herauszugeben.

[If the requirements of section 683 are not met, the principal is obliged to disgorge to the gestor everything he obtains through the management according to the provisions on the restitution of unjustified enrichment.]

The same rule is enshrined in the French Code Civil (but not in the Italian Codice Civile):

Art. 1301–5 C.civ.:

437 There is an exception if the services of the gestor are rendered within his or her professional capacity. This is drawn from an analogy to § 1877 Abs. 3 BGB. The rule underlines how civil law has always accepted the objective value of conduct of one imposed on another unilaterally even without prior agreement, other than English law (see pp. 26–27 and 82–84).

Si l'action du gérant ne répond pas aux conditions de la gestion d'affaires mais profite néanmoins au maître de cette affaire, celui-ci doit indemniser le gérant selon les règles de l'enrichissement injustifié.

[If the manager's action does not meet the conditions for the management of another's affairs but nevertheless benefits the principal, he must indemnify the manager according to the rules of unjust enrichment.]

The justification of this rule is not evident. From a normative perspective, it is questionable why a person should be able to oblige another (the "principal") to disgorge anything at all by virtue of a prohibited and unwelcome interference.[438] At least, it seems that the disgorgement of a resulting enrichment should be restricted to the amount of the expenditure incurred by the gestor.[439] Otherwise, the illegitimate manager of another's affairs would be better off than the legitimate gestor. But the wording does not indicate a cap,[440] and in accordance with that, the prevailing opinion in Germany rejects any such restriction.[441]

The course for this somewhat surprising enrichment claim under §§ 684, 812 BGB has been set in the Middle Ages. It was decisively influenced by the principle of unjust enrichment. The Pomponian prohibition to benefit from another's loss was perceived as an equitable maxim that had the power to correct the strict law (*rigor iuris*). Without such corrective powers, no remedy could have been granted. This was because the Justinian Code, aiming to settle an ancient dispute between classical Roman jurists, had explicitly ruled out any claims in favour of an officious intermeddler who had disregarded an express prohibition:

CJ.2.18.24: Imperator Justinianus

Si quis nolente et specialiter prohibente domino rerum administrationi earum sese immiscuit, apud magnos auctores dubitabatur, si pro expensis, quae circa res factae sunt, talis negotiorum gestor habeat aliquam adversus dominum actionem. Quam quibusdam pollicentibus directam vel utilem, aliis negantibus, in quibus et salvius iulianus fuit, haec decidentes

438 Likewise Stevens, p. 175. It is as doubtful why the "principal" should be obliged towards a third party, but see *Watteau v Fenwick* [1893] 1 QB 346.
439 This is the minority view in Germany, MünchKommBGB/F. Schäfer, 9th edn. 2023, § 684 para. 8; Jauernig/Mansel, 18th edn. 2021, § 684 para. 1
440 Contrast § 996 BGB, below p. 128.
441 BGH WM 1967, 1147, 1148; Erman/Dornis, 17th edn. 2023, § 684 para. 5; Loyal JZ 2012, 1102, 1198. Inter alia, it can be argued that the principal has always the option to authorise the conduct of the gestor to reduce the award to the amount of the agent's actual outlay. The argument that a restrictive interpretation based on a purposive approach is not appropriate where the law allows other options to mitigate harshness is familiar to Common Lawyers, too, see *Ricketts v Ad Valorem Factors* [2003] EWCA Civ 1706, at paras. 14 et seq., 19 (per Mummery LJ). But see also *ESS v Sully* [2005] EWCA Civ 554, at para. 84 (per Arden LJ as she then was) for the limits of the "options-argument".

sancimus, si contradixerit dominus et eum res suas administrare prohibuerit, secundum iuliani sententiam nullam esse adversus eum contrariam actionem, scilicet post denuntiationem, quam ei dominus transmiserit nec concedens ei res eius attingere, licet res bene ab eo gestae sint.

[Scott: 24. *The Emperor Justinian to John.*

Where **anyone has interfered with the administration of the affairs of another, against the consent of the owner of the property, who has even forbidden him to do** so, a doubt is entertained by certain eminent authorities whether such a person has a right to bring suit against the said owner to recover expenses which he had incurred with reference to it; and some of them declare that a direct or an equitable action can be brought by him, and others (among whom was Salvius Julianus), deny that this can be done, but now **We, in deciding the question**, and in accordance with the opinion of Julianus, **order that if the owner of the property was opposed to the other transacting his business, and forbade him to do so, he can bring neither a direct nor an equitable action against him;** that is to say, after notice had been given him by the owner that he did not authorize him to attend to his affairs, even though he may have done so advantageously.]

However, this prohibition was called into question after the reception of Roman law in the Middle Ages. At the beginning, it was only a minority of commentators, amongst them Martinus Gosia, one of the famous "four doctors of Bologna" whose teachings were later summarised in the glossa Romana of Accursius.[442] His main argument was the prohibition of unjust enrichment. Support for a claim could also be derived from the following reference in the Digest:

D.3.5.5.5 (Ulpianus 10 ad ed.)
Sed et si quis negotia mea gessit non mei contemplatione, sed sui lucri causa, labeo scripsit suum eum potius quam meum negotium gessisse (qui enim depraedandi causa accedit, suo lucro, non meo commodo studet): sed nihilo minus, immo magis et is tenebitur negotiorum gestorum actione. ipse tamen si circa res meas aliquid impenderit, **non in id quod ei abest, quia improbe ad negotia mea accessit, sed in quod ego locupletior factus sum habet contra me actionem.**

[Scott – citing the passage in a deviating way as D.3.5.6.3 – Julianus, Digest, Book III.) Where anyone transacts my business, not through consideration for me but for the sake of profit, Labeo held that he was rather attending to his own affairs than mine; for he aims at his own advantage and not at mine, if he acts for the purpose of personal gain. Nevertheless, there is all the more reason that he should be liable to a suit based on business transacted. If, however, he has expended anything while attending to my business, he will be entitled to an action against me; not for what he has lost, since he was guilty of bad faith in meddling in my affairs, but merely to ascertain the amount by which I am enriched.]

---

442 The others were Bulgarus, Jacobus de Boragine and Hugo de Porta Ravennate. On a side note: Porta Ravennate (today Piazza di Porta Ravegnana) is the name of the place where the famous "Two Towers" of Bologna are located.

Here, the gestor is allowed to claim even though he did not intend act for the benefit of the principal but for his own ("sui lucri causa"). The reason is the enrichment of the principal ("in quod ego locupletior factus sum habet contra me actionem"). According to that, the gestor cannot claim his outlay but is allowed to skim of the enrichment of the principal instead. Some commentators argued that what was right for the illoyal and selfish gestor of D.3.5.5.5, should also be right for someone who had only tried to help when the principal acted irrationally.[443]

However, it took very long time before a claim for enrichment stemming from a prohibited interference became the law, and that only happened in some (not all) civilian jurisdictions. The reason was the weight of the explicit prohibition in C.2.18.24.[444] The unjust enrichment argument created a conflict of equity versus strict law that most commentators tried to avoid. They preferred to allow exceptions where adherence to the strict rule seemed unsustainable. One such exception was assumed where irrational prohibitions by the principal were apparently caused by insanity or anger in the heat of the moment. It was discussed in relation to two almost identical cases, set in Bologna and Barcelona:[445]

> A stubbornly refuses to pay the municipal real estate tax. This refusal is threatened by a (harsh) sanction: the demolition of the house. When the day has come to execute the sanction, a friend of A pays the tax on his behalf under his fierce protest and thus saves the house.

Cases like this[446] eventually paved the way for the enrichment claim in case of a prohibited but useful *negotiorum gestio*, as it has been codified in § 684 BGB and Art. 1301–5 C.civ. Other ways around the strict prohibition of C.2.18.24 were proposed,[447] and some have made it into the Civilian Codes, too, as for example the reference by one author to the public interest ("ne ciuitas deformaretur ruinis"

443 Hallebeek, in Schrage (ed.), pp. 72–73; Zimmermann, pp. 875–879. However, others held that the enrichment in such a case was not unjust because the gestor only had himself to blame for acting against the prohibition.

444 See Hallebeek, in Schrage (ed.), p. 120: The provision was not generally derogated.

445 Hallebeek, in Schrage (ed.), pp. 72–73. The case set in Bologna is discussed by Azo (A. Belloni, Le questioni civilistiche des secolo XII, Frankfurt am Main, 1989, pp. 127–130. The house belongs to Titius and the friend who pay is called Sempronius. The case set in Barcelona is discussed by Pilius, see Nicolini, Pilii Medicinensis, Quaestiones sabbatinae, 1946, pp. 23–27.

446 Similar cases were discussed by the postglossators, for example the payment against the will of a friend to free him from the debtor's tower; or a payment which is made against the will of a criminal although it spares him the capital punishment. See Hallebeek, in Schrage (ed.), p. 76.

447 According to Hallebeek, in Schrage (ed.), p. 74, Pierre de Belleperche argued in his commentary that C.2.18.24 was only applicable if the gestor acted against a prohibition of unnecessary (as opposed to necessary) management of the principal's affairs.

– the city should not be defaced by ruins).[448] These approaches were closer to the strict law. They are reminiscent of the piecemeal development of Common Law agency of necessity.[449] It is even possible to detect an efficiency story here. Enrichment from prohibited interference will often prove that the prohibition by the principal was objectively stupid. It would be more efficient to let the manager allocate the resources, create value and reap the benefits.[450] But whatever the reasons, it is beyond doubt that in the course of the centuries the majority view has continuously shifted towards the minority position of once. The "higher law" of Pomponian unjust enrichment trumped the black letter law.

b) The enrichment claim for building on another's land

The rules on building of another's land are the second example to show how *negotiorum gestio* and unjust enrichment shaped (others might think: deformed) Civil Law. The starting point was D.12.6.33 where any *condictio* of the possessor against the owner to claim compensation for improvements was denied for lack of a *negotium.*[451] Instead, the possessor was reduced to a lien to retain possession until he was reimbursed by the owner.

The legal situation has changed considerably since then. In Germany, the relationship between the illegitimate possessor of tangible property (land and movable) is regulated in the §§ 985–993 BGB, the so-called *Eigentümer-Besitzer-Verhältnis* or "EBV" (= owner – possessor – relationship). It contains the *rei vindicatio* (§ 985 BGB) and the follow-up claims that may arise between (§§ 987–993 BGB). German law grants the bona fide possessor (as said: of land or movables) a right to claim reimbursement for necessary expenditure like e.g. repair costs:

> § 994 BGB:
> Der Besitzer kann für die auf die Sache gemachten notwendigen Verwendungen von dem Eigentümer Ersatz verlangen.
>
> [The possessor may claim compensation from the owner for necessary expenditures made on the property.]

448 Hallebeek, in Schrage (ed.), p. 74 attributes this argument, gleaned from D.43.8.2.17 and D.43.8.7., to the commentary on C.2.18.24 by Pierre de Belleperche. A public interest exception is e.g. codified in Germany (§ 679 BGB) and Italy (Art. 2031 C.C.), but not in France.

449 Originating in Admirality and commercial law, see e.g. *The Gratitudine* (1801) 3 C. Rob 240; *Arthur v Barton* (1840) 6 M.– & W 138; *Mertens v Winnington* (1794) 1 Esp 112; but contrast the restrictive approach in *Hawtayne v Bourne* (1841) 7 M. & W. 595.

450 Erman/Dornis, BGB, 17th edn. 2023, § 684 para. 5.

451 Hallebeek, in Schrage (ed.), pp. 77 et seq.

This right is independent of any surviving enrichment. It is similar to a the right of an agent or a *negotiorum gestor* who acts according to the interest of the principal. It might well be explained as an agency of necessity that the possessor performs on behalf of the owner. By contrast, if the expenditure is not necessary to maintain the property of the owner, the reimbursement will be capped to the extent of the owner's enrichment by the expenditure (§ 996 BGB).[452]

> § 996 BGB:
> "Für andere als notwendige Verwendungen kann der Besitzer Ersatz nur insoweit verlangen, als ... Wert der Sache durch sie noch zu der Zeit erhöht ist, zu welcher der Eigentümer die Sache wiedererlangt."
>
> [For expenditures other than necessary ones, the owner may claim compensation only to the extent that ... the value is still increased by them at the time when the owner regains possession of his property.]

The right to reimbursement under § 994 or § 996 can be enforced actively via a claim under § 1001 BGB (provided that the owner retained possession or authorised the expenses), not only via a right to retention under (§ 1000 BGB) that works as defence against the *rei vindicatio* of the owner under § 985 BGB – the remainder of the classical Roman solution of the lien.

> However, it must be noted that the German Supreme Court does *not* grant any right to reimbursement in the case of a newly erected building on another's land.[453] From the perspective of legal history, this solution marks more than a U-turn because it even falls back behind the restrictive Roman law where at least a lien had been granted. The highly contentious jurisdictions rests on the ground that due to the massive increase in value of the land, indemnifying the possessor for the expenses could expropriate the owner.[454]

It is interesting to see how the Roman restriction to a lien has been overturned in favour of a claim to reimbursement that now flanks the right to retention in the

452 This contrasts with the predominant solution under § 684 BGB, see p. 124.
453 BGHZ 41, 157, 159; BGHZ 41, 341, 346; BGH NJW 1996, 52. The doctrinal arguments are that erecting a building on another's land is not a "Verwendung" (= defined as an expenditure serving the property) but an "Aufwendung" (= an investment changing the property), and that the more specific rules of the §§ 994 et seq BGB bar the application of the more general enrichment law (§ 812 BGB). Less restrictive *Yeoman's Row v Cobbe* [2008] UKHL 55.
454 For the opposing view Canaris, JZ 1996, 62 who wants to award a so-called Aufwendungskondiktion under § 812 I 1 2. Alt. BGB (p. 281). The advantage of this approach is that the enrichment claim will not be awarded before the increase in value of the land has actually been realised by the owner. This solution rests on the modern doctrine of "Aufdrängungsschutz" (= protection against the unilateral imposition of enrichment). See below, pp. 282–283.

German Code (§§ 1000, 1001 BGB). Again, the driver was the *negotiorum gestio* in combination with the notion of unjust enrichment. Building on another's land could be seen as unauthorised management of another's affairs. The proponents of this view would "substitute" the required intent to obligate the principal ("animus gerendi") by the fact that the act of the "gestor" was beneficial to the owner (so-called "negotiorum gestio ipso gestu" or "ipsa re").[455] The link between *negotiorum gestio* and unjust enrichment in D.3.5.5.5. was again a key argument. Like in the case of the prohibited interference, the equity of unjust enrichment was used to surpass the *rigor iuris* of the "written law" (here of D.12.6.33) – a view that was again opposed by the majority of writers.[456] The detailed account given by Jan Hallebeek reads like an oracle, a premonition of centuries of future debates. The solution proposed by Martinus Gosia was met with the full force of the "sloppiness of thought"-criticism. It was said polemically that he had made up an action "ex sua ficta" or "ex falsa equitate."[457] In part, this harsh criticism may have been caused by his view that even a mala fide possessor should have an enrichment claim.[458] But again, why should a mala fide possessor who confers an enrichment on the owner be worse off than an officious intermeddler who confers an enrichment on someone who expressly forbade him to act.

As it turned out, Martinus Gosia was simply a bright mind way ahead of his time. All that original outrage against his teachings could not prevent the demise of the classical restriction to a lien. Centuries later, a case came up where a bona

455 For the exact arguments exchanged in favour and against this highly contentious solution see Hallebeek, in Schrage (ed.), pp. 80–81 and 82–86. Again, Martinus Gosia carried the torch of unjust enrichment.

456 Hallebeek, in Schrage (ed.), pp. 82–86 and 118–119.

457 See in particular Hallebeek, in Schrage (ed.), p. 84. Several commentators even admonished him in writing next to the passage D.12.6.33 which they felt Martinus had disrespected: "*audi, domine Martine*". See ibid, p. 84 Fn. 107.

458 Hallebeek, at p. 81 with Fn. 84 and p. 82 with Fn. 87; this solution is also found in the Brachylogus, see Böcking (ed), Corpus legum sive Brachylogus iuris civilis, 1829, at p. 38 (Liber II, Tit. VIII – De accessione), see https://archive.org/details/bub_gb_VigtAAAAYAAJ/page/38/mode/2up. On that fundamental medieval work see Fitting, Über die Heimat und das Alter des sogenannten Brachylogus, 1880 (reprint 2019), assuming that it served as a textbook for legal studies in Orléans (at pp 16–18).

The opposing majority of the contemporary jurists presumed that a mala fide possessor who was building on another's land was making a gift – a fiction that did however not sit easily with D.3.5.5.5, cf. Hallebeek, in Schrage (ed.), p. 83 and 84–86.

In later times, the distinction between bona fide and mala fide possessors became more and more central. Today, German law grants indemnification for necessary expenditures to a mala fide possessor according to the rules of the *negotiorum gestio* (§ 994 Abs. 2 BGB), but denies any other claims for expenditure, including those based on unjustified enrichment, cf. Jauernig/Berger, BGB, 18th edn. 2021, Vorbem. zu §§ 994–1003, Rn. 7.

fide possessor had, ill-advised by his lawyer, not exerted his lien and thus forfeited compensation. Why should that pure technicality, a merely innocent mistake, spare the owner and cost the possessor the well-deserved reimbursement? The new spirit was that a remedy had to be granted. And this time, the argument of unjust enrichment prevailed. [459] Once again, the juggernaut had been set into motion. Afterwards, it could not be stopped any more.

In the process of codification, the modified, enrichment-infused solutions for building on another's land and prohibited interference were either enacted directly (e. g. Art. 555 C.civ. on building on another's land[460]) or immersed in the general provisions of the *rei vindicatio* (§§ 985–1003 BGB) and the *negotiorum gestio* (§§ 677–687 BGB; Art. 1301–1301–5 C.civ.; Art. 2028–2032 C.C.). Today, they are often no longer discernible as unjust enrichment.[461] But it was the ancient link between *negotiorum gestio* and enrichment in D.3.5.5.5 that profoundly shaped civilian enrichment law.[462] That happened in a way that was not open to the Mosaic enrichment claims. English law has always severely restricted restitution of unrequested benefits, be it for edifices wrongfully erected on another's land or for misdirected services (Zach the window cleaner mistakenly administers his service to 34 Wellington Street instead of 36 Wellington Street).[463] This restraint is based on the same ground that Julian put forward: there is no prior agreement between the parties. This antecedent meeting of minds is called "*negotium*" by Julian, "request" under a quantum meruit or "acceptance" by Robert Stevens.[464] If it lacks, the defendant cannot be held to account for any "benefit" because there is no mutual consent that the doings of one party are of money's worth to the other. However, the acceptance of a general claim in unjust enrichment has the potential to undermine the traditional English principles regarding unrequested benefits and remote beneficiaries, as is discussed above p. 24 and below p. 189.

---

459 See Hallebeek, in Schrage (ed.), p. 92, referring to Paulus Castensis, In secundam Digesti Veteris partem, 1533, ad D.12.6.33

460 See also Cass. 3e civ. 9–9–2021 n° 20–15.713 FS-B, clarifying that this rule only covered the erection of new buildings.

461 But see Cass. 3e civ. 9–9–2021 n° 20–15.713 FS-B on the Romain "theorie des impenses" that has not been codified but is generally accepted and may give rise to a claim in negotiorum gestio or unjust enrichment. See also Aufwendungs- and Verwendungskondiktion in Germany (below p. 282).

462 Hallebeek, in Schrage (ed.), pp. 106–108 and 117–120.

463 See above p. 26; further *Falcke v. Scottish Imperial Insurance Co* (1888) 34 ChD 234 (CA), 248 (per Bowen LJ.); *Yeoman's Row v Cobbe* [2008] UKHL 55; Stevens, pp. 37–38, 160, 175–176.

464 This resonates with the *acceptio sine causa* that civil lawyers employed for the – obsolete – classification as quasi-contractual, cf. v. Glück, Die Pandekten nach Hellfeld, Vol 13/1, pp. 209–210.

6 The *actio de in rem verso (utilis)* and unjust enrichment in civil law

Reinhard Zimmermann counted the *actio de in rem verso* to the "Roman institutions that stimulated the advance towards a broadly based enrichment liability." Still, it is the widely "unknown unknown" in the English debate on unjust enrichment. There has always been awareness of the *condictiones*, but much less of the "version claim" and its similarity – French lawyers might even say: identity – with the Pomponian sentence.[465] As said in the beginning, not all civilian enrichment laws embrace the Pomponian claim. Likewise, civil law was and continues to be split on the merits of the *action de in rem verso.* Jurisdictions which adhered to the view that the *actio de in rem verso* was immersed in the general enrichment claim of Pomponius (France, Italy) preserved its content to the present day whereas jurisdictions adopting the opposing view of an independent cause of action (Germany, Austria) laid it to its grave for good.

The journey of the *actio de in rem verso* in Europe has poignantly been described as "history of a misunderstanding of the institute or misuse of the term" ("Geschichte eines Missverständnisses des Instituts oder Missbrauchs des Begriffs") by *Tiziana Chiusi.*[466] Understanding the reasons why is complicated. Nevertheless, comprehension is essential for English unjust enrichment as it is standing at the crossroads and will have to choose between Pomponius' "super-eminent equity" and Savigny's "direct shift of wealth/value".

a) The actio de in rem verso and the actio de in rem verso utilis in the Roman sources

The basic notion of the version claim is that investment of one for the benefit of another is subject to restitution. This idea has become so central to civilian enrichment thinking that even the explicit prerequisite of a "negotium" in the D.12.6.33 (Iulianus 39 Dig.) was overcome and an enrichment claim for a claimant who had built on another's land would generally be granted. As seen in the previous chapter, this development was initiated by references to D.3.5.5.5 and the Pomponian sentence in the teachings or Martinus Gosia.[467] Later, D.12.1.32 was cited to support a general rule that restitution will lie if money of the claimant enriched the defendant.[468] But the foremost manifestation of this principle is found in the classical *actio de in rem verso* of D. 15.3. This action was extended beyond its original

465 Zimmermann, p. 878.
466 Chiusi, p. 1.
467 Hallebeek in Schrage (ed.), p. 82.
468 Hallebeek in Schrage (ed.), p. 92.

boundaries by imperial enactment in C.4.26.7.3.[469] Together with the Pomponian sentence, the expansive *actio de in rem verso utilis* of the Digest became the prime driver for enrichment claims against remote recipients. By contrast, traditional English law does not allow any "version claims" against remote beneficiaries of a transaction.[470]

The original *actio de in rem verso* is located in D.15.3. It had its origins in the classical period of Roman law. It belonged to the so-called "*actiones adiecticiae qualitatis*" (= "adjected or added actions").[471] Those were legal instruments created to compensate the peculiar restrictions of legal capacity under Roman law. First, it was not permissible to act openly on behalf of others as undisclosed agent ("alteri stipulari nemo potest").[472] Second, persons who were subject to the paternal power of the *paterfamilias* ("qui alienae potestati subiecti sunt"[473]) lacked legal capacity to act on their own behalf. As a result, the members of a Roman patrician household (wife, sons, slaves, employees) could neither hold property on their own nor oblige the *paterfamilias* by acting in his name as disclosed agents. Roman law did however accept undisclosed agency and allowed dispositions of the principal's property by other persons.[474] This facilitated trading by the legally "incapacitated" members of the household on behalf of the principal. That option created the necessity for the specific "*actiones adiecticiae qualitatis*".

This array of legal instruments brought the law in line with the economic reality. Particularly, it allowed family members (typically sons or slaves) to run their own businesses. The specific legal tool at hand for that purpose was the *peculium*, described in great depth in D.15.1. "de peculio". The peculium was a separated fund of assets that legally still belonged to the paterfamilias, but could be used for the business by the son or slave. Liability under the *actio de peculio* was restricted to the value of the *peculium* ("dumtaxat de peculio"[475]). It was a precursor of trading

469 Zimmermann, p. 879. Text and translation below in the text.
470 *Costello v MacDonald* [2011] EWCA Civ 930, [2011] 3 WLR 1341 following the Australian case of *Lumbers v W Cook Builders Pty Ltd* [2008] HCA 27, 232 CLR 635; Stevens, p. 42. But see below pp. 191 et seq.
471 In depth Wacke, ZRGRA 111 (1994), 280; cf. further Kaser, Das römische Privatrecht I – Das römische, das vorklassische und klassische Recht 2 (1971), at p. 605;
472 D.45.1.38.17 (Ulpianus 49 ad Sabinum); cf. further Kaser, Das römische Privatrecht I – Das römische, das vorklassische und klassische Recht 2 (1971), at p. 260; Honsell, Römisches Recht, 2010, pp. 32–33; Lange, ZRGRA 73 (1956), 279.
473 D.15.1.1. (Ulpianus 29 ad edictum).
474 Kaser, Das römische Privatrecht I – Das römische, das vorklassische und klassische Recht 2 (1971), at p. 260
475 D.15.1.5.1. (Ulpianus 29 ad edictum).

with limited liability,[476] just as the *actio de in rem verso* was a precursor of piercing the veil – and fulfils this function until the present day.[477] The *actio de in rem verso* came into play once the *peculium* was used up ("nihil in peculio habent").[478] But this was under the strict proviso that the owner had actually benefitted from the conduct of the business:

> D.15.3.1 (Ulpianus 29 ad edictum): "Si hi qui in potestate aliena sunt nihil in peculio habent, … tenentur qui eos habent in potestate, si in rem eorum quod acceptum est conversum sit, quasi cum ipsis potius contractum videatur."
>
> [If those who are subject to the power of another have nothing in the peculium, those who have power over them will be held liable as if they had contracted themselves if what had been received was converted for the benefit of their goods.]

In the Codex Justinianus, the *actio de in rem verso* was extended in the most decisive way. The claim now covered the acts of "free" third parties who were neither subject to another's power nor acting under restricted capacity ("cum libero agente").

> C.4.26.7.3 (Imperatores Diocletianus, Maximianus)[479]
>
> Alioquin si cum libero rem agente eius, cuius precibus meministi, contractum habuisti et eius personam elegisti, pervides contra dominum nullam te habuisse actionem, nisi vel in rem eius pecunia processit vel hunc contractum ratum habuit.
>
> [Blume: "If, on the other hand, you contracted with a free person who transacted the business of the man whom you mention in your petition, relying on the former, you can see that you

476 Hansmann/Kraakman/Squire, Incomplete Organizations: Legal Entities and Asset Partitioning in Roman Commerce (2014); also Hansmann/Kraakman/Squire, Law and the Rise of the Firm (2006).
477 The most famous example being the arrêt Boudier in France, see p. 157.
478 But note also the opposing view of the "Regresstheorie" (= doctrine of reimbursement), see below p. 135.
479 The Codex Justinianus attributes the enactment to the Imperatores Diocletianus and Maximus in 293 A.D. They were the leader and deputy leader of the Roman tetrarchy that was introduced by emperor Diocletian in that very year. However, there has been debate whether the extension of the action beyond the boundaries of classical Roman law had originally been ordered at the time of the tetrarchy, or whether it was wilfully added by the jurists of Justinian in the course of the compilation. There was suspicion that both the word "libero" and the part "nisi vel in rem eius pecunia processit" have been inserted later, cp. Otto Lenel, Das Ediktum Perpetuum, 1928, p. 297. That does however not affect the pivotal role the passage played in the history of enrichment law. Also, it must be observed that claiming inaccuracies and falsifications was one trick of old to get rid of "disliked" Roman authority.

> have no right of action against the principal, unless the money was used for his benefit, or he ratified the contract.]

After the reception, the so extended claim became known under the name *actio de in rem verso utilis.*[480] It lay for any benefits that accrued to the assets of a third person by acts or dealings between other parties. Henceforth, it bore two characteristic features: the benefit of the principal and the futility of the claim against the agent ("nihil in peculio habet"). They are paradigmatic for the leap frogging function that the version claim is still fulfilling in those jurisdictions that have embraced it as enrichment claim, most notably France and Italy.[481] For a proposition of an alternative principle ("no liberality at another's expense") that may be underlying such claims as well as *Menelaou* see below p. 200.

b) The legal nature of the *actio de in rem verso* between *negotiorum gestio* and unjust enrichment

The legal nature of the action in C.4.26.7.3 has been subject to intensive debate from the beginning of the reception in medieval Europe. The views were split between an *actio negotiorum gestio* (Irnerius; Azo), a *condictio sine causa ex equitate* (Jacques de Revigny), a *condictio certi utilis* in the wake of D.12.1.32; but for Bulgarus and Roffredus Beneventanus, it was the *actio de in rem verso utilis.*[482] While that term prevailed, the legal nature of the version claim remained contentious. The glossators had already marked the basic frontlines of the opposing opinions. One view assumed an agency-related remedy similar to the *negotiorum gestio.* Others saw the claim based on enrichment. The two antagonists fought out their battle over the centuries. The Digest was inconclusive. There were surely passages that mentioned the necessary benefits of the *dominus* in terms of enrichment ("locupletior"[483]). On the other hand, the *actio de in rem verso* was closely connected with

---

480 See only Zimmermann, p. 879 et seq; Coing, Europäischen Privatrecht 1500–1800, 498–502; Chiusi, p. 1–2; Kupisch, Versionsklage, pp. 57 et seq.

481 But also e.g. in the Czech republic, cf. Dostalik, Actio de in rem verso. An Unwanted Continuity. The Doctrine of versio in rem in the Austrian Civil Code and Interwar Legal Discussion in Czechoslovakia, Krakowskie Studia z Historii Państwa i Prawa 2022; 15 (2), 203–214; available at: https://dspace5.zcu.cz/bitstream/11025/49673/1/Dostalik_KSzHPiP_15%282%292022.pdf.

482 *Roffreddus Beneventanus* and *Bulgarus*, Hallebeek in Schrage (ed.), p. 103; de Chiusi, p. 1; Roffreddus, Tractatus libellorum, Argentorati 1502, pars 1, fol. 18.

483 See for example D.15.3.2. (Iavolenus 12 ex Cassio, denying the claim for lack of enrichment): "Qui nummis acceptis servum manumisit, agi cum eo de in rem verso non potest, quia dando libertatem locupletior ex nummis non fit."

the peculiar "agency" under the *peculium.* It did not generally address all people who were made richer, or whose assets were enhanced by the acts of others.

This debate is key to the different shapes of Civilian unjustified enrichment laws. Germany was a particular stronghold of the agency approach. It was vigorously defended in the dying days of the *ius commune* by Andreas von Tuhr whose analysis has shaped the perception of the *actio de in rem verso* for the time to come.[484] His fundamental treatise had the tell-tale subtitle "zugleich ein Beitrag zur Lehre von der Geschäftsführung" [= at the same time a contribution on the doctrine of management of another's affairs].[485] According to his "Regreßtheorie"[486] (= doctrine of reimbursement[487]) that he opposed to the "Bereicherungstheorie" (= doctrine of enrichment), the *actio de in rem verso* was based on the agent's claim of reimbursement against his principal.[488]

For the contrary enrichment view, the claim for the versum was explained by the Pomponian principle that nobody be enriched by another's detriment.[489] One consequence of emphasising the enrichment of the principal instead of its relation to the agent was that the action could be extended to cover two party situations. If the claim is not based on the existence of an agency-relation, but rests on "no benefit from another's detriment", it cannot make a difference whether the money of the claimant was used for the benefit of a third party (the "principal") or directly for the benefit of the counter party (the "gestor"). This led to a material shift in the perception of the *actio de in rem verso.* Claims for reimbursement of the "versum"

D.15.3.6. (Tryphoninus): "Nam si hoc verum esset, etiam antequam venderet rem peculiarem, de in rem verso teneretur, quia hoc ipso, quod servus rem in peculio haberet, locupletior fieret, quod aperte falsum est."

484 Chiusi, p. 6.

485 von Tuhr, Actio de in rem verso – zugleich ein Beitrag zur Lehre von der Geschäftsführung, 1895.

486 So named by v. Tuhr, p. 1.

487 Meaning the claim for reimbursement.

488 Cf. v. Tuhr, pp. 1 et seq. The focal point of the discussion was the question whether or not the agent *always* had a claim to reimbursement against the principal. For the agency view, the answer was in the affirmative. But this was at odds with the passage where Ulpian said that the *actio de in rem verso* only stepped in when the peculium was repleted ("nihil in peculio", D.15.3.1.). If there was always the reimbursement claim at the hands of the agent, how could there ever be "nothing in the peculium". The answer given by v. Tuhr, p. 130, was that the actio de in rem verso was based on the agent's right to reimbursement, not on the enrichment of the principal. It followed that – contrary to the enrichment theory (and D.15.3.10.6, for that matter) no surviving enrichment was required.

489 For the older views: Leyser, Meditationes ad pandectas, Lipsiae, 1717, specim. 130 med. 8; Kind, Quaestiones forenses, Lipsiae 1792, tom. I cap. 35; for the 19the century, Mandry, Das Familiengüterrecht, Vol. II, 1876, pp. 454 et seq.

were allowed within bipartite relations, for example by I 13 § 262 PrALR.[490] We will see in the following text how this "diversion" fuelled the civilian (mis)conception that every expenditure for another's benefit *as such* constitutes a recoverable enrichment, regardless of any unjust factor.

The academic debate on the legal nature of the *actio de in rem verso* became of considerable practical consequence when the codifications emerged. The jurists of the *usus modernus* had not immersed the *actio de in rem verso (utilis)* in the general enrichment claim.[491] There was no need to do so since the Roman legal sources were directly at hand. The *actio de in rem verso* had a free-standing legal basis even though the jurists were of course aware that it fitted under the overarching "brocade" that there be no benefit from another's loss. In this context, we must also remember the deep-rooted reservations against the vague "super-eminent equity" of Pomponius that already Martinus Gosia had faced.

The diverging opinions shaped the first codifications. Under the Ancien Régime, France had been extremely hostile to the *actio de in rem verso.* Claude de Ferrière stated in 1677: "Cette action est inutile en France."[492] The highly influential Pothier saw the *condictio indebiti* as the only case of unjust enrichment. To him, the *actio de in rem verso* was not a claim in unjust enrichment.[493] For that reason, the original Code Civil of 1804 only contained the *condictio indebiti* (Art. 1376 old C.civ.) but neither a general enrichment claim[494] nor the *actio de in rem verso.*[495] This contrasted with the Prussian Allgemeine Landrecht and the Austrian ABGB of 1812 that both contained a general *actio de in rem verso* (§§ 1041–1043 ABGB; ALR I 13 § 262). None of these Codes contained a general enrichment claim though.[496]

It was at this point of time that the underlying disputes on the legal nature of the version claim suddenly resurfaced in two different ways. In Prussia and Austria, the provisions of the *actio de in rem verso* covered two party situations.[497]

---

490 Zimmermann, pp. 881–882; Kupisch in Schrage (ed.), p. 268.
491 See Kupisch, Versionsklage, p. 18–19; Chiusi, p. 2.
492 Claude de Ferrière, La Jurisprudence du Digeste, Paris, 1677, annotations to D.15.3. Chiusi, p. 194.
493 Grauer, Die ungerechtfertigte Bereicherung im französischen Privatrecht, 1939, p. 7–8; Ferid-Sonnenberger, Das französische Zivilrecht II, 2nd edn. 1986, S N 1, p. 427; Chiusi, p. 194.
494 Chiusi, p. 194; Zimmermann, pp. 883–884; Mélodie Combot, pp. 54 et seq.
495 However, the Code civil of 1804 contained a range of provisions that were perceived as specific cases of the *actio de in rem verso.* That laid the basis for its general acceptance in the arrêt Boudier, see in detail below, pp. 139 et seq.
496 The situation was clear for Austria, but less clear under the Prussian ALR, see Chiusi, p.5.
497 Kupisch in Schrage (ed.), p. 268; Zimmermann, p. 883. Indeed, the controversy about the scope of the condictiones and the actio de in rem verso played out exactly in the reverse. As a rule, the

That resonated with the enrichment view, in particular D.12.1.32,[498] and allowed jurists to recognise the *condictio sine causa* in those Codes (that had *not* been codified).

> A.L.R. I 13 § 262:
>
> "Derjenige, aus dessen Vermögen etwas in den Nutzen eines Andern verwendet worden, ist dasselbe entweder in Natur zurück, oder für den Werth Vergütung zu fordern berechtigt."
>
> ["The person from whose property something has been used for the benefit of another is entitled either to have it returned in kind or to claim remuneration for its value." – by Deep-L]
>
> Similarly § 1041 ABGB that however points to the negotiorum gestio because it is independent of a surviving enrichment.

But the most interesting part is the final twist that caused the split within civilian enrichment. The leading proponents were Germany and France. In the last quarter of the 19th century, the German codification was well on its way. In accordance with Savigny, but also with the Code Civil of 1804, the Pomponian sentence had been discarded and unjust(ified) enrichment had been restricted to the *condictiones*. In addition, and also in accordance with the Code Civil, the decision had been taken not to enshrine the *actio de in rem verso (utilis)* in the BGB. With those two related legislative decisions the sentence of Pomponius seemed overcome in civil law.

At the same time, the development took a U-turn in neighbouring France when the Cour de Cassation decided the arrêt Boudier in 1892. It ruled that the general enrichment claim, in the shape of the Pomponian sentence, was part of French law despite it not having been codified. And it held that this general enrichment claim embraced the *actio de in rem verso*, despite it not having been codified either. Thus, it did not only claim a late victory for the enrichment view of the *actio de in rem verso*. It even used the principle of unjust enrichment as the direct basis for the claim. That was unheard of under the *usus modernus* of the Roman sources.[499] At the end of the day, the Cour de Cassation had allowed two dead corpses to pull each other by the straps out of the grave. And they went on to thrive for ever after!

---

actio de in rem verso required three parties (agent, principal and contracting party), but was extended by some jurists to the two parties between the enrichment took place, thus disposing of the middleman (agent). By contrast, the condictio would naturally be directed against the other party of the failed transaction, but could, according to some, exceptionally, reach out to remote beneficiaries under D.12.1.32.

498 Above, p. 115.

499 Kupisch in Schrage (ed.), p. 250 with fn. 52.

A grave consequence of this development was the extension of the general enrichment claim to remote beneficiaries – we could speak of the "leap frogging function". But the enrichment approach of the Cour de Cassation also provided new doctrinal means to restrict the claim and avoid overreach. They were more flexible than under the agency approach. This is best exemplified contrasting the arrêt Boudier to a judgement of the then newly established *Reichsgericht* (German Imperial Court) on the *actio de in rem verso* in the PrALR I 13 § 262.[500] The facts of the Imperial Court case of 1880 (RGZ 1, 159) were as follows:

> The claimant had sold fertiliser to a customer who used it on fields that solely belonged to his wife. After the death of the husband, his estate was insufficient to cover the purchase prize. The vendor sued the widow of the deceased because the fertiliser had been used for her benefit.

This might appear to be a case of the *actio Pauliana.* But it was tried on the codified *actio de in rem verso* of the PrALR. The *Reichsgericht* awarded the claim.[501] In doing so, it rejected the approach of the Preußische Obertribunal (= Prussian Supreme Tribunal) that restricted the *actio de in rem verso* to two party situations.[502] Following the jurisdiction of its predecessor, the *Reichsoberhandelsgericht* (ROHG = Imperial Supreme Commercial Court), the Reichsgericht saw no basis for the exclusion of three party situation. That the PrALR did not require an intermediate agent, did not mean that it excluded those cases altogether.[503] To hold otherwise would have been at odds with the historic roots of the *actio de in rem verso* in Roman law.

The judgement removed any opportunity to curtail the version claim for the sake of commercial certainty. The application of the remedy in three-party situations opens the door for extensive leapfrogging to mitigate insolvency risks. To deem someone agent for that purpose, it sufficed that his acts were beneficial to another. As shown in the Helmstedt case above p. 114 (that had however been solved under enrichment law, i. e. the Pomponian principle and D.12.1.32), multiple benefits of third parties may commonly occur in trade relations. This cannot suffice to create new "principals" only for the purpose to get into the pockets of third parties outside the contractual relations of the claimant. Any yet, there was no discernible way to deny those claims. ALR I 13 § 277 only required that there was no

500 RG Judgement of 03.02.1880 IVa 502/79, RGZ 1, 159.

501 The RG cites R.O.H.G., Entscheidungen des Reichsoberhandelsgerichts, Band (Vol.). 3 Nr. 78 p. 377 and Bd. 11 Nr. 47 S. 136.

502 Preußisches Obertribunal, Striethorst Archiv (= Theodor Striethorst, Archiv für Rechtsfälle, die zur Entscheidung des königlichen Obertribunals gelangt sind), Band (Vol.) 10, p.142; Band 77, p. 70; Band 87, p. 283; Band 73, 155; Entscheidung (des königlichen Obertribunals), Band 56, 114.

503 The Court cites the provisions ALR I. 17 § 236; I. 1 §. and 324 II. 2 §. 126 for its view.

contract between claimant and defendant.[504] The existence of a contract between claimant and agent or agent and defendant was of no relevance.

A different situation arises under the enrichment framework of the Cour de Cassation in the arrêt Boudier.[505] The enrichment approach also reaches out beyond the parties of the contract. But it knows various ways to restrict the claim in order to align it with the necessities of trade and commerce, last not least the subsidiarity rule that is not uncommon with equitable remedies. These restraints haven been developed over time. They were not inherent in the original judgement that laid the basis for the claim. The process is the civilian paradigm of the successful metamorphosis of the Pomponian principle into hard law and could serve as a blueprint for current and future developments in English law.

7 The *actio de in rem verso*, cloaked in the Pomponian principle, turns into hard French law

The arrêt Boudier[506] is a veritable "merveille de la nature juridique". In one bold act the Cour de Cassation transformed the moral principle of Pomponius into "hard" French law. It did so only for one purpose: to justify the existence of the *actio de in rem verso* despite it not being codified. The Cour equates the *actio de in rem verso* directly with the Pomponian principle. This was his poignant and final answer to a question that had been debated for long time. It was neatly posed on the beginning of the annotations by the reporter Baudouin, avocat général à la Cour de cassation, in the Recueil Dalloz:[507]

> "A quel tire l'action de in rem verso est-elle accordée. De quelle cause procède-t-elle?"
>
> [On what grounds is the action de in rem verso granted? What is the cause of action?]

a) The earlier history of the *actio de in rem verso* in French law

The arrêt Boudier did not come "out of the blue skies". Rather, it marked the end of a long way from principle to law in France, first for the *actio de in rem verso* and

---

504 RGZ 1, 159, 160

505 Cour de Cassation, Chambre des requêtes, 15 Juin 1892, Julien Patureau-Miran C. Boudier, D.P. 92.1.569.

506 Cour de Cassation, Chambre des requêtes, 15 Juin 1892, Julien Patureau-Miran C. Boudier, D.P. 92.1.569.

507 At that time, the full title was: Dalloz (ed.), Jurisprudence Générale – Recueil Périodique et Critique de Jurisprudence, de Legislation et de Doctrine en Matières Civiles, Commerciales, Criminelles, Administratives et de Droit Public, abbreviated: D.P.

then for the sentence of Pomponius. Originally, French judges and academics accepted that the general *actio*[508] *de in rem verso* had not been codified and could therefore not be applied. Also, it was widely assumed that the *condictiones* were the codified expression of the Pomponian principle, with the *condictio indebiti* explicitly enshrined and all other *condictiones sine causa* covered by analogy.[509] This left no room for a general enrichment claim either.

But peu à peu, this apparently clear and unambiguous state of the law was called into question. One contributing factor is found in a line of cases that can be traced back to the early days of the Code Napoleon[510] and even beyond, to the law of the Ancien Régime.[511] They had one recurring issue: Parents had entered into contracts for the education of their children, but became insolvent and unable to pay the instructor. If the children had separate funds available, the instructor would turn to them for payment of his services on the grounds that they had benefitted from the education. From the very beginning in 1813, the Cour de Cassation honoured these claims.[512] But the exact legal basis remained unclear and contentious. In the first two decision of the Cour de Cassation, the première chambre created a kind of case law that seemed to be based on equitable considerations. In 1845, the chambre de requêtes opted for the *negotiorum gestio*

---

508 French lawyers speak of the action *de in rem verso*, i.e. they combine the Latin name with their own word "action". To avoid confusion, we prefer to stick with the Latin version, apart from references that are cited in the original language.

509 Gaston Rau, De la valeur, 1872, pp. 2, 13–15, 106, 120, 123 et seq. and particularly pp. 187 et seq. for the analogies. See in detail below p. 183.

510 See the account in the annotations to Cass req 17.3.57, D.P.57.1.149, at p. 150 sub note (1), containing numerous references. Cf. further Francois Terré/Yves Lequette, "Julien Patureau c/ Boudier", in Henri Capitant et al. (eds.), Les grands arrêts de la jurisprudence, Vol. 2, 12th edn. 2008, pp. 553 et seq.

511 Arrêt du Grand Chambre de Paris, 20.12.1750: The case was about a son who renounced the inheritance of his father, but was still held liable to pay the curator for the education he received from the tutor because he benefitted from it. The case is reported by Jean Baptiste Denisart, Collections des décisions nouvelles et de notions relative à la jurisprudence actuelle, vol 3, 5th edn. 1766, at p. 326: "Le Jeudi 20 Décembre, on a plaidé en la Grand chambre ... la question de savoir, si un fils qui avait renoncé à la succession de son père, pouvoit être contraint, nonobstant la renonciation, de payer les pensions dûes à un Curé, chez lequel il avoit reçu une partie de son éducation. La Sentence du Châtelet avoit jugé que la Renonciation du fils le libéroit des ses pensions. .... Sur l'appel, le Curé observa que l'éducation qu'il avoit donné à son élève, l'avoit conduit lui-même à la possession de quelques bénéfices dont il jouissoit. ... Par arrêt du dit jour 20 Décembre 1759, ... le fils condamné à payer ses pensions au Curé." Available at https://gallica.bnf.fr/ark:/12148/bpt6k206724d/f364.item.

512 The two leading cases were decided in 1813 and 1835, Cass civ D.A.1.348 and D.P. 35.1.566.

instead, thus overcoming lose references to equity.[513] But in 1857, the chambre de requêtes chose to support its decision by a reference to equity again: "Attendu que cette décision est conforme à l'équité et n'a rien de contraire à la loi."[514] [Whereas this decision is in accordance with equity and is not contrary to law]. In the annotation to that judgement, the issue was still reported as open and contentious among the lower courts.[515] The problem was that the requirements of the "quasi-contrat" of "gestion d'affaires"[516], i.e. the straightforward *negotiorum gestio* of Art. 1371–1375 C.civ 1804 (recast in 1301–1–5 C.civ 2016) were not met.[517] The cases looked more like the old *actio de in rem verso* that had been left out of the Code. But evidently, the underlying notion that benefits received from another must be accounted for had remained in the hearts and minds of French lawyers. Thus over time, the general *actio de in rem verso* found its way back into the new, codified law of France.[518]

All the while, French lawyers were well aware that the non-codification of the *actio de in rem verso* posed a major obstacle. True, the prohibition of the "deni de justice" in Art. 4 C.civ provided a general justification of judge-made law to close gaps in the law.[519] Nevertheless, the danger of undermining the legislator could not be ignored. The "arrêtiste"[520] Emile-Joseph Labbé (a follower of the enrichment approach) wrote in his seminal annotation to a case of the Cour de Cassation of 16 July 1889:[521]

> "[Nous ne pourrons] pas considerer comme ayant passé dans le droit français toutes les maxims du droit romain. Nous sommes régis et bournés dans notre horizon juridique par des codes et des lois écrits.
>
> [We cannot assume that all the maxims of Roman law have been incorporated into French law. Our legal horizon is governed and circumscribed by written codes and laws.]

The way around the problem was found by arguing that the Code had enshrined various specific applications of the *actio de in rem verso*. From those, the general

513 Cass req 18.6.1845, D.P. 45.1.290.
514 Cass req 17.3.57, D.P.57.1.149, at p. 151.
515 See the account in the annotations to Cass req 17.3.57, D.P.57.1.149, at p. 150 sub note (1).
516 See the definition of quasi-contrats in Art. 1300 C.civ 2016.
517 For a view on the issue through modern eyes see only Combot, n° 67, at pp. 72–73.
518 Cass req 17.3.57, D.P.57.1.149, at p. 150 sub note (1).
519 Goré, p. 36.
520 An author writing annotations on the arrêts of the Cour de cassation.
521 Labbé, S.90.1.97. The full name and title of the publication at that time was: (Jean Baptiste) Sirey, Journal des Audiences de la Cour de Cassation ou Recueil des Arrêts de ce Cour, en matières civiles et mixtes.

principle could be derived and directly applied as general claim: From principle to law! This had already been settled by the time of the arrêt Boudier.[522] The remaining question was that of the legal nature of the claim. In a fascinating way, the two approaches that had been contending the legal nature of the *actio de in rem verso* for centuries under the ius commune[523] resurfaced and proposed two competing solutions. The enrichment approach invoked the Pomponian principle as basis for the *actio de in rem verso*, whereas the agency approach classified it as an auxiliary remedy that supplemented the codified claims in cases of "abnormal" gestions d'affaires.[524]

The leading authority of the enrichment view (that finally prevailed) was the statement by Charles Aubry and Charles-Frédéric Rau:[525]

> "L'action de in rem verso, dont on ne trouve au Code civil que des applications spéciales,[526] doit être admise d'une manière générale, comme sanction de la règle d'équité, qu'il n'est pas permis de s'enrichir aux depens d'autrui, dans tous les cas où le patrimoine d'une personne se trouvant, sans cause légitime, enrichi au détriment de celui d'une autre personne, celle-ci ne jouirait, pour obtenir ce qui lui appartient ou ce qui lui est dû, d'aucune action naissant d'un contrat, d'un quasi-contrat, d'un délit ou d'un quasi-délit."[527]
>
> [The actio de in rem verso, of which only special applications are found in the Civil Code, must be generally accepted, as a sanction of the rule of equity that it is not permitted to enrich oneself at the expense of another, in all cases where the patrimony of a person is, without legitimate cause, enriched to the detriment of that of another person who does not have any action arising from a contract, a quasi-contract, a delict or a quasi-delict in order to obtain what belongs to him or what is due to him.]

The opposing agency approach was put forward by Demolombe in his fundamental treatise on the Code Napoléon. First, he presented the enrichment approach as one possible solution:

---

522 See below, p. 157.
523 See above, p. 134.
524 Cf. also the account of Goré, p. 32 et seq.
525 Aubry/Rau, Cours de droits civil francais: d'après la méthode de Zachriae, vol. 6, 4th edn. 1873, § 578, p. 246. Pior to the arrêt Boudier, that view was inter alia shared by Labbé, S.1.90.97.
526 Aubry/Rau cite in their footnote 9 the following provisions of the C.civ 1804: Art. 548, 554, 555, 556, 570, 571, 1241, 1312, 1437, 1864 and 1926.
527 Here, Aubry and Rau lay the basis for the subsidiarity of the claim, following the view of Zachariä whom they cite in footnote 10. Indeed, the Cours de droits civil by Aubry and Rau was originally a mere translation of the multivolume *Handbuch des französischen Zivilrechts* by Karl Solomo Zachariä von Lingenthal, 1st edn 1808–1809; see https://dlc.mpg.de/toc/mpirg_sisis_72942/1/. So in one peculiar sense, French unjust enrichment is also German-based.

Demolombe, n° 48: "Il est vrai que l'équité ne saurait, à elle seule, sous un regime de lois codifies comme le nôtre, devenir la source d'un droit ni d'une obligation, si l'application n'en est pas consacrée par une texte. Mais de nombreux textes consacrent cette maxime, l'une de plus sacrées, que nul ne peut s'enrichir aux depens d'autrui, et il n'y a, en une telle matière, rien d'excessif à dire que les textes qui la consacrent, en ont seulement des applications démonstratives, et doivent être etendues à tous les cas semblables."[528]

[It is true that equity alone cannot, under a system of codified laws such as ours, become the source of a right or an obligation unless its application is enshrined in a text. But many texts enshrine this maxim, one of the most sacred, that no one may enrich himself at the expense of others, and there is, in this matter, nothing excessive in saying that the texts which enshrine it have only demonstrative applications, and must be extended to all similar cases. [based on Deep-L]

But Demolombe chose not to follow the enrichment approach and opted for the alternative explanation of the agency approach:

Demolombe, t. (= vol) 8, n° 49, p. 46: "La seconde explication que, pour notre part, nous croyons devoir proposer, consiste à dire que l'action *de in rem verso,* quoique se trouvant en dehors des conditions du quasi-contrat de gestion d'affaires, n'en doit pas moin pourtant être considerée comme un action en quelque sort auxiliaire de l'action negotiorum gestorum lorsque, par une circonstance quelconque, le fait juridique, qui s'est produit, ne réunit pas toutes le conditions requises pour constituer le quasi-contrat de gestion d'affaires. Tel a toujours été, en effet, son charactère, d'apres les traditions les plus anciennes; et c'est là, certes, un argument considérable dans un sujet qui est entré, tout entier, dans nos lois modernes avec le cortège des règles romaines."

[The second explanation which, for our part, we think we should propose consists in saying that the action *de in rem verso*, although outside the conditions of the quasi-contract of gestion d'affaires, must nonetheless be considered as an action in some way auxiliary to the action *negotiorum gestorum* if, by some circumstance, the facts of the case that materialise do not meet all the conditions required to constitute the quasi-contract of gestion d'affaires. This has always been its characteristic, according to the most ancient traditions; and this is certainly a considerable argument in a subject which has entered our modern laws in its entirety with the procession of Roman rules.]

To support his point, Demolombe cited two passages from the Digest. The first to underpin his point that gaps in the law could be closed by judges[529] and the second

528 Approving the method of using analogies from code provisions (but not the enrichment approach), Petiton, D.P. I-89, 393: "Telle est bien la règle qu'il faut prendre pour base."
529 Demolombe, t.8, n° 49, p. 46 referring to D.1.3.12 (Julianus 15 Dig.): Non possunt omnes articuli singulatim aut legibus, aut senatus consultis comprehendi; sed cum in aliqua causa sententia eorum manifesta est, is, qui iurisdictioni praeest, ad similia procedere atque ita ius dicere debet. [Scott: All matters cannot be specifically included in the laws or decrees of the Senate;

to present Ulpian as authority that the *actio de in rem verso* had the character of a *negotiorum gestio.*[530] It lay for all "abnormal" cases of a *negotiorum gestio* ("gestion d'affaires anormale"[531]) where the acting person had no *animus gerendi*, but still conferred a benefit to another by objectively promoting that person's interests. The two classical examples are the erroneous management of another's affairs (where the acting person assumes to do her own business) and the intentional usurping of another's affairs (a thief who sells the stolen goods acts as if he was the owner).[532] In such cases, the quasi-contractual (and reciprocal!) actions of the gestion d'affaires[533] will not lie, and therefore, according to Demolombe, the action *de in rem verso* had to fill the gap.[534]

The approach of Demolombe was condoned by avocate-général Petiton in his annotation in the Recueil Dalloz to the Crédit foncier case of the Cour de cassation from 16 July 1899 (p. 145). In this case, the chambre de requêtes had denied a claim on the basis of the agency approach, and rightly so in the eyes of Petiton: [535]

> "La doctrine, ... n'a point hesité, par assimilation aux cas prévus dans le code civil, à accorder au gérant une action de in rem verso, pour se faire indemniser dans la mesure où il a fait profiter celui dont il a géré l'affaire."

---

but where their sense is clear in any instance, he who has jurisdiction of the same can apply it to others that are similar, and in this way administer justice.]

530 Demolombe, t.8, n° 49, p. 47, albeit without discussion of the contradictory Roman sources: D.15.3.3.2. (Ulpian 29 ad ed): "Et regulariter dicimus totiens de in rem verso esse actionem, quibus casibus procurator mandati vel **qui negotia gessit negotiorum gestorum haberet actionem** quotiensque aliquid consumpsit servus, ut aut meliorem rem dominus habuerit aut non deteriorem." [Scott: We state, as a general rule, that an action founded on the employment of property in the business of another will lie in those cases in which an agent would be entitled to an action on mandate, or a person who had transacted business without being empowered to do so, could bring suit on the ground of voluntary agency; and wherever the slave has consumed anything in order that the property of the owner might be improved, or not deteriorated.

531 Petiton, D.P. I 89, 393.

532 Demolombe, t. (=vol.) 8, n° 48, at p. 45 mentions only the first ("Vous avez, par exemple, croyant gérer votre propre affaire, géré l'affaire d'un autre" [For example, believing you were managing your own business, you managed someone else's business. Deep-L].

Petiton, D.P. I-89, 393, at p. 394 mentions both cases.

The German code excludes the erroneous management absolutely from the rules of the negotiorum gestio ("irrtümliche Eigengeschäftsführung, § 687 I BGB), but offers the "principal" an opt-in in usurpation cases ("angemaßte Eigengeschäftsführung", § 687 II BGB).

533 Art. 1372–1375 C.civ 1804 = (recast) Art 1301–1–5 C.civ 2016. See also Planiol, D. P. 91.1.49, at p. 50.

534 Demolombe, t. 8, n° 46 et seq., n°48, p. 45: "Il n'y a pas gestion d'affaires...Mail I peut y avoir lieu à l'action de in rem verso." [There is no negotiorum gestio ...But it may give rise to an action de in rem verso.] In this respect, Aubry and Rau concurred, see volume 4, 4th edn. 1872, § 441, p. 725.

535 D.P. I 89, 393 sub (1, 2 et 3), second column.

> [The doctrine, ... has not hesitated, by assimilation to the cases provided for in the Civil Code, to grant the manager an action in rem verso, to obtain compensation insofar as he has benefited the person whose business he has managed.]

After citing several references in addition to Demolombe, Petiton concludes: "On ne saurait qu'applaudir a cette solution"

By the time of 1890, the agency approach seemed to have won the day. However, the reasoning of the judgement was criticised from the perspective of the enrichment approach in a competing case note by Emile-Joseph Labbé in the Recueil Sirey.[536] Since the debate on this case presumedly turned the tide and marked the first step towards the arrêt Boudier, we have to analyse it in depth. This so much the more since the facts were similar to Banque Financière. In both cases, credit institutes had made the mistake of extending loans that they thought sufficiently secured while they were not – which benefitted third parties. But in Banque Financière, the claim, based on unjust enrichment, was awarded! And according to Labbé, the same should on principle have happened in France. He only defended the denial of the claim on grounds of the negligent mistake of the renowned bank.

b) The Crédit foncier case of 16 July 1889

Crédit foncier was a famous French real estate financier. They had given Paris its modern face by financing the transformation of the City led by Baron Hausmann in the 19th century. In the case decided by the Cour de cassation,[537] they had made an unseeming but costly mistake.[538]

Mr. Arazzat owned land that was encumbered by a first rank mortgage of 77.000 Francs in favor of two creditors. On second rank, his minor children held a legal mortgage.[539] The Crédit foncier agreed to lend 160.000 Franc to Mr. Arazzat. The loan agreement was made under the proviso that the 160.000 Franc should be secured by a first rank mortgage. For that purpose, the two secured creditors (Mme Nouguier and Mr Martin) holding claims for a combined 77.000 Francs had to be paid off first – and were paid off. However, here is where a fatal mistake was made.

---

536 Labbé, S.90.1.97. The full name and title of the publication organ at that time being: Jean Baptiste Sirey, Journal des Audiences de la Cour de Cassation ou Recueil des Arrêts de ce Cour, en matières civiles et mixtes.
537 Cass req D. P. 89.1.393.
538 For the following account, see Labbé, S.90.1.97 who started his annotation by saying: "Cette affaire offre un exemple d'une imprudence grave commise par les agents d'une administration..."
539 See Art 2398–2400 C.civ.

Under French law, a debt secured by a mortgage can be paid off by a third party.[540] It is not necessary that this party is the lower ranking mortgagee. The effect of the payment of the debt is legal subrogation of the payor to the position of the payee. The debt is not discharged, with the effect of the mortgage being extinct. Rather, the payor steps into the shoes of the old creditor by operation of law. This would have been the route to take for Crédit foncier as regards the tranche of the loan destined for the secured creditors. By following it, they would have held first rank mortgages for the amount of the discharged debts of 77.000 Francs.

However, Crédit foncier made the loan conditional on a first rank mortgage for the *whole* advance. Therefore, they insisted on the mortgage of the children being deleted – which explains why they did not seek to achieve priority over the legal mortgage of the children via legal subrogation. Indeed, Mr Arrazat managed to persuade the family council and an ad-hoc tutor to consent to the deletion. When that had been achieved, the whole amount of the loan was paid to a notary of Mr. Arrazat, who paid off the two secured creditors himself. As a consequence, both the first and second rank mortgages were extinct, and Crédit foncier was inserted as sole mortgagee over 160.000 Francs.

However, after the death of Mr. Arrazat, the children sued to have their legal mortgage reinstated – and succeeded. The mortgage was resurrected with retrospective effect. It followed that it now took priority over the mortgage held by Crédit foncier for their total claim of 160.000 Francs. In order to cut their imminent loss and to recover a part of their exposure, Crédit foncier brought a lawsuit against the children on the basis of an *actio de in rem verso*. They argued that the elevation of the children to first rank, as far as the amount of 77.000 Francs of old debt was concerned, was solely achieved with the money of the Crédit foncier. The children benefitted from their loss, and therefore, this benefit was to be restituted to them as "in rem versum".[541]

The decision of the Cour de cassation and the critical annotation by Labbé exemplify perfectly the difference between the agency and the enrichment approach. They also give some guidance on how to restrict an overreach of the leapfrogging by the versum claim.

The Cour denied the claim because it could not find the required legal or factual relation ("lieu de droit ou de fait") between the Crédit foncier and the chil-

540 Labbé, S.90.1.97.

541 According to Labbé "une thèse, non pas insoutenable, mais appuyés sur des raisonnements très subtiles."

dren.[542] That is why it felt unable to bring the case within the scope of the "abnormal" cases of the gestion d'affaires[543] where the *actio de in rem verso* had meanwhile been accepted. It was not only that the Crédit foncier did not have any *animus gerendi* to act in the children's affairs.[544] It did not even *objectively* act in the management of the children's affairs.[545] Rather to the contrary. By insisting on the deletion of the children's mortgage as condition for extending the loan to the father, it only pursued its own affairs. If anything, it had acted in the management of father's affairs by stipulating that the loan be passed on to the secured creditors. True, the children eventually benefitted from the transaction that at the time when it was executed had been so much against their vital interests. But the Cour did not consider the accidental conferral of the benefit as sufficient to create the necessary relation between claimant and defendant. This was in line with elder case law according to which neither the partnership nor the other partners could be held liable to repay the loan extended to one partner in his personal capacity, even though they all had benefitted from that loan because he used the funds in the interest of the partnership.[546]

The judgement was approved by Petiton who fundamentally rejected the principle of unjust enrichment as basis of the claim:[547]

> Les anciens adages de droit ne doivent être admis et appliqués aujourd'hui qu'avec une extrême prudence. Il ne faut pas oublier que nous vivons sous une législation codifiée, qui s'est efforcée de comprendre, dans ses textes, toutes les dispositions qui doivent nous obliger et nous régir.
>
> [The old legal adages should only be accepted and applied today with extreme caution. We must not forget that we live under codified legislation, which has undertaken to comprehend in its texts all rules that shall oblige and govern us.]

542 Cass req DP 89.1.393, at 395: "Attendu que de ce qui a été ci-dessus exposé il résulte qu'il n'a jamais existé entre le Crédit foncier et les enfants Arrazat aucun contrat, ni aucun quasi-contrat, ni un fait pouvant produire entre eux un lien de droit quelconque."

[Whereas it follows from the above that there has never existed between Crédit Foncier and the Arrazat children any contract, any quasi-contract, or any fact that could produce between them any legal relationship whatsoever]

Approving of this argument Petiton, DP 89.1.393, at p. 394.

543 I.e. the erroneous management and the intentional usurpation of another's affairs.

544 This was the very requirement of the "straightforward" gestion d'affaires that could be overcome in the "abnormal" cases by the actio de in rem verso.

545 Rather to the contrary, with a view to the deletion of their mortgage.

546 Civ cass, 16 Febr. 1855, D.P. 53.1.47. Petiton, D.P. 89.1.393, at p. 394.

547 Petiton, D.P. 89.1.393 against the view of Aubrey and Rau.

He went on to point out the specific applications of the *actio de in rem verso* that had found their way into the Code and concluded:

> Ces citations vérifient d'une façon complète la règle énoncée plus haut, comme étant celle invariablement suivie par le code civil, à savoir : que pour qu'il y ait lieu à l'action de in rem verso, il ne suffit pas qu'une partie ait recueilli un avantage prenant sa source dans l'agissement d'autrui; il faut qu'un lien de droit se soit établi entre les deux personnes dont l'une prétend agir contre l'autre; ...".
>
> [These quotations fully verify the rule set out above as being the one invariably followed by the Civil Code, namely that for an action in rem verso to arise, **it is not enough** for one party **to have received a benefit from the action of another**; a legal relationship must have been established between the two persons, one of whom claims to be acting against the other; ... DeepL]

The reasoning of the judgement was criticised by Labbé. After thoroughly laying the ground and explaining the misfortunate miscalculation of the bank, he argued that the Cour violated the principle of unjust enrichment. The Cour had failed to note that the children would not have been in their comfortable situation as first ranked security holder but for the moneys extended by Crédit foncier to pay off the old secured creditors. The principle of unjust enrichment was of higher equity and had the power and function to correct the law where necessary. Labbé referred to the *actio contraria* (see above, p. 122) that had been accepted by French law and concluded:

> Les juges français adopteraient sans aucun doute cette doctrine ; elle est une application de notre principe : il n'est pas juste de s'enrichir même au détriment d'un homme de mauvais foi.
>
> [French judges undoubtedly adopted this doctrine; it is an application of our principle: it is not right to enrich oneself even at the expense of a man of bad faith.]

At the heart of Labbé's argument lay the extension of a century-old idea of Martinus Gosia whose torch he thus carried forth: if an enrichment claim is available for benefits that were conferred by an "agent" who usurped another's affairs mala fide, it will have to lie *a fortiori* for a bona fide claimant who conferred such benefits unintentionally.[548]

However, the partnership case remained a high hurdle to jump. Labbé distinguished it from the Crédit foncier case by the following, interesting explanation:[549]

548 Labbé, S.90.1.97, at p. 98: "On serait tenté de tirer un argument a fortori de cette solution en faveur de Crédit foncier."
549 Labbé, S.90.1.97, at p. 99.

In the partnership case, the funds were extended to the free disposal of the partner in his private capacity. Since he could use them as he pleased, the fact that he used them for the benefit of the company was merely accidental and could not be qualified as a "versum" by the bank to the partnership.[550] By contrast, Crédit foncier extended the loan only subject to the proviso that the secured creditors had to be paid off first. Therefore, the advantage of the children was not accidental but consequential from the business that had been conducted. That is why the advantage could be seen as a "versum", whereas the advantage of the partnership could not. This argument deserves closer consideration because it might be able to explain the denial of restitution in cases of incidental benefits under English law as well (*Lowick Rose v Swynson*, below p. 198).

> Labbé, S.90.1.97, at p. 99: "La société n'a pas été en rapport avec l'auteur de prêt, ni au point de vue des intentions, ni au point de vue des faits, il n'y a pas de lien, de connexité entre l'avance faite par le tiers prêteur et l'enrichissement de la caisse social. Le profit tout accidentel de cette caisse, le prêteur ne l'a jamais eu en vue. – Voilà des espèces dans lesquelles manque la relation directe que justifié l'action *de in rem verso.* Au contraire ici le Crédit foncier a poursuivi maladroitement, mais certainement, le but, le résultat dont il se trouve que les mineurs profitent. Le Crédit foncier a fait un déboursé dont la conséquence directe est un avantage pécuniaire pour les mineurs."
>
> [There is no link or connection between the advance made by the third party lender and the enrichment of the company's assets. The lender never had the accidental profit of these assets in mind. – These are cases in which the direct relationship justifying the action *de in rem verso* is lacking. On the contrary, here Crédit Foncier has clumsily, but certainly, pursued the aim, the result from which the minors happen to benefit. Crédit Foncier has made a disbursement whose direct consequence is a pecuniary advantage for the minors.]

Taking a closer look at that intricate argument, it cannot fly under English law because it derives its power from the acceptance of the negotiorum gestio in France. To be sure, Labbé rejected the agency approach with the notion that the claimant had to act like an agent of the defendant's affairs and saw the *actio de in rem verso* as an enrichment claim based on the principle of Pomponius. That was also how he could find a way to condone the result reached by the Cour de cassation despite rejecting its reasoning. The grossly negligent mistake deprived the bank of its enrichment claim.[551] Nevertheless, Labbé too required the ominous "direct link" be-

550 Labbé, S.90.1.97, at p. 99.

551 Labbé, S.90.1.97, at p. 99 referring to Africanus, but this view was not supported elsewhere in the Digest and remained a minority position in the ius commune. The rule is hotly debated even after being introduced in the new Code Civil of 2016, Art. 1303–2, alinéa 2 C.civ: "L'indemnisation peut être modérée par le juge si l'appauvrissement procède d'une faute de l'appauvri." [Restitution may be moderated by the judge if the impoverishment is the result of fault on the part of the im-

tween enrichment and detriment. The Cour de cassation had denied that link in the case, but Labbé thought otherwise. For him, the necessary link was established by the fact that Crédit foncier had intentionally benefitted the minors – unlike the person who gave the loan to the partner, not knowing about the indirect benefit to the partnership. But with respect, this cannot be right because it suggests that the partnership case would have had to be decided differently, had the lender known about and intended the benefit of the partnership. Also, there is no ground to hold that the principle of Pomponius requires anything else than a causal link.

It follows that Labbé did *not* advocate the direct application of the Pomponian principle (contrary to the Cour in 1892). He did not propose a general enrichment claim. Had he, the partnership cases could not have been distinguished from Crédit foncier because it cannot be doubted that the loan to a partner caused the benefit of the partnership. If the claim is about reversal of unjust enrichment, showing enrichment must suffice.[552] This is not to say that there is no point in the accidental benefits argument.[553] But it cannot be directly derived from the sentence of Pomponius that prohibits to benefit from another's loss and therefore only requires loss and causal benefit. Labbé saw that. Thus, he referred to the Pomponian principle to support the correct application of the *actio de in rem verso*, not to apply it as a general enrichment claim in its own right. By requiring a specific legal relationship between claimant and defendant beyond mere causation, he basically reinterpreted and enlarged the agency approach.

Under this pretext, the enrichment view perceived the Pomponian sentence as the underlying moral rationale of the *actio de in rem verso*. That justified the generalisation of the *actio de in rem verso* beyond the specific cases in the Code. But the Pomponian sentence itself was NOT the claim. Rather, it was (again) employed as driver to modify the law, as an equitable tool of higher morality that corrected the harshness of strict law. Within the new framework of the French Code, the traditional role of the Pomponian enrichment principle in the ius commune[554] continued.

---

poverished party.] Cf. Dalloz, Code Civil annoté, 123th edn. 2024, Art. 1303–1303–4, Commentaire, B Les Changements, n°3.

552 See Planiol, D. P. 91.1.49, below in the text.

553 See Burrows, Restatement, pp. 54–55; accepted by *Revenue and Customs Commissioners v Investment Trust Companies* [2018] A.C. 275, at para. 52 (per Lord Reed).

554 See e.g. by the court of first instance, the tribunal civil de Corbeil, 31 dec 1884, reported D. P. 91.1.49, at p. 50 (the Lemaire case, in detail below p. 151) with reference to the provisions of Art. 555 C.civ (concerning the rights of a possessor subject to the rei vindicatio against the owner) and 1375 C.civ 1804 (concerning the claim to reimbursement in case of a gestion d'affaires) – which both did not sit easily: "...ce principe d'équité que nul doit s'enrichir aux depens d'autrui, base des art. 555

It is academic to muse about whether an analogy to the legal subrogation would have been a less invasive, more precise and convincing solution of the Crédit foncier case. There does not really seem to be a justification to make a difference whether the bank paid the mortage off directly or had the debtor pay the mortage off. But be that as it may. The critique of Labbé on the Crédit foncier case of 1889 was soon followed by a scathing critique of Planiol on the ensuing Lemaire-case of 1890, and eventually the Cour readjusted his position towards the enrichment view.

c) An aside: *Banque Financière* compared to Crédit Foncier

The case in Banque Financière was similar to Crédit foncier. Banque Fiancière agreed to extend a loan under the proviso of a security granted that did not exist in reality. The difference is that the security required by Banque was not the transfer of an asset or the granting of a mortgage, but merely a covenant that the other companies of the group accepted the priority of Banque's claim over any claims they might have and securities they might hold.

The problem of the case was that the assurance given by the directors of the parent company was not valid against and did not bind the other companies of the group. As a consequence, Banque lost out in the insolvency of the parent just as Crédit foncier. Thus, they sued the accidentally enriched companies of the group, just as Crédit foncier had sued the accidentally enriched children. But contrary to Crédit foncier, they succeeded.

The obvious difference is that Banque Financiére was openly decided under a direct enrichment claim. The four-stage-test is as easily satisfied as it would have been in Crédit foncier, had that case been decided under the Pomponian principle of "no benefit from a loss." The loss was with the bank, the benefit with the defendants (children; group members), and there was the same "unjustice". The banks had acted on a mistaken assumption of sufficient security – without which they would never have extended the loan and the defendants would never have reaped any benefits.

A more complicated issue is the reverse comparative test, namely whether the claim of Banque Fiancière would have been awarded under the French *actio de in rem verso* (as it stood before Boudiêr). It may be that the minor technical difference in the mode of securing the loan would have called for a different outcome. It could be said that the advantage derived by the other companies of the group from the cash flow of the not-sufficiently-secured loan did not stem from an investment for their benefit, like in the French partnership case. However, the difference

et 1375, trouve ici son application…" [the principle of equity that no person should be enriched at the expense of another, which is the basis of art. 555 and art. 1375, is applied here – Deep-L].

to the French partnership case is that the funds of Banque were deliberately directed to the company where they then indirectly benefitted the group members. These beneficiaries were accidental, but the investment decision was deliberate. The investment merely "went astray". That is why the loan of Banque could still be seen as a "versum" that was turned for the benefit of the group members. It would probably have been caught by the French *actio de in rem verso.* And the same is by the way true for the *Swynson* case, although the UK Supreme Court had denied the enrichment claim. The act that benefitted the defendant was a deliberate investment decision by the shareholder to recapitalize his ailing company (in detail p. 198). The loss of the damages claim was the accidental benefit that "turned" to the auditors from that investment.

By contrast, in the partnership case the funds of the loan were directed to the partner in his private capacity. They could not benefit the partnership before the debtor-partner had made an independent investment decision. The lending bank knew beforehand that this decision was up to the debtor alone. Therefore, it could not be argued that the investment of the lending bank was (accidently) turned to the third parties.

The only way to get to the pockets of the partnership and the other partners would have been via the argument from the Helmstedt case above (p. 114), based on the (presumed) rule of D.12.1.32: my money has got to you, so you must repay me. But that was NOT the state of French law in 1899. Otherwise, the partnership case would have been decided differently.

Trying to sum up Labbé's point, I should think that he saw the "versum" characterised by a subjective element: an intentional investment of the claimant that benefits another (in the Crédit foncier case: the loan to pay off the secured creditors that benefitted the children). If that rang true, it underpins the point that the *actio de in rem verso* is NOT identical with the general enrichment claim. That is because the objective situation of an enrichment caused by the loss of the claimant would not *per se* be sufficient to found the claim for the *versum.* The enrichment would have to stem from some kind of investment decision. That would by the way deliver an argument to kill the stamp case of Robert Stevens because the accidental destruction of A's stamp is not in any way an intentional investment into the assets of B.

d) The "last stand" of the *negotiorum gestio* view: the Lemaire case of 16 July 1890

As shown above, the general *actio de in rem verso* had been accepted as part of French law by 1890. As to the legal basis and nature, the dominant view was that this claim lay in cases of an "abnormal" gestion d'affaires and that it rested on an analogy to specific cases of the *actio de in rem verso* enshrined in the Code civil of 1804. After the Crédit foncier case of 1899, there was one last judgement that dealt with the loss of one party that turned into the profit of another, i.e. a "versum case", from the perspective of a *negotiorum gestio*. This arrêt rested even more firmly on the agency view of "versum" constellations. It was not based on the general *actio de in rem verso*, but on an *action directe* under the rules of the gestion d'affaires under Art. 1375 C.civ 1804. The judgement was delivered exactly one year after Crédit foncier, on the 16 July of 1890:

> Lemaire was the owner[555] of several plots of land in Paris.[556] He granted a lease for three years to the Société de la Seine. The Société had the right to develop the land and erect buildings as well as an option to acquire the land after three years. In case the option was not called, it was stipulated that the land would be repossessed by Lemaire without compensation for any works done or buildings erected.
>
> The Société contracted with the entrepreneur Lamoureux for the building works. It became insolvent when the financing of the project collapsed due to misrepresentations made by Lemaire to the lender.[557] Lamoureux turned to Lemaire for payment of the works. Lemaire invoked the contractual clause under which he owed no indemnity if the purchase failed.

The Cour de cassation, confirming the courts below, lost no time to set aside the "no compensation clause" since Lemaire had caused the failure of the transaction by his own doing.[558] However, the facts of the case did not fit under Art. 555 C.civ[559]

555 For the sake of simplification. Actually, he was the "acting" co-owner.
556 The lots were situated in the 18e arrondissement, north of Montmartre, in rue Hermel and rue des Baigneurs.
557 Lemaire had falsely claimed to take the loan to erect the buildings himself, falsely claiming that the representatives of the Société were his architects. By that, he had deprived the other parties of the contract of their rights, see Cour de cassation, D. P. 91.1.49, 50: "...Lemaire ne pet donc plus se prévaloir de la convention don't il a par sa faute, rendu les stipulations inutiles pour les autres parties qu'il a ainsi privées du droit qu'elles leur conferaient..." [Lemaire can therefore no longer rely on the agreement, the stipulations of which he has, through his own fault, rendered useless to the other parties, whom he has thus deprived of the right they would have had under the agreement]
558 Cass civ, 16. July 1890, D. P.91.1.49. Approving Planiol, D. P. 91.1.49 sub note 1.
559 The relevant passage of the law of "accession" in Art. 555 (3) reads: "Si le propriétaire du fonds préfère conserver la propriété des constructions, plantations et ouvrages, il doit, à son choix, rembourser au tiers, soit une somme égale à celle dont le fonds a augmenté de valeur, soit le coût des matériaux et le prix de la main-d'oeuvre estimés à la date du remboursement, compte tenu de l'état dans lequel se trouvent lesdites constructions, plantations et ouvrages."

[If the owner of the land prefers to retain ownership of the constructions, plantations and works [[sc. that the possessor has made under Art. 555 (1)]], he must, at his option, reimburse the third party either a sum equal to the increase in value of the land, or the cost of materials

because the works had not been executed by the possessor, the Société, but by a third party, the entrepreneur Lamoureux who acted on his contract with the Société. [560] The difference is inter alia marked by the fact that a possessor can hold his right to compensation against the *rei vindicatio* whereas Lamoureux could obviously not do that.[561]

At first sight, the quasi-contrat of gestion d'affaires in Art. 1372–1375 C.civ 1804 may have seemed unavailable due to the lack of *animus gerendi.* The builder intended to perform his contract with the tenant Société, not to manage the affairs of the owner Lemaire. But like under the ius commune,[562] the Cour trumped the lack of the subjective element via the objective enrichment that the owner received from the buildings[563] and assumed a *gestion d'affaires* by Société:

> D.91.1.49, at p. 51: "[Attendu] – Qu'il suit de la qu'en élevant sur les terrains loués des constructions don't le proprietair a seul profité, la Société a réellement, quoique involontairement et a son insu, géré l'affaire de Lemaire, et a le droit de lui réclamer le remboursement de toutes ses dépenses utiles. – Attendu que le tiers[564] qui a execute sur l'ordre du gérant des travaux don't le géré a retire le profit a lui-même pour le prix de ces travaux une action directe contre le géré;[565] – que l'action de Lamoureaux contre Lemaire était donc recevable.
>
> [[Whereas] – It follows from this that by erecting on the rented land buildings from which the owner alone benefited, the Société has actually, albeit involuntarily and without her knowledge, managed Lemaire's business, and is entitled to claim reimbursement from him for all

---

and labour estimated at the date of reimbursement, taking into account the condition of the said constructions, plantations and works. – Deep-L]

560 The Code civil speaks of a "tiers" (= third). But this only means the person having the possession of the property of the owner, see Planiol, D. P. 91.1.49: "L'art 555 était certainement inapplicable a'entrepreneur puisque cet article suppose que l'auteur de constructions détient le terrain... " [Art. 555 was certainly inapplicable to the contractor since this article presupposes that the building owner owns the land. Deep-L]. The appellants had accused the lower courts of wrongfully applying Art. 555 to found the claim. The Cour rejected this (D. P. 91.1.49, at p. 50.)

Note further that Art 554 C.civ. could not be applied either because the works were not done by the owner, using another's materials, but by the entrepreneur in his own capacity and using his own materials.

561 Planiol, D. P. 91.1.49.

562 See above, pp. 127 et seq.

563 Profoundly critical to this notion Planiol, D.91.1.49, left column: "Il ne nous semble nullement certain que le fait d'avoir élevé des constructions sur un terrain puisse constituer une gestion d'affaires..." [In our view, it is by no means certain that the fact of having erected buildings on a plot of land can constitute business management. ... Deep-L]

564 = Lamoureux.

565 See Art. 1375 C.civ 1804, but see also the rejection of that statement by Planiol below in the text.

useful expenses. – Whereas a third party who has carried out work on the order of the manager, from which the manager has derived a profit, has himself a direct action against the manager for the price of this work; – that Lamoureaux's action against Lemaire was therefore admissible.]

This is the reasoning and consequence of a pure agency approach to "versum" cases. The claim aims to reimburse expenses of Lamoureux, not to skim off the enrichment of Lemaire.[566] The procurement of the enrichment from Société to Lemaire substitutes the lack of the principal-agent relationship normally required by a *negotiorum gestio.* The basis of the claim is laid by the fictitious assumption that the Société had "in reality" (if unconsciously) managed the business of the owner Lemaire. This assertion is solely founded on the factual transfer of the benefit to the owner. This artificially construed *negotiorum gestio* serves to leapfrog the contract between Lamoureux and insolvent Société in that it bridges the gap to the factual beneficiary Lemaire

It might have been more persuasive to extend Art. 555 C.civ to cover the claims of builders and service providers who have improved another's property without themselves being in possession.[567] But be that as it may: the solution via Art 1375 C.civ 1804 that the Cour de cassation had chosen, was profoundly criticised by Marcel Planiol.[568] His argument reads like a tour de force through centuries of Roman law. He insisted emphatically that the doctrinal categories of unjust enrichment and *negotiorum gestio* must be strictly distinguished.[569] He accused the Cour of confounding those concepts.[570] In truth, the claim could only be based on the gen-

566 On the difference, see p. 123.
567 Despite the rejection by Planiol, D. P. 91.1.49, at p. 50, this idea is not far-fetched. In a well-known German case of 1960, an owner had sold a vehicle under reservation of title. The purchaser commissioned repair works that he did not pay for. When the owner aimed to repossess the vehicle, the garage successfully counter-claimed reimbursement under § 994 BGB (BGHZ 34, 122 = NJW 1961, 499; this solution is however contended, see MünchKommBGB/Raff, § 994 mn. 59). If the service provider in possession can claim reimbursement, why should the service-provider without possession not be able to do the same? If the underlying principle is the Pomponian sentence, as both the court of first instance, the Tribunal civil de Corbeil of 31 Dec 1884, reported D. P. 91.1.49 – 50, and Planiol assume, the fact of the possession should not make a difference at all.
568 Planiol, D. P. 91.1.49.
569 See above, p.15.
570 Planiol, D. P. 91.1.49: "nous craignons fort qu'on ait ici confondu le gestion d'affaires… avec la famille des obligations qui naissent d'un enrichissement sans cause." [We are very much afraid that the negotiorum gestio has been confused here… with the family of obligations arising from unjust enrichment.] In the following, several distinctions are elaborated, the most important being the argument that the action direct under Art 1375 C.civ 1804 could never compete with a contractual claim against the gérant (Société), see in the following text.

eral principle of unjust enrichment ("la famille des obligations ... qui naissent d'un enrichissement sans cause"[571]). At that point, Planiol merged the *actio de in rem verso* with the general enrichment claim:

> D. P. 91.1.49, sub notes 2, 3 et 4, left column: "Il y a une foule de cas das lesquels une personne, ayant retiré un profit pécunaire d'actes juridique ou de travaux accomplis par une autre personne, se trouve soumise à une obligation de restitution... Dans sa forme la plus générale, l'action qui sanctionne cette obligation porte le nom Latin de actio de in rem verso..."
>
> [There are a host of cases in which a person who has derived a pecuniary benefit from legal acts or works performed by another person is subject to an obligation of restitution... In its most general form, the action which sanctions this obligation bears the Latin name of actio de in rem verso....]
>
> And then, D.91.1.50, left column: "On eût ainsi appliqué à l'entrepreneur, non pas l'art 555 qui règle une hypothèse différente, mais le grand principe d'après lequel nul ne doit s'enrichir aux dépens d'autrui, principe qui n'est écrit nulle part en termes généraux, mais qui domine le droit tout entier et don't l'art 555 lu-même n'est qu'une application."
>
> [One should have applied to the entrepreneur not Art. 555, which governs a different situation, but the great principle according to which no one may enrich himself at the expense of another, a principle which is not written anywhere in general terms, but which dominates the entire law and of which Art. 555 itself is merely an application.]

To support his point that the claim of Lamourex against Lemaire was not, and could not be, an action directe under Art. 1375 C.civ, he made the following point: Under Art 1375 C.civ, the third party either has a claim against the gérant (Société) or the géré (Lemaire). If the gérant concluded the contract in the name of the principal, the géré would be obliged directly. If the gérant entered into contract in his own name, he would be obliged to the third party himself. In addition, there would be a claim to reimbursement against the géré as principal. But this claim was caught by the insolvency of Société. The third party (Lamoureux) had no way of availing himself of an action directe under the laws of the gestion d'affaires. Under Art. 1375, either the agent or the principal could be sued, never both.[572] But according to the Cour, Lamoureaux had a contractual claim against Société and a competing claim against Lemaire under Art 1375 C.civ 1804.

In my opinion, this was the strongest argument put forward against the agency approach because contrary to the usual flexibility and ambiguity of legal arguments, it proved the Cour de cassation wrong with mathematical precision. No surprise therefore that the Cour skipped the agency approach in favour of the enrichment approach merely two years later.

---

571 See citation in the previous footnote.

572 Planiol, D.91.1.49, at p. 50.

e) The amalgamation of *actio de in rem verso* and general enrichment claim by the arrêt Boudier of 15 June 1892

The arrêt Boudier completed the immersion of the *actio de in rem* verso within the general enrichment claim under the Pomponian principle.[573] This happened two years after Planiol had laid the ground with his fundamental critique of the Lemaire-case. Like in RGZ 1, 159 (above p. 138), the issue at stake was unpaid fertiliser:

> The claimant, Miran C. Boudier, had sold fertiliser to a tenant farmer. The lease was terminated when the farmer failed to meet his obligations. To settle part of his debts to the landowner, Julien Patureau, the tenant farmer transferred the crop still standing. Mr Boudier, not being paid for his supplies by the tenant farmer, sued the landowner (inter alia[574]) on the *actio de in rem verso* because his fertiliser had helped to produce the harvest that was now the landowner's. The main defence of the landowner was that he had not contracted with the supplier.[575]

The award was granted by the Tribunal civile de Chateauroux, 2 Dec 1890. This underpins that the "praeter legem" existence of a general *actio de in rem verso* was already widely accepted at that time. However, the legal nature and exact content of the claim remained contentious between the agency view and the enrichment approach. Drawing on these uncertainties, the appellants complained about a "fausse application de l'action *de in rem verso*".

The Cour de Cassation rejected the appeal on all grounds. It allowed the claim based on the general principle of unjust enrichment. In doing so, the Court did not only confirm the existence of the general *actio de in rem verso.* Rather, it immersed it in the Pomponian principle which it directly applied as general enrichment claim. The principle had been turned into hard law. The decisive passage is short and of utmost clarity. It reads as follows:

> "Attendu que cette action [sc. l'action de in rem verso] dérivant de principe d'équité qui defend de s'enrichir d'autrui et n'ayant été réglementée par aucun text de nos lois, son exercise n'est soumis à aucune condition déterminée; – Qu'il suffit, pour le rendre recevable, que **le demandeur allègue et offre d'ètablir l'existence d'un avantage qu'il aurait, par un sacrifice ou un fait personnel, procuré à celui contre lequel il agit.**"

> [Whereas this action derives from the principle of equity which forbids one from enriching oneself from another and has not been regulated by any text of our laws, its exercise is not subject to any specific condition; – That it is sufficient, in order to render it admissible, **that**

573 Cass req, D. P. 92.1.596, S.93.1.281, noted Labbé; for an earlier judgement based directly on Pompean enrichment see Cass req, 15 July 1873, DP 73.1.457.
574 There were other grounds ("pourvois") for appeal like e.g. the alleged misapplication of the French privity of contract rule (Art 1165 old C.civ that were all dismissed.
575 He would have been heard at a Common Law court, cf. *Costello v Macdonald* [2011] EWCA Civ 930, as well as before in France, Cass civ, 9 May 1853, D. P. 53.1.251, S.53.1.699!

> **the plaintiff alleges and offers to establish the existence of an advantage which he has, by a sacrifice or a personal act, procured for the person against whom he is acting.** – Deep-L]

After the previous attempts to establish the general *actio de in rem verso* as a remedy in the context of the *gestion d'affaires* had failed, the Court chose to apply the Pomponian sentence directly.[576] The result was the application of the *actio de in rem verso* in the guise of the general enrichment claim. In essence, this is a misnomer the consequences of which are felt to the present day. To be sure, the Cour de cassation may not have seen any other way out. If the objective fact of the benefit conferred on the defendant was the only reason to assume a (if abnormal) *gestion d'affaires,* the true principle at work seems to be the Pomponian sentence. This so much the more since after the codification, the Roman sources had lost any force as direct authority. Without backing of the Digest, the moral commandment "You must not benefit from my loss" carries more force[577] than the dubious rule of D.12.1.33 "You must repay me because my money has somehow found its way into your pocket".

Nevertheless, the new approach levelled the distinctive feature of the *actio de in rem verso:* the intention to invest value for the benefit of someone else. As has been shown, this intention was inherent in all versum cases, even if the person that actually benefitted was not necessarily the person whose benefit the claimant had intended to procure. There may have been disagreement about the exact content of this subjective link between claimant and the defendant in the Crédit foncier case of 16 July 1899, the Cour de cassation and Petiton adopting a narrower view than Labbé. However, both sides of the argument agreed on the principle. The mere causation of the benefit of the defendant by the loss of the claimant would not be sufficient to establish the claim in restitution.

This changed radically with the arrêt Boudier. The Cour de cassation only intended to provide a more persuasive doctrinal justification for the existence of the general *actio de in rem verso* that the legislator had abstained from codifying. But to give this new answer to the big question "A quel tire l'action *de in rem verso* est-elle accordée. De quelle cause procède-t-elle?"[578], the Cour de cassation turned the general equity of the Pomponian sentence into hard law.[579] In doing so, the Cour

576 Goré, p. 27. Note that this was not warranted by Labbé who had argued for the existence of the general *actio de in rem verso* and had merely used the Pomponian sentence as a guiding principle for the application, not as a direct cause of action, but certainly by Planiol who dismissed any notion of gestion d'affaires in his scathing criticism of the 16 July 1890 Lemaire-case.

577 Cf. Goré, p. 6: "une règle de haute moralité sociale".

578 Above p. 139.

579 See Goré, p. 101, n°98: "Un grand courant d'équité traverserait ainsi le droit."

stirred up a hornets' nest. It set aside the profound reservations of ancient French law that had never accepted the Pomponian sentence as an independent source of an obligation.[580] In the aftermath of the arrêt Boudier, it seemed to suffice that the benefit was caused by the loss of the claimant.[581] Robert Stevens' stamp case should succeed!

However, this state of the law was short-lived. The Cour de cassation soon recognised that the general enrichment claim was too wide and vague and started to restrict the Pomponian principle. This development was welcomed by the vast majority of French lawyers. In the influential work of Francois Goré, we read a detailed, approving account:[582]

> "Mais la formule était extrêmement dangereuse par son imprécision. Si elle avait triomphé, elle aurait marqué le début d'une insécurité juridique. Il n'y aurait plus eu de sécurité dans les affaires. Le principe consacré était en effet purement moral, donc par sa nature même, imprécis. Il ne donnait pas au juge de règle précise pour apprécier les circonstances où il y avait enrichissement aux dépens d'autrui. Le tribunal devait rechercher dans chaque cas si la morale exigeait un rétablissement. On aboutissait ainsi fatalement à l'arbitraire. Tel aurait estimé que la morale était lésée. Tel autre, avec la plus entière bonne foi, aurait été d'un avis différent."
>
> [But the formula was extremely dangerous because of its vagueness. If it had succeeded, it would have marked the beginning of legal uncertainty. There would no longer have been any certainty in business transactions. The principle enshrined was purely moral, and therefore by its very nature imprecise. It did not give the judge a precise rule for assessing the circumstances in which there was enrichment at the expense of others. The court had to consider in each case whether moral considerations required restoration. This inevitably led to arbitrariness. Some would have considered that morality had been wronged. Another, with the utmost good faith, would have taken a different view.]

Goré goes on to cite the French version of the "sloppiness of thought"-critique that had been formulated by André Rouast:[583]

> "L'enrichissement sans cause avec la formule de la Cour de cassation de 1892 aurait été une sorte de brûlot capable de faire sauter tout l'édifice juridique"
>
> [Unjust enrichment, as formulated by the Cour de cassation in 1892, would have been like a firecracker capable of blowing up the entire legal edifice.]

580 Cf. Goré, p. 6 and pp. 22–23.

581 Goré, p. 101 n°98.

582 Goré, p. 46, n° 51.

583 A. ROUAST, *Les obligations dont la source n'est ni le contrat ni la faute*, Répétitions écrites de droit civil approfondi et comparé, Les Cours de droit, Paris, 1933–1934, p. 78. Cf. Goré, p. 46–47, n°. 51.

The solution of the Cour de cassation was a continuous reduction of the general enrichment claim. Two major goal posts were the right to enrichment defense and the subsidiarity principle. Goré has applauded and promoted the curtailing of the general enrichment claim back to the *actio de in rem verso* throughout his book. And indeed, it seems that the safeguards installed by the Cour de cassation have achieved this aim and avoided a general equity "firecracker". Successful enrichment claims will normally lie where the old *actio de in rem verso* would have been available to leapfrog the insolvency of the other party of the contract.[584] While it may have appeared that the general enrichment claim so curtailed was of little practical relevance in France,[585] this suspicion is disproved by the recent PhD-thesis of Mai-Lan Dinh who accessed databases to analyse the astounding number of 4000 cases during 5 years prior to 2022.[586]

f) The doctrinal inconsistencies from amalgamating actio de in rem verso and unjust enrichment

Whether or not French legal practice has learned to live with the general enrichment claim: its doctrinal foundations remain dubious. This is because under the loose heading of the Pomponian sentence, two distinct legal instruments with diverging rationales were amalgamated. The *condictiones* were all based on the lack of a *causa.* With respect to failed transfers, their point was to overcome the principle of *volenti non fit inuria.*[587] This was achieved by the various specific condictiones (causa data causa non secuta; indebiti, ob turpem vel inustam causam; ob causam finitam), as it is achieved by the unjust factors.

By contrast, the *actio de in rem verso* has never been based on the lack of a causa. The original transfer of value to the *peculium* took place under a valid contract. The versum claim against the *pater familias* was only needed when the peculium was exhausted ("nihil in peculio"). True, the claim against the *pater familias* would only succeed if there had been a "versum" into his personal assets. But this was only relevant *within* the existing, mandate-like situation of the *peculium* where the *pater familias* had established a separate fund to enable his "agents" (sons, slaves) to trade. The unaccounted benefit of the "principal" was the reason to pierce the veil of his limited liability. This principle may at its time have reasonably been extended to any agency situation (pp. 133–134). But it will certainly be-

584 Cf. e.g. Cass req 11.9.1940, S.1941.1.121; Chiusi, p. 200.

585 Cf. Chiusi, p. 200–201; J. Carbonier, Droit Civil, 15th edn. 1991, p. 542–3.

586 Mai-Lan Dinh, L'Enrichissement injustifié en droit privé; État des lieux et perspectives, 2022, p. 30.

587 *Astley v Reynolds* (1731) 93 E. R. 939. See below, p. 264.

come overstretched if the indirect enrichment is *per se* deemed sufficient. And it is surely purely fictitious, a "legal lie" so to say, to argue that any agency relation arises from the mere conferral of a benefit from A to B. If A mistakenly destroys his stamp, he may enrich B, but he is not the agent of B. To hold otherwise would not be the interpretation, but the annihilation of the agency requirement. It would be redundant. The claim would merely be founded on the benefit. This is what happened in France. It made the Pomponian sentence look like the overarching principle.

However, the enrichment of the *pater familias* was never based on any lack of a *causa*, and rightly so. On closer looks, the principle of *volenti non fit inuria* should in truth **prevent** any claim for the *versum*. This is because the bankruptcy of the other party does not vitiate the contract. There is no lack of *causa*, no "unjust factor" attached to the original transaction entered into by the claimant. The only possible linkage to the "unjust factors" of the transaction-based *condictiones* would be the notion of *causa data causa non secuta* / failure of consideration because the performing party does not receive the counterperformance (= the payment). However, this cannot be accepted as an exception from *volenti non fit inuria* because the risk of insolvency is willingly incurred by a party performing in advance. Under the principle of *pacta sunt servanda*/sanctity of contract, the law must not relieve that party from this risk. It is outrageous to shift that risk to the door of innocent third parties.

Arguably, a modern justification for the *actio de in rem verso* could be found in the gratuity of the remote benefit that came out of the purse of the unpaid party of the contract. Generally speaking, it is a watertight legal principle to sanction gratuities at other people's expense. This was the basis of the Roman *actio Pauliana* and lives on in the avoidance provisions for fraudulent preferences that are found in all insolvency laws. It may as well serve as foundation for meritorious cases of enrichment claims versus remote recipients (see also below p. 200 as to English law). But to be sure, this is not how *enrichissement sans causa* / *injustifié* is seen at present.

At the end of the day, Planiol's plea for doctrinal clarity to avoid contradictory decisions is still unanswered. The Pomponian mist has drowned French law in the sea of equity. Let us listen to the recent words of Mélodie Combot:[588]

> Faute de concept bien identifié, et en l'absence de toute précision légale, les juges disposent de la plus grande liberté s'agissant de l'enrichissement injustifié et des quasi-contrats. Ils ne s'estiment notamment pas tenus par la conception renouvelée des quasi-contrats autour de l'enrichissement injustifié et conservent la faculté de découvrir de nouveaux quasi-contrats lors-

588 Mélodie Combot, Quasi-contrat et enrichissement injutifié, 2023, n° 249, p. 235.

qu'ils en ressentent le besoin, sans avoir à les rattacher à l'enrichissement injustifié. En dépit de la très grande plasticité de la notion, force est de reconnaître que la jurisprudence n'a pas fait un usage démesuré des quasi-contrats, la liste des quasi-contrats créés étant relativement courte. Leur utilisation demeure ponctuelle et imprévisible. Paradoxalement, la prudence relative des juges participe aussi à cette impression de désordre, car il reste difficile de déterminer dans quelles situations la jurisprudence fera usage des quasi-contrats, et ce qu'ils soient nommés ou innommés.

Si l'on ajoute à cela que les quasi-contrats innommés d'un jour ne le restent pas nécessairement toujours, la systématisation de cette source d'obligation devient quasi-impossible. Ainsi, l'évolution de cette source d'obligation est marquée par un certain chaos que ne risque malheureusement pas de dissiper l'ordonnance du 10 février 2016.

[In the absence of a clearly identified concept, and in the absence of any legal precision, judges have the greatest freedom as regards unjust enrichment and quasi-contracts. In particular, they do not consider themselves bound by the new concept of quasi-contracts based on unjust enrichment and retain the power to discover new quasi-contracts when they feel the need to do so, without having to link them to unjust enrichment. Despite the great versatility of the concept, it has to be admitted that the case-law has not made excessive use of quasi-contracts, the list of quasi-contracts created being relatively short. Their use remains ad hoc and unpredictable. Paradoxically, the relative caution of judges also contributes to this impression of disorder, as it remains difficult to determine in what situations case law will make use of quasi-contracts, whether they are named or unnamed.

If we add to this the fact that quasi-contracts which are innominate one day do not necessarily always remain so, it becomes almost impossible to systematise this source of obligation. Thus, the development of this source of obligation is marked by a certain chaos which, unfortunately, the Order of 10 February 2016 is unlikely to dispel. – DeepL]

The acceptance of the Pomponian sentence blurred the doctrinal principles of French law and prevented a clear scientific perception of the *actio de in rem verso.*[589] The restrictions of the enrichment claim established by the Cour de cassation are not convincing (subsidiarity, (p. 162) and even at odds with general principles of private law ("cause légitime", p. 168, "suum recepit", p. 176). French enrichment law split up and "disgorged" the condictiones (p. 182).

aa) The subsidiarity bar

The subsidiarity bar is an important restriction of the French general enrichment claim.[590] Since 2016, it is codified in Art. 1303–3 C.civ:

---

589 Also critical Zimmermann, p. 884.

590 See in great depth Goré, pp. 92 et seq.; Alexis Posez. La subsidiarité de l'enrichissement sans cause : étude de droit français à la lumière du droit comparé. Revue de droit international et de droit comparé, n° 2, 2014, 186 et seq. Cf. further the annotation in Dalloz, Code Civil annoté, Art 1303 n° 1: "***1. Caractère subsidiaire de l'action. Absence de toute autre action.*** L'action fondée sur

"L'appauvri n'a pas d'action sur ce fondement lorsqu'une autre action lui est ouverte ou se heurte à un obstacle de droit, tel que la prescription"

[The impoverished person has no action on this basis if another action is available to him or if such action is barred by a legal obstacle, such as limitation.]

The same rule had been laid down in Italy in the Code of 1942:

Art. 2042 Codice civile (Carattere sussidiario dell'azione): "L'azione di arricchimento non e' proponibile quando il danneggiato puo' esercitare un'altra azione per farsi indennizzare del pregiudizio subito."

[An action for enrichment may not be brought when the aggrieved party can bring another action to obtain compensation for the harm suffered.]

Originally, the subsidiarity rule was introduced by the Cour de cassation in two subsequent decisions in the years 1914 and 1915.[591] According to the approving account by Francois Goré, these judgements clarified that the Cour had only accepted the *actio de in rem verso* in the arrêt Boudier.[592] The passages read:

"Attendu que l'action de in rem verso, fondée sur le principe d'équité qui defend s'enrichir au detriment d'autrui, doit être admise dans tous les cas où le patrimoine d'une personne, se trouvant sans cause légitime enrichie aux dépens de celui d'une autre personne, celle-ci ne jouirait, pour obtenir ce qui lui est dû, d'aucune action naissant d'un contrat, d'un quasi-contrat, d'un délit ou d'un quasi-délit."

[Whereas the *actio de in rem verso*, founded on the principle of equity which forbids enrichment at the expense of another, must be admitted in all cases where the patrimony of a person, being enriched without legitimate cause at the expense of that of another person, the latter would not enjoy, in order to obtain what is owed to her, any action arising from a contract, a quasi-contract, a delict or a quasi-delict.]

---

l'enrichissement sans cause ne peut être admise qu'à défaut de toute autre action ouverte au demandeur; elle ne peut l'être, notamment, pour suppléer à une autre action que le demandeur ne peut intenter par suite d'une prescription, d'une déchéance ou forclusion ou par l'effet de l'autorité de la chose jugée ou parce qu'il ne peut apporter les preuves qu'elle exige ou par suite de tout autre obstacle de droit. Civ. 3e, 29 avr. 1971, n° 70–10.415 P: *R. 1970–1971, p. 37; Gaz. Pal. 1971. 2. 554.* V. aussi Com. 10 oct. 2000, n° 98–21.814 P: *D. 2000. AJ 409, obs. Avena-Robardet; RTD civ. 2001. 591, obs. Mestre et Fages* (action préalable possible contre les cautions) Civ. 1re, 26 sept. 2007, n° 06–14.422 P (action possible en paiement de salaire différé) 23 juin 2010: *cité note 17 ss. art. 270; JCP 2010, n° 1027, note Bonnet et Bosse-Platière* (demande présentée subsidiairement sur le fondement de l'enrichissement sans cause tendant aux mêmes fins que la demande de prestation compensatoire, laquelle avait été jugée irrecevable)." In Belgium: Art. 5.136. Cc.

591 Cass civ 12 May 1914, S.1918.1.11; Cass civ 2 March 1915, D.P.1920.1.102.; Goré, p. 47. ; cf. further Chiusi, p. 200; König, pp. 71 et seq. Recently confirmed Cass civ, 10 January 2024, n° 22-10.278.

592 Goré, pp. 44 et seq.

The Court replicated the words of Aubry and Rau[593] to circumscribe the subsidiarity.[594] Thus, it has been argued that the original inspiration for the subsidiarity rule stemmed from Prussian law[595] after Roman law had at best been inconclusive.[596] This is because the actio de in rem verso could be interpreted as a veil-piercing instrument that would only apply after the peculium was exhausted as well as a competing claim against the principal in a situation of undisclosed agency (of course, the claim being under the proviso that the principal had actually received the benefit from the undisclosed agent).

But be that as it may: Notwithstanding the contentious interpretation of the Roman *actio de in rem verso* to which we cannot contribute here, the subsidiarity rule certainly makes sense when assuming a "veil-piercing" rationale. Adopting that, the action would only lie if the peculium was exhausted ("nihil in peculio"). The claimant has to sue the other party of the contract first. Only if this lawsuit failed due to the bankruptcy of the "agent", it would become possible to sue his principal as remote beneficiary.

However, within the wider framework of a general enrichment claim, the subsidiarity principle takes on a completely different function. It is now supposed to curtail the wide and vague wording of the enrichment claim to prevent it from undermining the law.[597] But in *this* function, the subsidiarity bar is useless and merely serves as a fig leaf for judicial arbitrariness. I have put forward a similar criticism against the rule of last resort that the UK Supreme Court has introduced in *Prest v Petrodel*[598] in order to curtail the doctrine of piercing of the corporate

---

593 See Aubry et Rau, vol VI, 4th edn, § 548, explaining the subsidiarity of the actio de in rem verso.

594 Goré, p. 47.

595 According to Alexis Posez, Revue de droit international et de droit comparé, n°2, 2014, 186, at p. 189, the rule stemmed from the Prussian ALR I XIII § 277 and been imported via Zachariae whose treatise Aubry and Rau had originally translated.

596 See Alexis Posez, Revue de droit international et de droit comparé, n° 2, 2014, 186, 189 who assumes that the rule had never been received under Roman law.

597 Alexis Posez, Revue de droit international et de droit comparé, n°2, 2014, 186, at p. 192: "La condition de subsidiarité est pourtant incontournable, considérant que c'est précisément par elle que l'on évite que l'enrichissement sans cause devienne cette machine à faire sauter le droit que l'on évoque souvent depuis les mots prononcés après-guerre par Paul Esmein devant l'Association Henri Capitant." [The condition of subsidiarity is, however, unavoidable, given that it is precisely through subsidiarity that we can prevent unjust enrichment from becoming the machine for blowing up the law that has often been evoked since the words spoken after the war by Paul Esmein to the Association Henri Capitant.]

598 *Prest v Petrodel Ressources* [2013] UKSC 34.

veil.[599] In the following, I will re-elaborate with a view to the general enrichment claim.

The primary reason why rules of "last resort" or "subsidiarity" are not apt to contain overly wide and vague remedies is because the problematic cases are rarely those where there is another remedy available. It is easy to understand that in such cases, the general enrichment claim must be barred in order not to upset and undermine specific limitations of those remedies.[600]

The actual problem in terms of vagueness will however arise in cases that are covered by the too wide wording of the Pomponian enrichment claim but *not* by any other remedy, like for example Robert Stevens' stamp case. The fact that there is no specific remedy might indicate a gap in the law that must be closed.[601]

However, this is only one side of the story. The absence of any established legal rule may likewise mean that the law does not want to provide for a remedy in that case – a negative decision that must not be undermined by awarding an enrichment claim on loose equitable considerations.[602]

---

599 Schall, ECFR 2016, 476, at pp. 471–473. But note that there is the additional unclarity whether the rule of last resort is triggered by other remedies against third parties or only those against the defendant.

600 In that sense now Corte di Cassazione, sezione III civile; ordinanza 20 febbraio 2023, n. 5222, Foro Italiano 3/2023, 719, at p. 724 (on this case, see in more detail below, p. 185).

In accordance with that rationale, French law distinguishes "factual obstacles" of claims against third parties (that do not bar the *actio de in rem verso*) from "legal obstacles" (that do), cf. Dalloz, Art. 1303–3, n° 3: "L'action *de in rem verso* ne peut être introduite pour suppléer à une autre action qui se heurte à un obstacle de droit. Com. 16 mai 1995, n° 93–14.709 P: *Rev. sociétés 1996. 95, note Gerschel; RTD civ. 1996. 160, obs. Mestre; BJS 1995. 757, note Le Cannu* (interdiction, pour les administrateurs de sociétés, des rémunérations autres que celles prévues par l'art. 107 de la L. du 24 juill. 1966, devenu C. com., art. L. 225–44) Com. 2 nov. 2005: *D. 2005. AJ 2943, obs. A. Lienhard* (inopposabilité à la procédure des actes accomplis par le débiteur dessaisi)."

601 Goré, at p. 35–36: "On est bien en présence d'une lacune. Une solution juridique est indispensable et le droit positif n'en fournit pas. C'est a cette constatation qu'aboutissent tous les civilistes francais contemporains. Le principe de la restitution de l'enrichissement aux depens d'autrui est imposé directement par la notion de justice en vertu de l'article 4 du Code civil." [There is a gap here. A legal solution is essential and positive law does not provide one. This is the conclusion reached by all contemporary French civil lawyers. The principle of restitution of enrichment at the expense of others is imposed directly by the notion of justice under article 4 of the Civil Code.]

602 This problem is also recognized by Goré, p. 102, however without proposing a way forward: "C'est donc en droit francais, l'admission d'un principe general postérieur à des réglementations particulières d'applications de ce principe qui pose le problème des rapports de la notion d'enrichissement injuste avec les règles juridiques édictées par le législateur." [In French law, therefore, it is the acceptance of a general principle subsequent to the specific rules of application of that principle which raises the problem of the relationship between the concept of unjust enrichment and the legal rules enacted by the legislator.]. Cf. further Goré, pp 47–48.

This issue cannot simply be solved by arguing that the text of the provision (or the test devised by the jurisdiction, for that matter) embraces the case. Just as the law may be too narrow and must be extended by analogies *in consimili casu*, it may be too wide and must be restricted by teleological interpretation. This is common knowledge of European lawyers since the sanctity of the wording had been overcome in the *causa Curiana* of 94 B.C.[603] In a French stamp case, one might e.g. argue that the enrichment was not caused by any vitiated transfer, that there was no misdirected investment, or that there was no value "taken" by the defendant. But whatever arguments could be brought to support or reject an enrichment claim in a French stamp case, one thing is crystal clear: The subsidiarity bar has nothing to contribute at all. If anything, it disguises the true reasons for the decision.

This is confirmed by an analysis of the following case that, according to Francois Goré, rightly closed a gap in the law.[604] It is structurally similar to the stamp case and exemplifies the danger of random arbitrariness posed by the general enrichment claim:

> To save the (valuable) house of B from a fire, the firefighters tear down the (less valuable) house of A. The Tribunal of Vannes holds B enriched at the expense of A and awards compensation.[605]

603 This famous case was fought in Rome between the jurist Scaevola and the orator Crassus. It concerned the intertrepeation of the will of one Coponius who had stipulated: "If a son is born and dies before adolescence, Curius shall be the heir." When Coponius died, no son had been born at all. Thus the legal heir argued that he should inherit because the stipulation in favour of Curius did not cover that case. But Crassus won the day by arguing that the true intent of Coponius was to endow Curius if he had now sons himself.

In that historical moment, the law may have become more sound and just but also more prone to the rethoric sophistry of petty lawyers. And so it remained, see Honsell, Die rhetoirschen Wurzeln der juristischen Auslegung, ZfPW 2016, 106, in particular at pp. 111–113; Wieacker, The Causa Curiana and Contemporary Roman Jursiprudence, Irish Jurist (1967), Vol. 2, No. 1, pp. 151 et seq. The fundamental discussion of the vices and virtues for legal interpretation was initiated by the work of Johannes Stroux, Summum Ius Summa Inuria (1926); cf. on this e.g. A. Schiller, Roman Law – Mechaisms of Development (1978), pp. 572–579; John W. Vaughn, "Law and Rhetoric in the Causa Curiana", Classical Antiquity Vol 4 n°2 (1985), 208.

604 Goré, at p. 36. On the same page, Goré reports another example for a gap in the law to be closed by the general enrichment claim: a freshwater company used a pipe that one of its members had installed at its own expense to distribute Fresh water to others. No charge had been contracted for. The Cour de cassation forced the company to indemnify the member to the extent it drew benefit from the latter's expenses, Cass req, 11 Dec 1928, D.P. 1929.1.18. But this case is less alien to enrichment law because it seems to be about taking value – a situation that had always been sanctioned by the condictio furtiva and the condictio sine causa.

605 Tribunal de paix Vannes, 26 January 1927, D.H.1927.535. Cf. the Austrian rule in §1043 ABGB, too.

The outcome is generally accepted in European private law.[606] The problem is that this is the only discernible difference to the stamp case about which Robert Stevens forcefully claims that no jurisdiction should award it.[607] In both cases, the property of one is damaged. This detriment directly causes the unjust(ified) enrichment of the other.[608] That being so, the solution cannot be found by applying the Pomponian sentence. Other considerations are at work under the surface. They are merely glossed over by resorting to the enrichment argument.

For starters, it is true that the firefighter case rested upon a lacuna that French law inherited from Roman law.[609] It is a well-known topic of European legal comparison.[610] The issue at stake is the possible justification of damaging a lesser good for saving a higher good. In Germany, it is called *rechfertigender Notstand* (= "justifying state of emergency"[611]). German law further distinguishes between *defensiver Notstand* (= "defensive state of emergency") in § 228 BGB and *aggressiver Notstand* ("aggressive state of emergency") in § 904 BGB.[612] The former relates to situations where the property of another is damaged or destroyed because it posed a danger. The latter refers to the situation of the firefighter case where the source of the danger for the higher good is not the damaged property but something else. The provision reads as follows:

> § 904 BGB: "Der Eigentümer einer Sache ist nicht berechtigt, die Einwirkung eines anderen auf die Sache zu verbieten, wenn die Einwirkung zur Abwendung einer gegenwärtigen Gefahr notwendig und der drohende Schaden gegenüber dem aus der Einwirkung dem Eigentümer entstehenden Schaden unverhältnismäßig groß ist. Der Eigentümer kann Ersatz des ihm entstehenden Schadens verlangen."

> [The owner of a thing is not entitled to prohibit the influence of another person on the thing if the influence is necessary to avert a present danger and the imminent damage is dispropor-

---

606 See in depth Amalia Diurni: Schädigende Nothilfe – Haftungszurechnung im Europäischen Privatrecht, ZEuP 2006, 583.

607 To be sure, the unjust factors of English law would differ as well, being mistake in the stamp case and maybe compulsion in the firefighter case. But this is a minor side note in this context.

608 In the stamp case, the increase in value of the defendant's property; in the firefighter case, the aversion of a decrease in value of the defendant's property.

609 Diurni, ZEuP 2006, 583, 584. Note that the Belgium Cour de cassation closed that gap in 1987, Cour cass., 2e chambre, 13.5.1987, Revue critique juridique belge 1989, 588, noted De Nauw, La consacration jurisprudentielle de l'état de nécessité (pp. 593 et seq).

610 For an account, see Diurni, ZEuP 2006, 583 et seq.

611 The officially approved translation of § 904 BGB merely speaks of "necessity", cf. https://www.gesetze-im-internet.de/englisch_bgb/englisch_bgb.html#p4427.

612 At first sight, it may look odd to describe a "state" as aggressive, but it means that the protective measure is not adressed "defensively" against the originator of the danger.

tionately great in relation to the damage the owner stands to suffer as a result of the influence. The owner may require compensation for the damage they suffer.]

The gist of the German rule is that the destruction of A's house is justified under the proviso that he is **compensated** for his loss. The law does not spell out who is to pay that compensation, but the prevailing doctrine would not hold acting persons (the firefighters) liable but the beneficiary (the owner of the saved house, B).[613]

This outcome is in line with the decision found in France. But the solution cannot be derived from the moral prohibition to benefit from another's loss. There are various other, more refined considerations at stake. They centre on the acceptance and limits of utilitarianism, the necessity of compensation for expropriation, the question of proportionality etc., and lead to complex balancing exercises. All this is disguised by the Pomponian brocade and the ill-fitting concept of subsidiarity. If the firefighter case is awarded simply because of the moral prohibition to benefit from another's loss, how could the stamp case be denied?

In such cases, the subsidiarity principle cannot but conceal judicial arbitrariness ("sloppiness of thought"!). If anything, the solution under the moral enrichment principle, restricted by the subsidiarity bar, would have to be in the reverse: the stamp case would have to be awarded because B clearly benefits from the loss of A (immoral!) and no other remedy is available. By contrast, the firefighter case should probably have been denied. If French law did not accept any justification under the heading of *aggressiver Notstand*, the firefighters would be liable in tort law to owner A. If that was true, they should be able to claim an indemnity from the owner B under the rules of *gestion d'affaires* because they incurred the tort liability voluntarily during the management of B's affair to save his house. That being so, the subsidiarity principle bars a direct enrichment claim of A versus B because A can sue the firefighters who can sue B.[614]

bb) The defence of "cause legitime" (= "right to enrichment")

The next criticism is directed to the first important restriction of the arrêt Boudier, namely that the enrichment claim would not succeed if the defendant was "enti-

613 BGHZ 6, 102.

614 It may even be that a direct *negotiorum gestio* claim could be construed by arguing that it was house owner A, not the firefighters, who managed the affairs of B. German law would not allow this because one cannot manage affairs by mere passivity. However, where would be the difference if A had destroyed his house himself to save B? Or if A had issued the firefighters to do so? If A was the gerens in those two cases, it would be hard to see why the actions of the firefighters could not be attributed to him anyway, in order to create a direct claim from A to B under the more apt heading of a *negotiorum gestio* instead of the Pomponian brocade?

tled" to the enrichment. It was introduced in the arrêt Bouche-Pech.[615] The case concerned the purchase of clothes by a wife Mme Bouche-Pech, that could not be paid by her bankrupt husband.[616] When the vendor Jovalier tried to sue the wife on grounds of her benefitting from the transaction, the Cour held that she was not enriched since she was entitled to be maintained by her husband.[617]

> "Attendu que ... il n'est pas permis de considérer la femme comme s'étant enrichie du montant d'une fourniture dont le mari était tenu vis-à-vis elle."
>
> [Whereas ... it is not permissible to consider the wife as having been enriched by the amount of a supply for which the husband was liable to her. Deep-L]

Soon afterwards, the arrêt Leloup[618] confirmed the rule, albeit on a different reasoning. A rural worker (Leloup) sued the owner of the land (Lutier) after not being paid by the tenant (Pré), based on the fact that Lutier had taken half of the harvest – which was supposed to be the settlement of Lutier's own claims against Pré under the lease. Again the Cour dismissed the claim owing to the fact that Lutier had contracted for the benefit. But now, the argument was that the enrichment of Lutier was based on a cause légitime.

The reasoning of the Cour de cassation in the arrêt Bouche-Pech had avoided a self-contradiction after having stated in the arrêt Boudier that the enrichment claim had no other requirements than detriment of the claimant and resulting enrichment of the defendant. Denying the enrichment by netting the benefit received by the third party with the value given for it seemed to be in line (see also p. 306), whereas asking for a causa or allowing a defence of *suum receipt* / good consideration *ex iure tertii* openly introduced an additional requirement and "qualified" the central statement of the arrêt Boudier.[619] Therefore, it was really only when the doctrinal approach changed from denying the enrichment to accepting the de-

---

615 Cass. civ 7 July 1896, D. P. 1898.1.18. See also König, Bereicherungsanspruch, pp. 31 et seq.; Chiusi, pp. 198–199.

616 Under Art. 1998 C.civ 1804, the husband was deemed party of the contract concluded by his wife.

617 According to Chiusi, p. 198, this was in line with Roman law. But if the wife was seen as the "agent", the vendor should have had an *actio de peculio* against her, whereas if she was the principal, the *actio de in rem verso* should have succeeded irrespective of any obligations of the "agent" (husband) towards her. For "netting" the enrichment also Burrows, The Law of Restitution, p. 46 fn. 8.

618 Cass civ. 10.10.1898. D.1899.1.105; Chiusi, p. 199; König, pp. 31 et seq.

619 That doctrinal consistency was however only superficial. First, netting the benefit received from one party with the discharge of the debt to a third party is just another technical method to the same end and therefore meets the same criticism from the privity of contract. Second, the argument is also circular, see in more detail below on the related issue of the *suum recepit* rule.

fence of "cause légitime" that the French *actio de in rem verso*, clothed in the Pomponian prohibition of benefit from another's detriment, turned into "enrichissmeent sans cause", now "injustifié".

Today, it is settled that the enrichment claim is defeated by a "cause legitime" of the defendant's enrichment. That being so, claims for the "versum" against owners by parties who had contracted with tenants, leaseholders etc. are regularly dismissed.[620] That is surely important for commercial certainty. However, on closer looks, it is not sustainable from the doctrinal perspective. The reason is the **privity of contract**, or to speak more broadly, the **relativity of obligations.** In a three-party-situation, the defence of cause légitime violates the basic structure of private law.

A contract only binds the parties to it. Legal obligations only exist between the debtor and the creditor. A contract between two private parties must not work at the expense of a third party. But this is exactly what happens by allowing the defence of "cause legitime". It explicitly contradicted the rule formerly laid down in the old **Art. 1165 C.civ 1804:**

> "Les conventions n'ont d'effet qu'entre les parties contractantes; elles ne nuisent point au tiers, et elles ne lui profitent que dans le cas prévu par l'article 1121."[621]
>
> [Contracts have effect only between the parties; they are not harmful to third parties, and they benefit them only in the circumstances set out in article 1121.][622]

First of all, the criticism raised here must be distinguished from the argument that the *actio de in rem verso* itself violated Art. 1165 C.civ 1804. That point had been argued but rightly refuted by the Cour de cassation in the arrêt Boudier:[623]

> "Attendu que s'il est de principe que les conventions n'ont d'effet qu'entre les parties contractantes et ne nuisent point aux tiers, il est certain ce principe n'a pas eté méconnu par le jugement attaqué; qu'en effet, cette décision n'a point admis, comme le prétend le pourvoi, que le demandeur pouvait être oblige envers les défendeurs éventuels à raison d'une fourniture d'engrais chimiques faite par ces derniers à un tiers, mais seulement à raison du profit per-

---

620 Chiusi, p. 199.; König, pp. 43 et seq.

621 Art. 1121 C.civ contained the exception of contracts for the *benefit* of third parties.

622 Art 1121 C.civ 1804 regulated contracts for the benefit of third parties ("stipulation pour autrui"). The rule is now found, recast in modern language, in Art 1205 C.civ 2016: "On peut stipuler pour autrui. L'un des contractants, le stipulant, peut faire promettre à l'autre, le promettant, d'accomplir une prestation au profit d'un tiers, le bénéficiaire. Ce dernier peut être une personne future mais doit être précisément désigné ou pouvoir être déterminé lors de l'exécution de la promesse. "

623 Cass reg, 15 June 1891, D. P. 92.1.596, S.93.1.281, noted Labbé.

sonnel et directe que ce même demandeur a retiré de l'emploi de ces engrais sur ses propres terres."

[Whereas it is a matter of principle that agreements have effect only between the contracting parties and do not harm third parties, it is certain that this principle was not disregarded by the judgment under appeal; that, in fact, this decision did not admit, as the appeal claims, that the plaintiff could be obliged towards the eventual defendants by reason of a supply of chemical fertilisers made by the latter to a third party, but only by reason of the personal and direct profit that this same plaintiff derived from the use of these fertilisers on his own land.]

However, the reasoning of the Cour does not defeat the critical point made here. It is surely true that the claim of Boudier against Patureau was not founded on the contract between Boudier and the tenant. But the argument does not hold in the reverse. The claim of Leloup against Lutier is solely rejected because of the latter's contractual entitlement vis-à-vis Pré. Therefore, this defence is undeniably in the most direct way based on the contract between Lutier and Pré. This could not be reconciled with the old Art. 1165 that prohibited the contract from having *any* legal effect vis-à-vis Leloup. The judgement violated the basic civilian maxime "res inter alios acta aliis neque nocere, neque prodesse potest" enshrined in the old Art 1165 C.civ 1804.

It must of course be noted that in the revised Code civil of 2016, the text was recast and the rule appears modified. It now reads more precisely, but it is also narrowed down. Art 1199 C.civ 2016 merely states:

"Le contrat ne crée d'obligations qu'entre les parties."

[Contracts only create obligations between the parties.]

In this new version, the text of the provision does not appear to be violated any more because from a purely technical perspective, Leloup did not become "obliged" to Lutier. Nor did of course the marriage oblige the vendor to maintain the wife of the husband. However, it still holds true that admitting the "cause légitime defense" on grounds of a right against a third party militates against the basic principles of private law. The privity of contract stems from the fact that party autonomy enables private persons to create "binding law" in between them. But on the flip side, it is self-evident that the "law" so created can only have effect to the parties of the respective agreement. That is why the critique put forward here cannot be countered by reference to the new Art. 1200 C.civ 2016 either.

"Les tiers doivent respecter le situation juridique crée par le contrat."

[Third parties must respect the legal position created by the contract.]

Whatever the content of any duty to "respect the judicial situation created by a contract" between others may mean: The fact that A owed a payment to B cannot justify that B keeps a benefit at the expense of C. The "law" that allocates the sum of money to B is a legal bond that only exists between A and B. C is not subject to it. If A sells the land of B to C, B will not have to accept that C should be now entitled to hold the land. So why should Leloup remain unpaid for the benefits he conferred merely to honour another's (Pré's) debt to Lutier from the lease or the vendor unpaid for the clothes because they were owed by the husband to his wife?

One might argue that there are exceptions to "nemo dat quod non habet" in many jurisdictions that allow a bona fide acquisition of another's title. Would that not indicate that there are generally accepted exceptions to the privity of contract? The answer is: No. Wherever a jurisdiction allows a bona fide acquisition of titles, this is not because the contract is endowed with absolute power against third parties. Rather, the rules on bona fide purchase are a legal instrument to promote commercial certainty by granting protection to innocent parties. They allow the general public to rely on prima facie entitlements. The justification for protection is therefore not the conclusion of the contract between the pseudo-owner and the third party, but that the true owner allowed the pseudo-owner to convey the impression of being the legitimate owner. Typically, the true owner has loosened the grip on his property voluntarily by leaving possession to the pseudo-owner who then abuses the trust of the owner by taking his place.[624] The principle at work in jurisdictions with a bona fide acquisition of titles can be paraphrased as "Retrieve your trust where you left it." The negative consequences of the breach of trust must hit the owner as "trustor" instead of innocent third parties. The same idea is inherent in the admission of "bona fide purchase for value" in English trust law. So the prerequisite of giving value has undoubtedly the effect that another's property can be bought while it cannot be received as a gift.[625] But this is not

---

624 Cf. §§ 932 et seq. BGB, with the notable exception of bona fide acquisition where the possession was lost without the consent of the owner (§ 935 BGB).

625 N.B. that in essence, German law restricts the bona fide acquisition of another's title to purchase for value, too. But the mechanism works differently. The acquisition of the title is solely governed by §§ 932–935 BGB and will only require good faith, not the giving of value. But the title so acquired by the purchaser can only be held for good if value had been given for it. If it was obtained gratuitously, the previous owner is allowed to claim the (re)transfer of the title under enrichment law (§ 816 I 2 BGB – note that this is an action ad personam, not ad rem). By contrast, if the third party has given value, the owner can only sue the vendor to recover the purchase prize (according to the minority view: the objective value of the property) under § 816 I 1 BGB.

These rules are also in the middle of the German equivalent of waiver of torts. Stolen property can never be acquired in good faith under German law (§ 935 BGB). But the owner can validate the transfer of title retrospectively (*Genehmigung* under § 185 II BGB), thus "waiving" the *rei*

due to any absolute power of the contract, but because private law, in a kind of proportionality principle, restricts its protection to those who need it most.

By contrast, neither the landworker Leloup nor the vendor of the clothes have done anything that makes them less worthy of protection in the eyes of the law than the owner Lutier or the wife. Rather to the contrary. If the husband was broke, how could the wife expect be maintained by a third party. Rather, she should wear her old clothes. If Pré was broke, why should Leloup bring in the harvest for free. I would argue that Lutier should have used his own hands for that.

Again, the problems highlighted here are caused by the amalgamation of the *actio de in rem verso* with the Pomponian sentence. The doctrinal reshuffle of the arrêt Boudier transplanted the concept of "cause" from the *condictiones* into the alien surroundings of the *actio de in rem verso* where it cannot work. The *actio de in rem verso* has never aimed to undo failed transactions. It was thus not concerned with the existence or lack of a causa. Its purpose was to allow leapfrogging when the peculium was exhausted ("nihil in peculio") but the *pater familias* had derived a lasting benefit from the transactions of the son or slave: a benefit that was not accounted for by the master. If anything, this required a valid contract between the claimant and the manager of the pecuilum. Otherwise, there would be nothing to claim, neither from the peculium nor from the *pater familias.*

The requirement of a (lack of) causa is the feature of the *condictiones.* The *condictiones* concern failed transaction and thus relate to a direct shift of value, whereas the *actio de in rem verso* is concerned with three party situations.

> Goré, p. 13, n°15: "Ajoutons enfin que non seulement les condictiones sine causa supposaient un negotium mais aussi un enrichissement ayant eu lieu aux dépens d'autrui d'une manière directe entre le patrimoine du demandeur et celui du défendeur. Autrement dit, elles ne sanctionnaient pas l'enrichissement dû à l'intervention juridique d'un tiers. C'était au contraire cet enrichissement que sanctionnait l'action de in rem verso."
>
> [Finally, it should be added that not only did the condictiones sine causa presuppose a negotium, but also an enrichment which took place at the expense of another person in a direct manner between the assets of the plaintiff and those of the defendant. In other words, they did not sanction enrichment due to the legal intervention of a third party. On the contrary, it was this enrichment that was sanctioned by the action in rem verso.]

The search for a "causa" or "cause" only makes sense where the direct shift of value takes place. It is not compatible with the three-party-situation of the *actio*

---

vindicatio under § 985 against the purchaser and claiming the purchase prize from the vendor instead.

de in rem verso. Therefore, it leads to logical inconsistencies. Take a chain of sales. A sells a good to B, and B sells it on to C.[626] Originally, A held the property. Now C is the owner. Shall the law require two causes to justify the shift? If so, the invalidity of the contract of B and C could allow the recovery to the original owner A who performed on a valid contract? Conversely, if one cause sufficed, why should the valid contract between B and C bar recovery by A who had performed on a non-existing obligation? For a detailed account of the complicated solution of tripartite cases, see below p. 176 (suum receipt) and p. 303.

The observation that the requirement of a "causa" in the sense of the *condictiones* is a misfit for the *actio de in rem verso* is confirmed by the historical shape of both instruments in the Digest and the *ius commu*ne. It has only been blurred under the broad brush of the Pomponian sentence. Against this background, it is not coincidental that there is no general consensus on the meaning of "cause" in French unjust enrichment.[627] The majority of authors assumes the clear-cut legal definition in line with the realm of the *condictiones.* For this view, the rebranding of French enrichment law from "enrichissement sans cause" to "enrichissement injustifié" seems consequential. However, a minority of writers understand sans cause in an equitable way. Following their approach, French enrichment law should rather be labelled as "enrichissement injuste". If we understand the Pomponian sentence as a moral principle of higher equity, which was the view of the French jurists of the nineteenth century and accords with centuries of evolution under the ius commune, this would be the more correct approach.

These uncertainties are testimony that the commandment of Planiol to keep the scientific notions of the law clear[628] has not been complied with yet. And as so clairvoyantly foretold by him, this immediately leads to contradictions and irreconcilable decisions. Dismissing any idea that fertiliser could be a "higher" ingredient than human labour, it is hard to see why the claim of unpaid Boudier against the owner who received a part of the crops on his claim against the tenant was awarded whereas the claim of unpaid Leloup against the owner who received a part of the crops on his claim against the tenant was denied. Also, the dismissal of the vendor's claim against the wife in 1898 was at odds with the older judgements in favour of the unpaid instructors where the French Courts had disallowed the defence that the children were owed an education by their parents.[629]

626 Note that this chain can be multiplied by numerous links, as often happens in business practice.

627 For the various competing explanations see Goré, pp. 87–92.

628 Above p. 15.

629 Above, p. 140.

If we take the original *actio de in rem verso* of Roman law as paradigm, it seems to describe a situation where the benefit of the *pater familias* (i.e. the justification for leapfrogging the restriction to the peculium) was received without giving extra value for it.[630] But the French enrichment cases are inconclusive on this point. For example, in one case an enrichment claim was awarded for a plaintiff who had lost his clients due to a non-competition clause for which he had not been compensated.[631] By contrast, the Tribunal civ. Seine did not care for any value given for the benefits when it ruled that a donation was a cause légitime that excluded the enrichment claim.[632] But this judgement seems outdated under the new Code civil that does not look at the justification from the perspective of the defendant ("(un)just retention"), but from the perspective of the claimant.

> Art. 1303–2 C.civ:
> "L'enrichissement est injustifié lorsqu'il ne procède ni de l'accomplissement d'une obligation par l'appauvri ni de son intention libérale."
>
> [The enrichment is unjustified where it does not result from the fulfilment of an obligation by the impoverished person or from his liberal intention".]

But be that as it may. It is noteworthy that the lack of value given for the benefit by the defendant did not help the claimant in a rerun of the Lemaire case (above p. 152).[633] The only difference to the original case of 16 July 1890 had been that this time, the identical stipulation that all buildings erected on the land would accrue to the owner without compensation at the end of the lease was deemed valid and could be invoked. Based on this, the Cour de cassation held that the owner was entitled to the enrichment and did not have to answer the unpaid builder's claim for his benefits. But the claimant had not given any value for those benefits and it is therefore hard to see why the position of the poor unpaid builder from whose loss the owner benefitted should be worse. The validity of the contractual clause is the only difference. To allow this defence means to allow an *exceptio ex iure tertii.*

---

630 Albeit it must be taken into account that the pater familias had provided the funds to set up the peculium in first place.

631 Com. 9 oct. 2007, n° 05–14.118: JCP 2007. II. 10211, noted N. Dissaux; CCC 2007, n° 298, observed M. Malaurie-Vignal; D. 2008. 388, noted D. Ferrier; RJDA 2008. 335, noted H. Kenfack.

632 Trib. Civ. Seine, 22.2.1913, G.P. 1913.1.634.; Chiusi, p. 199 text with fn. 39: An expensive barrel of wine had been bought from wine merchant Moreau by M. Massif who had him send it directly to Demoiselle Robert. When Massif could not pay, Moreau addressed the Desmoiselle – and failed. This is at odds with the weakness of gratuities. Critical therefore Detlef König, Bereicherungsanspruch, pp. 58–59. The judgement seems to rest on chivalry rather than doctrine.

633 Civ. 3^{e}, 28 mai 1986, n° 85–10.367 P.

The latter judgements are particularly hard to comprehend from the merits, but also from the doctrinal perspective. This is because with no value given, nothing diminishes the enrichment of the defendant. But the value given in the form of the discharge of the claims from the lease/from family law had been the explicit reason for Cour de cassation to deny the enrichment claims in the first restricting case, the arrêt Bouche-Pech.

The analysis demonstrates the danger of conflating the concepts of leapfrogging under the *actio de in rem verso* with restitution of failed transactions under the *condictiones sine causa* in the name of the generic catch-all heading of Pomponian unjust enrichment. This was possible because the Pomponian sentence, unlike the *condictiones*, never explicitly referred to the lack of a *causa* and therefore was not reduced to it. However, introducing it as a defence in the guise of "cause légitime" only highlights the unresolved issue of melting different doctrinal concepts into one catch-all claim. The fusion of the systematically distinct Roman legal bases, the *condictiones sine causa*, and the *actio de in rem verso* under the heading of the equitable principle of Pomponius led to the inconsistencies shown here. This is confirmed by the observation that the same issues arise under the similarly structured enrichment law of Italy.[634]

To me, it would seem more appropriate and in line with the historic evolution to restrict the leapfrogging *actio de in rem verso* under French law to remote recipients who have a benefit passed on from a failing debtor without giving value. The legal principle at work would be that liberality has to come out of the pockets of the donor and not at the expense of third parties.[635] This is akin to the principle of the *actio Pauliana* and also reflected in the avoidance provisions of many insolvency laws. It sits well with the observation that many versum cases have an air of fraudulent preferences.[636]

cc) An aside on *suum recepit*

For sake of accuracy, it is appropriate to discuss the defence of *suum recepit* at this stage. Strictly speaking, this was not a defence against the *actio de in rem verso*, but against a *condictio indebiti*. Nevertheless, it must be introduced here because it also covered three-party-situations. It must be understood how these situations

634 See the thorough account of Shida Galletti and Charles Mitchell, "Arricchimento senza causa: a comparative introduction" RLR (2015): 1–20.

635 Cf. also the German provision on gifts that states in § 516 BGB: "Schenkung aus dem Vermögen" (see in detail below p. 200).

636 See in particular the two fertilizer cases, the French arrêt Boudier and the Prussian case of RGZ 1, 157 (above, p. 138 and p. 157).

that occur under a direct shift of value approach are to be distinguished from the cases of the *actio de in rem verso* and why there is legitimate scope for the defendant to argue that has got what was due to him from a third party. This so much the more since the same defence has been accepted in the guise of "good consideration" or "discharge for value" in common law enrichment.[637]

The Roman rule is a derivative of the generic "suum cuique" principle at the beginning of the Digest[638] and says in essence that there is no restitution from someone who received his due.

> D.12.6.44: Repetitio nulla est ab eo, qui suum recepit, tametsi ab alio, quam vero debitore solutum est."
>
> [There is no recovery from him who has received what was due to him, even if it has been given in discharge **by** somebody other than the true debtor.

The first part of this rule seems very basic and self-evident. If your debtor paid you, why should you be obliged to return the payment? However, it may still be better to spell this out since the pure Pomponian principle, only looking at detriment and benefit and neglecting the causa, could even be (ab)used as a tool to correct exchanges under valid but "unfair" contracts.[639]

In our context, the second part of the rule ("tametsi ab alio...) is of prime interest because it appears to contradict the argument derived above from the privity of contract / relativity of obligations. However, on closer looks, the "suum recepit" rule has less bearing as one might assume at first. We will see that it is restricted to the specific situation where the payor willfully "adopted" the indebtedness to the creditor by paying in lieu of the debtor (cf. § 4 VE, below p. 305). The modern paradigm is the liability insurer paying on the debt of the tortfeasor. The classic case of English law is *Aiken v Short*[640] where the plaintiff bank had bought property from one Carter that was encumbered with a charge. In order to release that charge, the bank paid on the debt of Carter to his creditor (Short). The bank

---

637 *Aiken v Short* (1856) 1 H&N 210; *Barclay v Simms* 1980] 1 QB 677; *Lloyds v Independent* 1998] EWCA Civ 1853; cf. Schall, RLR 2004, 110, 112 et seq.

638 D 1.1.10 pr. (Ulp. 1 reg.): "Justitia est constans et perpetua voluntas jus *suum cuique* tribuendi." [Scott: Justice is the constant and perpetual desire to give to everyone that to which he is entitled.] Cf. von Kübel, pp. 33 et seq. = Schubert, pp. 693 et seq.

639 In France, the Cour de cassation firmly rejected that attempt (but it is telling that the case even got there), Com. 23 oct. 2012, n° 11–25.175 P: *D. 2012. 2598.*

In England, despite Goff & Jones, 12-20, a similar attempt has been reported in which Islington Bourough tried to rectify its contract with Antony Zomparelli, see The Times, 16 Feb 2019: "Owner told to pay Ł 360,000 or lose flat after council missed a bedroom."

640 *Aiken v Short* (1856) 1 H&N 210; see also Stevens, pp. 43–44.

was mistaken since Carter had had no title to the collateral. But that was just a disappointed motive which did not alter the fact that the bank had achieved its primary purpose: the discharge of Carter's debt with Short. That is why the creditor was allowed to keep the payment. *Suum recepit!*

The rule does not bar restitution simply because the benefit was owed to the recipient by a third party. It bars recovery because the payor (the liability insurer, the plaintiff bank) bargained as third party with the creditor (victim; Short) for the discharge of the debtor (tortfeasor; Carter). The payor subjects himself to the claim of the creditor against the debtor. The discharge of the obligation of the debtor can only become the *causa* for his payment because he adopts it as such.

The restriction of the rule to payments of third party debts cannot be derived from the wording of the rule itself. But it becomes obvious in the "counter rule" that allowed restitution if the payor falsely assumed to be obliged to the payee whereas in truth, a third party was the debtor.

> Dig **12.6.65.9:** Indebitum est. . . si id, quod alius debebat, alius quasiipse debeat, solvat."
>
> [It is not due to the recipient .. if that what is owed by the one is paid by the other as if owed by himself.

If the payor does not freely choose the third party debt as causa for his payment to the creditor, the existence of a claim against a third party is not enough to justify the retention of the benefit by the creditor. The same is true under common law. In *Colonial Bank v Exchange Bank of Yarmouth,*[641] a payment was misdirected into the wrong bank account. The bank where the funds ended up had a good claim against the account holder. Nevertheless, it could not keep the money. Restitution was ordered because of the mistake notwithstanding the good claim. The same happened in *Barclays v Simms.*[642]

So when does a legal reason / *causa* vis-à-vis a third party exclude the *condictio indebiti* / action for money had and received and when does it not? In light of the principle of privity of contracts/relativity of obligations, the answer must be that the payor deliberately made his payment on the debtor's obligation towards his creditor. Thereby the payor subjects himself to a *causa* that exists between the payee and a third party: the claim of the creditor against the debtor. The doctrinal situation is exactly described by Pollock C.B.: "the defendant (= Short) had a perfect right to receive the money from Carter, and the bankers paid for him."[643]

641 (1885) 9 App Cas 84 (PC).

642 *Barclays Bank Ltd v W J Simms, Son and Cooke (Southern) Ltd* [1980] 1 QB 677, [1979] 3 All ER 522.

643 *Aiken v Short* (1856) 1 H&N 210, at p. 214.

The same notion "to make the payment for the debtor" was expressed in a provision that had been proposed as § 4 of the pre-draft (see below p. 305).

As just pointed out: The classic paradigm is the liability insurer. The insurance contract obliges the company to indemnify the insured party. Comes the insurance case, the insurer will be paying the debt of the tortfeasor to the victim. In case the insurance contract is void, the company will not be able to recover the payment from the victim because that debt had existed and was validly discharged. The payor gave the payee what was due to him: *suum recepit.* This does not violate the core principles of privity of contract and party autonomy. To the contrary: Party autonomy allows people to bargain for whatever legal purpose they seek to achieve. One of those possible purposes is to discharge another's debt. The *suum recepit* rule only keeps the payor to that bargain. The flip side of the bargain is that in case the tort liability does not exist, the *condictio indebiti* will lie at the hands of the insurer because he paid *sine causa.*[644]

It is another question whether the rule of *suum recepit* / good consideration / discharge for value is apt to provide security of receipt in banking law. In my opinion, this is not the case because unlike the liability insurer, a bank does not normally bargain for the discharge of the customer's debt to the recipient.[645] *Aiken v Short* was a truly exceptional case where the plaintiff bank had a vital interest to achieve the discharge of Carter's (= the customer's) debt in order to release the encumbrance on its property. In all other "everyday cases", the bank is not concerned with the reason for the payment. It is neither interested nor obliged to indemnify its customer. Therefore, it does not willingly subject itself to the obligation of its customer vis-à-vis the payee.

That being so, one might ask if the agnostic stance of the bank could be construed as intent to subject itself to *any* reason of the payment issued by its customer? This may be an enticing idea on its surface, seemingly providing encompassing security of receipt. But if the bank really adopted any reason for the customer's payment as its own, the flipside would be that it would always be up to the bank (and never to the customer) to recover the money if the debt does not exist or the consideration of the payment fails etc. This is not the law anywhere, nor should it be. But if it is true that the bank does not subject itself to the reason for the customer's payment, it cannot be held to the discharge of the customer's debt under general principles of private law.

This is not to say that the decision in *Lloyd's v Independent* is "wrong". But neither the Roman *suum recepit* rule nor its common law twin good consideration /

644 BGHZ 113, 62.
645 See already Schall, RLR 2004, 110, at p. 115.

discharge for value are able to explain these cases in a persuasive way because they are circular. If the discharge can only work if no restitution is granted (*Barclays v Simms, Colonial Bank v Exchange Bank of Yarmouth*), restitution cannot be denied because the discharge is granted. For the same reason, the alternative approach of netting the benefit received from the claimant with the discharge[646] obtained vis-à-vis the third party is bound to fail.

But deferring the correct shape of the law of restitution of bank transfers to later (p. 303), the foregoing analysis shows that the *suum recepit* rule cannot be called to aid in support of the "cause légitime"-defence of French enrichissement sans cause. If A sells clothes to B or works for B, there is no basis to argue that he also subjects himself to B's obligations to C. But as shown above, this would be necessary because the mere fact that a benefit is due to the enriched person from a third party does not suffice to create a bar to recovery.

To conclude this side glance with a final observation. It is generally true that the *condictiones* relate to direct shifts of value whereas the *actio de in rem verso* extends to remote recipients in three party situations, as Francois Goré has said. There are however two provisos to be made. First, the shift of value must be understood in a normative way and equated with the performance. Otherwise, the claim of "directness" will be misleading (in more detail pp. 246–247).

Second, as just seen, the restriction of enrichment claims to direct shift of value does not prevent *all* three-party situations. However, it considerably narrows down the scope for problematic constellations. They do not occur in any of the common situations where benefits from commercial transactions spread on, like in the chain of sales or in the Helmstedt-case of the loan (p. 114). There is no open door for leapfrogging insolvency risks. Rather, the complexities of tripartite situations are reduced to scenarios where one transfer simultaneously discharges two obligations.

First and foremost, this is the case of the liability insurer: the payment to the victim discharges the tort liability of the insured as well as the duty of the insurance company to indemnify the insured.[647] It is also the case of a payment to the assignee. This becomes particularly clear if the assignment had been made by the assignor to secure the repayment of a loan to the assigne. The payment will not only discharge the debtor, but at the same time settle the loan of the assignor.

As last example, take the following case: I order 6 bottles of Channel Island Gold Foil milk at "Milk and More" in the following way: 5 bottles are to be deliv-

646 For this alternative mode of construction p. 306; Burrows, The Law of Restitution, p. 46 fn. 8.
647 The simultaneous transfer of two benefits is overlooked by Lionel Smith, Restitution: A New State?, p. 105, who asks "If a guarantor pays the debt and sues the primary debtor, is he seeking restitution?" If he acted on a void contract with the debtor, the answer is: yes.

ered directly to my door step, but 1 bottle is to be placed in front of next door. Thereby, I want to return the bottle that our neighbour Evelyn lent us the weekend before. The delivery of the bottle to Evelyn's door will settle the milkman's duty to sell the bottle to me as well as my duty to return the bottle to Evelyn in one single act.

Let us take this example one step further and assume that I did not pay my order in advance, as required by the t's & c's of "Milk and More", but the milkman did not notice it before placing the 5 + 1 bottles on the door steps in Wellington Street. Who would deny him the right to take all bottles back immediately after he found out about his mistake (maybe rung by his wife from home), knowing that had he found out before, he would never have delivered the bottles? If this is so, why should he not be able to reclaim the bottle from Evelyn one minute after she had opened the door and taken it into her house? This confirms the observation made above regarding *Lloyds v Independent,*[648] namely that the widely accepted rules on the restitution of mistaken bank transfers are much more questionable than currently assumed. Arguably, this is because the doctrinal structure of such triangular transfers had not been comprehended exactly yet, neither by civil nor by common law (see also below, pp. 303 et seq.).

To sum up: There are three-party situations that cannot be avoided under a performance-based direct-shift-of-value approach. The principles of party autonomy and freedom of contract allow us to create obligations and transfer values. But they also facilitate the divergence of the subsequent transfers from the original contracts. We can pay other people's debts, assign our claims, create obligations for the benefit of third parties and short-cut payments and deliveries like in the milkman case. This results in transfers that simultaneously relate to more than one "causa", any of them being a direct shift of value in the eyes of the law and potentially subject to unjust factors. The solution of those cases is complicated because the system of the *condictiones* has been coined to two-party situations, and so are the English unjust factors under the action for money had and received. We will come back to discuss possible solutions below (p.303). For the time being, it suffices to distinguish the three-party situations in the context of a direct shift of value from the far greater number of three-party situations under the *actio de in rem verso* in the following examples.

Example 1 (Helmstedt case, p. 114, Crédit foncier case, p. 145): If the bank disbursed a loan to the customer who pays off the debts himself, there is only one direct shift of value from the perspective of the bank. This is the payment to its

648 *Lloyds Bank plc v Independent Insurance Co Ltd* [1998] EWCA Civ 1853.

customer. The remote recipients who benefit from the funds cannot be reached but for the *actio de in rem verso.*

Conversely, if the bank paid off the (secured) creditors directly, they would be the recipients of the payment. That being so, the first direct shift of value would occur from the bank to the creditors. At the same time, the customer receives the discharge of his debts. The indemnity is the second direct shift of value that flows from the same transaction (the payment). It is located between bank and customer. Thus, the payment from bank to creditor creates two simultaneous shifts of value that relate to two different contractual obligations. As an aside, we notice that the payment to the creditor must be deemed as a disbursement of the loan to the customer because it is self-evident that the customer (and not the actual recipients of the payment) will be liable to repay the loan. This cannot happen if the loan was never disbursed to him.

Example 2: If my employee paints the wall of my customer, he works for me. He is under my instruction and at my disposal, even though he may appear to create direct benefits for my customer. The *actio de in rem verso* is the only way for him to reach into the pockets of my customer.

By contrast, if I send my employee to work for a befriended painter for a few days because I have no work for him myself, he performs his duties under our service contract to a third party and the shift of value takes place between those two, like the bottle of milk delivered from the milkman to Evelyn.

dd) The consequent doctrinal alienation of *condictiones*

A fundamental consequence of the arrêt Boudier is the doctrinal split of traditional enrichment law. During the evolution under the *ius commune*, the *condictiones* had always been the integral core part of enrichment law. Today in France, the *répétition de l'indu* is under a different heading of quasi-contrat (Art. 1302 C.civ)[649] and follows different rules than *enrichissiement injustifié* (Art. 1303 C.civ).[650]

The roots for this split predate the Code civil.[651] The soil was already fertilized by the French concept of *cause juste* that has just been expelled from the revised Code civil of 2016. Under this concept, devised by the great jurisconsulte Jen Domat (1625–1696), any transaction not based on a *cause juste* was deemed a nullity.[652] If

649 Mélodi Combot, Quasi-contrat et enrichissement injutifié, 2023, n° 104 – pp 112–113 and n° 238 et seq, pp. 226 et seq. Likewise e.g. in Belgium, Art. 5.133. and 5.135. Cc.

650 Mélodi Combot, Quasi-contrat et enrichissement injutifié, 2023, n° 240 – p. 227.

651 The following passage draws from the account of Goré, pp. 22 et seq.

652 Domat. Liv. I, Tit. I, Sec. I, No. 5.; cf. Planiol, Droit Civil, Tome II, 1931, Sec. 1029 et seq.; Robert L Henry, "Cause in the Civil Law and Consideration in the Common: Much Ado About Nothing", 29 Kentucky Law Journal 4 (1941), 369, 370 et seq.

one followed the view that the *condictio* generally required a valid transfer ("datio", "negotium"),[653] the new doctrine of *cause juste* basically abolished this kind of action. Instead, the right to restitution was derived directly from the fact of the nullity ("restitutio in integrum").

However, the Code of 1804 enshrined the répétition de l'indu which translated the *condictio indebiti*. It was generally understood that the overarching principle of the claim was the Pomponian sentence.[654] Therefore, it was the arrêt Boudier that finally broke up civilian enrichment law. The identification with the *actio de in rem verso* has alienated the Pomponian sentence from the *condictiones*. This effect is demonstrated by a time line of French references:

In 1872, Gaston Rau elaborated in his PhD-thesis that all *condictiones* were applied under French law. This was true to the expressly enshrined répétition de l'indu as well as to the other *condictiones* that were applied by way of analogy.[655] According to him, this was based on the Pomponian sentence:

> Gaston Rau, p. 204: "..nous semble avoir établi d'une manière complète l'exactitude de la règle … une condictio est possible dans tous ces cas; et ainsi il est juste de dire que: chaque fois qu'une personne s'est enrichie aux dépens d'autrui, au moyen, d'un payment fait sans cause …, elle est soumise à une action en repetition."
>
> […it seems to us to have established in a complete manner the exactness of the rule … a *condictio* is possible in all these cases; and therefore it is right to say that: whenever a person has enriched himself at the expense of another, by means of a payment made without cause …, he is subject to an action en répétition."

The PhD-thesis of Gaston Rau did not *expressis verbis* rule out that there were other practical applications of the Pomponian principle under French law. But con-

653 Cf. e. g. Gaston Rau, De la valeur pratique de la maxime nemo cum damno alterius locupletior fieri debet en droit Romain – De l'action en répétition de l'indu et de quelques autres actions analogues en droit francais, 1872, at p. 25–26. This view, widespread as it was in the past, is from today's standpoint neither compatible with the *condictio furtiva* / *condictio sine causa* nor with the *condictio* relating to services, see Gaston Rau, ibid., pp. 95 et seq. But that does not change how things were seen in the past.

654 Pothier, Traité de prêt de consomption, n° 140: "Le fondement de cette obligation est cette règle d'équité naturelle: "Jure nature equum est neminem cum alterius detrimento et injuria fieri locupletiorem"; also cited by Gaston Rau, De la valeur, p. 140; but contrast Goré, p. 24–25 who assumed that Pothier only linked the (abnormal) *negotiorum gestio* with the Pomponian sentence – in order to explain the non-inclusion of the general enrichment claim in the Code Civil of 1804.

655 Gaston Rau, De la valeur, pp. 123 et seq., pp. 187 et seq. Rau classified them as the *condictiones sine causa (including causa data causa non secuta,* see p. 189, and -without naming it that way – the *condictio ob causam finitam,* see p. 194, text with fn. 4 and 5) and the *condictiones ex turpem vel iniustam causam,* pp. 195 et seq.

sidering that Gaston Rau had inter alia analysed the *actio de in rem verso* and the *actio contraria* in the first part on Roman law,[656] it is at least safe to say that he conceived the répétiton de l'indu / *condictio indebiti* and its analogous extensions as the central, but more likely even the only rules of French law that were based on the Pomponian sentence.

In 1890, Planiol wrote that both the *condictiones* in the guise of the répétiton de l'indu and the *actio de in rem verso* are exemplifications of that principle, the *conditiones* being more specific while the *actio de in rem verso* being more generic. This statement is already a precursor that paved the way to the equation of the *condictio sine causa* with the *actio de in rem verso.* But for the time being, it still kept "the family together":

> Planiol, D.P.91.1.49: "Il y a une foule de cas dans lesquels une personne, ayant retiré un profit pécuniaire d'actes juridiques ou de travaux accomplis par une autre se trouve soumise à une obligation de restitution. Dans sa forme la plus générale, l'action qui sanctionne porte le nom latin d'actio de in rem verso, bien connu de tous ceux qui se sont occupés de droit romain. Dans certains cas, l'enrichissement procuré sans cause à autrui est accompagné de circonstances caractéristiques, qui se reproduisent toujours les mêmes, et qui ont permis d'établir dans cette grande famille des variétés facilement reconnaissables. Tels sont les faits qui donnaient naissance, en droit romain, à la condictio indebiti, à la condictio ob rem dati, et à quelques autres condictiones, et lui chez nous encore donnent lieu à des actions en restitution auxquelles nous donnons souvent, pour plus de commodité, leurs anciens noms latins."
>
> [There are many cases in which a person who has derived a pecuniary benefit from legal acts or work performed by another is subject to an obligation to make restitution. In its most general form, the action for restitution bears the Latin name *actio de in rem verso*, well known to all those who have studied Roman law. In some cases, unjust enrichment of another person is accompanied by characteristic circumstances which are always the same, and which have made it possible to establish easily recognisable varieties within this great family. These are the facts which gave rise, in Roman law, to the condictio indebiti, the condictio ob rem dati, and some other condictions, and which still give rise in our law to actions for restitution to which we often give their old Latin names for convenience.]

The arrêt Boudier was the doctrinal breaking point. After it had equated the *actio de in rem verso* with the general enrichment claim, the Pomponian principle became separated from the *condictiones.* The "quasi-contrat" of the "répétititon de l'indu" was now distinguished from the claim for "enrichissement sans cause". That remained so after the recast Code civil had enshrined it as "enrichissement injustifié" in the Art.1303 – 1303 – 5 juxtaposed to the répéititon de l'indu in Art. 1302 – 1302 – 3. One major consequence of the two separate regimes is that the defence of disenrichment is subject to different rules, with only the "enrichissement

656 Gaston Rau, pp 36 et seq. and pp. 65 et seq.

injustifié" following the wide understanding of the general disenrichment defence (p. 57). Looking back to the Roman roots of the *condictiones* and the *actio de in rem verso*, and bearing in mind the contradictions surrounding the subsidiarity principle and the "cause légitime"-defence, it is difficult not to perceive this split regime as testimony of a fundamental doctrinal error.

French law consequently follows through on the separation of the *condictiones* / répétition de l'indu and the *actio de in rem verso* / general enrichment claim. This contrasts with the current legal situation in Italy, although the beginnings show a parallel pattern.[657] The Codice civile of 1865 followed the Code civil and only contained the *condictio indebiti.* This led to similar debates about the admissibility or not of the "azione de in rem verso" and its legal nature.[658] They ended with the new Codice civile of 1942 enshrining the Pomponian principle as general enrichment claim in Art. 2041 CC. Like in France, that claim was originally understood as merely circumscribing the Roman *actio de in rem verso utilis.*[659] However, Italian jurists adopted an understanding of the general enrichment claim as sweeping clause that covered all enrichment cases beyond the *condictio indebiti.* The other specific condictiones that had not been codified were not applied by way of analogy to the *condictio indebiti,* but immersed in the general claim.[660]

On the one hand, the Italian approach may look more in line with the notion of the general enrichment claim. On the other hand, the inconsistencies of the amalgamation of the *actio de in rem verso* and the Pomponian sentence are felt even harder within that framework. That is shown in a recent case that the third section of the Corte di Cassazione decided to refer to the President of the Corte with the aim to assemble the united sections to overhaul its jurisdiction:[661]

A company (FIM) held buildable land in the municipality of Tavagnacco. But the administration changed, and the land was zoned down to agricultural. The company did not seek legal protection because of assurances by the mayor that the change would only be of temporary nature. Subsequently, the community entered into a scheme with the municipality of Udine that obliged it to bury high volt-

---

657 See Chiusi, pp. 201 et seq.

658 Like France, Italy originally favoured the alignment to the *negotiorum gestio* (gestione d'affari), Chiusi, p. 201–202. The enrichment view started to spread in the jurisdiction of the Courts at the end of the nineteenth century, see Cass. Torino, 19 Dec 1897, Giur. Tor. 1898, 40; Cass. Firenze ,24 Feb 1898, Foro it. 1898 I 322.

659 Ruggiero/Maroi, Instituzioni di diriito privato, Vol II, 2nd edn 1954, p. 474; Chiusi, p. 202.

660 Trimarchi, p. 27 with more references for the prevailing opinion and the dissenting minority view; cf. also Chiusi, p. 207.

661 Corte di Cassazione, sezione III civile; ordinanza 20 febbraio 2023, n. 5222, Foro Italiano 3/2023, 719 et seq.

age cables under that land. FIM offered to bury the cables at her own expense (150.000 EUR) in exchange for re-establishing the old zoning plan and rendering the land buildable again. The cables were laid, but Tavagnacco broke its word and the zoning plan remained. FIM brought an action to assert pre-contractual liability of the community. Alternatively, it based the claim on unjust enrichment. The court of first instance dismissed the claim for pre-contractual liability for lack of proof, but allowed the claim for unjust enrichment. On appeal by the municipality, however, the Court of Appeal of Trieste held the claim for unjust enrichment was barred by residuality. The third section of the Corte agrees with the Court of appeal, but sees itself hindered to reject the appeal because of the restrictive interpretation in the previous jurisdiction of the Corte where it was held that the residuality bar would only apply if an "azione tipica" (= "typical action" arising from the contract or specific legal provisions, but not from general clauses[662]) was available.

From a purely technical perspective, the view of the third section of the Corte seems convincing. The very function of the residuality bar is to avoid the outflanking of legal restrictions on competing actions. However, the fact that the bar should apply in that case only underscores the doubts about the doctrinal classification of the action in question. This is because the case is a straightforward example of a *causa data causa non secuta*. From a teleological perspective, it *must not* be barred just because the also alleged *culpa in contrahendo* cannot be proved. The claim rests solely and directly on the fact that money was spent for an (agreed) purpose that did not materialise. Like in all cases of failure of consideration, that per se

662 See in detail Corte di Cassazione, sezione III civile; ordinanza 20 febbraio 2023, n. 5222, Foro Italiano 3/2023, 719, 721: "La tesi su cui fa affidamento la ricorrente è la seguente. L'azione di arricchimento è residuale solo rispetto ad azioni basate sul contratto o sulla legge (si dice altresì che si tratta di azioni tipiche). Invece se l'azione alternativa è basata su una clausola generale, allora la sua disponibilità non preclude di agire con l'azione di arricchimento. Si legge in Cass. 4620/12, *Foro it.*, Rep. 2012, voce *Arricchimento senza causa*, n. 12, che: "secondo la giurisprudenza di questa corte, questa condizione preclusiva si verifica quando la parte può esercitare, contro l'arricchito o contro altre persone, un'azione tipica, che trovi titolo in un contratto o nella legge (Cass. n. 20747 del 2007, *id.*, Rep. 2007, voce cit., n. 26; n. 11067 del 2003, *id.*, Rep. 2003, voce cit., n. 31; n. 16340 del 2002, *ibid.*, n. 33)"“
[The argument relied on by the plaintiff is as follows. The enrichment action is only residual with respect to actions based on contract or law (it is also said to be typical actions). On the other hand, if the alternative action is based on a general clause, then its availability does not preclude an action of enrichment. It is stated in Cass. 4620/12, *Foro it.*, Rep. 2012, voce *Arricchimento senza causa*, n. 12, that: "according to the jurisprudence of this court, this preclusive condition occurs when the party can exercise, against the enriched party or against other persons, a typical action, which finds its title in a contract or in the law (Cass. n. 20747 del 2007, *id.*, Rep. 2007, voce cit., n. 26; n. 11067 del 2003, *id.*, Rep. 2003, voce cit., n. 31; n. 16340 del 2002, *ibid.*, n. 33).]

suffices to found the claim. It is not necessary to tell any story of fraud, even if there was one. This would only be required for the claim in damages which might then bring further-reaching compensation that covered for example reliance losses in the context of developing and advertising the land. But a fault-based action cannot be the exclusive remedy to simply get one's investment back if the consideration failed. To give another example: Who would deny me the *condictio sine causa* against a person who drank up my Coke simply because I cannot prove that he did so purposely or at least negligently? Should that be sufficient reason to spare him paying for my Coke?[663] I think not.[664]

The case pending before the Corte is paradigmatic for the serious consequences of the unresolved doctrinal frictions caused by the amalgamation of *the actio de in rem verso* with the general enrichment claim. They originated in France. From a historical perspective, the specific *condictiones* had never been subject to any residuality rule – and rightly so, as has just been shown. The subsidiarity bar has no role to play where the issue at stake is that of a (lack of a) causa for a direct shift of wealth. Accordingly, German enrichment law never introduced a rule of residuality.[665] By mixing up the *condictiones* with the *actio de in rem verso* in the bowl of the Pomponian enrichment claim, this insight got lost in Italy and the *condictiones* were accidentally subjected to the subsidiarity that is in truth only apt for the real *actio de in rem verso.*

8 Summary

At the beginning of the 18th century, the first great codifications emerged. They seemed to bring the demise of the Pomponian sentence. None of these codes laid down a general enrichment claim that prohibited to benefit from another's

663 Note however that this example only works in a civil law environment because lack of default would exclude tort liability, whereas under the common law tort of conversion liability would be strict.

664 In the same sense Gaston Rau, De la valeur pratique, at p. 107: "Contre celui-ci, l'équité exigeait un recours; comment en effet laisser quelqu'un dépouiller un tiers par ses propres actes?" [Equity demanded a remedy against him; how could anyone allow a third party to be robbed by his actions?]

665 For sake of accuracy, it should however be mentioned that the prevailing opinion of German jurists assumes priority of performance-related over non-performance related enrichment claims. This looks similar to the subsidiarity bar of enrichment law, but it is not. It is merely based on the technical argument that there can only be the one or the other kind of enrichment and that this must be judged from the perspective of the defendant. Besides, this view is not persuasive, but this cannot be elaborated here. Cf. instead Schall, Leistungskondiktion, pp. 92 et seq.

loss, while all contained the *condictio indebiti*. The *actio de in rem verso* was enshrined in Prussia and Austria, if not closely tied to the Roman paradigm but extended to two-party situations. A century later, the BGB would follow the French example and exclude both the Pomponian sentence and the *actio de in rem verso*, but include all *specific condictiones* and the *condictio sine causa* as small sweeping clause (on this next). If we only looked at the written laws, Pomponius would have died. The only faint reminder being the defence of disenrichment that had been generalised to all *condictiones* in Germany (§ 818 III BGB).

However, the Cour de cassation resurrected the Pomponian principle in France in the arrêt Boudier. From there it spread into other Francophile jurisdictions of Europe, the largest being Italy and Spain. This complemented the parallel emergence of the law of unjustified enrichment in Germany. In a certain sense, the Cour de cassation had anticipated the French-German axis that works as driver in modern Europe. As a result, all civil laws today contain a law of unjust(ified) enrichment as separate and independent source of obligations.

This is well known. It is less well-known that the resurrection of Pomponius was based on judicial overreach. The original aim in France had been to introduce a general *actio de in rem verso utilis*. It was felt that the Code civil contained enough specific claims for the "versum" that the establishment of the general principle was justified in the name of Art. 4 C.civ that prohibited any "deni de justice". This aim had already been accomplished by the end of the 19th century. The *actio de in rem verso* was generally accepted and applied in Courts all over the country, last but not least the Tribunal de Chateauroux, the court of first instance in the Boudier-case. The only open question was the exact doctrinal basis of the claim. After the once predominant *negotiorum gestio* approach had encountered profound criticism (most notably Labbé in the Crédit foncier case and Planiol in the Lemaire case), the Cour de cassation opted for a doctrinal reshuffle. In the arrêt Boudier of 1892, it delivered the simple equation: *actio de in rem verso* = Pomponian prohibition to benefit from another's loss = general enrichment claim. The moral principle of Pomponius had – for the first time – turned into hard law.

By this operation, the Cour de cassation and its suitors in other jurisdictions boldly put aside centuries of reservations of European jurists against using the Pomponian principle as direct cause of action. The Romans had never used it in that way.[666] Nor did the glossators or the postglossators. Rather, as has been shown above, the Pomponian sentence was perceived as a moral principle that handed an equitable tool to correct the strict law. Martinus Gosia was the first to make extensive use of the Pomponian principle for that purpose. And it took

666 See e.g. Gaston Rau, pp. 8–9; Zimmermann, p. 852.

much time, long after his death, before the gist of his teaching eventually gained the upper hand (with the most fertile ground interestingly found in France where centuries later the Pomponian principle would resurge). True, the jurists of the usus modernus began to resort to the Pomponian sentence in their attempt to give contours to the *condictio sine causa specialis.* But the omission from the first codifications showed that this way of thinking was far from generally accepted at the turn of the 19th century.

The arrêt Boudier therefore profoundly changed the traditional role of the Pomponian sentence. The elevation from a moral principle to guide and correct the interpretation of the strict law to a directly applicable cause of action caused severe frictions. The traditional view "too wide and vague" soon held true and forced the Cour de cassation to develop restrictions, most notably the "cause légitime" and the rule of residuality. They may have made the general enrichment claim administrable for legal practice. But they are subject to considerable doubts under the general principles of private law. While a rule of residuality cannot really solve the issue of overreach (stamp case), the *cause légitime* is a doctrinal mix-up of the *actio de in rem verso* and the *condictiones sine causa.* The actio de in rem verso was never based on the lack of a causa, and the concept cannot work in the three party situations typically covered by it.

This is far from saying that equitable remedies can never work as independent "cause of action". But they work differently from strict legal rules. Under the Pomponian brocade, two relatively clear, developed and distinct actions of strict law, the specific *condictiones* and the *actio de in rem verso,* were amalgamated and then topped up with a loose equitable element. This led to frictions that can, in my opinion, no more be solved in a consistent way than a circle be squared. Of course, there is no doubt that the wisdom of the judges in the civil law jurisdictions that followed the French enrichment approach can always be relied upon to achieve reasonable outcomes (as has e. g. been proven in the firefighter case, above p. 166). But a different issue is whether to say "I cannot tell you for sure what unjust enrichment means but I do know it when I see it" really satisfies jurists who agree with Planiol that the law should be understood and practiced as a science.

This critique weighs so much heavier since the Pomponian notion of unjust enrichment has potential to reach far beyond the rare "freak cases" of paying non-existing debts or building on another's land. The Harvard Law Review has given a vivid impression of that. Did not fossil-based industrialization cause man-made climate change? Is therefore not the whole Western world enriched at the expense of the climate victims who predominantly live in the poorer countries of the Global South. If agile human rights lawyers apply Pomponius to this scenario, neither "cause légitime" nor subsidiarity will be of any help. A more structured way forward would arguably have to start with distinguishing the different actions and remedies that are immersed within the general claim:

- The condictiones with their requirements of direct shift of value and lack of causa;
- The *actio de in rem verso* with its leapfrogging function, arguably restricted to gratuitous remote recipients in alignment with the actio Pauliana (p. 200);
- The equitable element of a remedy that may be called upon to fill gaps in the law and avoid a deni de justice (Art. 4 C.civ).

In those latter cases that are purely based on the moral principle not to benefit from another, the application of the general enrichment claim would differ from its "strict law" foundations. To grant an award, the benefit of one party from the loss of another would be necessary but not sufficient. Additional considerations are necessary to balance out whether or not the loss of the claimant be compensated by the enriched defendant.

But be that as it may. The aim of this comparative book is not to invade French law on how to best cope with the heritage of Pomponius. But it must certainly show the way the principle of unjust enrichment has worked from past to present. For English law, the conclusion from the foregoing chapters is to consider carefully whether Pomponius can provide the appropriate guide line for the direct application of the general enrichment claim – this so much the more since England has never felt any desire for having something like the *actio de in rem verso.* The principle no benefit from a loss is too vague and wide to apply word by word. This has been demonstrated by the stamp case, and the argument can be multiplied at will. But as said on that occasion in the beginning, unjust enrichment is not a field of law that can be applied from the dictionary. For French law, the paradigm of the general enrichment claim has always been the *actio de in rem verso.* But this is not the "official" guiding line of the interpretation. It is not the cause, but the effect of the interpretation. This is to be criticised because it blurs the rationale and shape of the enrichment claim. To put it frankly: The turning of the Pomponian sentence into hard law only appears to work in France and Francophile jurisdictions because it is not the general equity of Pomponius, but mainly the clear-cut *actio de in rem verso* that is applied as unjust enrichment.

IV The Pomponius-related extension beyond direct shifts of value and its incompatibility with English unjust enrichment

1 The irreconcilable contradiction of *Banque Financière / Menelaou* and *Costello*

The adoption of Pomponius was directly connected to the extension of the English enrichment claim to remote recipients. The first strong indicator is the similarity of *Banque Financière*[667] and the French *Crédit foncier* case of 1889[668] that has been set out above (p. 151). Just like in the French case, the first question – and arguably the better solution – would have been whether to extend the traditional subrogation rule to cover that case by way of analogy. But both France and England opted for the alternative way to go down the route of unjust enrichment. For France, this was consequential because of its strong affinity to the *actio de in rem verso* that survived both the Ancien Regime and the Napoleonic Codes. For England, it was not because there had never been any comparable claim to remote recipients, openly purporting to leapfrog insolvency risks. The *actio de in rem verso* is rightly rejected as incompatible with common law.[669] But the general enrichment claim based on Pomponius naturally encompasses this claim against remote beneficiaries. That is why its adoption by English common law causes irreconcilable doctrinal frictions. Let us not forget that prior to the arrêt Boudier, *Costello v. MacDonald* was the Law of France, too.[670]

a) *Banque Financière*

The case of *Banque Financière* concerned a refinancing transaction that went wrong. Like in the Crédit foncier case, there would have been a straight forward way to go that would not have posed any problems. But owing to the intended circumvention of Swiss regulatory law, this path was not open.

Banque Financière wanted to refinance (in part) a loan by another bank (RTB). That loan was secured by a first charge. Had Banque Financière simply lent the money to Parc with the purpose to pay off the secured debt to RTB, it would

---

667 *Banque Financière v Parc (Battersea) Ltd* [*1998*] UKHL 7; [1999] AC 221; [*1998*] 1 All ER 737
668 Cass req DP 89.1.393.
669 Restatement (Third), § 4 cmt. B; Andrew Kull, James Barr Ames and the Early Modern History of Unjust Enrichment, 25 Oxford J. Leg. Stud. 297, 313 (2005); Caprice L Roberts, The Restitution Revival, Washington & Lee Law Rev. 1027, 1044 (2011). Criticising the actio de in rem verso as erroneous from the historical perspective Chiusi, pp. 1 et seq. and ff. p. 193 ("somewhat provocative ").
670 Cass civ, 9 May 1853, DP 53.1.251, S.53.1.699.

have been subrogated to the first charge and everything would have been fine. The problem that arose was twofold. First, the loan was not made to Parc but to an intermediary, one Mr Herzig, as conduit-pipe. Second, the advance of the funds was not made subject to any provision of collateral by Parc, but only to the "express condition" that all other intragroup loans would be subordinated to the repayment of Banque Financière. This "promise" was given by the parent in a "postponement letter". The complicated detouring structure was chosen in order to avoid disclosure obligations under Swiss banking regulation that would otherwise have arisen.

The problem of the case was that the parent did not fulfil its "promise". The priority of Banque's claim was never executed vis-à-vis the other companies of the group. When the Omni group collapsed a few months after the transaction, Omnicorp Overseas Limited (OOL), a sister company of Parc, successfully recovered 10 Mio £ on an intra-group loan. That loan had been secured by a second charge. It had ranked behind the loan of RTB that had been paid off with the funds of Banque Financière. Against this, Banque Financière invoked equitable subrogation arguing that otherwise, OOL would be unjustly enriched at their expense. While the Court of Appeal rejected this, the House of Lords accepted the remedy. They might have achieved this by extending the scope of traditional equitable subrogation to cases of "economic claim redemption".[671] But they did not.[672] Instead, they applied equitable subrogation directly as remedy against unjust enrichment under the four-stage-test. By doing so, they extended unjust enrichment to remote recipients. This will be shown next.

b) The acceptance of unjust enrichment against remote beneficiaries

The enrichment claim of Banque Financière against OOL is directed against a remote recipient. This becomes clear if we contrast it with the direct enrichment

671 What happened in the case was in its economic substance not different from the standard cases of subrogation. It does not matter whether security is granted "positively" (e.g. by collateral) or negatively (e.g. by negative pledge clauses). The purpose of the parties in such cases is not to create an unsecured loan, unlike in *Paul v. Speirway Ltd.* [1976] Ch. 220. To hold otherwise misreads the bargain.

The Court of Appeal had denied subrogation also because Banque Financiére would have got something they did not bargain for. However, the same was true for the second lender, Mr Mynor, in *Chetwynd v. Allen* [1899] 1 Ch. 353 as far as the mortgage over the riding school of Mr Chetwynd was concerned.

672 The judgement of Lord Hoffmann comes closest to simply extending the scope of standard equitable subrogation. But he also argues that equitable subrogation in general is based on unjust enrichment: "But the term is also used to describe an equitable remedy to reverse or prevent unjust enrichment which is not based upon any agreement or common intention of the party enriched and the party deprived."

claims that would have lain against Parc and its parent, Omni Holdings AG. Such claims were useless due to the insolvency. But they would have been the only actions available if enrichment actions are limited to direct shifts of value.

The direct shift of wealth in *Banque Financiére* was the 10 Mio £ loan of the bank to the Parc (Battersea) Limited.[673] The purpose was to refinance 10 Mio of a loan from another bank (RTB). As security, the parent company of Parc, Omni Holdings AG had issued a "postponement letter" where it promised to halt the collection of any intragroup loans to Parc until the full repayment to Banque Financière. This basically amounts to contractual subordination. But the promise was not honoured. When the Omnigroup including Parc went into insolvency a few months later, the second rank secured loan of OOL was put back into the money with the funds provided by Banque Financière. When Banque Financière asserted their priority under the postponement letter, it transpired that the parent company had failed to procure the consent of OOL to the subordination of their loan in favour of Banque Financière.

Under a direct shift of value approach, this can only be an unjust enrichment case between Banque Financière and Parc or Omni Holdings. The failure of the repayment of the loan amounts to a total failure of consideration. But this enrichment claim can only hit insolvent Parc. Alternatively, one might argue that there was a total failure of consideration vis-à-vis the parent Omni Holdings AG. The contractual agreement was not entirely clear. According to Lord Hoffman, the promise

673 For regulatory reasons, this loan had to go through one Mr Herzig. This was however deemed irrelevant for the solution by Lord Steyn: "The loan to Mr. Herzig was a genuine one spurred on by the motive of avoiding Swiss regulatory requirements. But it was nevertheless no more than a formal act designed to allow the transaction to proceed. It does not alter the reality that OOL was enriched by the money advanced by BFC via Mr. Herzig to Parc. To allow the interposition of Mr. Herzig to alter the substance of the transaction would be pure formalism."

On the irrelevance of agents interposed as "conduit-pipes" cf. further *Continental Caoutchouc and Gutta Percha Co v Kleinwort, Sons & Co* (1904) 90 LT 474, at p. 476 (per Collins MR): "On the other hand, it is equally clear that an intermediary who has received money for the purpose of handing it on to a third party, and has handed it on, is no longer accountable to the sender. In such case he is a mere conduit-pipe, and has not had the benefit of the windfall." and at p. 477 (per Romer LJ): "When the mistake in fact was discovered the plaintiffs became entitled to recover the moneys from the defendants, unless the defendants could show that they had received the moneys as agents, and before notice of the mistake had parted with them to their principle, or so dealt with them by mandate of their principle as to render it unjust to call upon them to repay the moneys to the plaintiffs."

Further than English law, German law zooms out conduit-pipes completely even before they pass their receipt on, cf. BGH BKR 2021, 516: no enrichment claim against wife who received her husband's overpaid commissions on her private account – although the husband (other than the son-in-law) did not even have access to that account!

by Omni Holdings AG in the postponement letter to subordinate competing intra-group loans to Banque Financière's claim was an "express condition" of the advance. But according to Lord Steyn, Parc was not aware of the postponement letter. So it seems to have been an arrangement between bank and parent. Lenders normally require companies to promise collateral for the extension of a loan. That promise may also be given by a parent, shareholder or director. Instead of collateral, "negative" security can be given as well. Negative pledge clauses are a common example. Contractual subordination of shareholder or intra-group loans is a similar means to the same end. Seen from that angle, the failure of the parent to procure the promised priority of Banque Financiére amounts to a total failure of consideration because Banque received a (now valueless) unsecured claim instead of the secured claim it had bargained for. But an enrichment claim against Omni Holdings AG would not have helped either since the whole group was insolvent.

If enrichment claims were strictly limited to direct shifts of value, that would have been it. The flaw in the transaction is located between Banque Financière and Parc / Omni Holdings AG. The contentious issue of piercing the corporate veil aside, the failure of the agreement should be of no consequence for any third party under the general principles of party autonomy. Private people can create rights and obligation by their consensus – but not at the expense of anybody else.

It is only with the help of the Pomponius that any enrichment of the other subsidiaries within the group can come into the line of fire. This is what happened to OOL. Benefits from the partial refinancing of the RTB loan accrue to OOL. This opens the case for a Pomponian enrichment claim based on the detriment of another's loss (as had happened in the civilian Helmstedt case above p. 114): Banque Financière suffered a loss. The beneficiary of this loss is OOL because, as Lord Steyn said, "the repayment of 10 Mio £ of the loan pro tanto improved OOL's position as chargee." The benefit of OOL is caused by the loss of Banque Financière. The unjust factor is the mistaken assumption of Banque Financière to be secured under the postponement letter when it handed out the funds.[674] As a result, the House of Lords held that the unjust enrichment of OOL can be recovered by Banque Financière via the remedy of equitable subrogation. But this line of argument collides with *Costello v MacDonald.*[675]

---

674 It should be noted that under the German failure of purpose approach (see below, pp. 309 et seq.), no unjust factor vis-à-vis the subsidiaries would lie because the bank did not pursue any purpose towards them.

675 *Costello v MacDonald Dickens and Macklin [2011]* EWCA Civ 930; see also *Brown & Davis Ltd v Galbraith* [1972] EWCA Civ J0426–2 (an insurer had the car of its customer repaired after an acci-

c) The collision with *Costello v MacDonald*

In *Costello v MacDonald*, builders (MacDonald Dickens & Macklin) had contracted with a company (Oakwood) for works carried out on the land of Mr. and Mrs Costello who owned Oakwood.[676] When Oakwood did not (and could not) pay, the builders turned to the Costellos to recover their unjust enrichment. They, too, had suffered a loss (non-payment of the works). The Costellos had been enriched by those works (improvement of their land). The unjust factor could be seen in the unconscionability of the Costellos hiding behind the corporate veil to get the benefit for free.[677] Alternatively, it might have been the mistaken assumption of Oakwood's readiness / ability to pay.

The county court had accordingly allowed the enrichment claim of the builders against the couple. On appeal of the Costellos, a unanimous Court of Appeal rejected the claim. There is not much to add to the reasons given by Lord Justice Elverton:

> Para. 4: "The issue of principle on the appeal is whether Mr and Mrs Costello can be held liable in restitution for unjust enrichment when the services of the respondents from which they have benefited were given pursuant to a contract between a third party, Oakwood, and the respondents."
>
> Para. 15: "There can be no doubt that Mr and Mrs Costello have benefited from, or in restitutionary terms, have been enriched by, the work carried out by the respondents on the Site."
>
> Para. 20: "The submission gives rise to two points of legal principle. The first is whether, in terms of causation, Mr and Mrs Costello's enrichment can be said to have been at the expense of the respondents. In one sense, of course, it was. The respondents have provided the services which have benefited Mr and Mrs Costello, and for which they expected to be paid, but they have not been paid. On the other hand, those services were provided solely because of, and pursuant to a contract between the respondents and Oakwood. Mr and Mrs Costello have been enriched because Oakwood has allowed the benefit of the contract to be conferred on them. The benefit has, in that way, come directly from Oakwood and only indirectly from the respondents. The question is whether the respondents should be permitted to leapfrog Oakwood in order to claim against Mr and Mrs Costello."
>
> Para. 21: "The second point of principle is whether a restitutionary claim should be allowed to undermine the contract between Oakwood and Mr and Mrs Costello, that is to say the way in which the parties chose to allocate the risks involved in the transaction. The parties arranged the transaction as one in which legally enforceable promises were made only between Oak-

---

dent but failed to pay. The claim against the owner of the car was denied) and the Australian case *Lumbers v W Cook Builders Pty Ltd* [2008] HCA 27, 232 CLR 635.

676 Note that no issue of piercing the corporate veil was raised – and probably could not have been. *Prest v Petrodel* [2013] UKSC 32 decided that veil-piercing would basically only be available if a pre-existing liability was evaded. That is not what the Costellos did.

677 Note that this line of argument was rejected by the Court of Appeal.

> wood and the respondents, even though the benefit of the contract was to be conferred on Mr. and Mrs. Costello. The obligation to pay for the respondents' services, and so the risk of non-payment, was contractually confined to Oakwood. If a claim was permitted directly against Mr and Mrs Costello, it would shatter that contractual containment."
>
> Finally, at para. 23: "**I am clear.. that the unjust enrichment claim against Mr. and Mrs. Costello must fail because it would undermine the contractual arrangements between the parties**, that is to say the contract between the respondents and Oakwood and the absence of any contract between the respondents and Mr and Mrs Costello. **The general rule should be to uphold contractual arrangements** that have defined and allocated and, to that extent, restricted their mutual obligations, and, in so doing, **have** similarly **allocated and circumscribed the consequences of non-performance.**"

In denying the claim against the beneficiaries of the works, *Costello* followed highest authority. This is important to note because otherwise, any conflict with the House of Lords in *Banque Financière* would be dissolved by rank.

> *Costello v MacDonald*, Para. 24: "In *Hampton v Glamorgan* [1916] AC 13 the appellant was a subcontractor who carried out work for a school built for the respondent pursuant to a lump sum contract between the respondent and the main contractor. The main contractor having failed to pay and having become insolvent and unable to pay, the appellant sued the respondent for the unpaid balance of his fee. The House of Lords held that, as the main contractor had not acted as the respondent's agent, the appellant could not recover from the respondent."[678]

---

678 Lord Justice Elverton also relied on *PanOcean Shipping Co Ltd v Creditcorp Ltd, The Trident* [1994] 1 WLR 161. This is in so far correct as that judgement was also based on the argument not to stir up the contractual agreements (per Lord Goff, at pp. 164–166). However, Creditcorp was directly enriched by the payment of PanOcean. The direct receipt of a payment by an assignee cannot be qualified as remote enrichment without drifting into an insolvable paradox (see also p. 312 and p. 319). These difficulties can only be overcome by understanding that every performance is the direct shift of value to be undone. Otherwise, the interpretation of "at the expense" will run loose.

As to the role of "at the expense" see *Banque Financière De La Cité v. Parc (Battersea) Ltd and Others* [1998] UKHL 7 = 1 AC 221, 237 (per Lord Clyde); *Uren v First National Home Finance Ltd* [2005] EWHC 2529, para. 24; *The Investment Trust Companies* v HMRC [2017] UKSC 29; calling for flexibility that is however hard to entertain at law *Relfo Ltd v Varsani* [2014] EWCA Civ 360; *Lowick Rose LLP v Swynson Ltd* [2017] UKSC 32; [2018] AC 313 at para. 22; *Dargamo Holdings Limited v Avonwick Holdings Limited* [2021] EWCA Civ 1149, at para. 56.

See also the clear position expressed by Burrows, *A Restatement of the English Law of Unjust Enrichment*, 2012, p. 44: "The defendant's enrichment is at the expense of the claimant if the benefit obtained by the defendant is … directly from the claimant rather than by way of another person."; id., *Restitution*, p. 69 ff..

Laying the foundations Peter Birks, "At the expense of the claimant: direct and indirect enrichment in English law", in: Johnston & Zimmermann, *Unjustified Enrichment*, 2002, p. 494; id.,

If *Costello* is right, *Banque Financière* must be wrong. The two cases can neither be distinguished nor reconciled under a general claim in unjust enrichment. In both cases, valid contracts between two parties exist. Macdonald contracted for works with Oakwood. Banque Financière extended a loan (via Mr Herzig) to Parc. In both cases, benefits accrue to a third party. The works improve the land of the Costellos. The funds from the loan are used to pay off RTB and thereby revaluate the second rank claim of OOL. In both cases, the contract is breached. Oakwood did not pay the work. Parc did not repay the loan (and Omni Holdings AG did not remove the priority of the subsidiaries' claims). In both cases, the contractual arrangements define the mutual obligations and thereby "allocate and circumscribe the consequences of non-performance". It follows that in both cases, the contractual arrangements must not be undermined.

Costello explicitly rejected leapfrogging via a claim in unjust enrichment. This very argument would have stood in the way of the subrogation in *Banque Fiancière.* The only discernible differences were pure technicalities: *Costello* concerned a contract for work whereas *Banque Financière* was about a loan. In *Costello,* the plaintiffs brought a money claim to reverse the unjust enrichment whereas in *Banque Financière,* the remedy was subrogation. But if the basis for the award is the four stage test of unjust enrichment, these points do not justify any different treatment.

This is not to say that *Banque Financière* cannot stand at all. As indicated above, there would have been as good arguments to extend the remedy of subrogation as in Crédit foncier.[679] In Crédit foncier, it should not have mattered if the loan was paid off directly or if the funds to do so were channelled through the pockets of the debtor. English law would not have made that distinction to award subrogation. But it contained another trap that should have been overcome. In *Banque Financière,* it should not have made a difference whether the envisaged security was to be provided "positively" as collateral or guarantee or "negatively" by negative pledge clauses or contractual subordination.

But be all that as it may: the solution of *Banque Fiancière* cannot be based simply on the unjust enrichment by benefitting from another's loss without contradicting *Costello,* and doing so irreconcilably. If the four-stage test suffices to trigger a remedy, it must do so in both cases. So much the more since the issue replicated in *Menelaou.*[680] The Bank of Cyprus had made the following bargain with the parents:

Unjust Enrichment, S. 89 ff.; cf. further Virgo, pp. 104 et seq.; in German: Solomon, pp. 213 et seq.; Rademacher, at p. 32.

679 Above p. 145.

680 *Bank of Cyprus UK Ltd v Menelaou* [2015] UKSC 66.

release of the "old" charge over the land that was to be sold on in turn for granting a "new" charge over the land that was to be acquired. The parents breached the contract and did not procure the new charge. The children reaped the benefits because the newly bought land was gifted to them without encumbrance. Applying Pomponian enrichment, the bank can recover the unjust enrichment from the children. But following the argument in *Costello*, the bank can have no claim because the contractual risk allocation must not be undermined.

The reason for the conflicting case law is the overreach of the Pomponian principle. The only cure is to renege on it and to restrict enrichment claims to direct shifts of value. Lord Justice Elverton considered doing so, but eventually abstained.

> Para. 22: "...I do not propose, therefore, to examine further whether the appeal should be allowed simply on the basis that there can be no claim against Mr. and Mrs. Costello for unjust enrichment since that enrichment was only indirectly from the respondents."

The judicial self-restraint was necessary because the precedents were (and are) not clear. However, the restriction of enrichment claims to direct shifts of value is the better approach *pro futuro*. The test for this is: Should *Costello* have had a different outcome if MacDonald & Co had been able to rescind the contract? Or if the contract had been invalid from the outset? The answer must surely be no. The flaw of the transaction, i.e. the unjust factor, only plays out between the parties of the invalid contract. There is no case for restitution against the remote recipient. As just said above with regard to French law: The contract between A and B is of no consequence for C. Its existence cannot explain *why C should keep the enrichment.* Conversely, its absence cannot explain *why C should disgorge the benefit to A.*

d) The direct shift of value in *Lowick Rose v Swynson*

The need for a strict directness requirement is also confirmed by *Lowick Rose* v *Swynson.*[681] This is a difficult case because the solution of the antecedent legal issue, the extinction or not of the damages claim in the course of the restructuring, is fraught with difficulties. The case concerned the liability claim of a company (Swynson) against its accountants (now Lowick Rose, originally "HMT") who had breached their contractual duty of care negligently. Swynson, owned by Mr. Hunt, ran a vulture fund. It had financed the MBO of a medical company (Evo) via a SPV, EMSL. The loans extended for that purpose to the EMSL became ailing because the target Evo was less viable than the financial due diligence had shown.

681 *Lowick Rose LLP (in liquidation) v. Swynson* Ltd [2017] UKSC 32.

Eventually, the transaction was refinanced in the following way. Mr. Hunt took on the ailing loan personally. For that purpose, he extended a new loan to EMSL that was used to pay off the debt to Swynson. But as it turned out, Mr Hunt had shot himself into the foot because when the debt to Swynson had been repaid, the damage to the company was healed and the claim against the accountants extinct. As a result, the Lowick Rose were relieved from their liability.

On a side note, this issue was very contentious and with respect, the solution of the Supreme Court cannot entirely convince. From an economic perspective, the transaction amounted to the assignment of an ailing claim to the shareholder in return for the full nominal value. That is a transaction at an undervalue, just in the reverse of the normal direction. It does not (unlawfully) return capital to the shareholder but injects fresh capital. After the financial crisis, this had been done multiple times by private actors as well as states. Foul assets were disposed with "bad banks". Such rescue transfers must not have erased claims in damages against reckless directors and officers.

As a result from the Supreme Court's assumption, the accountants were enriched by the "disappearance" of the damages claim. This happened at the expense of Mr. Hunt who had given full value for the "damaged" claim, with a view to later recovery of his loss via the damages claim. That was a mistaken assumption because, as just shown, the damages claim had actually become erased by the transfer. The benefit of the accountants was caused by the loss of Mr Hunt. It was of course incidental. This was the ground on which the Supreme Court denied the enrichment claim. But that cannot be the right ground. If funds are wired to the wrong person's bank account, that person's enrichment is as incidental as that of the accountants. But this is no reason to deny restitution. The better argument to deny the claim is the indirectness of the enrichment. The direct shift of value was the payment for the foul claim. The accountants were not the recipients of this transfer.

2 The origin of remoteness – *Lipkin Gorman v Karpnale*

Modern English law of unjust enrichment was rolled out in *Banque Financière*. But the precursor that initiated the development was *Lipkin Gorman*.[682] Not only did it introduce the language of unjust enrichment and the characteristic defence change of position / disenrichment previously denied in the law of restitution. Arguably, the enrichment claim was directed against a remote beneficiary. If we "pierce

682 *Lipkin Gorman (a firm) v Karpnale Ltd* [1991] 2 AC 548.

the veil" of tracing and following,[683] we may recognise an overarching rationale that binds together *Lipkin Gorman, Banque Financière* and *Menelaou:* the restitution of gratuities on the backs of third parties.

Leaving aside the tracing exercise in *Lipkin Gorman*, direct shifts of value took place (a) between the bank and Cass when the bank transferred the title to the cash that Cass had withdrawn from the solicitors' account[684] and (b) between Lipkin Gorman and Cass when Cass traded in their book money for the cash. Under both perspectives, the Casino (Karpnale) was a remote recipient. Since gambling contracts were generally void prior to the Gambling Act 2005, it was also a volunteer.[685] A better explanation for *Lipkin Gorman* may therefore be found in the prohibition of gratuities at the expense of third parties. This aspect may help to explain the remote enrichment cases. On the flip side, it would also turn the tables on *Macdonald v Costello.* The decision looks far less persuasive once we realise that the Costellos received a gift from their company that was actually made out of the pockets of the company's creditor.

3 The "equitable element" inherent in wide unjust enrichment: no gratuity at the expense of third parties

Lipkin Gorman, Banque Financière and *Menelaou* have in common that they award enrichment claims against **remote** recipients whose benefits were gratuitous. These characteristics may be indicators for the existence of a legal principle in English law that has been detected and described by German lawyers as *Schwäche des unentgeltlichen Erwerbs* (i. e. the weakness of gratuitous receipts).[686] It is enshrined in a wide range of legal rules of both civil law and common law jurisdictions, most notably in the defences of "bona fide purchase for value"[687] or "good

---

683 "Following is the process of following the same asset as it moves from hand to hand. Tracing is the process of identifying a new asset as the substitute for the old", according to Lord Millet in *Foskett v McKeown* [2001] 1 AC 102.

684 Authority for this proposition is *Banque Belge pour l'Etranger v. Hambrouck* [1921] 1 K.B. 321. Contrast Stevens, pp. 207–208, assuming a direct shift from Lipkin Gorman to Karpnale because of joint tenancy of the funds.

685 *Lipkin Gorman (a firm) v Karpnale Ltd* [1991] 2 AC 548 (per Lord Goff).

686 Harke in BeckOGK BGB, § 525 mn. 14; Jens Koch in MünchKommBGB, Vol. 4/2, 9th edn. 2023, § 516 mn. 3 and § 528 mn. 2.

687 The defence is accepted in English case law and under statutory law, cf. e. g. s.241(2)(a) and (b); s.425(2)(a) and (b) IA 1986. In Germany, it is derived from the combination of §§ 932 – 934 BGB (bona fide acquisition of title) and § 816 I 1 BGB (no restitution to previous owner if title was acquired for

consideration", but also in manifold provisions of insolvency laws to avoid transactions detrimental to the creditors. The central idea underlying the weakness of gratuities is *en passant* expressed in the definition of a donation in § 516 BGB:

> § 516 I BGB: "Eine Zuwendung, durch die jemand **aus seinem Vermögen** einen anderen bereichert, ist Schenkung, wenn beide Teile darüber einig sind, dass die Zuwendung unentgeltlich erfolgt."
>
> [A transfer by which someone enriches another person **from their own assets** is a gift if both parties agree that the transfer is made free of charge – based on Deep-L]

This provision expresses the principle that gifts must come out of one's own pocket. They must not be made at somebody else's expense. That principle is strongly at work in insolvency law because the inability of the debtor to pay his debts is proof that the gift was made on the back of the creditors.[688]

The weakness of gratuitous receipts has historically been connected with the Pomponian principle of unjust enrichment. The tentative thesis put forward here is that preventing gratuity at the expense of third parties has been hidden under various legal remedies at common law as well as civil law and more importantly, that it has been the driver to apply the Pomponian principle directly. The two most ancient examples may be the *actio Pauliana* and the *actio de in rem verso.* These two remedies have later been covered by the equitable cloak of Pomponian unjust enrichment. The example of France has demonstrated both: The *actio de in rem verso* finally immersed in Pomponian enrichment. And it aimed at gratuities of third parties earned on the back of the claimants.

The unjust enrichment qualification is also true, if less known, for the *actio Pauliana.* Once upon a time, when Germany still believed in Pomponius, the *actio Pauliana* was perceived as an enrichment claim.[689] This notion of old is still reflected under current German insolvency law that protects innocent recipients of gifts with a change of position defence against the claw back by the liquidator:

---

value) and § 816 I 2 BGB (enrichment claim of the previous owner against the gratuitous acquirer of title).

688 Both the US Bankruptcy Coe and the Insolvency Act 1986 demand expressly that the gift was made in or led to the insolvency of the company: s.240(2)(a) and (b) IA 1986; 11. USC § 548(a)(1)(B)(i)(I) – as if otherwise, gifts from companies during the twilight period were a good thing happily to be accepted by the shortened creditors. The better approach is to render every gift in the twilight period challengeable, like is e.g. the case in Germany.

689 See the reference at v.Kübel, Motive zum Vorentwurf, p. 12 who himself had already reneged on Pomponius.

§ 143 II InsO: "Der Empfänger einer unentgeltlichen Leistung hat diese nur zurückzugewähren, soweit er durch sie bereichert ist. Dies gilt nicht, sobald er weiß oder den Umständen nach wissen muß, daß die unentgeltliche Leistung die Gläubiger benachteiligt."

[**The recipient of a gratuitous benefit only has to return it if he is enriched by it.** This does not apply as soon as the recipient knows or must know from the circumstances that the gratuitous benefit is detrimental to the creditors. – Deep-L]

The unjust enrichment stories of the *actio de in rem verso* and the *actio Pauliana* raise a suspicion. The sound principle "no gratuity on the back of third parties" has never been spelled out openly. It has been overlaid by remedies with a wider scope and other specifications. This is particularly true for the *actio Pauliana.* That action would typically target fraud: the hiding of assets with family and friends to save them from the creditors. That is why fraud is sought where the gratuity as such should be sufficient. This is not only so in civil law. The same idea surfaces recurrently under common law. For example, some important cases before *Macdonald v Costello* were argued on propriety estoppel and accordingly searched for unconscionable conduct (which the judges were surprisingly unable to find in *Macdonald v Costello*[690]). The same is true for insolvency law. The making of a gift at the expense of the creditors[691] is apparently not enough. It must also be done with malicious intent (e.g. s.423 IA 1986 – Transactions defrauding creditors; 11. USC § 548 – fraudulent transfers).[692] However, the reason for the specific provision to restore the gift is not really the fraud (there is not always malign intent) nor the *par conditio creditorum* (gifts have no creditors) but the fact that in reality, this gratuity came from the assets of the creditors. To accommodate this rationale, jurisdictions either resort to fictions like "constructive fraud" (cp. 11. USC § 548(a)(1)(B)) or sanction gifts / transactions at an undervalue[693] when made within a twilight period.[694]

The gratuity of the benefit of the remote recipient has carried the *actio de in rem verso,* too. As Labbé rightly said about the loss of Crédit foncier that benefitted the minors:[695]

"...ce dégrèvement est le résultat d'un déboursé fait par le credit foncier sans aucun espirit de donation."

690 How is it not unconscionable of the owners to force their company to give them precious presents at the expense of its creditors?

691 s.423(1)(a) IA 1986.

692 s.423(3) IA; likewise the *Vorsatzanfechtung* under § 133 InsO and preferences under s.239(5) IA 1986.

693 s.238 IA 1986 – Transactions at an undervalue; § 134 InsO – *Schenkungsanfechtung.*

694 s.240(1) IA: two years; 11. USC § 548(a)(1): two years; § 134 InsO: 4 years.

695 Labbé, S.90.1.97.

> [.. this decrease of assets is the result of a payment that was made by Crédit foncier without any liberal intention]

It must be borne in mind that to succeed the classic *actio de in rem verso* required the receipt of a benefit by the pater familias (p. 132). Again, the remedy was defined by other requirements and considerations (agency law, tripartite situations, "my money got to you so you have to restore it"). But when the *actio de in rem verso* immersed in the Pomponian principle, the gratuities at the expense of others became a case of unjust enrichment.

Now a new problem arose. It was no longer an issue that the gift *per se* was not enough to found the enrichment claim. Rather, the neuralgic point was that the principle "no benefit from another's loss" was too wide to apply directly in *other* cases – as the stamp case shows. This new problem can only by solved if "no gratuities at the expense of third parties" is recognised as starting point of the legal – or better: equitable – principle at work in these cases.

At the end of the day, it seems safe to say that the only *true* case, the very raison d'être of wide enrichment is undoing gratuities at the expense of third parties. The unfairness of the free benefit from the other's loss seems a perfectly fitting, probably the best or even the only justification for restitution. This case differs profoundly from the reversal of failed transfers and the recovery of value taken that are both restricted to the parties of the direct shift of value and can be explained by the lack or vitiation of consent. And not only does it differ in scope and rationale, but also in the shape and nature of the claim. As will be shown next, it is a close relative to the general issue when gratuities can be revoked. That topic poses problems that differ from non-consent cases and are ideally covered by equitable remedies.

4 The equitable issues surrounding the restorations of gifts

a) Gifts and disenrichment – a marriage of old

The close link between the Pomponian principle and the extension of enrichment claims to remote volunteers is no coincidence. From a historical perspective, the disenrichment defence is rooted in the restoration of gifts. This is where it is most persuasive. The starting point are two distinctive features of Roman law. The *rei vindicatio* and the illegality of gifts between spouses.[696] Under Roman law, spouses were not allowed to make gifts – basically a patriarchal rule that for-

696 D.24.1.1 (Ulp 32 ad Sab).

bade the husband / *pater familias* to syphon the family's fortune into the "wrong" pockets. Since the rule prevented title from passing, the illicit gift could be recovered by the *rei vindicatio*. However, if the asset was no longer existing, the *condictio sine causa* would lie and ask for surviving enrichment. It is right here that the *bona fide* recipient deserves – and was granted – protection. You may have to return the gift, sad as that may be. But you should not have to pay for the gift with your own money because you never agreed to pay for it. In other words: There was no **spending decision** you can – and must – be held to (see in detail pp. 295 et seq.).

It follows that if the gift was lost, no enrichment would survive and the wife could not be sued. If it was stolen, she would have to cede her potential claims against the thief (this is explicitly ordered by § 818 I BGB[697]) but otherwise left alone. To take a modern example, one containing a non-reciprocal benefit: if you have been overpaid pension for several years (e.g. 2.500 instead of 2.000 £), you may have adopted a certain life style in your justified faith on the availability of that monthly income. Why should you now be pushed into debt to make good what was clearly the mistake of the pension fund. However, if you adhered to a frugal lifestyle in order to save money for your children, you cannot be spared from returning the surplus. The overpayment still persists in your assets, so you are not disenriched, only disappointed.

By contrast, the defence of disenrichment has far less justification in the realm of failed transactions. *Fibrosa v Fairbairn*[698] shows that any deductions for work done or expenses spent would undermine the fact that the contractual promise has not been fulfilled and the agreed counter-performance has not been earned. Again, it is not coincidental that restitution of failed transactions has not been subject to a disenrichment defence for a long time in both common law and civil law. But there *is* a useful function in the reversal of failed transactions, and that is why both common and (German) civil law were right to extend the defence of disenrichment to these cases, too.

The key is the (lack of a) spending decision. Normally, I cannot claim that I have not become richer by a haircut because I received value. Full stop. My decision to invest into my looks does not swell my assets. But that does not allow me to

---

697 "Die Verpflichtung zur Herausgabe erstreckt sich auf die gezogenen Nutzungen sowie auf dasjenige, was der Empfänger auf Grund eines erlangten Rechts oder als Ersatz für die Zerstörung, Beschädigung oder Entziehung des erlangten Gegenstands erwirbt." [The **obligation to surrender extends** to the **benefits** derived as well as **to that which the recipient acquires** on the basis of a right obtained or **as compensation for the** destruction, damage or **dispossession of the item** originally obtained. – based on Deep-L]
698 [1942] UKHL 4.

deny that I actually received value – just like I could not deny that I am enriched by a purchase of apples only because I have eaten them up or let them perish in my fruit bowl. Change of position is not meant to save me from accounting for value I wanted to buy and actually received. It is meant to save me from paying for what I never intended to pay for. That is why its main function lies in the area of gratuities or non-reciprocal payments (life insurances; pensions).

Unjust enrichment offers following construction to uphold the spending decision. Since I would have cut my hair or bought the apples anyway, the receipt under the invalid contract spared me the expenses under a valid contract. But this is a detour that should not be necessary. Suffice to say that I received the value I wanted and must therefore account for it. Even though the contract may have been void, I must not deny that the exchange actually took place. Note that this does not mean the voidness of the contract is ignored. Since I only must account for the objective value of the service or the good I received, I will be relieved of a bad bargain (but lose a good bargain in the converse case).[699]

However, if I was incapable, or a minor, or led to believe that the haircut was a freebie, I did not make that decisive spending decision in a way that the law could hold me to it. Now the question arises: Did I get richer? The answer is: Yes, if I saved expenses I would otherwise have had to incur (because I would normally have gone to my hairdresser the next day, as I do every other week). No, if it was a random luxury (because my mother normally gives me a bowl cut).

The same solution applies to the exchange of goods. Assume the contract is invalid. I bought the car and crashed it into the bridge. Now I claim my money back under the *condictio indebiti* / action for money had and received under mistake. The vendor claims back the car. I cannot invoke disenrichment because I had received the value I bargained for (just like the hair cut). That was my spending decision, and I must stick to it. Subsequently driving the car into the bridge is not so different from eating up the apple and surely equates with letting the apples rot. It is something that only happened because I made a disposition concerning the use of the good I bought (I could have left the car in my garage and used public transport; I could have driven more carefully). By contrast, if I was defrauded by the vendor, the spending decision will not be held against me. Only now can I claim that I am not enriched anymore because I lost the car I bought. This is the solution that almost all German lawyers reach even if their arguments vary in detail.[700]

---

699 This is where German Bereicherungsrecht differs from German *Rücktrittsrecht* pursuant to §§ 346–354 BGB. The latter even upholds the contractually agreed values to execute the contract de facto. The reason for the difference is that in cases of § 346 BGB, the contract is valid.

700 Fundamental arguments were made by Flume, FS Niedermeyer, 1953, 103 = Studien, p. 27. See in detail below, pp. 295 et seq.

If we contemplate the disenrichment / change of position defence from this angle, it loses the air of a loose equity covering up for sloppiness of thought. The principles at hand become clear and can be translated into hard law, be it under strict law or equity. There is no more need for any comprehensive weighing and balancing the merits of the individual case.

The first rule is that spending decisions must be recognised and not be overturned by the law of unjust enrichment. That reduces the scope of disenrichment to a small circle of defendants: Volunteers plus everyone who cannot be kept to the spending decision made. In such cases, the focus shifts to the "natural enrichment". Here, the second rule comes into play: The claimant has induced trust of the defendant to keep what was received. Conversely, the defendant has done nothing wrong. Unjust enrichment is a liability based on a wrong state of things, not on conduct or even misconduct by the defendant. Therefore, the law does not "punish" the *bona fide* defendant with a duty to compensate the loss. The loss is shifted to the claimant because it would not have hit the defendant had the claimant not created trust.

That said, it should have become clear that we do not need the principle formulated by Pomponius to justify the defence of unjust enrichment. The refinement of concepts like estoppel (England) or the *Vertrauenshaftung* (Germany) could have led us there, too. This is not how it worked. It would be historically incorrect to "cancel" the decisive role of Pomponius-induced thinking in terms of equity. The equitable mindset of unjust enrichment was the driver that made the disenrichment defence grow into ubiquity.[701] But the exercise of reverse engineering assures us that we do not have to rely on this rationale any more. The defence of disenrichment in the sense of "not having benefitted from an act / event" is a legal concept that is not indivisibly linked to the moral principle not to benefit from another's loss. If leapfrogging the peculium via the *actio de in rem verso* was only justified by a benefit of the *pater familias*, the lack or loss of this benefit would necessarily bring the claim down. If the rule is "no benefit from a wrong", the claim to skim off such profits will only lie as long as ill-gotten gains remain in the hands of the wrongdoer. This holds true for profit skimming under both private and criminal law.[702] If the action of money had and received in Lipkin Gorman is based on following and tracing the title to the book money (see below pp. 216 et seq.), it must fail if that title gets lost. If the *rei vindicatio* is based on possession without entitlement, it must cease to apply if the defendant loses possession.

701 Also Zimmermann, p. 900.

702 As to skimming of criminal profits under German § 73 I StPO, see the disenrichment defence in the old § 459 g V StPO. The provision was modified in 2021 without changing the core content, see BGH NZG 2024, 596, 599.

The first reason why gifts must be in the centre of the disenrichment defence has thus become clear. The defendant / recipient did not make a spending decision that the law must keep him to in order to avoid the shifting of the negative consequences to the claimant.

b) Most reasons for reversing gifts are of equitable nature

The other reason why gifts and equity are closely related is the fact that the common or garden unjust factors do not really explain the reversal of gratuities. Starting point here is the thesis that the general unjust factor at the bottom of unjust enrichment is the failure of purpose, mirrored in the common law failure of consideration. In case of a gift, there is no consideration so that this will not apply. The same is true for mistake if it is understood, as it should be from the historic perspective, as liability mistake. The only conceivable application would be a payment or transfer on a deed that was somehow invalid(ated) so that in truth, no liability arose under it. One might counter that mistake is not reduced to liability mistake, and that it is therefore *the* unjust factor to cover mistakes.[703] But that does not hold true either because simple unilateral mistakes do not suffice. I cannot return and demand the pound coin back from the beggar just because I need it for the trolley, having mistakenly assumed I'd have another coin with me. This is not in doubt.[704] The first authority was the statement of Linley L.J. in *Ogilvie v Littleboy:* [705]

> "Gifts cannot be revoked, nor can deeds of gift be set aside, simply because the donors wish they had not made them and would like to have back the property given. Where there is no fraud, no undue influence, no fiduciary relation between donor and donee,[17] no mistake induced by those who derive any benefit by it, a gift, whether by mere delivery or by deed, is binding on the donor. ... In the absence of all such circumstances of suspicion a donor can only obtain back property which he has given away by showing that he was under some mistake of so serious a character as to render it unjust on the part of the donee to retain the property given to him."

---

703 See e. g. Birke Häcker, "Mistaken Gifts after Pitt v Holt", (2014) 67 Current Legal Problems 333–372.

704 For another example cf. Burrows, Restatement, p. 66 example 7: Someone donates to the Red Cross mistakenly believing that the mayor and vicar have also made donations.

Contrast however the case that the collector has led the donator into the mistaken belief. According to an old judgment from Bavaria (that is however rejected by most criminal lawyers today), doing so will amount to fraud if the donator gives more than he had otherwise done, BayObLG Bay NJW 1952, 798.

705 *Ogilvie v Littleboy* (1897) 13 TLR 399 (CA), affirmed sub nom *Ogilvie v Allen* (1899) 15 TLR 294 (HL)

This was picked up and refined in the leading case from 2013, *Pitt v Holt*, at para 114 (per Lord Walker):[706]

> The fact that a unilateral mistake is sufficient (without the additional ingredient of misrepresentation or fraud) to make a gift voidable has been attributed to gifts being outside the law's special concern for the sanctity of contracts (O'Sullivan, Elliott and Zakrzewski, The Law of Rescission (2007) para 29.22):
>
> 'It is apparent from the foregoing survey that vitiated consent permits the rescission of gifts when unaccompanied by the additional factors that must be present in order to render a contract voidable. The reason is that the law's interest in protecting bargains, and in the security of contracts, is not engaged in the case of a gift, even if made by deed.'
>
> Conversely, the fact that a purely unilateral mistake may be sufficient to found relief is arguably a good reason for the court to apply a more stringent test as to the seriousness of the mistake before granting relief.

The reversal of gifts is shifted to equity, and the unjust factor of mistake is restricted to grave mistakes. The Supreme Court also delivered a formula to implement that restraint:

> *Pitt v Holt*, at para. 122 (per Lord Walker): "I would provisionally conclude that the true requirement is simply for there to be a **causative mistake of sufficient gravity**; and, as additional guidance to judges in finding and evaluating the facts of any particular case, that the test will normally be satisfied only when there is a mistake either as to the legal character or nature of a transaction, or as to some matter of fact or law which is **basic to the transaction.**
>
> …
>
> At para. 126: "The injustice (or unfairness or unconscionableness) of leaving a mistaken disposition uncorrected must be evaluated objectively, but with an intense focus (in Lord Steyn's well-known phrase in In re S (A Child) [2005] 1 AC 593, para 17) on the facts of the particular case."

There has an argument been made that *Pitt v Holt* only relates to equitable restitution.[707] But the recognition that a simple "but for"-test cannot suffice (see the trolley example above) applies with the same force to both law and equity. To be sure, gifts can be flawed in a similar way as contracts, e.g. if made by incapables or minors or induced by fraud. These cases will and should be covered by strict law, one way or another. The want of the transaction will normally prevent title from passing and shift the case to proprietary remedies (as to money see

706 *Pitt v Holt* (consolidated appeal with *Futter v Futter*) [2013] UKSC 26, [2013] 2 AC 108.
707 This argument was prominently made by former Chancellor and Master of the Rolls, Terence Etherton, 'The Role of Equity in Mistaken Transactions' (2013) 27 TLI 159.

below pp. 216 et seq.). That may bring the tort of conversion into play. A payment on a void deed can even found an action for money had and received for a (liability) mistake. But all those examples are rare and more or less academic.[708] At the very heart of restitution lie cases where it would be *unfair* to uphold the gift. And that is a matter of fairness.

Accordingly, equity takes care of these issues under English law. Take for example the unjust factor of "undue influence". As a label, it mingles with other unjust factors (mistake; failure of consideration; extortion) that are linked with the strict law action for money had and received that undo failed transactions. But in reality, it requires a completely different call. The lines must be drawn case by case on the merits. There can never be a clear-cut abstract distinction when a donation is duly influenced and when it is unduly influenced. This makes it a question of equity.[709] Once it is determined that the influence was undue, restitution will follow. But equity does not need a strict law action for this.

The thesis of a special law for gifts is confirmed by the comparative perspective to Germany.[710] The civilian construction of gifts as a *Vertrag* (= "contract" or rather, binding agreement) provides a different doctrinal explanation why one-sided motivational errors cannot be considered.[711] It brings *pacta sunt servanda* into play, while English law has to rely on *volenti non fit iniuria*. But the effect is similar.[712] Under both regimes, gifts cannot simply be cancelled. But if they

---

708 Cf. also Goff & Jones, 2011) para 9–110.

709 Birke Häcker, Mistaken Gifts after Pitt v Holt, (2014) 67 Current Legal Problems 333, holds a different view. According to her, *Pitt v Holt* should be used as a general guideline to restrain mistakes relevant for restitution. While it is true that that mistake under the "but-for"-test is too wide, the coherent solution is delivered by the failure of purpose approach (see below pp. 270–272). There are only three main purposes (causa solvendi / donandi / acquirendi). Their failure explains the unjust enrichment claims under strict law without need to balance the merits of the case. It follows that the only mistake relevant for restitution is a liability mistake. The restrictions of *Pitt v Holt* do not lead there. They are only apt for equity.

710 Cf. in detail, Birke Häcker, Mistaken Gifts after Pitt v Holt, (2014) 67 Current Legal Problems 333 (sub "A comparative side glance"); Pfeifer in Schmoeckel, Rückert and Zimmermann (eds), HKK BGB, Vol III/1, §§ 516–534 mn. 9–11.

711 Cf. Birke Häcker, ibid: The Austrian Code allows avoidance of gifts for unilateral errors of motivation under § 572 ABGB. In England, the remedy to undo such errors is equitable rescission, *Lady Hood of Avalon v Mackinnon* [1909] 1 Ch 476 – which underscores the point made here.

712 Cf. Hang Wu Tang, 'Restitution for Mistaken Gifts' (2004) 20 JCL 1 who draws from the seminal work of Marcel Mauss (in German: Die Gabe, 1954) to show that gifts were a form of exchange between families and tribes. Cf. Ehmann, Der Zweck der Leistungen, p. 14. Cf. further S Meier, 'Unjust Factors and Legal Grounds' in Johnston & Zimmermann (eds), Unjustified Enrichment 37, at pp. 43–54.

can, the reasons will be of equitable nature. The BGB contains two prominent cases where "pure"[713] gifts can be undone: the claw back provision for impoverishment of the donator under § 528 I 1 BGB (*Verarmung des Schenkers*) and the revocation of the gift for gross ingratitude of the donee under § 530 I BGB (*grober Undank*). Both claims to recover the gift from the donee are subject to the defence of disenrichment.

> § 528 I 1 BGB: "Soweit der Schenker nach der Vollziehung der Schenkung außerstande ist, seinen angemessenen Unterhalt zu bestreiten und die ihm seinen Verwandten, seinem Ehegatten, seinem Lebenspartner oder seinem früheren Ehegatten oder Lebenspartner gegenüber gesetzlich obliegende Unterhaltspflicht zu erfüllen, kann er von dem Beschenkten die Herausgabe des Geschenkes nach den Vorschriften über die Herausgabe einer ungerechtfertigten Bereicherung fordern."
>
> [Insofar as the donor is unable to support himself adequately after the gift has been executed and to fulfil his legal obligation to support his relatives, spouse, life partner or former spouse or life partner, he may demand that the donee **return the gift** in accordance with the provisions on the return of **unjust enrichment.** – Deep-L]
>
> § 530 I BGB: "Eine Schenkung kann widerrufen werden, wenn sich der Beschenkte durch eine schwere Verfehlung gegen den Schenker oder einen nahen Angehörigen des Schenkers groben Undanks schuldig macht."
>
> [A gift can be revoked if the donee is guilty of gross ingratitude through serious misconduct against the donor or a close relative of the donor.]
>
> § 531 II BGB: "Ist die Schenkung widerrufen, so kann die Herausgabe des Geschenks nach den Vorschriften über die Herausgabe einer ungerechtfertigten Bereicherung gefordert werden."
>
> [If the gift is revoked, the **return of the gift** can be demanded in accordance with the provisions on the return of **unjust enrichment.** – Deep-L][714]

It is evident that these rules are of equitable nature. Gross ingratitude of the recipient appears similarly unconscionable as undue influence. And it is not the defective will but considerations of fairness that lead to the impoverishment of the donator trumping the rule "No take backs!" or as the Germans say: "Geschenkt ist geschenkt – wieder holen ist gestohlen".[715] It is a specific application of the equi-

---

713 Note that there are two cases that do not qualify as "pure" gifts under German law: the *Schenkung unter Auflage* (§ 525 BGB) and the *unbenannte Zuwendung* of family law. They will be explained in the following text.

714 Note further that a binding promise to make a gift under § 518 I BGB (comparable to a deed) need not be honoured in case of impoverishment, *Einrede des Notbedarfs* (§ 519 BGB) = defence of urgent necessity.

715 "A gift is a gift – taking back means stealing."

table doctrine of *Wegfall der Geschäftsgrundlage* (§ 313 BGB),[716] the German adaption of the *clausula rebus sic stantibus* of Roman law.[717] It is of particular interest that § 528 I 1 BGB confirms the claim of a close link between the reversal of gifts and wide Pomponian enrichment to prevent gratuities at the expense of third parties. The claim in restitution does not only lie if "the donor is unable to support himself adequately after the gift has been executed", but also if he cannot "fulfil his legal obligation to support his relatives, spouse, life partner or former spouse or life partner". This means that the gift can also be reclaimed for the benefit of third parties. From that, it is only a small step to attack all gifts that leave the donor unable to fulfill his obligations because they are *gifts at the expense of third parties.*

Equity further governs the reversal of the so-called "unbenannte Zuwendung" (= unnamed grant). This is a term of German family law that describes gratuitous pecuniary advantages shifted between spouses or partners under the mistaken assumption of the permanence of the relationship. The failure of this assumption makes the transfer liable to be challenged under the rules of *Wegfall der Geschäftsgrundlage* pursuant to § 313 BGB.[718]

These observations underpin the thesis that most grounds for the recovery of gifts are of equitable nature. Moreover, the German rules confirm the proximity of those equitable causes of action to the disenrichment defence that mitigates the harshness that the consequent obligation to make restitution imposes on the defendant.

By contrast, the *Schenkung unter Auflage* under §§ 525–527 (= conditional gift) cannot be seen as a mere gift because the recipient is obliged to some kind of performance. Take the example that the family home is transferred from the parents to the children with an obligation to keep employing the house keeper or to grant a life estate. Such stipulations can either be enforced (§ 525 I BGB) or the gift can be revoked in case of non-performance (§ 527 BGB). Under German law, such agree-

---

716 MünchKommBGB/Koch, Vol 4–2, 9th edn. 2023, § 528 mn. 1 and § 519 mn. 1.

717 See in general MünchKommBGB/Finkenauer, Vol 3, 9th edn. 2020, § 313 mn. 20; *Finkenauer*, Stipulation und Geschäftsgrundlage, SZ Rom. Abt. 126 (2009), 305 (357); *Finkenauer*, La théorie de l'imprévision en droit allemand et le jugement de Salomon, in Mausen, Aequitas – Équité – Equity, 2015, 97; HKK/*Finkenauer* §§ 158–163 Rn. 11; *Zimmermann* AcP 193 (1993), 121, 136.

Note however that common law has become hostile to the idea of *clausula rebus sic stantibus* following the demise of *Solle v Butcher* [1950] 1 KB 671 in *Great Peace Shipping Ltd v Tsavliris (International) Ltd* [2002] EWCA Civ 1407.

718 Cf. Jauernig/Stadler, BGB, 19th edn. 2023, § 313 mn. 34. This equitable principle also offers a road to relief in the case of gifts from parents and in-laws that are frustrated by the breakdown of the relationship of their children, BGHZ 184, 190. A *condictio ob rem* may also lie, cf. already BGHZ 177, 193.

ments are construed as (conditional) gifts.[719] Under the wide "Carbolic smokeball consideration"[720] of common law however, it seems that in cases equivalent to § 527 BGB, an action for restitution could be based on failure of consideration.

5 Conclusions

England followed France. The acceptance of a general claim based on unjust enrichment imported the problem of indirect enrichment. The Pomponian principle "no benefit from another's loss" is wide enough to accommodate actions against remote beneficiaries. That is why it was able to absorb the *actio de in rem verso* in France and that is also the reason why it produced similar actions in England (cp. *Banque Financière* and Crédit foncier). Even without the dependence on the path laid by the historic precursor from ancient Rome, the deductions made under the principle led English common law to the same place as French civil law.

However, several Civilian codifiers had snubbed the *actio de in rem verso.* Common lawyers have never accepted it from the outset. This happened for good reasons. The extension of enrichment claims to remote beneficiaries collides with ironclad principles of private laws. It is therefore no coincidence that Pomponian unjust enrichment, likewise rejected by past codifiers of civil law, led English law into a conflict. Through the lenses of the four-stage test of unjust enrichment, *Banque Financière, Menelao* and *Costello* are irreconcilable. *Swynson* hardly fairs better. Pomponian unjust enrichment cannot solve these cases because it has no means to explain why one time, the benefit from another's loss triggers a remedy, while the other time, it does not. This is exactly the challenge that the stamp case mounts against unjust enrichment: arbitrariness.

Likewise, the sloppiness-of-thought-criticism seems confirmed. It only blurs the true rationale of the solutions. The enrichment remedies against the remote recipients in the three leading cases, *Lipkin Gorman, Banque Financière* and *Menelaou* were in truth all based on the prohibition of gratuities at the expense of third parties. To challenge such transactions is well established in all private laws since the *actio Pauliana,* even though the remedies to that end vary widely.

Seen from that angle, *Costello* of course becomes questionable. It may be based on an overstatement of the Salomon-principle that is held (too?) high amongst Eng-

719 The fine line drawn by German doctrine to distinguish such conditional gifts from exchange contracts is whether the counter-performance merely diminishes the value of the gift instead of creating a counterclaim laying a claim on the other assets of the donee; see Jauernig/Mansel, BGB, 19th edn. 2023, §§ 525–527 mn. 2)

720 *Carlill v Carbolic Smoke Ball Company* [1893] 1 QB 256.

lish corporate lawyers. Just as the separate legal personality of the company does not exclude parent liability under the tort of negligence,[721] it does not allow gratuitous shifts of wealth within the group at the expense of the creditors. In truth, cases like *Costello* or *Yukong Lines*[722] simply raise the question: What remedies of insolvency law were available? Why were they not applied? If it turns out that the remedies of insolvency law were no longer available because of procedural mistakes, limitation periods etc., that be it.

The Oakwood case may indeed have been wound up the wrong way. As a general rule, a company must not make gifts ("no cake and ales"!). The shareholders are only entitled to the balance sheet profit (s.830 CA 2006). Disguised returns of capital are unlawful.[723] Oakwood had procured the benefits from the works to the owners gratuitously.[724] That being so, Oakwood should have had a claim for restitution of the gift to the shareholders under mandatory corporate law that MacDonald & Co might have seized. When Oakwood did not pay, insolvency proceedings were due.[725] The liquidator would have clawed back the unlawful gift to the Costellos. Insolvency law provides additional remedies. The procurement of the benefit was liable to avoidance pursuant to s.238 IA 1986 (transaction at an undervalue). The remedy under s.423 IA 1986 (transactions defrauding creditors) could have been applied as well. It bites if the debtor (Oakwood) "makes a gift to the other person or he otherwise enters into a transaction with the other on terms that provide for him to receive no consideration" (s.423(1)(a) IA 1986). Also, even if piercing the corporate veil was rejected, a trust between the Costellos and their company could have been assumed along the lines drawn by the Supreme Court in *Prest v Petrodel.*[726] It is hard to see if and why none of this happened. But this is not a point to follow through here.

---

721 This was only recently recognised by the UK Supreme Court, see *Vedanta v Lungowe* [2019] *UKSC* 20 and *Okpabi v Royal Dutch Shell* [2021] *UKSC* 3. For the old, erroneous view see the judgement of the Court of Appeal in *Okpabi v Shell* [2020] EWCA Civ 191 that was unanimously overturned by the Supreme Court.
722 *Youkong Line Ltd of Korea v Rendsburg Inv. Corp of Liberia and others (n° 2)* [1998] 1 Lloyd's Rep. 322; [1998] 1 WLR 294; [1998] 4 All ER 82.
723 *Re Halt Garage (1964) Ltd* [1982] *3 All ER 1016; Aveling Barford Ltd v Perion Ltd* [1989] BCLC 626.
724 *Costello v MacDonald Dickens and Macklin* [2011] EWCA Civ 930, at para. 20: "Mr and Mrs Costello wished to use Oakwood, their corporate creature established purely for tax and financial purposes, merely as a conduit to make the payments due to the respondents. There was no contract between Mr and Mrs Costello and Oakwood, and Oakwood never provided them with any services." And at para 21: "Mr and Mrs Costello have been enriched because Oakwood has allowed the benefit of the contract to be conferred on them."
725 Since the order against Oakwood had not been appealed (*Costello v MacDonald Dickens and Macklin* [2011] EWCA Civ 930, at para. 12), unwillingness to pay a would have sufficed to trigger insolvency proceedings under s.123(1)(a) or (b) IA 1986.
726 *Prest v Petrodel Resources Ltd* [2013] AC 32.

It follows that if the principle of Pomponius continued to be applied as law, it should at least be subject to the same subsidiarity principle that we know from French, Italian and Spanish law. Unjust enrichment claims would lie but for the priority of specific remedies. Although this approach has been criticised above from a principled point of view because of its inherent arbitrariness (pp. 162 et seq.), it is the law in France, Italy and Spain and it works sufficiently well in the legal practice of these countries not to interfere with commercial needs.

Currently, English law cannot get there because unlike the aforesaid jurisdictions, it does not distinguish its general enrichment claim from the specific, strict law actions to undo failed transfers (in England the action for money had and received, on the Continent the *condictiones*). Instead, it amalgamates the strict law actions with the equitable principle. This leads to the bizarre situation where the general enrichment claim cannot be a subsidiary remedy because of the strict law components but should be a subsidiary remedy because of the equitable components. By contrast, enrichment claims to reverse direct shifts of value cannot be subsidiary.

If Pomponian unjust enrichment shall continue to be the law of England, that leaves two options on the technical level: either the cases of direct and indirect enrichment are distinguished within the general claim. The latter but not the former should then be subject to a rule of last resort. Or the actions and remedies in unjust enrichment are split and separated from each other. The traditional actions to reverse direct shifts of value (money had and received; *quantum meruit / valebat*) continue to be applied to those cases of unjust enrichment that civil lawyers cover with the *condictio indebiti / Leistungskondition / paiement de l'indu*. The general enrichment claim would not be conceived as a catch-all clause to include all those claims and remedies, but as a subsidiary sweeping clause to cover the remaining cases where it seems necessary to restitute unjust enrichment, particular against remote volunteers benefitting at the back of the claimant.

Finally, the comparative view has shown that both in England and in Germany, the reversal of gifts is a question of fairness / equity. The triggers are typically based on equitable grounds: undue influence; gross ingratitude; impoverishment. These grounds have in common that they do not give a clear case for restitution but must be weighed out against the justified trust of the donee who relied on the permanence of his receipt.

For many centuries, the disenrichment defence has been providing a viable tool to balance out the conflicting interests of the restitution for the donor and security of receipt for the donee, in a fair way. Whatever legitimate reasons to claw back a gift are to be accepted by a given jurisdiction: the *bona fide* recipient must be protected from damage suffered in the good faith on the permanence of the receipt. The consequence is disgorgement of surviving enrichment (including allowance for necessary expenses, if any), but no compensation from the defendant's purse if the value of the benefit has got lost. The defendant has not decided to spend money to have the benefit, and that is why he cannot be forced to spend money to return the benefit.

Protecting volunteers from any harshness of restitution is a core feature of unjust enrichment. This is a consideration that must be taken into account when musing if English law should use Pomponian enrichment to get to remote beneficiaries. The consequent application of disenrichment can balance out the conflicting interests of the parties in an appropriate manner. But it also comes with two downsides. First, it relies on a principle that cannot be applied directly without resulting in arbitrariness. Second, as French law has shown, the "equitable function" of unjust enrichment calls for a limiting rule of last resort. In particular, wide enrichment claims with a function equivalent to the civilian *actio de in rem verso* should be subsidiary in order not to undermine the specific remedies of written (insolvency) law. The better approach may therefore be to disengage both cause of action and defence from the Pomponian principle, for example by extending equitable subrogation in *Banque Fiancière* and *Menelaou* because of the economic similarity of the situations to a direct redemption or to allow the change of position defence to protect the defendant's faith in the permanence of the receipt that was created by the (if vitiated) transfer of the claimant, not because of the fairness or not of his or her enrichment. This would dispose of the criticisms or arbitrariness and sloppiness of thought. But it could still achieve the results that have been worked out with much effort over centuries.

6 Outlook on following part

The following part will show that German law of unjustified enrichment emerged from a similar error concerning the notion of enrichment that originated from the statements of Pomponius in the Justinian compilation. True, Savigny had ousted the Pomponian principle as a cause of action. As a consequence, Germany only received the *condictiones* to undo direct shifts of value /wealth *sine causa*.

However, the *condictiones* were subsequently wrapped up in soft enrichment paper. Like the action for money had and received, the traditional *condictiones* were not subject to a general defence of disenrichment. They only had a defence of "impossibility" if a specific chattel was to be returned but destroyed beforehand. This was necessary because unlike money had and received, the Roman *condictiones* were not restricted to (re)payments but allowed recovery in kind. But German jurists of the 19th century imported through the back door both the notion of disgorging the "enrichment" as the aim of the claim and the consequent defence of "disenrichment". Instead of rationalising the reasons when to allow or disallow the defence of disenrichment / change of position, they hid them behind the enrichment language. The result was the glittering concept of a *Bereicherungsrecht* that was said to be bound to general equitable considerations ("allgemeines Billigkeitsrecht") in a special manner ("in besonderer Weise").

The BGB was codified on this undercooked basis. All the *condictiones* were now said to reverse "unjustified enrichments". Accordingly, all *bona fide* defendants could invoke disenrichment (§ 818 III). This happened 100 years before the House of Lords took the same escape route in *Lipkin Gorman.* They dissolved the action for money had and received in the wider concept of unjust enrichment to solve a truly difficult case. Both jurisdictions misshaped and falsified the original actions to undo failed shifts of value by clothing it into wide equitable enrichment: Sloppiness of thought.

In Germany, the idea that restitution aimed at the unjust enrichment instead of the receipt of the benefit never stood on solid ground. If German lawyers actually searched for enrichments, they could not undo any invalid exchange because the purchaser has the car but gave the money while the vendor has the money but gave the car, i.e. on balance: No enrichment for no one. This is of course not the law in Germany today. Instead, both parties have to return the performance they received *sine causa.* But it took and still takes a lot of energy to overcome the original idea of the Code and reach the right conclusions *against* the misshaping of the law that the enrichment idea has produced. Arguably, *Werner Flume* was the first who managed to see clearly through the mess that Pomponius had created (see pp. 284 et seq.).

7 Annex: A comparative view on *Lipkin Gorman* as a hybrid of personal action and *rei vindicatio* for a sum of money

Lipkin Gorman introduced the defence of change of position / disenrichment and finally established the language of unjust enrichment to take over the law of restitution. It is the starting shot for unjust enrichment as *legal* principle that soon afterwards turned into directly applicable law. So much the more it is surprising that on closer analysis of the doctrinal foundation, it may not be an enrichment case at all. There is a vivid debate among common lawyers about this. The purpose of that Annex is to cast a comparative view on why the assertion of property rights to stolen cash works smoother than under civil law.

Under German law, property in stolen money gets lost quickly. In theory, a *rei vindicatio* for cash could lie under § 985 BGB. But in practice, this will not happen. First, title to cash will normally get lost by operation of law when it is mixed with other cash of the new possessor (§§ 948, 947 II BGB[727]). Second, the *rei vindicatio* under § 985 BGB only covers *bewegliche Sachen* (= chattels and cash), but not book money. Therefore, it does not apply to the "theft" of book money that happened in *Lipkin Gorman*. Also, it automatically ceases to exist when stolen cash is paid into a bank account and turns into a claim. To be sure, civil law accepts surrogation of property in specific cases.[728] Likewise, it can extend personal obligations to transfer specific items into the products of those items.[729] But none of that is available to keep the *rei vindicatio* alive. When the title to the stolen money is lost, the *condictio* will step in and recover the value taken from the previous owner. But in most cases, formal technicalities of German law will prevent effective restitution. In *Banque Belge*,[730] Mlle. Spanoghe would have been spared by German law simply because the money stolen by her sweetheart Hambrouck was paid into his bank account before passing it on to her. The direct claim

727 The prevailing doctrine assumes sole ownership of the new holder, OLG Frankfurt NJW-RR 1987, 310, 311; BeckOK BGB/Kindl § 948 mn. 7; contrast MünchKommBGB/Füller, Vol. 8, 9th edn. 2023, § 948 mn. 7–8: co-ownership).

728 In Germany, this happens in the case of the special joint property called *Gesamthandseigentum*. The main example had been partnership property, cf. the old § 718 II BGB that had been in force till 31.12.2023: "Zu dem Gesellschaftsvermögen gehört auch, was auf Grund eines zu dem Gesellschaftsvermögen gehörenden Rechtes oder als Ersatz für die Zerstörung, Beschädigung oder Entziehung eines zu dem Gesellschaftsvermögen gehörenden Gegenstandes erworben wird." [The company's assets shall also include what is acquired on the basis of a right belonging to the company's assets or as compensation for the destruction, damage or seizure of an object belonging to the company's assets. – DeepL]. Cf. further § 2018 I BGB (concerning estates).
From a technical perspective, the difference to following and tracing is that it is not remedial, i. e. the surrogation rule transfers the title by operation of law and with effect against all the world.

729 If the property sold gets destroyed, the purchaser can claim the insurance benefit (= *commodum ex re*). If it was sold to a higher bidder, the purchaser can claim the purchase prize under that other contract (*commodum ex negatione cum re*). See § 285 I BGB: "Erlangt der Schuldner infolge des Umstands, auf Grund dessen er die Leistung nach § 275 Abs. 1 bis 3 nicht zu erbringen braucht, für den geschuldeten Gegenstand einen Ersatz oder einen Ersatzanspruch, so kann der Gläubiger Herausgabe des als Ersatz Empfangenen oder Abtretung des Ersatzanspruchs verlangen." [If the debtor obtains a replacement or a claim for compensation for the object owed as a result of the circumstance on the basis of which he is not required to render performance in accordance with section 275 (1) to (3), the creditor may demand surrender of the object received as compensation or assignment of the claim for compensation.]

Note further that under German unjustified enrichment, only the *commodum ex re* can be claimed, § 818 I BGB: "Die Verpflichtung zur Herausgabe erstreckt sich auf die gezogenen Nutzungen sowie auf dasjenige, was der Empfänger auf Grund eines erlangten Rechts oder als Ersatz für die Zerstörung, Beschädigung oder Entziehung des erlangten Gegenstands erwirbt." [The obligation to surrender extends to ... that which the recipient acquires on the basis of a right obtained or as compensation for the destruction, damage or seizure of the item obtained.]

730 *Banque Belge pour l'Etranger v. Hambrouck* [1921] 1 K.B. 321; for the facts, see below in the text.

under § 816 I 2 BGB would have been lost, and the prolonged enrichment claim under § 822 is basically dead letter law.[731]

This is different with the action for money had and received. Unlike the Roman *condictiones*, the action for money had and received was not restricted to cases where title had passed. There was no competing *rei vinidcatio* it would have to be distinguished from and no need for an exception like the *condictio furtiva*.[732] The result was an easy-going personal action to vindicate a sum of money. This application is deeply rooted in the original, literal function of this count: the action for **money had an received for the use of the plaintiff** was perceived as a "trust of money".[733] It followed that the claimant could base an action for money had and received simply on saying: this money is mine, and you have to pay it over to me. Following and tracing were the means to facilitate that end. Pragmatic common law managed something that civil law, caught in its dependence on Roman paths, never could. This is demonstrated by the property-rights-based solution of *Lipkin Gorman* that will be explained in detail below.

a) The title to the money

The starting point of the House of Lords was that title to the cash had passed from the bank to Cass at the moment of the withdrawal.

> *Lipkin Gorman v Karpnale* (per Lord Goff) "...where a banker's cheque payable to a third party or bearer is obtained by a partner from a bank which has received the authority of the partnership to pay the partner in question who has, however, unknown to the bank, acted beyond the authority of his partners in so operating the account, the legal property in the banker's cheque thereupon vests in the partner. The same must a fortiori be true when it is not such a banker's cheque but cash which is so drawn from the bank by the partner in question."

This is not easy to understand because Cass blatantly abused his authority to draw on the firm's account. He could not have transferred the title to any cash from the cash register of the firm to himself. But it was the bank who transferred the title, and that is why it worked. Cass had authority to draw on the account and used it to strike the following bargain with the bank: release of Lipkin Gorman's claim on the money in the account ("book money") in exchange for paying out an equivalent

---

731 For the reasons, see below p. 228.

732 See above, pp. 118–119.

733 Baker in Schrage (ed.), at p. 48 with fn. 91, noting that the common law accepted equitable interests in money which eventually made it necessary to distinguish the action for money had and received from equitable trust of money, citing e.g. *Case v Roberts* (1817) Holt N.P. 500.

sum in cash. One might of course argue that the bank wanted to transfer the cash to the firm as the account holder, not to the authorised agent.[734] But the authority to dispose over the firm's bank account includes the right to convey book money to third parties. The same must be true for cash. If I draw on my grandmother's authority from her account, the money might be destined for her (e. g. to pay deliveries, hand out presents etc.) or it may be destined for me (e. g. to reimburse me for layouts I made). That is why the fact that I acted on the authority of my grandmother when disposing over the account does not preclude the question who received the title to the cash drawn from it. Since money has no earmark, the better solution is to assume transfer of title to the drawer in order to align the possession of and the title to the cash.

A similar issue arises under German banking law where the authority to draw from and make dispositions of another's bank account is called *Kontovollmacht.*[735] The construction is intricate. German law distinguishes *Vertretungsmacht*[736] under § 164, 167 BGB from *Verfügungsmacht*[737] under § 185 BGB. The former describes the power of agents to bind another person *in that person's name*, while the latter describes the power of agents to dispose of third parties' assets *in their own name.* This distinction seems to indicate that only the latter would allow the holder of a *Kontovollmacht* to receive title to the cash drawn in his or her *own name.* But as just pointed out, the authority to dispose of *the account* does *not* predetermine who receives the title in the case of a cash withdrawal. The disposition over the bank account is solely performed in the name and on behalf of the account holder. This must be so because otherwise, the bank would not be allowed to act on it. That is why the term *Kontovollmacht* is perfectly right. However, recipient of the disposition can be a third party. This is regularly the case with bank transfers.[738] It is likewise true for cash withdrawals by authorised agents. The title to the cash will normally be received by the agent in her own name. Only if it is made clear that the money is received on behalf of the account holder, the title will go there. This is a consequence of the so-called Offenkundigkeitsprinzip under § 164 II BGB.[739]

---

734 In a similar vein Stevens, p. 208, arguing with the joint tenancy of partnership law.
735 Compare Herresthal in MünchKommHGB, Vol. 6, 5th edn. 2024, Part A, mn. 260.
736 The power to act in another's same.
737 The power to dispose of another person's assets in the own name.
738 Sometimes however, transfers are not made to third parties but to other accounts of the holder, cp. e. g. *Colonial Bank v Exchange Bank of Yarmouth* (1885) 9 App Cas 84 (PC) where this went wrong.
739 § 164 II BGB reads: "Tritt der Wille, in fremdem Namen zu handeln, nicht erkennbar hervor, so kommt der Mangel des Willens, im eigenen Namen zu handeln, nicht in Betracht." [If the intention to act on behalf of another person is not recognisable, the lack of intention to act on one's own behalf does not come into consideration. – Deep-L]

> Therefore, German banking practice regularly attributes the title to the agent without further ado.[740]

After establishing the title of Cass, the House of Lords resorted to following and tracing to reallocate Cass' title to Lipkin Gorman. After that, it followed it into the surplus that the Casino had made from Cass' gambling.

> Lipkin Gorman (per Lord Goff): "It must follow a fortiori that the solicitors, as owners of the chose in action constituted by the indebtedness of the bank to them in respect of the sums paid into the client account, could trace their property in that chose in action into its direct product, the money drawn from the account by Cass."
>
> (per Lord Templeman): "There remained £154,695 which must have been money stolen from the solicitors. My conclusion is that the club has no right to retain stolen money received by the club from the thief. ... In the present case money stolen from the solicitors by Cass has been paid to and is now retained by the club and ought to be repaid to the solicitors. The solicitors will recover part of their stolen money and the club will only lose the winnings the club was not entitled to make out of the solicitors' money."

Lord Templeman furnished ample references to show that stolen money can be recovered from volunteers.[741] English law knows no conversion of money used as currency. *Nemo dat quod non habet* does not apply to money as currency either.[742] If stolen money was acquired bona fide for good consideration, it belongs to the new holder. However, if no consideration was given – as was the case be-

---

740 BGHZ 205, 334 = NJW 2015, 2725, 2726 mn. 27; BGH NJW-RR 1989, 834; NJW 1999, 2833 (citing § 164 BGB but speaking of "Verfügungsvollmacht"); Herresthal in MünchKommHGB, Vol. 6, 5th edn. 2024, Part A, mn. 260.

741 The cases exactly dealing with the recovery of stolen money from volunteers were *Miller v Race* (1758) 1 Burr. 452; *Clark v Shee and Johnson* (1774) 1 Cowp. 197 (where Lord Mansfield also cited *Golightly v. Reynolds* (1772) Lofft. 88 next to *Miller v Race*); *Banque Belge pour l'Etranger v. Hambrouck* [1921] 1 K.B. 321; *Transvaal & Delagoa Bay Investment Co. Ltd, v. Atkinson* [1944] 1 All E.R. 579; in the same sense for Australia *Black v. S. Freeman & Co.* (1910) 12 C.L.R. 105, albeit treating stolen money as (constructive) trust money.

Shoolbred v. Roberts [1899] 2 QB 560 was cited to support the argument that the mere fact of having been prepared to honour the wager does not entitle the club to retain the subsequent gains from gambling vis-à-vis the solicitors, and also for the proposition that paying up gambling debts is a gift in the eyes of the law – a gift made by Cass with stolen money.

Aubert v. Walsh (1810) 3 Taunt. 277 shed little light though because it concerned the withdrawal from a wager before it was closed, whereas Cass had completed the gaming. Likewise, *Hudson v. Robinson* (1816) 4 M. & S. 475 merely granted restitution for failure of consideration.

742 *Miller v Race* (1758) 1 Burr 452 = 97 ER 398 (per Lord Mansfield); on the background of this seminal case Fox, "Bone Fide Purchse and the Currency of Money" CLR (1996), 547.

cause gambling was treated as a gift prior to 2005 – the title did not get lost and the money could still be followed on the basis of the original property.

> *Miller v Race* (1758) 1 Burr. 452, at 457–458 (per Lord Mansfield): "So, in the case of money stolen, the true owner cannot recover it, after it has been paid away fairly and honestly upon a valuable and bona fide consideration: but before money has passed in currency, an action may be brought for the money itself."
>
> The same issue arose in *Clark v Shee and Johnson* (1774) 1 Cowp. 197, at pp. 199–200 (per Lord Mansfield) where the thief, a clerk, had used the money to buy tickets for an illegal lottery: "Where money or notes are paid bona fide, and upon a valuable consideration, they never shall be brought back by the true owner; but where they come mala fide into a person's hands, they are in the nature of specific property; and if their identity can be traced and ascertained, the party has a right to recover. ...
>
> Here the plaintiff sues for his identified property, which has come to the hands of the defendants iniquitously and illegally in breach of the Act of Parliament. Therefore they have no right to retain it; and consequently the plaintiff is well entitled to recover."

In *Lipkin Gorman*, the asset that was stolen by Cass was not the cash, but the "book money" of Lipkin Gorman, i.e. their claim against the bank.[743] The cash that the bank paid to Cass was merely the product of the book money. Lipkin Gorman traced their title into the cash. That allowed them to follow the cash to the Casino subsequently. The bank itself could not have traced because the cash was not stolen. The withdrawal was made on the authority of Cass. Contrast *Banque Belge v Hambrouck* where the bank itself traced the payment on the forged cheque because *that* payment was voidable for fraud.[744]

The facts of *Banque Belge v Hambrouck* as far as they matter here were as follows: Hambrouck forged cheques that he drew on his employer's (one Pelabon) account with Banque Belge. Hambrouck paid the cheques into his bank account at another bank (Farrows) who collected from Banque Belge. Later, Hambrouck withdrew money from his account at Farrow's and donated it to his mistress Mlle Spanoghe who paid it into her account at the London Joint City and Midland Bank. No

743 Note that the abstract authority to draw does not mean consent to each individual transaction. This was rightly recognised by the German Bundesgerichtshof in NJW 2015, 2725, 2727, mn. 20: "Die Kontovollmacht weist, anders als ein später widerrufener Überweisungs- oder Dauerauftrag, keinen Bezug zu einem konkreten Zahlungsvorgang auf." [Unlike a revoked transfer or standing order, the account authorisation is not related to a specific transaction.] Note further that under civil law, only movable property could be the object of theft, Zimmermann, p. 840 with fn. 39.

744 *Banque Belge pour l'Etranger v. Hambrouck* [1921] 1 K.B. 321,

other money ever went into that account.[745] Banque Belge was allowed to follow and trace the money it had paid to Hambrouck on the forged cheque into the remains of it in Mlle Spanoghe's bank account. That was possible even at law because tracing did no longer stop "at the doors of banks".[746]

Deviating from *Lipkin*, it is the bank (Banque Belge) not the account holder (Pelabon) who traces the money. The explanation is that Banque Belge had paid on a forged instrument and could avoid the title of Hambrouck for fraud.[747] That paved the way for tracing their money to the volunteer. In *Lipkin Gorman*, the bank had no claim because they were not defrauded or robbed in any way. The tracing could accordingly only be done by the solicitors.[748]

---

745 *Banque Belge pour l'Etranger v. Hambrouck* [1921] 1 K.B. 321, at p. 328 (per Bankes L.J.): "The money which the Bank seeks to recover is capable of being traced, as the appellant never paid any money into the Bank except money which was part of the proceeds of Hambrouck's frauds, and the appellant's Bank have paid all the money standing to the appellant's credit into Court, where it now is."

746 *Banque Belge pour l'Etranger v. Hambrouck* [1921] 1 K.B. 321, at p. 335 (per Atkin L.J.): "But if in 1815 the common law halted outside the bankers' door, by 1879 equity had had the courage to lift the latch, walk in and examine the books: *In re Hallett's Estate* (1880) 13 Ch D 696. I see no reason why the means of ascertainment so provided should not now be available both for common law and equity proceedings."

747 There was an issue whether title was void or voidable. Atkin L.J. assumed the latter, see *Banque Belge pour l'Etranger v. Hambrouck* [1921] 1 K.B. 321, at p. 332: "It does not appear to be necessary for this case to determine whether Hambrouck stole the money or obtained it by false pretences. At present it appears to me that the plaintiff Bank intended to pass the property in and the possession of the cash which under the operations of the clearing house they must be taken to have paid to the collecting bank. I will assume therefore that this is a case not of a void but of a voidable transaction by which Hambrouck obtained a title to the money until the plaintiffs elected to avoid his title, which they did when they made their claim in this action. The title would then revest in the plaintiffs subject to any title acquired in the meantime by any transferee for value without notice of the fraud."

748 Later, Pelabon allowed Banque Belge to debit his account. This was apparently based on an eventually successful argument of ostensible authority. Had that been clear from the beginning, Pelabon should have been able to follow and trace the money stolen from him by Hambrouck to the volunteer Spanoghe, just as Lipkin Gorman did. Interestingly, the Court of Appeal did not think that the debiting of Pelabon's account extinguished the claim of Banque Belge, as counsel for the defendant had argued. *Banque Belge pour l'Etranger v. Hambrouck* [1921] 1 K.B. 321, at p. 325 (per Bankes l.J.): "Whatever the position of the plaintiff Bank may have been in relation to their customer, M. Pelabon, in the event of the Bank being unable to recover the moneys which they had paid out when the cheques were presented to them for payment, it is I think clear that the moneys which were so paid out were the moneys of the plaintiff Bank which they were entitled to recover if they could. This conclusion disposes of the point raised by Mr. Warren that the action would not lie, because the Bank were, at the time of the trial, claiming that as between themselves and M. Pelabon the loss must fall upon him."

b) The remedies available

Tracing allowed Lipkin Gorman to identify a certain sum of money in the hands of Karpnale as their own property. The process is famously described by Lord Ellenborough in *Taylor v. Plumer:*[749]

> "...the property of a principal entrusted by him to his factor for any special purpose belongs to the principal, notwithstanding any change which that property may have undergone in point of form, so long as such property is capable of being identified, and distinguished from all other property. .... It makes no difference in reason or law into what other form, different from the original, the change may have been made, whether it be into that of promissory notes for the security of the money which was produced by the sale of the goods of the principal, as in *Scott v. Surman*[750] or into other merchandise, as in *Whitecomb v. Jacob,*[751] for the product of or substitute for the original thing still follows the nature of the thing itself, as long as it can be ascertained to be such, ..."[752]

Lipkin Gorman could show through tracing and following that the sum of money they claimed was the product of the stolen debt.[753] Lipkin Gorman could say: This (sum of) money is mine, so hand it over to me. The question then arises: what is the correct remedy to enforce that ascertained property right. Two options are available: the action for money had and received at law (money judgement), or a specific order in equity. An illuminating account has been delivered by Atkin L.J. in *Banque Belge v Hambrouck* where he had to explain and distinguish both options because the proceedings before him were unclear.[754]

> The course of the proceedings in this case is not quite clear. **The statement of claim alleges specifically that the money is the property of the plaintiffs which they are entitled to follow, and the relief asked is not for a money judgment against the defendants, but an order that the sum paid into Court, by the defendant Bank should be paid out to the plaintiffs.** In giving judgment however, the learned judge has treated the claim as one

---

749 [1815] 3 M. & S. 562, 574, referred to by Atkin L.J. in *Banque Belge pour l'Etranger v. Hambrouck* [1921] 1 K.B. 321, at pp. 334–335.
750 (1743) Willes 400.
751 (1711) 1 Salk. 160.
752 The reference is cut off here because the subsequent statement that a payment into a bank account *per se* stops tracing at common law appears overruled.
753 On a side note: with a view to money, be it book money or cash, the concept of tracing through products defeats the argument of mixed funds. If the funds can be divided, the product can be ascertained. That need not be the *same* cash. From that perspective, tracing of (sums of) money is indeed the same at law and in equity, the old distinction being overhauled. It would only be different if e.g. Mlle Spanoghe would have bought a precious jewel and paid in part with the stolen money and in part with her own. That could be where tracing at law ends (or does it attribute joint ownership?), whereas equity will surely find a way to recover.
754 *Banque Belge pour l'Etranger v. Hambrouck* [1921] 1 K.B. 321, at pp. 332–335.

> for money had and received, and the judgment entered is an ordinary judgment against the appellant on a money claim for 315 l. together with an order that the sum in Court should be paid out to the plaintiffs in part satisfaction. The two forms of relief are different, and though in this case there is no substantial difference in the result, the grounds upon which relief is based might have been material. ...
>
> If the question be the **right** of the plaintiffs **in equity** to follow their property, I apprehend that no difficulty arises. ... it appears to me that the plaintiffs were, on the grounds alleged in the statement of claim, entitled to a **specific order for the return of the money in question**, and, as it is now represented by the sum in Court, to payment out of Court of that sum.
>
> The question whether they are entitled to a **common law judgment** for money had and received may involve other considerations. I am not without further consideration prepared to say that every person who can in equity establish a right to have his money or the proceeds of his property restored to him, can, as an alternative, bring an action against the person who has been in possession of such money or proceeds for money had and received; still less that he can always bring trover or detinue. But the common law rights are large and are admirably stated in *Taylor v. Plumer*...[755]

It transpires that the most direct remedy to vindicate the traced property would have been a specific order to pay out the identified sum. In *Banque Belge*, that would have obviously been available since that sum had already been isolated and paid into court by the bank of the defendant.[756] This specific order is equivalent to an award under § 985 BGB.

Alternatively, the claimant is entitled to bring a common law action of money had and received to obtain a money judgement.[757] However, this does not seem to be an ordinary money judgement because the basis for this award, too, is the property in the money identified by the tracing exercise. The action for money had and received merely vindicates that property right. Like the parallel equity, it says this is mine so pay it over – a sort of *rei vindicatio* to a sum of money. This function is different from the Mosaic *condictiones*. It does not reverse an otherwise valid payment on grounds of unjust factors, but merely asserts the property of the owner as a "trust of money".[758] In this venerable function of old, it does exactly the same at

755 [1815] 3 M. & S. 562, 574, see above.
756 Under German law, the *Hinterlegung* (§ 372 BGB) is the equivalent instrument to relieve a debtor from his liability in the case of competing claimants.
757 German terminology would instructively speak of a *Geldherausgabeschuld* in the first case, and of a *Geldsummenschuld* in the second. This reflects the difference that in the first case, it is exactly *that* identified amount of money ("in a bag") that has to be handed over whereas in the second, the defendant owes a certain sum of money. If you are robbed of the bag of money, you are liberated. But even if you were robbed of *all* your money, the *Geldsummenschuld* will persist because, as they say in Germany, *Geld hat man zu haben* (one has to have money).
758 See above p. 218.

law as *Re Hallet's Estate*[759] and *Sinclair v Brougham*[760] do in equity – and is therefore also functionally equivalent to a claim under § 985 BGB. This sheds light on why a money judgement is possible even if due to the successful tracing exercise, title to the money never passed to the defendant. The defendant has just got to pay over the money held "for the use of the plaintiff". Who holds the title to the money, principal or agent, does not matter for granting this award.

c) Tracing and the principle of unjust enrichment

The afore-described hybrid function as a personal claim based on a property right, pragmatic as it is, nevertheless blurred the categories and left uncertainty over the doctrinal classification of both the personal action based on a property right *inter omnes* and the nature of following and tracing.

If we take the construction of following and tracing serious, the action for money had and received in this old line of cases may not be a claim in unjust enrichment at all because the argument of the claimant is not "You are enriched at my expense" but "You illegitimately hold my property in your hand". Since the title is still with the claimant, the defendant is not enriched at his expense but instead sort of "trespasses" by holding possession of the other's property. Leaving aside the civilian discussion on the existence of a *condictio possessionis:*[761] an enrichment of the defendant does not materialise before any value has been absorbed from the property of the claimant e.g. by way of consumption or conferral to a third party for valuable consideration.[762]

If the basis of the claim is simply the (traced and followed) property, not unjust enrichment, it would follow that there is no need for a defence of disenrichment / change of position either. If the money has been paid away, the property has left the hands of the defendant and the straightforward claim "this is mine" will fail for that reason alone.

If an action for money had and received merely vindicated the title, it has nothing to say about the remoteness of enrichment claims. A property-based per-

759 (1880) 13 Ch D 696.

760 [1914] AC 398.

761 If possession of an asset received *sine causa* can be claimed back by a *condictio*, the loss of possession might lead to a duty to compensate the value of asset under § 818 II BGB although that value is represented by the property right to the asset, not by the possession of it. German Courts have nevertheless accepted the *condictio possessionis*, but denied compensation of the value under § 818 II BGB, see BGHZ 198, 381 = NJW 2014, 1095, 1096, mn. 13–15.; RGZ 98, 131, 135; RGZ 115, 31, 34.

762 The enrichment claim for the last case granted by § 816 I 1 BGB under German law and "waiver of tort" under English law.

sonal action would be automatically attached to the property right and follow wherever that may go. Since the property right is valid against all world (*inter omnes*), the action to enforce it must knock at every door it might hide behind.

However, there are good reasons to qualify the claim in *Lipkin Gorman* as based on unjust enrichment, like the House did. A first indicator is that Lord Mansfield himself recognised the claim as the "liberal action" closely related to equity that he had rolled out in *Moses v Macferlan.*[763]

> *Clark v Shee and Johnson* (1774) 1 Cowp. 197, 199: "This is a liberal action in the nature of a bill in equity; and if, under the circumstances of the case, it appears that the defendant cannot in conscience retain what is the subject matter of it, the plaintiff may well support this action"

But unlike in *Moses v Macferlan*, there is no talk of specific unjust factors (that would tie the claims to direct enrichments). We simply learn that the action lies where the defendant cannot in conscience retain what he got. This reads very much like the equitable general clause of the *condictio sine causa*, even if Pomponius himself is (again) not cited. It sounds very similar to the dubious civilian stretching of the *condictio sine causa* in D.12.1.32 that laid the ground for confounding the *condictiones* with the *actio de in rem verso* – **my money got to you so you have to pay me back** (above p. 115). Viewed from that angle, it is not really surprising that Lipkin Gorman paved the way for enrichment claims to remote recipients.

Confirmation that *Lipkin Gorman* must be about unjust enrichment can also be derived from the *mala fide* test. The Casino would have had to repay all of Lipkin Gormans' money had they known that Cass stole it. Formally, this was explained by Lord Mansfield that cash received *male fide* remained property of the claimant and could be demanded back.[764] But the same would be true for *all* cash that was received *without* consideration. All of it was still Lipkin Gorman's money when it came into the hands of Karpnale. The "repayments" made by the Casino on the gambling wins of Cass were no consideration but a gift[765] because

763 (1760) 2 Bur 1005.

764 *Clark v Shee and Johnson* (1774) 1 Cowp. 197, 200: "Where money or notes are paid bona fide, and upon a valuable consideration, they never shall be brought back by the true owner; but where they come mala fide into a person's hands, they are in the nature of specific property;"

765 *Lipkin Gorman v Karpnale* [1988] UKHL 12 (per Lord Goff): "It follows, as I have said, that the casino, by accepting the bet, does not thereby give valuable consideration for the money which has been wagered by the gambler, because the casino is under no legal obligation to honour the bet. Of course, the gambler cannot recover the money from the casino on the ground of failure of consideration; for he has relied upon the casino to honour the wager – he has in law given the money to the casino, trusting that the casino will fulfil the obligation binding in honour upon it and pay him

prior to 2005, gambling contracts were invalid and the Casino gave no value. The same would be true if the legal title of Cass would have been construed as being held on trust for Lipkin Gorman in answer to his disloyal conduct as the firm's agent.[766] Karpnale could only become "equity's darling" by giving value.

The original result of the tracing exercise must therefore have been that Karpnale had received the title to *all* cash that was stolen from Lipkin Gorman. If they were subsequently entitled to reduce their liability under the action for money had and received by deducting the repayments made to Cass even though they were gifts, this was only because of their being *bona fide* opened the defence of change of position / disenrichment.

This argument could still be construed in a more refined way. One could discern two different causes underlying the action of money had and received: the first cause of the action could simply be based on the persisting property right (as described above). It follows that right wherever it goes. The second cause could be based directly on unjust enrichment. It would (only) bite as soon as one of the holders of possession actually converts the value of the property to herself by consumption or transfer for value. This would clearly constitute a direct shift of value without consent of the owner. Indeed, any defendant down the line who eventually consumes the property does so at the expense of the owner. (Only) This second part of the claim would be subject to the disenrichment defence for bona fide recipients.

Finally, it could be argued that the remedy of following and tracing is itself based on the principle of unjust enrichment. To that debate of learned common law writers, I would only like to add the following qualification. If the principle of unjust enrichment is defined by the Pomponian sentence that nobody shall benefit from another's loss, it would naturally extend to remote recipients – as following and tracing does. But again, the criticism would be that the Pomponian interpretation falls short of explaining when to apply the principle directly and when not to (stamp case!). That has been the point of this book all along. By contrast, if unjust enrichment is based on Savigny's direct shift of value / wealth, the enrichment classification would find it hard to explain following beyond the first enrichee (Cass).

---

if he wins his bet – though **if the casino does so its payment to the gambler will likewise be in law a gift.**"

766 In that sense *Lipkin Gorman* (per Lord Goff), however noting that this was not argued before the Courts.

d) Final observations: Too narrow German Law

In *Lipkin Gorman*, German law could only have awarded a personal action in unjust enrichment because title to the cash drawn from the account would have been transferred at the counter on a valid (not forged) *Kontovollmacht*.[767] This excludes the *rei vindicatio* under § 985 BGB. The exact basis of the enrichment claim would have depended on who had received title from the bank.[768] Had it been the solicitors, they could have sued the Casino under § 816 I 2 BGB. The availability of this action would have come down to the distinction whether the gambling was legally prohibited (therefore illegal and void)[769] or whether it was just unenforceable due to being a wager.[770] In the former case, but not the latter, the BGH would have equated the transaction with a gift and applied § 816 I 2 BGB.[771] In Lipkin Gorman, the contract may not have been illegal, but was surely void.[772] It follows that a direct enrichment action against Karpnale would have lain had Lipkin Gorman received the title from the bank.

Conversely, if Cass had got the title, the standard enrichment claim could have only been directed to Cass under § 812 I 1 2. Alt. BGB ("in sonstiger Weise") as *Eingriffskondiktion*. A Leistungskondiktion under § 812 I 1 1. Alt. BGB would not have been available since Lipkin Gorman did not want to make a performance to Cass. Granting a general authority to draw from a bank account does not render every withdrawal into a performance made by the account holder.[773] The reason is that the authority does not specify the purpose for which it was given. So we cannot derive the purpose of the performance from it. That is why an abusive withdrawal constitutes a case of taking value without consent, even though it is legally valid owing to the authorisation. Under German law Cass would have had to restore the book money taken from Lipkin Gorman's account via the *Eingriffskondiktion*.

With Cass being the direct recipient, the Casino was only the remote beneficiary of the funds taken from Lipkin Gorman. Remote beneficiaries are beyond the reach of German actions in unjustified enrichment. The only direct action for Lipkin Gorman against the Casino would have been the exception under § 822 BGB.

---

767 See above p. 219.
768 See above p. 218.
769 BGHZ 37, 363 = NJW 1962, 1671; but cf. academics criticising that a void contract is not a voluntary gift, e.g. Schlosser, JuS 1963, 141, 143.
770 Cp. § 762 I 1 and 2 BGB; BGHZ 47, 393 = NJW 1967, 1660
771 BeckOK BGB/Wendehorst, 1.2.2024, § 816 mn. 9.
772 *Lipkin Gorman v Karpnale* [1991] 2 AC 548 (per Lord Templeman): "For present purposes, however, it does not seem to me to matter whether the contract upon which the defendant relies as affording consideration for receipt of stolen money is illegal as provided by the Lottery Act 1772 or void as provided by the Gaming Act 1845."
773 BGHZ 205, 334 = NJW 2015, 2725, 2726 mn. 27

But this provision is so heavily (overly!) restricted that it merely marks dead letter law in Germany. It allows leapfrogging the direct recipient of an unjust enrichment in order to address a donee if the enrichment claim against the direct beneficiary (Cass) fails *only* owing to the gift being made.[774] This is only the case if the direct recipient of the unjust enrichment can invoke disenrichment on the grounds of passing on the benefit to a volunteer. This does not normally happen because making the gift from another's funds saves own expenses. § 822 can only bite if the gift to the done is a luxury the donor would not have afforded without faith in the receipt. Moreover, *mala fide* recipients can never invoke the defence of disenrichment. Since Cass was stealing the book money, § 822 BGB could not have got off the ground. This may seem doubtful because it affords unmerited protection to donees.[775] Nevertheless, German doctrine has always been reluctant to extend § 822 BGB because of its adamant rejection of the *actio de in rem verso.* Thereby, it secures the priority of insolvency law and avoids bypassing the estate.[776]

Based on the House's assumption that Cass received title, German law of unjustified enrichment would have been of no avail to Lipkin Gorman. The reason is the non-acceptance of following and tracing into products in order to prolong the *rei vindicatio.* As has been shown, the re-allocation of the title to the money to Lipkin Gorman that had been achieved by following and tracing their stolen book money led to a situation where their enrichment claim against Karpnale (if it is one) formally remained within the scope of a direct shift of value – even though in substance, it was a claim against a remote volunteer. Basing the cause of action on following and tracing of property enables the personal action of money had and received to transgress the frontiers that are normally determined by the transactions between the parties. However, it remains a personal action to enforce the property right.[777] The money tracing enrichment action is a positive feature of English law compared to German law because it allows to reach out beyond formalistic legal boundaries to reach volunteers like Mlle. Spanoghe or the Casino. It is an exotic hybrid grown on English soil where people say that the best roses bloom. For the purposes of this book, it is important to note it has blossomed without the fertiliser of Pomponius. The claim vindicates "lost" values unilaterally and irrespective of legal title. It precludes "finders keepers"!

774 BeckOK BGB/Wendehorst, 1.2.2024, § 822 mn. 9.
775 Critical to the narrow interpretation Schall, Leistungskondiktion, p. 63.
776 BeckOK BGB/Wendehorst, 1.2.2024, § 822 mn. 10.
777 Depending on how serious the claim "This is my money" is taken at law, it is arguable that it can or cannot be brought against an insolvent defendant.

V The true shape of unjust enrichment: Savigny's direct shift of value unlocks the rationale of restitution

1 The ousting of the Pomponian principle by the direct shift of wealth/value (unmittelbare Vermögensverschiebung) in Germany

a) The discovery of the direct shift of wealth/value concept by *Friedrich Carl von Savigny*

Friedrich Carl von Savigny was the father of the concept of the direct shift of value. His great work, *System des heutigen Römischen Rechts*, published in 1841, was driven by a desire to thoroughly analyse all Roman-based law of the time in order to prepare the codification in Germany.[778] This led him to search for the principle underlying the Roman *condictiones.* In the third volume, he had already dismissed the notion of the Pomponian sentence that there be no enrichment from another's loss as too wide and too vague to be applied directly.

> Savigny, III, p. 451: "Dieſe Regel iſt indeſſen ſo allgemeiner und unbeſtimmter Natur, daß ſie eine unmittelbare Anwendung auf die Beurtheilung praktiſcher Rechtsfragen gar nicht zuläßt..."
>
> [However, this rule is of such a general and vague nature that it does not allow for a direct application to the judgement of practical legal questions... – DeepL]

Savigny argued for example that under Pomponius any (objectively) too expensive purchase would have to be undone because the vendor's gain came from the buyer's loss or that any gain made by a competitor would have to be disgorged, even if made in the course of fair competition.[779]

In the fifth volume, *Savigny* analysed the Roman *condictiones* and claimed a different underlying principle. According to *Savigny,* **all *condictiones*** were claims to reverse a **direct shift of wealth / value**[780] (= *unmittelbare Vermögensverschiebung*) from one person's assets to another's.

> *Savigny,* V. p. 564: "Grund und Bedingung der Condictionen iſt die ... Bereicherung des gegenwärtigen Schuldners aus dem Vermögen des Glaubigers, welche jetzt wieder rückgängig gemacht werden ſoll.
>
> [The reason for and condition of the *condictiones* is the enrichment of the current debtor from the creditor's wealth ..., which is now to be cancelled]

---

778 As set out by Savigny, Vom Beruf unsrer Zeit für Gesetzgebung und Rechtswissenschaft, 1814, p. 83

779 Savigny, III, p. 451–2.

780 As to the terminology, see above pp. 28–29.

The value that had been shifted had to be returned if and because it was without legal reason (*sine causa*). The starting point for *Savigny's* analysis was the repayment of a loan (*pecuniam creditam*)[781] which had been the paradigm of the *condictiones* in the Digest.[782] Today, we view the repayment of a loan as based on a promise and embark on a discussion whether or not there is a thing like "contractual restitution".[783] For Savigny however, the termination of the loan rendered the money in the hands of the defendant *sine causa* and therefore founded the *condictio.*[784] All other *condictiones*, e.g. the *condictio indebiti, ob causam datorum, sine causa* and *ob injustam causam*, i.e. the "true" cases of unjustified enrichment from today's viewpoint, were developed from this basis.[785] They all shared the common feature that the transaction either lacked a causa from the outset (*condictio indebiti*) or lost it later on,[786] like in the original case of the terminated loan or in the cases of the *condictio ob causam finitam* and the *condictio causa data causa non secuta*). This equating of original and subsequent missing of the *causa* explains why civilian enrichment laws have no difficulty with retrospectivity – unlike common law.[787] The shared roots of civil and common enrichment laws in the Mosaic *condictiones* indicate that common law should not be troubled either. The key to the solution is the failure of purpose approach (see below pp. 270–272).

---

781 Savigny, V, p. 511: "Um jenes Prinzip zu finden, gehe ich von der Zergliederung eines einzelnen Rechtsgeschäfts aus, aus welchem sicher eine Condiction entspringt, nämlich des Darlehens, welches ich daher als Ausgangspunkt der ganzen Untersuchung nehmen will."

[In order to find that principle, I start from the dissection of a single legal transaction, from which a *condictio* certainly corresponds, namely the loan, which I will therefore take as the starting point of the whole investigation]

782 See the first title of the twelfth book, D. 12.1.0: "de rebus creditis, si certum petetur, et de condictione."

783 In the affirmative Birks, Unjust Enrichment, 2005, p. 11 and 25; in the negative Burrows, The Law of Restitution, 3rd edn. 2011, pp. 12–13. For France in the affirmative Marie Malaurie, Les Restitutions en Droit Civile, 1991, pp. 23 et seq.

784 Savigny, V, p. 526: Es kommt nämlich darauf an, daß dem Übergang eines Rechts aus einem Vermögen in ein anderes die causa entzogen ſey, oder ſtets gefehlt habe; ſo iſt es bey dem Darlehen nach der Kündigung, oder bey dem irrig bezahlten indebitum.

[The point is that the transfer of a right from one property to another is deprived of causa, or has always lacked causa; so it is with the loan after cancellation, or with the wrongly paid indebitum – DeepL]

785 Savigny, V, p. 521.

786 Savigny, V, p. 526: Es kommt nämlich darauf an, daß dem Übergang eines Rechts aus einem Vermögen in ein anderes die causa entzogen ſey, oder ſtets gefehlt habe;

[The point is that the transfer of a right from one property to another is deprived of causa, or has always lacked causa;

787 This distinctive feature of the causa approach is advocated for English law under the heading of "absence of basis", Birks, Unjust Enrichment, 2005, pp. 101 et seq.; contrast Stevens, pp. 104–105.

The payment of money was the paradigm for the shift of value. But this did not necessarily mean that a voluntary transfer of title from the claimant to the defendant had to take place. The *condictiones* also applied to cases where the defendant had "taken" value by converting the title of the claimant for his benefit.[788] This did not only cover outright theft, where the *condictio furtiva* was the primary remedy, but also cases where property had been entrusted for safekeeping, but later was converted by the defendant in breach of that "trust".[789] The *condictio* was generally seen as a substitute making up for the loss of the *rei vinidcatio.*[790]

This line of thought is reminiscent of the view that the English action for money had and received is linked to transfers of title[791] – which is correct from the historic perspective of the different bases (namely *quantum meruit*),[792] but may have been overcome by *Lipkin Gorman v Karpnale* where the House seemed fairly agnostic to the question whether or not title had passed from the Bank to Cass and confirmed the very English *rei vindiactio* of a sum of money (above, pp. 216 et seq.).

By contrast, as just shown, the *condictiones* did *not* require any antecedent transfer of title (*datio*) from the claimant to the defendant. They covered the consumption of another's property. They did not even require any loss of title as they

788 Savigny, V, p. 552: "Wenn der Dieb gestohlenes Geld in seinen Nutzen verwendet, oder den gestohlenen Weizen aufzehrt, so bereichert er sich ohne Rechtsgrund auf Kosten des Bestohlenen, der sein Eigenthum durch Zerstörung der Sache verliert, und für Fälle dieser Art ist die allgemeine condictio sine causa völlig ausreichend." ["If the thieve uses stolen money for his benefit, or eats up the stolen wheat, he is enriched without legal ground at the expense of the of the victim, and for cases of this kind the general condictio sine causa is completely sufficient."]

At the passage cited, Savigny explained the need for the exceptional and additional *condictio furtiva* (pp. 551–554). It was the only *condictio* available together with the *rei vinicatio.* The aim of this exception was to deny the thief the opportunity to defeat the *rei vindicatio* simply by using up or mixing the stolen assets, e. g. money, Savigny, p. 553; on the exceptional character of the *condictio furtiva* see also von Kübel, Motive zum Vorentwurf des Bereicherungsrecht, p. 1; published in: *Schubert* (ed.), Die Vorentwürfe der Redaktoren zum BGB, Recht der Schuldverhältnisse, Teil 3, Besonderes Schuldrecht II, 1980, p. 661; cf. further Zimmermann, pp. 839–841.

789 Savigny, p. 518: "In unmittelbarer Entwicklung schließen sich an das Darlehen diejenigen Fälle an, worin dem Andern eine Sache ohne Übertragung des Eigenthums anvertraut worden ist, er aber das Eigenthum des Gebers eigenmächtig zerſtört, und ſich dadurch bereichert hat."

790 Savigny, V, pp. 514–515 and p. 518, referring inter alia to L. 11 § 2 R.C. (12,1) = D. 12.1.11 2. (Ulpianus libro 26 ad edictum): … Vindicari nummi possunt, si extant "exstant", aut, si dolo malo desinant possideri, ad exhibendum agi: quod si sine dolo malo consumpsisti, condicere tibi potero; and L. 29 de condi. indeb. (12.6.) = D. 12.6.29 (Ulpianus libro secundo disputationum): "… Et si quidem exstant nummi, vindicabuntur, consumptis vero condictio locum habebit."

791 Peter Watts, A Property Principle and a Services Principle [1995] RLR 49; contrast Stevens, pp. 80–82.

792 Baker in Schrage (ed.), pp. 33 et se.; pp. 47 et se.

covered the restitution of services and user.[793] That may have been under debate in the ius commune, but it was no longer under debate when the German codification was under way. Savigny and, following him, von Kübel, the Erste Kommission and the Zweite Kommission were unequivocal on this.

To hold otherwise was the (unfortunately common) misconception of German lawyers in later times. They were led to believe that Savigny's concept meant a "*gegenständliche Vermögensverschiebung*", i.e. the transfer of a real, tangible asset like property, [794] and applied the general enrichment claim of § 812 I 1 BGB accordingly. This misconception left the law of unjustified enrichment with massive inconsistencies and gaps that were exploited by Walter Wilburg to rip the concept of the direct shift of wealth apart (pp. 254 et seq.).

Some blame for this must be addressed to Savigny himself. It is surely true that Savigny saw the transfer of an asset (money) that had to be reversed as the paradigm of the *condictiones*. But it is far less clear if this meant that a prior *datio* from claimant to the defendant was a legal requirement. Probably not, because he had analysed the sources thoroughly and was therefore well aware of the cases of consumption, services and user. But we do not have to delve into this because whatever he thought about the *datio*, he introduced the decisive modification of that rule – the qualification that made the principle work where it would otherwise fail. Other than all the later (mis)interpreters of the direct shift of wealth requirement, Savigny had explained why the Roman *condictiones* also covered services as shift of wealth. True, he should have used "value" instead (p. 29 and p. 235). But still: In a passage that has attracted (too) little scholarly attention, Savigny referred to the money's worth of services which allowed them to be equated with money.

Savigny, V, p. 523: "Ja sogar eine Arbeit, die geleistet wird, weil man dazu irrigerweise verpflichtet zu sein glaubte, kann die Kondiktion begründen, insofern sich die Arbeit auf einen bestimmten Geldwert zurückführen, also mit einer gezahlten Geldsumme vergleichen lässt."[795]

["Indeed, even works which were conducted because one erroneously believed an obligation to exist to this effect can cause a claim of enrichment, insofar as the works were linked to a

793 D. 12.6.26 (Ulpianus ad edictum):

794 For this criticism, that can in truth only be held against the misinterpretation of the direct shift of value / wealth, not against Savigny's teachings, see for example *Ellger*, Bereicherung durch Eingriff, 2002, p. 58: "Die strikte Einhaltung dieses Erfordernisses schließt den Bereicherungsausgleich aus, in denen es um die Bereicherung aus nichtkörperlichen Gegenständen geht"; likewise *Maximilian Wolf*, Bereicherungsausgleich bei Eingriffen in höchstpersönliche Rechtsgüter, 2017, pp. 112 et seq.

795 Referring to L. 26 § 12 = D. 12.6.26 (Ulpianus ad edictum)

particular pecuniary value, which is to say that they can be compared to a particular sum of money."]

This is an important observation to understand the direct shift of wealth/value in Savigny's unjustified enrichment. **Money and money's worth are treated equally.** It is a central pillar of the normative foundation pp. 262 et seq. To the criticism that Robert Stevens has formulated against the transfer of value approach under English unjust enrichment: "If at your request I sing a song for you, nothing is transferred to you."[796] Savigny would answer: You are right if your singing is of no value for me. But if your singing is money's worth because you are a singing flower or a pop star whom I hired, you give value to me.

Savigny equated the rendering of a valuable service to the payment in order to fit the Roman rule that (the value of) services could be claimed back by a *condictio* into his approach of the *unmittelbare Vermögensverscheibung* = direct shift of wealth. This cannot be criticised as a mere fiction. A fiction is an outright "legal lie", like in the Oxonian story of the Dean's dog,[797] or in the Civilian anecdote of the succulent roast that was baptized "carp" by the monk ("Ego te baptizo carpam") before it was eaten during Lent. But the equation of money and money's worth does not tell a lie, but a truth: the objective value of services. The provider who renders a service gives something valuable ("that he must be paid for"), and the recipient receives something valuable ("that he must pay for"). Imagine the procurement of the benefit as that one moment captured by Michelangelo's "Godly spark": The piano concert, the haircut, the surgery, the song by the singing flower, the use of the hired car or building. It is exactly that moment of receiving something valuable that constitutes the shift of wealth/value for unjust enrichment, just as is the payment, the assignment or the conveyance. This value need not come out of the purse of the claimant, and it need not go into the purse of the defendant. If that point is missed, the law drowns in quicksand.

Correctly understood, Savigny's principle defines and confines the claims in unjust enrichment: **Procuring and receiving money or money's worth is the relevant shift of value. The recipient, and only the recipient, is enriched "at the expense" of the performing party – who is therefore the right claimant for the restitution of the failed transaction.**[798]

Thus, Savigny's shift of wealth/value leads directly to the "performance-based" approach of the *condictio indebiti* that prevails in Germany today. *Every* party mak-

---

796 *Stevens*, LQR (2018) 573, at p. 583.
797 The college rules prohibited keeping of dogs in the college. The Dean had a dog. In order to allow this, a subparagraph in the college rules ordered that the Dean's dog was deemed a cat.
798 Motive II, 830.

ing a performance to another can demand restitution of the performance (or its value) from the recipient if he has performed *sine causa* = without legal reason.

To reiterate the point on taxonomy made in the beginning (pp. 29–30): The *unmittelbare Vermögensverschiebung* = "direct shift of wealth" and the "direct shift of value" of English unjust enrichment mean essentially the same. But on closer looks, direct shift of value describes Savigny's concept even more precisely than he did himself, and that difference probably had decisive effects for the later distraction of German unjustified enrichment. The point is not about translation. English law may offer various more or less fitting options for *Vermögen:* assets, wealth, fortune. But German law has a direct correspondent to value: *Wert.* And this is exactly the word *Savigny* should have used, too. All *condictiones* are primarily concerned with the return of the very value given or taken. They do not require that the assets of the claimant are depleted or that the assets of the defendant are swollen. To the contrary: this is irrelevant to found the enrichment claim. Services neither deplete nor swell the assets. But they must be refunded because value has been shifted. The stamp destruction decreases the wealth of one and increases that of the other. But there is no restitution because no value has been shifted. Pomponius did not get that. Nor did the BGB in § 812. Savigny got it, but did not describe it precisely enough. He used the requirement *aus dem Vermögen* = out of the assets/the wealth of the claimant and searched for a *Vermögensverschiebung* = shift of wealth. But this terminology indicates that an actual transfer of assets from A to B must have taken place (*gegenständliche Vermögensverschiebung*). And that was exactly how later jurists interpreted it – and led the law astray. The right approach would have been to require a direct shift of value at the expense of the claimant = *unmittelbare Wertverschiebung auf Kosten des Gläubigers.*

b) The adoption of Savigny's direct-shift-of-wealth/value concept by the *Vorentwurf* and the *Erste Entwurf*

Savigny's view of unjustified enrichment as direct shift of wealth/value *sine causa* gained constantly ground in nineteenth century Germany. By the time Franz-Philipp von Kübel wrote the *Vorentwurf* (Pre-draft) of the BGB, it had become almost generally accepted that unjustified enrichment consisted of the *condictiones* only, and that those *condictiones* aimed to return a direct shift of value that lacked legal reason.[799] The *Vorentwurf* ("pre-draft") and the *Erste Entwurf* ("first draft") of the

799 See the explanation in the "motives" of the pre-draft by *von Kübel,* Motive zum Vorentwurf des Bereicherungsrechts, p. 1: "Das römische Recht hat eine besondere Art von Klagerechten geschaffen, vermöge welcher Etwas zurückgefordert werden kann, was … ohne Grund von dem

BGB rested firmly on Savigny's principle. They rejected both the Pomponian principle and the *actio de in rem verso* as basis of unjust enrichment.[800]

> Motive II, 829: "Die Vorschriften des Entwurfs über die Bereicherung beruhen nicht auf dem in der früheren gemeinrechtlichen Theorie missverständlich aufgestellten und gehandhabten Billigkeitssatze, niemand dürfe sich mit dem Schaden eines anderen bereichern, noch auf dem ähnlichen, der preußischen Versionsklage zugrunde liegenden Prinzip, dass derjenige, aus dessen Vermögen etwas in den Nutzen eines anderen verwendet worden war, dasselbe ... zurückzufordern ... berechtigt sei..."
>
> [The provisions of the draft on enrichment are not based on the equitable principle, misleadingly established and applied in the earlier theory of the ius commune, that no one may enrich himself with the damage of another, nor on the similar[801] principle underlying the Prussian *actio de in rem verso* action, that he from whose property something had been used for the benefit of another was entitled to reclaim the same...]
>
> Von Kübel, p. 3: "Früher wurde unter Berufung auf missverstandene oder allgemeine Quellenaussprüche ... die Grundlosigkeit des Erwerbs mit Rücksicht auf den allgemeinen Billigkeitssatz bestimmt, dass niemand sich mit fremden Schaden bereichern solle und so diese Klagen lediglich als ein Ausdruck jenes völlig vagen und keiner sicheren Anwendung fähigen Grundsatzes selbst bezeichnet. ... Dieser Satz, so unrichtig er ist..."
>
> [In the past, with reference to misunderstood or general source statements ... the groundlessness of the acquisition was determined with regard to the general principle of equity, that no one should enrich himself with another's detriment, and thus these actions were described merely as an expression of that completely vague principle itself, which is incapable of any certain application. ... This principle, incorrect as it is....]

Vermögen des einen in das eines anderen gelangt ist, die condictiones sine causa in ihren verschiedenen Gestaltungen."

[Roman law created a special type of right of action by means of which something can be reclaimed that ... has passed without cause from the property of one person to that of another, the condictiones sine causa in their various forms.

The motives are published in: Schubert (ed.), Die Vorentwürfe der Redaktoren zum BGB, Recht der Schuldverhältnisse, Teil 3, Besonderes Schuldrecht II, 1980, pp. 661 et seq.

800 Contrast a last stand of the old view: Georg Wilhelm August Sell, "Über den Grundsatz des römischen Rechts, dass niemand mit oder aus dem Schaden eines andern sich bereichern dürfe", Versuche im Gebiete des Zivilrechts, 1st Part, Gießen, 1833, p. 14; against him von Kübel, at p. 3.

801 Note a little twist here: The motives only recognised a "similar" principle for the *actio de in rem verso*. According with the predominant view of 19th century Germany (pp. 134 et seq.), they saw it as related to the negotiorum gestio and therefore rejecting its introduction into the BGB after those provisions, not in the context of enrichment law, see Motive II, 871–873. By contrast, according to von Kübel, p. 7–8 (= Schubert, p. 667–668), the *actio de in rem verso* of Prussian ALR was seen as based on Pomponian principle, mirroring the prevailing doctrine at that time.

Instead of the Pomponian principle, *Vorentwurf* and E I accepted the direct shift of wealth/value as general feature of the condictiones:

> Motive II, 830: "Ist durch einen den Vermögensübergang an sich begründenden Akt das Vermögen des einen gemindert und das des anderen vermehrt und fehlt hierzu ein rechtlicher Grund, so hat jener gegen den letzteren den persönlichen Anspruch auf Zurückgewährung des ohne Rechtsgrund Empfangenen und nur gegen den letzteren. Der die Kondiktion begründende Tatbestand ist grundsätzlich ein unmittelbar zwischen den Benachteiligten und dem Bereicherten eingetretener; gegen Dritte besteht der Kondiktionsanspruch nicht."
>
> [If the wealth of one person is reduced and that of the other increased by an act which in itself constitutes a transfer of wealth/value, and if there is no legal reason for this, the latter has a personal claim against the former for restitution of what he has received without legal reason, and only against the latter. The fact giving rise to the *condictio* is generally one that has occurred directly between the disadvantaged and the enriched; the claim does not lie against third parties."]

The principle of direct shift of wealth/value became the basis of German unjustified enrichment. The performance-based *condictiones* were all structured as personal claims of the performing party against the recipient. The *Vorentwurf* proposed detailed provisions to recover shifts of value including services and user.[802] Subsequently, the *Erste Entwurf* streamlined these rules on editorial grounds and immersed the restitution of services / user in an abstract formulation:

> 739 E I: "Ist die Herausgabe durch die Beschaffenheit des Geleisteten ausgeschlossen… hat der Empfänger den Wert zu vergüten."
>
> [If restoration is excluded by the nature of what has been provided… the recipient must pay the value.]

The pre-draft consisted of 28 provisions.[803] At centre stage were the performance-based *condictiones*, the *Leistungskondiktionen*. As their Roman predecessors, they concerned cases where the performance had either been made without legal reason (= *ohne Rechtsgrund / sine causa*) or where the legal reason subsequently got lost. The claim for repayment of a loan, the original *condictio* of Roman law for Savigny, was no longer seen as an enrichment claim. It had moved to the law of obligations and became § 607 BGB a.F.[804] The draft contained the *condictio indebiti* (§ 1 VE), the *condictio ob causam datorum* (§ 14 VE), the *condictio ob turpem cau-*

---

802 § 10 VE (services) and § 11 VE (user).

803 On the drafting process see also *Schubert*, "Windscheid und das Bereicherungsrecht des ersten Entwurfs", Zeitschrift der Savigny-Stiftung für Rechtsgeschichte, 1975, Vol. 92, 186, at 191 et seq.

804 Since 2002, the law of loan contracts is subdivided: The claim for repayment of money (§ 498 I 2 BGB) and the claim for repayment of loans in kind (§ 607 I 2 BGB).

sam (§ 18). The final chapter on the restitution of enrichments *sine causa* (= "Rückforderung wegen grundlosen Habens") added four more actions to recover performances that failed for specific reasons (§§ 23–26 VE), [805] the most important being the *condictio ob causam finitam* in § 26 VE. It concluded with the *condictio sine causa specialis* a sweeping clause for non-performance related enrichments in § 27 VE.

All *Leistungskondiktionen* were structured according to the following pattern: The claimant was the performing party ("Wer ... geleistet hat"). The defendant was the recipient ("Empfänger") of the performance. The claimant could primarily demand restitution of the subject-matter of the performance *in natura* ("das Geleistete"). If that was impossible, the value of the performance could be claimed. That was expressed by § 6 III VE for goods and by § 10 VE for services and user. Both the natural and the value-based restitution were under the proviso that the defendant was still enriched (§ 5 VE), unless he was mala fide (§ 12 VE).

The *Erste Entwurf* essentially followed this structure, but reduced the number of performance-related by cutting out §§ 23–25 VE, only keeping the *condictio ob causam finitam.* The relevant provisions are shown in the following. We start with the performance-related Leistungskondiktionen. It is of vital importance to note that the text of these provisions contained no additional requirement of "aus dem Vermögen" (= "out of the wealth/assets") or "auf Kosten" (= at the expense) because under Savigny's system, that was not necessary. *Every* performing party that transferred money's worth *sine causa* to another *automatically* earned the right to restitution, namely:

- **the *condictio indebiti:***

> § 737 **E I:** "Wer zum Zweck der Erfüllung einer Verbindlichkeit eine Leistung bewirkt hat, kann wenn die Verbindlichkeit nicht bestanden hat, von dem Empfänger das Geleistete zurückfordern."
>
> [A **person who has rendered a performance** for the purpose of discharging a liability may, if the liability did not exist, reclaim from the **recipient** what has been rendered.]

805 § 23 VE concerned performances by a minor and performances violating a legal prohibition. § 24 VE allowed the recovery of performances made under contracts that later were nullified with retrospective effect by way of *Anfechtung*, a functional equivalent of rescission. § 25 VE concerned performances that were made to attain legally impossible purposes. § 26 VE concerned performances that were made on a temporary causa that later got either lost or deleted with retrospective effect and named the case of damages that had been paid before the cause of the damages ceased to exist.

§ 1 VE: "Wer einem Anderen Etwas zur Erfüllung einer ihm hierzu obliegenden Rechtsverbindlichkeit geleistet hat, kann das Geleistete von dem Empfänger zurükfordern, wenn eine Verbindlichkeit nicht bestanden hat. ..."

[A **person who has rendered something** to another **as a performance** for discharging a legal obligation incumbent on him may **reclaim the performance** from the **recipient** if an obligation did not exist.]

– the *condictio causa data causa non secuta:*

§ 742 E I: "Wer unter der ausdrücklich oder stillschweigend erklärten Voraussetzung des Eintritts oder Nichteintritts eines künftigen Ereignisses oder eines rechtlichen Erfolges eine Leistung bewirkt hat, kann, wenn die Voraussetzung sich nicht erfüllt, von dem Empfänger das Geleistete zurückfordern."

[A **person who has rendered a performance** on the express or implied precondition of the occurrence or non-occurrence of a future event or of a legal result may, if the condition is not fulfilled, **recover** from the **recipient** what has been rendered.]

§ 14 VE: "Hat Jemand, ohne hierzu durch einen zweiseitigen Vertrag verpflichtet zu sein, aus einem erlaubten Grunde unter der ausdrücklich erklärten oder aus den Umständen sich ergebenden Voraussetzung des Eintritts eines künftigen Ereignisses einem Anderen Etwas geleistet, so ist er, sofern dieses Ereignis nicht eintritt, das Geleistete von dem Empfänger zurückzufordern berechtigt."

[If **someone**, without being obliged to do so by a contract, **has rendered something as a performance** to another for a permissible reason under the expressly declared or from the circumstances resulting precondition of the occurrence of a future event, he is entitled to **reclaim what he has rendered from the recipient** if this event does not occur.]

– the *condictio ob causam finitam* (§ 745 E I; § 26 VE):

§ 745 E I: "Wer eine Leistung aus einem Rechtsgrunde bewirkt hat, welcher später weggefallen ist, kann von dem Empfänger das Geleistete zurückfordern."

[A person who has **rendered** a **performance** for a legal reason which has subsequently ceased to exist may **reclaim the performance** rendered **from the recipient.**]

§ 26 VE: "Hat Jemand einem Anderen aus einem vorübergehenden, nach der Leistung weggefallenen Rechtsgrunde oder aus einem nach der Leistung mit rückwirkender Kraft vernichteten Grunde Etwas geleistet, so ist der Geber berechtigt, Rückerstattung des Geleisteten von dem Empfänger zu fordern. ..."[806]

806 The ensuing second sentence of § 26 added the example of the fullo (D.12.7.3): "Insbesondere ist derjenige, welcher für eine ihm anvertraute und ihm abhanden gekommene Sache einem Anderen Ersatz geleistet hat, insoweit, als der Schaden später wegefallen ist, Rückerstattung zu fordern berechtigt." [In particular, a person who has paid compensation to another for a thing entrusted to

[If someone has **made a performance** to another person for a temporary legal reason that ceased to exist after the performance was made or for a reason that ceased to exist with retroactive effect after the performance was made, **the giver** shall be entitled to **demand restitution of the performance from the recipient.** ...]

– **the *condictio ob turpem vel inustam causam*** (§ 747 E I; § 18 VE):

§ 747 EI: "Ist von dem Empfänger einer Leistung durch deren Annahme nach dem Inhalte des Rechtsgeschäfts gegen die guten Sitten oder die öffentliche Ordnung verstoßen worden, so kann der Geber das Geleistete zurückfordern."

[If the **recipient of a performance** has violated morality or public policy by accepting it with regard to the content of the transaction, the **giver** may **reclaim** the **performance.**

§ 18 VE: "Hat Jemand um eines künftigen Erfolges willen aus einer sittlich verwerflichen Ursache Etwas angenommen, so ist der Geber zur Rückforderung berechtigt, ohne Unterschied, ob der erwartete Erfolg eingetreten ist oder nicht."

[If **someone has accepted something** for the sake of a future success out of a morally reprehensible reason, the **giver** is entitled to **reclaim** the **benefit**, regardless of whether the expected success has occurred or not.][807]

The more **abstract requirement of "aus dem Vermögen"** (= out of the wealth/assets) or **"auf Kosten"** (= at the expense) was **only necessary** to determine the claimant in the residual, **non-performance based enrichment cases** that were covered by the *condictio sine causa specialis* (§ 748 E I; § 27 VE):

§ 748 E I: "Derjenige, aus dessen Vermögen nicht kraft seines Willens oder kraft seines rechtsgültigen Willens ein anderer bereichert worden ist, kann, wenn hierzu ein rechtlicher Grund gefehlt hat, von dem anderen die Herausgabe der Bereicherung fordern."

[The person from whose property another person has been enriched **not by virtue of his will (consent) or by virtue of his legally valid will (consent)** may, if there was no legal reason for doing so, demand the restitution of the enrichment from the other person.]

§ 27 VE: "Derjenige, **aus dessen Vermögen** etwas ohne seinen Willen in das Vermögen eines anderen gekommen ist, kann, wenn ein rechtlicher Grund hierzu von Anfang an nicht vorhanden war oder derselbe später weggefallen ist, von letzterem Rückerstattung verlangen."

[The person **from whose "wealth"/assets/property** something has come into the **"wealth"/assets/property** of another without his "will"/consent may, if a legal reason for this did not exist from the beginning or if this reason has subsequently ceased to exist, demand restitution from the latter.]

---

him and lost by him is entitled to claim restitution to the extent that the damage has subsequently ceased to exist.]

807 Note that this provision does not use "performance" yet, but nevertheless refers to purposeful giving ("for the sake of a future success").

The condictiones *sine causa specialis* were the only actions that expressly required a direct shift of value "out of the assets" or "wealth" of the claimant into those/that of the defendant. That requirement was derived from the underlying principle of all *condictiones.* However, with a view to the later developments that derailed the German principle, it is important to note that § 27 VE and § 748 E I were not a large general clause catching *all* cases of unjustified enrichment but a small sweeping clause to catch the few remaining cases. The claim was expressly reduced to shifts of value that had taken place **without any consent** on the side of the claimant ("ohne dessen Willen"). This excluded all performance-based claims where the consent was merely flawed because the purpose of the performance failed. The Leistungskondiktionen followed a clear pattern: claimant = performing party; defendant = recipient of the performance; object of restitution = the performance *in natura* or its value. There was no requirement that the claim had to come "out of the assets/the wealth" (= *aus dem Vermögen*) or "at the expense" (= *auf Kosten*) of the claimant.

Both drafts clearly show the **dichotomy of *Leistungskondiktionen* and *Nichtleistungskondiktion.*** The former are pinned to the performance, the latter to the direct shift of wealth/value. Nevertheless, the road to the dichotomy of performance-based and non-performance-based enrichment in Germany was rocky because it had got lost in the final version of the BGB. While this was partly due to sloppy drafting, as we will see below, it must be mainly attributed to the fact that German lawyers never fully appreciated that the giving and receiving of money's worth (or the taking of it) *per se* meant the direct shift of value of *Savigny's* principle. Instead, they searched for a "real" shift of value ("gegenständliche Vermögensverschiebung") that could not be found at all for services and that would only derail the enrichment claim where money or goods were transferred in multi-party situations. This approach was bound to fail. But when it did, people generally assumed the principle was wrong while it had only been misapplied. Thus, when the works of Wilburg and von Caemmerer finally led to the establishment of the Roman *condictiones,* with a delay of 60 years after the BGB had entered into force, this was misconceived as the defeat of Savigny's principle rather than the triumph it actually was.

In truth, the application of the *condictio indebiti* within the framework of § 812 I 1 BGB does not only confirm Savigny's principle. On closer looks, German law even depends on Savigny's explanation why the *condictiones* covered services. German law defines a *Leistung* (= performance) as *bewusste und zweckgerichtete Mehrung fremden Vermögens* – which translates as "deliberate and purposeful **in-**

crease of another's wealth".[808] There is no doubt amongst German jurists that services qualify as a performance in that sense. And yet, this long-standing definition is not apt to cover services or user.[809] The explanation why the recipient of a service enjoys an "increase of his wealth" is given by Savigny: the service is money's worth. That is why some leading commentators have started to propose alternative definitions like the *zweckgerichtete Hingabe von Vermögensvorteilen* (= purposeful transfer of pecuniary advantages)[810] *or the Verschaffung eines Vorteils* (= procurement of an advantage).[811] They rightly focus on the transfer of money's worth instead of demanding an increase in the defendant's wealth/assets. But this is not generally accepted in Germany, and anyway, the modifications only come down to the direct shift of value of Savigny and English law – albeit adding a special emphasis on the purpose of the transaction that bodes well for English law, too (see the normative foundation below, pp. 266 et seq.).

c) The direct shift of value dissolves the *condictio indebiti* in the general enrichment claim

The clear picture of German law of unjustified enrichment got lost in the final version of the Code.[812] This was caused by the decision of the Second Commission to start the chapter with a general enrichment claim ("große Generalklausel"). The final version of § 812 I 1 BGB allowed an interpretation that did not only immerse the clear-cut *Leistungskondiktion* within the general enrichment claim, but also falsified its content. That mislead the *Einheitslehre* (= unity doctrine) into a deficient interpretation which nevertheless prevailed for more than 60 years. When this was finally corrected by the *Trennungslehre* (= separation doctrine) and, following Wilburg and von Caemmerer, the pure and simple *Leistungskondiktion*, without recourse to the "at the expense", requirement was re-established in Ger-

---

808 The Bundesgerichtshof has constantly adhered to this definition, BGHZ 40, 272 (277); 50, 227 (231, 232); 56, 228 (240); 72, 246 (248 f.); NJW 2004, 1169.

809 NK-BGB/Prinz v. Sachsen Gessaphe, § 812 Rn. 15. One counter-argument is the notion of *Ersparnisbereicherung:* by receiving the service without legal reason, the defendant is said to spare the expenses of buying the service under a valid contract. But this is not only complicated, but misses the point. Spared expenses only become relevant to determine enrichment from services that were not requested, i. e. where the defendant did *not* make a spending choice to which he can be held. If he did, he simply received the value of the service, not a construed enrichment from sparing other expenses.

810 MüKoBGB/Schwab, 8th edn. 2020, § 812 Rn. 347.

811 BeckOKBGB/Wendehorst, 1.8.2023, § 812 Rn 38.

812 Also critical Zimmermann, pp. 887–888: no "legislative masterpiece".

many in the late 1960ies, it was generally assumed that this was an achievement that defied and defeated the unified principle of unjustified enrichment.[813]

> *Wilburg*, p. 23: "Die einheitliche Grundlage der Bereicherungsansprüche ist durch den Misserfolg der Bereicherungsdogmatik widerlegt."
>
> ["The uniform basis of the enrichment claims is falsified by the failure of the doctrine of unjustified enrichment" (i.e. the direct shift of wealth)]

In truth however, the *Trennungslehre* just corrected the misapplication of the direct shift of wealth/value. This is a technical interpretation exercise. It can be shown by tracing the process step by step.

aa) The general enrichment claim in the counter-draft of the *Reichsjustizkommission:* blurring the equation "performance = direct shift of value" is the first nail in the coffin of Savigny's uniform principle

The starting point for the demise of the direct shift of value concept was a new counter-draft for the law of unjustified enrichment. It was drawn up by the *Vorkommission des Reichsjustizamtes* and put before the Second Commission as a preferable alternative to the First Draft.

Dropping the entire first draft was a harsh measure. The background was the rejection of the *Lehre von der Voraussetzung* (= doctrine of precondition). This doctrine had been developed by Bernhard Windscheid to explain the lack of legal ground (*sine causa*). Windscheid was the most eminent disciple of Savigny and member of the First Commission. He took a very active role in the codification of the BGB. So great was his influence that the first draft was nicknamed "kleiner Windscheid" because it was said to mirror his *Lehrbuch der Pandekten.* Unsurprisingly, the first draft also followed his theory in the provisions of the *condictio causa data causa non secuta* (§ 742 E I). It had actually already been adopted by von Kübel's pre-draft (§ 14 VE; for the texts see above). But after fierce criticism by Otto Lenel,[814] the notion of *Voraussetzung* was dropped in favour of the more precise concept of (the failure of) the *Leistungszweck* (= purpose of the performance). The reason was that the distinction between a unilateral *Voraussetzung* and irrelevant motives was too unclear. The purpose of the performance offered a clearer solution that the Second Comission chose to follow (on the normative foun-

813 It is interesting to note that the same assumption (defeat of the principle by the separate reading of § 812 I 1 BGB) is made by the opposing view. The (ever fewer) supporters of the uniform enrichment principle think that it commands the interpretation of § 812 I 1 BGB as general enrichment claim, see *Flume*, AcP 199 (1999), 1, 35 = Studien, p.197 *Wilhelm*, pp. 98 et seq.

814 Lenel, AcP 74 (1889), 213; contra: Windscheid, AcP AcP 78 (1892), 161; re: Lenel, AcP 79 (1892), 49.

dation see below, pp. 266 et seq.). This led to the resignation of Windscheid from the Commission. He would not live to see the BGB but died in 1892.

The counter draft that was put in the place of the first draft defined all performance-related *condictiones* by the failure of their purpose (§ b, see below). More importantly for the purposes of this book, instead of starting with the *condictio indebiti* (as § 1 VE and § 737 E I), it formulated a general enrichment claim in § a. The aim was to put the general principle of unjustified enrichment on top, like had also been done in the Swiss Code.[815] It is interesting to note that von Kübel had deliberately abstained from putting the general clause at the beginning for fear that its vagueness would cause misinterpretations.[816] How very right history would prove him!

The general clause of the *Vorkommission* of the *Reichsjustizamt* read:

> § a: "Hat jemand aus dem Vermögen eines anderen etwas ohne rechtlichen Grund erlangt, so ist er dem anderen zur Herausgabe des Erlangten verpflichtet."
>
> [If somebody has received something without legal reason out of the wealth/assets of another, he is obliged to make restitution of the received to the other.]
>
> § b "Eine Leistung kann wegen mangelnden rechtlichen Grundes zurückgefordert werden, wenn sie ohne Zweckbestimmung erfolgt oder die Zweckbestimmung nichtig ist, oder wenn der bestimmte Zweck nicht erreicht oder später weggefallen oder der Art ist, daß der Empfänger durch die Annahme der Leistung gegen ein gesetzliches Verbot oder gegen die guten Sitten verstößt"
>
> [A performance may be reclaimed for lack of legal reason if it is made without a determination of purpose or if the determination of purpose is null and void, or if the determined purpose is not achieved or subsequently ceases to exist or is of such a nature that the recipient, by accepting the performance, violates a legal prohibition or offends against morality.]

The enrichment action is formulated from the perspective of the debtor. The defendant is the "jemand" who must have obtained ("erlangt") something ("etwas"), i.e. the enrichment, out of the wealth/assets ("aus dem Vermögen") of another, i.e. the claimant. The provision neatly transposes the principle of direct shift of wealth/value from the claimant to the defendant.

---

815 Art. 62 OR: The provision essentially equals that of Art 70 OR 1881 to which the German lawmakers referred. Von Kübel, p. 9 assumed that this rule translated the obsolete Pomponian principle – just as many think about § 812 I 1 BGB.

816 Von Kübel, p. 15 (= Schubert, p. 675): "Obgleich nach dem Entwurfe die sämtlichen Kategorien der Kondiktionen auf das kaum erwähnte Prinzip zurückzuführen sind, so vermeidet er es doch, dasselbe in einem besonderen Paragraphen an die Spitze zu stellen; es wäre dies mit der Gefahr vager und missbräuchlicher Anwendung verbunden..."

Next came a provision that enlisted the reasons that would render a performance *sine causa.* It was centred throughout on the notion of the (failure of the) *Zweck* (purpose) or the performance instead of the *Lehre von der Voraussetzung.* Nevertheless, it confirmed that restitution is triggered unilaterally. The purpose is set by the performing party. It is a question of debate whether every purpose must be agreed with the recipient before its achievement can provide a legal reason. But the determination of purpose (*Leistungszweckbestimmung*)[817] remains a one-sided act. The Second Commission was as clear as the First Commission and von Kübel that the **reason for restitution** (not: for keeping the benefit) was **unilateral.** This remained so even though the provision of § b was later dropped for editorial reasons:

> Protokolle II, 2950–2951 = Mugdan II, 1173: "Der Rechtsgrund der Leistung bilde darnach materiell einen Bestandteil des Leistungsgeschäftes, die Leistung werde nur um des Zweckes willen gemacht und könne deshalb auch nicht unter Ablehnung der Zweckbestimmung entgegengenommen werden; eine ohne Zweckbestimmung erfolgte Leistung sei ein von vornherein unvollständiges Geschäft und dürfe auch nur als solches vom Empfänger behandelt werden, eine Leistung, deren Zweck nichtig oder nicht zustande gekommen sei oder später wegfalle, entbehre des Rechtsgrundes und könne nicht aufrechterhalten bleiben."
>
> [The legal reason of the performance materially formed an integral part of the transaction, the performance was only made for the sake of the purpose and could therefore not be accepted by rejecting the purpose; a performance made without a purpose was an incomplete transaction from the outset and could only be treated as such by the recipient, a performance whose purpose was void or did not come about or subsequently ceased to exist was devoid of legal basis and could not be maintained.]

Thus, a failure to agree on the purpose leads to restitution under German law – contrary to Robert Stevens who is adamant that without acceptance of the performance/purpose, no restitution should lie under common law.[818] But as already said above: *Moses v Macferlan* imported the unjust factors of the "Mosaic condictiones", and with them came the unilateral justification of claims in unjust enrichment to England, alien to general common law as that may be. However, as set out in the introduction (pp. 25–27), this does not preclude a counter-rule barring restitution. That makes particular sense in cases where "restitution" essentially means enforcing the contract, like the restitution of services and user.

Taken together, §§ a and b of the counter-draft still showed the dichotomic structure of unjust enrichment. The content of § b indicated that failed perform-

---

817 See in detail Chris Thomale, Leistung als Freiheit, 2012, pp. 5 et seq. and pp. 163 et seq.; Sascha Beck, Die Zuordnungsbestimmung im Rahmen der Leistung, 2006.

818 Stevens, p. 46; contrast Burrows, A Defence of Unjust Enrichment, 78 (3) CLJ 521 (2019).

ances must be restored. But the clear structure of the *Leistungskondiktionen* under the pre-draft and the first draft got lost. Their specific requirements became immersed in the general claim. Instead of the recipient of the performance, the defendant was "somebody who has received something" and instead of the performing party, the claimant was the person "out of whose wealth/assets" that something had been received. True, it would have still been possible to apply the general enrichment claim in a way that achieved the same outcome. Both Savigny and von Kübel had recognised that this was possible. Otherwise, the direct shift of value could not have been the underlying principle! Nevertheless, the creation of the general claim has sowed the seed of destruction to the principle because it blurred the clear and necessary notion that **every performance** of money of money's worth **as such** qualifies as the direct shift of value of the Roman *condictiones.* This can be shown in the following example of **multiple perfomances underlying one natural act:**

A paints the house of B under a service contract.

As shown above, p. 235, this valuable service is a direct shift of value for Savigny because it transfers money's worth to the recipient. However, the simple natural act of painting the door need not merely be a performance of a service contract with B. It could as well relate to a multitude of contracts. By A's act of painting,
- A could perform on his labour contract with his employer E,
- E could perform as subcontractor for M as main contractor,
- M could perform on his service contract with the subtenant S,
- S could perform his obligations under the tenancy agreement with mesne tenant T,
- T could perform on his tenancy agreement with landlord and owner C.

In this variant of the example, the same natural act relates to a multitude of performances. Each of these performances can trigger an enrichment claim (from A to E, from E to M, etc.) if it is defective. Obviously, it is still possible to explain each of these performance as a shift of value because every performing party transferred money's worth to the respective recipient. However, it is as evident that the enrichment claim must never follow any "direct shift of wealth" *instead* of the performance. That would only make sense if the "direct shift of wealth" was different from the performance, whereas *it is* the performance. A rule pointing to the shift of value *instead* of the performance would lose track. It would indicate a different, "natural" meaning for shift of value. From a natural perspective, value can hardly be shifted more directly than from the brush of the painter into the wall of the owner[819] Thus, the only enrichment claim in our extended example would lie between employee A and owner C. This cannot be right and it is not the law, neither in Germany nor in England.[820]

The search for a "real shift of value in kind" is even setting a false fire where real values are transferred under contracts. If A transfers land to C, this could be done in fulfilment of an obligation arising from their contract. But it could as well be done in fulfilment of a chain of 2 sales contracts entered into by A and B, and B and C. Again, a multitude of enrichment claims relate to the multitude of performances. It is irrelevant whether the seller owns the property before he procures the transfer to his buyer, likewise if the buyer receives the property himself before passing it on, as long as every party eventually got what it bargained for. And yet, if the legal rule requires a direct shift of value instead of a performance, it is highly likely to be interpreted in a "natural" way, only looking at the direct transfer between A and C.

These examples confirm: every performance *as such* must be understood as "direct shift of value". Otherwise, the general enrichment claim will derail. It is wrong to search for a "real transfer of value" (*gegenständliche Vermögensverschiebung*) instead of the performance. A general enrichment claim blurs the simple, clear and necessary equation "valuable performance = shift of value". That is why the counter-draft of the *Reichsjustizamt*, ignoring the wise reservations of von Kübel, has pushed German unjustified enrichment towards the abyss. It was the Second Commission's subsequent failure to combine that general enrichment claim with the traditional headings of the *condictiones* in § 812 I 1 and 2 BGB that finally pushed the direct shift of value over the edge.

bb) The general enrichment claim in the final version of § 812 I 1 BGB

(1) Step one: the extension from "out of the assets/wealth" to "at the expense"

The Second Commission accepted the view that the general principle of unjustified enrichment should be stated at the beginning. Also, it followed the rejection of the *Lehre von der Voraussetzung.*[821] Thus, its first recorded decision was to replace the First Draft by the counter-draft.[822]

---

819 Schall, Leistungskondiktion, 2003, p. 46 with fn. 207.

820 As to the UK, see *Costello v MacDonald* [2011] EWCA Civ 930, [2011] 3 WLR 1341; above pp. 195 et seq.

821 Protokolle II, 2953 = Mugdan II, 1174: "…für deren Beibehaltung niemand in der Kommission eingetreten sei…" […for the retention of which no one had argued in the Commission…]

822 Protokolle II, 2940 = Mugdan II, 1170.

Immediately after that, the Second Commission opted for the first material change to the text of the counter-draft. It replaced "aus dem Vermögen" (= out of the assets/wealth) by "auf Kosten" (= at the expense).[823] To justify the amendment, the Second Commission discussed several cases where "aus dem Vermögen", understood in the sense of "out of the assets/wealth" of the claimant", was seen as too narrow.[824] It is enough to look at the easily accessible bona fide transfer of title[825] to get the gist of the argument.

Under German law, A can transfer the property of owner X to a bona fide recipient B.[826] If this transfer was based on a sale, the owner has no enrichment claim against B, but only against A for disgorgement of the purchase price[827] (§ 816 I 1 BGB –equivalent to waiver of tort). By contrast, if the transfer of title was based on a gift (§ 516 BGB), the owner can reclaim the retransfer of the title directly from B under § 816 I 2 BGB. But what if the contract (sale) between A and B was void? Who is to have the enrichment claim against B? A or X? The answer is crystal clear:

- The performance to B is made by A. But it does not come "out of the assets" of A. Rather, B receives the property out of the assets of X.
- Still, B does not have any right to keep the performance.
- Thus, the Second Commission wanted A to have the enrichment claim.

> Protokolle II, 2942 = Mugdan II, 1171: "Wer etwas ohne rechtlichen Grund erlangt habe, erlange in vielen Fällen mehr als der Benachteiligte hatte, ... er ... werde durch seinen gutgläubigen Erwerb ... sofort Eigentümer der Sache, die er ohne rechtlichen Grund von einem Nichteigentümer erlangt habe. In diesen Fällen müsse er herausgeben, was er erlangt habe, nicht blos, was der andere Teil verloren habe, was aus dem Vermögen des Benachteiligten an ihn gelangt sei."
>
> [A person who has acquired something without legal reason in many cases acquires more than the disadvantaged party had, ... by virtue of his acquisition in good faith, he immediately becomes the owner of the thing which he has acquired without legal reason from a non-owner. In these cases, he had to hand over what he had obtained, not merely what the other party had lost, what had come to him from the property of the disadvantaged party.]

---

823 For the amended version, see below p. 251.
824 Protokolle II, 2941–2943 = Mugdan II, 1170–1171.
825 At common law, there is no bona fide transfer of legal title (*nemo dat quod non habet*), but equitable titles can be defeated by a bona fide purchase for value.
826 For chattels, the provisions are under §§ 929, 932–934 BGB – the bona fide acquisition of title is excluded if the good was lost or stolen (§ 935 BGB). The provisions referring to the bona fide transfer of land are §§ 873, 925, 892 BGB.
827 BGHZ 29, 127; by contrast, the prevailing doctrine would only grant the objective value and leave any gains with the transferor, Medicus/Petersen, mn. 722 et seq.

The decision of the German legislator is the right one. It confirms the principle as laid out above. Unjustified enrichment is about reversing failed performances, i. e. a shift of value from A to B. It is not concerned whose assets were naturally enriched and disenriched by the performance. The direct transfer of the title from the owner A to the bona fide purchaser C is of no consequence for the claim. It does not matter whether the performance depleted the assets of A. What is true for services, holds as well for money and goods.

The normative justification is that between A and B, the performance belongs to A. B has no right to keep it, so why should the enrichment claim of A be defeated by invoking the alleged ownership of X? There must be no *exceptio ex iure tertii.* That is why it is persuasive to grant the *Leistungskondiktion* to A irrespective of the question of ownership. This could not be expressed by the requirement "aus dem Vermögen" (= out of the assets) because those words would inevitably divert the enrichment claim from A to X. Not so under the requirement "at the expense". It is apt to cover the right of A to bring the enrichment claim. Plus, it is apt to explain why this should be so. A has procured the contractual performance to B. He would have to be paid under the contract (if valid), and he has to account to whomever he received the performance from. That is why the performance to B was made "at the expense" of A even though it came out of the assets of X. This is the law in Germany, and rightly so. It follows that "at the expense" in § 812 I 1 BGB must never be interpreted as meaning "out of the assets" of the claimant.[828]

The reasons given for the extension to "at the expense" show that the Second Commission was aware that (1) *every* claimant, including a performing party, had to show that the defendant was enriched at his expense under the general claim, and (2) that this concept did not mean a "real" shift of value from the assets of a to those of B.[829]

---

828 This is constantly denied by the minority views of the Einheitslehre (unity doctrine), see e. g. Wilhelm, Rechtsverletzung und Vermögensentscheidung, 1973, pp. 109 et seq.; Kupisch, JZ 1985, pp. 193 et seq.

829 This is also confirmed by the other examples, one of them being the *Erbverzicht* (§ 2346 BGB), i. e. the contractual renunciation of the inheritance by the prospective heir for the benefit of another. The *Erbverzicht* is a contract between the *Erblasser* (= testator) and his next of kin and/or spouse by which the latter waive their legal right to inherit in absence of a will (*gesetzliches Erbrecht*). As a consequence of the *Erbverzicht,* title to the estate will pass by the spouse/next of kin and directly accrue to the beneficiary of the renunciation so that the "real" shift of value takes place between the latter and the deceased. Background: Under German law, title to the estate passes to the heir automatically ex lege in the event of death (§ 1922 BGB). There is no need for acceptance by the heir, only a right to reject (§ 1942 BGB). The Erbverzicht will prevent the passing of the estate from the outset. That is why the value shifted to the beneficiary could not be said to

But at the expense" was also vaguer and wider and left leeway for many interpretations. As shown above, it would have easily accommodated both the Pomponian principle of no benefit from another's loss and the version claim. The Second Commission did not realise the danger because the new version accorded with the terminology of legislation, doctrine and court practice of the time.[830] It is quite remarkable that German lawyers were so convinced by the 19th century rejection of these principles that they never tried to revive them under the wider wording, and even more so that this remained the case after they had lost their faith in Savigny's concept of direct shift of value. But loyalty was not kept entirely. The vagueness of the wording allowed Fritz Schulz to corrode the direct shift of value approach and develop his *Rechtswidrigkeitstheorie*, claiming that in § 812 I 1 BGB, the principle of "no benefit from a wrong" had entered German law through the back door.[831] True, this was eventually rejected.[832] But not by re-affirming the direct shift of value, but by burying it in favour of Wilburg's newly created *Eingriffskondiktion* – which is little else but a modified *Rechtswidrigkeitstheorie* granting restitution for wrongs, but only for those wrongs that violate a right that (allegedly) allocates the benefit to the claimant (see below pp. 254–256).

Notwithstanding that, even after the Second Commission had replaced "aus dem Vermögen" with "auf Kosten", it would still possible to read the general claim of § a in the correct way, namely that **every** performing party had a claim to recover a failed performance from the recipient – as had always been the case since Savigny discovered the direct shift of value. This changed with the next move of the Commission. It was the moment when German unjustified enrichment was finally derailed. We will see that it happened accidentally and unconsciously in the course of an editorial change.

(2) Step two: The misshapen "clarification" of the general enrichment claim and the uncalculated repercussion of derailing the general enrichment claim

The Second Commission did not like § b of the counter-draft. This provision had defined the lack of causa by various defects of the *Zweckbestimmung* (determination of purpose), ranging from its lack or invalidity to the failure of the determined purpose. The Second Commission accepted the *Zweckbestimmung* in principle be-

---

have come "out of the assets" of the renouncing party. Nevertheless, that party had to be the right claimant, cf. Protokolle II, 2942 = Mugdan II, 1171.

830 Protokolle II, 2943 = Mugdan II, 1171.

831 *Schulz*, AcP 105 (1909) 473 et seq.

832 See only *Ellger*, Bereicherung durch Eingriff, 2002, pp. 89 et seq, 128 et seq.

cause it was better suited than Windscheid's *Lehre von der Voraussetzung* to distinguish the legally relevant disappointment of the performing party from irrelevant motives. But it refrained from stating a wholesale definition. The Commission did not "feel that it could express all the cases of a lack of legal ground." This is not really illuminating because the §§ 812 BGB *do* actually contain *all* cases where performances lack legal ground. We cannot know the Commission's reasons to tarry for sure. What we know is that the Second Commission decided to skip § b. However, it also felt that after skipping § b, it would be necessary to find an alternative way to **emphasise performance-related enrichment** within the framework of the general claim because those were the paradigm cases. That is why § a changed into today's § 812 I 1 BGB.

§ a (after "at the expense" amendment):

> Hat jemand **auf Kosten eines anderen** etwas ohne rechtlichen Grund erlangt, so ist er dem anderen zur Herausgabe des Erlangten verpflichtet.
>
> [If a person has obtained something **at the expense of another** without legal reason, he is obliged to hand over what he or she has obtained to the other person.]
>
> § 812 I 1 BGB
> Wer **durch die Leistung eines anderen** oder **in sonstiger Weise auf dessen Kosten** etwas ohne rechtlichen Grund erlangt hat, ist dem anderen zur Herausgabe verpflichtet. Diese Verpflichtung besteht auch dann, wenn der rechtliche Grund später wegfällt oder der mit einer Leistung nach dem Inhalt des Rechtsgeschäfts bezweckte Erfolg nicht eintritt.
>
> [Anyone who has obtained something without legal reason **through the performance of another or in any other way at the latter's expense** is obliged to hand it over to the other. This obligation exists even if the legal reason later ceases to exist or the success intended with a performance according to the content of the legal transaction does not occur.]

The general clause of § a turned into the extended first sentence of § 812 BGB where the perfomance-based claim, the *condictio indebiti* (*durch die Leistung eines anderen*), is named next to the sweeping claim for enrichments in other ways (*in sonstiger Weise*). The second sentence adds the *condictio ob causam finitam* and the *conditio causa data causa non secuta.* They do not play a role in the discussion to be looked at here. For the following argument, the focus is entirely on the first sentence.

The change from "Hat jemand ... erlangt" to "Wer ... erlangt hat" is purely technical. It removes the prior conditional structure of the sentence.[833] The decisive

833 It seems the same minimal change of the grammatical structure would be possible in English, namely from If someone received...., he is obliged to make restitution" to "Anyone (or older: He) who has received ... is obliged to make restitution.

change is the **addition of the two alternatives.** It is therefore put in bold print. The sentence now names two ways of how to get something at the expense of another: "Durch Leistung (= through performance) or "in sonstiger Weise" (= in another way). This addition aims to express that under the principle of direct shift of value, enrichments can come as performances (*condictio indebiti* etc) or in other ways (*condictio since causa specialis*) So far, so good. This does not contradict the axiom that every performance marks a direct shift of value. The problem arises if we take a closer look at the exact requirements that the claimant has to plead to found a performance-related enrichment action. Here, we notice a material change brought about by the merely editorial amendment. We remember that the right claimant is the performing party

Under the general enrichment claim of § a (as amended in the course of the consultations), the performing party would have had to plead that the defendant is enriched "at its expense". To do so, it could have referred to Savigny and show the giving of money or money's worth. If the claimant performed money's worth to the recipient, the latter's enrichment comes at the claimant's expense.

Under § 812 I 1 BGB, this clear picture was lost to an ambiguity. From a grammatical perspective, the sentence can be read in two ways with relation to performances. The "at the expense" requirement could be either read into the performance cases (uniform interpretation), or left out of them ("split interpretation").

> Split interpretation: "Wer **durch die Leistung eines anderen** [oder in sonstiger Weise auf dessen Kosten] etwas ohne rechtlichen Grund erlangt hat, **ist dem anderen zur Herausgabe verpflichtet.**
>
> Uniform interpretation: "Wer **durch die Leistung eines anderen** [oder in sonstiger Weise] **auf dessen Kosten** etwas ohne rechtlichen Grund erlangt hat, **ist dem anderen zur Herausgabe verpflichtet.**

The fatal flaw is this: The idea of the general enrichment claim based on the direct shift of value is that it covers all enrichment cases, performance-related as well as non-performance related. Thus, it seems that "at the expense" surely must apply to both variants, as proposed by the uniform reading.[834]

834 For this widespread conclusion cf. e. g. Schäfer, Das Bereicherungsrecht in Europa, 2000, p. 299 whose argument overlooks the fact that the performance-based condictiones of *Vorentwurf* and *Erster Entwurf* were based on the same principle but did NOT contain the "at the expense" requirement. Suffering from the same flaw is the argument of Wilhelm, Rechtsverletzung, 1973, pp. 103–104; against his view already Schall, p. 12 fn. 52.

To date, no legal writer has undertaken to deliver a plausible explanation for the material divergence between the earlier drafts and the uniform reading of § 812 I 1 BGB. The reason is that there is none.

However, on closer looks it turns out that, quasi by coincidence, the split reading of the sentence describes correctly that *every* performing party can claim restitution of the performance if it failed – which is right under the direct shift of value principle of the *condictiones* and was expressly stated by both pre-draft and first draft. This situation is aggravated by the fact that **only** the split reading can achieve the correct outcome. The uniform reading, although seemingly imperative because of the legislator's aim to put a general enrichment claim to the top of the chapter, cannot correctly transpose the right of *every* performing party to claim restitution. Instead, it creates an additional requirement under which the performance to the defendant had to be made "at the expense" of the claimant. But every performance comes automatically "at the expense" of the claimant because every performance *per se* is a direct shift of value. Therefore, the additional "at the expense" requirement falsifies the enrichment claim.

The split reading of § 812 I 1 BGB clearly expresses that the defendant who has been enriched by the performance of another must make restitution to that other!

> "Wer **durch die Leistung eines anderen** ... etwas ohne rechtlichen Grund erlangt hat, ist **ihm** zur Herausgabe verpflichtet."
>
> [Anyone who has obtained something without legal reason **through the performance of another**, is obliged to make restitution to him..]

By contrast, the uniform reading of § 812 I 1 BGB seems to impose an additional requirement that the performance must have been made at the expense of the claimant:

> "Wer **durch die Leistung eines anderen ... auf dessen Kosten** etwas ohne rechtlichen Grund erlangt hat, ist ihm zur Herausgabe verpflichtet."
>
> [Anyone who has obtained **through performance of another at his expense** something without legal ground, is obliged to make restitution to him]

If we read the additional "at the expense" requirement into the performance -based enrichment claims, it can only be understood as a restriction. Contrary to the split reading, it is no longer enough for the claimant to show that he has made the performance. He also has to show that he made the performance at his expense. That *inevitably* diverts the claim from the performance. It falsified *Savigny's* principle because according to him, *every* performance is a direct shift of value *per se*. By contrast, the uniform reading of § 812 I 1 made it almost impossible to argue that the enrichment claim must lie with every performance. Instead, it seemed that the natural transfer is relevant. But this is wrong, as has been shown above both for the painting of the wall (p. 246) and for the direct transfer of the property (bona fide purchase, pp. 248–249). The Second Commission itself has decided that in the case of a bona fide acquisition for value **sine causa**, the enrichment claim should be at the hands of the performing party and not at the hands of the owner who lost the title. That was the reason to extend "out of the assets to "at the expense". The uniform reading that relates "at the expense" as additional requirement of the performance-based claims undermines this decision. It indicates that rendering a performance of money's worth is not enough. In addition, it requires that the performance must also come "at the expense" of the performing party. But that does not make sense. It can only be a restriction. If this restriction was to be taken seriously, the performing party that transferred title bona fide to the recipient could not have the claim in unjust enrichment. But as shown above, German law wants the performing party to have the claim in order to avoid defences *ex iure tertii*. That leaves but two options: If the restriction does *not* bite in the bona fide case, it is meaningless and better left completely. If it does bite, it falsifies the law. The laws of logic prove the fallacy of the uniform reading with mathematical accuracy!

To sum up: The "natural" view of "at the expense" is misleading because it points to wider effects in the wealth of the parties while these are irrelevant to establish the claim. The decisive notion is the **transfer of money or money's worth.** The act of performance itself is the direct shift of value to be reversed, the "Godly spark". To lose that focus derails the enrichment actions because it shifts attention to the irrelevant "real" shift of value (*gegenständliche Vermögensverschiebung*), i. e. painting the colour from brush to wall, transferring the money from bank to recipient. Any *"real"* shift of value deviates from the parties of the performance. It was the starting reason that led to the failure of Savigny's principle. Jurists did not recognise the performance as paradigm for direct shifts of value any more. As a consequence, they could not understand how to apply the *condictio sine causa specialis* correctly. That will be shown next.

2 The demise of the general enrichment claim in § 812 I 1 BGB – the rise of the *Trennungslehre* following *Walter Wilburg* and *Ernst von Caemmerer*

a) The doctrinal shift from *Einheitslehre* (= unity doctrine) to *Trennungslehre* (= separation doctrine)

The uniform reading of the general enrichment claim in § 812 I 1 BGB destroyed the cognition that every performance is a direct shift of value simply for the giving and receiving of money or money's worth. This falsified the enrichment claim. The failure of this concept was inevitable, the following account a chronicle of a death foretold.

The decline started in the year 1934 when Walter Wilburg wrote his fundamental criticism of German unjustified enrichment.[835] He made two major points against the concept of "real direct shift of wealth" that are both very similar to the criticism put forward by Robert Stevens against unjust enrichment. First, he argued that the direct shift of wealth could not explain tripartite performance cases in a persuasive way.[836] At that time, it had already been established that the customer, not the bank, should normally have the enrichment claim against the recipient of the bank transfer. We come back to this remarkable way of arguing from the presumed result instead of from the wording of the law in great detail below (p. 303). But suffice here to say that everybody agreed on the result. However, it was basically impossible to bring this result in line with the requirement of the *gegenständliche Vermögensverschiebung* because the real transfer of value took undoubtedly place from bank to recipient. *Wilburg's* answer was the split reading of § 812 I 1 BGB, pinning the enrichment claims to the performance *instead* to the shift of wealth. Based on this premise, he argued that only the customer had made a performance to the bank because only the customer pursued the purpose of the discharge vis-a-vis the recipient. In turn, the bank only performed vis-à-vis the customer because by following the instruction of the customer, it only pursued the purpose of the transaction vis-à-vis the customer. This became the standard solution of bank cases in Germany and is almost generally accepted to the present day.

The other focal point of Wilburg's scathing criticism was the availability of the enrichment claim in cases of unauthorised use of another's intellectual property right. In a similar vein as Robert Stevens again, he claimed that this could not be a shift of value because nothing was transferred from the claimant to the defendant.[837] He proposed instead to accept the *"Eingriffskondiktion"* as the paradigm case of a *Bereicherung in sonstiger Weise.* Instead of searching for a shift of value, it was based on the alternative explanation that the defendant derived his enrichment from an unlawful interference (= *Eingriff*) with another's right. Modifying Fritz Schulz's *Rechtswidrigkeitstheorie*[838] however, Wilburg argued that the enrichment claim was not triggered by *any* wrong suffered by the claimant, but only though the interference with such rights that "allocated" to the claimant the benefit taken by the defendant (*Recht mit* ***Zuweisungsgehalt***). A good ex-

---

835 *Wilburg*, "Die Lehre von der Ungerechtfertigten Bereicherung", Festschrift der Universität Graz, 1934.

836 *Wilburg*, pp. 108 et seq. and 113 et seq.; cp. *Stevens*, LQR (2018) 573, at p. 583 for a performance-based explanation of *Aiken v Short.*

837 *Wilburg*, pp. 97 et seq.; cp. the same argument brought by *Stevens*, (2018) LQR, 573, at 583. For the counter argument, see already above, at p. 234.

838 Fritz Schulz, System der Rechte auf den Eingriffserwerb, AcP 105 (1909), 473.

ample of how this concept works to restrict the enrichment claim is the sub-lease by the tenant. If the sublease is not authorised, it does not only breach the tenancy agreement, but also violates the property right of the landlord. But since the property is already let, the property right cannot allocate to the landlord the rent paid by the subtenant to the tenant, too. The tenant derives a benefit from a wrong against the landlord. But *this* benefit is not allocated to the landlord who therefore cannot demand disgorgement of the enrichment from the wrong.[839]

In 1954, Ernst von Caemmerer wrote "Bereicherung und Unerlaubte Handlung" in the *Festschrift für Ernst Rabel*. In this seminal work, he condoned all fundamental theses of Walter Wilburg: The rejection of the general enrichment claim based on the direct shift of value under the uniform reading of § 812 I 1 BGB, the division instead of § 812 I 1 into the 1st and 2nd alternative, covering performance-based and other enrichment claims under the split reading, the "tucking" of the performance to the person vis-à-vis its purpose is pursued and the *Eingriffskondiktion* for unlawful interference with rights that allocated benefits to the claimant. He added two more non-performance-based enrichment claims to cover traditionally accepted cases: the *Aufwendungskondiktion* would cover the (mistaken) improvement of another's property. The *Rückgriffskondiktion* would compensate for the (even officious!) discharge of another's debt.

Since then, the *Trennungslehre* (= separation theory) was on the rise. The new doctrinal approach was taken up and further developed by leading scholars in text books, such as the seminal text book "Schuldrecht II" by Josef Esser[840] or the treatise "Ungerechtfertigte Bereicherung" by Dieter Reuter and Michael Martinek.[841]

In 1970, the *Bundesgerichtshof* finally adopted the new interpretation. The occasion was a highly complicated tripartite case where a supplier had delivered materials to a building site in the mistaken belief that the owner had ordered them, while the owner had good reasons to believe that the main contractor had ordered the materials. The case is famous to date because the *Bundesgerichtshof* protected the owner in his mistaken assumption beyond the disenrichment defence and shielded him (some might argue: *contra legem*) completely from any enrichment claim of the mistaken supplier. The exact reasoning is still highly contentious, but this is immaterial for present purposes except for one undebated fact: the pre-

---

839 BGHZ 131 ,297 (306); BGH NZM 2014, 582; annotated by Riehm JuS 2014, 940. For the criticism of this solution see below, pp. 276–277.

840 Esser, Schuldrecht, Band 2, Besonderer Teil, 4th edn. 1971, § 100 I, pp. 337 ff.

841 Reuter/Martinek, Ungerechtfertigte Bereicherung, 1983.

vious *Einheitslehre* was officially given up in favour of the *Trennungslehre*.[842] The modern German law of unjustified enrichment was born.

b) The current structure of the law of unjustified enrichment in Germany

Under the modern *Trennungslehre* (= separation doctrine), German law of unjustified enrichment is subdivided into performance-based enrichment claims (*Leistungskondiktionen*) and enrichment in other ways (*in sonstiger Weise*). The starting point for the separation doctrine is the split reading of § 812 I 1 BGB, the former general enrichment claim. This is usually equated with the view that *Savigny's* direct shift of value is **not** the overarching principle of the *condictiones* and does not play any role for the interpretation of these actions, neither the performance-related nor the non-performance-related ones.

Every *Leistungskondiktion* is attached to the "relation of performance" (*Leistungsverhältnis*). Performance (= *Leistung*) is defined as *bewusste zweckgerichtete Mehrung fremden Vermögens* (p. 241 and p. 268). The performing party is the party that sets that purpose (*Zweckbestimmung*). The recipient is the person vis-à-vis the purpose is pursued. This will normally be the recipient of the "natural" performance (money, goods, services). However, as seen above in the bank cases, the natural transfer (funds from bank to payee) can deviate from the performance relations (bank – customer and customer – payee).

The lack of legal ground can either be defined objectively or subjectively. One could say that the causa (= reason) of a performance is the objective existence of a debt under a valid contract (= objective theory of legal ground). However, this rule can also be described from a subjective perspective: The performance is made for the purpose of discharging the debt (= *solvendi causa*). The achievement of that purpose justifies the transfer as legal ground (= subjective theory of legal ground), whereas the failure of the purpose triggers restitution for lack of legal ground. The debate between the objective and the subjective theory of legal ground is mainly academic. This is because it is generally agreed that a valid performance *cum*

---

842 BGHZ 40, 272 – Elektrogerätefall even went so far as to provide a new reasoning for an earlier, similar case (BGHZ 30, 36) that had at the time been decided under the shift of value approach. The prior case was a twin of *Jones v Waring & Gillow* [1926] AC 670 (HL), with the only difference that the fraud related to the delivery of the goods, not to the payment. A supplier was led to believe in a contract to deliver building materials. When he discovered the fraud, he sued the landlord in unjust enrichment. The BGH rejected his claim. The modern argument was that from the landlord's perspective, the performance was made by the fraudster, not the supplier. In an earlier case (RGZ 98, 64), the claim was denied for disenrichment (approving Flume, AcP 199 (1999) 1, at 28 et seq.). By contrast, the House of Lords allowed the claim of Jones against Waring & Gillow.

causa depends on a link between the objective existence of the debt and the purpose of the performing party to discharge this debt. The objective existence of the debt as such is not enough to justify the performance:

> A sends the bill to B. It is payable into his account at B-Bank. B accidentally pays into A's account at N-Bank. The debt is not discharged because the payment is not made as required (§ 362 I BGB).[843] Despite the objective existence of the debt, the payment is *sine causa.* A can still sue B for payment. In turn, B can sue for restitution of the payment for lack of legal ground.

Note that the exact legal solution of that case is usually "hidden" because A is happy to have the money and anyway, B would be able to set off his enrichment claim. But this does not mean that the original payment was made *cum causa.* This will become obvious if the payment gets lost (e.g. due to the failure of N-Bank) and A brings the defence of *Entreicherung* (= disenrichment, i.e. change of position).

The causes of action relating to performances are the traditional *condictiones* of Roman law:

- the *condictio indebiti* in § 812 I 1 1. Alt. BGB and § 813 I BGB;[844]
- the *condictio ob causam finitam* in § 812 I 2 1. Alt. BGB (for subsequent loss of legal ground),[845]
- the *condictio causa data causa non secuta* in § 812 I 2 2.Alt. BGB (for failure of the agreed purpose of the performance)

---

843 Larenz/Canaris, § 67 III 1, pp. 136–137. In England, the law seems to be the same, *Colonial Bank v Exchange Bank of Yarmouth* (1885) 9 App. Cas. 84 (PC).

844 § 813 BGB extends the *condictio indebiti* to cases where the debt was valid but the debtor would not have had to pay because he could have invoked a permanent defence. In these cases, the *causa solvendi* fails because it is only technically achieved, but in reality, the performance amounts to a gift.

845 This action typically relates to performances, but not necessarily so, see Protokolle II, 2956 = Mugdan II, 1173–1174: "Prot. II, 2956 = Mugdan II, 1173–1174: Logisch richtiger sei es ferner, die Herausgabe wegen späteren Wegfalls des Rechtsgrundes nicht als eine Spezialanwendung des in § a aufgestellten allgemeinen Rechtsprinzipes anzusehen, sondern sie diesem als eine selbständige Kategorie an die Seite zu stellen, **um so** mehr als sich **Fälle der cond. ob causam finitam** denken ließen, in welchen die Bereicherung **nicht auf einer Leistung des Rückforderungsberechtigten beruht.** [Furthermore, it was logically more correct not to regard restitution due to the subsequent cessation of the legal ground as a special application of the general legal principle established in § a, but to place it alongside it as an independent category, all the more so as **cases of cond. ob causam finitam** could be conceived **in which the enrichment was not based on a performance** by the person entitled to restitution.]

However, such cases are rare and therefore, the *condictio ob causam finitam* under § 812 I 2 1. Alt. BGB is normally counted towards the *Leistungskondiktionen.*

- the *condictio ob turpem vel inustam causam* in § 817 Satz 1 BGB (for immorality or illegality of accepting the performance)

The main cause of action for non-performance-related enrichments is § 812 I 1 2. Alt. BGB covering all enrichments that occurred "in sonstiger Weise" (= in another way) without legal ground.[846]
- *Eingriffskondiktion*
- *Aufwendungskondiktion*
- *Rückgriffskondiktion*

These three causes of action follow the taxonomy introduced by Wilburg and von Caemmerer. Later, German doctrine has added the *Direktdurchgriffskondiktion* as a fourth case. But this term as such is not equally accepted.[847] It describes the direct claim of the bank against the payee that will exceptionally lie if the transfer cannot be attributed to any instruction by the customer (e.g. because the instruction was revoked, illusory or forged). Under English law, the equivalent is the direct claim under *Barclays v Simms*. For German lawyers, this claim cannot be a *Leistungskondiktion* because the bank does not pursue the purpose of the transfer vis-à-vis the payee, but only vis-à-vis the customer – who, in this case, does not receive anything (for a more detailed account including the criticism see below pp. 303 et seq.).

The actions under § 812 I 1 2. Alt. BGB are supplemented by two specific rules regulating the enrichment claims in case of a valid transfer of another's title in § 816 I 1 and 2 BGB. They are generally perceived as sub-variants of the *Eingriffskondiktion*. If good title is transferred for value, the enrichment claim for the previous owner is directed against the transferor (§ 816 I 1 BGB).[848] There will be no claim against the acquirer. The bona fide purchaser for value is protected and allowed to keep his title. His enrichment is thus justified by an objective legal ground. By contrast, if good title is acquired by a volunteer, the owner can sue him for restitution of his property under § 816 I 2 BGB. There is an academic debate on whether the first or the second sentence marks the rule/the exception. The answer is that the valid transfer of another's title simultaneously enriches the re-

846 See MüKoBGB/Schwab, § 812 mn. 278 et seq (Eingriffskondiktion); mn. 355 et seq. (Aufwendungskondiktion); mn. 389 et seq. (Rückgriffskondiktion); mn. 100 (Direktdurchgriffskondiktion)
847 For example, MüKoBGB/Schwab, § 812 mn. 100 assumes an *Aufwendungskondiktion*; BeckOKBGB/Wendehorst, § 812 mn. 105 et seq. speaks more generally of a *Zuwendungskondiktion*.
848 There is a debate whether the owner can only recover the value of his lost property or demand the disgorgement of the full purchase price paid to the transferor by the acquirer, for the latter the prevailing view, BGHZ 29, 157; contrast Medicus/Petersen, Bürgerliches Recht, 28th edn. 2021, mn. 722 et seq.

cipient and the transferor (the latter because it allows him to "use up" the owners value)

Unlike the *condictio sine causa specialis* in the pre-draft and the first draft, the enrichments "in sonstiger Weise" under § 812 I 1 2. Alt. BGB are not explicitly reduced to enrichments that occur **without** will of the claimant. That is why German doctrine does not apply any such restriction. However, it will be shown below that it should (pp. 264–265, 273 et seq., 282 et seq.). The reason is the general principle of *volenti non fit inuria.*

c) Fundamental criticism of the modern German approach to unjustified enrichment: the legacy of Wilburg's fallacy

The starting point for criticising the modern law of unjustified enrichment in Germany are **two fundamental flaws** in Wilburg's successful attack on the general enrichment claim. To be sure, he was right to criticise the interpretation of § 812 by the prevailing doctrine of the time, the *Einheitslehre* with its misunderstanding of the direct shift of wealth (*unmittelbare Vermögensverschiebung*), attaching performance-based enrichment claims to "real" shifts of wealth/value instead of the performance. However, Wilburg believed to disprove the direct shift of value principle, while in truth, he had only disproved the misapplication of § 812 I 1 BGB.

The first flaw in the argument was that Wilburg presented the split reading and the consequent re-establishment of the *Leistungskondiktion* in lieu of the general enrichment claim as defeat of the direct shift of value.[849] In truth, as has become clear by now, the split reading was just the rectification of a misinterpretation that was caused by the sloppy drafting. The Second Commission did not realise that under the uniform reading of § 812 I 1 BGB, the editorial insertion "*durch Leistung eines anderen oder in sonstiger Weise auf dessen Kosten*" accidentally caused a material change of the law it has merely meant to clarify. The extension derailed the *Leistungskondiktion* by diverting it from *every* performance relation and attaching it to an alleged "real shift" (*gegenständliche Vermögensverschiebung*). Dropping the general enrichment claim in favour of the split reading was indeed the right answer to that. But this correction did not defeat the direct shift of value principle but was commanded by it! – as Wilburg might have found out by analysing the *Erste Entwurf* and the accompanying motives (so-called historical interpretation[850]) and answer the question why that draft contained *Leistungskondiktionen*

849 Wilburg, p. 23.
850 A permissible method under German law.

that exactly corresponded to his own proposal and sold them as the paradigm of the direct shift of value.

Second, Wilburg referred to the example of using another's intellectual property without consent and made his point that there was no shift of wealth. While this was a case of "taking value", he could as well have referred to services, as Robert Stevens did.[851] Again, he was right to hold that objection against the old doctrine of the "real" shift of wealth. But again, he erred in holding them against the concept of Savigny that was transposed by von Kübel. If **giving and receiving money's worth** is the direct shift of value for the *Leistungskondiktionen*, the taking of money's worth is the corresponding shift for the enrichment in other ways (*condictio sine causa specialis*). It is actually trivial to see that someone who uses another's intellectual property without consent takes money's worth – and must account for that **forced shift of value** in unjust enrichment. Just as anyone who dodges the fare, sneaks into a concert, forces labour or squats a building.

The simple logic of this explanation will prove superior to alternative attempts that explain non-performance based enrichment as wrong- or tort-based. This will be shown in the course of the ensuing normative justification of Savigny's system. For the time being, a recent English case shall demonstrate this point.[852] A school stopped paying the rent for a building after it emerged that the lease was void (*ultra vires*).[853] But it continued to use the building. This was a case of taking value. The leasing company did not make a performance because it knew that there was no contract. The school simply took the use, probably because it thought (with some justification on the facts) that it had already paid more than enough for it. The unjust enrichment of the school is exactly the same before and after knowing that the lease was invalid. Before, the enrichment (use of the building) was transferred by the leasing company, afterwards, it was taken by the school. But in both cases, it would have taken a valid lease to shift the value of the use in an unassailable way to the school.

---

851 Stevens, (2018) LQR, 573, at 583.

852 *School Facility Managements Limited and others v Governing Body of Christ the King College and another* [2021] EWCA Civ 1053.

853 The reason being that the true colour of the contract was a prohibited financial lease and not a permissible operating lease.

VI The normative foundation of unjust enrichment claims to reverse direct shifts of value

The following passage is Janus-faced. It draws conclusions from the development of unjustified enrichment in Germany and proposes them to English unjust enrichment. The methodological justification is the common basis on a direct shift of value, the widely corresponding unjust factors after the transplant from the "Mosaic *condictiones*" and the identity of the underlying principles of party autonomy and *volenti non fit inuria.*

The legal principles and the cases to support them are abstract and destined to go both ways. Nevertheless, the arguments of existing concepts (and misconceptions) concerning e.g. the German *Eingriffskondiktion* cannot be ignored but must be challenged to build a persuasive construction of unjust enrichment.

The basis for my normative argument is the principle of Savigny. I am convinced that it showed the right path to overcome Pomponius and reach a clear, rational law of unjust enrichment. It had a good start with the *Vorentwurf* drafted by von Kübel and adopted by the *Erste Kommission* in the *Erste Entwurf.* The problem is that, as shown before, Germany has lost its way since, while England has not even been aware yet of the possibility (and necessity!) to bypass Pomponius. As a consequence, the normative argument must be fighting on two fronts at the same time. This is particularly gruesome in the areas where the concept of Savigny and von Kübel is merely the starting point to develop solutions. The main example is the *condictio sine causa specialis* that has been subdivided into the sub-categories *Eingriffskondiktion*, the *Aufwendungskondiktion* and the *Rückgriffskondiktion* by the modern German apostates of Savigny. Also, the concept of failure of purpose must and will be further refined to deliver better and more precise answers.

1 Party autonomy and *volenti non fit inuria:* the uniform foundation of enrichment claims for giving or taking value

The access to the normative foundation of unjust(ified) enrichment is revealed by the two drafts preceding the final version of the §§ 812 BGB: the *Vorentwurf* of the redactor Franz Philipp von Kübel and the *Erste Entwurf* drafted by the *Erste Kommission.* It is preferable to rely on those earlier drafts because they show the clear-cut dichotomic picture, whereas the final version of the §§ 812 BGB was riddled with ambiguity that eventually brought the old doctrine down (above, pp. 242 et seq.). *Vorentwurf* and *Erster Entwurf* saw every "performance", i.e. the purposeful transfer of money or money's worth (services) as direct shift of value and the failure of the purpose of that transfer as unjust factor. They added the shifts of value without consent that were covered by the *condictio sine causa specialis* (§ 27 VE; § 748 E I). The resulting sum is the essence of unjust(ified) enrichment. But why is this so?

The answer is party autonomy. The starting point is a dictum by *Samuel Stoljar* who said:[854]

> "Indeed a basic theme running through our law is that . . . *things or money cannot validly pass from one person to another without the former's sufficient consent* either before or after the event."

If we extend this statement from "things and money" to "money and money's worth", we have exactly the rule that commands reversal of unjust enrichment:

> **Money or money's worth cannot validly pass from one person to another without the former's sufficient consent.**

2 The justification for equating money and money's worth

The equation of money and money's worth has already been recognised by Savigny (p. 233).[855] Money and money's worth rank principally equal for the law[856] and for the economy (GDP). But there are differences, and it is important to analyse whether they can be of consequence.

One difference is that money is *transferred*, while the value of services, user &ct. is *created* while they are performed.[857] But that difference does not warrant different treatment under unjust enrichment. It is not important that the assets of one are depleted and those of the other are swollen because unjust enrichment looks at the transfer of the value itself (p. 234).

Another difference is the grade of **negotiability** of various assets/values. Most goods that are acquired by a purchase or by services to an end are as freely trade-

854 Stoljar, Quasi-Contract, 2nd edn 1989, p. 6.

855 Savigny, System des heutigen Römischen Rechts, Vol. V, p. 523, referring to L. 26 § 12 = D. 12.6.26 (Ulpianus ad edictum).

856 Cf. e. g. s.582(1) CA 2006: Shares ...may be paid up by money or money's worth."; s.238(4)(b) IA 1986: "the company enters into a transaction with that person for a consideration the value of which, in money or money's worth, is significantly less than the value, in money or money's worth, of the consideration provided by the company."

857 That will normally happen *pro rata temporis*, i. e. every minute I work for you or let you use my property, that objective value is created for you and flows to you. But note that in case of a service to an end, no value will be received before the service (or severable parts of it) is completed, as was rightly recognised in the *Fibrosa* case.

able as money from a legal perspective. But they must find buyers. User is tradeable in theory, too (sub-lease), but that is not standard practice. Services are not transferable at all. Does lack of negotiability eclipse their value? The answer is no, just as it would be for non-assignable claims and shares &ct. Otherwise, one would not pay for them.

However, there is yet another difference. Services and user "**evaporate**". The haircut, the piano concert, the singing flower, the hotel room, the boat hire: they all dissolve on receipt, without leaving a trace of value in the assets of the recipient.[858] That is why the balance sheet does not see assets acquired, but expenses, i.e. losses incurred. Does *this* change the perception of a shift of value? Again, the answer is no. Nobody would deny the monetary value of your nightly kebab at St. Giles even though it is surely gone with the first bite you take, probably already when you grab it with your hands. The non-preservability of the value cannot alter or eradicate the fact that the recipient has enjoyed something valuable at the moment he received what he bargained for. The dissolution of the value at the very moment of its receipt does not render the benefit that has been obtained gratuitous. The spending decision of the defendant cannot be denied or reset only because it was – from an economic perspective – a very bad one that did not make the defendant richer but poorer. It follows that the equation of money and money's worth is spot on for unjust ernichment.

3 Party autonomy and *volenti non fit iniuria*

Intentional shifts of value are governed by party autonomy. This principle is typically equated with freedom of contract. But it is wider because it means the general **freedom to dispose of one's belongings** (e.g. by discharging debts, making gifts, giving up property), but also **of one's time, actions and activities.** If such dispositions bring objective value to others, they must be carried by the flawless will of the disposing party. The flip side is being bound to the dispositions. Again, *pacta sunt servanda* is the most prominent, but not the only aspect. Neither simple gifts nor derelictions nor favours done to another rest on a binding contract. No consideration was given. Yet, they cannot be revoked. I cannot suddenly reclaim the pound from the beggar or charge a fare from the hitchhiker whom I gave a ride. To give another example: I take care of the vegetation on a strip of land at the backside of my neighbour's house because it is me, not him who

858 Notable exception: value enhancing or preserving services like repairs, renovations, improvements &ct.

would have to suffer the sight of decay. So I cut, I mow, I weed, and I even plant some nice flowers (that forthwith become the property of my neighbour). Again, there can be no restitution. A similar example discussed in England is the "grudging gift". The neighbour upstairs benefits from the neighbour downstairs heating the flat.[859]

The rule in all these cases is *not*, and never has been, that the benefit must be justified by a legal reason – or else disgorged. Rather, the basic rule is that no benefit accruing to others from the voluntary dispositions, acts or omissions of a person can be recovered because of ***volenti non fit inuria.***[860] People can never complain for having their way.

Volenti non fit inuria is the main preventor of enrichment claims. Recovery can only lie where there is either no consent at all, or where the autonomous will of the individual is invalidated in the eyes of the law.

If *volenti non fit inuria* ceases to apply, this fact *per se* commands the reversal of the transfer or usurpation of the value. Restitution springs directly from the wont of will. Party autonomy is violated. That is why the law must correct the wrongful state that party autonomy disapproves of. The enrichment claim is based on the lack or vitiation of consent of the claimant.[861] This foundation is as one-sided as the principle of *volenti non fit inuria* from which it exempts. It is not contingent on any (mis)conduct of either party.

4 The different challenges for performance-based and non-performance based enrichment claims ("giving value" and "taking value")

The law of unjust enrichment rests on the **uniform principle** set out above (p. 263). It covers both cases of "giving value" and cases of "taking value" without legal reason.[862] Nevertheless, it faces different challenges in the two scenarios.[863] In the first case, the claim must obviously be attached to the parties of the failed transaction, i. e. the transferor of the benefit and the recipient, whether that act is called "performance", "paiement"/"pagamento" or "shift of value". The main ques-

859 Peter Birks, Unjust Enrichment, p. 158–160; Stevens, p. 32.
860 This was first recognised by English judges, *Astley v Reynolds* (1731) 93 E.R. 939; see also Schall, Leistungskondiktion, p. 83.
861 That becomes most obvious under the draft *condictio causa data causa non secuta* in § 742 E I (see below). That provision has been formulated under the influence of the *Lehre von der Voraussetzung* (= doctrine of condition) by Bernhard Windscheid (a famous disciple of Savigny).
862 On principle also Kupisch, JZ 1985, 163, at 164.
863 Similarly Kupisch, JZ 1985, 163, at 164.

tion is under what circumstances the natural will of the transferor was invalidated in the eyes of the law. The task is to distinguish acceptable triggers of restitution from one-sided motives and assumptions that must be of no consequence. The task is complicated by the fact that the accepted triggers for restitution are one-sided as well.[864] The best answer to date is the generalisation of the **failure of the purpose of the performance**, as developed by the German *Zwecklehre* (= doctrine of purpose, pp. 270–272).

The no-consent cases pose different questions. It is clear that restitution must be granted for taking value. But it is not always as obvious as with me drinking up your Coke between which parties and to what extent an enrichment claim should lie. This is because it is not possible to attach the claim to the intentional transfer or "performance". While we look for alternative anchors, we ask ourselves: Does the enrichment claim require a wrong? (like the theft in the *condictio furtiva*).[865] Can only holders of violated property rights claim restitution? Will *every* infringement of such a right trigger a claim? Is the claim directed against the wrongdoer or against the beneficiary of the wrong (A mistakenly fed the horse of B with the grass of C)? Does it skim off all gains from the wrong, or is it restricted to value shifted from the claimant (if any)? The answers can be derived from the paradigm of the performance, too. Since the law requires flawless consent for valid shifts of value, the task is to define which enrichments would have to be consented by others. The key question is which benefits taken by one would have to be bargained for with another. That might be termed a "meant-to-be performance". It describes the relevant shift of value in the "taking value"-scenarios.

5 The purpose of transfers of value

The paradigm of unjust enrichment has always been the failed payment. Since Roman times, the *condictio* lay to claim back money paid to discharge on a non-existing debt (*condictio indebiti*) or for some other purpose that did not materialise (*condictio causa data causa non secuta*). In Germany, the recognition of the relevance of the purpose for unjust enrichment has been inexorably connected with adopting the term *Leistung* (= performance) to describe intentional transfers.

---

864 That marks a difference to contract law where motives are one-sided, whereas conditions must be agreed.

865 But cf. Zimmermann, pp. 839–841 who shows how Romans stretched the action to all "unjust having". That anticipated the function of the *condictio sine causa specialis*.

a) The alignment of enrichment claims to the "performance" in Germany

The act of a "payment" became generalised to any "transfer of value", be it money, property or money's worth (user, services). In some jurisdictions, this was achieved by a wide "interpretation" of the term "payment" ("paiement", Art. 1302 C.civ; "pagamento", Art 2033 C.C.).[866] In Spain, the Código Civil repeatedly refers to "el pago indebido" (cp. Art 1896, 1897 cc). But the provision at the beginning speaks more generically about the "receipt of something that could not be demanded" (Art. 1895 cc: "Cuando se recibe alguna cosa que no había derecho a cobrar, y que por error ha sido indebidamente entregada, surge la obligación de restituirla").

In the German BGB, the abstract term of *Leistung* (= performance") was transplanted from contract law to enrichment law to describe all intentional shifts of value. The original meaning of performance is **doing what is required by a legal obligation**, in order to discharge that obligation. Pursuant to § 241 I 1 and 2 BGB, "performance" is the act or omission that can be claimed from the debtor "by virtue of the obligation" ("Kraft des Schuldverhältnisses..."). According to § 362 I BGB, this obligation will be discharged if the performance is made. This resonates well with the general use of *Leistung* in the German language that indicates both an achievement and something that *must* be achieved. It accords with the common law understanding of performance as well as with the taxonomy of Italian use of "prestazione" in the Art. 1174 et seq. C.C. The strict connection of "performance" and (existing) "obligation" became however loosened under the BGB. German law transferred the term "performance" to the law of unjustified enrichment. This enlarged the meaning because it also encompasses transfers that are not owed (invalid contracts) or not even presumably owed like donations or the "performances" to achieve an agreed purpose under § 812 I 2 2. Alt. BGB (*causa data causa non secuta*, see above p. 72).

The German *Leistungskondiktionen* are built around and rest on the notion "performance". The long and short of it is that **every performance of money or money's worth constitutes a direct shift of value**, as has been set out above.[867] It follows that it is *always and only* the performing party who can demand restitution of the failed performance. And it is always and only the direct recipient who is liable for restitution. In other words: restitution is restricted to the parties of the failed performance and to the money or money's worth trans-

866 For the wide scope see Art. 1302–1 in conjunction with Art. 1352–1352-9 C.civ.; Art. 2037 C.C.
867 This is the point that was – and still is – missed by followers of the uniform doctrine, e.g. Kupisch, JZ 1985, 163 et seq.

ferred.[868] This can be directly inferred from the drafts of *von Kübel* and the *Erste Kommission* (pp. 235 et seq). After the final version of § 812 I 1 BGB had blurred the picture, the *Leistungskondition* was reinstated by the modern *Trennungslehre* (= doctrine of separation), albeit without recognizing that the performance was the paradigm shift of value (see pp. 242, 254 and 260).

Leistung / performance is traditionally defined as *bewusste und zweckgerichtete Mehrung fremden Vermögens* (= conscious and purposeful increase in another's wealth).[869] The emphasis of this definition lies on the purpose of the performance. It is the key to unlock the question what circumstances do invalidate the wilful transfer in a way that the bar of *volenti non fit inuria* can be overcome.

For German law, the notion of the "performance" has been the original focal point for the *Leistungskondiktionen*, and is so again after the demise of the *Einheitslehre* and the subsequent rise of the *Trennungslehre.* This is so because it is the taxonomy of the German Act. However, since every "performance" (in the German sense) is a **direct transfer of value**, the direct shift of value approach of English law catches the same. The recognition of purposes of transfers is not tied to the use of the specific German term "performance" either. It is derived from a general philosophical observation that is expressed in the paroemia ***nihil est sine ratione*** – nothing happens without a reason. Human intent is driven by the pursuit of purposes. The task of the law of unjust enrichment is to explain the achievement or failure of which purposes is relevant for restitution. This is equally true for German performances and for common law transfers of value – as the unjust factor of failure of consideration indicates.

b) The failure of purpose as the overall unjust factor

aa) The paradigm of the *causa solvendi*

For Savigny, the principle of all Roman *condictiones* was to reverse direct shifts of wealth without legal reason (*sine causa*). The drafts of von Kübel and the Erste Kommission started to express the lack of a legal reason in the performance-based claims more precisely. The leading provision was the *condictio indebiti* that was defined by the failure of the purpose to discharge the obligation (*causa*

868 For a performance-based approach under English law Stevens, The Laws of Restitution, 2022, p. 29 et seq.

869 The Bundesgerichtshof constantly adheres to this definition, BGHZ 40, 272 (277); 50, 227 (231, 232); 56, 228 (240); 72, 246 (248 f.); NJW 2004, 1169. For criticism see NK-BGB/Prinz v. Sachsen Gessaphe, § 812 Rn. 15; MüKoBGB/Schwab, 8th edn. 2020, § 812 Rn. 347; BeckOKBGB/Wendehorst, 1.8.2023, § 812 Rn 38.

solvendi).[870] The normative justification was explained by von Kübel in the motives of his pre-draft:

> v. Kübel, S. 16 = Schubert, S. 676: "Wer nämlich zahlt, um einer bestimmten Verbindlichkeit zu genügen (solvendi causa), hat eben damit in deutlich erkennbarer Weise als seine Absicht und seinen Willen erklärt, dass er nur zahle, um diese Verbindlichkeit zu erfüllen, dass er nicht leisten würde, wenn eine Verbindlichkeit hierzu nicht bestände... . ... Die Rücksichtnahme auf die erkannte wahre Absicht und die aus dem Willen resultierende Zweckbestimmung (das aequum et bonum) hat dazu geführt, in solchen Fällen dem Leistenden ein persönliches Forderungsrecht ... auf Wiederherstellung ... zu geben."
>
> [Whoever pays in order to meet a certain obligation (solvendi causa) has thereby declared in a clearly recognisable manner as his intention and his will that he only pays in order to fulfil this obligation, that he would not pay if an obligation to do so did not exist.... . ... The consideration of the recognised true intention and the purpose resulting from the will (the aequum et bonum)[871] has led in such cases to grant a personal claim to the payer ... for restoration.]

The "consideration of the recognised true intention" ("Die Rücksichtnahme auf die erkannte wahre Absicht") leaves no choice but restitution. The claimant made the performance for the discharge. If the discharge fails, the performance must be returned because the claimant did not want to make a gift.[872] To hold otherwise falsifies the will of the claimant and violates party autonomy.

bb) Failure of the *causa solvendi* instead of (liability) mistake

The failure-of-purpose explanation of the *condictio indebiti* made the liability mistake as a precondition of the claim redundant.[873] To be sure: The principle of *volenti non fit inuria* excludes an enrichment claim if the claimant *knew* that he was

870 See above, § 737 E I: "Zum **Zweck der Erfüllung** einer Verbindlichkeit..." (= **for the purpose of discharging** a liability); § 1 VE: "Wer .. zur Erfüllung einer ... Rechtsverbindlichkeit geleistet hat..." [= A person who... has rendered a performance for discharging a ... legal obligation...].

871 Note the similar reference to the *aequum et bonum* by Lord Mansfield in *Moses v Macferlan:* "This kind of equitable action, to recover back money, which ought not in justice to be kept, is very beneficial, and therefore much encouraged. It lies for money which, **ex aequo et bono**, the defendant ought to refund..." (see already F.L. Schäfer, p. 574–575).

However, whereas von Kübel explains the failure of purpose as the concrete reason for restitution, Lord Mansfield's reference is connected with a loftier description ("ought not in justice to be kept", "ought to refund") that is only specified by the following examples ("money paid by mistake; or upon a consideration which happens to fail"...).

872 See also Labbé, S. 90.1.97, above p. 201.

873 Cp. § 812 I 1 1. Alt. BGB; already § 1 VE and § 737 E I. By contrast, Savigny held the liability mistake for indispensable, based on the Romans sources; see Savigny, Vol III, pp. 447 et seq.

not obliged to perform (cp. § 814 BGB[874]). But beyond those cases, the decisive flaw of the transaction is not the error of the claimant but the failure of the purpose (above p. 98). The failure of the purpose calls for restitution not only because it renders the transaction useless but also because leaving the benefit with the recipient would falsify the will of the claimant who did not want to make a gift.

The advantage of the failure of purpose explanation becomes obvious if contracts are rescinded with retrospective effect (no error at the time of performance; likewise in the SWAP-cases, p. 272). Also, if I paid a non-existent debt despite harbouring serious doubts, for example because I did not want to risk litigation or an entry in the debtor register, I have not erred but a claim in restitution must lie nevertheless – or else the law creates a gift where there was none.

This shows that dropping the mistake of law bar was but a foreshadowing. Mistake seeks to explain restitution as invalidation of the consent at the moment of the transfer. But that cannot be the reason because if the consent was actually vitiated by the mistake, the respective transaction would have to be invalidated – which it is not. Moreover, if mistakes vitiated the will of the performing party, any unilateral misapprehension of the claimant would be liable to invalidate transfers, provided it was a but-for-cause for the performance.

In truth, the principle of *volenti non fit inuria* is not trumped because the legal act to perform is invalid, but because the performance makes no sense. German law was therefore right to skip the liability mistake as precondition of the *condictio indebiti* and turn to the failure of purpose explanation. English law should follow suite with "mistake" because the unjust factors of *Moses v Macferlan* are the same. English law took the other turn when it departed from liability mistake (*Kelly v Solari*) to general mistake in *Aiken v Short* and *Barclays v Simms.* But this may have to be revisited after a thorough understanding of the performances and purposes pursued in tripartite cases (see below p. 303, also as to mistake in relation to gifts, p. 200).

cc) The extension of the concept of failure of purpose to all performance-based *condictiones* in the §§ 812 BGB

The first draft of the BGB was skipped on the way to the final version of the BGB because the *Lehre von der Voraussetzung* was rejected (p. 243). The Second Commission replaced it with the *Zweckbestimmung* (= determination of the purpose)

874 "Das zum Zwecke der Erfüllung einer Verbindlichkeit Geleistete kann nicht zurückgefordert werden, wenn der Leistende gewusst hat, dass er zur Leistung nicht verpflichtet war...."

[A payment made for the purpose of discharging an obligation may not be reclaimed if the person making the payment knew that he was not obliged to make the payment ....

of the *Leistung* (performance). This has rightly been interpreted as an evolution (instead of a rupture) by the followers of the *Zwecklehre.*[875] It was done to distinguish the legally relevant purpose from irrelevant personal motives for the transaction. The determination of the purpose is a (unilateral) legal act that is set by the performing party (although this may be done with a view to be agreed by the recipient). The purpose of the performance is legally relevant because keeping the performance despite its failure would falsify the legal meaning of the transaction, creating a gift where there was no liberal intent. That distinguishes it from mere motives, even if those are clearly recognisable. The *Lehre von der Voraussetzung* could not define this as clearly. The wedding ring cannot be returned after being jilted at the altar because the purchase is useless, but it is still a purchase. The buyer paid the ring and acquired title to and possession of it.

dd) The *Zwecklehre* (causa-doctrine) as key to distinguish the purpose of the performance from motivations

Not achieving the purpose of the transaction is a notion that can be generalised to explain why performances fail and must be undone. But extending this approach beyond the obvious case of the *causa solvendi* requires a clear distinction between relevant purposes and irrelevant motives, expectations and assumptions. Assume I balance my negative bank account because I want to secure goodwill for a new loan request – that is nevertheless rejected by the bank. The true purpose of my action has failed, but I cannot recover because I achieved the discharge when I paid my due.

A theory to distinguish relevant purposes from irrelevant motives is the *Zwecklehre* (causa-doctrine). It has been developed by Hugo Kreß[876] who built on fundaments of Roman law laid by jurists like Savigny. This theory has well-founded, coherent views on a wide range of connected doctrinal issues related to the creation and the discharge of obligations. To give one example: English lawyers know the difference between a sale and a contract to sell. By contrast, most German lawyers think that if I buy a bun at the baker's, the handing over of the bun simultaneously creates and discharges the obligation to deliver the bun under § 433 I 1 BGB, i. e. that there are only contracts to sell. The *Zwecklehre* strongly opposes that assumption.[877] That is a minority view, but it is more persuasive. The

---

875 Ehmann, Die Lehre vom Zweck als Entwickelung der Voraussetzungslehre, FS Beuthien, 2009, 37 = https://www.uni-trier.de/fileadmin/fb5/prof/eme001/FS-Beuthin_die_lehre_vom_Zweck.pdf.

876 Hugo Kreß, Lehrbuch des Schuldrechts, 1929 (reprint 1974), § 5; he was followed by Hermann Weitnauer who forcefully promoted that school of thought.

877 Ehmann, Der Zweck der Leistungen, p. 14–15.

dominant German view has already been proven wrong because otherwise, the *condictio indebiti* would be the only enrichment claim required under modern law. For the purposes of this book, it is not possible to do all the intricate arguments of the *Zwecklehre* justice. I will therefore restrict myself to explain the failure of the three purposes that distinguish irrelevant mistakes (cf. again pp. 36, 74, 84, 91–92; 98; 107–108 and 245–246).

ee) The three purposes of the performance ("drei Classen der Leistungszwecke")

Savigny has shown us that there are only three reasons to make transfers: to acquire ("do ut des"), to donate and to discharge:[878]
- *causa acquirendi*[879]/ Austauschzweck / purpose of exchange
- *causa donandi* /Liberalitätszweck / purpose of liberality
- *causa solvendi* /Erfüllungszweck / purpose of discharge

These three basic purposes can be further qualified and subdivided according to the different character of contractual exchanges. For example, the purpose to give security (*causa fiduciae*) is an additional, preliminary stage of the *causa solvendi.* A security is originally granted for securing the debt, but also for the discharge of the debt on maturity. There are only the three basic purposes. They are the pillars of the concept. If they are achieved, all is well. If they fail, the transfer makes no sense and must be restored. This logic applies under any private law that is built on the freedom of contract and party autonomy. Deviating from German orthodoxy, I would argue that most payments on debts pursue a double purpose: a payment on a sale only pursues the *causa acquirendi* (receipt of the quidproquo)), while the payment on a contract to sell pursues both the *causa solvendi* and the *causa acquirendi* (pp. 105–106). The failure of the consideration "discharge" explains why restitution lay in the closed swaps.[880] Conversely, only the failure of the purpose "compensation" can explain why the damages could be recovered from the fullo after the toga had resurfaced (pp. 106–108).

878 Friedrich Carl v. Savigny, Obligationenrecht als Theil des heutigen Römischen Rechts, 2. Bd. Berlin 1853, § 78, p. 251. Approving Ehmann, Der Zweck der Leistungen, pp. 8–11 with an account of the debate.

879 Savigny spoke of the *causa credendi* to describe that the giver believed in receiving the counter-performance. But the term is too fraught with connotations to loans, and was therefore dropped, Ehmann, Der Zweck der Leistungen, p. 2–6.

880 *Kleinwort Benson v Lincoln City Council* [1999] 2 AC 349 as opposed to *Westdeutsche Landesbank Girozentrale v Islington LBC [1996] AC 669*; in depth Birks, pp. 108 et seq.

6 The enrichment claim for "taking value"

a) The basic principle at work

The basic principle of the enrichment claim for taking value is easy to access:

- To ride on the train, you have to pay the fare.
- To go into a concert, you have to buy a ticket.
- To have someone work for you, you must pay him a wage.
- As tenant, you have to pay rent.

If the underlying contracts are invalid, the performance must be reversed. If this is impossible due to the nature of the performance, the objective value must be restored. This will normally amount to paying for the train ride, the concert, the work, the use. This is because you should have bargained for that value under a valid contract. Otherwise, you cannot keep it because you did not receive a gratuity.

If you take the value by dodging the fare, sneaking into the concert, forcing the labour or squatting, the same logic applies. Taking the value may not be a direct transfer of value, since transfer indicates wilful conduct. But it is still a "direct shift of value" that must be reversed, too.[881] It follows that you have to pay for the train ride, the concert, the work because you have taken a value you should have bargained for. The claimant is the party who would have contracted with you. The "meant-to-be-performance" directs the enrichment claim in non-performance cases in analogy to the way the performance directs the *Leistungskondiktionen.*

On a side note: The most famous German case of "taking value" is the so-called *Flugreisefall:*[882] A minor boarded a flight from Munich to Hamburg. In Hamburg, he did not disembark but hid in it to make the subsequent flight to New York – from where he was taken back directly by the carrier after being denied entry to the US. The carrier successfully demanded the costs for the flight to New York in unjust enrichment (§§ 812, 818 I BGB) and for the flight back home under *negotiorum gestio* (§§ 683, 679 BGB). One of the many doctrinal issues surrounding the case was whether the enrichment claim for the value of the intercontinental flight was a performance-based *Leistungskondiktion* or an *Eingriffskondiktion.* The *Bundesgerichtshof* assumed the former. They argued that the carrier had the general intention to perform the transport service to every person on board of the plane. This is debatable because the case certainly looks more like one of "taking value" (*Eingriff*). If the intruder had escaped entry barriers, e.g. by jumping over them or digging through the soil in Glastonbury, it could hardly be assumed that the organiser wanted to perform his services (flight, train

881 BeckOKBGB/Wendehorst, § 812 Rn. 110; Schall, Leistungskondiktion, p. 76 et seq.

882 BGHZ 55, 128 = NJW 1971, 609.

ride, concert, etc.) even to persons who did not comply with the entry procedure. But be that as it may: the *Flugreisefall* certainly shows that the difference between failed transfers and cases of taking value can be fairly little.[883] Savigny perfectly meets this point by explaining both from the same basic principle.

On the practical side, there is a different level of urgency with respect to enrichment claims for taking value in Germany and England. This may have influenced the historical evolution, particularly the decision not to accept the unjust factor of "no consent" that was carrying the *condictio sine causa specialis.* For starters, German damages claims fail if the defendant can show that the claimant would not have sold the value that was taken. A fitting example is the unauthorised (ab) use of the picture of a stately gentleman rider in his golden years for an advertisement to sell some libido-enhancing product.[884] He would NEVER have agreed to this use of his picture. That is why no causal loss results from the infringement of the right in his picture. This problem can be overcome under common law where "Wrotham Park damages" are awarded to the victim on the basis of a reasonable hypothetical bargain even if the parties would never have agreed on one.[885] However, this may be an enrichment claim in disguise anyway. It measures and reverses the objective value taken, not any causal loss.

A similar picture emerges with respect to the recovery of stolen value. The tort of conversion covers both the function of the *rei vindicatio* (return of the stolen good) and the *condictio furtiva/sine causa specialis* (return of the value taken). But torts are normally dependent on misconduct and require default, at least negligence. If I treat my property as my property, this conduct is perfectly legal. If I treat another's property as mine because I cannot know that I am not the lawful owner, I do not commit a tort with intent. What counts is not the intentional treatment of the thing as mine, but the complete innocent, not even negligent lack of knowledge that I am not allowed to do so because it belongs to another. No civil lawyer would treat a *bona fide possessor* as tortfeasor, and while the functional indispensability of this standard construction of the tort of conversion is obvious, it seems to be yet another enrichment claim for taking value in disguise.

883 Cf. Medicus/Petersen, Bürgerliches Recht, 28th edn. 2021, mn. 665 who concede this point.
884 BGHZ 26, 349 – Herrenreiterfall. The case was not about enrichment. It is famous with every German law student because the BGH allowed immaterial damages against the express wording of the BGB by arguing that higher constitutional law commanded effective protection of the personality (*allgemeines Persönlichkeitsrecht*).
885 *Wrotham Park Estate Co Ltd v Parkside Homes Ltd* [1974] 1 WLR 798.

b) The superiority of the direct shift of value to the current approach of the *Eingriff in ein Recht mit Zuweisungsgehalt* (= violation of a right that allocates values)

Wilburg was wrong to drop the direct shift of wealth for *condictio sine causa specialis.* [886] His alternative concept of the *Eingriffskondiktion* is based on the encroachment of rights that allocate values (*Eingriff in Rechte mit Zuweisungsgehalt*). But that merely describes the relevant direct shift of value less precisely and distorts it thus, like the shadows on the wall of Plato's cave are distorted from reality. Wilburg fell for a typical lawyers trap: the fallacy of the typical case (see in more detail p. 279). The traditional cases of the *condictio sine causa specialis* were all violations of the owner's property right: Using up, commingling or selling another's property. It is true that property rights (including IP) allocate the use and all the gains coming from the property to the owner (cp. § 903 BGB). But the decisive point to establish a claim in unjustified enrichment is the **identification of the value taken** by the defendant and to be restored the claimant. And contrary to Wilburg's Eingriffskondiktion, this identification is **not** necessarily **dependent** on the **violations of rights** of the claimant.

If you evaded the barriers and bouncers and successfully sneaked into the Capital Summertime Ball in Wembley Stadium, you certainly trespass on the property of Wembley Stadium Ltd. You may also violate the copyrights of the performing artists. But all that is irrelevant. The crucial point is that you took value from the organiser of the event, Capital Radio. You should have bought your ticket from them instead of sneaking in. *That* is why Capital Radio must have the enrichment claim against you. It is a consequence of the contractual arrangements between all the parties involved and has nothing to do with anyone's property rights in the music, the concert or the stadium.

The enrichment claim cannot depend on whether any wrong or tort against Capital Radio can be construed, e.g. because they registered their festival as trade mark, because the musicians gave them a license and the license is seen as IP right instead of a mere contractual right,[887] because organisers are granted

886 For the same view BeckOKBGB/Wendehorst, § 812 Rn. 110; already Schall, Leistungskondiktion, pp. 67 et seq.

887 That is the prevailing position in Germany, BGHZ 180, 344, 353 Rn. 20 = NJW-RR 2010, 186– Reifen Progressiv; confirmed BGHZ 185, 291, 302, Rn. 29 = NJW 2010, 2731– Vorschaubilder; MüKoBGB/Wagner, 8th edn. 2020, § 823 Rn. 322; but contrast e.g. *McGuire*, Die Lizenz, 2012, pp. 582 et seq, denying any property position for the taker of a licence.

IP-protection in their own right,[888] or because the lawful possession of the organiser enjoys legal protection *inter omnes* akin to a property right.[889] Any such construction would only multiply the possible claimants. Looking for a wrong/tort *cannot* lead to the right claimant because it *cannot* explain why the wrongs against Wembley Stadium Ltd and the artists are irrelevant, as they surely have to be.

German lawyers would object that the violation of a right *per se* is not a sufficient basis for the *Eingriffskondiktion* anyway. *Wilburg* (rightly) rejected, or rather: restricted the *Rechtswidrigkeitstheorie* of Fritz Schulz that would have amounted to restitution for wrongs in the English sense. The restriction imposed by Wilburg was that the violated right must also **allocate** the respective value received by the defendant to the claimant (*Zuweisungsgehalt des Rechts*). Otherwise, the defendant could not receive any value resulting from the encroachment of that right. But for starters, the search for the "allocating content/power of the violated right" does little else than rephrase the search for a direct shift of value. If anything, it should have been sold as an evolution of, not an anti-thesis to Savigny's concept by Wilburg, instead of an evolution of the *Rechtswidrigkeitstheorie* that basically rephrased the second part of the ousted Pomponian principle.[890] Even more importantly, Wilburg's theory misses the direct shift of value beyond the standard cases. This is shown by the well-known German solution of the unauthorised sublease by the tenant.

Under German law, a tenant requires authorisation by the landlord if he intends to sublet the property (§ 540 I BGB). A sublease without prior authorisation (e.g. via Airbnb) does not only breach the tenancy agreement, but also violates the property right of the landlord. Despite that, the *Bundesgerichtshof* rightly denied the enrichment claim of the landlord against the tenant to disgorge the whole amount of the unlawful rental income.[891] The Court argued that the property

---

888 This is the case for concerts or other cultural events in Germany, § 81 UrhG, but not (yet) for sports events (see Heermann: Leistungsschutzrecht für Sportveranstalter de lege ferenda?, GRUR 2012, 791) or other merely commercial events.

889 That is the partly case under German law where *berechtigter unmittelbare Besitz* is protected like property, see RGZ 59, 326; BGHZ 32, 194 = NJW 1960, 1202, 104; MüKoBGB/Wagner, 8th edn. 2020, § 823 Rn. 324.

890 D.50.17.206 (Pomp. 9 var. lec.): "Iure naturae aequum est neminem fieri cum alterius detrimento et **iniuria** locupletiorem" [Under natural law it is fair that nobody shall become enriched from another's detriment or **injury**.]

891 BGHZ 131, 297 (306); BGH NZM 2014, 582; annotated by Riehm JuS 2014, 940.

right of the landlord does not allocate the rental income of the tenant because the landlord cannot rent the property twice. Insofar, the result is correct.[892]

But the solution is incomplete because the authorisation to sublet is normally granted in return for a rent increase that compensates the higher use and risk (cp. § 553 II BGB). This value has been taken from the landlord when the tenant was subletting without authorisation. It must be restored by an enrichment claim. This is even so if the landlord would never have agreed to the sublease because if suffices that there is a market and a market value for such authorisations. The right to demand the increase stems from the contract, not from the property right. This fits the general picture that all claims in unjust enrichment react to violations of the principle of party autonomy (above p. 262). Again, the property right of the landlord and its allocational powers did not guide to the solution but blurred it. The landlord will often be the owner but this is not necessarily so. There may be a chain of leases, and the lessor entitled to the increase may be just one link in that chain.

The irrelevance of the violation of (property) rights, even of those having allocating powers, is also confirmed by the following inverse tests:

> If A breaks into his absent neighbour's flat to better peep on the couple living on the other side of the street, he is creepy and a trespasser, but not taking value because there is no market for such "benefits".
>
> By contrast, if A breaks into that flat to watch the coronation parade, he is taking value because, as the coronation cases testify, there is a market for renting out rooms with a view for that purpose.

In both cases, A violates the property of the owner. The property right surely allocates the value of the use to the owner. But this is not the answer to the cases. The right answer is that in the first example, no value was taken, whereas in the se–cond, it was. The distinction hinges on the question whether there existed a market for the value taken. As von Kübel rightly wrote with respect to services: It does not depend whether the claimant would have sold the service as long as there is an

892 By contrast, if § 812 I 1 2. Al.t BGB was applied according to the principle of "no benefit from a wrong", as proposed by Fritz Schulz' Rechtswidrigkeitstheorie (AcP 105 (1909), 473), the tenant would have to disgorge his unlawful rental income completely.

Note further that French law reaches the result of no benefit from a wrong via the route of civil damages, thus avoiding the tricky enrichment issue, cf. e.g. The Times, Monday October 29 2018, https://www.thetimes.com/world/us-world/article/tenant-gets-46-000-bill-for-letting-flat-on-airbnb-g2prrww8f.

objective market.[893] I only beg to add that the same must be true in the converse case that it is a "freaky" kind of service that is not generally offered for money, but is so by the claimant. Claus-Wilhelm Canaris has rightly denied an enrichment claim of the land owner against someone who climbs a tree in his garden to watch a football match in the neighbouring stadium.[894] This must however change if the owner has a habit to sell the access to his tree on match days, but the climber sneaks in without paying.

All these examples underpin that the enrichment claim for taking money's worth must be applied irrespective of the violation of rights ("wrongs", "torts"), even of those rights that allocate benefits to the claimant. The lasting truth at the core of the *Eingriffskondiktion* – that you would expect in an almost generally accepted doctrinal concept – is the cognition that the law **allocates objective benefits of money's worth** that can be taken by others and must be restored.[895] But the precise test for this is whether there was a market for the benefit in question, and who would have been the right person to sell it to the defendant. To determine this, the facts must be examined in an encompassing way. Any existing contractual relations have to be taken into consideration, not only property or other *inter omnes* rights. The correct question to ask is always whether an objective value has been taken, and from whom. If I trespass on a building site to use the Toi-Toi, I do not take value. If I jump over or slip under the pay barrier of the toilets of the motorway service station, I take value, either from the owner of the service station or from the company servicing the toilets.

The benefit is attained **"at the expense"** of the claimant if and because he would have been the person to charge the defendant for it. That being so, the **meaning** of "at the expense" turns out to be the **same** for **performance-based**

---

893 von Kübel, p. 46 (= Schubert, p. 706): "Hervorzuheben ist nur, dass es nicht darauf ankommt, ob gerade der Leistende solche Dienste gegen Entlohnung zu leisten pflegt, sondern ob überhaupt solche Dienste und Handlungen im heutigen Verkehr gegen Lohn geleistet werden."

It should be noted that the passage only speaks of performances because under the structure of the pre-draft, § 10 VE directly related to the *condictio indebiti* in § 1 VE. However, the same principle was by way of cross-reference applied to determining the value taken under the *condictio since causa specialis.*

In *Victoria Park Racing & Recreational Grounds v Taylor* (1937) 58 CLR 479, no value was taken from the organisers under this rationale because the organisers of spectacles sell places only in their stadiums, grandstands, event zones &ct. Against a claim for the "stolen spectacle" also Lionel Smith, Restitution: A New Start, in Devonshire/Havelock (eds.), p. 91, at p. 101.

894 Larenz/Canaris, Schuldrecht II/2, p. 173.

895 For this allocation-based interpretation of "at the expense" see already *Heck*, Grundriss des Schuldrechts, 1929 (reprint 1994), § 141, 5; picked up by *Guangyu Fu*, Das Causa-Problem im deutschen Bereicherungsrecht, 2010, p. 132.

and non-performance-based enrichment. And why should it not? In both cases, there is a direct shift of value. In neither case can the claimant charge the defendant for the benefit under a contract. But in both cases, party autonomy commands that the benefit should have been paid for to the claimant.

c) *Der Fehlschluss vom Faktum auf die Norm* (= the fallacy to see the typical case as legal rule)

The right to charge for benefits will often be, but is not necessarily, tied up to the ownership of rights. That is why the *Eingriffskondiktion* of German law is an unfinished concept of insufficient precision. It can be understood as an example of an old fallacy that lawyers worldwide tend to fall for again and again: the mistaken conclusion from the typical case to the legal rule, in German: ***Der Fehlschluss vom Faktum auf die Norm.*** Sometimes, lawyers recognise this beforehand and are able to avoid it. An example of this is the genesis of the seminal Salomon-case about the separate legal personality of a company.

The typical case of a 19th century company were large stock corporations, not *Aaron Salomon's* de-facto one man company. That is why the lower Courts did not accept the legal personality and limited liability of that atypical company which they regarded as fraud (*fraus legis*). But the House of Lords recognised that the legal rules of how to set up a company were not confined to the typical case and accepted the existence of the Aaron Salomon & Co Ltd.[896] Something similar happened in Germany with the acceptance of the GmbH & Co KG. Typical partnerships or limited partnerships have always consisted of natural persons. However, there was nothing in the German HGB to prohibit a company from becoming a member of a partnership, nor companies from forming a partnership (OHG) or limited partnership (KG) without any natural person involved. That is why the *Reichsgericht* allowed the construction of a GmbH & Co KG on the 4th of July 1922[897] – even though that clearly undermined the idea that partnerships must at least have one fully liable partner as opposed to limited liability companies.

But German jurists did not see through that old fallacy in the context of enrichment law. The ousted *Einheitslehre* had assumed that a real transfer of wealth for the assets of one to the other (*gegenständliche Vermögensverschiebung*) was necessary because of the original case of the mistaken payment. I take the cash from my purse and give it to you. But this law came from a time where services were owed not paid (family, slaves) and bank transfers were unknown. Moreover, even the Romans had already understood that the value of services or user could

896 *Salomon v A Salomon* & Co Ltd [1896] UKHL 1, [1897] AC 22.
897 RGZ 101, 106.

be reclaimed, despite there being no transfer of any title (*datio*).[898] That led the way to the direct shift of value.

The doctrine of *Eingriffskondiktion* replicated the mistake to build the rule on the typical case. Admittedly, this fallacy was particularly hard to realise because almost all cases of "taking value" amount to the encroachment of another's property, intellectual property or similar property-like legal positions under German law[899] that are valid *inter-omnes*, not only *inter partes* like obligations.[900] Indeed, this is not coincidental. It is a dominant[901] purpose of creating rights *inter omnes* to allocate the value of the right to their exploitation to the holder. The historic evolution of intellectual property is testimony to that. But not only that. The lines drawn by the existence of an intellectual property right also work the other way. Ideas are not protected, so there can be no enrichment claim for exploiting them without the consent of the originator. So it is understandable that Wilburg attempted to draw the line for unjustified taking value in accordance with the existence of *inter omnes* rights, and that von Caemmerer concurred.

However, the existence of absolute rights is only one part of the picture. On the one hand, not all encroachments of such rights carry enrichment claims (climbing the tree for the football game). And if they do, they may point to the wrong claimants (concert case). On the other hand, shifts of value can occur where no right is violated. To conclude, this point will be underscored by the example of a Bitcoin exchange raid.

d) The example of the Bitcoin exchange raid

German law does not (as yet) accept a property right in crypto currencies (Bitcoin).[902] If a Bitcoin exchange is hacked (Mt Gox), the victim will have no *Eingriffs-*

898 Note that along the same lines, the ius commune had also been adamant to brand the *condictio furtiva* as exception. While that was true in one aspect, it again missed the point and misled further conclusions. The exceptional feature was merely that this *condictio* was not barred even though the claimant might still have the title (pp. 118–121). But clearly, this did *not* mean that every *condictio* required that the claimant had transferred his *own asset* to the defendant, as again the cases of services and user underline.

899 One example is the *berechtigte Besitz* = lawful possession.

900 Germans call such positions "absolute rights", meaning that they work against everyone, as opposed to "relative rights" like obligations that only bind creditor and debtor, but no one else. That is why only absolute rights are protected under § 823 I BGB.

901 Not the only one, as rights to personality, to data protection, to Habeas Corpus &tc shall also shield from non-pecuniary disadvantages.

902 Prevailing opinion, Omlor ZHR 183 (2019) 294, at 310; Weiss: Die Rückabwicklung einer Blockchain-Transaktion, NJW 2022, 1343, 1345. The reason is that the value of intrinsic tokens does not exist beyond the blockchain so that it cannot be held by any owner. But contrast Walter: Bitcoin,

kondiktion against the "thief" to recover the value that was taken from him without consent. But an enrichment claim *must* lie, and the reason is that the thief has taken something that he would have had to bargain and pay for. Party autonomy commands the restoration of the value.

> Cf. the strong argument of *Alexander Weiss*, NJW 2022, 1343, 1346, Rn 27: "Dass im Zusammenhang mit diesem Tatbestandsmerkmal [sc. "auf dessen Kosten] zum Teil von einem Eingriff in eine *Rechts*position die Rede ist, kann dabei nicht ernsthaft zum pauschalen Ausschluss der Eingriffskondiktion bei Blockchain-Transaktionen führen. Diese Begrifflichkeit ist wohl eher der Vorstellung geschuldet, es gebe keine Vermögenspositionen außerhalb des Rechts. Dass dem nicht so ist, zeigt gerade die Blockchain-Technologie. Indes kann weder dem Wortlaut ("auf dessen Kosten" statt "durch Rechtsverlust") noch dem Sinn und Zweck (Unmittelbarkeit und Zurechnung) des Tatbestandsmerkmals eine Beschränkung auf Rechtspositionen entnommen werden."
>
> [The fact that in connection with this legal element [sc. "at the expense"] there is sometimes talk of an encroachment on a legal position cannot seriously lead to a blanket exclusion of the *Eingriffskonditkion* for blockchain transactions. This terminology is more likely due to the idea that there are no property positions outside of the law. Blockchain technology shows that this is not the case. However, neither the wording ("at its expense" instead of "through loss of rights") nor the sense and purpose (immediacy and attribution) of the element of the offence imply a restriction to legal positions.]

There is nothing to add to what Alexander Weiss says.[903] To conclude:

The enrichment claim must address a direct shift of value. If objective value is taken, it must be restored to the person who should have sold it. That achieves the right result without further ado. It is neither necessary nor sufficient to show encroachment of a right. The construction of any rights, property-like positions etc will never solve the issue coherently and completely. Even if German law recognised property rights in crypto currencies,[904] what about the theft of developed "characters" in massive(ly) multiplayer online role-playing games (MMORPG),[905] &ct. The attachment to an encroachment of a right is a fallacy derived from the

---

Libra und sonstige Kryptowährungen aus zivilrechtlicher Sicht, NJW 2019, 3609; Johannes Arndt, Bitcoin-Eigentum, 2021, calling for recognition as property.

Under common law, crypto-currencies are personal property as a specific locus of monetary value.

903 The alignment with the position taken here is not coincidental. Weiss refers to BeckOKBGB/Wendehorst, § 812 Rn. 110 who in turn refers to Schall, Leistungskondiktion, pp. 67 et seq.

904 As proposed e.g. by Arndt, Bitcoin-Eigentum, 2021.

905 The objective value is beyond doubt, cf. https://en.wikipedia.org/wiki/Massively_multiplayer_online_role-playing_game sub "economics" or virtual economy.

typical case. It misapplies the enrichment claim in the same way as attaching it to a "real" shift of wealth.

7 Direct shift of value, volenti non fit inuria and "imposed enrichment" (aufgedrängte Bereicherung) under the Aufwendungskondiktion and Rückgriffskondiktion

Despite the demise of the unmittelbare Vermögensverschiebung, the principle of a direct shift of value still governs two specific non-performance-related enrichment claims of German law: The *Aufwendungskondiktion* and the *Rückgriffskondiktion.*

- The *Aufwendungskondiktion* applies if A makes expenditure for the benefit of B. Paradigm: A builds on the land of B (but see p. 128).
- The *Rückgriffskondiktion* if A pays the debt of B to C.

In both cases, there is a direct shift of value from A to B: the improvement of the land; the discharge.[906] The typical feature of *both* cases under German law is that the benefits can be conferred behind the back of the beneficiary.[907] That raises the issue of "imposed enrichment" (*aufgedrängte Bereicherung*). This is aggravated by the fact that the final version of § 812 I 1 BGB omitted the "without consent" element of the *condictio sine causa specialis.*[908] As a consequence, it seems that A can deliberately impose not only the enrichment, but also the enrichment claim on B. To come back to the above example where I planted flowers on my neighbour's strip of land to enjoy the nice view.[909] After they faded, I can knock on the door and demand payment of the objective value.

The prevailing assumption that such a claim could principally be justified[910] is a remainder of the dye-hard notion of the *actio de in rem verso:* my money came to you so you have got to account to me (p. 115). No unjust factor required. But the *actio de in rem verso* has no place in German law. What is right for three party situation is also right for two party situations. The principle of *volenti non fit iniu-*

---

906 Note that the payment of another's debt leads to a typical tripartite constellation where two direct benefits are transferred simultaneously: the discharge of B and the payment to C. On the follow-up issues arising from this see already above pp. 176–182 and in more detail below pp. 303 et seq.

907 By contrast, under English law, the debt of another cannot be discharged without that other's consent, Stevens, p. 157.

908 See p. 260.

909 See p. 264.

910 Cf. MünchKommBGB/Schwab, Vol 7, 9th edn 2024, § 812 mn. 364.

ria prohibits my enrichment claim for the value of the flowers. This would have been the law under § 27 VE; § 748 E I, so it must be the law under § 812 BGB.

This is not to say that no claim for imposed enrichments can lie at all. Germany has historical reasons not to be as principally hostile as England towards imposed enrichments.[911] Rather, a proportionate solution can be steered via the defence of disenrichment. If the owner cannot demand removal of the building,[912] there will nevertheless be no enrichment claim as long as the owner does not make use of the building. This shall prevent the "expropriation" of the owner via an enrichment claim that is forced upon him by an imposed enrichment. However, if the owner uses the building to generate income (e.g. bei letting; by selling the land at the higher value), the *Aufwendungskondiktion* of the claimant who erected the building will liven up.

That solution is persuasive under but one proviso. Any enrichment claim must first overcome *volenti non fit inuria*, or else there can be no restitution. The scenarios of the *Aufwendungskondiktion* do not concern performances. A does not want to transfer value to B, but to him-/herself. One cannot perform to oneself,[913] as little as one can be obliged to oneself. Nevertheless, *nihil est sine ratione* applies to the actions of A. The purpose pursued by A is a *causa acquirendi*. A intends to acquire a building on his land. If the land does not belong to A but B, his purpose fails – and justifies restitution.

The conclusion for Germany should be to restrict the *Aufwendungskondiktion* and the *Rückgriffskondiktion* to cases where the enrichment occurs without consent of the claimant because the *causa acquirendi* as the purpose of the investment failed. Otherwise, there can be at most a claim under a *negotiorum gestio contraria* (§§ 684, 812 BGB).[914]

The conclusion for England would be that building on another's land will carry an award under the general enrichment claim if and because it is a direct shift of value from A to B that is flawed by an unjust factor. If A built erroneously on another's land, the investment for the own benefit is frustrated by the failure of the *causa acquirendi* (or according to orthodoxy: by a mistake). This enrichment claim is subject (a) to any proprietary rights to demand removal of the building from the land and (b) to the defence of unjust enrichment.[915]

---

911 See above pp. 121 et seq.

912 In particular, a bona fide possessor will be protected from any tortious or other liability to remove the building under § 993 I BGB.

913 But see *Colonial Bank v Exchange Bank of Yarmouth* (1885) 9 AppCas 84 (PC).

914 Schall, Leistungskondition, pp. 88 et seq.

915 Too restrictive *Yeoman's Row v Cobbe* [2008] UKHL 55.

VII The normative foundation of defences under the direct shift of value approach

1 Direct shift of value and disenrichment

a) The extension to all *condictiones* under German law as explained by *von Kübel*

The defence of disenrichment (change of position)[916] is the logical flipside of the principle of unjust enrichment. An enrichment can only be unjust if it still exists. No enrichment – no unjust enrichment. The Pomponian principle is the originator of all laws of unjust enrichment. It introduced the language of enrichment and the inherent concept of an obligation to disgorge that is based on the state of the defendant's wealth, without any reliance on personal blame. Conversely, it followed that disenrichment extinguished this liability, what was a welcome feature in order to protect bona fide recipients.

However, the plain and simple argument for accepting the defence of disenrichment as flipside of an enrichment claim breaks down as soon as unjust enrichment is not justified any more by the Pomponian principle not to be enriched (*locupletior*) from another's detriment.

All the more it is remarkable that German law, after rejecting Pomponius outright, still adopted the defence of disenrichment. Moreover, deviating from the first natural law codifications, it extended this defence to all *condictiones*. In the 18th century, the doctrine of the ius commune had not accepted a general defence of unjust enrichment. Relief was only granted if restitution of a specific asset had been owed and become impossible. By contrast, money was always to be returned. The Code Civil freeze-framed this earlier view in Art. 1352 – 1352 – 9 C.civ:[917]

> Art 1352 C.civ: La restitution d'une chose **autre que d'une somme d'argent** a lieu en nature ou, lorsque cela est impossible, en valeur, estimée au jour de la restitution.
>
> [The restitution of a thing **other than a sum of money** is made in kind or, where this is impossible, in value, estimated on the day of restitution.]

---

916 There are technical differences between civilian disenrichment and common law change of position, cp Mélodie Combot, Quasi-contrat et enrichissement injustifié, 2023, n° 167 et seq. These differences do not matter in the present context. On change of position in general, cf. e. g. Stevens, pp. 354 – 374. Burrows, Restatement, pp. 117 et seq.; see also *Cheese v. Thomas* [1994] 1 WLR 129 (CA); *Haugesund Kommune v. Depfa ACS Bank* [2010] EWCA Civ 579.

917 For an account of the diverging rules on disenrichment see Mélodie Combot, Quasi-contrat et enrichissement injustifié, 2023, n° 240 who builds on this difference an argument that the action en répétition de l'indu is not based on the wider principle of Pomponian unjust enrichment – which is true, following Savigny.

This is the same rule that applied to restitution under common law prior to *Lipkin Gorman.*[918] In 19th century Germany, it had been vigorously defended by Erxleben.[919] But the prevailing opinion moved on. The debate is accounted for by von Kübel who followed the prevailing opinion.[920] Somewhat surprisingly in light of the rejection of Pomponius, he justified his decision by ample reference to the to the *aequum et bonum*, i.e. considerations of higher equity (see in detail p. 295). The references to higher equity are remarkable in light of the rejection of Pomponius. It would not do justice to discard them as an attempt to justify a law without having achieved its complete intellectual penetration. Rather, they reveal a basic notion that is of even higher interest in the comparative context, in particular since they connect to a part of Lord Mansfield's speech in *Moses v Mcferlan.*[921]

The starting point is a primeval conception of property. The owner of chattel or land can transfer his/her property. But (s)he cannot be forced to dispose of it. This is still the common law today. It was equity, administered by the chancellor, representing Godly justice on behalf of the King, that had to devise means to get around that rule under the laws of England, starting with the trust and ending with specific performance.

From the common law perspective, unjust enrichment shows characteristic features of an equitable remedy. However, common law unjust enrichment does not re-transfer titles, while civil law does not have any problems with forcing the owner to convey property in order to perform contractual or legal duties. The references to equity blurred the true rationale of the enrichment claims in both common and civil law.[922] As a consequence, the search for it began here and there. As far as the foundation of the claims is concerned, both sides have progressed considerably. In England, the way led from Lord Mansfield's "eternal justice"[923] to the introduction of the theory of implied promise, its rejection in favour of unjust enrichment with the various unjust factors, culminating in acceptance of the general claim. After all these periods, the law is still oddly infused by the Pom-

918 *Baylis v Bishop of London* [1913] 1 Ch 127.

919 Erxleben, Die Condictiones sine Causa, Vol I, 1850, pp. 182 et seq.

920 Von Kübel, pp. 35–42. Cf. further Zimmermann, pp. 895–901; Flume, FS Niedermeyer, 1953, p. 103, at 140 et seq = Studien, p. 59.

921 The speech was cited above, p. 66. Mélodie Combot, Quasi-contrat et enrichissement injustifié, 2023, n° 77 also notes that Lord Mansfield refers to equity in general, not to unjust enrichment specifically.

922 Critical to the abandoning of a clear rationale by referring to general equity Mélodie Combot, Quasi-contrat et enrichissement injustifié, 2023, e.g. n°234 and n° 249.

923 *Marriot v Hampton* 101 Eng. Rep. 669 (K. B. 1797).

ponian principle not to benefit from another's detriment even though that was never received by Lord Mansfield.

By contrast, 19th century Germany had already overcome Pomponius and the *actio de in rem verso* in favour of the direct shift of value approach with the cardinal unjust factor failure of purpose. But the justification of the disenrichment defence was in its infancy. It was not before the groundbreaking article by Werner Flume, "Der Wegfall der Bereicherung in der Entwicklung vom römischen zum geltenden Recht", Festschrift für Hans Niedermeyer, 1953, that this myth was rationalised. The key cognition was the relevance of the spending decision. The findings of Werner Flume may be interesting for English law that has just really started to explore the issue after the acceptance of change of position 1991, particularly if English law wants to escape the clutches of Pomponius, as it should. Before we revisit the evolution to a modern rationale of disenrichment, starting with the Motive by von Kübel where we find first concrete guidance beyond equitable considerations, let us first have a look how the odd survival of Pomponian equity within German unjustified enrichment thinking disturbed the codification and subsequently, the application of the §§ 812, 818 BGB in Germany.

b) The original misconception of § 812 BGB (in particular: the *Saldotheorie*)

aa) The "enrichment" of the defendant as the "Erlangte etwas" of § 812 I 1 BGB

When the BGB entered into force on 1 January 1900, the predominant view was that § 812 I 1 was a general clause that allowed the claimant to demand from the defendant disgorgement of the enrichment made at his or her expense. The "Erlangte Etwas" (literally translated as "obtained something") was not merely the benefit (money or money's worth) that the defendant had received. Rather, it was understood as the "enrichment" of the claimant. This required a calculation that took into consideration the entire wealth, i. e. the sum of the assets of the defendant. It followed that the claimant did not only have to show the conferral of a benefit, but a resulting enrichment of the defendant. For example, it would not suffice that a service rendered to the defendant was money's worth (haircut). It would have been necessary to show that the defendant was actually "enriched" from the haircut. This is obviously not obvious because the assets of (legal) persons do not swell by receiving services. If anything, they are depleted by the payments due for the services. They appear as expenses in the profit and loss account, as every accountant well knows. To find an enrichment from services, jurists have devised following argumentative trick. They assume that the defendant would have had the hair cut anyway. That is why the receipt of the haircut under the void contract saved him the expenses of entering into a valid contract for a haircut. Generally speaking, all necessary expenses must be made anyway. That is why receiving necessary expenses under an invalid contract will always amount to an enrichment. The defendant saves the expenditure for a valid contract for the services etc. This saving is the foundation to assume the defendant's enrichment (*ersparte Aufwendungen*). As the BGH[924] explained in 1971, it was not enough that the debtor of the enrichment claim had obtained a valuable service (money's worth) but also that ...

> ... der Bereicherungsschuldner auch dementsprechende Ausgaben erspart habe. Das war in den damaligen Rechtsstreitigkeiten ... vorauszusetzen, da es um Dienstleistungen .. ging, die der Bereicherungsschuldner benötigte und von denen deshalb anzunehmen war, daß er sie sich auf jeden Fall zum üblichen bzw. angemessenen Entgelt anderweitig beschafft hätte, zumal er über sie bereits entgeltliche Verträge abgeschlossen hatte.
>
> [... the debtor had also saved corresponding expenses. This was to be assumed in the legal disputes at the time ..., as it concerned services ... which the debtor needed and of which it could therefore be assumed that he would in any case have procured them elsewhere for the usual or reasonable remuneration, especially since he had already concluded contracts for them for a fee. – DeepL]

The interpretation of the "Erlangte Etwas" as the enrichment of the defendant sat well with the text of § 818 III BGB. According to the original reading, this provision went hand in hand with § 812 I 1 BGB. The enrichment claim would only lie when the defendant was enriched. It would cease to lie if the defendant was no longer enriched.

> § 818 III BGB:
> Die Verpflichtung zur Herausgabe oder zum Ersatz des Wertes ist ausgeschlossen, soweit der Empfänger **nicht mehr** bereichert ist.
>
> [The obligation to disgorge or to compensate the value is excluded insofar as the recipient is **no longer** enriched.]

However, the doctrinal interpretation of the "Erlangte etwas" began to change in the second half of the twentieth century. In 1960, the BGH decided a pre-war case that had been dragging on well into the new Bundesrepublik: A had promised consulting services to the owner of a company in order to rationalise its business. The promised fee was 50 % of the savings, but maximum 60.000 Reichsmark = 6.000 DM. The contract had been avoided for *arglistige Täuschung* pursuant to §§ 123, 142 I BGB (= fraudulent misrepresentation). Having lost his contractual claim, A sued in unjust enrichment. He argued that the total amount of the savings had been 139.000 Reichsmark = 13.900 DM and claimed restitution of that total amount as un-

924 BGHZ 55, 128 = NJW 1971, 609, 610 – Flugreisefall.

just enrichment. The BGH dismissed the action on grounds of § 242 BGB because it contradicted *bona mores* that the claimant should be awarded for his deceit with a higher remuneration than the contract would have given him. But in addition to that compelling main argument, the Court also delivered doctrinal elaborations on the object of an enrichment action for services:[925]

> Die Revision meint anscheinend, die Beklagte müsse dem Kläger den Gesamtwert der von ihm im Betrieb der Beklagten herbeigeführten Ersparnisse und Wertsteigerungen ersetzen. Das trifft jedoch nicht zu. Der Umstand, daß die Rationalisierungstätigkeit des Klägers Dauerersparnisse und Wertsteigerungen im Unternehmen der Beklagten herbeigeführt hat, löst nicht einen Bereicherungsanspruch des Klägers gegen die Beklagte in der vollen Höhe dieser Ersparnisse und Wertsteigerungen aus.
>
> "Erlangt" (§ 812 BGB) hat die Beklagte die ihr vom Kläger geleisteten Dienste. Ihre Bereicherung findet daher ihren Ausdruck in dem Wert dieser Dienste (§ 818 II BGB). Der Wert der Dienste ist mit ihrer üblichen und angemessenen Vergütung zu bemessen.
>
> [The appeal apparently believes that the defendant must compensate the plaintiff for the total value of the savings and increases in value that he brought about in the defendant's business. However, this is not the case. The fact that the plaintiff's rationalisation activities brought about permanent savings and increases in value in the defendant's company does not give rise to a claim for enrichment by the plaintiff against the defendant in the full amount of these savings and increases in value.
>
> The defendant has "obtained" (§ BGB § 812 BGB) the services rendered to it by the plaintiff. Her enrichment is therefore expressed in the value of these services (§ 812 II BGB). The value of the services is to be measured at their usual and reasonable remuneration. – Translated with DeepL.com (free version)]

This new approach to the obtained benefit was finally confirmed in the seminal *Flugreisefall* (see above p. 273). The BGH was forced to clarify the law that was in doubt from two sides. On the one hand, the lower Court had concluded from the jurisdiction just mentioned that there could be no disenrichment where money's worth had been obtained. Enjoyment of the service meant receipt of the value by the defendant. That value could not get lost any more (unlike money or assets). On the other hand, the view that the total enrichment, not the specific benefit was the "obtained something" under § 812 was still deeply entrenched.

The BGH struck a compromise. The Court accepted that the specific benefit (service, user) was the "obtained something" but insisted that in addition, (dis)enrichment had to be tested under § 818 III BGB and that to this end, the saved expenditure test was to be applied. In the context of the enrichment test, the BGH went beyond the wording and ruled that it did not matter whether the defendant

925 BGH JZ 1960, 603 = BeckRS 1960, 31186313; cfd. BGHZ 36, 321 = NJW 1962, 807.

became subsequently *dis*enriched or whether he has *not* been *en*riched from the outset. Thus, the Court transferred the question of the defendant's overall enrichment completely from a requirement of the claim to the defence of disenrichment (now better called: non-enrichment). They did so to avoid the inconsistency that mala fide defendants could escape liability by claiming not to be enriched from the outset (background: Only the defence of § 818 III BGB is barred to mala fide defendants).

BGHZ 55, 128 = NJW 1971, 609, at pp. 610–611: Der Revision ist allerdings zuzugeben, daß sich das Berufungsgericht für seine Ansicht, der Beklagte hafte als Empfänger einer ihrer Natur nach nicht rückgabefähigen Leistung auf deren Wert unabhängig davon, ob die Leistung zu einer Vermögensvermehrung oder der Ersparnis von Aufwendungen geführt habe, zu Unrecht auf die Rechtsprechung des erkennenden Senats beruft. ...

Die Rechtsprechung hat im Gegenteil stets den Standpunkt eingenommen, daß von einer Bereicherung im Sinne der §§ 812 ff. BGB in der Regel nur gesprochen werden kann, wenn und soweit der Bereicherte eine echte Vermögensvermehrung, und sei es allein durch die Ersparnis von Aufwendungen, erfahren hat.

Andernfalls wäre in Frage gestellt, ob dem allgemein anerkannten obersten Grundsatz des Bereicherungsrechts immer Geltung verschafft werden könnte, wonach die Herausgabepflicht des Bereicherten keinesfalls zu einer Verminderung seines Vermögens über den Betrag der wirklichen Bereicherung hinausführen darf

Zu Recht wird von einem Teil des Schrifttums (*von Caemmerer*, Festschrift für Rabel, Bd. I, S. 368; *Kleinheyer*, JZ 61 473, 474 *Larenz*, Schuldrecht, 9. Aufl., § 64 II, S. 393) besondere Aufmerksamkeit dem Umstand gewidmet, daß die Bereicherungsansprüche nach bürgerlichem Recht primär auf “das Erlangte” oder dessen Wert gerichtet sind. Tatsächlich ist in den §§ 812 ff. BGB – von der Überschrift abgesehen – zunächst stets nur vom “Geleisteten” oder “Erlangten” die Rede, und zwar noch in den Abs. 1 und 2 des § 818 BGB. Erstmals in § 818 *Abs. 3* (und dann wieder in den §§ 820 Abs. 2, 822) BGB wird der Begriff der “Bereicherung” verwendet als Maßstab für die Begrenzung der Haftung nach den vorangehenden Vorschriften, denen diese Begrenzung deshalb schlechthin eigen ist.

Damit erscheint es aber durchaus angebracht, ja sogar geboten, Grundsätze, die für die Frage des eventuellen *späteren Wegfalls* einer Bereicherung aufgestellt worden sind, bei gleicher Interessenlage auf die Beurteilung zu übertragen, *ob* eine Bereicherung überhaupt eingetreten ist. Das muß zumindest dann geschehen, wenn dadurch Ungereimtheiten innerhalb des Bereicherungsrechts gelöst werden können, die entstünden, wollte man für den späteren Wegfall einer Bereicherung andere Voraussetzungen fordern als für ihr Fehlen von Anfang an, obgleich für eine verschiedene Behandlung keine einleuchtenden Gründe erkennbar sind.

Wird nun aber – wie dargelegt – einem Bereicherungsschuldner, der den fehlenden Rechtsgrund beim Empfang kennt, im allgemeinen versagt, sich auf den späteren Wegfall einer einmal vorhandenen Bereicherung zu berufen, so ist nicht einzusehen, warum es ihm gestattet sein soll, unter den gleichen Voraussetzungen schon die Entstehung einer Bereicherung zu leugnen. Das muß jedenfalls dann gelten, wenn die in Frage stehende Bereicherung – wie hier – in der Ersparnis von Aufwendungen für außergewöhnliche Dinge besteht, die sich der Bereicherungsschuldner sonst nicht leisten würde oder sogar leisten könnte.

[However, the appeal must be conceded that the Court of Appeal wrongly refers to the case law of the recognising Senate for its view that the defendant, as the recipient of a benefit which by its nature cannot be returned, is liable for its value irrespective of whether the benefit led to an increase in assets or the saving of expenses. ...

Case law has always taken the contrary view that enrichment within the meaning of §§ 812 et seq. BGB can generally only be said to exist if and insofar as the enriched party has experienced a genuine increase in assets, even if only through the saving of expenses.

Some of the literature (*von Caemmerer*, Festschrift für Rabel, Bd. I, S. 368; *Kleinheyer*, JZ 61 473, 474 *Larenz*, Schuldrecht, 9. Aufl., § 64 II, S. 393) rightly pays particular attention to the fact that claims for enrichment under civil law are primarily directed at "the thing obtained" or its value. In fact, §§ 812ff. BGB – apart from the heading – initially only refers to "what was paid" or "what was obtained", and this is still the case in paras. 1 and 2 of § 818 BGB. The term "enrichment" is used for the first time in § 818 para. 3 (and then again in §§ 820 para. 2, 822) BGB as a standard for the limitation of liability according to the preceding provisions, which are therefore inherently characterised by this limitation.

That being so, it seems entirely appropriate, indeed even necessary, to transfer principles that have been established for the question of the possible subsequent cessation of an enrichment to the assessment of whether an enrichment has occurred at all ... [to] resolve inconsistencies within the law of enrichment that would arise if one were to demand different conditions for the subsequent cessation of enrichment than for its absence from the outset, although there are no obvious reasons for a different treatment. ...

If – as explained above – a debtor who is aware of the lack of legal grounds upon receipt is generally denied the right to invoke the subsequent cessation of an enrichment once it has arisen, it is not clear why he should be permitted to deny that an enrichment has already arisen under the same conditions. This must apply in any case if the enrichment in question – as here – consists in the saving of expenses for extraordinary items which the debtor of the enrichment would otherwise not or could not afford. – Translated with DeepL.com (free version)]

This doctrinal reshuffle is in line with the modern approach of the separation doctrine. § 812 I 1 BGB is not a general claim to reverse enrichment. Rather, the sentence "hides", within its wide wording, the *condictio indebiti* as specific claim. The object of the *condictio indebiti* is to reverse the performance, not any subsequent "causal enrichment" in the assets of the plaintiff. The defence of disenrichment / non-enrichment only looks at the general wealth of the defendant to determine whether he still holds on to the value of the performance (= surviving enrichment). The modern rationale for doing so will be explained below. But it is certain that it is not to be based on the Pomponian principle of "no enrichment from another's loss". Contrary to what the Court assumed in the *Flugreisefall* (and still insists on to the present day), it has nothing to do either with unjust enrichment being a field of law that is "particularly subject to equitable considerations" ("*das Gebot der Billigkeit, dem das Bereicherungsrecht in besonderem Maße unterliegt*").[926]

bb) The Saldotheorie

One lasting inheritance of the enrichment approach to the "obtained something" was the judicial creation of the *Saldotheorie*. The search for the enrichment allowed a very specific answer to a problem that English lawyers would call restitutio in integrum the impossibility of which creates a bar to rescission. It is worth taking a look at for two reasons: First, it is an instance of an enrichment-based solution that should be better overcome with a rationalisation beyond Pomponius. Second, the *Saldotheorie* has recently drawn the attention of the English judiciary.[927]

The starting point is that the Roman *condictiones* were not well equipped to deal with the impossibility of restitutio in integrum. However, Roman lawyers were not unaware of the problem. But it primarily arose in the context of sales law. The *actio redhibitoria* allowed the buyer to demand back the purchase price of faulty goods.[928] But for the claim to be awarded, the buyer had to show that he had given back the goods. If he could not do that due to his own fault, no *actio redhibitoria* would lie. However, if he was unable to do so because of *force majeur*, a fiction that the goods were returned would come to his aid.[929] The rationale was to punish the vendor. This is obsolete in modern private law. However, the rule can still be explained. The normal rule is *casum sentit dominus*, i.e. the loss lies where it falls. But the buyer would not have incurred that loss because he would not have bought the good had he known about its faultiness. That is why the *Zufallsgefahr* (risk of coincidence)[930] is shifted from the buyer to the vendor.

The paradigmatic solution of Roman sales law concerned restitution, but not unjust enrichment. It has already been shown above (pp. 74–75 and 77–79) that path dependence made us perceive these cases of failure of the *causa acquirendi*

926 BGHZ 55, 128 = NJW 1971, 609, 611 referring to BGHZ 36, 232, 235 = NJW 1960, 580.

927 *School Facility Managements Limited and others v Governing Body of Christ the King College and another* [2021] EWCA Civ 1053.

928 Zimmermann, pp. 311 et seq.

929 The name of this is fiction was "mortuus redhibetur" because in practice, the cases concerned slaves who died due to illness. Cp. also the rule of Code Hamurabi, above p. 74.

930 This is the term German lawyers use to describe the risk of becoming unable to perform an obligation to deliver something in kind, without any negligent misconduct that would render the debtor liable in damages). It is discussed in the context of the concept of "impossibility". On the roots of that Zimmermann, pp. 859–860; Christian Wollschläger, Die Entstehung der Unmöglichkeitslehre, 1971.

as belonging to the law of contract. And so is the law in Germany today.[931] By contrast, "pure" unjust enrichment did not deal with that. In the case of the builder who did not build, there is no counter performance to be returned. Likewise, in the case of the payment on a non-existing debt where the "consideration" for the payment was the discharge. It must be remembered that contract law was underdeveloped in those times. Not every exchange was supposed to rest on an exchange of binding promises. The long and short of it is that the *condictiones* did not take into consideration the "restituability" of the counter-performance. Nor did the §§ 812 et seq BGB when they entered into force 1.1.1900. That led to following situation:

> A sells a car to B. B crashes the car into the bridge. It turns out that the contract was invalid (what no party knew at the time). The solution under black letter law would be as follows:[932]
>
> B has a claim against A to return the payment of the purchase prize under § 812 I 1 1. Alt. BGB due to lack of legal reason. A would like to counter-claim for the value of the car under § 812 I 1. Alt., 818 II BGB. But B can invoke the defence of disenrichment under § 8181 III BGB because he was bona fide recipient of the car that is now destroyed without leaving any surviving enrichment in the assets of B. This solution does not depend on any negligence or not of B when crashing the car.[933]

This solution was soon perceived as unfair because B can shift the consequences of his stupidity onto A. But unlike in the sales cases, A was not necessarily responsible for the invalidity of the contract. Claims in unjust enrichment require no fault on either side. It would be odd if someone who has no control over the asset should bear the consequences of its mishandling. *Casum sentit dominus!*[934]

---

931 For a recent academic push to transfer the sales law solution that governs German *Rücktrittsrecht* by way of analogy into the law of unjustified enrichment see Medicus/Petersen, mn. 228 et seq.

932 Today, this solution is – somewhat irritatingly – called the (non-modified) *Zwei-Kondiktionen-Lehre* although it just follows from the literal application from the provision. But as Flume, FS Niedermeyer, 1953, 103, at p. 161 = Studien, p. 77 rightly said: "Es wäre geradezu ein Verstoß gegen die Würde des positiven Rechts, wenn man ihm irgendwelche Theorie gleichstellen wollte." [It would be an offence to the dignity of the positive law if any theory were to be equated with it].

933 It should however be noted that any claims against a third party causing the accident (or the proceeds therefrom) would have to be ceded to the vendor under § 818 I BGB.

934 But again, contrast Flume, FS Niedermeyer, 1953, 103, at p. 171 = Studien, p. 86: " Von dem Satz: casum sentit dominus, muss man sich im geltenden Kondiktionsrecht, das den Anspruch abstrakt am Vermögen des Empfängers orientiert, frei machen." [The sentence: casum sentit dominus, must be abandoned in the current law of unjustified enrichment which orients the claim abstractly to the assets of the recipient.– based on DeepL]

Against that background, German judges devised an ingenious solution that was based on the older assumption that § 812 I 1 BGB was a claim for disgorgement of the overall enrichment. They argued that in the example above, A is not enriched either. This is because he lost his counter-claim against B!

Normally, there would have been two assets in the balance sheet of A: the cash / book money from the payment of the purchase prize and the counter-claim under § 812 I 1 for the car or the value of the car (§ 818 II). If A loses out on the counter-claim because B is disenriched, A will be disenriched, too, because his balance sheet has been diminished simultaneously by B's loss. The loss of B is the loss of A. As a result, B does not owe any restitution to A, but A does not owe any restitution to A either.

BGHZ 53, 144 = NJW 1970, 656:

Wird ein gegenseitiger Vertrag angefochten, so entbehren die beiderseitigen Leistungen des rechtlichen Grundes. Sie sind herauszugeben. Voraussetzung ist aber, wie sich aus § 818 Abs. 3 BGB ergibt, daß der Empfänger noch bereichert ist. Ob noch eine Bereicherung vorhanden ist, ist grundsätzlich nicht isoliert für die einzelne Leistung zu betrachten (so die ältere Zweikondiktionen-Theorie), sondern beurteilt sich danach, ob unter Berücksichtigung der Gegenleistung für eine Partei noch ein Überschuß bleibt (Saldotheorie, allgemein anerkannt, anders nur noch *Flume*, Festschrift für Niedermeyer S. 103). An einem solchen Überschuß kann es namentlich dann fehlen, wenn eine der Leistungen untergegangen ist oder an Wert verloren hat. Nach der Saldotheorie ist dann nicht nur der Empfänger der untergegangenen oder entwerteten Leistung in dem entsprechenden Umfang nicht mehr bereichert; er kann auch diesen Verlust nicht auf den anderen Teil überwälzen und von diesem die dort noch vorhandene Gegenleistung herausverlangen ohne Rücksicht darauf, daß er selbst nichts mehr zu bieten hat. Wer also einen Bereicherungsanspruch geltend macht, trägt das Risiko, daß sowohl seine Leistung noch beim Gegner ist als auch die von ihm selbst empfangene Leistung noch vorhanden ist.

[If a mutual contract is avoided, the mutual performances will be without legal reason. They must be returned. However, as follows from Section 818 (3) BGB, the prerequisite is that the recipient is still enriched. Whether there is still enrichment is generally not to be considered in isolation for the individual performance (according to the older two-*condictiones* theory), but is assessed according to whether, taking into account the consideration for one party, there is still a surplus (*Saldotheorie*, generally accepted, contrast only Flume, Festschrift für Niedermeyer p. 103). Such a surplus may be lacking in particular if one of the benefits has been lost or has lost value. According to the *Saldotheorie*, not only is the recipient of the lost or devalued performance no longer enriched to the corresponding extent; he also cannot pass on this loss to the other party and demand from him the consideration still available there regardless of the fact that he himself has nothing more to offer. Whoever asserts a claim for enrichment therefore bears the risk that both his performance is still with the other party and the performance he himself has received is still available. – Translation based on DeepL.com (free version)]

This solution rests on the thesis that in the case of invalid contracts, all costs and benefits incurred and received by the parties are netted by operation of law. The mutual claims are amalgamated to one single claim that lies at the hands of the party who has the surplus after the netting exercise. That rule was introduced by the Reichsgericht (= German Imperial Court) in RGZ 54, 137. After the war, the Bundesgerichtshof immediately followed suit:

> BGHZ 1, 75, 80 = NJW 1951, 270, 271:
>
> Oberster Grundsatz des Bereicherungsrechtes ist es, daß die Herausgabepflicht der Bereicherten keinesfalls zu einer Verminderung seines Vermögens über den Betrag der wirklichen Bereicherung hinaus führen darf (§ 818 Abs. 3 BGB). Der Bereicherungsanspruch ist daher nach st. Rspr. von vornherein in sich auf den Betrag beschränkt, der sich bei einer Gegenüberstellung der erlangten Vorteile und erlittenen Nachteile als Überschuß zugunsten des Empfängers ergibt (sog. Saldo-Theorie, RGZ 94, 94, 253; 105, 29; 106, 4, 7; 141, 312).
>
> [The overriding principle of the law of unjust enrichment is that the obligation of the enriched party to surrender his assets may under no circumstances lead to a reduction of his assets beyond the amount of the actual enrichment (§ 818 para. 3 BGB). According to established case law, the claim for enrichment is therefore limited from the outset to the amount that results as a surplus in favour of the recipient when comparing the advantages gained and the disadvantages suffered (so-called *Saldo-Theorie*, RGZ 94, 94, 253; 105, 29; 106, 4, 7; 141, 312). – based on DeepL]

The rule is still applied by German Courts today, subject to exceptions[935] that will be dealt with later. But it has always been subject to fierce criticism by German doctrine. This criticism is not directed against the outcome, but against the construction based on the net enrichment. The case where this has been demonstrated is the *Vorleistung* (= advance performance).[936]

> If B had not yet paid the car in the example above, the solution via "cross-disenrichment" will fail. Again, A cannot get back the car nor the value of it because B is disenriched (§ 818 III BGB). But A cannot force B to pay for the car either. Disenrichment is only a defence. It would bar the claim of B against A to restitute the purchase price, but it cannot give A any

---

935 BGHZ 53, 144 = NJW 1970, 656: non-application in case of fraudulent misrepresentation if defendant was not guilty of negligence; BGHZ 57, 137: non-application in case of fraudulent misrepresentation if defendant caused the accident negligently, but diminution of the buyer's enrichment claim to recover the purchase price under § 242 BGB due to the own carelessness (critical e.g. Medicus / Petersen, mn. 299); BGHZ 78, 216: non-application if the devaluation of the asset is caused by its faultiness.

936 Medicus / Petersen, mn. 226; the fundamental criticism was formulated by Flume, FS Niedermeyer, 1953, 103, at p. 162 and 167 = Studien, p. 78 and 83; reiterated by Flume, Wegfall der Bereicherung, AcP 194 (1994) 427 = Studien, p. 115; id., Festgabe 50 Jahre BGH, 2000, Vol I, 525, at pp. 536–545 = Studien, pp. 102–111; id., ZIP 2001, 1621; id., JZ 2002, 321 = Studien, p. 248.

claim against B to make that payment. In the case of the performance in advance, A would have to bear the consequences of B's stupidity.

The jurisdiction adhered to the solution of the *Saldotheorie* despite the academic criticism. But while it is certainly true that performing in advance typically comes with higher risks, these risks concern the insolvency of the other party and can be mitigated by collateral. It has nothing to do with the odd shift of the *Zufallsgefahr* via § 818 III in the cases of invalid exchange contracts. That is why German doctrine has promoted different solutions.[937] Their common ground is to deny the defence of disenrichment to the buyer on teleological grounds instead of assuming counter-disenrichment. This solves the advance performance cases in the appropriate way. But more importantly for the purposes of this book, it lays bare the true rationale of the non-enrichment / disenrichment defence, thus overcoming the need to rely on Pomponian considerations of general equity.

c) A modern normative justification of disenrichment

aa) The core argument by von Kübel

The key to a modern, post-Pomponian rationale for the defence of disenrichment can already be found in the passage where von Kübel justified its extension to all enrichment claims:

> von Kübel, Motive, p. 38 = Schubert, p. 698: "Die Klage wurde ex aequo et bono, vom höheren Gesichtspunkt der Billigkeit und des materiellen Rechts aus gegeben, gegen das formelle Recht, wonach der formell unanfechtbare Rechtserwerb unumstößlich wäre (vergl. Windscheid § 424 R. 3). Dies ist als Prinzip der Klage auch noch im heutigen Recht und für das heutige Rechtsbewusstsein anzuerkennen. Die Tendenz bei der *condictio indebiti* geht nicht auf vollständige formelle und materielle Annullierung des bereichernden Rechtsvorganges selbst. ... Die Rücksicht auf das *aequum et bonum*, die Billigkeit und höhere Gerechtigkeit, muss nach beiden Seiten wirken; beiden Teilen ist mit gleichem Maß zu messen und es kann und darf der formell vollendete, aber materiell nicht gerechtfertigte Erwerb des Empfängers eines *indebitum* deshalb nur insoweit rückgängig gemacht werben, als solches ohne Schaden des Letzteren geschehen kann. Dem entspricht vollkommen, wenn der Empfänger Alles das, aber auch nur das heraus zu geben hat, um was er aus des Leistenden Vermögen um die Leistung bereichert ist."
>
> [The action was given *ex aequo et bono*, from the higher point of view of equity and substantive law, against the formal law, according to which the formally unchallengeable legal title

937 With different arguments en detail Flume, FS Niedermeyer, 1953, 103, at pp. 159 et seq. = Studien, pp. 76 et seq.; Larenz/Canaris, Schuldrecht II/2, 13th edn. 1994 § 73 III 7; Wendehorst, Anspruch und Ausgleich, 1999, p. 382; Staudinger/Kaiser/Sittmann-Haury, 2022, Vor § 346 ff., mn. 34.; Medicus /Petersen, mn. 225–235.

> would be irrevocable (cf. Windscheid § 424 R. 3). This is still to be recognised as the principle of the action in today's law and for today's legal consciousness. The tendency of *condictio indebiti* is not towards complete formal and material annulment of the enriching legal process itself. ... Consideration of the *aequum et bonum*, equity and higher justice, must work on both sides; both parts are to be measured equally, and **the formally completed but materially unjustified acquisition of the recipient of an *indebitum* can and may therefore only be reversed insofar as this can be done without harm to the latter.** This corresponds perfectly if the recipient has to return everything, but also only that by which he is enriched from the performing party's assets by the performance.

If we peel off the talk of equity, von Kübel's core argument is the following: **The law allows the performing party to make good its disappointment – but not at the cost of damaging the other party, the recipient.**

This sound principle also governs the avoidance of contracts for error (§§ 119–121 BGB). German law enables a party who suffered from certain kinds of error[938] to annul the contract for under §§ 119, 120 BGB in connection with § 142 BGB (similar to common law rescission). But it in turn it obliges this party to make good any reliance loss of the other party (§ 122 BGB). Party autonomy allows you to correct your error, but not at the detriment of the other party.[939] The defence of disenrichment works similarly – if not synchronously because, as will be shown below with the example of the dog and the ruined carpet, the concept may be narrower than reliance loss.

The true reason for the disenrichment defence is therefore that unjust enrichment is not fault-based on either side. It enforces party autonomy if a benefit was received that is not covered by *volenti non fit iniuria* because there was no consent or because the purpose failed. But the flipside is that the recipient did nothing wrong either, other than receiving the benefit. That is meant by "justice works both ways" – and that applies with double force in the context of exchanges.

The explanation given by von Kübel focusses on performances. And indeed, the explanation that the law allows the transferor to make good the error, but not for the damage of the recipient is particularly persuasive. But on closer looks, the disenrichment defence is likewise justified in no consent cases if value is taken by innocent defendants. Normally, taking value will constitute a tort and trigger damages. But tort claims usually require default. Without default, there will be no claim and the loss will lie where it falls. If unjust enrichment nevertheless steps in to reverse that shift of value, it must not ignore this fundamental

938 § 119 I 1. Alt. BGB: Erklärungsirrtum; § 119 I 2. Alt. BGB: Inhaltsirrtum; § 119 II BGB: Irrtum über verkehrswesentliche Eigenschaften.

939 This is only different if avoidance is based on § 123 BGB because the party seeking it was deceived (arglistige Täuschung) or coerced (widerrechtliche Drohung).

decision of the law. That is why the innocent defendant deserves protection. Here too, justice works both ways. Just imagine little Lord Fauntelroy being dispossessed by the true heir who was previously unknown but suddenly resurfaced out of the blue.[940] Should the poor little Lord repay years and years of rent for Dorincourt where he would never have lived otherwise? [941]

The case for the defence of unjust enrichment was well argued by von Kübel, even if framed within and hidden under general equitable considerations. But this does not yet illuminate the exact content and particularly the limits of the defence. In this respect, German doctrine is infinitely indebted to Werner Flume. And maybe English doctrine will be, too. True, Werner Flume drew heavily from the Romans sources that have never been accepted as authority nor persuasive authority for common law. Nevertheless, it is advisable to consider his conclusions because they concern the same issues arising under similar claims that rest on a common doctrinal foundation – unlike e.g. French enrichment law that rests firmly on Pomponius and therefore bases both claim and defence on general equitable considerations (like e.g. the fault of the party).

bb) The *Vermögensentscheidung* (spending decision) limits disenrichment (*Werner Flume*)

The starting point of Flume's well-founded argument was the restriction of disenrichment. He did not accept all the disadvantages that had a causal connection to the enrichment but excluded those that were based on decisions of the recipient that were made independent from the enrichment. The consequences of a *Vermögensentscheidung* (= spending decision) of the defendant that was made independent of the trust on the receipt of the benefit must not be shifted to the claimant.

> Flume, FS Niedermeyer, 1953, 103, at p. 152 = Studien, p. 70:
> Es gilt also, bei der Frage des Wegfalls der Bereicherung danach zu unterscheiden, was von den Veränderungen im Vermögen des Kondiktionsschuldners, die in ursächlichem Zusammenhang mit dem als ungerechtfertigte Bereicherung Empfangenen aufgetreten sind, dem Vermögenszugang und was der Person des Empfängers zuzurechnen ist.

940 The movie with Sir Alec Guinness as the old cantankerous Lord who is mellowed by his sweet little grandson is hardly known in England, but became hugely successful in Germany where the airing around 24 December is now an integral part of our Christmas culture. The high point is when the alleged true heir turns out to be of lesser provenance so that the position of the little Lord is saved.

941 Note that under civilian systems, the major part of this protection is traditionally afforded by the rules privileging bona fide possessors of chattel or land vis-à-vis the owner.

[When considering the question of the loss of enrichment, a distinction must therefore be made as to **which of the changes in the assets of the defendant,** which occurred in causal connection with the unjust enrichment received, **are attributable to the receipt of the benefit** and **which are attributable to the person of the recipient.** – based on DeepL]

The leading textbook example of the time was the invalid gift of the dog.[942] Doubtlessly, if the dog dies, the recipient will be disenriched.[943] But what if the dog bites into a valuable carpet. The defendant has surely suffered a loss that was caused by the gift of the dog. Should that loss be held against the enrichment claim? According to Flume, the answer must be in the negative. The defendant suffered the damage not because of his trust on the validity of the gift, but from his decision to keep the dog and thereby run the risk of damages to his property. The destruction of the carpet is the consequence of the defendant's free *Vermögensentscheidung* (spending decision). This decision is not related to the *sine causa*-receipt because it has nothing to do with the validity or not of the gift, nor with any trust invested to it by the defendant. The damage could have happened with any other dog the defendant chose to keep. The same is true for expenditure made with respect to the keeping of the dog (tax, insurance). It may only be different if the recipient made expenditure specifically with a view to the "strength of the wealth after the gift" ("Stärke des Vermögens durch den causalosen Vermögenszugang"). That would be e.g. the case if the dog was so particularly precious that the recipient chose to buy insurance for the value or the vet costs. This shows that disenrichment is similar in principle, but far from fully congruent with the concept of reliance loss. It is narrower because reliance loss is a claim for damages, and damages require personal responsibility for the breach of the promise whereas unjust enrichment does not.

In the next step, Flume distinguished between gifts and exchanges.

Flume, FS Niedermeyer, 1953, 103, at p. 157 = Studien, p. 74
Entscheidend scheint uns bezüglich des Schicksals des sine-causa-Erlangten für die Frage der Bereicherungsminderung nach § 818 III zu sein, ob der Empfänger den Erwerb erlangt hat im Hinblick auf eine sein Vermögen mindernde Gegenleistung, die das Äquivalent des Empfangenen sein soll, … oder ob der Empfang nicht im Kontakt mit der Vereinbarung einer solchen Gegenleistung steht.

[With regard to the fate of the sine-causa receipt, it seems to us to be decisive for the question of the reduction of enrichment under § 818 III whether the recipient has obtained the acquisition with regard to a counter-performance reducing his assets, which is supposed to be the

942 Ernst, in Flume, Studien, Einleitung, p. 12; Flume, FS Niedermeyer, 1953, 103, at pp. 155–156; Wilburg, p. 119
943 Ernst, in Flume, Studien, Einleitung, p. 12.

equivalent of what was received, ... or whether the receipt is not connected to the agreement of such a consideration. Based on DeepL]

A benefit that is not "bought" by an equivalent counter-performance (i. e. gifts, but also payments on pensions, benefits, life insurances, lottery tickets) enriches the recipient without reservation. Every spending decision that is linked to that payment can lead to disenrichment. The test to be passed is whether the spending decision would have been made anyway (so that the recipient spared expenditure of his "own" money) or whether the decision was only taken because the defendant relied on the increased state of wealth. This refers to the so-called "luxury expenditure" like e. g. choosing a first class flight instead of economy, displaying generosity induced by the benefit, generally leading a better lifestyle, etc. In that context, Flume expressly applauded the Austrian OGH. Even though Austria's time-honoured Code had not contained a general disenrichment defence for the *condictio indebiti*, the Court allowed it in the case of an overpayment of wages (OGH 23.04.1929, Präs 1025/28, publ. SZ 11/96).

By contrast, parties of an exchange do not normally take decisions because they rely on having become wealthier. To the extent that performance and counter-performance are of equal value, each side basically just chooses to restructure its assets. Both sides of the bargain knew that they would have to pay for the benefit. From the perspective of *both* parties, the exchange was supposed to be balance sheet neutral – a mere asset swap. None of the parties made any decisions specifically because they relied on having become richer by the receipt of the respective benefits (payment; asset). That is why the decision to buy a car may well lead to a financial loss due to an accident. But it is a spending decision of the same quality as the decision to keep the dog. It has nothing to do with the reliance on the receipt of a benefit that increases the wealth of the recipient. Since the rationale of disenrichment does not apply, the defence does not apply. *Cessante ratione legis cedit lex.* The subsequent loss of the performance (or the counter-performance) must not be deducted as disenrichment. It follows that every party carries the risk of subsequent loss of this benefit itself and cannot shift it back to the other party.

Flume, FS Niedermeyer, 1953, 103, at p. 165 = Studien, p. 81
Wenn jemand mit seinem Willen einen gegenseitigen Vertrag schließt, so fällt er damit – auch wenn der Vertrag nichtig ist – die vermögensmäßige Entscheidung, daß er statt des Vermögenswertes seiner Gegenleistung die ihm zu erbringende Leistung haben will. Die Konsequenzen dieser Entscheidung muß er tragen, denn er ist es, der die Entscheidung gefällt hat.

[If someone concludes a mutual contract with his will, he thereby makes the spending decision – even if the contract is null and void – that he wants the performance to be rendered to him as part of his assets instead of the counter-performance. He must bear the consequences of this decision, because it is he who has made the decision.]

The solution must only be different if one party cannot be held to its spending decision. The generally accepted cases are contracts that are avoided due to fraudulent misrepresentation and contracts entered by minors or incapables. Another, however more contentious example of an invalid spending decision may be the German case BGHZ 78, 216: After the sale was avoided for an error about its age, a harvester could only be returned in a devalued state due to a default (for which the vendor would have been liable had the contract still been valid). It may be said that the spending decision to exchange money for the harvester was not valid because the buyer would not have made it had he known about the default.

cc) Conclusion

Flume solved the cases of the Saldotheorie within the legal framework of the disenrichment / non-enrichment defence. However, he abstained meticulously from any reference to loose equitable considerations. Instead, he painted a clear and persuasive picture of the true rationale, scope and limits of disenrichment. This was a decisive step to finish the ousting of Pomponius that German law had only half managed in the nineteenth century.

Following Flume, the defence of disenrichment should play no role in the reversal of contracts. It should be limited to situations where the recipient of the benefit has not made any spending decision to get that benefit. Examples are: gifts, annuities, life insurance payments, imposed benefits (cleaning another's shoes), but also requests for benefits by incapable or deceived persons, because of a kind of "super-nullity" of such legal acts that prohibit the attachment of any legal consequences to them.

It can be demonstrated in the following steps:

Performing a service is a shift of value because the recipient gets money's worth.

Why is it irrelevant that the service evaporates immediately and there is no surviving enrichment in the assets of the recipient? It does not alter the fact that something valuable had been requested and received. If that fact was ignored, the transfer of value would not be reversed but turned into a gift instead. To prevent that from happening, the law must keep the defendant to his decision to spend money on the service. That is why the balance sheet of the defendant does not play any role before, on or after the receipt of the service. The same is true for goods.

Transfer of ownership is a shift of value because the recipient gets money's worth.

I buy a car. I drive it. It gets destroyed in an accident. At first, my assets were increased from receiving the ownership of the car. The balance sheet remained neutral because of the asset swap (money for car). After the accident, my assets are depleted and the balance sheet shows a loss. Why is this irrelevant? The increase in my assets does not matter because it did not matter in the case of the service either. Since this is so, the decrease does not matter either. What matters is that I received money's worth. If I cannot return the asset in kind, I must return the value of the asset like I had to return the value of the service. To hold otherwise, turns the sale into a gift. It shifts the consequences of my spending decision (to buy a car, to use it and to risk losing it) to the other party of the contract. That must not happen in unjust enrichment. That is the difference to the civilian remedies of sales law that worked in such way that purchasers of faulty goods were relieved of the risk of loss that was shifted back to the vendor. This is justified because the vendor is responsible for the good and the purchaser would not have assumed the risk if he had known about the fault.[944] The risk is allocated by the law for the default with the valid contact. By contrast, unjust enrichment invalidates the contractual obligations and agreements. But it does not as such invalidate the spending decisions.

It follows from the afore-said that any other investments of the parties prior or subsequent to the execution of contracts are irrelevant, too. If the buyer sold on the good too cheap, it cannot be deducted from the value to be reversed to the vendor. If the vendor had to overpay to get the asset, it cannot be deducted from the payment to be reversed to the buyer. The same is true for all investment decisions made to procure or create the asset.

That is why no deductions from the upfront payment were to be accepted in *Fibrosa*. As the BGH and Flume rightly argued: without the upfront payment, there would have been no basis to claim these costs.[945] Why should the agreement of an upfront payment for purposes of liquidity change this? It can only be different if the upfront payment is made in return for a part delivery, like is often the case in large building projects. In these cases, the payor has received value in return, and must account for that. This would have been the better reasoning to solve the case of the ultra vires financial lease, too. The school did not only receive

944 § 346 III Nr. 3 BGB; BeckOGKBGB/Schall, § 346 mn. 8 et seq. The rule is rooted in Roman law ("mortuus redhibetur") where it had a penal function for the vendor that is obsolete in modern European private law. For the reasons given in the text, the tendencies in modern German doctrine to align unjust enrichment with the recast rules of risk bearing under the *Rücktrittsrecht* (§§ 346 II and III BGB) cannot be condoned (contra Medicus/Petersen, mn. 228 et seq.).

945 BGH II ZR 295/51, Beck RS 1952, 31203092; Flume, FS Niedermeyer, 1953, 103, at p. 162–163 = Studien, p. 79.

the user. Under the financial lease that the arrangement truly was, it had also received the procurement of the building.[946] The 5,8 Mio £ paid by the leasing company to acquire the building were therefore not to be deducted under the heading of change of position. Rather, they were the objective value of the procurement of the building that the school received from the leasing company. Without it, the school would have had to teach on the meadow.

If the normal spending decisions of the recipient are recognised as beyond the reliance protected by disenrichment / change of position, most issues in the context of disenrichment and counter-performance will dissolve. In the context of contracts, they only revive if there is a super-nullity invalidating not only the contract, but also the spending decision. That is basically the case of incapacity, deceit or extortion. In these cases, the party cannot be held to the objective value of the performance it requested and received. Rather, the actual situation of the assets will be the starting point of the consideration. The service evaporates. The car is destroyed. In both cases, no enrichment survived. But in these constellations, too, value judgements are to be made. It is possible for example to show that expenses were saved because the service was needed (doctor's treatment of an incapable person).

The appropriate field for the defence are gifts and overpayments on annuities, maintenance, bonuses, pension payments, life insurances &ct. The examples can be traced back to Roman times as the true basis of the defence of disenrichment[947] – which btw confirms that 19th century Germany was right to extend the defence to all enrichments claims including those for money. In these cases, there is no spending decision to which the defendant must be kept. To the contrary, there are spending decisions to which the defendant was induced by the claimant's mistake and from which he therefore has to be relieved. Due to the reliance on the payments, the defendant will normally adopt a certain life style that cannot retrospectively be reset. Reliance is also the key to allocate the loss between two innocent victims of a fraud, like in *RE Jones v Waring & Gillow.* Only if the defendant delivered goods, released security or otherwise diminished his assets in reliance on the receipt of the payment, he can invoke disenrichment.[948]

946 *School Facility Managements Ltd v. Christ the King College* [2021] EWCA Civ 1053. For German law, see Canaris, AcP 190 (1990) 446. The issue is contentious, but the diverging view also accepts that user is of higher market value under a financial lease due to the financing element.
947 Flume, FS Niedermeyer, 1953, 103, at pp. 115 et seq = Studien, pp. 37 et seq.
948 Flume, AcP 199 (1999) 1, at pp. 28 et seq.; RGZ 98, 64 - Bierkutscherfall.

2 Security of receipts in three party situations: suum receipt / good consideration, disenrichment and other arguments

The final point of the analysis has become one of the most contentious and fraught issues of unjust enrichment under German law: The persuasive solution of three-party-situations. As explained in the first touch upon the subject above (pp. 176–182), the starting point was the *suum receipt* rule of Roman law that was mirrored in the "good consideration" / "discharge for value" defence of common law.[949]

It has been shown that from the perspective of party autonomy / privity of contract this rule is only justified where the payor aims to discharge another's debt. By pursuing the discharge of that debt, the payor adopts it as the *causa solvendi* of the own performance. The payor makes the payment in lieu of the debtor, i. e. "für letzteren", as the proposed provision of § 4 VE would expressly have stated (see below, sub a). The same was true in the English case of *Aiken v Short.*[950] That is the decisive reason why the payment is subjected to the privity of the obligation between the debtor and creditor. It has already been explained that this solution cannot be applied to bank transfers because the bank is not interested in the reason of the customer to make the payment and therefore does not adopt it as reason for the own performance. The bank does not pay "in lieu of the customer". Rather, it directs the funds owed to its customer to a third party according to the instructions. That is why the discharge of the bank's obligation towards the customer is the *causa solvendi*, not the discharge of the customer's obligation vis-à-vis the recipient of the book money.

Nevertheless, the ill-fitting and hardly explicable defence *ex iure tertii* was applied in many jurisdictions, civil law as well as common law, in the context of bank transfers because it came in handy to enforce a policy of "security of receipts". But when Germany started disbelieving the unity doctrine, this happened also because academics had begun to harbour serious doubts and searched for alternative explanations for the three-party-situations. That search continues to date,[951] due to another misconception that will be set out below and has nothing to do with the Pomponian principle.

For the purposes of deconstructing enrichment, it is interesting to observe in a first step how the receipt was repackaged into the concept of a general enrichment claim.

---

949 Cf. Schall, Three Party Situations in Unjust Enrichment, RLR 110 (2004).

950 *Aiken v Short* (1856) 1 H&N 210, at p. 214 (per Pollock C.B.): "the defendant (= Short) had a perfect right to receive the money from Carter, and the bankers paid for him."; see already pp. 177–178.

951 For a recent example cf. Bartels, Der Bereicherungsausgleich im verbundenen Geschäft unter § 358 Abs. 4 Satz 5 BGB, JZ 2024, 478.

a) Disenrichment as an alternative to *suum receipt?*

The misleading effect of the general enrichment approach can be demonstrated by reference to a (subsidiary) proposal by *Bernhard Windscheid* to codify tripartite performances. As already noted above, Windscheid was one of the leading German private lawyers of his time. He took an active role in the codification of the BGB. As said, the first draft was nicknamed "kleiner Windscheid" before he was ousted because the *Lehre von der Voraussetzung* was rejected (p. 243).

The pre-draft by von Kübel contained a single rule on tripartite performances:

> § 4 VE: "Hat jemand an den Gläubiger eines Dritten für letzteren geleistet, um damit eine Verbindlichkeit gegen den Dritten zu erfüllen, so kann er, auch wenn diese Verbindlichkeit nicht bestand, das Geleistete von dem Empfänger nicht zurückfordern, ausgenommen wenn dieser das Nichtbestehen der Verbindlichkeit und die Absicht des Leistenden, solche zu erfüllen, gekannt hat."
>
> [If someone made a performance to the creditor of a third party in lieu of the latter, in order to discharge a liability owed to that third party, he cannot, even though that liability did not exist, recover the performance from the recipient (i. e. the creditor), except he knew about the non-existence of the liability and the purpose of the performing party to discharge it.

The provision was primarily an attempt to transpose the Roman rule of *suum recepit* which basically said that a performance made by someone in lieu of the debtor cannot be recovered from the recipient creditor because the creditor has got his due:[952] "Repetitito nulla est ab eo qui suum recepit, tametsi ab alio quam vero debitore solutum est."[953]

In a triangle of A – B – C, this means that A pays the debt that B owes to C. If the debt of B is discharged, A cannot reclaim from C even if he had no reason to make the payment for B (because he did not owe it to B). *Suum receipt!*

As said above (p. 177), this is the scenario of the liability insurer. The liability insurer A pays the damages claim on behalf of the tortfeasor B ("für letzteren" = in lieu of the latter, as § 4 VE states) to the tort victim C. The insurance company pays because it is obliged to do so under the insurance contract with the customer. If the tort liability does not exist, the insurer can recover because the *causa solvendi* was not achieved.[954] Conversely, if the insurance lapsed, the insurer had no reason to make the payment vis-à-vis the insured party (B) but still cannot recover from the creditor (C) because the *causa solvendi* vis-à-vis the creditor was achieved.

---

952 Von Kübel, pp. 33–34 (= Schubert, pp. 693–694).

953 D.12.6.44 (Paulus 14 ad plaut.) See already *Schall*, RLR 2004, 110, 128; above p. 177.

954 BGHZ 113, 62; approving Jakobs, NJW 1992, 2524, at the same time criticising more complicated, differentiating approaches advocated by Canaris, NJW 1992, 868 and to some extent also Martinek, JZ 1991, 395.

However, the last part of § 4 also introduced a novel exception from *suum receipt* that had hitherto been unknown. If the recipient of the payment knew that the payor had discharged the debtor in the mistaken belief of being obliged to do so, he should not be allowed to retain his due.

During the sessions of the First Commission, § 4 VE was (rightly) criticised. Windscheid successfully proposed to skip it (see below). However, he also made a subsidiary proposal how the complete solution should look like. Due to the success of his primary motion to skip § 4 VE, this subsidiary motion did not come to fruition. Nevertheless, the proposal is interesting because it demonstrates the misunderstanding of the general enrichment claim. The passage in the protocols of the sessions of the First Commission reads as follows:[955]

> Zu § 4 des Entwurfs… war beantragt:
>
> …
>
> 2. den § zu streichen, wenn aber eine Bestimmung aufgenommen werden solle, diese in hinreichender Allgemeinheit etwa so zu fassen:
>
> "Leistet der vermeintliche Schuldner auf Anweisung des vermeintlichen Gläubigers einem Dritten, so steht ihm das Rückforderungsrecht nicht gegen den Dritten sondern gegen den vermeintlichen Gläubiger zu."
>
> "Leistet dem vermeintlichen Gläubiger auf Anweisung des vermeintlichen Schuldners ein Dritter, so steht das Rückforderungsrecht nicht dem Dritten, sondern dem vermeintlichen Schuldner zu."
>
> eventuell hinzuzufügen
> " Leistet der vermeintliche Schuldner auf Anweisung des vermeintlichen Gläubigers dem vermeintlichen Gläubiger des Anweisenden, so kann er das Geleistete von diesem letzteren zurückfordern."
>
> [Regarding § 4 of the draft… was requested:
>
> …
>
> 2. to delete the section, but if a provision is to be included, it should be worded in sufficiently general terms as follows:
>
> "If the alleged debtor pays a third party on the instructions of the alleged creditor, the right of recovery shall not be against the third party but against the alleged creditor."
>
> "If a third party makes payment to the alleged creditor on the instructions of the alleged debtor, the right of recovery is not due to the third party but to the alleged debtor."

---

955 Protokolle der [ersten] Kommission zur Ausarbeitung des Entwurfs eines Bürgerlichen Gesetzbuches, Sitzungen vom 20. Dezember 1882 bis zum 13. April 1883, Seiten 1497–2003, at pp. 1500–1501; made available by Werner Schubert online at https://rwi.app/iurisprudentia/de/bgb/documents/static/722952/pages/5?zoom=0.80623586978610981 (p. 1500) https://rwi.app/iurisprudentia/de/bgb/documents/static/722952/pages/6?zoom=0.41795267489711935 (p. 1501).

possibly to be added
" If the alleged debtor pays the alleged creditor's alleged creditor on the instruction of the alleged creditor, he may reclaim what he has paid from the latter."]

Windscheid did not oppose the *suum recepit* rule. Rather, he completed it and clothed the explanation differently, by reference to who shifted the unjustified enrichment from his assets:

In the case of *suum receipt*, the recipient (C) was **not enriched** because he paid for the receipt of the money from A with the discharge of his debt against B.

It followed that the enrichment claim of A had to lie against the former debtor B because he had been unjustly enriched by the discharge of his debt to C while the payor was depleted.

The converse case was that the obligation of the payor A towards B existed, but the obligation of B towards C did not exist. In that case, A could not have an enrichment claim. Although A made the payment, the enrichment of C did not come out of the assets of A because they were not depleted. The balance sheet of A remained unchanged as the payment to C was set off with the discharge of the debt to B. Rather, the enrichment of C came out of the assets of B who "paid" for it with losing his claim against A.

Finally, in the (highly academic) case that both debts did not exist (in German doctrine: *Doppelmangel* = "double defect"), the payor A must recover the performance directly from the payee C because only the payee is enriched and only the payor is depleted. The debtor B neither gains nor loses anything.

It is obvious that the solution proposed by *Windscheid* did not focus on the performance at all. Instead of recognising every performance as direct shift of value, he drowned in the quicksand of searching "enrichments" and "depletions". But those enrichments flounder around the triangle dependent on the existence and the discharge of the debts involved. We might denounce this as "enrichment seesaw". This is undoubtedly wrong. As explained above, the Second Commission insisted on the wider wording "auf Kosten" / "at the expense" instead of "aus dem Vermögen" / "out of the assets" because it wanted to make sure that the claim would lie with the performing party even if it transferred another's property to a bona fide purchaser for value (p. 248). This was done to deprive the defendant of defences *ex iure tertii.* The fact that the property actually came out of the assets of A does not strengthen the case of C to keep the benefit vis-à-vis B. But under the solution proposed by Windscheid, this is exactly what would happen. In the last constellation of the *Doppelmangel,* B would be denied an enrichment claim even though he has made a performance without legal reason to C! This was not acceptable. The *Doppelmangel* became the academic test case and eventually the driver that drove the enrichment approach out of the door. German writers developed a solution that secured B's right to claim in unjust enrichment even in the *Doppelmangel*-scenario and argued forthwith about the best reasoning to achieve this outcome. At the end of the day, the answer was the performance-based approach. And in principle, this can only be approved. However, before we revisit that development, let us see how the initiative of Windscheid panned out.

As said, the First Commission opted against any codification. They deemed the solution of *suum recepit* correct, but incomplete. Moreover, they opposed the new and unprecedented *mala fide* exception. All in all, they abstained from overregulation and preferred to leave the solutions of the other constellations for academia and practice to develop (see bold print):[956]

> Der §. 4 behandeln nur einen einzelnen Fall der Betheiligung eines Dritten bei der Leistung. Der hervorgehobene Fall biete aber für die Beurtheilung gerade die geringsten Schwierigkeiten. Es könne keinem Zweifel unterliegen, daß in demselben der Dritte welcher geleistet habe, gegen den Empfänger die condictio indebiti nicht habe, wohl aber einen Anspruch habe gegen den befreiten Schuldner. Dies noch besonders zu bestimmen, sei daher entbehrlich. Anders verhalte es sich freilich mit der auf den Fall der mala fides des Empfangers sich beziehenden Schlußbestimmung. Die letztere habe einen positiven Charakter, nach den allgemeinen Grundsätzen wurde gegen den Empfänger die condictio indebiti nicht Platz greifen, sondern nach Beschaffenheit der Umstände nur der Anspruch auf Schadensersatz ex delicto begründet sein. Es fehle an genügenden Gründen, durch eine positive Vorschrift zum Nachtheil des Empfängers ein Anderes zu bestimmen. **Anlangend die übrigen Fälle der Betheiligung eines Dritten, so sei es vorzuziehen, auch in Ansehung ihrer sich jeder besonderen Vorschrift zu enthalten und ihre Beurtheilung der Praxis und Wissenschaft zu überlassen.**
>
> [Section 4 only deals with a single case of the involvement of a third party in the performance. The emphasised case, however, offers the least difficulties for the assessment. There can be no doubt that in this case the third party who has performed does not have the condictio indebiti against the recipient, but does have a claim against the exempted debtor. It was therefore unnecessary to specify this. The situation is different, however, with the final provision relating to the case of mala fides of the recipient. The latter had the character of a new overriding law; according to the general principles, the condictio indebiti was not applicable against the recipient, but according to the nature of the circumstances only the claim for damages ex delicto was justified. There were no sufficient grounds to determine otherwise by a positive provision to the detriment of the recipient. **With regard to the other cases of the involvement of a third party, it is preferable to refrain from making any special provision and to leave their judgement to practice and science.** – based on DeepL]

---

956 Protokolle der [ersten] Kommission zur Ausarbeitung des Entwurfs eines Bürgerlichen Gesetzbuches, Sitzungen vom 20. Dezember 1882 bis zum 13. April 1883, Seiten 1497–2003, at pp. 1502; made available by Werner Schubert online at https://rwi.app/iurisprudentia/de/bgb/documents/static/722952/pages/7?zoom=0.9000225383950602.

One cannot but conclude that German judges and unjust enrichment lawyers have taken the assignment in the last sentence close to their hearts. Three party situations in unjust enrichment have become a strong candidate for the most debated issue of German private law.[957] It remains yet to be seen whether the same will happen under common law.[958]

957 For seminal cases of the BGH, see e.g. BGHZ 30, 36; 40, 272; 50, 227; 55, 176; 58, 184; 61, 289; 66, 362; 66, 372; 67, 75; 69, 186; 72, 246; 105, 362; 87, 393; 88, 232; 113, 62; 205, 334; BGH NJW 1984, 1456; NJW 2016, 2260; NJW 2016, 3027; BKR 2021, 516; For a random selection of academic literature, without being in the least complete, leaving inter alia out all commentaries and general textbooks: Marietta Auer, Neuanfang beim Bereicherungsausgleich in Dreipersonenverhältnissen, ZfPW 2016, 479; Claus-Wilhelm Canaris, Der Bereicherungsausgleich im Dreipersonenverhältnis, 1. Festschrift für Karl Larenz, 1973, p. 799; id., Der Bereicherungsausgleich bei Zahlung des Haftpflichtversicherers an einen Scheingläubiger, NJW 1992, 868; id., Die Rückkehr der Praxis zur Regelanwendung und der Beruf der Theorie im Recht der Leistungskondiktion, NJW 1992, 3143; Ernst von Caemmerer, Bereicherungsansprüche und Drittbeziehungen, JZ 1962, 385; Werner Flume, Zum Bereicherungsausgleich bei Zahlungen in Drei-Personen-Verhältnissen, NJW 1991, 2521 = Studien, p. 233; Werner Flume, Die Zahlungszuwendung im Anweisungs-Dreiecksverhältnis und die Problematik der ungerechtfertigten Bereicherung, NJW 1984, 464 = Studien, p. 220; Werner Flume, Der Bereicherungsausgleich in Mehrpersonenverhältnissen, AcP 199 (1999), 1 = Studien, p. 165; Werner Flume, Die Zahlung des Putativschuldners, JZ 1962, 281 = Studien, p. 215; Hassold, Zur Leistung im Dreipersonenverhältnis, 1981; Christian H. Jahn, Der Bereicherungsausgleich im Mehrpersonenverhältnis dargestellt anhand der Rückabwicklung von Werk- und Dienstleistungen, 2014; Horst-Heinrich Jakobs, Die Rückkehr der Praxis zur Regelanwendung und der Beruf der Theorie im Recht der Leistungskondiktion, NJW 1992, 2524; Kamionka, Der Leistungsbegriff im Bereicherungsrecht, JuS 1992, 845; Berthold Kupisch, Gesetzespositivismus im Bereicherungsrecht, 1978; Stephan Lorenz, Bereicherungsrechtliche Drittbeziehungen, JuS 2003, 729 and *839*; Michael Martinek, Der Bereicherungsausgleich bei veranlaßter Drittleistung auf fremde nichtbestehende Schuld, JZ 1991, 395; Sonja Meier, Die Leistung durch Dritte in historisch-vergleichender Perspektive, ZfPW 1 (2015) 103; Dieter Reuter & Michael Martinek, Ungerechtfertigte Bereicherung, Teilband 2, 2. Aufl. 2016; Alexander Schall, Leistungskondiktion und Sonstige Kondiktion auf der Grundlage des einheitlichen gesetzlichen Kondiktionsprinzips, 2003; id., Abrüstung der Bereicherungsdogmatik Im Dreipersonenverhältnis, JZ 2013, 753; Franz Schnauder, Grundfragen zur Leistungskondiktion bei Drittbeziehungen, 1981; Franz Schnauder, Die Sonderrechtsprechung zum Bereicherungsausgleich im neuen Zahlungsdiensterecht, JZ 2016, 603; Dennis Solomon, Der Bereicherungsausgleich in Anweisungsfällen – Rechtsvergleichende Untersuchung zum deutschen Recht und zu den Rechtsordnungen des Common Law, 2004; Stolte, Der Leistungsbegriff: Ein Gespenst des Bereicherungsrechts?, JZ 1990, 220; Chris Thomale, Leistung als Freiheit, 2012; Hermann Weitnauer, Zum Stand der Lehre von der Leistungskondiktion, NJW 1979, 2000; Christiane Wendehorst, Anspruch und Ausgleich, 1999; Walter Wilburg, Die Lehre von der Ungerechtfertigten Bereicherung, in: Festschrift der Universität Graz, 1934, p. 1; Jan Wilhelm, Rechtsverletzung und Vermögensentscheidung als Grundlagen und Grenzen des Anspruchs aus ungerechtfertigter Bereicherung, 1973; id., "Upon the Cases" bei der Leistungskondiktion in Dreiecksverhältnissen, JZ 1994, 585; Joachim Wolf, Der Stand der Bereicherungslehre und ihre Neubegründung, 1980.

b) The modern German solution: construction of a chain of enrichment claims (A – B and B – C) under a performance-based approach

aa) The *Anweisungslage* as test case and starting point

Today, the standard case of the three-party-situations in the academic discussion is the *Anweisungslage* (= literally: "instruction situation").[959] It describes a situation where B instructs his (presumed) debtor A to make the payment to B's (presumed) creditor C. This sounds like the payment on the debt of a third party (*Drittzahlung*) that would have been regulated by the once proposed draft provision of § 4 VE (p. 304). But it is not. In the *Anweisungslage*, the payor (A) does not make the payment to C in lieu of B on B's (presumed) debt, but acts under instruction of B to discharge his own (presumed) debt to B by surrendering the performance to a third party. This situation is governed by § 362 II BGB that orders for the debtor to be discharged, the payment to the third party must be authorised under § 185 BGB by the creditor.[960]

> § 362 II BGB
> Wird an einen Dritten zum Zwecke der Erfüllung geleistet, so finden die Vorschriften des § 185 Anwendung.
>
> [If payment is made to a third party for the purpose of discharge, the provisions of § 185 shall apply]

For an understanding of the immeasurable burdens that this field of law imposes on German law students see only the textbook of Gursky/Linardatos, 20 Probleme aus dem Bereicherungsrecht, 7th edn. 2023, pp. 1–78 and 97–104, explaining (only) 8 central problems of three party situations and delivering on average 5 elaborate arguments for each of the various solutions to each of the various problems debated over the decades.

958 Cf. Birks, Unjust Enrichment, 2nd edn. 2005, pp. 90–91; id., At the expense of the claimant: in: Johnston & Zimmermann, *Unjustified Enrichment*, 2002, p. 494; Burrows, Law of Restitution, 2011, pp. 213–214; Stevens, pp. 42–46; Goff & Jones 3-56–3-90.

For attempts to raise the interest of common law in the intricacies of the German solutions see Sonja Meier, Mistaken Payments in Three-Party-Situations: a German View of English law [1999] CLJ 56; Alexander Schall, Three Party Situations in Unjust Enrichment, RLR 110 (2004).

959 It must be noted that there is also a specific *Anweisungslage* regulated under the §§ 783–792 BGB. This specific constellation differs slightly from the general paradigm of the Anweisungslage in unjust enrichment. First, the instruction by B cannot be given to his debtor (A), but must be handed over in written form (!) to the recipient (C) who will then be entitled to claim the performance from A on behalf of B (cf. § 783 BGB). Also, the legal terminology of §§ 783–792 BGB differs slightly from the general *Anweisungslage* as test case for unjustified enrichment (as to that latter meaning, see only recently BGH BKR 2021, 516). However, some important discussions about the viability of the dominant solution have been and still can be drawn from the provisions in §§ 783–792 BGB.

960 The authorisation can be given to the payor or to the third party or to both (example for the latter is the specific *Anweisungslage*, § 783 BGB).

The other situation is governed by § 267 I BGB that principally[961] allows payment by a third party debt without authorisation of the debtor.

> § 267 I BGB
> Hat der Schuldner nicht in Person zu leisten, so kann auch ein Dritter die Leistung bewirken. Die Einwilligung des Schuldners ist nicht erforderlich.
>
> [If the debtor does not have to perform in person, a third party may also effect the performance. The debtor's consent is not required.]

To put it concisely:

Anweisung: the debtor performs *causa solvendi* to a third party instead of his creditor.

Drittzahlung: a third party performs instead of the debtor *causa solvendi* to the creditor.

This clear doctrinal distinction can get slightly blurred. First, it may be that the third party is obliged to the debtor to make the performance as *Drittleistung* to his creditor, so that the third party, too, appears to act under instruction, like in the instruction cases. Leading unjust enrichment lawyers have therefore labelled it "veranlasste Drittleistung" (= induced/instructed third party performance) and argue to solve it analogous to the *Anweisungslage*, i. e. "restitution over the corner" (= via B) instead of a direct claim A – C.[962]

Second, in the case of § 362 II BGB the creditor issuing the instruction to his debtor may be indebted himself to the third party (so-called *Anweisung auf Schuld*, §§ 787, 788 BGB). In that case, many assume that *only* B *performs* to C, while A acts merely as agent of C when surrendering the money /asset. This view is the basis for the chain of enrichment claims in the *Anweisungslage* that is almost generally accepted in Germany today (p. 312). That assumption is inter alia entrenched in the Directive (EU) 2015/2366 on payment services[963] that only sees the customer (= B) as the "payor" who makes the payment to the recipient (= C) whereas the bank is the payer's payment service provider (cf. e.g. Art. 73). Irrespective of the Directive, this assumption rings true for banking law. It may be the better explanation for *Lloyds v Independent*.[964] It is the solution that Stevens advocates.[965] The bank performs the

---

961 The exception is regulated in § 267 II: if the debtor disapproves of the payment, the creditor may reject it (but need not do so).

962 Particularly Canaris, NJW 1992, 868 and 3143 against BGHZ 113, 62.

963 As to the liabilities in light of this Linardatos, Das Haftungssystem im bargeldlosen Zahlungsverkehr, 2013.

964 *Lloyds Bank plc v Independent Insurance Co Ltd* [1998] EWCA Civ 1853.

service to its customer, and the customer performs the payment to the recipient. In case of non-authorisation, the performance of the bank fails and the apparent performance of the customer is non-existent. Then, the bank has to collect the money directly. This is the law of Germany[966] and the law of England (*Barclays v Simms*[967]), provided that the recipient has not changed position in reliance on the receipt (e.g. limitation period). The almost generally accepted view amongst German lawyers is that there cannot be any enrichment claim of the customer because he must not be burdened with any consequences of the non-authorised transaction.[968]

However, the neat explanation of the banking cases is a peculiarity that is also justified by the need for security of receipts. It is not a natural given, as the criticism of the "suum receipt"-rule / good consideration case above has shown ("Evelyn's case" of the milk bottle, pp. 180–181). To the contrary, we will see on page 322 that the generalisation of that assumption is the very fallacy that haunts German doctrine to date because it prevents the detection of the real location of the performances. The argument will be based on § 788 BGB. The provision shows that **both A and B make the performance to C!**

bb) The new solution of the *Anweisungslage* (chain of enrichment claims) and the shift from direct shift of value (unity doctrine) to the performance-based approach of the separation doctrine

After the solution of tripartite situations via the "enrichment seesaw" (p. 306) was rejected, the new approach to solve the *Anweisungslage* was a chain of enrichment claims. (Only) A has the enrichment claim against B, and (only) B has the enrichment claim against C. The debate now shifted to the correct explanation of this outcome. This proved particularly difficult for the old unity doctrine that (principally correct) searched for a "direct shift of wealth", but mistook that to be the "actual" shift of wealth (*gegenständliche Vermögensverschiebung*) instead of the performance and therefore should have ended up with only the enrichment claim

---

965 Stevens, LQR (2018) 573, at p. 583. But the references to *Aiken v. Short* and *MacDonald v Costello* are not spot on, see for the reasons above pp. 176 et seq, 181–182 (example 1 and 2).

966 BGHZ 205, 377 = NJW 2015, 3093. The BGH leaves open whether this result necessarily follows from the Directive on payment services (at para. 22). However, in light of cases like ECJ C-625/21 – Gupfinger no attempt to undermine the duty of the bank to immediately refund the debit entry on the account (Art. 73) by allowing the bank to sue the customer in unjust enrichment will get off the ground in Luxembourg.

967 *Barclays Bank Ltd v W J Simms, Son and Cooke (Southern) Ltd* [1980] 1 QB 677.

968 But contrast Foerster, AcP 213 (2013), 405; ID., BKR 2015, 473 who assumes joint and several liability of the bank and the recipient to restore the funds to the customer.

from A to C, following the money. Thus, it required considerable efforts, pull-ups, twists and turns for the unity doctrine to reach the chain-claims-solution that Germans would call "Rückabwicklung übers Eck" (= reversal over the corner), i.e. from C to B to A instead of directly from C to A.

These efforts culminated in a paradox: B was said to effect a "unmittelbare Vermögensverschiebung durch indirekte Leistung" towards C (= a "direct shift of wealth via an indirect performance").[969] This oxymoron became one of the two focal points of Walter Wilburg's general attack on the unity doctrine (*Einheitslehre*).[970] He argued that the direct shift of wealth could not be the solution because it evidently led into that paradox. The shift of wealth would always be directly from A to C and contradict the need to have a chain of enrichment claims. He concluded that the requirement "at the expense" should play no role for the reversal of performances and advocated the split reading of § 812 I 1 1. Alt. BGB (see p. 255). The reason to grant the enrichment claims to A versus B and to B versus C was that A only performed to B, and B only performed to C.

Wilburg based this assumption on the purpose of the performance.[971] A pursued the *causa solvendi* vis-à-vis his creditor B, and B pursued the *causa solvendi* vis-a-vis his creditor C. The modern separation doctrine (*Trennungslehre*) with its purpose-oriented definition of performance (*finaler Leistungsbegriff*) was born.[972] Its basic principles are almost generally accepted by German Courts and academics. One of them is the counter-exception of the direct enrichment claim A – C in cases where the instruction cannot be attributed to B.[973] This is in line with the Art. 73 of the Directive (EU) 2015/2366 on payment services that requires immediate refunding of unauthorised payments to the customer (p. 310).

The victory of the separation doctrine over the unity doctrine was a stunning event. It does not happen very often that a jurisdiction so completely and profoundly changes the hitherto uniform interpretation and application of its codified law. From today's perspective, we tend to rationalise ex-post the shift of theory in

---

969 Cf. von Mayr, Der Bereicherungsanspruch des deutschen Bürgerlichen Rechts, 1903, pp. 211 et seq.

970 Wilburg, pp. 108 et seq, 113 et seq.

971 Wilburg, p. 113.

972 Kötter, AcP 153 (1953), 195; Josef Esser, Schuldrecht BT, 4th edn. 1971, § 100 I, pp. 337 et seq.; Reuter-Martinek, Ungerechtfertigte Bereicherung, 1983, § 4 II, pp. 80 et seq.; Weitnauer, FS von Caemmerer, 1971, 255; Schnauder, Grundfragen, pp. 21 et seq, 59 et seq.; Schlechtriem, ZHR 149 (1985), 327, 340; Solomon, pp. 35 et seq.

The new doctrine was recognized in BGHZ 40, 272 and has been accepted ever since.

973 In recent times BGHZ 205, 377 = NJW 2015, 3039; prior to the Directive (EU) 2015/2366 on payment services, the issue had been more problematic, cf. e.g. BGHZ 61, 289; 66, 362; 111, 382; NJW 1994, 2357.

the so-called *bereicherungsrechtliche Wende,*[974] the "turnaround of enrichment law". We do understand the plain and simple performance-based explanation by Wilburg and we may join him in ridiculing the "direct shift of value via indirect performance". But in truth, the law is full of fictions and analogies, sometimes ill-fitting like the cash payment analogy, sometimes apt and enlightening like Savigny's equation of paying money and performing money's worth. Lawyers tend to apply them permanently without further ado, most of the time subconsciously. Also, we must note that civil lawyers generally consider themselves bound by the legislator to a large extent. The will of the German legislator to instigate § 812 I 1 BGB as general claim to cover all enrichment cases was clear and loomed large. Against that background, my personal guess is that what happened back then can also be understood as the seizure of a welcome opportunity to move away from the law and cases of the pre-war period and create something new and better. A similar, and similarly astonishing development had taken place in the area of the *Rücktrittsrecht* where the bold theory of the *Rückgewährschuldverhältnis* entered the scene and took over in no time.

At this stage, we could close our observations with a classical draw. Robert Stevens argues for a performance-based approach and is principally confirmed by the comparative perspective to the fundamental developments of unjustified enrichment in Germany after Wilburg and von Caemmerer. But that is not to say that the direct shift of value approach is wrong. As argued above, if we understand Savigny correctly, it will show that **every performance is a direct shift of value.** That is why the performance-based approach is not opposed to the direct shift of value, but translates and executes it perfectly. It confirms the basic approach of unjust enrichment rather than disproving it, as long as the central point is understood that the performance necessarily overlays any natural transfer of wealth (cf. the example of painting a wall, p. 246).

However, academic sincerity requires to lay open the fierce and well-founded criticism that has been put forward against the performance-based approach in Germany. It has made the topic the hell for students it is today. And it has the potential to shed doubts on the viability of the performance-based approach if (1) the alternative explanations were more persuasive (which they are not) and (2) there was no simple explanation for the infinite problems (which there is).

974 The term was coined by *Dieter Medicus* in his fundamental text book Bürgerliches Recht but has since disappeared in later editions.

cc) The criticism of the performance-based approach in Germany

To key to the criticism against the performance-based solution of the tripartite situations is to understand the artificiality of the solution: The money goes from A to C, but the performances are said to have taken place from A to B and B to C. Even if you agree with the outcome, as almost all German lawyers do, this still begs for an explanation. The strong point of the criticism is that this explanation has not been found yet. The weak point is that the alternative explanations offered by the main critics are not persuasive either. The surprising solution of the riddle is that the situation of the performances in the basic *Anweisungslage* has been misconceived; the chain of enrichment claims actually deviates from the location of the performances (pp. 322–323).

(1) The criticism by Caus-Wilhelm Canaris: *Abschied vom Leistungsbegriff*

After the successful takeover of German enrichment law by the separation doctrine, culminating in the acceptance by the *Bundesgerichtshof* in BGHZ 40, 272, it did not take long for the first critic to emerge. In 1973, Claus-Wilhelm Canaris launched a massive and potentially deadly attack in the first *Festschrift Karl Larenz*, his academic father, where he demanded the immediate farewell from the newly established doctrine of the *finale Leistungsbegriff* ("Abschied vom Leistungsbegriff").[975] This fundamental paper was important for German doctrine, but also for me personally as reading it marked the beginning of my doctorate with the author. It is written in a clear and sharp language that left no more room for the short and tempting, but overly simplified explanation that Walter Wilburg had tried to give by invoking the the purpose of the performance. Canaris put the new doctrine to the test – and it was found wanting. He made it clear that the final chapter of unjust enrichment was far from written yet and ushered in a new round of debate. Without his clairvoyant critique, we might have stood as silly *novarum rerum cupidi*, admiring and never doubting the emperor's new clothes.

To understand the core point of the critique, we must remind ourselves of Wilburg's thesis to solve the *Anweisungslage:*

975 Canaris, Der Bereicherungsausgleich im Dreipersonenverhältnis, 1 Festschrift für Karl Larenz, 1973, 799, at p. 857; also Larenz/Canaris, SchuldR BT II § 70 vor I, p. 199; V 1a, p. 238; VI 2, pp. 248–249. In the same vein Harder, JuS 1979, 76–77; *Kupisch*, Gesetzespositivismus, pp. 14 et seq., pp. 63 ff.; *id.*, FS v. Lübtow, 1980, 501, at p. 545; *Wilhelm*, Rechtsverletzung, 1973, 107 et seq. (143). Less sceptical for example Lorenz, JuS 2003, 839, 845. Working on bettering the solution inter alia Thomale, Leistung als Freiheit, 2012, pp. 163 et seq.; *Stolte*, JZ 1990, 220, 221.

A is instructed by his creditor B to render the money he owes directly to C because B owes the same amount to C. The money is transferred directly from A to C.

The "natural" shift of value goes directly from A to C (the money). Yet Wilburg says that A performs to B, while (only) B performs to C. If we ask why, Wilburg answers that the purpose of the transaction is pursued in these relations. A pursues the purpose of his payment, the *causa solvendi*, vis-à-vis his creditor B, while B pursues the purpose of his payment, the *causa solvendi*, vis-à-vis his creditor C. But what if we are not satisfied yet and ask again: Why? This question is the key to unravel the issue and find the wrong turn.

For starters, let us return to § 362 II BGB:

Wird **an einen Dritten zum Zwecke der Erfüllung** geleistet, so finden die Vorschriften des § 185 Anwendung.

[If payment is made **to a third party for the purpose of discharge**, the provisions of § 185 shall apply]

The provision describes in clear words that the payor makes the performance to a third party for the purpose of discharge. The third party is C. C receives the performance by A, and this is not done by A haphazardly or coincidentally, but *causa solvendi.* It follows that the performance is made from A to C. It should be noted that contrary to what the elders thought, this does not preclude a parallel performance by B to C. This is confirmed by § 788 BGB and will be explained in detail next. For the time being, suffice to say that already the wording of § 362 II BGB indicates that the thesis of Wilburg was wrong. The *causa solvendi* is pursued vis-à-vis C, not B. But words can be twisted into almost any direction in the hands of good lawyers, and so you might still argue that the fact that the performance is made *causa solvendi* to a third party does not say that the *causa solvendi* is pursued vis-à-vis the third party. This is indeed the view of basically all German jurists. If this was so, we still have to answer why? Why does the *causa solvendi* deviate from the natural performance in *this* specific case.

True, performance is a normative concept that is not bound to natural shifts of value. This is well argued and easily understood in the painting of the wall case (p. 246). But that does not answer the question here. If we search for a reason to justify the diversion of the *causa solvendi* from the natural shift of value, there are only three possible reasons:

- The objective fact that B is the (presumed) creditor of A, and C is the (presumed) creditor of B.
- The objective fact that the parties of the contracts that give birth to the claims are A and B and B and C.

– A may be free to choose the direction of the *causa solvendi* by setting the *Leistungszweckbestimmung* (vis-a-vis B or C)

None of those reasons will prove persuasive. But they characterise the differences of the argumentative approaches underlying the superficially unanimous solution of the *Anweisungslage.*

The most convincing aspect for Wilburg's solution is that only B is the creditor of A. That is why it seems that (contrary to § 362 II BGB) A still pursues the *causa solvendi* vis-à-vis his creditor by giving the performance to a third party authorised to receive it. B is the only one who can force A to perform, just as C is the only one who can force B to perform. That argument carries the German solution to the present day. It also impressed Robert Stevens.

However, it was here that Canaris launched his attack. His argument stems directly from the German Code. There is a variation of the specific *Anweisungslage* regulated under §§ 783 – 792[976] that seems to defeat Wilburg's argument. It is called *angenommene Anweisung.* The decisive rule is found in the first part of the first section of the paragraph. It must be remembered that in this constellation, the law speaks of A as the "instructed person" and of C as the "recipient of the instruction" because the instruction by B must be given in written form to C in order to authorise him to claim from A on behalf of B. For the sake of clarification, the letters A, B and C are inserted in the translation based on DeepL:

> § 784 I BGB
> "Nimmt der Angewiesene die Anweisung an, so ist er dem Anweisungsempfänger gegenüber zur Leistung verpflichtet; ..."
>
> "If the person instructed (= A) accepts the instruction (= by B), he is obliged to pay the recipient of the instruction (= C); ..."

According to § 784 I BGB, C acquires an own personal claim against A by the latter's acceptance of the instruction. This is a common feature in the law of cheques / bills of exchange / promissory notes where the specific *Anweisung* under § 783 BGB belongs to. This claim stands next to the original claim of B against his debtor A.

In this case, the thesis A that pursues the *causa solvendi* vis-à-vis B, and only vis-à-vis B, is obviously not true anymore. Canaris concluded that the true reason for addressing the enrichment claim to B was the contract between A and B, not the (purpose of the) performance. He argued that enrichment claims in tripartite

976 For the minor differences to the general *Anweisungslage* see above, p. 309. They do not matter in this context.

situations must follow the contracts (even if invalid) and gave three good reasons:[977]

- To preserve the chosen allocation of the insolvency risk:
  A must not leapfrog B via a direct claim against C if B is insolvent. Conversely he must not bear the risk of C's insolvency since he had chosen to contract with B.
- The prohibition of defences *ex iure tertii:*
  A must not face defences that C derives from his contract with B.
- The preservation of contractual defences:
  Conversely, C must be protected from being sued by A in order to preserve his defences against B as the other party of his contract.

The reasons have become widely accepted as underlying rationale for the complex solution of three-party-situations. However, the predominant opinion amongst German jurists did not follow the far-reaching suggestion of Canaris to say farewell to the performance-based solution ("Abschied vom Leistungsbegriff") and to openly correct the law of unjustified enrichment ("Rechtsfortbildung") in order to attach the enrichment claims generally to the parties of the contracts. Instead, they imported the criteria into the performance-based approach in order to rationalise it. This approach can always produce results. However: Beyond the simple paradigm of the *Anweisungslage*, it has never produced any results that were able to reconcile the deep rifts between German jurists in academia and Courts.

The reason is the overdrive of artificiality that starts with denying a performance from A to C in the *angenommene Anweisung.* To be sure, there are arguments to be made. For example, many enrichment lawyers argue that the additional claim under § 784 BGB at the hands of C has a merely supportive function. It is not supposed to alter the direction of the enrichment claims so that the chain of enrichments claims still prevails over the direct claim A – C. Along the same lines, doubts are raised whether such an "abstract" claim[978] at the hands of C is a relevant claim for the purposes of unjust enrichment at all. But since the claim of C under § 784 I BGB can be enforced and discharged, the *causa solvendi* cannot be denied.

To cut the endless (and largely futile) debates short, let us look at two examples that show clearly where German doctrine has ended up by applying the *finale Leistungsbegriff.*

---

977 Larenz/Canaris, II/2, pp. 249 et seq.

978 As to the concept of abstract claims like §§ 780, 781 BGB and their special connection with enrichment law via § 812 II BGB, see p. 108.

The first example is the *Vertrag zugunsten Dritter* under § 328 BGB.[979] In that situation, one party of the contract promises to another to render a performance to a third party. The right to claim the performance can lie with the third party (§ 328 I BGB), with the other party of the contract (§ 335 I BGB), or with both. Where should one assume the *causa solvendi?*

Let us look at the various options, all of them are found in commentaries, articles and judgements:

- Should restitution follow the right to claim the performance? Then it would have to shift depending on who has the claim, and even duplicate in the case of two competing claimants !
- Should the payor choose freely to whom he performs in order to determine from whom he wishes to claim restitution, if the case comes? On what rationale could such a free choice be justified in the context of restitution by operation of law?
- Should restitution always follow along the (presumed) contracts? But then would not Canaris be right and the *finale Leistungsbegriff* be wrong?
- Should restitution always follow the actual performance from A to C? But then, why here and not in the *Anweisungslage?*

It is obvious that there cannot be any convincing answer. That is what Canaris had said, and that has remained true in the fifty years since his great attack. German law lives in denial of this – at the expense of the students who are tormented with all the various explanations given for the inexplicable. The disaster of German doctrine culminated in the case of an assignment.

> BGHZ 105, 362 = NJW 1989, 900 (*Feuerversicherungsfall*)
> A was an insurance company with which B had contracted for a fire insurance. B assigned the (presumed) insurance claim for a fire as collateral on his debt to the innocent C. A harboured suspicions about the fire but could not prove them, so had to pay out to C. Later, it turned out that the fire had actually been set by B. The insurance claimed back the payment from C.

The solution seems plain and simple. A paid to their presumed creditor *causa solvendi.* The discharge failed because the claim did not exist. A should be able to recover from C. Nevertheless, the BGH denied the claim. They assumed that A had pursued the purpose of their payment vis-à-vis their customer B, not vis-à-vis the presumed creditor C. That is why the payment to C was legally made to B.

979 The English equivalent is of far younger age, introduced only 25 years ago in the *Contracts* (Rights of *Third Parties*) Act 1999.

To support that solution, the Court made use of the criteria developed by *Canaris* and transplanted them into the *finale Leistungsbegriff.*[980] By doing so, the BGH ended up with an outcome that sits well with *Pan Ocean.*[981] In that case, the House of Lords denied an enrichment claim (for failure of consideration) against an assignee, too. Today, this case is viewed as an "impeccable source" for the priority of contract over unjust enrichment.[982] The claim in unjust enrichment must not stir up the contractual agreements. This had following background: Pan Ocean had agreed a charterparty with the shipowner. The owner assigned the claims under the charterparty to Creditcorp as collateral. The hire was prepaid but not earned. The House concluded that Pan Ocean was nevertheless bound to address the owner for restitution under the contract, not the assignee for failure of consideration. A main argument was the commercial practice to set off overpayments by adjusting future instalments that should not be undermined by an enrichment claim against the assignee. However, it could be argued equally well that the netting arrangement is not undermined, but merely inoperative if the hire was not paid to the other party of the contract but to an assignee. Pan Ocean would clearly have had the enrichment claim for failure of consideration against the owner next to the contract. Under general principles of private law, it does not seem right that the assignment to Creditcorp should deprive Pan Ocean of this right, so much the more since debtors cannot veto assignments.[983]

---

980 BGHZ 105, 362 = NJW 1989, 900, 901 sub 2 b: "Gesichtspunkte der Risikoverteilung und des Vertrauensschutzes sprechen ebenfalls dafür, daß die Kl. sich wegen der Rückforderung ihrer Versicherungsleistung nicht an die Bekl. halten kann." [Aspects of risk distribution and the protection of legitimate expectations also speak in favour of the plaintiff not being able to hold on to the defendant because of the reclaim of her insurance benefit. – DeepL]

981 *Pan Ocean Shipping Co Ltd v. Creditcorp Ltd (THE "TRIDENT BEAUTY").* [1994] 1 Lloyds Report 365.

982 *Barton v Morris* [2023] UKSC 3, at paras. 90–91 (per Lady Rose); Stevens, p. 45; on the relation between contract and unjust enrichment see also *Dargamo Holdings v Avonwick Holdings* [2021] EWCA Civ 1149, at paras. 65–76 (per LJ Carr).

For the corresponding priority of contract rule under French law see the much commented case Com. 23 oct. 2012, n° 11–25.175 P: *D. 2012. 2598, observed Delpech; ibid. 2862, noted Dissaux; ibid. 2013. 732, observed Ferrier; RTD civ. 2013. 114, observed Fages; RLDC 2013/103, n° 5034, noted Bringuier-Fau* 23 oct. 2012, n° 11–21.978 P: *D. 2012. 2862, noted Dissaux; ibid. 2013. 732, observed Ferrier; RTD civ. 2013. 114, observed Fages; RDC 2013. 641, observed Grimaldi.*

For a different interpretation of *Pan Ocean* as a rule against double recovery see Schall, RLR 2004, 110, at pp. 121–122.

983 In principle of the same opinion Stevens, p. 45 who however goes on to argue on the next page (p. 46) that in this exceptional case, the assignment of the debt had not conferred the property to Creditcorp yet because the debt had not been earned. He concludes that this is why the payment was actually made to the owners, not to Creditcorp. But with respect, the fact that the payment was

At the same time, the BGH decided in another, less prominent case in the contrary direction.[984] The case concerned an overpayment to the assignee. Here it was said that the enrichment claim had to be directed against the assignee (C) because the pressure to make the overpayment came from him, not from the assignor / other party of the contract (= B). That is why the Court assumed that the purpose of the performance was pursued vis-à-vis C, not B!

At the end of the day, the performance in tripartite situations other than the two generally consented cases of the *Anweisung* and the *angenommene Anweisung* can be found anywhere and be predicted by no one. That is the law of Germany under the performance-based approach.[985] German Courts openly admit this: [986]

> Bei der Behandlung von bereicherungsrechtlichen Vorgängen verbieten sich schematische Lösungen. Vielmehr sind nach gefestigter höchstrichterlicher Rechtsprechung in erster Linie die Besonderheiten des einzelnen Falls für die sachgerechte bereicherungsrechtliche Abwicklung zu beachten.
>
> [Schematic solutions are not permitted when dealing with transactions under unjust enrichment law. Rather, according to established supreme court rulings, the particularities of the individual case must be taken into account first and foremost for the appropriate settlement under unjust enrichment law.]

In other words: The Supreme Court of Germany is not able to tell from our codified law whether the milkman should reclaim the bottle of milk from me or from my neighbour Evelyn.

(2) The criticism by Jan Wilhelm: "Upon the cases!"

The arbitrariness of the *finale Leistungsbegriff* was also called out in a scathing criticism by *Jan Wilhelm.* In his seminal article, he used the title as pun drawing

---

flawed by an unjust factor can not change the person of actual recipient. If anything, it supports the claim against Pan Ocean because if Robert is right, Creditcorp was only the apparent creditor and Pan Ocean had paid to the wrong recipient – an evident case for restitution against Creditcorp.

984 BGH NJW 1989, 161; criticising that reasoning Kohler, WM 1989, 1630; Wilhelm, JZ 1994, 585, 591.

985 Critical, demanding a solution deductible from the codified law, e.g. MünchKommBGB/Schwab, Vol 7, 9th edn. 2024, § 812 mn. 52–53; *Solomon,* Der Bereicherungsausgleich in Anweisungsfällen, 2004, p. 109; *Stolte,* JZ 1990, 220, 221.

986 OLG Saarbrücken, NJOZ 2012, 1966, 1967 referring to the permanent statements in the jurisdiction of the Bundesgerichtshof, e.g. BGH NJW 1999, 1993, 1994. The statement became common knowledge amongst German enrichment lawyers. The original quote was made by von Caemmerer, JZ 1962 385, 386. It was taken up by BGHZ 50, 227 = NJW 1968, 1822 and repeated in many three party cases over the decades, cf. e.g. BGHZ 105, 362 = NJW 1989, 900, 901; BGHZ 58, 184 = NJW 1972, 864; BGHZ 61, 289, 292 = NJW 1974, 39; BGHZ 72, 246, 250 = NJW 1979, 157; BGHZ 87, 393, 396 = NJW 1983, 2499; BGHZ 88, 232, 235 = = NJW 1984, 483.

on one of the many anecdotes about the peculiar "literal German-English" applied by former German Bundespräsident Heinrich Lübke (1894–1972) who was said to bring a toast to the women present at a banquet by saying: "Upon the ladies".[987] Wilhelm showed that the purpose-based approach could be used to cover any given result. But his criticism ebbed away because the solution he proposed did not convince either. It is still worth considering because it is similar to a solution proposed under English law.

Wilhelm, building on the teachings of his academic father Werner Flume, is one of the few remaining proponents of the uniform reading of § 812 I 1 BGB (though not of the old doctrine of direct shift of value). It follows that he applies the at – the – expense requirement to performance-based enrichment claims. To show that the payment to C is made at the expense of B (instead of A), he argues that A, by following the instruction of B, gave B what he wanted. That is why B has to account for the benefit in relation to A and that is why B performs at his own expense to C.[988]

To be sure, the explanation why B has received the value from A seems persuasive at first sight. Similar arguments have been made under English law in *Coutts v Stock* [989] and by Peter Birks who framed it as cash payment analogy (= to look at the wiring of funds as a cash payment by the bank to the customer and the customer to the recipient).[990] However, the problem is that Wilhelm cannot explain why this artificially construed enrichment should cancel out the actual flow of the enrichment directly from A to C. To put it differently: Why apply a cash payment analogy where we have a direct wiring of funds. We can understand why the direct transfer of the asset is not a performance for Wilburg. But Wilhelm does not want us to look for the performance. He wants us to look for the location

---

987 Wilhelm, JZ 1994, 858 with fn. 7. Other internet sources speak of "upon the women" and ascribe the sentence to Walter Scheel who used it as a fun-take on "Lübke-English" in a reception for the singer Juliette Gréco in 1968; see https://www.reisegeschichte.de/doku.php?id=wiki:luebke-englisch. Btw: Wilhelm primarily used that title to connect his article with the paper of Jakobs, ZIP 1994, 10 who had demanded "better" case law from the BGH (at p. 14).

988 Wilhelm, Rechtsverletzung und Vermögensentscheidung, 1973, 109 et seq. See also Flume, AcP 199 (1999), 1 = Studien, p. 165.

989 [2000] Lloyds Report 14, at p. 17; see also *Agip (Africa) Ltd v Jackson* [1990] Ch 265, 283, 292 (per Millett J) with regard to accounts in credit.

990 Birks, At the expense of the claimant: direct and indirect enrichment in English law, in: Johnston & Zimmermann, *Unjustified Enrichment*, 2002, 494, at p. 503; but contrast Schall, RLR 2004, 110, at p. 120: "fragile fiction". For an explanation by way of analogy to chain transfers cf. further Kupisch, Gesetzespositivismus, at pp. 20 and 23; id., FS v. Lübtow, 1980, 501, at pp. 505 and 515–516; MünchKomm/Lieb, Vol 5, 4th edn. 2004, § 812 mn. 36.

of the unjustified enrichment at the expense of another. On that premise, why construe an enrichment that deviates from the actual transfer at all?

dd) A little spin to put the performance-based approach right

Contrary to the views of adamant critics like Canaris and Wilhelm, the performance-based approach is to be approved. Contrary to what the proponents of the modern separation doctrine assume, this follows directly from Savigny's principle. That is evidenced by the *Vorentwurf* of von Kübel and the *Entwurf* of the *Erste Kommission.* Both contain the performance-based *condictiones* without requiring that the performance be made "out of the assets" / "at the expense" of the performing party. Also, it is true that performances are characterised by their purpose of which there are only three: *causa solvendi*; *causa acquirendi*; *causa donandi.*

So what went wrong? Why has the solution of tripartite cases drowned in shiftsand of arbitrariness and legal uncertainty.

The answer is surprisingly simple: Wilburg mistook the location of the performances in the *Anweisungslage.* It has already been shown that the wording of § 362 II BGB points to the third party (= C) as recipient of the performance *causa solvendi.*[991] It follows that C receives the money / asset under two headings: as performance of his debtor B (as everybody assumes), but also as performance of B's debtor A. This is expressed in the wording of § 788 BGB that states that C receives the performance from B at the moment that he receives the performance from A, not already at the time when A accepts the instruction of B (= *angenommene Anweisung*, § 784 BGB, see above p. 316).[992]

991 On the following, see already Schall, JZ 2013, 753; id., Leistungskonditkion, at pp. 21 et seq.; widely consenting Marietta Auer, Neuanfang beim Bereicherungsausgleich in Dreipersonenverhältnissen, ZfPW 2016, 479.

992 Schall, Leistungskondiktion, p. 22. Franz Schnauder, Grundfragen, pp. 105 et seq.; id., AcP 187 (1987) 142, at p. 171) has argued that the chain of enrichment claims is the only possible solution of the Anweisungslage because C cannot receive two performances at the same time. But the law says otherwise! So does *Banque Belge* by also accepting a claim of Pelabon (p. 222 fn. 748)

There is another common case to underpin my point: B assigns his claim against A to C as collateral for his debt. The loan is terminated and B demands payment from A in order to collect the collateral. In this case, there is no doubt that the payment by A discharges his own debt to C as well as the debt of B to C. One and the same payment has two legal reasons vis-a-vis two different parties.

As a consequence, it is not only true that the same natural act can relate to a multitude of performances (painting the house, above p. 246), but also that it can relate to more than one performance in the hand of the recipient.

> § 788 BGB:
> Erteilt der Anweisende die Anweisung zu dem Zwecke, um seinerseits eine Leistung an den Anweisungsempfänger zu bewirken, so wird die Leistung, auch wenn der Angewiesene die Anweisung annimmt, erst mit der Leistung des Angewiesenen an den Anweisungsempfänger bewirkt.
>
> If the instructing party (= B) issues the instruction for the purpose of effecting a performance to the recipient of the instruction (= C), **the performance** [sc. of B to C] **is only effected when the instructed party (= A) makes the performance to the recipient of the instruction** (= C), even if the instructed party (= A) has accepted the instruction.

As a consequence, both A and B make the performance to C based on their respective purposes. If the purpose of A fails, he can claim back the performance in unjust enrichment. If the purpose of B fails, B can claim back the performance in unjust enrichment. In the academic case that both purposes fail, both can claim as "joint creditors". C will be liberated by paying back to either A or B.

That solves Evelyn's case on page 180 in a persuasive way. If the milkman notices his error (that the milk is not paid yet) before Evelyn collects the bottle, he can immediately take it back. If he notices it after Evelyn took the bottle in, he can ring her bell and demand it back. Contrary to widespread assumption, this claim cannot be barred merely because I owe Evelyn (no suum receipt / good consideration, see pp. 176–182). Conversely, if *I* did not owe the bottle of milk because my wife had already paid it back, it is only me who can claim back the bottle from Evelyn. The milkman cannot because he paid his due – and was duly discharged.

The results in plain and clear solutions compared to the German mess. The claim to reverse a performance always follows the performance. It always lies between the performing party and the recipient.

This is also true for bank cases. Insofar Robert Stevens may be right to say: The bank performs its service to the customer. Only the customer performs to the recipient. The artificially construed shift of value that constitutes the performance will normally overlay the natural shift of value from bank to recipient because the law reverses performances, not natural shifts. Since the customer receives the performance, the recipient of the payment is merely indirectly enriched from the performance of the bank. That was the true core of the old view that assumed a direct shift of wealth via an indirect performance.

However, it also follows that if the customer (= B) does not receive the performance (=banking service to wire the funds) because he did not authorise the transfer, the addressee of the funds (= C) becomes the direct recipient of the payment instead of the customer. In that case, the bank must turn to C for restitution. This is the law in England and Germany (*Barclays v Simms*; BGHZ 205, 377).

C Conclusion: The principles of unjust enrichment

At the end of the book, it must be asked whether the title is a misnomer since it has now become clear that there is not only one principle of unjust enrichment. There are two! The first and best known is the Pomponian sentence that nobody shall be enriched from somebody else's loss (*neminem fieri locupletior cum alterius detrimento debet*). The second and less known is Savigny's principle that all *condictiones* are based on a direct shift of wealth / value without legal reason (*sine causa*).

The first principle gave birth of the law of unjust enrichment. It overarched the specific actions of Roman law and created, in a process that spanned over centuries, a new field of law with its own idiosyncratic language. The concepts of enrichment, disenrichment and unjustness are living as witnesses of a great idea that was cast into words by a bright Roman jurist named Sextus Pomponius almost 2000 years ago (of whom we know not much else). The first who fell for their charm were the compilators of Justinian. Many others followed over the centuries, starting with the glossator Martinus Gosia, the jurists of Southern France, Canon lawyers and natural lawyers all over the Holy Roman Empire. But nowhere became this notion so wholeheartedly embraced than in France where the Cour de Cassation introduced this principle as binding law in 1892. This started a belated wave that washed through many European jurisdictions and re-established a claim in which none of the great codifications had had any interest at all. It is one of the ironies of this history that the path to the arrêt Boudier had been paved by Aubry and Rau who drew from the German jurist Zacharia in advocating the *actio de in rem verso*, whereas in Germany, both the sentence of Pomponius and the *actio de in rem verso* were dismissed the 19th century and eradicated by the codification of the BGB. It is equally ironic that the open and zealous disrespect for Pomponian enrichment displayed by the fathers of the BGB did not hinder Germany from expanding the Pomponian disenrichment defence to all *condictiones* and invoke the specific equity of unjust enrichment for doing so.

Nevertheless, the title of the book is not a misnomer because there is only one viable principle of unjust enrichment. It is the principle of the direct shift of value without legal reason that was formulated by Savigny in the 19th century. The vaguer and wider principle of Pomponius does not work because it cannot be applied as law. Savigny has stated it and Robert Stevens' stamp case confirms it. The apparent objection that it is the law of France and others can be overcome by showing (a) that France actually only adopted the (also specific) *actio de in rem verso utilis*, (b) that other applications are kept at bay by an ill-fitting and intellectually challenge-

https://doi.org/10.1515/9783110754452-003

able subsidiarity bar and (c) that there is nevertheless a legal uncertainty. This is caused by the paradox to simultaneously use the Pomponian principle as "super-eminent equity" to correct the strict law (as happened over centuries since the reception of Roman law) and as overarching rationale of strict law actions that shall be directly applied as law.[993]

The narrow enrichment principle of the direct shift of value without legal reasons is the right one because it serves the "vital interest in keeping the scientific notions of law as pure as possible", as Planiol had demanded. The principle was carved out by Savigny directly from the *condictiones* in the Digest. It was adopted for the BGB by Franz-Philipp von Kübel: Money or money's worth cannot pass from one to another without sufficient consent. The consent can either lack completely (cases of "taking value") or be invalidated by the failure of the purpose of a transfer (cases of failed performances). As the *Zwecklehre*, founded by Hugo Kreß and carried forth by Hermann Weitnauer, Horst Ehman, Franz Schnauder and others has taught us time and time again, there are only three primary purposes to make performances, as opposed to the infinite number of ulterior motives; the *causa acquirendi*, the *causa solvendi* and the *causa donandi*. If they are not achieved, the performance does not make sense. That is why a claim to reverse the performance must lie by operation of law (not by any implied promise), while unilateral mistakes and disappointments of personal motives are – and must be – as irrelevant as they are under contract laws. This rationale for claims in unjust enrichment is as universal as the principle of party autonomy of which it is the logical flipside.

Savigny has shown that all Roman *condictiones* can be reduced to the common denominator of the direct shift of value without legal reason. That is the fundament of German unjustified enrichment. The same must be true for English unjust enrichment because Lord Mansfield, in a bold move of legal transplanting, merged an action that was of similar abstract nature as the Roman *condictio* (the count for money had and received under *indebitatus assumpsit*) with the causes of action of the specific, "Mosaic" *conditiones* (*indebiti* = mistake; *causa data causa non secuta* = failure of consideration; *ob turpen vel iniustam causam* = extortion). Like cases must be treated alike, and that is why the same reasons for restitution can be led back to the same principle.

Contrary to the principle of Pomponius, the principle devised by Savigny works well and can be turned in to law. It only came into disrepute in Germany because due to the sloppy drafting of the final version by the Second Commission,

---

993 In the same vein Mélodie Combot, Quasi-contrat et enrichissement injustifié, 2023, n°234, at p. 223.

it was misread. Most authors connected it to real shifts of value. Some even mistook it for the old Pomponian equity requiring loss of the claimant.[994] That fallacy made it liable to challenge. The attack by Walter Wilburg broke through after the war when it was condoned by Ernst von Caemmerer.[995] It rightly brought down the old misinterpretation and established the correct shape of unjustified enrichment as already *Vorentwurf* and *Erster Entwurf* would have had it. A separate reading of § 812 I 1 BGB took over that saw on the one side the performance-based *Leistungskondiktionen* that lie between performing party and recipient and reverse the performance *sine causa* (not any consequential enrichments obtained through the performance). On the other side, there are the enrichments that are in other ways ("in sonstiger Weise") obtained "at the expense of the claimant".

However, the fact that this dichotomic structure actually transposes the enrichment law envisaged by Savigny and von Kübel has never been understood in Germany. Full of *cupiditas novarum rerum*, German jurists discarded Savigny's striking analysis of the *condictiones.* As a consequence, they did not see that every performance is a direct shift of value at the expense of the performing party simply because the performing party (and no one else) is to be paid for it.[996] This statement is completely independent of whether the performance was made out of the assets of the claimant – and rightly so because it simply does not matter whether the performance on the obligation creates value instead of transferring it (haircut vs. conveyance) or whether it is made by use of another person's property. It only matters that the performance of money' or money's worth came from the claimant. That is why Josef Esser did *not* hit the nail on the head when he famously said that the §§ 812 BGB are ***Be****reicherungsrecht*, not ***Ent****reicherungsrecht* (= enrichment law, not disenrichment law).[997] This statement is only true insofar as (1) the claimant does not have to suffer a loss[998] and (2) "at the expense" does not apply as an additional (restrictive) requirement of the *Leistungskondiktion.* But the first point is only true because German law does not accept Wrotham

994 This is particularly true for the leading critics *Wilburg* and *von Caemmerer.* See Wilburg, pp. 97 et seq., e.g. at p. 101 talking about apparent loss ("scheinbarer Schade"); von Caemmerer, FS Rabel, Vol 1, 1954, 333, at p. 337: "Die Versuche, eine einheitliche Formel zu finden, … laufen vielfach nur darauf hinaus, den Satz dass sich niemand mit dem Schaden eines anderen bereichern dürfe, in anderen Worten zu umschreiben." [The attempts to find a uniform formula … often only amount to circumscribing the sentence that no one may enrich himself with the damage of another in other words.]

995 von Caemmerer, FS Rabel, Vol 1, 1954, 333.

996 Schall, pp. 19–20.

997 Josef Esser, Schuldrecht BT, 4th edn. 1971, § 104 I 1, at p. 363 and § 104 II 1b, at p. 370.

998 MünchKommBGB/Schwab, vol 7, 9th edn. 2024, § 812 mn. 5.

Park damages,[999] and the second is only true because *every* performance of money or money's worth is necessarily made at the expense of the performing party. It does not mean that claimants should be allowed to skim off values from the defendants that did not, in the eyes of the law, come "from" them.[1000] As von Kübel rightly said:[1001]

> Jede Kondiktion setzt einen Vermögenswert voraus, der vom Kläger auf den Beklagten überging, auf Kosten des ersteren dem letzteren zu Gute gekommen ist; ohne das kann von einer Bereicherung und also auch von einer Kondiktion keine Rede sein.
>
> [Every *condictio* presupposes a value that has been transferred from the plaintiff to the defendant and has benefited the latter at the expense of the former; without this, there can be no question of enrichment and therefore also of a *condictio*. based on DeepL]

The claimants of a *Leistungskondiktion* are "depleted" by the failure of their performance that renders their act of giving senseless. The giving (or losing) at one's own expense is the reason that entitles the claimant to restitution because the necessary consent lacks or is flawed by the failure of the purpose. There can be no "enrichment" claim without that reason or else, German law would be "Kangaroo law" that randomly grants claims to skim off increases in wealth that are deemed unfair. But German law does not require anyone to "justify" the level of his wealth, but only his receipts. This is because as said: party autonomy wants money or money's worth to be transferred under the unflawed will of the person that is competent to transfer it (p. 263).

Failing to understand the performance as direct shift of value, German jurists could not see either the perfect blueprint that this paradigm provided for the enrichment in other ways.[1002] The question is simply whether the defendant took without consent any value that he should have bargained for with the claimant, i.e. money or money's worth that he should have received as performance with legal reason (*cum causa*). The determination of such a "hypothetical bargain" is the only necessary and apt test for enrichment claims under § 812 I 1 2. Alt. BGB.

Add to that the misreading of the location of the performances in the paradigmatic *Anweisungslage:* instead of a chain of performances, as assumed by most

---

999 This is an odd and probably wrong decision of German lawyers. If I dodge the fair in an empty train, the damage of the train operator is simply that I did not pay what I owed. The same if I sneak into a hotel room for the night. It is completely irrelevant if the train or the hotel were fully booked. Contrast however the Flugreisefall BGHZ 55, 128 (p. 273).

1000 Flume, AcP 199 (1999), 1, 3 et seq. = Studien, pp. 166 et seq.; Wilhelm, pp. 107 et seq.; the criticism by Wilburg, p. 23 is not persuasive.

1001 Motive VE, p. 46 = Schubert, p. 706.

1002 Schall, pp. 67 et seq.

German jurists, the law says that C receives both a performance from A and a performance from B (§ 788 BGB). This corresponds with current English law that assumed a transfer from bank to recipient both in *Barclays v Simms* and *Lloyds v Independent* and only distinguished both cases by the acceptance or rejection of the good consideration defence. It follows that by paying, the bank effects a direct shift of value (= performance) to the recipient. But simultaneously, the customer renders a performance to the recipient as well. Otherwise, his debt could not be discharged and "good consideration" would be non-existent.

At first sight, it may have seemed odd, maybe even bothersome, to reiterate highly specific, much-debated and hopelessly contentious doctrinal issues of German law at great length and depth in a comparative law book. But the necessity to do so should have become clear by now. Since English law of unjust enrichment, with its direct shift of value, shares the basic structure of unjustified enrichment after Savigny, while diverging from French unjust enrichment that basically enshrined the *actio de in rem verso* so alien to England, it was important to show the validity of Savigny's principle despite its unanimous disposal by German jurists of the twentieth century. That erroneous disposal turned out to be the reason why German law of unjustified enrichment has become such a notoriously complicated topic, despite the fundamentals being widely (and correctly) agreed today. All those problems can be explained and have been explained. It should therefore not deter English law to choose the right direction of the performance-based approach. The rule of enrichment law must be a **strict restriction to direct shifts of value** because this is the relation where the law requires a valid contract as basis for the transfer. The direct shift of value is embodied in the paradigm of the performance: every performance of money or money's worth is a direct shift of value. If the performance fails its purpose (= the uniform unjust super-factor), it will be recovered from the recipient. No one else must be concerned.

That is not to say that claims to recover benefits from remote recipients are necessarily always unsustainable. But they cannot be explained by unjust enrichment. The narrow unjust enrichment of Savigny does not cover them, while the wide unjust enrichment of Pomponius cannot be applied as law. The true principle at work is the prohibition of gratuities at the expense of third parties. This notion, well-known from the *actio Pauliana*, may allow jurisdictions leaning to wide French-style enrichment law to curtail its inherent arbitrariness.[1003] Claims to recover gratuities may well lie against remote recipients. Even though they are no

1003 For a criticism of the state of French unjust enrichment see Mélodie Combot, Quasi-contrat et enrichissement injustifié, 2023, n° 249, p. 235.

enrichment claims, a defence of disenrichment / change of position can be administered.[1004]

Werner Flume has shown that the defence of disenrichment / change of position does not need to rely on the "supereminent equity" of Pomponius. Rather, the defence finds its clear rationale in protecting reliance of bona fide recipients on their gains. This must not be mistaken with a damages claim to compensate reliance losses. Disenrichment merely relates to such losses incurred by the reliance on gains of which the defendant justifiably assumed not to have to pay for, e.g. gratuities or other non-reciprocal benefits like insurance or pension payments (*Kelly v Solari*).

In a combined effort over the span of two centuries, Friedrich Carl von Savigny, Franz Philipp von Kübel, Werner Flume and the *causa*-doctrine of the school of thought founded by Hugo Kreß have demystified the "supereminent equity" of Pomponian unjust enrichment and produced a principle that can work perfectly well as hard law despite its abstract language. By rationalising the reasons for awarding restitution and accepting the defence of disenrichment / change of position, they achieved a persuasive framework for a modern law of (narrow) unjust(ified) enrichment based on Savigny's principle to restore direct shifts of value that took place without legal reason. Since Lord Mansfield transplanted the central features of unjust enrichment from civil law to common law, their findings are of consequence for English law, too. They should therefore guide the interpretation of the law both in England and in Germany. My prediction is that the laws of unjust enrichment will then become as easy and accessible as they should be and always have been.

1004 Cf. e.g. § 134 II 1 InsO: Der Empfänger einer unentgeltlichen Leistung hat diese nur zurückzugewähren, soweit er durch sie bereichert ist. [The recipient of a gratuitous benefit only has to return it if he is enriched by it.]

Evans, Translation of Robert Joseph Pothiers Treatise on the Law of Obligations, or Contracts, Volume II, 1806

as the exceptions to this observation unquestionably are, it cannot be denied that it is too fashionable to sneer at a deviation from the beaten track of practical authority, as the result of pedantry and ostentation; but although, limiting the range of professional arguments to *Impey's Practice*, and the *Index* to the *Term Reports*, might possibly be found to diminish the trouble, without detracting from the profits of individuals, the majority of the profession would assuredly be unwilling to confine themselves within such narrow trammels.

But if there is any subject to which the doctrine of an universality of principle peculiarly applies, it is that of reclaiming money unduly paid; not only upon the ground that there is no subject in its nature, more wholly referable to the general rules of natural justice, as distinct from the laws founded upon local habit or municipal institution, but also upon the more favourite ground of precedent itself. It will be generally agreed that the system of law upon this subject, as administered in *England*, is chiefly to be deduced from the determinations of Lord *Mansfield*, and that the few cases respecting it of an earlier date are not of sufficient importance to form any regular system. But Lord *Mansfield's* own views upon the subject are peculiarly referable to the principles of universal jurisprudence, as illustrated and embodied in the *Roman* law, and the whole series of his conduct respecting it is a continued precedent of his recurrence to those principles. In the leading case of *Moses* v. *Macfarlane*, in which he embraced the earliest opportunity that occurred to him, of giving an exposition of the grounds and nature of the action for money had and received, he enters diffusely into the general doctrine respecting it, and states several principles which have ever since been looked up to as the standard of authority (even by those who think that in the particular application of these principles, he did not allow sufficient consequence to others by which they ought properly to have been restricted and controuled.) But it will scarcely be contended that he found the materials of his exposition in any preceding volume of *Reports*; whereas a very slight comparison will evince the source of it to have been the judicial wisdom of ancient *Rome*:

This kind of equitable action to recover money, which ought not in justice to be kept, is very beneficial, and therefore much encouraged. It is only for money which, ex æquo et bono, the defendant ought to refund.	Hæc condictio ex bono et æquo introducta, quod alterius apud alterum sine causa deprehenditur, revocari consuevit. l. 66. ff. Lib. 12. Tit. 6. de Cond. Indeb.
It does not lie for money paid by the plaintiff, which is demanded of him as payable in point of honour and honesty, though it	Naturales obligationes non eo solo æstimantur, si actio aliqua earum nomine competit; verumetiam eo si soluta pecunia re-

https://doi.org/10.1515/9783110754452-004

could not have been recovered from him by any course of law.

peti non possit. ff. Lib. 44. Tit. 7. de Oblig. et Actio. l. 10. Lib. 46. Tit. 1. de fide jussoribus, l. 16. § 3.

Naturaliter etiam servus obligatur, et ideo si quis ejus nomine solvat, vel ipse manumissus ex peculio, repeti non poterit. l. 13. de Condictione Indebiti. ff. 12. Tit. 6.

Naturale autem debitum in hac causa pro vero debito habetur, eoque etsi exigi non potest; solutum tamen non repetitur. Vinnius. Ad. Inst. Lib. 3. Tit. 28. 4. 6.

As in payment of a debt, barred by the statute of limitations.

Julianus verum debitorem post litem contestatam, manente adhuc judicio, negabat solventem repetere posse: quia nec absolutus nec condemnatus repetere posset, licet enim absolutus sit, natura tamen debitor *permanet*. l. 60. de Cond. Indeb.

Or contracted during his infancy.

Huc item plerique referunt exceptionem Senatus Consulti Macedoniani; nam et filius familias si mutuam pecuniam acceperit, et pater familias perperam solverit, non repetit. Vinnius. Quoniam, naturalis obligatio manet. ff. Lib. 14. Tit. 6. de Sct. Maced. l. 9. 10.

It lies for money paid by mistake.

Quod indebitum per errorem solvitur, aut ipsum aut tantumdem repetitur, l. 7. de Cond. Indeb.

Is cui quis per errorem non debitum solvit, quasi ex contractu debere videtur. Inst. Lib. 3. Tit. 28.

Or upon a consideration which happens to fail.

The whole title in the digest, de *Condictione Causa data, Causa, non secuta*, is an amplified view of this proposition.

Or for money got by imposition, express or implied, or extortion, or oppression.	Si quis dolo malo aliquem induxerit, aut metu illato coegerit, ut promitteret non possum adduci ut credam, solutum ex his causis retineri posse. Vinnius. Ex ea stipulatione, quæ per vim extorta esset, si exacta esset pecunia, repetitionem esse constat. ff. Lib. 12. Tit. 5. de Cond. ob Turp. vel Injust. Caus. l. 7.
Or an undue advantage taken of the plaintiff's situation, contrary to laws made for the protection of persons, under these circumstances.	Si naturalis obligatio jure civili improbata sit, aut destituta juris civilis auxilio, qualis est mulieris intercedentis. l. 16. § 1. ad Sct. Maced. prodigi promittentes, l 6. de Verb. Oblig. pupilli sine tutoris contractu, licet hæc admittunt accessiones, ea non attendetur et perinde repetitio datur, ac si quod ex causa solutum est nullo jure debitum esset. Vinnius, 22.
In one word the gift of this action is that the defendant, upon the circumstances of the case, is obliged by the ties of natural justice and equity, to refund the money.	Hoc natura æquum est neminem cum alterius detrimento, fieri locupletiorem. l. 14. de Cond. Indeb.
The damages recovered in the case of *Dutch* v. *Warren*, shew the liberality of this kind of action: for though the defendant received considerably more, yet the difference only was retained against conscience, and therefore the plaintiff ex æquo et bono could recover no more,	agreeably to the rule of the Roman law: Quod condictio indebiti non datur ultra quam locupletior est factus qui accepit.

The case of *Smith* v. *Branley*, *Doug.* 696. also affords a very clear instance of a similar parallel:

If an act is itself immoral, or a violation of the general laws of public policy, there the party	Ubi dantis et accipientis turpitudo versatur, non posse repeti dicimus: veluti *si pecunia*

paying shall not have this action, for where both parties are equally criminal against such general laws, potior est conditio defendentis.

detur ut male judicetur. l. 3. de Cond. ob Turp. vel Injust. Caus.

But there are other laws which are calculated for the protection of the subject, against oppression, extortion, deceit, &c. If such laws are violated, and the defendant takes advantage of the plaintiff's condition or situation, then the plaintiff shall recover.

Quotiens autem solius accipientis turpitudo versatur, Celsus ait repeti posse: veluti si tibi dedero *ne mihi injuriam facias.* l. 4. ibid.

But it may be said, that however apposite all the reasonings deduced from *D'Aguesseau* and *Vinnius* might be to have shewn, *a priori*, what the decision ought to have been, whatever influence the discussion now submitted to the public might have had, if it had been presented as an argument to the court, the subject is now at rest and concluded by authority, and that any reasoning of a private individual respecting the grounds of that conclusion, must be not only unavailing but impertinent.

But however little encouragement the discussions of a private individual, respecting legal subjects, have received, or are likely to receive, the reasons which militate against the offering such discussions to the public, seem to be much more numerous on the score of prudence than on the principles of propriety. The law, like every other subject, may be regarded as a matter either of practical information, or of scientific inquiry; if a doctrine which is merely the speculative opinion of an individual, should be conveyed to the public in such a manner as to be susceptible of producing an erroneous impression, that it was admitted in judicial practice, much inconvenience might arise, and much censure would be reasonably incurred. Or if an individual should pronounce a peremptory decision, in opposition to principles established by judicial authority, he would be fairly liable to the imputation of presumption. But in suggesting grounds, and reasons, in support of a difference of opinion fairly stated, every reader is left to the exercise of his own judgment, upon the correctness of the premises and their accordance with the conclusion. To support a general and indiscriminate objection to this course of proceeding, it must be assumed that the reasoning which is offered is satisfactory and correct; for if either the premises are erroneous in themselves, or inadequate to the conclusion which is deduced from them, an objection arises of a very different nature from that of a presumptuous arraignment of established authority. Perhaps, in some cases, an examination of any subject may escape reprehension even whilst the result of it is not assented to, as, by exciting

Sources Unjust Enrichment

Albers, Gregor; Patti, Francesco Paolo; Perrouin-Verbe, Dorothée: Causa contractus: Auf der Suche nach den Bedingungen der Wirksamkeit des vertraglichen Willens / Alla ricerca delle condizioni di efficacia della volontà contrattuale / À la recherche des conditions de l'efficacité de la volonté contractuelle, Beiträge zum ausländischen und internationalen Privatrecht, Vol. 137, 2022

Alder, John:Restitution in public law: bearing the cost of unlawful state action, Cambridge University Press, Legal Studies, Vol. 22, Iss. 2 (2002) 165 – 184

American Law Institute: The Restatement of The Law Third: Restitution and Unjust Enrichment, 2 Vol., ALI, 2011

Ames, Dean: The History of Assumpsit, Harvard Law Review, Vol. 2, 1888 – 1889

Arndt, Johannes: Bitcoin-Eigentum: Zur Notwendigkeit rechtlicher Zuweisung außer-rechtlicher außer-subjektiver Vermögenspositionen durch subjektive Rechte, Schriften zum Recht der Digitalisierung, Vol. 9, Mohr Siebeck, 2021

Aubry, Charles; Rau, Charles FrédéricCours de droits civil francais: d'après la méthode de Zachriae, Vol. 4, 4th edn., 1872

Aubry, Charles; Rau, Charles Frédéric: Cours de droits civil francais: d'après la méthode de Zachriae, Vol. 6, 4th edn., 1873

Auer, Marietta: Neuanfang beim Bereicherungsausgleich in Dreipersonenverhältnissen, ZfPW 2016, 479

Baker, John Hamilton: New Light on Slade's case, The Cambridge Law Journal, Vol. 29, Iss. 1 (1971) 51 – 67

Baldus, Christian; Brückner, Bettina; Burgmair, Alice: Münchener Kommentar zum Bürgerlichen Gesetzbuch: BGB, Band 8: Sachenrecht §§ 854 – 1296, WEG, ErbbauRG, CH Beck, Vol. 8, 9th edn., 2023

Ball, Eli: Enrichment at the Claimant's Expense. Attribution Rules in Unjust Enrichment Oxford: Hart Publishing, 2016

Baloch, Tariq: Unjust Enrichment and Contract, Oxford: Hart Publishing, 2009

Bant, Elise: Payment Over and Change of Position: Lessons from Agency Law, Lloyd's Maritime and Commercial Law Quarterly (2007), 225 – 245

Bant, Elise: The Change of Position Defence, Lloyd's Maritime and Commercial Law Quarterly Journal (2007), 129 – 271

Bant, Elise; Barker, Kit; Degeling, Simone: Research Handbook on Unjust Enrichment and Restitution, Elgar, 2020.

Barker, Kit: After Change of Position: Good Faith Exchange in the Modern Law of Restitution in: Peter Birks (ed), Laundering and Tracing, Oxford , 1995, 191 – 215

Barker, Kit: Bona Fide Purchase as a Defence to Unjust Enrichment Claims, Restitution Law Review, Vol. 7 (1999), 75 – 91

Barker, Kit; Grantham, Ross: Unjust Enrichment, Sydney, 2008

Bartels, Klaus: Der Bereicherungsausgleich im verbundenen Geschäft unter § 358 Abs. 4 Satz 5 BGB, JuristenZeitung (JZ) 2024, 478

Bartolini, Francesca: La causa del contratto dal Codice civile del 1942 ai giorni nostri in: Gregor Albers, Francesco Paolo Patti, Dorothée Perrouin-Verbe, Causa contractus, Mohr Siebeck, 2022

Beatson, Jack: "Restitution of Taxes, Levies and Other Imposts: Defining the Limits of the Woolwich Principle", Law Quarterly Review, Vol. 109 (1993), 401

https://doi.org/10.1515/9783110754452-005

Beatson, Jack: The Use and Abuse of Unjust Enrichment: Essays on the Law of Restitution, Clarendon Press, 1991
Belloni, Annalisa: Le questioni civilistiche del secolo XII. Da Bulgaro a Pillio da Medicina e Azzone, Ius Commune, 43rd edn., 1989
Birks, Peter: An Introduction to the Law of Restitution, Clarendon Press, 1989
Birks, Peter: Unjust Enrichment, Oxford University Press, 2nd edn., 2005
Birks, Peter: At the expense of the claimant: direct and indirect enrichment in English law, in: Johnston & Zimmermann (eds.), Unjustified Enrichment, 2002, 494
Birks, Peter: Misdirected Funds: Restitution from the Recipient, Lloyd's Maritime and Commercial Law Quarterly (1989) 296–341
Birks, Peter; Rose, FrancisLessons of the Swaps Litigation, Routledge, 2000
Birks, Peter; Rose, Francis: Restitution and Equity Vol. 1: Resulting Trusts and Equitable Compensation, Informa Law from Routledge, 2000
Birks, Peter; Yin, Chin Nyuk: On the Nature of Undue Influence in: Jack Beatson and Daniel Friedmann, Good Faith and Fault in Contract, Oxford: Clarendon Press, 1995
Böcking, Eduard: Corpus legum sive Brachylogus iuris civilis, 1829, availabl at: https://archive.org/details/bub_gb_VigtAAAAYAAJ/page/38/mode/2up
Boosfeld, Kristin: Gewinnausgleich. Vergleichende und systematisierende Gegenüberstellung der französischen, niederländischen und englischen Tradition, Mohr Siebeck, 2015
Bryan, Michael: Recovering Misdirected Money from Banks: Ministerial Receipt at Law and in Equity in: Francis Rose, Restitution and Banking Law, Informa Law from Routledge, 1998, 161
Burrows, Andrew: The Law of Restitution, Oxford University Press, 3rd edn., 2011
Burrows, Andrew: A Restatement of the English Law of Unjust Enrichment, 2012
Burrows, Andrew: Absence of Basis: The New Birksian Scheme in: Andrew Burrows, Lord Alan Rodger, Mapping the Law: Essays in Memory of Peter Birks, Oxford University Press, 2006
Burrows, Andrew: At the Expense of the Claimant: A Fresh Look, Restitution Law Review, Vol. 25 (2018), 167
Burrows, Andrew: A New Dawn for the Law of Illegality in: Alan Bogg, Sarah Green, Illegality after *Patel v Mirza*, Bloomsbury Publishing, 2020
Burrows, Andrew: Essays on the Law of Restitution, Legal Studies, Oxford: Clarendon Press, 1991
Burrows, Andrew: Free Acceptance and the Law of Restitution, Law Quarterly Review, Vol. 104 (1988), 576
Burrows, Andrew: Is there a defence of good consideration? in: Charles Mitchell, William Swadling, The Restatement Third: Restitution and Unjust Enrichment, 2013, 165–184
Burrows, Andrew: Lord Rodger of Earlsferry Mapping the Law: Essays in Memory of Peter Birks, Oxford University Press, 2006
Burrows, Andrew: The Australian Law of Unjust Enrichment: Has the High Court Lost its Way? in: Elise Bant; Matthew Harding (eds.), Exploring Private Law, Cambridge University Press, 2010, 67–85
Burrows, Andrew: Understanding the Law of Obligations: Essays on Contract, Tort and Restitution, Oxford: Hart Publishing, 1998
Burrows, Andrew; McKendrick, Ewan; Edelman, James: Cases and Materials on the Law of Restitution, Oxford University Press, 2nd edn., 2006
Canaris, Claus-Wilhelm: Der Bereicherungsausgleich im Dreipersonenverhältnis, in: Paulus, Gotthard; Diederichsen, Uwe; Canaris, Claus-Wilhelm, Festschrift für Karl Larenz zum 75. Geburtstag, 1973, 799

Canaris, Claus-Wilhelm: Das Verhältnis der §§ 994 ff. BGB zur Aufwendungskondiktion nach § 812 BGB: Zugleich eine Besprechung der Entscheidung des BGH vom 29.9.1995 – V ZR 130/94, JuristenZeitung (JZ) 1996, 344
Canaris, Claus-Wilhelm: Der Bereicherungsausgleich bei Zahlung des Haftpflichtversicherers an einen Scheingläubiger, Neue Juristische Wochenschrift (NJW) 1992, 868
Canaris, Claus-Wilhelm: Noch einmal: Die Rückkehr der Praxis zur Regelanwendung und der Beruf der Theorie im Recht der Leistungskondiktion, Neue Juristische Wochenschrift (NJW) 1992, 3143
Capitant, Henri/ François Terré/Yves Lequette: Les grands arrêts de la jurisprudence, Vol. 2, 12th edn., 2008
Carbonier, Jean: Droit Civil, Presses Universitaires de France (PUF), 15th edn., 1991
Chambers, Robert: Resulting Trusts, Clarendon Press, 1997
Chambers, Robert: Integrating Property and Obligations in: Andrew Robertson, The Law of Obligations: Connections and Boundaries, Oxford: Hart Publishing, 2004, 127
Chambers, Robert: Is There a Presumption of Resulting Trust? In: Charles Mitchell, Constructive and Resulting Trusts, Oxford: Hart Publishing, 2010, 267–287
Chambers, Robert: Two Kinds of Enrichment in: Philosophical Foundations of the Law of Unjust Enrichment, Oxford Univerity Press, 2009, 242–278
Chambers, Robert; Mitchell, Charles; Penner, James: Philosophical Foundations of the Law of Unjust Enrichment, Oxford, 2009
Chiusi, Tiziana: Die actio de in rem verso im römischen Recht, Münchener Beiträge zur Papyrusforschung, Iss. 91, 2001
Cohen, Henry: Harvard Law Review, Vol. 45, Iss. 8, Jun., 1932, 1333–1364
Coing, Helmut: Europäischen Privatrecht 1500–1800, Verlag C.H. Beck, Vol. 1, 1985
Coke, Edward: The Reports of Sir Edward Coke In Thirteen Parts, Moore Dublin, 6th Report, 1796
Combot, Mélodie: Quasi-contrat et enrichissement injustifié, LGDJ, 2023
Contreas Aguirre, Sebastián: Restitution and Corrective Justice in the Aristotelian Scholastic Tradition: The Contribution of Francisco Suárez (1548–1617), Caurensia, Vol. 15, 2020, 221–254
Contreras Aguirre, Sebastián: Hugo Grotius and the Scholastic Tradition, Espíritu, Vol. 71, Iss. 163, 2022
Cope, Malcolm: Proprietary Claims and Remedies, Sydney: The Federation Press, 1997
Cornish, William et al.: Restitution: Past, Present and Future, Oxford: Hart Publishing, 1998
Dagan, Hanoch: The Law and Ethics of Restitution, Cambridge University Press, 2004
Dalla Massara, Tommaso: Die causa des Vertrages im Denken des Aristoteles – zu den Ursprüngen einer Idee in: Gregor Albers, Francesco Paolo Patti, Dorothée Perrouin-Verbe, Causa contractus, Mohr Siebeck, 2022
Dannemann, Gerhard: The German Law of Unjustified Enrichment and Restitution: A Comparative Introduction, Oxford, 2009
Dannemann, Gerhard: Unjust Enrichment as Absence of Basis: Can English Law Cope? in: Andrew Burrows and Lord Alan Rodger, Mapping the Law: Essays in Memory of Peter Birks, Oxford, 2006, 363
Dalrymple, James, 1st Viscount of Stair: Institutions of the Laws of Scotland, 1681 (1981 edn.)
Dawson, John Philip: Unjust Enrichment: A Comparative Analysis, 1951
Dawson, John Philip: Negotiorum Gestio: The Altruistic Intermeddler, Harvard Law Review, Vol. 74, 1961, 817
Dawson, John Philip: Unjust Enrichment – a Comparative Analysis, 1951, reprinted 1999
De Ferrière, Claude: La Jurisprudence du Digeste, Paris, 1677

De Nauw, Alain: La consacration jurisprudentielle de l'état de nécessité, R.C.J.B., 1989
De Ruggiero, Roberto; Maroi, Fulvio: Instituzioni di diriito privato, Vol. 2, 2nd edn., 1954
Degeling, Simone; Edelman, James: Unjust Enrichment and Commercial Law, 2008
Denisart, Jean Baptiste: Collections des décision nouvelles et de notions relative à la jurisprudence actuelle, Vol 3, 5th edn., 1766, available at: https://gallica.bnf.fr/ark:/12148/bpt6k206724d/f364.item
Demolombe, Charles: Traité des Engagements qui se forment sans convention: des contrats et des obligations conventionelles en général, tome (= Vol.) 8, = Cours de Code Napoleon, tome (= Vol.) 31 Rue de Fleurus 9, Paris, 1882
Dietrich, Joachim: Restitution: A New Perspective, Annandale, 1999
Diósdi, György: Gaius der Rechtsgelehrte in: Hildegard Temporini at al., Aufstieg und Niedergang der Römischen Welt – Rise and Decline of the Roman World, De Gruyter, Vol. 15, 1976
Diurni, Amalia: Schädigende Nothilfe – Haftungszurechnung im Europäischen Privatrecht, ZEuP 2006, 583
Domat, Jen: Les Loix Civiles Dans Leur Ordre Naturel, Tome 1 (Vol. 1), rue St Jacques, Paris, 1689
Dostalík, Petr: Actio de in rem verso-An Unwanted Continuity-The Doctrine of versio in rem in the Austrian Civil Code and Interwar Legal Discussion in Czechoslovakia, Krakow Studies in State and Legal History, Vol. 15, Iss. 2, 2022, 203–214, available at: https://dspace5.zcu.cz/bitstream/11025/49673/1/Dostalik_KSzHPiP_15%282%292022.pdf
Doyle, Matthew: Unjust enrichment and Corrective Justice, Vol. 62 No. 2, Toronto law Journal (2012) 229–254
Douglas, Simon: The Nature of Conversion, Cambridge Law Journal Vol. 68, No. 1 (2009), 198–223
Du Plessis, Jacques: The South African Law of Unjustified Enrichment, Juta, 2012
Du Plessis, Jacques: Labels and Meaning: Unjust Factors and Failure of Purpose as Reasons for Reversing Enrichment by Transfer, Edinburgh Law Review 18.3 (2014): 416–43
Dyson, Andrew; Goudkamp, James; Wilmot-Smith, Frederick: Defences in Unjust Enrichment, Oxford: Hart Publishing, 2016
Edelman, James: Change of Position: A Defence of Unjust Disenrichment, Boston Law Review, Vol. 92, (2012), 1009–1033
Edelman, James: Restitution of (Property) Rights in: Elise Bant and Michael Bryan, Principles of Proprietary Remedies, Thomson Reuters Australia, 2013, 37–54
Edelman, James: The Meaning of Loss and Enrichment in: Robert Chambers, Charles Mitchell, James Penner, Philosophical Foundations of the Law of Unjust Enrichment, Oxford University Press, 2009, 211–241
Edelman, James; Bant, Elise: Unjust Enrichment, 2nd edn., Hart, 2016
Edelman, James; Degeling, Simone: Unjust Enrichment in Commercial Law, Thomson Reuters Australia, 2008
Edelmann, James: Change of Position: A Defence of Unjust Enrichment, Boston University Law Review, Vol. 92 (2012), 1009–34
Ehmann, Horst: Der Zweck der Leistungen und Leistungsversprechen, 1–42; https://www.uni-trier.de/fileadmin/fb5/prof/eme001/causa-Vigoni_2.pdf
Ehmann, Horst: Zur causa-Lehre, JuristenZeitung (JZ) 2003, 702
Ehmann, Horst: Die Lehre vom Zweck als Entwicklung der Voraussetzungslehre, Festschrift Beuthien, 2009, available at: https://www.uni-trier.de/fileadmin/fb5/prof/eme001/FS-Beuthin_die_lehre_vom_Zweck.pdf

Ehmann, Horst: Zu den Arten der Rechtsgründe von Leistungen und Leistungsversprechen in: Gregor Albers, Francesco Paolo Patti, Dorothée Perrouin-Verbe, Causa contractus, Mohr Siebeck, 2022

Ellger, Reinhard: Bereicherung durch Eingriff: Das Konzept des Zuweisungsgehalts im Spannungsfeld von Ausschließlichkeitsrecht und Wettbewerbsfreiheit, Mohr Siebeck, 2002

Elliott, Steven; Haecker, Birke; Mitchell, Charles: Restitution of Overpaid Tax, Oxford: Hart Publishing, 2013

Esser, Josef: Schuldrecht Besonderer Teil, Vol. 2, 4th edn., C.F. Müller, 1971

Evans, William David: A Treatise on the Law of Obligations or Contracts (Pothier on Contracts), Vol. 2, The Lawbook Exchange Ltd, 1806

Feenstra, Robert; Zimmermann, Reinhard: Das römisch-holländische Recht: Fortschritte des Zivilrechts im 17. und 18. Jahrhundert, Duncker und Humblot, Vol. 7, 1992

Ferid, Murad; Sonnenberger, Hans Jürgen: Das französische Zivilrecht II, Verlagsgesellschaft Recht und Wissenschaft, 2nd edn., 1986

Finkenauer, Thomas: Stipulation und Geschäftsgrundlage, Zeitschrift der Savigny-Stiftung für Rechtsgeschichte (SZ), Romanistische Abteilung, Vol. 126 (2009), 305

Finn, Paul: Essays on Restitution, Law Book Company, 1990

Finnis, John: The Fairy Tale's Moral, Law Quarterly Review, Vol. 115 (1999), 170

Fitting, Hermann: Über die Heimat und das Alter des sogenannten Brachylogus, 1880; reprint DeGruyter, 2019

Flume, Werner: Studien zur Lehre der ungerechtfertigten Bereicherung (hrsg. von Wolfgang Ernst), Mohr Siebeck, 2003

Flume, Werner: Wegfall der Bereicherung, in Festschrift für Hans Niedermeyer zum 70. Geburtstag, 1953, 103 = Studien, 27

Flume, Werner: Anwendung der Saldotheorie im Fall der Nichtigkeit eines Grundstück-Kaufvertrags nach § 138 Abs. 1 BGB wegen verwerflicher Gesinnung des Käufers, Zeitschrift für Wirtschaftsrecht (ZIP) 2001, 1621 = Studien, 242

Flume, WernerDie ungerechtfertigte Bereicherung nach dem Bürgerlichen Gesetzbuch als eine Rechtsfigur der Bereicherung, in Canaris, Claus-Wilhelm; Heldrich, Andreas; Hopt, Klaus j.; Roxin, Claus; Schmidt, Karsten; Widmaier, Gunter, 50 Jahre BGH, Festgabe der Wissenschaft, Vol. 1, 2000, 525 = Studien, 92.

Flume, Werner: Der Bereicherungsausgleich in Mehrpersonenverhältnissen, AcP 199 (1999), 1 = Studien, 165

Flume, Werner: Die Rückabwicklung nichtiger Kaufverträge nach Bereicherungsrecht – Zur Saldotheorie und ihren "Ausnahmen", JuristenZeitung (JZ) 2002, 321 = Studien, 248

Flume, Werner: Die Zahlungszuwendung im Anweisungs-Dreiecksverhältnis und die Problematik der ungerechtfertigten Bereicherung, Neue Juristische Wochenschrift (NJW) 1984, 464 = Studien, 220

Flume, Werner: Zum Bereicherungsausgleich bei Zahlungen in Drei-Personen-Verhältnissen, Neue Juristische Wochenschrift (NJW) 1991, 2521 = Studien, 233

Foerster, Max: Nicht autorisierte Zahlungsvorgänge und Ausschlussfrist des § 676b Abs. 2 BGB – Ausgleich in Anweisungsfällen, Archiv für die civilistische Praxis (AcP), Vol. 213 (2013), 405–442

Fombad, Charles Manga: The Principle of Unjust Enrichment in International Law, The Comparative and International Law Journal of Southern Africa, Vol. 30, Iss. 2 (1997), 120–130

Foster, Elisabeth Read: "Proceedings in Parliament, 1610. Vol. I, The House of Lords'", Yale University Press, Vol. 11, 1966

Fox, David: Bona Fide Purchase and the Currency of Money, Cambridge Law Journal, Vol. 55, Iss. 3 (1996) 547–565
Fridman, Gerald; McLeod, James: Restitution, 2nd edn., Toronto, 1992
Friedman, Wolfgang: The Principle of Unjust Enrichment in English Law, Canadian Bar Review, Vol. 16 (1938), 243
Fu, Guangyu: Das Causa-Problem im deutschen Bereicherungsrecht, Peter Lang, 2010
Gamauf, Richard: Vindicatio Nummorum: eine Untersuchung zur Reichweite und praktischen Durchführung des Eigentumsschutzes an Geld im klassischen Römischen Recht, Habilitationsschrift, Wien, 2001
Goré, François: L'enrichissement aux dépens d'autrui, Dalloz, 1949
Grantham, Ross; Rickett, Charles: Enrichment and Restitution in New Zealand, Bloomsbury, 2000
Grauer, Fritz: Die ungerechtfertigte Bereicherung im französischen Privatrecht, Winter, 1939
Grotius (De Groot), Hugo: De iure belli ac pacis libri tres, Nicolas Boun Paris, 1625
Grotius, Hugo: Inleydinge tot de Hollantsche Rechtsgeleertheit, Book III, The Hague, 1631
Gsell, Beate; Krüger, Wolfgang; Lorenz, Stephan: Beck-Online Großkommentar zum BGB(constantly updated)
Gursky, Karl-Heinz; Linardatos, Dimitrios: 20 Probleme aus dem Bereicherungsrecht, 7th edn., Franz Vahlen, 2023
Gutteridge, Harold Cooke; David, R. J. A.: The doctrine of unjustified enrichment, Cambridge Law Journal, Vol. 5 (1933–1935), pp.204–229
Habersack, Mathias; Papier, Hans-Jürgen; Raude, Karin: Münchener Kommentar zum Bürgerlichen Gesetzbuch: BGB, Band7: Schuldrecht -Besonderer Teil IV §§ 705–853, Vol. 7, CH beck, 9th edn. 2024
Häcker, Birke: Causa und Consideration: Ein historischer Dialog in: Gregor Albers, Francesco Paolo Patti, Dorothée Perrouin-Verbe, Causa contractus, Mohr Siebeck, 2022
Häcker, Birke: Consequences of Impaired Consent Transfers: A Structural Comparison of English and German Law, Mohr Siebeck, 2009
Häcker, Birke: Mistaken Gifts after Pitt v Holt, Current Legal Problems (CLP), Vol. 67, Iss. 1 (2014), 333–372
Hansmann, Henry; Kraakman, Reinier; Squire, Richard: Law and the Rise of the Firm, Harvard Law Review Vol. 119, Iss. 5 (2006), 1333–1403
Hansmann, Henry; Kraakman, Reinier; Squire, Richard: Incomplete Organizations: Legal Entitiesand Asset Partitioning in RomanCommerce, European CorporateGovernance Institute (ECGI) – Law Working Paper No. 271/2014, Yale Law &Economics Research Paper No. 511, 2014
Harvard Law Review: Developments in the Law: Unjust Enrichment, Vol. 133 (2019–2020), 2062
Hassold, Gerhard: Zur Leistung im Dreipersonenverhältnis, CH Beck, 1981
Hau, Wolfgang; Poseck, Roman: Beck-Online Kommentar, Bürgerliches Gesetzbuch (constantly updated)
Hausmaninger, Herbert; Gamauf, Richard: A Casebook on Roman Property Law, Oxford University Press, 2012
Heck, Philipp: Grundriss des Schuldrechts, Tübingen, Mohr, 1929
Hedley, Steve: Farewell to Unjustified Enrichment? – A Common Law Response, Edinburgh Law Review, Vol. 20, Iss. 3 (2016), 326–337
Heermann, Peter: Leistungsschutzrecht für Sportveranstalter de lege ferenda?, GRUR 2012, 791
Herresthal, Carsten; Brink, Ulrich; Einsele, Dorothee: Münchener Kommentar zum HGB, Band6: Bankvertragsrecht, Vol. 6, CH Beck, 5th edn.,2024

Herresthal, Carsten; Stoffels, Markus, Magnus, Robert: Staudinger, BGB, Eckpfeiler des Zivilrechts, OttoSchmidt – De Gruyter, 8th edn., 2022
Honsell, Heinrich: Römisches Recht, Springer, 7th edn., 2010
Honsell, Heinrich: Die rhetorischen Wurzeln der juristischen Auslegung, ZfPW 2016, 105
Ibbetson, David: Assumpsit and Debt in the early Sixteenth Century: the Originis of the Indebitatus Count, The Cambridge Law Journal, Vol. 41, No. 1 (1982), 142–161
Ibbetson, David: Sixteenth Century Contract Law: Slade's Case in Context, Oxford Journal of Legal Studies, Vol. 4, Iss. 3 (1984), 295–317
Jaffey, Peter: The Nature and Scope of Restitution, Bloomsbury, 2000
Jahn, Christian Hendrik: Der Bereicherungsausgleich im Mehrpersonenverhältnis – dargestellt anhand der Rückabwicklung von Werk- und Dienstleistungen, Mohr Siebeck, 2014
Jakobs, Horst Heinrich: Die Rückkehr der Praxis zur Regelanwendung und der Beruf der Theorie im Recht der Leistungskondiktion, Neue Juristische Wochenschrift (NJW) 1992, 2524
Jansen, Nils: Gesetzliche Schuldverhältnisse: eine historische Strukturanalyse, AcP 216 (2016), 112–233
Jansen, Nils: Die Korrektur grundloser Vermögensverschiebungen als Restitution? Zur Lehre von der ungerechtfertigten Bereicherung, Zeitschrift der Savigny-Stiftung für Rechtsgeschichte (SZ), Romanistische Abteilung 120 (2003), 106
Jansen, Nils: Farewell to Unjustified Enrichment?, Edinburgh Law Journal, Vol. 20 (2016), 123–148
Johnston, David; Zimmermann, Reinhard: Unjustified Enrichment: Key issues in Comparative Perspective, Cambridge University Press, 2002
Jones, Gareth: Goff & Jones: The Law of Restitution, Sweet & Maxwell, 7th edn., 2007
Kaiser, Dagmar; Sittmann-Haury, Stephanie: Julius von Staudingers Kommentar zum Bürgerlichen Gesetzbuch – Buch 2 (= Vol. 2): Recht der Schuldverhältnisse, Otto Schmidt – DeGruyter, 2022
Kaser, MaxIus honorarium und ius civile, 1984, Zeitschrift der Savigny-Stiftung für Rechtsgeschichte (SZ): Romanistische Abteilung, Vol. *101 (1984), 1–114*
Kaser, Max: Das römische Privatrecht I – Das römische, das vorklassische und klassische Recht, CH Beck, 2nd edn., 1971
Kaser, Max; Hackl, Karl: Das Römische Zivilprozessrecht, C.H. Beck, 1997
Kind, Johann: Adam Gottlieb Jo Adami Theophili Kindi. ...Quaestiones forenses – Observationibus Ac Praesertim Decisionibus Sax. Supremi Provocationum Tribunalis, Liipsiae, Caspari FritschVol. 1, 1792; https://www.digitale-sammlungen.de/de/view/bsb10396962?page=1
Klenner, Hermann: Savigny's Research Program of the Historical School of Law and Its Intellectual Impact in 19th Century Berlin, The American Journal of Comparative Law, Vol. 37, Iss. 1 (1989)
Krebs, Peter/Baldus, Christian (Hrsg.): Summum ius, summa iniuria, Boorberg, 1995
Kohler, Jürgen: Archiv für die civilistische Praxis (AcP) 208 (2008), 417–450
Kohler, Jürgen: Rücktrittsrechtliche Bereicherungshaftung, JuristenZeitung (JZ) 2002, 682
Köndgen, Johannes: Innovationen im Vertragsrecht als Folge der Pandemie, JuristenZeitung (JZ) 2022, 990
Koppensteiner, Hans-Georg; Kramer, Ernst: Ungerechtfertigte Bereicherung, 2nd edn., DeGruyter, 1988
Kortmann, Jeroen: Altruism in Private Law: Liability for Nonfeasance and Negotiorum Gestio, The Modern Law Review, Vol. 69, Iss. 2 (2005), 285–287
Krebs, Thomas: Restitution at the Crossroads: A Comparative Study, Cavendish, 2001
Kreß, Hugo: Lehrbuch des Allgemeinen Schuldrechts, Scientia-Verlag, 1929 (reprint 1974)
Kull, Andrew: James Barr Ames and the Early Modern History of Unjust Enrichment, Oxford Journal of Legal Studies, Vol. 25, No. 2 (2005), 297–319

Kupisch, Berthold: Die Versionsklage. Ihre Entwicklung von der gemeinrechtlichen Theorie des. 17 Jahrhunderts bis zum österreichischen Allgemeinen Bürgerlichen Gesetzbuch, Winter, 1965
Kupisch, Berthold: Gesetzespositivismus im Bereicherungsrecht: Zur Leistungskondiktion im Drei-Personen-Verhältnis, Duncker & Humblot, 1978
Kupisch, Berthold: Leistungskondiktion bei Zweckverfehlung – Teil 2 – Zum causa-Problem im Zivilrecht, JuristenZeitung (JZ) 1985, 163
Labbé, Joseph-Émile: Annotation to Cass req of 16 July 1889 – Crédit foncier, S. ("receuil Sirey") 90.1.97
Lange, Hermann: "Alteri stipulari nemo potest" bei Legisten und Kanonisten, Zeitschrift der Savigny-Stiftung für Rechtsgeschichte, Romanistische Abteilung (SZ or ZRGRA), Vol. 73 (1956), 279–306,
Larenz, Karl; Canaris, Claus-Wilhelm: Lehrbuch des Schuldrechts, Vol. II/2, CH Beck, 13th edn. 1994
Law Commission: The Illegality Defence: Law Commission Report, GOV.UK, Law Com No 320, 2010
Lenel, Otto: Die Lehre von der Voraussetzung (im Hinblick auf den Entwurf des Bürgerlichen Gesetzbuches), Archiv für die civilistische Praxis (AcP) 74 (1889), 213–239
Lenel, Otto: Nochmals die Lehre von der Voraussetzung, Archiv für die civilistische Praxis (AcP) 79 (1892), 49–107
Leyser, Augustin: Meditationes ad pandectas, Lipsiae, 1717
Leyser, Augustin: Meditationes ad pandectas II, Lipsiae, 1723
Liebs, Detlef: The History of the Roman condictio up to Jusitinian in: Neil MacCormick, Peter Birks, The legal mind – essays for Tony Honoré, Oxford University Press, 1986
Linardatos, Dimitrios: Das Haftungssystem im bargeldlosen Zahlungsverkehr, Nomos, 2013
Lodder, Andrew: Enrichment in the Law of Unjust Enrichment and Restitution, Oxford: Hart Publishing, 2012
Lord Bankton, Andrew Macdowall: An Institute of the Laws of Scotland in Civil Rights: With Observations Upon the Agreement Or Diversity Between Them and the *Laws* of England, Stair Society, Vol. 1, 1751
Lord Terence Etherton: The Role of Equity in Mistaken Transactions, Transnational Law Institute, Vol. 27 (2013), 159
Lord Kames, Henry Home: The Principles of Equity, printed for A. Millar, London, and A. Kincaid & J. Bell, Edinburgh,1767
Lord Donald James Nicholls of Birkenhead: Knowing Receipt: The Need for a New Landmark in: William Cornish et al., Restitution: Past, Present and Future, Oxford: Hart Publishing, 1998, 231–246
Lord Wright of Durley: Sinclair v Brougham in: Lord Wright of Durley, Legal Essays and Addresses, Cambridge University Press, 1939
Lorenz, Stephan; Horn, Norbert: Julius von Staudingers Kommentar zum Bürgerlichen Gesetzbuch mit Einführungsgesetz zu §§ 812–822, De Gruyter, 15th edn., 2007
Loyal, Florian: Der fremdnützige Leistungszweck, JuristenZeitung (JZ) 2012, 1102
MacCormick, Neil; Birks, Peter: The legal mind – essays for Tony Honoré, Oxford University Press, 1986
Maddaugh, Peter; McCamus, John: The Law of Restitution, 2nd edn., 2004
Magnus, Robert: Diskussionsbericht zum Referat von Nils Jansen, Archiv für die civilistische Praxis (AcP), Vol. 216, Iss. 1–2, 2016, 234–238
Malaurie, Marie: Les Restitutions en Droit Civile, Cujas, 1991
Mandry, Gustav: Das gemeine Familiengüterrecht mit Ausschluss des ehelichen Güterrechtes, Laupp, Vol. 2, 1876

Manthe, Ulrich: Gaius Institutuiones – Die Institutionen des Gaius, 2nd edn., Wissenschaftliche Buchgesellschaft Darmstadt, 2015; https://portal.dnb.de/opac.htm?method=simple Search&cqlMode=true&query=idn%3D1073849864
Markesinis, Basil: Foreign Law and Comparative Methodology: A Subject and a Thesis, Bloomsbury, 1997
Markesinis, Basil; Lorenz, Werner; Dannemann, Gerhard: The German Law of Obligations: Volume I, The Law of Contracts and Restitution: a Comparative Introduction, Clarendon Press, 1997, 710–770 (with cases 771–816)
Martinek, Michael: Der Bereicherungsausgleich bei veranlaßter Drittleistung auf fremde nichtbestehende Schuld – Besprechung des BGH-Urteils vom 28.11.1990 – XII ZR 130/89, in: JuristenZeitung (JZ) 1991, 395
Mason, Keith; Carter, John; Tolhurst, Greg: Restitution Law in Australia, 2nd edn., LexisNexis Butterworths, 2008
McGuire, Mary-Rose: Die Lizenz: Eine Einordnung in die Systemzusammenhänge des BGB und des Zivilprozessrechts, Mohr Siebeck, 2012
McInnes, Mitchell: Restitution: Developments in Unjust Enrichment, LBC Information Services, in association with Deakin University, Deakin Law School Legal Resources Project; Wm W. Gaunt & Sons [distributor], Sydney, 1996
McInnes, Mitchell: The Canadian Law of Unjust Enrichment and Restitution, 2nd edn., LexisNexis Canada, 2014
McKendrick, Ewan: Frustration, Restitution and Loss Apportionment, Clarendon Press, 1991
McKendrick, Ewan: The Further Travails of Duress in: Andrew Burrows and Lord Alan Rodger, Mapping the Law: Essays in Memory of Peter Birks, Oxford University Press, 2006
McKendrick, Ewan: Total Failure of Consideration and Counter-Restitution: Two Issues or One? in: Peter Birks, Laundering and Tracing, Clarendon Press, 1995, 243–60
McKendrick, Ewan: Work Done in Anticipation of a Contract Which Does Not Materialize in: William Robert et al., Restitution: Past, Present and Future, Oxford: Hart Publishing, 1998
Mead, Geoffrey: Free Acceptance: Some Further Considerations, Law Quarterly Review, Vol. 105 (1989), 460
Medicus, Dieter; Petersen, Jens: Bürgerliches Recht, Vahlen, 28th edn., 2021
Meier, Sonja: Irrtum und Zweckverfehlung, Mohr Siebeck, 1999
Meier, Sonja: Die Leistung durch Dritte in historisch-vergleichender Perspektive, ZfPW 2015, 103
Meier, Sonja: Mistaken Payments in Three-Party-Situations: a German View of English law, Cambridge Law Journal, Vol. 58, Iss. 3 (1999), 567–603
Meier, Sonja: No Basis: A Comparative View in: Andrew Burrows and Lord Rodger of Earlsferry, Mapping the Law: Essays in Memory of Peter Birks, 2006
Meier, Sonja: Restitution After Executed Void Contracts in: Peter Birks and Francis Rose, Lessons of the Swaps Litigation, Routledge, 2000, 168
Meier, Sonja: Unjust factors and legal grounds in: David Johnston, Reinhard Zimmermann, Unjustified Enrichment: Key issues in Comparative Perspective, Cambridge University Press, 2002, 37–75
Meier, Sonja; Zimmermann, Reinhard: Judicial development of the law, error iuris and the law of unjustified enrichment, Law Quarterly Review, Vol. 115 (1999), 556
Mitchell, Charles: Unjust Enrichment, in: Andrew Burrows, Principles of the English Law of Obligations, Oxford University Press, 2015

Mitchell, Charles; Mitchell, Paul; Watterson, Stephen Goff & Jones: Unjust Enrichment, 10th edn.,Sweet & Maxwell, 2022

Mitchell, Charles; Swadling, William: The Restatement of Restitution Third: Restitution and Unjust Enrichment – Critical and Comparative Essays, Oxford: Hart, 2013

Mitteis, Ludwig: Operae officilaes and operae fabriles, Zeitschrift der Savigny-Stiftung für Rechtsgeschichte, Romanistische Abteilung (ZRGRA) Vol. 23, (1902), 143

Mugdan, Benno: Die gesammten Materialien zum Bürgerlichen Gesetzbuch für das Deutsche Reich", Band 2 (Vol. 2), R. v. Deckers Verlag, Berlin, 1899 [= Mugdan II]; https://collections.thulb.uni-jena.de/servlets/MCRFileNodeServlet/HisBest_derivate_00010709/Band%202.pdf; contains (with diverging page-numbers)

Motive zu dem Entwurfe eines *Bürgerlichen Gesetzbuches* für das Deutsche Reich, Band II, Recht der Schuldverhältnisse, J. Guttentag (D. Collin), Berlin, Leipzig, 1888

Nair, Aruna: "Mistakes of Law" and Legal Reasoning: Interpreting Kleinwort Benson v Lincoln City Council in Robert Chambers, Charles Mitchell, James Penner, Philosophical Foundations of the Law of Unjust Enrichment, 2009, 373 – 93

Nicolini, Ugo: Pilii Medicinensis Quaestiones sabbatinae, Saggio di edizione, Modena: Università degli Studi, 1946

O'Sullivan, Dominic; Elliott, Steven; Zakrzewski, Rafal: The Law of Rescission, 2nd edn., Oxford, 2014

Oetker, Hartmut; Berger, Klaus Peter: Münchener Kommentar zum Bürgerlichen Gesetzbuch, Vol. 4/2, 9th edn., 2023

Oetker, Hartmut; Berger, Klaus Peter; Franzen, MartinMünchener Kommentar zum Bürgerlichen Gesetzbuch: BGB, Band 4/2: Schuldrecht – Besonderer Teil I, 2. Halbband: §§ 481 – 534, Finanzierungsleasing, Vol 4/2, 9th edn., 2023

Omlor, Sebastian: Kryptowährungen im Geldrecht, Zeitschrift für das gesamte Handelsrecht und Wirtschaftsrecht (ZHR), Vol. 183 (2019), 294

Palmer, George: The Law of Restitution, Boston and Toronto: Little, Brown and Company, 1978

Pascal, Robert A.: Book Review "The Doctrine of Unjustified Enrichment In The Law of The Province of Quebec [McGill Legal Studies No. 2] by George S. Challies, Wilson and Lafleur, 2nd edn., 1952", Vol. 14, Iss. 3, (1954), 734

Pavlicek, Antonin: Zur Lehre Von Den Klagen aus Ungerechtfertigter Bereicherung, Manz, 1878

Perrouin-Verbe, Dorothée: Causa and the Requirements of Valid Contracts, Max Planck Private Law Research Paper No. 22/24, posted 5 Dec 2022, last updated 15 Dec 2022; https://papers.ssrn.com/sol3/papers.cfm?abstract_id=4268473

Petiton, avocate général à la Cour de cassation: Annotation to Cour de Cassation, Chambre des requêtes (Cass req) of 16 July 1889 – Crédit foncier, DP(Dalloz périodique)89.1.393

Planiol, Marcel: Annotation of Cour de Cassation, Chambre civile (Cass civ) of 16 July 1890 – Lemaire, DP.(Dalloz périodique)91.1.49

Planiol, Marcel; Ripert, George: Traité Élémentaire de Droit Civil – conforme au programme officiel des facultés de droit, tome 2 (Vol. 2), 20 Rue Sufflot (5e arr.), Paris, 1931

Posez, Alexis: La subsidiarité de l'enrichissement sans cause: étude de droit français à la lumière du droit comparé. Revue de droit international et de droit comparé, 2014, 185 – 246

Postema, Gerald J.: Classical Common Law Jurisprudence, Part I, Classical Common Law Jurisprudence, Oxford University Commonwealth Law Journal, Vol. 1, (2002), 155 – 180

Pothier, Robert Joseph: Traité des contrats de prêt de consomption, 2nd edn., Cosse & Marchal, Paris, 1861

Pothier, Robert Joseph: Traité des obligations, Paris, 1761

Protokolle der [ersten] Kommission zur Ausarbeitung des Entwurfs eines Bürgerlichen GesetzbuchesSitzungen vom 20. Dezember 1882 bis zum 13. April 1883, pages 1497 – 2003, at 1500 – 1501, available by Werner Schubert online at: https://rwi.app/iurisprudentia/de/bgb/documents/static/722952/pages/5?zoom=0.80623586978610981 (p. 1500), https://rwi.app/iurisprudentia/de/bgb/documents/static/722952/pages/6?zoom=0.41795267489711935 (p. 1501)

Puchta, Georg Friedrich: Vorlesungen über das heutige römische Recht, B. Tauchnitz, Vol. 1, 1847; https://www.digitale-sammlungen.de/de/view/bsb10623970?page=,1

Rabel, Ernst: Grundzüge des römischen Privatrechts, Darmstadt: Wissenschaftliche Buchgesellschaft, 1955

Rai, Ruchir: The Principle of Unjust Enrichment, January 2012; https://papers.ssrn.com/sol3/papers.cfm?abstract_id=2353502

Rau, Gaston: De la valeur pratique de la maxime nemo cum damno alterius locupletior fieri debet en droit Romain – De l'action en répétition de l'indu et de quelques autres actions analogues en droit francvais, 1872

Reuter, Dieter; Martinek, Michael: Ungerechtfertigte Bereicherung, J.C.B. Mohr, 1st edn., 1983

Reuter, Dieter; Martinek, Michael: Ungerechtfertigte Bereicherung, Vol. 1/2, 2nd edn., 2016

Ridge, Pauline: Third Party Volunteers and Undue Influence, Law Quarterly Review, Vol. 130 (2014), 112 – 130

Riehm, Thomas: Schuldrecht und Sachenrecht: Nutzungsersatzanspruch gegen Mieter und Untermieter nach Beendigung des Mietverhältnisses, JuS 2014, 940

Roffredus Beneventanus: Solemnis atque Aureus Tractatus libellorum Domini Rofredi Beneventani super utraque censura cum suis fructuosissimis questionibus et eorundem decisionibus exquisitissimis, Argentorati: impr. Io. Grüninger exp. Petri Drach Spieres, 1502

Rouast, André: Les obligations dont la source n'est ni le contrat ni la faute, Répétitions écrites de droit civil approfondi et comparé, Les Cours de droit, Paris 1933 – 1934

Ruggiero, Roberto de; Maroi, Fulvio: Instituzioni di diriito privato, Giuseppe Principato, Vol II, 2nd edn. 1954

Rush, Michael: The Defence of Passing On, Oxford: Hart Publishing, 2006

Saccoccio, Antonio: Si certum petetur. Dalla condictiones dei veteres alle condictiones giustinianee, Giuffrè 2002

Saint German, Christopher: The Doctor and Student, or Dialogues between a Doctor of Divinity and a Student in the Laws of England containing the Grounds of those Laws together with Questions and Cases concerning the Equity thereof, 1518, Based on the 1874 edition. Revised and corrected by William Muchall, Gent.; https://lonang.com/wp-content/download/DoctorAndStudent.pdf

Schall, Alexander: Abrüstung der Bereicherungsdogmatik im Dreipersonenverhältnis, JuristenZeitung (JZ) 2003, 753

Schall, Alexander: Corona-Krise: Unmöglichkeit und Wegfall der Geschäftsgrundlage bei gewerblichen Miet- und Pachtverträgen, JuristenZeitung (JZ) 2020, 388

Schall, Alexander: Leistungskondiktion und Sonstige Kondiktion auf der Grundlage des einheitlichen gesetzlichen Kondiktionsprinzips, Verlag C.H. Beck, 2003, 83 – 91

Schall, Alexander: The New Law of Piercing the Corporate Veil in the UK, European Company and Financial Law Review (ECFR), Vol. 13, Iss. 4, 2016, 476

Schall, Alexander: Three-Party Situations in Unjust Enrichment Epitomised by Mistaken Bank Transfers, Restitution Law Review (RLR), Vol. 12, 2004, 110

Schiller, Arthur: Roman Law: Mechanisms of Development, Walter de Gruyter, 1978

Schlosser, Hans: Die Exegese aus der deutschen Rechtsgeschichte, JuS 1963, 141
Schmoeckel, Mathias; Rückert, Joachim; Zimmermann, Reinhard: Historisch-kritischer Kommentar zum BGB,Mohr Siebeck, Vol. 1, 2003
Schmoeckel, Mathias; Rückert, Joachim; Zimmermann, Reinhard: Historisch-kritischer Kommentar zum BGB,Mohr Siebeck, Vol. 3, 2013
Schnabel, Christian: Der solutionis causa adiectus im Römischen Recht, Münchener Beiträge zur Papyrusforschung, Vol. 110, 2015
Schnauder, Franz: Die Sonderrechtsprechung zum Bereicherungsausgleich im neuen Zahlungsdiensterecht, JuristenZeitung (JZ) 2016, 603
Schnauder, Franz: Grundfragen zur Leistungskondiktion bei Drittbeziehungen, Schriften zum Bürgerlichen Recht, Vol. 67, 1981
Schrage, Eltjo: Unjust Enrichment: a Comparative Legal History of the Law of Restitution, 2nd edn., Duncker & Humblot, 1999
Schrage, Eltjo: Unjust Enrichment and the Law of Contract, Kluwer Law International, 2001
Schubert, Werner: Die Vorentwürfe der Redaktoren zum BGB, Recht der Schuldverhältnisse Teil 3, Besonderer Teil II, DeGruyter, 1980
Schubert, Werner: Windscheid und das Bereicherungsrecht des ersten Entwurfs, Zeitschrift der Savigny-Stiftung für Rechtsgeschichte, Romanistiche Abteiling Vol. 92 (1975), 186
Schulz, Fritz: System der Rechte auf den Eingriffserwerb, Archiv für die civilistische Praxis (AcP), Vol. 105 (1909), 1–488
Schulze, Reiner; Dörner, Heinrich; Ebert, Ina: Bürgerliches Gesetzbuch, Handkommentar, 12th edn., 2024
Scott, HelenRestitution of Extra-Contractual Transfers: Limits of the Absence of Legal Ground Analysis, Restitution Law Review (RLR), Vol. 14, Iss. 1 (2006), 93
Scott, HelenUnjust Enrichment in South African Law: Rethinking Enrichment by Transfer, Oxford: Hart Publishing, 2013
Seavey, Warren; Scott, Austin: Restatement of Restitution Reporters Notes, American Law Institute, 1937
Sell, Georg Willehelm August: Über den Grundsatz des römischen Rechts, dass niemand mit oder aus dem Schaden eines andern sich bereichern dürfe, Versuche im Gebiete des Zivilrechts, 1st Part, 1833
Sheehan, Duncan: Negotiorum gestio: A Civilian Concept in the Common Law?, The International and Comparative Law Quarterly, Vol. 55, Iss. 2 (2006), 253–280
Sherwin, Emily: "*Restitution* and Equity: An Analysis of the Principle of *Unjust Enrichment*" *(2001)* Cornell *Law* Faculty Publications 847
Simpson, Alfred William: A History of the Common Law of Contract, Clarendon Press, 1975
Sir Kim Lewison: Under the Influence, Restitution Law Review (RLR) Vol. 19 (2011), 1
Sirks, Adriaan Johan Boudewijn; Mausen, YvesAequitas: équité, equity, Presses de la Faculté de Montpellier, 2015
Skelton, Andrew: Restitution and Contract, Informa Law from Routledge, 1998
Smith, Lionel David: The Law of Tracing, Clarendon Press, 1997
Smith, Lionel David: "Unjust Enrichment, Property and the Structure of Trusts", Law Quarterly Review, Vol. 116 (2000), 412–444
Smith, Lionel David: Unjust Enrichment: Big or Small? in: James Edelman; Simone Degeling, Unjust Enrichment in Commercial Law, Thomson Reuters Australia, 2008, 35–52

Smith, Lionel David: Restitution: A new Start? In: Devonshire, Peter; Havelock, Rohan, The Impact of Equity and Restitution in Commerce, Bloomsbury, 2018

Smits, Jan: The Principle of Unjust Enrichment and Formation of Contract: The Importance of a Hidden Policy Factor, European Review of Private Law, 2006

Soergel, Hans-Theodor: Bürgerliches Gesetzbuch mit Einführungsgesetz und Nebengesetzen, Vol. 5/3, Kohlhammer, 13th edn., 2010

Solomon, Dennis: Der Bereicherungsausgleich in Anweisungsfällen – Rechtsvergleichende Untersuchung zum deutschen Recht und zu den Rechtsordnungen des Common Law, Mohr Siebeck, 2004

Sorge, Christoph: Verpflichtungsfreier Vertrag als Rechtsgrund. Das Rechtsgeschäft der *condictio ob rem* gemäß § 812 Abs. 1 p. 2 2. Alt. BGB jenseits von Erfüllungszwang und Markttausch, V&R unipress Göttingen, 2017

Stadler, Astrid: Gestaltungsfreiheit und Verkehrsschutz durch Abstraktion, Mohr Siebeck, 1996

Stevens, Robert: When and Why does Unjustified Enrichment Justify the Recognition of Proprietary Rights? Boston University Law Review, Vol. 92, Iss. 3 (2012), 919

Stevens, Robert: Is there a Law of Unjust Enrichment? In: Simone Degeling; James Edelman, Unjust Enrichment in Commercial Law, Thomson Reuters Australia, 2008, 11

Stevens, Robert: The Laws of Restitution, Oxford University Press, 2023

Stevens, Robert: The Unjust Enrichment Disaster, Law Quarterly Review, Vol. 134 (2018), 573

Stevens, Robert: Three Enrichment Issues, in: Andrew Burrows and Lord Rodger of Earlsferry, Mapping the Law: Essays in Memory of Peter Birks, Oxford University Press, 2006

Stoljar, Samuel Jacob: Quasi-Contract, Law Book Company, 2nd edn., 1989

Stoljar, Samuel Jacob: Mistake and Misrepresentation: A Study in Contractual Principles, Sweet and Maxwell, 1986

Stroux, Johannes: Summum ius summa inuria: Ein Kapitel aus der Geschichte der interpretatio iuris, Teubner, 1926

Stürner, Rolf; Berger, Christian: Jauernig Bürgerliches Gesetzbuch, Kommentar, 19th edn., 2023

Swadling, William: The Limits of Restitutionary Claims: A Comparative Analysis, British Institute of International and Comparative Law, 1997

Swadling, William: Ignorance and Unjust Enrichment: The Problem of Title, Oxford Journal of Legal Studies, Vol. 28, Iss. 4, (2008) 627

Swadling, William: Rescission, Property, and the Common Law, Law Quarterly Review (2005) 123

Swadling, William: Undue Influence: Lessons from America? in: Charles Mitchell, William Swadling, The Restatement of Restitution Third: Restitution and Unjust Enrichment – Critical and Comparative Essays, Oxford: hart Publishing, 2013, 111–131

Swadling, William: Unjust Delivery in: Andrew Burrows and Lord Rodger of Earlsferry, Mapping the Law: Essays in Memory of Peter Birks, 2006, 277–298

Swadling, William; Jones, Gareth: The Search for Principle: Essays in Honour of Lord Goff of Chieveley, Oxford University Press, 2000

Tang, Hang Wu: Restitution for Mistaken Gifts, Journal of Constitutional Law, Vol. 20 (2004), 1

Thomale, Chris: Leistung als Freiheit, Mohr Siebeck, 2012

Trimarchi, Pietro: L'arricchimento senza causa, Giuffré, 1962

Varvaro, Mario: Der Glücksstern Niehburs und die Institutionen des Gaius, Jedermann-Verlag Heidelberg, 2nd edn., 2014

Vaughn, John: Law and Rhetoric in the Causa Curiana, Classical Antiquity Vol. 4, Iss. 2, (1985), 208–222

Vinnius, Arnolius: In quatuor libros institutionum imperialium commentarius academicus et forensis, Zieger/Lehmann, Herbornae, 1699, available at: http://tudigit.ulb.tu-darmstadt.de/show/51-4583/0001/thumbs
Vinnius, Arnoldus: Selectarum Quaestionum Juris libri II quibus additaë sunt Simonis Vinnii Arnoldi filii orationes duae, Elzevir, 1672; https://archive.org/details/ned-kbn-all-00004580-001
Virgo, Graham: The Principles of the Law of Restitution, Oxford University Press, 3rd edn., 2015
Visser, Daniel: Unjustified Enrichment, Juta, 2008
von Bar, Christian; Swann, Stephen: Principles of European Contract law: Unjustified Enrichment, Sellier European Law Publisher, 2010
von Caemmerer, Ernst: Bereicherungsansprüche und Drittbeziehungen, JuristenZeitung (JZ), 1962, 385
von Glück, Christian Friedrich: Ausführliche Erläuterung der Pandecten nach Hellfeld, ein Kommentar, Dreizehnten Teils Erste Abteilung (= Vol. 13/1), Palm'sche Verlagsbuchhandlung, 1811; https://www.digitale-sammlungen.de/de/view/bsb10565513?page=,1
von Glück, Christian Friedrich: Ausführliche Erläuterung der Pandecten nach Hellfeld, ein Kommentar, Dreizehnten Teils Erste Abteilung (= Vol. 13/1), 2nd edn. (unchanged), Palm'sche Verlagsbuchhandlung, 1843; https://www.digitale-sammlungen.de/de/view/bsb10565483?page=,1
von Kübel, Franz Philipp: Achter Titel; Schuldverhältnisse aus ungerechtfertigter Bereicherung, published by Schubert, Die Vorentwürfe der Redaktoren, Vol III/2, 1980, 655–670 Entwurfsvorlage = Schubert, 655–659 Motive VE (Vorentwurf), 1–90 = Schubert, 661–750
von Lingenthal, Karl Solomo Zachariä: Handbuch des französischen Zivilrechts, 1st edn., 1808–1809, available at: https://dlc.mpg.de/toc/mpirg_sisis_72942/1/
von Lingenthal, Karl Solomo ZachariäHandbuch des französischen Civilrechts, Vol 3, 4th edn., 1837
von Savigny, Friedrich Carl: System des heutigen Römischen Rechts, Vol III, Bei Veit & Comp. Berlin, 1840; https://www.deutschestextarchiv.de/book/view/savigny_system03_1840?p=7
von Savigny, Friedrich Carl: System des heutigen Römischen rechts, Vol. V, Bei Veit & Comp. Berlin, 1841; https://www.deutschestextarchiv.de/book/view/savigny_system05_1841?p=7
von Savigny, Friedrich Carl: Obligationenrecht als Theil des heutigen Römischen Rechts, 2nd edn., Bei Veit & Comp. Berlin, 1853; https://www.digitale-sammlungen.de/de/view/bsb10565884?page=5
von Savigny, Friedrich Carl: Vom Beruf unsrer Zeit für Gesetzgebung und Rechtswissenschaft, Mohr und Zimmer, 1814
von Tuhr, Andreas: Actio de in Rem verso – zugleich ein Beitrag zur Lehre von der Geschäftsführung, Mohr (Siebeck), 1895
Wacke, Andreas: Die adjektizische Klagen im Überblick. Erster Teil: Von der Reeder- und der Betriebsleiterklage zur direkten Stellvertretung, Zeitschrift der Savigny-Stiftung für Rechtsgeschichte, Romanistische Abteilung (SZ or ZRGRA) 111 (1994), 280
Walter, Andreas: Bitcoin, Libra und sonstige Kryptowährungen aus zivilrechtlicher Sicht, Neue Juristische Wochenschrift (NJW) 2019, 3609
Watts, Peter: A Property Principle and a Services Principle, Restitution Law Review, Vol. 3, (1995) 49–70
Watts, Peter: Property and "unjust enrichment": cognate conservators, New Zealand Law Review (1998), 151–162
Watts, Peter: Unjust Enrichment – the Potion that Induces Well-meaning Sloppiness of Thought, Current Legal Problems, Vol. 69, Iss. 1, (2016), 289–325
Webb, Charlie: Reason and Restitution: A Theory of Unjust Enrichment, Oxford University Press, 2016
Wegmann Stockebrand, Adolfo: Obligatio re contracta, Mohr Siebeck, 2017

Weinzierl, Karl: Die Restitutionslehre der Frühscholastik, Max Hueber Verlag, 1936
Weiss, Alexander: Die Rückabwicklung einer Blockchain-Transaktion, Neue Juristische Wochenschrift (NJW) 2022, 1343
Weitnauer, Hermann: Zum Stand der Lehre von der Leistungskondiktion, Neue Juristische Wochenschrift (NJW) 1979, 2000
Wellspacher, Moriz: Versio in rem: Eine Studie zu den Problemen der Rechtsentwicklung und Gesetzes-Interpretation auf Grundlage des Österreichischen Rechtes, 1900; reprint Forgotten Books, 2018
Wendehorst, Christiane: Anspruch und Ausgleich, Jus Privatum, Mohr Siebeck, Vol. 37, 1999
Westermann, Harm Peter; Grunewald, Barbara; Maier-Reimer, Georg: Erman, BGB-Kommentar, 17th edn., 2023
Whittaker, SimonContractual Purpose in English Contract Law in: Gregor Albers, Francesco Paolo Patti, Dorothée Perrouin-Verbe, Causa contractus, Mohr Siebeck, 2022
Wieacker, Franz: Privatrechtsgeschichte der Neuzeit unter besonderer Berücksichtigung der deutschen Entwicklung, Vandenhoeck u. Ruprecht, 1952, 2nd edn., 1967
Wieacker, Franz: The Causa Curiana and Contemporary Roman Jursiprudence, Irish Jurist, Vol. 2, Iss. 1 (1967), 151–164
Wieling, Hans Josef; Finkenauer, Thomas: Bereicherungsrecht, Springer, 2nd edn., 2020
Wilburg, Walter: Die Lehre von der ungerechtfertigten Bereicherung nach österreichischem und deutschem Recht, Festschrift der Universität Graz, Leuschner and Lubensky, 1934
Wilhelm, Jan: Rechtsverletzung und Vermögensentscheidung als Grundlagen und Grenzen des Anspruchs aus ungerechtfertigter Bereicherung, Röhrscheid, 1973
Williams, Rebecca: Unjust Enrichment and Public Law: A Comparative Study of England, France and the EU, Bloomsbury, 2010
Wilmot-Smith, Frederick: Contract and Unjust Enrichment in the High Court of Australia, Law Quarterly Review, Vol. 136 (2020), 196–201
Wilmot-Smith, Frederick: Reconsidering "Total" Failure, The Cambridge Law Journal, Vol. 72, Iss. 2 (2013), 414–436
Wilmot-Smith, Frederick: Replacing Risk-Taking Reasoning, Law Quarterly Review, Vol. 127 (2011) 610–630
Wilmot-Smith, Frederick: Should the Payee Pay?, Oxford Journal of Legal Studies, Vol. 37, Iss. 4 (2017), 844–861
Windscheid, Bernhard Joseph Hubert: Die Lehre des römischen Rechts von der Voraussetzung, Buddeus, 1850
Windscheid, Bernhard Joseph Hubert: Die Voraussetzung, Archiv für die civilitische Praxis (AcP) 78 (1892), 161–202
Windscheid, Bernhard Joseph Hubert: Zur Lehre des Code Napoleon von der Ungültigkeit der Rechtsgeschäfte, Buddeus, 1847, 270
Windscheid, Bernhard Joseph Hubert: Lehrbuch des Pandektenrechts, Band 2 (Vol. 2), Literarische Anstalt Rütten & Loening, 1887; https://books.google.de/books?id=DAwPAAAAYAAJ&pg=PA420&hl=de&source=gbs_toc_r&cad=2#v=onepage&q&f=false
Wolf, Joachim: Der Stand der Bereicherungslehre und ihre Neubegründung, Heymanns, 1980
Wolf, Maximilian: Bereicherungsausgleich bei Eingriffen in höchstpersönliche Rechtsgüter, Nomos, 2017
Worthington, Sarah: Reviewed Work: Proprietary Interests in Commercial Transactions, Oxford Journal of Legal Studies, Vol. 18, Iss. 2 (1998) 363–379

Zachariä, Karls: Solomo (see von Lingenthal)

Zimmermann, Reinhard: The Law of Obligations: Roman Foundations of the Civilian Tradition, Oxford University Press, 1996

Zimmermann, Reinhard: Grundstrukturen eines Europäischen Bereicherungsrechts, Mohr Siebeck, 2005

Zimmermann, Reinhard: Unjustified Enrichment – the Modern Civilian Approach, Oxford Journal of Legal Studies, Vol. 15, 1995, 403

Zweigert, Konrad: Rechtsvergleichung als universale Interpretationsmethode, Rabels Zeitschrift für ausländisches und internationales Privatrecht, Vol. 15, Iss. 1 (1949 – 50), 5 – 21

Table of Cases (Common Law)

Agip (Africa) v Jackson [1991] Ch. 547 321
Aiken v Short (1856) 1 H & N 210, 156 ER 1180 **177**, **178**, **179**, 255, 270, 303, 311
Allcard v Skinner (1887) 36 Ch D 145 (CA) 50, 93
Arthur v Barton (1840) 6 M.– & W 138 127
Astley v Reynolds (1731) 2 Str 915, 93 E.R. 939 49, **66**, 69, 94, **95**, 160, 265
Aubert v Walsh (1810) 3 Taunt. 277 220
Australian Financial Services and Leasing Pty Ltd v Hills Industries Ltd [2014] HCA 14; (2014) 253 CLR 560, (2014) 88 AJLR 552 54
Aveling Barford Ltd v Perion Ltd [1989] BCLC 626 213

Bank of Cyprus UK Ltd v Menelaou [2015] UKSC 66, [2016] AC 176 1, 17, 38, **197**, **198**
Banque Belge pour l'Etranger v. Hambrouck [1921] 1 KB 321 200, **217**, 220, **221**, **222**, **223**
Banque Financière de la Cite´ v Parc (Battersea) Ltd [1998] UKHL 7, [1999] AC 221 1, 3, 15, 17, 35, 53, 55, 191, 196
Barclays Bank Ltd v W J Simms, Son and Cooke (Southern) Ltd [1979] 3 All ER 522, [1980] 1 QB 677 178, 259, 270, 311, 323
Barnes v Eastenders Cash & Carry plc [2014] UKSC 26, [2015] AC 1 1, 53, 71, 74, **75**, **82**, 88, **92**
Barton v Armstrong [1976] AC 104 (PC) 50
Barton v Morris [2023] UKSC 3 1, 35, 37, **39**, 54, 71, 74, **75**, 81, 86, 87, 319
Baylis v Bishop of London [1913] 1 Ch 127 (CA) 50, 285
Bell v Lever Bros [1931] UKHL 2, [1932] AC 161 78, **89**, **90**, **91**
Benedetti v Sawiris [2013] UKSC 50, [2014] AC 938 1, 35, 53, 54
Black v S. Freeman & Co. (1910) 12 CLR. 105 220
Bofinger v Kingsway Group Limited [2009] HCA 44, (2009) 239 CLR 269 (HCA) 54
Bonnell v Fowke (1657) 1 Sid. 4 49
Brown and Davis Ltd v Galbraith [1972] EWCA Civ J0426-2 194

Carlill v Carbolic Smoke Ball Company [1893] 1 QB 256 212
Case v Roberts (1817) Holt N.P. 500 49, 218
Chandler v Webster [1904] 1 KB 493 50, 87
Cheese v Thomas [1994] 1 WLR 129 284
Chetwynd v Allen [1899] 1 Ch. 353 194
Clark v Shee and Johnson (1774) 1 Cowp. 197, 98 ER 1041 71, 201, 221, 226
Colonial Bank v Exchange Bank of Yarmouth, Nova Scotia [1885] 9 App Cas 84 (PC) 178, 180, 219, 258, 283
Continental Caoutchouc and Gutta Percha Co v Kleinwort, Sons & Co [1904] 90 LT 474 193
Costello and another v MacDonald Mackling and Dickens [2011] EWCA Civ 930, [2011] 3 WLR 1341, [2012] QB 244 132, 157, **194–202**, 213, 247
Crédit foncier v Arrazat Cass req DP 89.1.393 16, 40, **143–151**

Dargamo Holdings Ltd and another v Avonwick Holdings Ltd and others [2021] EWCA Civ 1149, [2022] 1 All ER (Comm) 1244 23, 24, 27, 35, 37, 39, 40, 52, 54, 71, 74, 76, 86, **87**, 88, 196, 319
Donoghue v Stevenson [1932] AC 562 34

ESS v Sully [2005] EWCA Civ 554 124

Fairchild v. Glenhaven Funeral Services Ltd [2002] UKHL 22 23
Falcke v Scottish Imperial Insurance Co [1886] 34 ChD 234 130
Farah Constructions Pty Ltd v Say-Dee Pty Ltd [2007] HCA 22 54
Fibrosa Spolka Akcyjna v Fairbairn Lawson Combe Barbour Ltd [1942] UKHL 4, [1943] AC 32 50, **51**, **52**, 70, 75, 76, 85, 88, 204

https://doi.org/10.1515/9783110754452-006

Foskett v McKeown [2001] 1 AC 102 200
Framson v Delamere (1595) Cro El. 458 49

Gilbert v Ruddeard (1607) Dyer (Treby edn., 1688) 272 68
Giles v Edward (1797) 7 Term rep 181 50
Great Peace Shipping Ltd v Tsavliris (International) Ltd [2002] EWCA Civ 1407 25, 86, 90, 211
Green v Biddle (U.S.) 8 Wheat. 1, 83 = 5 L Ed 547, 567 (1823) 52

Hampton v Glenmorgan [1916] AC 13 196
Haugesund Kommune v Depfa ACS Bank [2010] EWCA Civ 579, [2012] QB 549 284
Hawtayne v Bourne (1841) 7 M. & W. 595 127
Holman v Johnson (1775) 1 Cowp 341 95
Holt v Markham [1923] 1 KB 504 38, 90
Home Office v Dorset Yacht Co Ltd. [1970] UKHL 2, [1970] AC 1004 34
Hudson v Robinson (1816) 4 M. & S. 475 220

International News Service v Associated Press, 248 U.S. 215 (1918) 17
Investment Trust Companies (in liquidation) v Revenue and Customs Commissioners [2017] UKSC 29, [2018] AC 275 1, 24, 38, 53, 54, 196
Investment Trust Companies (in liquidation) v HMRC [2015] EWCA Civ 82 53
Investment Trust Companies (in liquidation) v HMRC [2012] EWHC 458 (Ch) 53

Kelly v Solari (1841) 9 M & W 54, 152 ER 24 50, 270, 329
Kleinwort Benson v Lincoln CC [1999] 2 AC 349 (HL) 97
Krell v Henry (1903) 2 KB 740 87

Lady Hood of Avalon v Mackinnon [1909] 1 Ch 476 209
Lipkin Gorman v Karpnale Ltd [1988] UKHL 12, [1991] 2 AC 548 5, 17, 24, 25, 53, 68, 116, **199**, 200, 206, 212, **216**, **217–229**, 232, 285
Lloyds Bank plc v Independent Insurance Co Ltd [1998] EWCA Civ 1853, [2000] 1 QB 110 177, 181, 310
Lowick Rose LLP (in liquidation) v Swynson Ltd [2017] UKSC 32, [2018] AC 313 1, 17, 35, 53, 54, 149, 152, 196, **198–199**
Lumbers v W Cook Builders Pty Ltd (in liquidation) [2008] HCA 27, (2008) 232 CLR 635 54, 132, 195

Magee v Pennine Insurance Co. [1969] 2 QB 507 90
Management Services v Lloyds Bank Plc [2013] EWCA Civ 1415 53
Marriot v Hampton 101 Eng. Rep. 669 (1797) 285
Mertens v Winnington (1794) 1 Esp 112 127
Miller v Race (1758) 1 Burr 452, 97 ER 398 220
Morris v Burroughs (1737) 1 Atk. 398 66
Morris-Garner and another (Appellants) v One Step (Support) Ltd [2018] UKSC 20 20
Moses v Macferlan (1760) 2 Bur 1005, 97 ER 676 5, 6, 16–18, 22, 24, 40, 49, 50, 55, 56, 61, **65–70**, 80, 84, 95, **103–221**, 226, 245, 269, 270, 285

National Carriers Ltd v Panalpina (Northern) Ltd [1981] AC 675 86

Ogilvie v Allen (1899) 15 TLR 294 (HL) 207
Ogilvie v Littleboy (1897) 13 TLR 399 (CA) 207
Okpabi v Royal Dutch Shell [2021] UKSC 3 213
Okpabi v Royal Dutch Shell [2020] EWCA Civ 191 213
Orakpo v Manson Investments [1978] AC 95 53

Pan Ocean Shipping Co Ltd v Creditcorp Ltd (The Trident Beauty) [1994] 1 Lloyds Report 365, [1994] 1 WLR 161 86, **319**, **320**
Patel v Mirza [2016] UKSC 42, [2017] AC 467 (SC) 95, 96
Paul v Speirway Ltd. [1976] Ch. 220 192
Pitt v Holt [2013] UKSC 26, [2013] 2 AC 108 207–209
Prest v Petrodel Resources Ltd [2013] UKSC 34, [2013] AC 32 33, 95, 164, 195, 213

Re Hallett's Estate (1880) 13 Ch D 696 222

Re Halt Garage (1964) Ltd [1982] 3 All ER 1016 213
RE Jones Ltd v Waring & Gillow Ltd [1926] AC 670 (HL), *1926*] All ER Rep 36 257, 302
Relfo Ltd (in liq) v Varsani [2014] EWCA Civ 360 53, 54, 196
124
Rowland v Divall [1923] 2 KB 500 50, 75, 78
Roxborough v Rothmans of Pall Mall Australia Ltd [2001] HCA 68, [2001] 208 CLR, 516 24, 54, 75, **90–91**

Salomon v A Salomon & Co Ltd [1896] UKHL 1, [1897] AC 22 179
Samsoondar v Capital Insurance Co Ltd' [2020] UKPC 33, [2021] 2 All ER 1105 1, 35, 54
School Facility Managements Limited and others v Governing Body of Christ the King College and another [2021] EWCA Civ 1053 12, 16, 23, 24, 261, 291, **301–302**
Sharma v Simposh Ltd [2011] EWCA Civ 1383 88, 91
Shoolbred v Roberts [1899] 2 QB 560 220
Sinclair v Brougham [1914] AC 398 9, 50–52, 68, 70, 71, 102, 225
Slade v Morley (1602) B. & M. 420 60
Solle v Butcher [1950] 1 KB 671 25, 86, 90, 211
Supreme Court of Canada, Kingsway Investments v New Brunswick (Department of Finance) (2007) 1 SCR 3 114
Swynson Ltd v Lowick Rose LLP [2015] EWCA Civ 629 53

Taylor v Caldwell [1863] EWHC QB J1, (1863) 3 B. & S. 826 50, 69, 86
Taylor v Laird (1856) 25 LJ Ex 329 26
Taylor v Plumer [1815] 3 M. & S. 562 223, 224
TFL Management Services v Lloyds Bank Plc [2013] EWCA Civ 1415 53
The Gratitudine (1801) 3 C. Rob 240 127
Tinsley v Milligan [1993] UKHL 3, [1994] AC 340 96
Transvaal and Delagoa Bay Investment Co. Ltd v Atkinson [1944] 1 All E.R. 579 220

United Australia v Barclays Bank [1941] AC 1 51
Uren v First National Home Finance Ltd [2005] EWHC 2529 196
Vedanta v Lungowe [2019] UKSC 20 213

Voris v Lampert 446 P.3d 284 (Cal. 2019) 4

Watteau v Fenwick [1893] 1 QB 346 124
Westdeutsche Landesbank Girozentrale v Islington LBC [1996] AC 669 272
Whitecomb v Jacob (1711) 1 Salk 160 223
Woolwich Building Society v Commisioners of Inland Revenue [1993] AC 70 69, 20, 274, 326–327

Yeoman's Row v Cobbe [2008] UKHL 55 **102**, 128, 283
Youkong Line Ltd of Korea v Rendsburg Inv. Corp of Liberia and others [1998] 4 All ER 82, [1998] 1 WLR 294, [1998] 1 Lloyd's Rep. 322 213

Bei Fragen zur Produktsicherheit wenden Sie sich bitte an:
If you have any questions regarding product safety, please contact:

Walter de Gruyter
Genthiner Straße 13
10785 Berlin
productsafety@degruyterbrill.com